THE BEST TEST PREPARATION FOR THE

GRE®

GRADUATE RECORD EXAMINATION®

PHYSICS TEST

Joseph J. Molitoris, Ph.D.
Professor of Physics
Muhlenberg College
Allentown, PA

Research & Education Association
Visit our website at
www.rea.com

Research & Education Association
61 Ethel Road West
Piscataway, New Jersey 08854
E-mail: info@rea.com

The Best Test Preparation for the
GRE® PHYSICS TEST

Year 2006 Printing

Printed in the United States of America

Library of Congress Control Number 2002117188

International Standard Book Number 0-87891-848-5

C06

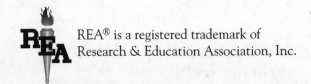

CONTENTS

INTRODUCTION

GRE PHYSICS REVIEW

1 CLASSICAL MECHANICS

2 ELECTROMAGNETISM

3 ATOMIC PHYSICS

4 THERMODYNAMICS

FOUR PRACTICE EXAMS

ABOUT RESEARCH & EDUCATION ASSOCIATION

Founded in 1959, Research & Education Association is dedicated to publishing the finest and most effective educational materials—including software, study guides, and test preps—for students in middle school, high school, college, graduate school, and beyond.

REA's Test Preparation series includes books and software for all academic levels in almost all disciplines. Research & Education Association publishes test preps for students who have not yet entered high school, as well as high school students preparing to enter college. Students from countries around the world seeking to attend college in the United States will find the assistance they need in REA's publications. For college students seeking advanced degrees, REA publishes test preps for many major graduate school admission examinations in a wide variety of disciplines, including engineering, law, and medicine. Students at every level, in every field, with every ambition can find what they are looking for among REA's publications.

REA's series presents tests that accurately depict the official exams in both degree of difficulty and types of questions. REA's practice tests are always based upon the most recently administered exams, and include every type of question that can be expected on the actual exams.

REA's publications and educational materials are highly regarded and continually receive an unprecedented amount of praise from professionals, instructors, librarians, parents, and students. Our authors are as diverse as the fields represented in the books we publish. They are well-known in their respective disciplines and serve on the faculties of prestigious high schools, colleges, and universities throughout the United States and Canada.

We invite you to visit us at *www.rea.com* to find out how "REA is making the world smarter."

ACKNOWLEDGMENTS

In addition to our author, we would like to thank Larry B. Kling, Vice President, Editorial, for his overall guidance, which brought this publication to completion; Pam Weston, Vice President, Publishing, for setting the quality standards for production integrity and managing the publication to completion; Alicia Shapiro and Mark Zipkin for coordinating revisions; R.D. Murphy, Ph.D., and James L. Love, M.S., M.A.T., for their review for technical accuracy; Catherine Battos for her editorial contributions; and Wende Solano for typesetting the original manuscript.

About the Book

This book provides an accurate and complete representation of the Graduate Record Examination in Physics. The four practice exams and review section are based on the format of the most recently administered GRE Physics Exam. Each exam is two hours and fifty minutes in length and includes every type of question that can be expected on the actual exam. Following each exam is an answer key, complete with detailed explanations designed to clarify the material for the student. By studying the review section, completing all four exams, and studying the explanations which follow, students can discover their strengths and weaknesses and thereby become well prepared for the actual exam.

About the Test

The Graduate Record Examination in Physics is offered three times a year by the Educational Testing Service, under the direction of the Graduate Record Examination Board. Applicants for graduate school submit GRE test results together with other undergraduate records as part of the highly competitive admission process to graduate school. The GRE tests are intended to provide the graduate school admissions committee with a means of evaluating your competence in certain subject areas. Scores on the test are intended to indicate mastery of the subject matter emphasized in an undergraduate program.

The test consists of about 100 multiple-choice questions, some of which are grouped in sets and based on such materials as diagrams, experimental data, graphs, and descriptions of physical situations. Emphasis is placed on the ability to grasp fundamental principles of physics as well as the ability to apply these principles. Most test questions can be answered on the basis of a mastery of the first three years of undergraduate physics. Emphasis is placed on the following major areas of physics and occur in the percentages indicated. These percentages reflect the relative emphasis placed on these topics in most undergraduate curricula.

1. Fundamentals of electromagnetism, including Maxwell's equations (18%)
2. Classical mechanics (20%)
3. Atomic physics (10%)
4. Quantum mechanics (12%)
5. Physical optics and wave phenomena (9%)

6. Special relativity (6%)
7. Thermodynamics and statistical mechanics (10%)
8. Laboratory methods (6%)
9. Advanced topics: Lagrangian and Hamiltonian mechanics, solid state physics, nuclear and particle physics and miscellaneous (9%)

About the Author

Dr. Joseph Molitoris is a professor of Physics at Muhlenberg College in Allentown, Pennsylvania, where he teaches introductory and advanced physics. His teaching responsibilities include courses in General Physics, Modern Physics, Mechanics, Advanced Mechanics, Statistical Physics, and Nuclear Physics.

After receiving his Bachelor of Science degree in Physics from Massachusetts Institute of Technology, Dr. Molitoris went on to receive his Master of Science degree in Mathematics from the University of North Florida. He was awarded a doctorate in Physics from Michigan State University. His post-doctoral work was performed as a fellow of the Alexander von Humboldt Foundation in Frankfurt, Germany.

About the Review

The review in this book is designed to further your understanding of the test material. It includes techniques you can use to enhance your knowledge of physics and to earn higher scores on the exam. The review includes extensive discussions and examples to refresh your knowledge. Topics covered in the review are:

Classical Mechanics

- Vectors
- Linear Motion
- Two-Dimensional Motion
- Newton's Laws
- Momentum
- Energy and Work
- Harmonic Motion

- Collisions
- Lagrangian Mechanics

Electromagnetism

- Electric Fields
- Capacitors
- Current and Resistance
- Circuits
- Magnetism
- Maxwell's Equations and Electromagnetic Waves

Atomic Physics

- Rutherford Scattering
- Atomic Spectra
- The Bohr Atom
- The Laser

Thermodynamics

- Temperature
- Coefficient of Thermal Expansion
- Heat capacity, Specific Heat and C_P
- Heat of Vaporization and Heat of Fusion
- Conduction, Convection and Radiation
- Heat, Work and the Laws of Thermodynamics
- Entropy

Quantum Mechanics

- Wave Functions and Equations
- Schrödinger's Equation
- Potential Wells and Energy Levels
- Harmonic Oscillator
- Reflection and Transmission by a Barrier

Special Relativity

- Time Dilation and Length Contraction
- Dynamics
- Lorentz Transformations

Optics and Wave Phenomena

- Mechanical Waves
- Ray Optics
- Thin Lenses
- Interference
- Diffraction

Scoring the Exam

Two types of scores are obtained from your results on the GRE Physics examination: a raw score and a scaled score. The raw score is determined first and is then converted into the scaled score.

To determine the raw score, a number of things must be done. The following equation represents the process:

$R - W/4$ = Raw Score (round off if necessary)

First calculate the total number of wrong (W) answers. Next, calculate the total number of right (R) answers. Unanswered questions are not counted. At this point, divide the total number of wrong answers by four and subtract this result from the total number of right answers. This adjustment is made to compensate for guessing. Finally, take the last result and round it off to the nearest whole number, which will be the raw score.

To determine the scaled score, find the number that corresponds to the raw score in the table on the following page.

It is important to note that the raw score can vary slightly and still result in the same scaled score. This is because various forms of the test may be administered.

For more information, please visit the official GRE Web site at www.gre.org.

GRE Physics — Total Score

Raw Score	Scaled Score	Raw Score	Scaled Score
84–100	990	41–42	670
83	980	40	660
81–82	970	39	650
80	960	37–38	640
79	950	36	630
77–78	940	35	620
76	930	33–34	610
75	920	32	600
73–74	910	30–31	590
72	900	29	580
71	890	28	570
69–70	880	26–27	560
68	870	25	550
67	860	24	540
65–66	850	22–23	530
64	840	21	520
63	830	20	510
61–62	820	18–19	500
60	810	17	490
59	800	16	480
57–58	790	14–15	470
56	780	13	460
55	770	12	450
53–54	760	10–11	440
52	750	9	430
51	740	8	420
49–50	730	6–7	410
48	720	5	400
47	710	4	390
45–46	700	2–3	380
44	690	1	370
43	680	0	360

GRE PHYSICS REVIEW

CHAPTER 1

CLASSICAL MECHANICS

A. VECTORS

A vector is a measure of both direction and magnitude. Vector variables are usually indicated in **boldface**, or with an arrow, such as $\vec{v}$.

THE COMPONENTS OF A VECTOR

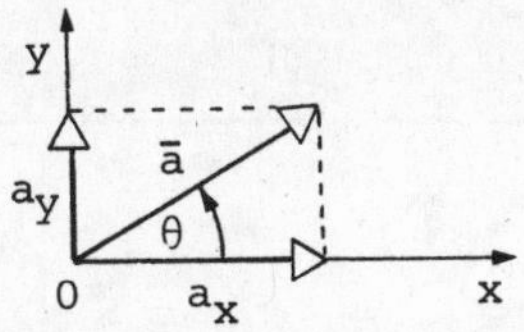

a_x and a_y are the components of a vector a. The angle θ is measured counter-clockwise from the positive *x*–axis. The components are formed when we draw perpendicular lines to the chosen axes.

The Formation of Vector Components on the Positive *X* – *Y* axis

The components of a vector are given by

$$\boldsymbol{a}_x = \boldsymbol{a}\cos\theta$$

$$\boldsymbol{a}_y = \boldsymbol{a}\sin\theta$$

A component is equal to the product of the magnitude of vector *A* and cosine of the angle between the positive axis and the vector.

The magnitude can be expressed in terms of the components

$$|\boldsymbol{a}| = \sqrt{\boldsymbol{a}_x^2 + \boldsymbol{a}_y^2}$$

Finally the angle θ is given by

$$\theta = \tan^{-1}\frac{\boldsymbol{a}_y}{\boldsymbol{a}_x}$$

Like scalars, which are measures of magnitude, vectors can be added, subtracted and multiplied.

To add or subtract vectors, simply add or subtract the respective x and y coordinates. For example,

a – **b** implies $a_x - b_x = c_x$,

$a_y - b_y = c_y$

Therefore, **C** is the difference of **a** and **b** and is given by $c = \sqrt{c_x^{\,2} + c_y^{\,2}}$.

There are 2 forms of multiplication: the dot product and the vector, or cross product. The dot product yields a scalar value:

$$\mathbf{a} \cdot \mathbf{b} = ab \cos \theta$$

The Cross Product of two vectors yields a vector:

$$\mathbf{a} \times \mathbf{b} = \mathbf{c}$$

and

$$|\mathbf{c}| = ab \sin \theta$$

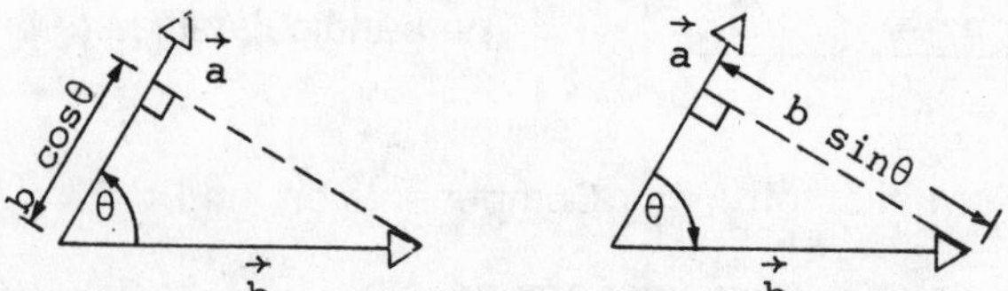

(a) Dot Product (b) Cross Product

Vector Multiplication

The direction of the Vector Product **a** × **b** = **c** is given by the "Right-Hand Rule":

1) With **a** and **b** tail-to-tail, draw the angle θ from **a** to **b**.

2) With your right hand, curl your fingers in the direction of the angle drawn. The extended thumb points in the direction of **c**.

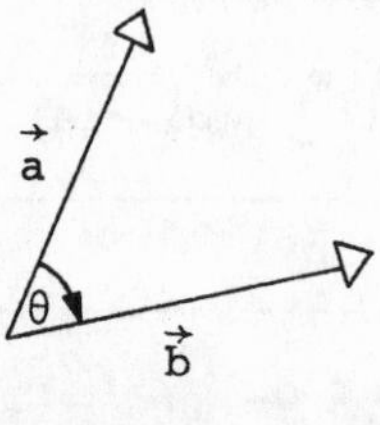

The direction of the vector product,
c = **a** × **b** (| **c** | = *ab* sin θ), is into the page.

Properties of the Cross Product:

$\mathbf{a} \times \mathbf{b} = -\mathbf{b} \times \mathbf{a}$

$\mathbf{a} \times (\mathbf{b} + \mathbf{c}) = (\mathbf{a} \times \mathbf{b}) + (\mathbf{a} \times \mathbf{c})$

$c(\mathbf{a} \times \mathbf{b}) = (c\mathbf{a}) \times \mathbf{b} = \mathbf{a} \times (c\mathbf{b})$, where c is a scalar.

$|\mathbf{a} \times \mathbf{b}|^2 = A^2B^2 - (\mathbf{a} \cdot \mathbf{b})^2$

B. LINEAR MOTION

Any object in motion has an average and an instantaneous velocity:

a) Average Velocity

$$V = \frac{\Delta x}{\Delta t} = \frac{x_2 - x_1}{t_2 - t_1} \qquad \text{units}: \frac{\text{meters}}{\text{sec}}$$

b) Instantaneous Velocity

$$V = \lim_{\Delta t \to 0} \frac{\Delta x}{\Delta t} = \frac{dx}{dt} = v(t) \qquad \text{units}: \frac{\text{meters}}{\text{sec}}$$

Just as the average and instantaneous velocities are the rate of change of position with respect to time, acceleration is the rate of change of velocity with respect to time.

$$\frac{dx}{dt} = \mathrm{v}\,; \quad \frac{d\mathrm{v}}{dt} = \mathrm{a}$$

From this, the following basic kinematic equations of motion can be derived:

1. $v = v_0 + at$

2. $v^2 = v_0^2 + 2a(x - x_0)$

3. $x = x_0 + v_0 t + {}^1/_2\, at^2$

4. $x = x_0 + {}^1/_2\,(v_0 + v)\mathrm{t}$

where v_0 and x_0 are initial values.

C. TWO-DIMENSIONAL MOTION

For two-dimensional, or planar, motion, simply break the velocity and acceleration vectors down into their x and y components. Once this is done, the preceding one-dimensional equations can apply.

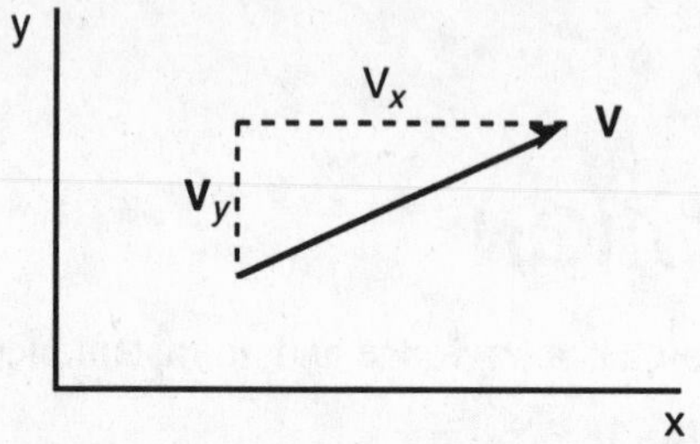

A special case of two-dimensional motion is **Uniform Circular Motion**. For a particle to be held on a circular path, a radial force must be applied. This acceleration is called **centripetal acceleration.**

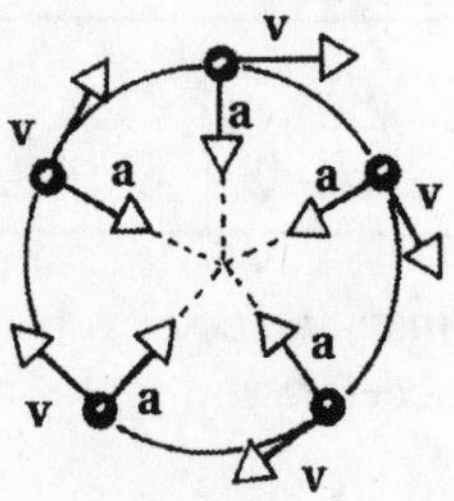

Centripetal Acceleration

$$\mathbf{a} = \frac{v^2}{r}$$

where a = Acceleration
v = Tangential Component of Velocity
r = Radius of the Path

For uniform circular motion, a can also be written as

$$\mathbf{a} = \frac{4\pi^2 r}{T^2}$$

where T, the period or time for one revolution, is given by

$$T = \frac{2\pi r}{v}$$

The tangential component of the acceleration is the rate at which the particle speed changes; for uniform circular motion this acceleration is zero.

When dealing with circular motion or other situations involving motion relative to a central force field, it is often appropriate to use polar coordinates, where the position is a function of radius and angle (r, θ).

In the case of three dimensions, the coordinates become (r, θ, z), where the z-coordinate is identical to the respective cartesian z-coordinate. This is known as the cylindrical coordinate system.

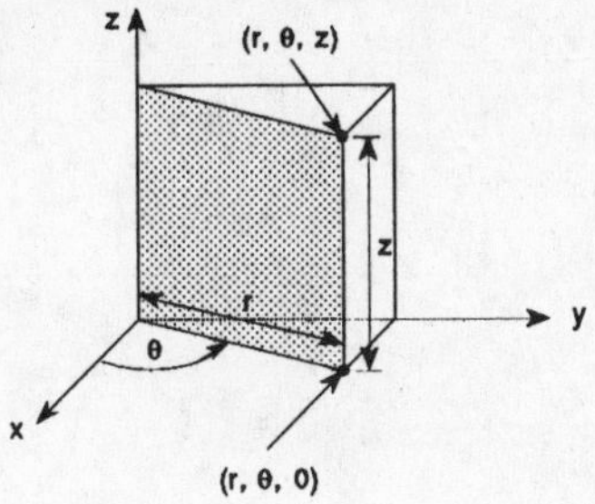

In describing two-dimensional motion, α represents angular acceleration

$$\left(\frac{d\,\omega}{dt}\right)$$

and ω represents angular velocity

$$\left(\frac{d\,\theta}{dt}\right)$$

If angular acceleration, α, is constant, then equations correlating to those previously stated for linear motion can be shown to apply as given in the table below.

Comparison of Rotational and Linear Motion Equations

Rotational Motion	Linear Motion Equivalent
$\alpha = \text{constant}$	$a = \text{constant}$
$\omega = \omega_0 + \alpha t$	$v = v_0 + at$
$\theta = \dfrac{\omega_0 + \omega}{2}\, t$	$x = \dfrac{v_0 + v}{2}\, t$
$\theta = \omega_0 t + {}^1/_2\, \alpha t^2$	$x = v_0 t + {}^1/_2 a t^2$
$\omega^2 = \omega_0^2 + 2\,\alpha\theta$	$v^2 = v_0^2 + 2ax$
θ_0, θ = initial and final angular displacements	
ω_0, ω = initial and final angular velocities.	

Another type of coordinate system used is the spherical coordinate system, with components (ρ, ϕ, θ).

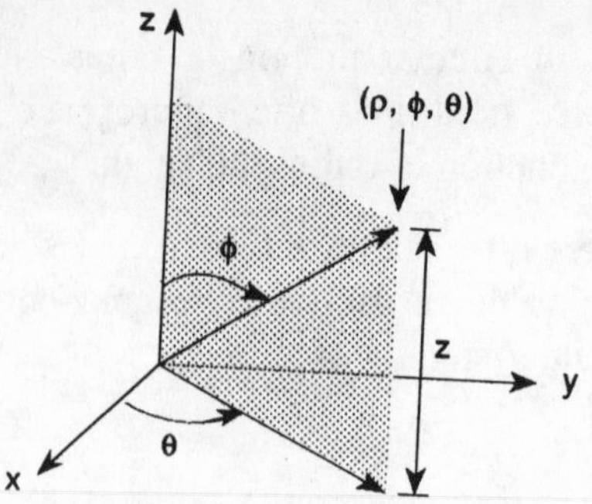

$r = \rho \sin \phi$ $\quad$ $x = r \cos \theta$ $\quad$ $x = \rho \sin \phi \cos \theta$

$z = \rho \cos \phi$ $\quad$ $y = r \sin \theta$ $\quad$ $y = \rho \sin \phi \sin \theta$

$\theta = \theta$ $\quad$ $z = z$ $\quad$ $z = \rho \cos \phi$

D. NEWTON'S LAWS

First Law

Every body remains in its state of rest or uniform linear motion, unless a force is applied to change that state.

Second Law

If the vector sum of the forces **F** acting on a particle of mass *m* is different from zero, then the particle will have an acceleration, **a**, directly proportional to, and in the same direction as, **F**, but inversely proportional to mass *m*. Symbolically

$$\mathbf{F} = m\mathbf{a}$$

Units: Newtons = $^{kgm}/_{s^2}$

(If mass is constant)

Third Law

For every action, there exists a corresponding equal and opposing reaction, or the mutual actions of two bodies are always equal and opposing.

Newton's Laws all refer to the effects of forces on particles or bodies. These forces are often represented with vectors and can be added/subtracted vectorially. In addition, certain mathematical operations can be used on vectors to obtain components, unit vectors, directional cosines, and resultants.

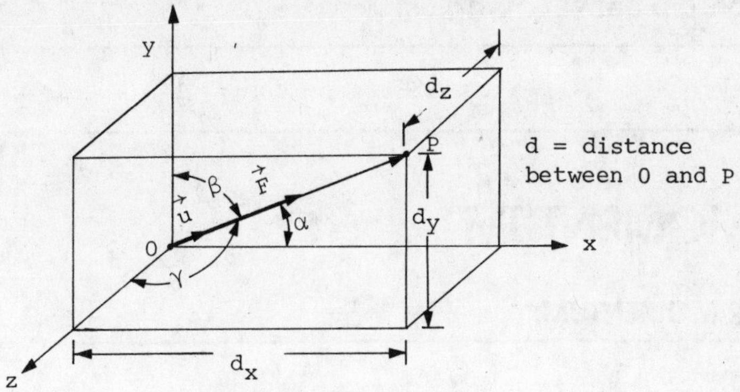

$$\mathbf{OP} = d_x\mathbf{x} + d_y\mathbf{y} + d_z\mathbf{z}$$

Unit Vector:

$$\mathbf{u} = \frac{\mathbf{OP}}{OP} = \frac{1}{d}\left(d_x\mathbf{x} + d_y\mathbf{y} + d_z\mathbf{z}\right)$$

Force F:

$$\mathbf{F} = F\mathbf{u} = \frac{F}{d}\left(d_x\mathbf{x} + d_y\mathbf{y} + d_z\mathbf{z}\right)$$

Components:

$$F_x = \frac{Fd_x}{d}, \quad F_y = \frac{Fd_y}{d}, \quad F_z = \frac{Fd_z}{d}$$

Distance:

$$d = \sqrt{d_x^{\,2} + d_y^{\,2} + d_z^{\,2}}$$

Directional Cosines of F:

$$\alpha = \cos^{-1}\frac{d_x}{d}$$

$$\beta = \cos^{-1}\frac{d_y}{d}$$

$$\gamma = \cos^{-1}\frac{d_z}{d}$$

Unit Vector Expressed in Terms of Angles:

$$\mathbf{u} = \cos\alpha\,\mathbf{x} + \cos\beta\,\mathbf{y} + \cos\gamma\,\mathbf{z}$$

Relationship Between Angles:

$$\cos^2\alpha + \cos^2\beta + \cos^2\gamma = 1$$

E. MOMENTUM

LINEAR MOMENTUM:

$$p = mv \qquad \text{units: } \frac{\text{kg}\cdot\text{m}}{\text{sec}}$$

where p = linear momentum of particle
m = mass of particle
v = velocity of particle

NEWTON'S SECOND LAW

$$\mathbf{F} = \frac{d\mathbf{p}}{dt} = \frac{d(m\mathbf{v})}{dt}$$

where $\mathbf{F}$ = the net force on the particle.

LINEAR MOMENTUM OF A SYSTEM OF PARTICLES

Total Linear Momentum

$$\begin{aligned} P &= \sum_{i=1}^{n} p_i = p_1 + p_2 + \ldots + p_n \\ &= m_1 v_1 + m_2 v_2 + \ldots + m_n v_n \end{aligned}$$

where $\mathbf{P}$ = total linear momentum of system
$\mathbf{p}_i$, m_i, $\mathbf{v}_i$, = linear momentum, mass, and velocity of ith particle, respectively.

Newton's Second Law for a System of Particles (Momentum Form).

$$\mathbf{F}_{\text{ext}} = \frac{d\mathbf{P}}{dt}$$

where $\mathbf{F}_{\text{ext}}$ = sum of all external forces

Momentum is conserved. The total linear momentum of the system remains unchanged if the *sum* of all forces acting on the system is zero.

According to Newton's 2nd Law:

$$\frac{d\mathbf{P}}{dt} = \sum F_{ext} = 0$$

ANGULAR MOMENTUM:

Vector Equation

$$\mathbf{L} = \mathbf{r} \times \mathbf{P} = \mathbf{I}\omega \qquad \text{Units: } {kgm^2}/{s}$$

Scalar Equation

$$l = rP \sin\theta$$

where
- $\mathbf{L}$ = Angular momentum
- $\mathbf{r}$ = Radius vector from axis of rotation to $\mathbf{p}$
- $\mathbf{p}$ = Linear momentum vector
- $\mathbf{I}$ = Moment of inertia about axis of rotation
- ω = Angular velocity

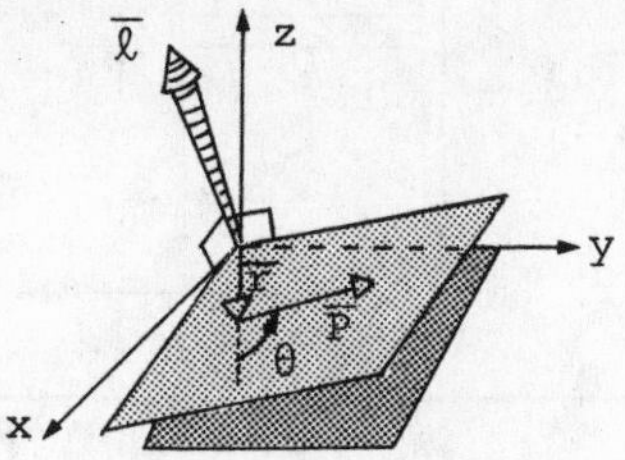

Angular Momentum

Note that these two equations are equivalent with producing a vector result that is perpendicular to the plane formed by **r** and **p**, as shown in the figure. Using cross-product form, the magnitude is found by

$$L = rp \sin\theta$$

with the direction and sense given by the right-hand rule.

For the second form, the same result is achieved with

$$L = I\omega$$

where I is the moment of inertia about any selected axis of rotation and is defined by

$$I = \int r^2 dm$$

and is a measure of rotational inertia.

Torque

Torque can be defined as

$$\tau = \mathbf{r} \times \mathbf{F} \qquad \text{Units: Nm}$$

and is a vector with magnitude given by cross-product operation and direction/sense as determined by the right-hand rule. An equivalent form is

$$\tau = {}^{d\mathbf{L}}\!/_{dt}$$

Determination of I:

Integration Method

Area — General Formula:

$$I = \int_A s^2 \, dA$$

where s = Perpendicular distance from the axis to the area element.

EXAMPLE:

For a Rectangular Area

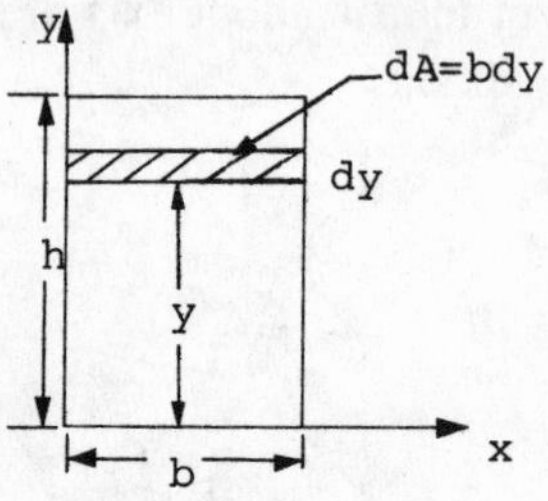

$$I_x = \int_0^h by^2 \, dy = \frac{1}{3} bh^3$$

This is the moment of inertia with respect to an axis passing through the base of the rectangle.

Moments of Inertia of Masses:

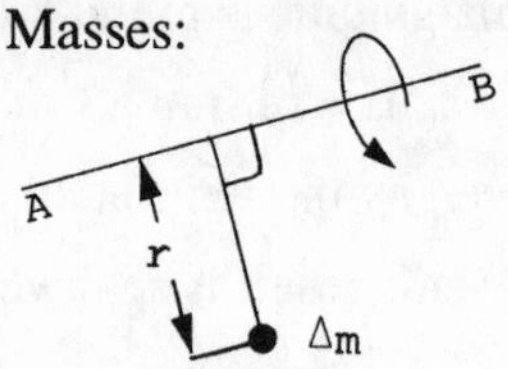

$$I = \int r^2 \, dm$$

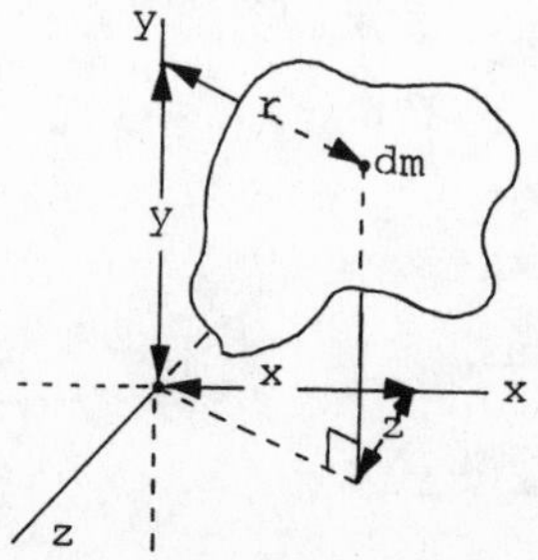

In Polar Coordinates, the polar moment of Inertia is noted as J.

Polar Moment of Inertia:

$$J_0 = \int r^2 \, dA$$

In terms of rectangular moments of inertia:

$$J_0 = I_x + I_y$$

The Radius of Gyration can be determined once the moment of Inertia and the Area are known.

$$I_x = k_x^2 A; \quad I_y = k_y^2 A$$

Rectangular component form:

$$k_x = \sqrt{\frac{I_x}{A}}$$

$$k_y = \sqrt{\frac{I_y}{A}}$$

Polar form:

$$k_0 = \sqrt{\frac{J_0}{A}}$$

Relation between rectangular component form and polar form:

$$k_0^2 = k_x^2 + k_y^2$$

Masses

$$I = k^2 m$$

$$k = \sqrt{\frac{I}{m}}$$

Impulse and Momentum

Impulse-Momentum Method — An alternate method to solving problems in which forces are expressed as a function of time. It is applicable to situations wherein forces act over a small interval of time.

Linear Impulse-Momentum Equation:

$$\int_1^2 \mathbf{F}\, dt = \text{impulse} = m\mathbf{v}_2 - m\mathbf{v}_1$$

Ideal impulse produces an instantaneous change in momentum and velocity of the particle without producing any displacement.

$$M\mathbf{v}_1 + \Sigma\mathbf{F}\,\Delta t = M\mathbf{v}_2$$

Any force which is non-impulsive may be neglected, e.g., weight, or small forces.

F. ENERGY AND WORK

The work done by a force **F** through a displacement $d\mathbf{r}$ is defined:

$$dw \equiv \mathbf{F}\cdot d\mathbf{r} \text{ in Joules. (SI units)}$$

Over a finite distance from point 1 to point 2:

$$W_{1-2} = \int_1^2 \mathbf{F}\cdot d\mathbf{r}$$

Work-Energy Principle

Kinetic energy for a particle of mass M and velocity v is defined as

$$\text{K.E.} = \frac{1}{2}mv^2$$

Kinetic energy is the energy possessed by a particle by virtue of its motion.

Principle of Work and Energy — Given that a particle undergoes a displacement under the influence of a force **F**, the work done by **F** equals the change in kinetic energy of the particle.

$$W_{1-2} = (\text{KE})_2 - (\text{KE})_1$$

Results of the Principle of Work and Energy:

A) Acceleration is not necessary and may not be obtained directly by this principle.

B) The principle may be applied to a system of particles if each particle is considered separately.

C) Those forces that do not contribute work are eliminated.

Kinetic Energy and Newton's Law:

$$F = mv\,\frac{dv}{dx} = \frac{d}{dx}\,(\mathrm{KE})\,,$$

where KE = a function of x.

(This applies only in an inertial reference frame.)

Power and Efficiency

Power is defined as the time-rate of change of work and is denoted by dw / dt,

$$\text{Power} = \frac{dw}{dt} = \mathbf{F} \cdot \mathbf{v}$$

Mechanical Efficiency:

$$\eta = \frac{\text{Power out}}{\text{Power in}}$$

NOTE: η is *always* < 1.

Potential Energy

Potential Energy ≡ The stored energy of a body or particle in a force field associated with its position from a reference frame.

If PE represents potential energy,

$$PE = mgh$$

$$U_{2-1} = (PE)_1 - (PE)_2$$

A negative value would indicate an increase in Potential Energy.

Types of Potential Energy include:

Gravitational Potential Energy:

$$\mathrm{PE}_g = -\,G\,\frac{M_1 M_2}{r}$$

Spring Potential Energy:

$$\mathrm{PE} = \frac{1}{2}\,ky^2$$

Conservation of Energy

Conservative Case

For a particle under the action of conservative forces:

$$(KE)_1 + (PE)_1 = (KE)_2 + (PE)_2 = E \qquad (1)$$

The sum of kinetic and potential energy at a given point is constant.

Equation (1) can be written as:

$$E = \frac{1}{2}mv^2 + (\text{PE})$$

The Potential Energy must be less than or equal to the Total Energy.

In a conservative system, if $PE = E$, then velocity = *0*.

In a non-conservative system, relating potential and kinetic energy with the non-conservative force $\mathbf{F}'$

$$d(\text{PE} + \text{KE}) = \int \mathbf{F}' \cdot d\mathbf{r}$$

1) The direction of $\mathbf{F}'$ is opposite to that of $d\mathbf{r}$.

2) Total energy E decreases with motion.

3) Friction forces are nonconservative.

G. HARMONIC MOTION

Simple Harmonic Motion — Linear motion of a body where the acceleration is proportional to the displacement from a fixed origin and is always directed towards the origin. The direction of acceleration is always opposite to that of the displacement.

Equation of motion

$$mx'' + kx = 0$$

or

$$x'' + p^2x = 0 \qquad (2)$$

where $p^2 = k/m$.

General Solution of Equation (2)

$$x = c_1 \sin pt + c_2 \cos pt$$

where c_1 and c_2 may be obtained from initial conditions.

An alternate form of Equation (2)

$$x = x_m \sin(pt + \phi)$$

where x_m = the amplitude, and
ϕ = the phase angle.

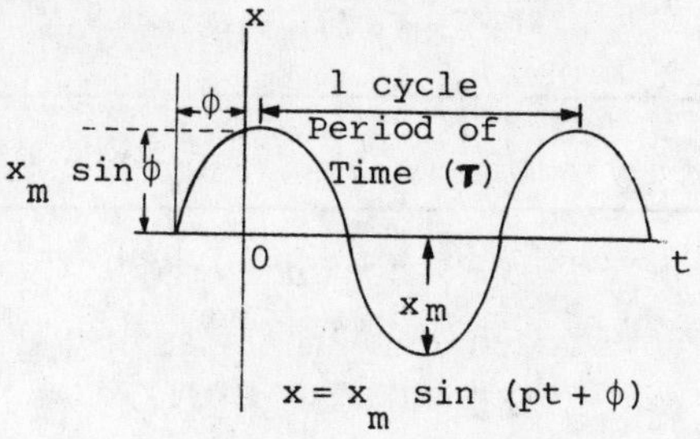

Period = T = $2\pi / \omega$
Frequency, $f = 1 / T = \omega / 2\pi$

For small angles of vibration, the motion of a simple pendulum can be approximated by simple harmonic motion.

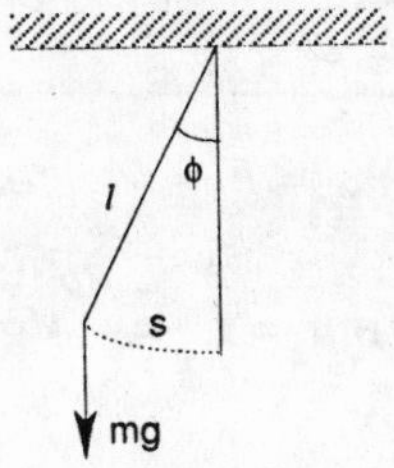

For small angles of vibration,

$$\phi = s / l$$

Equation of Motion:

$$\phi'' + \frac{g}{l}\phi = 0$$

The solution is:

$$\phi = \phi_0 \cos(\omega_0 t + \alpha_0)$$

where $\omega_0 = \sqrt{g/l}$

ϕ_0 = max amplitude of oscillation
α_0 = phase factor

The period of oscillation is:

$$T_0 = \frac{2\pi}{\omega_0} = 2\pi\sqrt{\frac{l}{g}}$$

The Spherical Pendulum refers to the simple pendulum-like arrangement, but with motion in 3-dimensions.

The equations of motion become:

$$x'' + (g / l)x = 0$$

$$y'' + (g / l)y = 0$$

with solutions:

$$x = A \cos(\omega t + r)$$

$$y = B \cos(\omega t + \delta)$$

where $\omega = \sqrt{g/l}$

On the x–y plane, the motion is an ellipse.

Spherical Coordinates — More accurate than the previous solution.

Equations of Motion:

$$ma_r = F_r = Mg \cos\theta - T$$

$$ma_\phi = F_\phi = -Mg \sin\phi$$

$$ma_{\phi\theta} = F_{\phi\theta} = 0$$

In spherical coordinates:

$$\phi'' - \psi'^2 \sin\phi \cos\phi + g \sin\phi = 0$$

$$\frac{1}{\sin\phi}\frac{d}{dt}(\alpha' \sin^2\phi) = 0$$

Forced (Driven) Harmonic Oscillator.

For periodic driving force:

Equation of Motion:

$$\frac{d^2x}{dt^2} = -\omega^2 x + \frac{F_0}{m}\cos\omega_f t$$

where ω_f = driving frequency
F_0 = max. magnitude of the driving force.

The solution will be equal to the sum of the complementary solution and the particular solution.

$$X = \underbrace{A\cos\omega t + B\sin\omega t}_{X_c} + \underbrace{\frac{F_o / m}{\omega^2 - \omega_f^{\,2}}\cos\omega_f t}_{X_p}$$

Resonance occurs when $\omega_f \approx \omega$.

Damped Oscillator.

A common damping force is

$$\mathbf{F} = c\frac{dx}{dt}$$

If an object's motion is damped in this manner, then the equation of motion is:

$$m\frac{d^2x}{dt^2} + c\frac{dx}{dt} + kx = 0$$

$$a_1 = \frac{-c}{2m} - \sqrt{\left(\frac{c}{2m}\right)^2 - \frac{k}{m}}$$

$$a_2 = \frac{-c}{2m} + \sqrt{\left(\frac{c}{2m}\right)^2 - \frac{k}{m}}$$

The critical damping coefficient is defined as

$$C_{\text{critical}} = 2m\sqrt{\frac{k}{m}}$$

Now, three cases must be considered with respect to C_{critical}:

A) If $c > C_{\text{critical}}$, a_1 and a_2 are both real, the motion is nonoscillating, and the system is overdamped. The general solution is given by

$$x = Ae^{a_1 t} + Be^{a_2 t}$$

B) If $c = C_{\text{critical}}$, $a_1 = a_2$ and the system is critically damped with general solution:

$$x = (A + Bt)e^{-\left(\frac{C_{\text{critical}}}{2m}\right)t}$$

C) If $c < C_{\text{critical}}$ a_1 and a_2 are complex and imaginary and the system is underdamped with the solution given by:

$$X = E\left[e^{-(c/2m)t}\sin\left(\sqrt{\frac{k}{m}-\left(\frac{C}{2m}\right)^2}\,t+\psi\right)\right]$$

where constants A, B, E and ψ are determined from initial conditions. The graph representing the above equation is shown in the following figure.

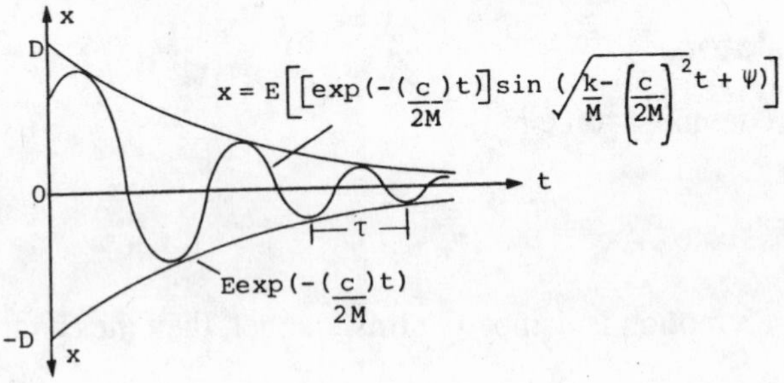

Damped Force (Driven) Vibration.

The equation of motion becomes:

$$m\frac{d^2x}{dt^2}+c\frac{dx}{dt}+kx = F\sin\omega t$$

Assuming $X_p = A\sin(\omega t-\psi)$

$$A = \frac{F/k}{\sqrt{\left[1-\frac{4m^2\omega^2}{C^2_{\text{critical}}}\right]^2+\left[\frac{4m\omega C}{C^2_{\text{critical}}}\right]^2}}$$

$$\psi = \tan^{-1}\left[\frac{c\omega/k}{\left(1-\frac{m\omega^2}{k}\right)}\right]$$

NOTE: Angle ψ is the phase difference between the resulting steady-state vibration and the applied force.

The magnification factor is defined as:

$$\text{Magnification factor} = \frac{A}{F/k} = \frac{1}{\sqrt{\left[1-\frac{4m^2\omega^2}{C^2_{\text{critical}}}\right]^2+\left[\frac{4m\omega c}{C^2_{\text{critical}}}\right]^2}}$$

and the graph is shown in the following figure. Resonance occurs only when the damping is zero and the frequency ratio is one.

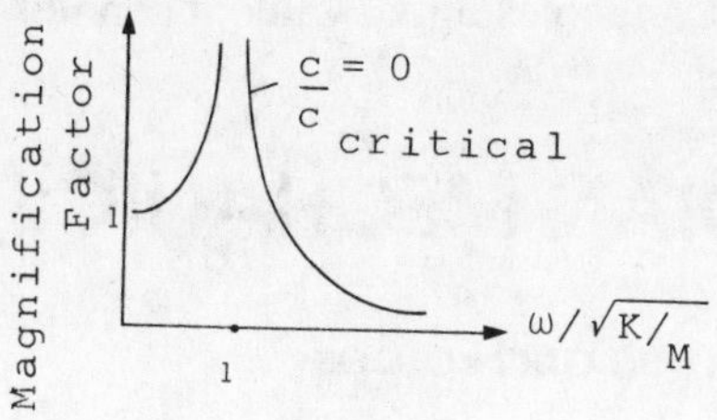

H. COLLISIONS

When kinetic energy, is conserved, the collision is **Elastic**. Otherwise, the collision is said to be **Inelastic.**

A) For an Elastic collision,

$$\frac{1}{2}m_1v_{1_i}^2+\frac{1}{2}m_2v_{2_i}^2=\frac{1}{2}m_1v_{1_f}^2+\frac{1}{2}m_2v_{2_f}^2$$

B) For an inelastic collision, some kinetic energy is transformed into internal energy. However, linear momentum is still conserved. If the two bodies stick and travel together with a common final velocity after collision, it is said to be completely inelastic. From conservation of momentum, we have

$$m_1v_{1_i}+m_2v_{2_i}=(m_1+m_2)v_f$$

Collisions in Two and Three Dimensions

Since momentum is linearly conserved, the resultant components must be found and then the conservation laws applied in each direction.

A) The x–component

$$m_1v_{1_i}=m_1v_{1_f}\cos\theta_1+m_2v_{2_f}\cos\theta_2 \qquad \text{(i)}$$

B) The y–component

$$m_2v_{2_i}=m_1v_{1_f}\sin\theta_1+m_2v_{2_f}\sin\theta_2 \qquad \text{(i)}$$

where θ_1 = the angle of deflection, after the collision, of mass m_1.
θ_2 = the angle of deflection, after the collision, of mass m_2.

C) For three dimensions, there would be an added z–component and an added angle, θ_3.

For the above cases, i denotes initial value; f denotes final value.

I. LAGRANGIAN MECHANICS

Generalized Coordinates and Forces

The position of a particle is described by employing the concept of a coordinate system. Given, for example, a coordinate system such as the spherical or the oblate spherical coordinates, etc., a particle in space may be characterized as an ordered triple of numbers called coordinates.

A constrained particle in motion on a surface requires two coordinates, and a constrained particle on a curve, requires one coordinate to characterize its location.

Given a system of m particles, 3M coordinates are required to describe the location of each particle. This is the configuration of the system. (If constraints are imposed on the system, fewer coordinates are required.)

A rigid body requires six coordinates — three for orientation and three for the reference point, to completely locate its position.

Generalized coordinates — A set of coordiantes, $q_1, q_2, \ldots, q_m$, equal to the number of degrees of freedom of the system.

If each q_i is independent of the others, then it is known as holonomic.

The rectangular coordinates for a particle expressed in generalized coordinates:

$x = x(q)$	Motion on a curve (one degree of freedom),
$x = x(q_1, q_2)$ $y = y(q_1, q_2)$	Motion on a surface (two degrees of freedom),
$x = x(q_1, q_2, q_3)$ $y = y(q_1, q_2, q_3)$ $z = z(q_1, q_2, q_3)$	Spatial motion (three degrees of freedom).

Small Changes in Coordinates:

$$\delta x = \frac{\partial x}{\partial q_1}\delta q_1 + \frac{\partial x}{\partial q_2}\delta q_2 + \frac{\partial x}{\partial q_3}\delta q_3$$

$$\delta y = \frac{\partial y}{\partial q_1}\delta q_1 + \frac{\partial y}{\partial q_2}\delta q_2 + \frac{\partial y}{\partial q_3}\delta q_3$$

$$\delta z = \frac{\partial z}{\partial q_1}\delta q_1 + \frac{\partial z}{\partial q_2}\delta q_2 + \frac{\partial z}{\partial q_3}\delta q_3$$

For a system of m particles in generalized coordinates:

$$\delta x_i = \frac{\partial x_i}{\partial q_k}\delta q_k \qquad k = 1, 2, \ldots, m \quad 1 < i < m$$

$$\delta y_i = \frac{\partial y_i}{\partial q_k}\delta q_k \qquad k = 1, 2, \ldots, m \quad 1 < i < m$$

$$\delta z_i = \frac{\partial z_i}{\partial q_k}\delta q_k \qquad k = 1, 2, \ldots, m \quad 1 < i < m$$

expressed in tensor notation.

Generalized Forces:

Work done $\qquad \delta w = \mathbf{F} \cdot \delta \mathbf{r} = F_i \cdot \delta x_i$

For one particle, $\qquad 1 < i < 3$

and for m particles, $\qquad 1 < i < 3m$

In terms of generalized coordinates:

$$\delta w = F_i \frac{\partial x_i}{\partial q_k}\delta q_k$$

or

$$\delta w = Q_k \delta q_k, \quad \text{where } Q_k = F_i \frac{\partial x_i}{\partial q_k}$$

and is known as the generalized force.

Conservative Systems

Forces expressed in terms of the potential energy function:

$$F_i = \frac{-\partial v}{\partial x_i},$$

where v is the potential energy.

In terms of the generalized force,

$$Q_k = -\frac{\partial v}{\partial x_i}\frac{\partial x_i}{\partial q_k} = -\frac{\partial v}{\partial q_k}$$

LAGRANGE'S EQUATION

For a system, kinetic energy KE is

$$T = \text{KE} = \frac{1}{2} m_i x'^{2}_i \qquad i = 1, 2, \ldots, 3M$$

where $$x'_1 = \frac{\partial x_i}{\partial q_k} q'_k + \frac{\partial x_i}{\partial t} \qquad k = 1, 2, \ldots, M$$

The Lagrange equation of motion using the equations above is:

$$\frac{d}{dt}\left(\frac{\partial T}{\partial q'_k}\right) = Q_k + \frac{\partial T}{\partial q_k} \qquad k = 1, 2, \ldots, M$$

or if the motion is conservative and if the potential energy is a function of generalized coordinates, then the equation becomes

$$\frac{d}{dt}\left(\frac{\partial T}{\partial q'_k}\right) = \frac{\partial T}{\partial q_k} - \frac{\partial v}{\partial q_k} \qquad k = 1, 2, \ldots, M$$

Lagrange's Function (*L*)

$L = T - V$ where T and V are in terms of generalized coordinates.

Lagrange's Equation in Terms of L

$$\frac{d}{dt}\left(\frac{\partial L}{\partial q'_k}\right) = \frac{\partial L}{\partial q_k} \qquad k = 1, 2, \ldots, M$$

Lagrange's equation for non-conservative generalized forces:

If $$Q_k = Q' - \frac{\partial v}{\partial q_k},$$

where Q' is non-conservative, then Lagrange's equation becomes

$$\frac{d}{dt}\frac{\partial L}{\partial q'_k} = Q'_k + \frac{\partial L}{\partial q_k},$$

and is useful, for example, when frictional forces are present.

General Procedure for Obtaining the Equation of Motion:

A) Choose a coordinate system.

B) Write the kinetic energy equation as a function of these coordinates.

C) Find the potential energy, if the system is conservative.

D) Combining these terms in Lagrange's equation results in the equation of motion.

Lagrange's Equations with Constraints

Holonomic Constraint — Constraints of the form

$$\frac{\partial q}{\partial q_k}\,\delta q = 0$$

Non-holonomic Constraint — Constraints of the form

$$h_k\,\delta\,q_k = 0$$

Differential equations of motion by the method of undetermined multipliers: (The Non-Holonomic Case)

Multiply the equation by a constant λ and add the result to the integrand of

$$\int_{t_a}^{t_b}\left[\frac{\partial L}{\partial q_k}-\frac{d}{dt}\frac{\partial L}{\partial q'_k}\right]\delta q_k\,dt = 0$$

Select λ such that the terms in brackets equals zero,

$$\frac{\partial L}{\partial q_k}-\frac{d}{dt}\frac{\partial L}{\partial q'_k}+\lambda h_k = 0 \quad (k = 1, 2, \ldots, m)$$

$$h_k q'_k = 0$$

There now exist $m + 1$ equations to obtain $m + 1$ unknowns, i.e., $(q_1, q_2, \ldots, q_n, \lambda$.

This technique may be employed with moving constraints or with several constraints by having corresponding undetermined coefficients with corresponding h's in the Lagrangian equations.

CHAPTER 2

ELECTROMAGNETISM

A. ELECTRIC FIELDS

Definition of an Electric Field

$$\mathbf{E} = \frac{\mathbf{F}}{q_0} \qquad \text{Units: } {}^{\text{N}}\!/_{\text{coul}}$$

where $\mathbf{E}$ = Electric Field
$\mathbf{F}$ = Electric Force
q_o = Positive Test Charge

1. COULOMB'S LAW

By definition, the force between two point charges of arbitrary positive or negative strengths is given by the Coulomb's law as follows:

$$F = \frac{Q_1 Q_2}{4\pi \varepsilon_0 d^2}$$

where
Q_1 and Q_2 = positive or negative charges on either object in coulombs.
d = distance separating the two point charges.
ε_0 = permittivity in free space
= 8.854×10^{-12} F/m

NOTE: $\varepsilon = \varepsilon_0 \varepsilon_r$ for media other than free space, where ε_r is the relative permittivity of the media.

The force F can be expressed in vector form to indicate its direction as follows:

$$\mathbf{F} = \frac{Q_1 Q_2}{4\pi\varepsilon_0 d^2}\, \mathbf{a}_d$$

The unit vector $\mathbf{a}_d$ is in the direction of d

$$\mathbf{a}_d = \frac{\mathbf{d}}{|\mathbf{d}|} = \frac{\mathbf{d}}{d}$$

Naturally, Q_1 and Q_2 can each be either positive or negative. As a consquence of this, the resultant force can be either positive (repulsive) or negative (attractive).

2. GAUSS'S LAW

Gauss's law states that the net electric flux passing out of a closed surface is equal to the total charge within such surface.

Hence, since

$$d\psi = \mathbf{D} \cdot d\mathbf{s}$$

$$\psi = \int \mathbf{D} \cdot d\mathbf{s}$$

and by Gauss's law,

$$\psi_{\text{net}} = \oint_s \mathbf{D} \cdot d\mathbf{s} = Q_s$$

where Q_s is the total number of charges enclosed by the surface.

Application of Gauss's Law

The following spherical surface is **chosen** to enclose a given charge to be determined: Q_S

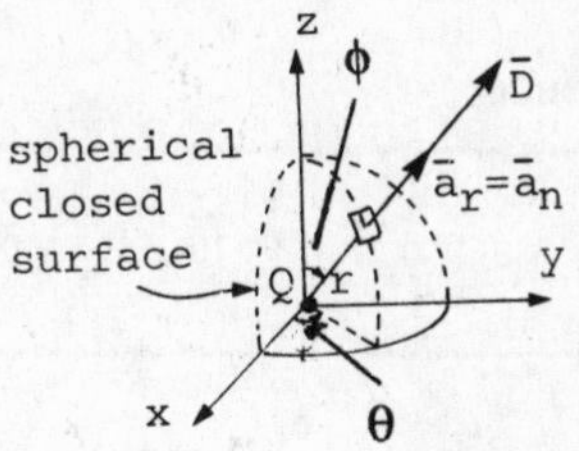

Applying Gauss's law:

The charge Q_S enclosed by the spherical surface is

$$Q_s = \oint_s \mathbf{D} \cdot \mathbf{ds}$$

where ds in this case is equal to $4\pi r^2$ (**NOTE**: r is the radius of the sphere). Hence,

$$Q_S = D4\pi\, r^2$$

and

$$\mathbf{D} = \frac{Q_s}{4\pi r^2} \cdot \mathbf{a}_r$$

Since electric field intensity **E** is equal to

$$\frac{Q}{4\pi\varepsilon_0 d^2}\, a_d$$

and d is equal to r in this case, then $\mathbf{D} = \varepsilon_0\mathbf{E}$.

Some hints for choosing a special Gaussian surface:

A) The surface must be closed.

B) D remains constant through the surface and normal to the surface.

C) D is either tangential or normal to the surface at any point on the surface.

It is easier in solving a problem if we can choose a special Gaussian surface. In other words, this surface should be chosen to conform to the flux at any given point on the closed surface about the charge.

3. ELECTRIC POTENTIAL, ENERGY AND WORK

Electric Potential Difference

$$V_B - V_A = \frac{W_{AB}}{q_0} \quad \rightarrow \text{units: Volts}$$

where
V_B = Electric Potential at Point B
V_A = Electric Potential at Point A
W_{AB} = Work Done by External Force
q_0 = Electrical Test Charge

More generally:

The potential difference between two points p and p', symbolized as $V_{p'p}$ (or $\phi p'p$) is defined as the work done in moving a unit positive charge by an external force from the initial point p to the final point p'.

$$V_{p'p} = -\int_{p}^{p'} \mathbf{E} \cdot d\mathbf{L} = V_{p'} - V_p$$

The unit for potential difference is the Volt (V) which is Joules/coulomb.

B. CAPACITORS

The Capacitance of two oppositely charged conductors in a uniform dielectric medium is

$$C = \frac{Q}{V_0} \qquad \text{Units: Farads} = \text{coul}/v$$

where Q = the total charge in *either* conductor.
V_0 = the potential difference between the two conductors.

EXAMPLE:

Capacitance of the parallel-plate capacitor:

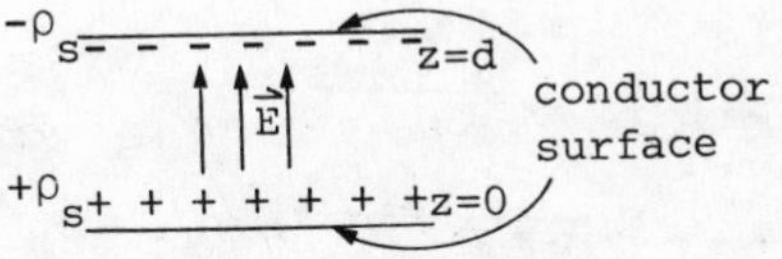

$$\mathbf{E} = \frac{\rho_s}{\varepsilon} \mathbf{a}_z$$

ε is the permittivity of the homogeneous dielectric

$$\mathbf{D} = \rho_s \cdot \mathbf{a}_z$$

On lower plate:

$$D_n = D_z = \rho_s$$

D_n is the normal value of **D**.

On upper plate:

$$D_n = -D_z$$

V_0 = The potential difference

$$= -\int_{\text{upper}}^{\text{lower}} \mathbf{E} \cdot d\mathbf{L}$$

$$= -\int_d^0 \frac{\rho_s}{\varepsilon}\, d_z = \frac{\rho_s d}{\varepsilon}$$

$$C = \frac{Q}{V_0} = \frac{\varepsilon s}{d}$$

$$Q = \rho_s S \text{ and } V_0 = \frac{\rho_s d}{\varepsilon}$$

considering conductor planes of area S are of linear dimensions much greater than d.

Total energy stored in the capacitor:

$$W_E = \frac{1}{2}\int_{\text{vol}} \varepsilon E^2\, dv = \frac{1}{2}\int_0^S\int_0^d \frac{\varepsilon\rho_s}{\varepsilon^2}\, dz\, ds$$

$$W_E = \frac{1}{2} CV_0^2 = \frac{1}{2} QV_0 = \frac{1}{2}\frac{Q^2}{C}$$

Multiple dielectric capacitors

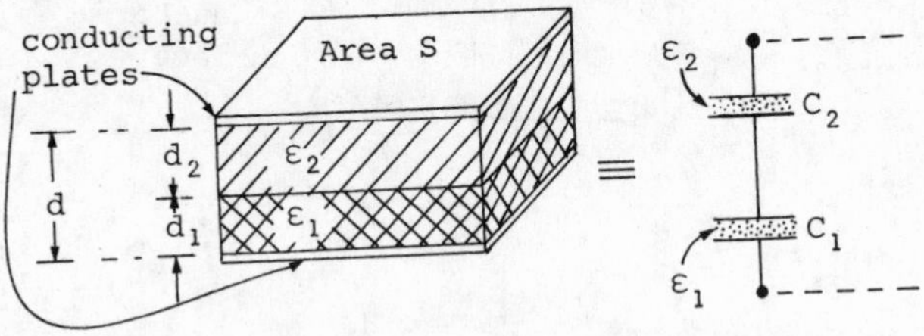

A parallel-plate capacitor containing two dielectrics with the dielectric interface parallel to the conducting plates; $C = 1/\{ (d_1/\varepsilon_1 S) + (d_2/\varepsilon_2 S) \}$.

$$C = \frac{1}{\left(\frac{1}{C_1}\right) + \left(\frac{1}{C_2}\right)}$$

where $\quad C_1 = \dfrac{\varepsilon_1 S}{d_1}$

$$C_2 = \frac{\varepsilon_2 S}{d_2}$$

V_o = A potential difference between the plates

$= E_1 d_1 + E_2 d_2$

$$E_1 = \frac{V_0}{d_1} + \left(\frac{\varepsilon_1}{\varepsilon_2}\right) d_2$$

ρ_{s_1} = The surface charge density $= D_1 = \varepsilon_1 E_1$

$$= \frac{V_0}{\left(\frac{d_1}{\varepsilon_1}\right) + \left(\frac{d_2}{\varepsilon_2}\right)} = D_2$$

$$C = \frac{Q}{V_0} = \frac{\rho_s \cdot S}{V_0} = \frac{1}{\left(\frac{d_1}{\varepsilon_1 s}\right) + \left(\frac{d_2}{\varepsilon_2 s}\right)} = \frac{1}{\left(\frac{1}{C_1}\right) + \left(\frac{1}{C_2}\right)}$$

C. CURRENT AND RESISTANCE

DEFINITIONS

Current:

$$i = \frac{dq}{dt} \text{ amperes}$$

where i = Electric Current
q = Net Charge
t = Time

Current Density and Current:

$$\mathbf{j} = \frac{i}{A} \text{ Amperes/ m}^2$$

where $\mathbf{j}$ = Current Density
i = Current
A = Cross-sectional Area.

Mean Drift Speed:

$$\mathbf{v}_D = \frac{\mathbf{j}}{ne}$$

where v_0 = Mean Drift Speed
$\mathbf{j}$ = Current Density
n = Number of atoms per unit volume.

Resistance:

$$R = \frac{V}{i} \quad \text{Ohms } (\Omega)$$

where R = Resistance
V = Potential Difference
i = Current

Resistivity:

$$\rho = \frac{E}{\mathbf{j}} \quad \text{Ohm–meters } (\Omega\,\text{m})$$

where ρ = Resistivity
E = Electric Field
$\mathbf{j}$ = Current Density

Power:

$$P = VI = I^2 R = \frac{V^2}{R} \quad \text{Watts (w)}$$

where P = Power
I = Current
V = Potential Difference
R = Resistance

D. CIRCUITS

Electromotive Force, *EMF*(ε)

$$\varepsilon = \frac{dw}{dq}$$

where ε = Electromotive Force
w = Work Done on Charge
q = Electric Charge

Current in a Simple Circuit

$$i = \frac{\varepsilon}{R}$$

where i = Current
ε = Electromotive Force
R = Resistance

Resistances:

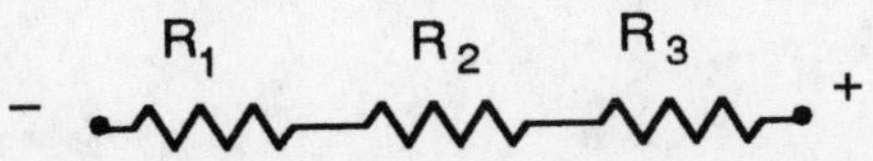

$$R_{\text{Total}} = (R_1 + R_2 + R_3)\ \Omega \text{ (in series)}$$

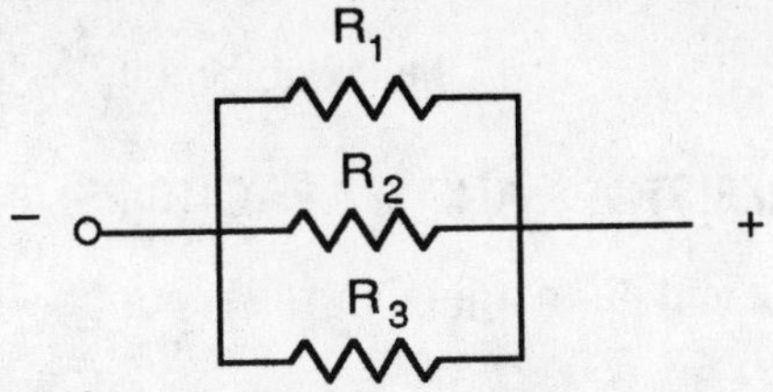

$$\frac{1}{R_{\text{Total}}} = \left(\frac{1}{R_1} + \frac{1}{R_2} + \frac{1}{R_3}\right) \text{ (in parallel)}$$

The Loop Theorem

$$\Delta V_1 + \Delta V_2 + \Delta V_3 \ldots = 0$$

For a complete circuit loop

EXAMPLE

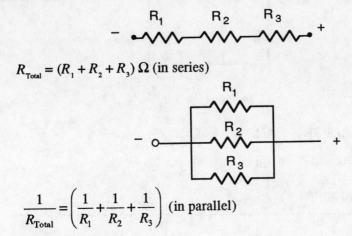

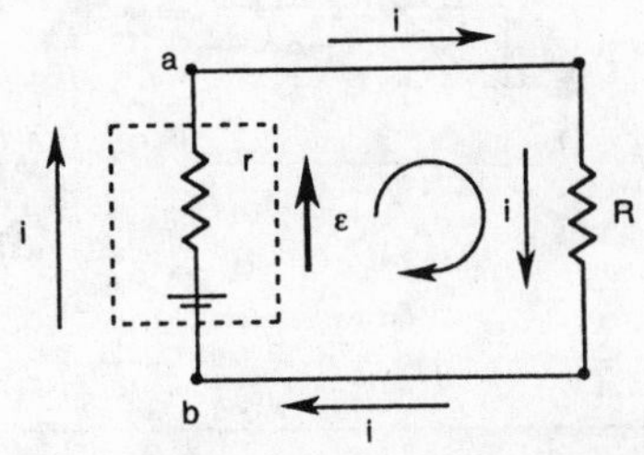

Simple circuit with resistor

$$V_{ab} = \varepsilon - iR = + ir$$

Then $$\varepsilon - iR - ir = 0$$

NOTE: If a resistor is traversed in the direction of the current, the voltage change is represented as a voltage drop, $-iR$. A change in voltage while traversing the *EMF* (or battery) in the direction of the *EMF* is a voltage rise $+\varepsilon$.

Circuit With Several Loops

$$\sum_n i_n = 0$$

EXAMPLE

$$i_1 + i_2 + i_3 = 0$$

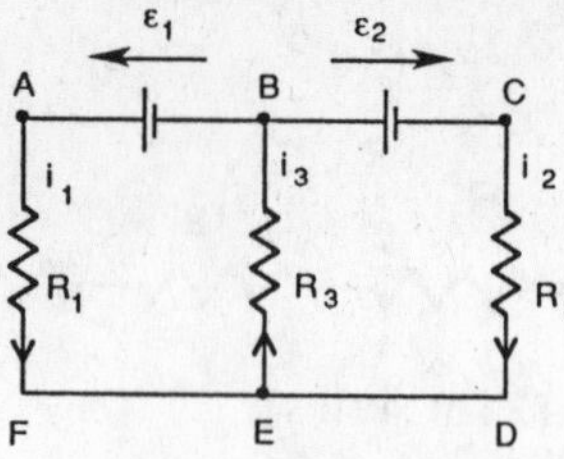

Multiloop circuit

RC CIRCUITS (RESISTORS AND CAPACITORS)

RC charging and discharging

Differential Equations

$$\varepsilon = R\frac{dq}{dt} + \frac{q}{C} \quad \text{(Charging)}$$

$$O = R\frac{dq}{dt} + \frac{q}{C} \quad \text{(Discharging)}$$

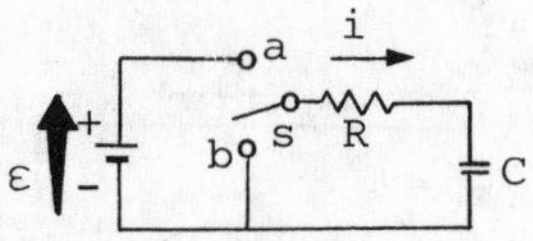

An RC circuit

Charge in the Capacitor

$$q = (C\varepsilon)\left(1 - e^{\frac{-t}{RC}}\right) \quad \text{(Charging)}$$

$$q = (C\varepsilon)\, e^{\frac{-t}{RC}} \quad \text{(Discharging)}$$

Current in the Resistor

$$i = \left(\frac{\varepsilon}{R}\right) e^{\frac{-t}{RC}} \quad \text{(Charging)}$$

$$i = -\left(\frac{\varepsilon}{R}\right) e^{\frac{-t}{RC}} \quad \text{(Discharging)}$$

where e = 2.71828 (Exponential Constant)

KIRCHOFF'S CURRENT LAW

The algebraic sum of all currents entering a node equals the algebraic sum of all currents leaving it.

$$\sum_{n=1}^{N} i_n = 0$$

KIRCHOFF'S VOLTAGE LAW (SAME AS LOOP THEOREM)

The algebraic sum of all voltages around a closed loop is zero.

THEVENIN'S THEOREM

In any linear network, it is possible to replace everything except the load resistor by an equivalent circuit containing only a single voltage source in series with a resistor (R_{th} Thevenin resistance), where the response measured at the load resistor will not be affected.

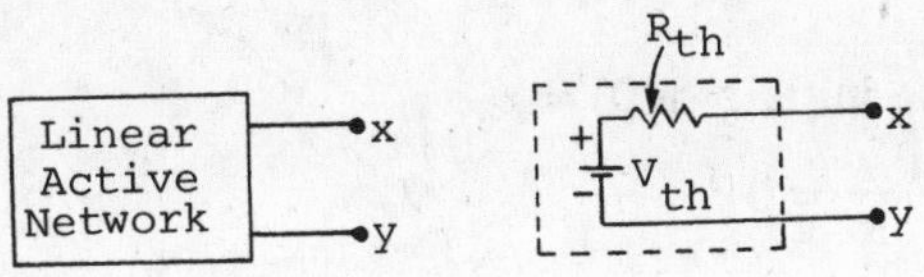

Procedures to Find Thevenin Equivalent:

1) Solve for the open circuit voltage V_{oc} across the output terminals.

$$V_{oc} = V_{th}$$

2) Place this voltage V_{oc} in series with the Thevenin resistance which is the resistance across the terminals found by setting all independent voltage and current sources to zero. (i.e., short circuits and open circuits, respectively.)

RLC CIRCUITS AND OSCILLATIONS

These oscillations are analogous to, and mathematically identical to, the case of mechanical harmonic motion in its various forms. (AC current is sinusoidal.)

SIMPLE RL AND RC CIRCUITS

Source Free RL Circuit

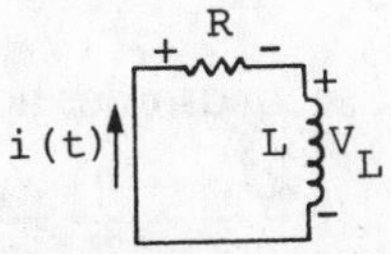

Properties: Assume initially $i(0) = I_0$.

A) $v_R + v_L = Ri + L\frac{di}{dt} = 0.$

B) $i(t) = I_0 e^{-Rt/L} = I_0 e^{-t/\tau}$, τ = time constant $= \frac{L}{R}$

C) Power dissipated in the resistor =

$P_R = i^2 R = I_0^2 Re^{-2Rt/L}$.

D) Total energy in terms of heat in the resistor =

$W_R = {}^1/_2 LI_0^2$.

Source Free RC Circuit

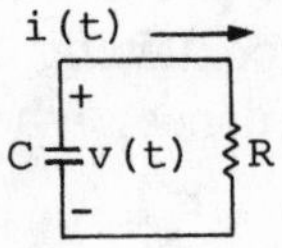

Properties: Assume initially $v(0) = V_o$

A) $C\frac{dv}{dt} + \frac{v}{R} = 0.$

B) $v(t) = v(0)e^{-t/RC} = V_o e^{-t/RC}.$

C) $\frac{1}{C}\int_{-\infty}^{t} i(\tau)\,d\tau + i(t)R = 0$

$i(t) = i(0)e^{\frac{-t}{RC}}$

THE RLC CIRCUITS

Parallel RLC Circuit (source free)

Circuit Diagram:

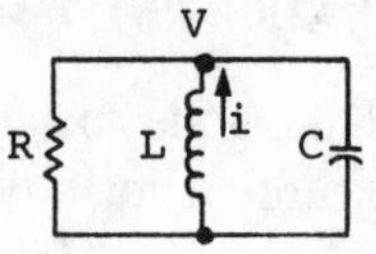

KCL equation for parallel RLC circuit:

$$\frac{v}{R} + \frac{1}{L}\int_{t_0}^{t} v\,dt - i(t_0) + C\frac{dv}{dt} = 0;$$

and the corresponding linear, second-order homogeneous differential equation is

$$C\frac{d^2v}{dt^2} + \frac{1}{T}\frac{dv}{dt} + \frac{v}{L} = 0.$$

General Solution:

$$V = A_1 e^{S_1 t} + A_2 e^{S_2 t},$$

where

$$S_{1,2} = \frac{-1}{2RC} \pm \sqrt{\left(\frac{1}{2RC}\right)^2 - \frac{1}{LC}}$$

or

$$S_{1,2} = -\alpha \pm \sqrt{\alpha^2 - \omega_0^2};$$

where α = exponential damping coefficient neper frequency

$$= \frac{1}{2RC}$$

and ω_0 = resonant frequency

$$= \frac{1}{\sqrt{LC}}$$

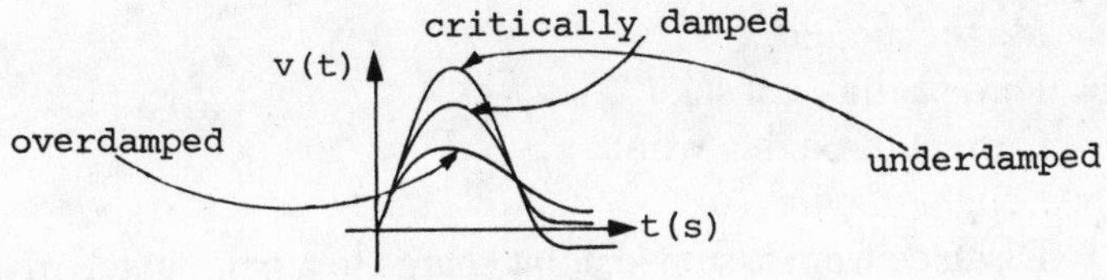

COMPLETE RESPONSE OF RLC CIRCUIT

The general equation of a complete response of a second order system in terms of voltage for an RLC circuit is given by,

$$v(t) = \underbrace{V_f}_{\text{forced response}} + \underbrace{Ae^{S_1 t} + Be^{S_2 t}}_{\text{natural response}}$$

(i.e., constant for DC excitation)

NOTE: *A* and *B* can be obtained by

1) Substituting v at $t = 0^+$

2) Taking the derivative of the response, i.e.,

$$\frac{dv}{dt} = 0 + S_1 A\, e^{S_1 t} + S_2 B\, e^{S_2 t}$$

where $\frac{dv}{dt}$ at $t = 0^+$ is known.

E. MAGNETISM

Force in a magnetic field

$$\mathbf{F}_b = q\mathbf{v} \times \mathbf{B}$$

where $\mathbf{F}_b$ = Force on particle due to field
q = Charge on particle
$\mathbf{v}$ = Velocity of particle
$\mathbf{B}$ = Magnetic field

THE BIOT-SAVART LAW

$$dB = \frac{\mu_0 i}{4\pi} \frac{\sin \theta dl}{r^2}$$

where $\mathbf{B}$ = Magnetic field
μ_0 = Permeability constant
i = Current through a wire
l = Length of wire
r = Distance from assumed point charge to a point in the magnetic field
θ = Angle between r and the direction of the element

NOTE:

$$\mu_0 = 4\pi \times 10^{-7} \frac{T \cdot m}{A}$$

Integral form:

$$\mathbf{B} = \frac{\mu_0 i}{4\pi} \oint_c \frac{d\mathbf{l}' \times \mathbf{a}_R}{r^2}$$

where primed terms refer to points along the source of the field.

AMPERE'S LAW

The line integral of the tangential component of **B** is exactly equal to the current enclosed by that path.

$$\oint \mathbf{B} \cdot d\mathbf{L} = I$$

Curl of a Vector Field.

The curl of any vector is defined as a vector where the direction is given by the right-hand rule and the magnitude is given by the limit of the quotient of the closed line integral and the area of the enclosed path as the area approaches 0.

$$(\text{curl } \mathbf{H})_n = \lim_{\Delta s_n \to 0} \frac{\oint \mathbf{H} \cdot d\mathbf{L}}{\Delta s_n}$$

Δs_n is the area enclosed by the closed line integral, and n is any component; this is normal to the surface enclosed by the closed path.

STOKE'S THEOREM

$$\oint_l \mathbf{F} \cdot d\mathbf{l} = \int_S (\nabla \times \mathbf{F}) \cdot ds$$

F is any vector field, s is a surface bounded by l. It gives the relation between a closed line integral and surface integral.

By using the Divergence Theorem and Stoke's theorem we can derive a very important identity:

$$\nabla \cdot \nabla \times \mathbf{A} \equiv 0$$

where **A** = is any vector field.

MAGNETIC FLUX AND MAGNETIC FLUX DENSITY

$B = \mu_0 H$, B is the magnetic flux density in free space.

Unit of B is webers per square meter (wb / m^2) or Tesla (T) a new unit.

$\mu_0 = 4\,\pi \times 10^{-7}$ H/m (permeability of free space)

H is in amperes per meter (A/m).

$$\oint_S \mathbf{B} \cdot d\mathbf{s} = 0$$

This is Gauss's law for the magnetic field

$$\nabla \cdot \mathbf{B} = 0$$

after application of the divergence theorem. This is the fourth and last equation of Maxwell.

FARADAY'S LAW

Faraday's Law can be stated as follows:

$$\text{emf} = \oint \mathbf{E} \cdot d\mathbf{L} = -\frac{d\phi}{dt}\,(v)$$

The minus sign is by Lenz's Law which indicates that the induced e.m.f. is always acting against the changing magnetic fields which produce that e.m.f.

Faraday's law describes the relationship between Electric and Magnetic Fields.

INDUCTANCE (L)

$$L = \frac{N\phi}{I} = \frac{\text{Total flux linkage}}{\text{current linked}}$$

Unit of inductance is H which is equivalent to wb / A.

Applications

Inductance per meter length of a coaxial cable of inner radius a and outer radius b.

$$L = \frac{\mu_0}{2\pi} \ln \frac{b}{a} \text{ H/m.}$$

A toroidal coil of N turns and IA,

$$L = \frac{\mu_0 N^2 s}{2\pi R}$$

where R = Mean radius of the toroid.

Different expressions for inductance:

$$L = \frac{2W_H}{I^2}$$

$$L = \frac{\int_{\text{vol}} \mathbf{B} \cdot \mathbf{H} \, dv}{I^2}$$

$$= \frac{1}{I^2} \int_{\text{vol}} \mathbf{H} \cdot (\nabla \times \mathbf{A}) \, dv$$

$$L = \frac{1}{I^2} \left[\int_{\text{vol}} \nabla \cdot (\mathbf{A} \times \mathbf{H}) \, dv + \int_{\text{vol}} \mathbf{A} \cdot (\nabla \times \mathbf{H}) \, dv \right]$$

$$L = \frac{1}{I^2} \int_{\text{vol}} \mathbf{A} \cdot \mathbf{J} \, dv$$

$$L = \frac{1}{I^2} \int_{\text{vol}} \left(\int_{\text{vol}} \frac{\mu \mathbf{J}}{4\pi R} \, dv \right) \cdot \mathbf{J} \, dv$$

Mutual inductance between circuits 1 and 2,

$$L_{12} = \frac{N_2 \cdot \phi_{12}}{I_1}$$

where N = the number of turns

$$L_{12} = \frac{1}{I_1 I_2} \int_{\text{vol}} (\mu \mathbf{H}_1 \cdot \mathbf{H}_2)\, dv$$

$$L_{12} = L_{21}$$

F. MAXWELL'S EQUATIONS AND ELECTROMAGNETIC WAVES

MAXWELL'S EQUATIONS

Maxwell's equation in differential form:

$$\nabla \times \mathbf{E} = -\frac{\partial \mathbf{B}}{\partial t}$$

$$\nabla \times \mathbf{H} = \mathbf{J} + \frac{\partial \mathbf{D}}{\partial t}$$

$$\nabla \cdot \mathbf{D} = \rho$$

$$\nabla \cdot \mathbf{B} = 0$$

Auxiliary equations relating **D** and **E**:

$$\mathbf{D} = \varepsilon \mathbf{E} \qquad \mathbf{D} = \varepsilon_0 \mathbf{E} + \mathbf{P}$$

$$\mathbf{B} = \mu \mathbf{H} \qquad \mathbf{B} = \mu_0 (\mathbf{H} + \mathbf{M})$$

$$\mathbf{J} = \sigma \mathbf{E} \qquad \mathbf{J} = \rho \mathbf{U}$$

Lorentz force equation

$$\mathbf{F} = \rho(\mathbf{E} + \mathbf{U} \times \mathbf{B})$$

Maxwell's equations in integral form:

$$\oint \mathbf{E} \cdot d\mathbf{L} = -\int_s \frac{\partial \mathbf{B}}{\partial t} \cdot d\mathbf{s}$$

$$\oint \mathbf{H} \cdot d\mathbf{L} = I + \int_s \frac{\partial \mathbf{D}}{\partial t} \cdot d\mathbf{s}$$

$$\oint_s \mathbf{D} \cdot d\mathbf{s} = \int_{\text{vol}} \rho \, dv$$
$$\oint \mathbf{B} \cdot d\mathbf{s} = 0$$

These four integral equations enable us to find the boundary conditions on **B**, **D**, **H** and **E** which are necessary to evaluate the constants obtained in solving Maxwell's equations in partial differential form.

ELECTROMAGNETIC WAVES

Maxwell's Equations in Phasor Form:

$$\nabla \times \mathbf{H}_s = j\omega \varepsilon_0 \mathbf{E}_s$$
$$\nabla \times \mathbf{E}_s = -j\omega \mu_0 \mathbf{H}_s$$
$$\nabla \cdot \mathbf{E}_s = 0$$
$$\nabla \cdot \mathbf{H}_s = 0$$

Wave equations:

$$\nabla \times \nabla \times \mathbf{E}_s = \nabla(\nabla \cdot \mathbf{E}_s) - \nabla^2 \mathbf{E}_s = -j\omega\mu_0 \nabla \times \mathbf{H}_s$$
$$= \omega^2 \mu_0 \varepsilon_0 \mathbf{E}_s = -\nabla^2 \mathbf{E}_s .$$

$$\nabla^2 \mathbf{E}_s = -\omega^2 \mu_0 \varepsilon_0 \mathbf{E}_s$$

$$\nabla^2 E_{xs} = \frac{\partial^2 E_{xs}}{\partial x^2} + \frac{\partial^2 E_{xs}}{\partial y^2} + \frac{\partial^2 E_{xs}}{\partial z^2}$$
$$= -\omega^2 \mu_0 \varepsilon_0 E_{xs}$$

For

$$\frac{\partial^2 \mathbf{E}_{xs}}{\partial y^2} = \frac{\partial^2 \mathbf{E}_{xs}}{\partial z^2} = 0$$

i.e., E_{xs} independent of x and y.

This can be simplified to

$$\frac{\partial^2 \mathbf{E}_{xs}}{\partial z^2} = -\omega^2 \mu_0 \varepsilon_0 E_{xs}$$
$$E_x = E_{x_0} \cos\left[\omega(t - z\sqrt{\mu_0 \varepsilon_0})\right]$$

and

$$E_{x'} = E_{x'_0} \cos\left[\omega(t + z\sqrt{\mu_0 \varepsilon_0})\right]$$

E_{x0} = value of E_x at $z = 0, t = 0$.

Velocity of the traveling wave:

To find the velocity U, let us keep the value of E_x to be constant; therefore

$$t - z\sqrt{\mu_0 \varepsilon_0} = \text{constant}.$$

Take differentials; we have

$$dt - \frac{1}{U} dz = 0$$

$$\frac{dz}{dt} = U$$

in free space.

$$\text{Velocity of light} = U = \frac{1}{\sqrt{\mu_0 \varepsilon_0}} = 3 \times 10^8 \text{ m/s}$$

$$\text{Wave length} = \lambda = \frac{U}{f} = \frac{2\pi U}{\omega}$$

The field is moving in the Z direction with velocity U. It is called a traveling wave.

Form of the ***H*** field:

If $\mathbf{E}_s$ is given, $\mathbf{H}_s$ can be obtained from

$$\nabla \times \mathbf{E}_s = -j\omega \mu_0 \varepsilon_0 \mathbf{H}_s$$

$$\frac{\partial E_{xs}}{\partial z} = -j\omega \mu_0 \mathbf{H}_{ys}$$

$$= E_{x_0}(-j\omega\sqrt{\mu_0 \varepsilon_0})e^{-j\omega\sqrt{\mu_0 \varepsilon_0} z}$$

$$H_y = E_{x_0}\sqrt{\frac{\varepsilon_0}{\mu_0}} \cos\left[\omega\left(t - z\sqrt{\mu_0 \varepsilon_0}\right)\right]$$

$$\frac{E_x}{H_y} = \frac{\mu_0}{\varepsilon_0}$$

is a constant where

$$\eta = \sqrt{\frac{\mu}{\varepsilon}}$$

where η = The intrinsic impedance: It is the square root of the ratio of permeability to permittivity and is measured in Ω.

$$\eta_o = \sqrt{\frac{\mu_0}{\varepsilon_0}} = 377\Omega$$

η_0 = η of free space.

The term *uniform plane wave* is used because the *H* and *E* fields are uniform throughout any plane, *Z* = constant, and it is also called a transverse electromagnetic (TEM) wave since both the *E* and *H* fields are perpendicular to the direction of propagation.

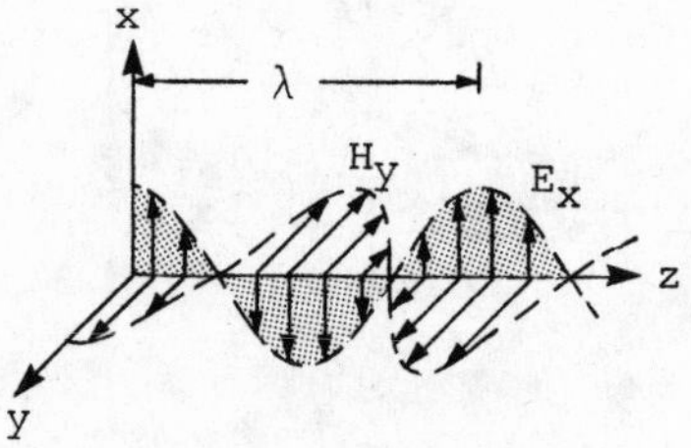

A uniform TEM wave.

CHAPTER 3

ATOMIC PHYSICS

A. RUTHERFORD SCATTERING

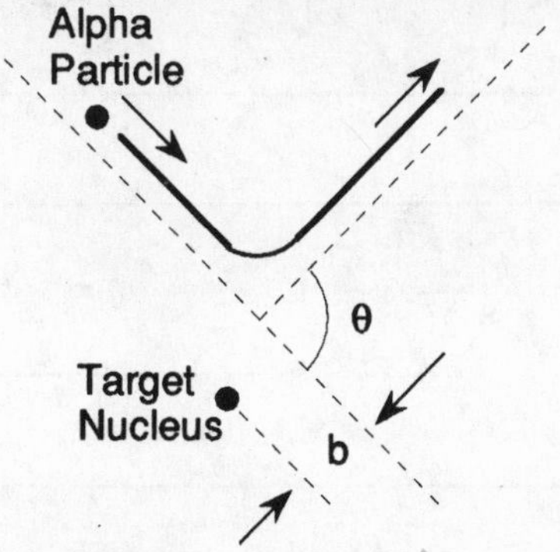

Θ is the scattering angle and *b* is the impact parameter

In this collision, it is assumed that the nucleus has sufficient mass as to not be moved by the alpha particle. In this case, the energy of the alpha particle stays the same. It follows that the **magnitude** of the momentum remains constant

$$P_1 = P_2 = mv$$

Therefore by the Law of sines:

$$\frac{\Delta p}{\sin\theta} = \frac{mv}{\sin\dfrac{\pi - \theta}{2}}$$

Solving for the change in momentum:

$$\Delta p = 2mv\sin\left(\frac{\theta}{2}\right)$$

It can also be shown that the scattering angle θ can be determined by the equation:

$$\cot\frac{\theta}{2} = \frac{4\pi\varepsilon_0 k}{Z_n e^2} b$$

where k = the alpha particle energy.

B. ATOMIC SPECTRA

When an atomic gas is excited, it emits radiation at certain specific wavelengths. This produces the gas' **emission line spectrum.**

When white light (all wavelengths) is passed through a gas, the gas will absorb certain specific wavelengths of the light. This produces the **absorption line spectrum.**

Wavelengths in atomic spectra fall into **spectral series.** There are 5 such series and 5 similar equations:

Lyman Series

$$\frac{1}{\lambda} = R\left(\frac{1}{1^2} - \frac{1}{n^2}\right) \qquad n = 2, 3, 4, \ldots$$

Balmer Series

$$\frac{1}{\lambda} = R\left(\frac{1}{2^2} - \frac{1}{n^2}\right) \qquad n = 3, 4, 5, \ldots$$

Paschen Series

$$\frac{1}{\lambda} = R\left(\frac{1}{3^2} - \frac{1}{n^2}\right) \qquad n = 4, 5, 6, \ldots$$

Brackett Series

$$\frac{1}{\lambda} = R\left(\frac{1}{4^2} - \frac{1}{n^2}\right) \qquad n = 5, 6, 7, \ldots$$

Pfund Series

$$\frac{1}{\lambda} = R\left(\frac{1}{5^2} - \frac{1}{n^2}\right) \qquad n = 6, 7, 8, \ldots$$

In general, series k is

$$\frac{1}{\lambda} = R\left(\frac{1}{k^2} - \frac{1}{n^2}\right) \qquad n = k + 1,\ k + 2,\ k + 3,\ \ldots.$$

R is known as the Rydberg constant.

$$R = 1.097 \times 10^7\ \text{m}^{-1}$$

C. THE BOHR ATOM

Classical physics is not adequate in describing the atom, due to the fact that in order to resist falling into the nucleus, an electron would have to whirl rapidly around the nucleus using the pull as centripetal acceleration. This motion would cause the electron to radiate electromagnetic energy, thereby rendering the system unstable. A quantum solution must therefore be sought.

Hydrogen Atom (1 electron)

If viewed classically, the required electron velocity for stability, not considering electromagnetic generation would be

$$v = \frac{c}{\sqrt{4\pi\varepsilon_0 mr}}$$

The DeBroglie wavelength for any object in motion is

$$\lambda = \frac{h}{mv}.$$

∴ Orbital electron wavelength

$$\lambda = \frac{h}{e}\sqrt{\frac{4\pi\varepsilon_0 r}{m}}$$

The conditions for stable orbit can be described as the situation when the circumference of the orbit contains an integral number of DeBroglie wavelengths.

A condition for orbit stability

$$n\lambda = 2\pi r_n \quad n = 1, 2, 3, \ldots$$

with possible radii

$$r_n = \frac{n^2 b^2 \varepsilon_0}{\pi m e^2} \quad n = 1, 2, 3, \ldots$$

The aforementioned spectra correspond to differing discrete energy levels, 1 level for each electron radius r_n. Using the theory of the Bohr atom, an explanation of spectral series can be found.

$$E_n = -\frac{e^2}{8\pi\varepsilon_0 r_n} \quad (E = \frac{1}{2}mv^2 + \frac{kqq}{r})$$

Substituting r_n it can be shown that

$$E_1 = -\frac{me^4}{8\varepsilon_0^2 h^2}$$

and that

$$E_n = \frac{E_1}{n^2}$$

The Bohr model can be used to derive accurately the value of the Rydberg constant.

Note, however, that the Bohr theory is not in fact a complete and accurate description of what is occurring, and is limited in its applications. For a more complete and accurate picture, Quantum Mechanics must be used.

D. THE LASER

Light Amplification by Stimulated Emission of Radiation

Properties

1. The light is coherent. (Waves are in phase)
2. Light is nearly Monochromatic. (One wavelength)
3. Minimal divergence.
4. Highest intensity of any light source.

Many atoms have excited energy levels which have relatively long lifetimes. (10^{-3} s instead of 10^{-8} s). These levels are known as **metastable.**

Through a process known as **population inversion**, the majority of an assembly of atoms is brought to an excited state.

Population inversion can be accomplished through a process known as **optical pumping**, where atoms of a specific substance, such as ruby, are exposed to a given wavelength of light. This wavelength is enough to excite the ruby atoms just above metastable level. The atoms rapidly lose energy and fall to the metastable level.

Ruby

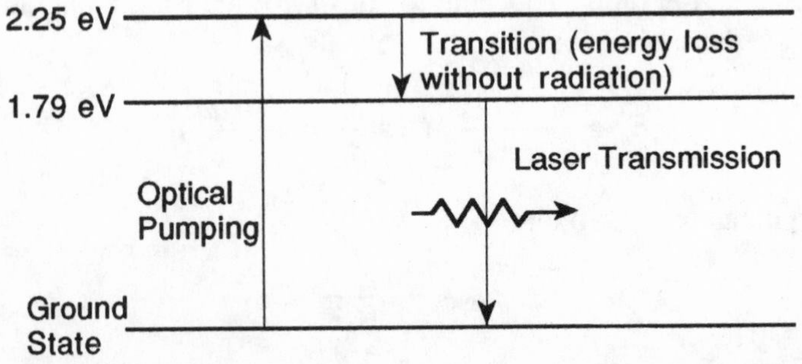

Once population inversion has been obtained, **induced emission** can occur from photons dropping from an excited metastable state to ground state. The photons have a wavelength equal to the wavelength of photons produced by each individual atom. The radiated light waves will be exactly in phase with the incident waves, resulting in an enhanced beam of coherent light. Hence the familiar Laser effect.

CHAPTER 4

THERMODYNAMICS

A. TEMPERATURE

The average kinetic energy possessed by the molecules of a body is referred to as its temperature. The zeroth law of thermodynamics states this more formally as:

> There exists a scalar quantity called temperature, which is a property of all thermodynamic systems (in equilibrium states), such that temperature equality is a necessary and sufficient condition for thermodynamic equilibrium.

The two main scales in use for measuring temperature are the Celsius (formerly known as **Centigrade**) and the Kelvin scales. On the Celsius scale, water boils at 100° (1 Atm) and freezes at 0°. The 100 equal divisions between these two points determine the size of the Celsius degree, and from this, the points above 100 and below zero can be determined. When a temperature is shown followed by a degree sign, but without an abbreviation to show the scale used (e.g., 25° instead of 25°C.), it is presumed to be a Celsius temperature. The degrees on the Kelvin scale are the exact same size as those on the Celsius scale. Kelvin, however, starts at absolute zero, hence it has no negative temperatures. A temperature in Kelvin is never reported with the degree sign (e.g., 300 K). To convert Kelvin to Celsius, simply subtract 273.15 from the Kelvin temperature. Put mathematically,

$$C = K - 273.15.$$

For example, 300 K would be

$$(300 - 273.15) = 26.85° \text{ C}.$$

Converting from Celsius to Kelvin is just the opposite of this. Two older scales of temperature measurement, Fahrenheit and Rankine, are not often used, and hence need not be learned.

B. COEFFICIENT OF THERMAL EXPANSION

As a substance is heated, its molecules vibrate faster and move further apart, or the material is said to expand. This phenomenon is much more pronounced in gases than in liquids and solids. If the material is a solid, and one of its dimensions is much more pronounced than the other two (e.g., a rod), a coefficient of linear expansion, α_l, can be determined, i.e., a value to determine the increase of the material in that one dimension only. For all other materials, a coefficient of volume expansion, α_v, is used.

For solids, the α_v is equal to three times the α_l. For liquids and solids the α_v will vary somewhat with the temperature, for gasses (at constant pressure) it is usually equal to 0.00367/°C.

EXAMPLE

The α_v for glycerin is 5.1×10^{-4} / °C. If 25.62 liters of glycerine are heated from 25° to 125°, what will its new volume be?

$$V = V_0 + (V_0 \cdot \alpha_v \cdot \Delta T),$$

where V = the new volume
V_0 = the initial volume, and
ΔT = the change in temperature.

ΔT can be calculated as 125 – 25 = 100. Putting everything into an equation, we get

$$V = V_0 + (V_0 \cdot \alpha_v \cdot \Delta T)$$

$$= 25.62 + (25 \cdot 62 \cdot 5.1 \times 10^{-4} \cdot 100)$$

$$= 26.93 \text{ liters.}$$

The same method is used for the linear coefficient of expansion.

EXAMPLE

The α_l for aluminum is 2.4×10^{-5} / °C. If an aluminum needle is 20 cm long at 350 K, how long will it be at 100 K?

The formula, much like the above, is

$$L = L_0 + (L_0 \cdot \alpha_l \cdot \Delta T)$$

or

$$L = 20 + (20)\,(2.4 \times 10^{-5})\,(-250)$$

$$= 19.88 \text{ cm.}$$

Note that in this instance, the ΔT is negative, hence the value decreases.

C. HEAT CAPACITY, SPECIFIC HEAT AND C_p

The heat gained or lost by a body can be quantisized in its ability to do work. The unit commonly used nowadays is the Joule, which is defined as the enegy required to move a force of one Newton the distance of one meter. Older, and out-dated units include the calorie and British Thermal Unit (BTU). The ratio of the change in heat (ΔQ) to the temperature change (ΔT) in an absorbing body is called the heat capacity, of C. Mathematically

$$C = \Delta Q / \Delta T.$$

EXAMPLE

A statue made of a metal alloy has a heat capacity of 55.8 Joules/°C. How many Joules of energy will have to be absorbed to raise its temperature from 25° to 100°?

$$T = 100 - 25 = 75°,$$

$$C = \Delta Q / \Delta T,$$

or
$$55.8 = \Delta Q / 75,$$

or
$$\Delta Q = 55.8 \times 75 = 4{,}185 \text{ Joules},$$

or
$$4.185 \text{ kJ}.$$

A more useful value is the specific heat, or c. Specific heat is defined as heat capacity per unit mass of body, or

$$c = \Delta Q / (m\Delta T),$$

where m = the mass of the object.

At ordinary temperatures and ordinary temperature ranges, specific heats can be considered constant. However, it must be specified if the specific heat is measured with constant pressure (c_p) or constant volume (c_v). For gasses,

$$c_p - c_v = R / M,$$

where R = the universal gas law constant (8.314 J/mole °C), and
M = the molecular weight of the gas

Sometimes specific heats are given in J/mole °C, rather than the standard J/gram °C, hence the units need to be inspected carefully.

EXAMPLE

The c_p for lead is 0.1277 J/gm °C, and for water it is 4.186 J/gm °C. If a lead block of 75.00 grams is placed in 200.0 grams of water at 25.00°, and the final temperature of the water and lead is 28.11°, what was the initial temperature of the lead? (Assuming no heat is lost to the surroundings.)

The fact that both c_p's are given in J/gm °C saves us the trouble of doing any conversions. The Joules lost by the lead will be equal to the number of Joules gained by the water, or

$$J_{Pb} = J_{H_2O}.$$

This can be restated as:

$$(\Delta T \cdot c_p \cdot m)_{Pb} = (\Delta T \cdot c_p \cdot m)_{H_2O}.$$

The c_p's and m's for each are given, the ΔT's can be calculated. For water, $\Delta T = 28.11 - 25.00 = 2.11°$. For lead, the initial temperature is not known, it will be assigned the value X, hence $\Delta T = X - 28.11$. Putting these values into the above equation, we obtain:

$$(X - 28.11)\,(0.1277)\,(75.00) = (3.11)\,(4.186)\,(200.0).$$

Performing the indicated operations we get:

$$2{,}603.7 = 9.578X - 269.2,$$

solving for X yields $X = 299.95°$, which was the initial temperature of the lead.

D. HEAT OF VAPORIZATION AND HEAT OF FUSION

When a substance changes state, e.g., from a liquid to a gas, energy is absorbed by the substance without change in temperature. For example, for water at 100° to change to steam at 100°, it must absorb 2,260 Joules per gram of water. This value is known as the **Heat of Vaporization**, (L_v) and is unique for each substance.

The melting of a solid involves a similar process, Joules are absorbed by the substance, but rather than an increase in temperature, there is a change of physical state. Ice at 0°, to melt to water at 0°, must absorb 335 Joules per gram. This value, again unique for each specific substance, is known as the **Heat of Fusion**, (L_f).

EXAMPLE

For mercury the boiling and freezing points are 358° and –39°, respectively. The L_v and L_f are 2197 J/gm and 11.7 J/gm, respectively. The c_p for liquid mercury is 0.138 J/gm °C. How much energy would have to be lost by 1.00 kg of Hg vapor at 358° to become solid Hg at –39°?

To calculate this, one needs to find: 1) The Joules to convert one kg of Hg vapor to one kg of liquid Hg. 2) The Joules lost to cool one kg of Hg from 358° to –39°. 3) The Joules lost to convert one kg of liquid Hg to one kg of solid Hg. Put mathematically,

$$[m \cdot L_v] + [m \cdot c_p \cdot \Delta T] + [m \cdot L_f]$$

$$= [1{,}000 \cdot 297] + [1{,}000 \cdot 0.138 \cdot 398] + [1{,}000 \cdot 11.7]$$

$$= [297{,}000] + [54{,}924] + [11{,}700]$$

$$= 406{,}848 \text{ Joules} = 407 \text{ kJ lost}$$

Had the mercury been heated to change it from a solid to a liquid and then to a gas, the procedure would have been just the opposite, and we would have been adding Joules. If a material changes directly from a solid to a gas (e.g., carbon dioxide), a similar term, **Heat of Sublimation,** (L_s) is used, just as L_v and L_f

E. CONDUCTION, CONVECTION AND RADIATION

Heat can travel from one body to another by three processes: conduction, convection and radiation. In conduction, one body is physically in contact with another, and the heat travels directly. The thermal conductivity of a material tells how easily it can transport heat. Metals are usually good at this. Steel, for example, has a thermal conductivity of 4.60×10^{-2} kJ/sec·meter·°C, whereas asbestos has a value of 8.37×10^{-5} kJ/sec·meter·°C.

EXAMPLE

Compare how much heat is transmitted per second by a steel plate 1.00 cm thick, and a surface area of 5,000 cm², and a temperature of 300° on one side, and 25° on the other, to how much heat is transmitted by an asbestos plate of equal dimensions under the same conditions.

$$\text{Heat Transfer} = \text{Thermal Conductivity} \cdot \text{Area} \cdot (T_1 - T_2) \,/\, \text{thickness}$$

For the steel plate this gives

$$(4.6 \times 10^{-2})\,(0.500)\,(275/0.0100) = 632.5 \text{ kJoules/sec.}$$

Note that cm² and cm were converted to m² and m. For the asbestos plate we get

$$(8.37 \times 10^{-5})\,(0.500)\,(275/0.0100) = 1.151 \text{ kJoules/sec.}$$

Convection simply involves heating the air molecules around an object, which then travel, via air currents, to another object where they impart their acquired energy by collisions.

Radiation involves the transfer of heat by photons, which can pass through a vacuum. A black body is one that absorbs all radiant energy that falls upon it, and emits radiation perfectly. The Stefan-Boltzmann equation states that E, the watts of power radiated by a black body, is equal to the Stefan constant (δ) times the fourth power of the absolute temperature, times the surface area, A, or

$$E = A\delta T^4.$$

The value of δ is 5.67×10^{-8} Watts/m^2·K^{-4}. A black, cubic body, 25.0 cm on the side is heated to 325°C. At what rate is energy radiated from its surface? First the surface area of the cube must be determined. Converting cm to m, we get $0.250^2 \times 6 = 0.375$ m^2 = A. The absolute temperature is 325 + 273 = 598 K. Putting these into the equation,

$$E = A\delta T^4.$$

yields $$E = (0.375)\,(5.67 \times 10^{-8})\,(598)^4 = 2{,}719 \text{ Watts}.$$

F. HEAT, WORK AND THE LAWS OF THERMODYNAMICS

THE FIRST LAW OF THERMODYNAMICS

Recall that work is defined as a force acting through a distance, and is measured in the same units as heat. Therefore, one might correctly conclude that a transfer of heat can be made to do work. The First Law of Thermodynamics states that there is a constant amount of energy in the universe, which can be neither created nor destroyed; it can only change its form. It is this change from one form to another that we observe and call work. Expressed mathematically, we have

$$\Delta U = Q - W$$

where ΔU = the change in energy of a system,
W = the energy spent in doing useful work, and
Q = any energy added to the system.

If $Q > W$, the energy remains within the system, i.e., work was done on the system. If $Q < W$, energy was lost by the system, and work was performed. When gasses are heated at a constant volume the added energy increases the internal energy of the molecules. However, when it is heated at constant pressure, the internal energy of the molecules is increased, but in addition, work is done by expanding the gas against the walls of its container. (Hence the different values for gases of c_p and c_v). Under isobaric conditions (constant pressure):

$$Q = \mathrm{m}c_p\,(T_2 - T_1),$$

where m = the mass of the gas
and W = (density) · $(V_2 - V_1)$,
where V = the volume of the gas.

Work is also defined as

$$W = \mathrm{m}(c_p - c_v)\,(T_2 - T_1)$$

in such a system. In a constant volume process (isovolumic) $W = 0$, hence,

$$Q = \Delta U = mc_v (T_2 - T_1).$$

In an isothermal process (constant temperature) $\Delta U = 0$, hence, $Q = W$. An adiabatic process is one in which heat is not transferred to or from the system. As a result, $Q = 0 = \Delta U + W$. Hence, $\Delta U = -W$.

THE SECOND LAW OF THERMODYNAMICS

The Second Law of Thermodynamics states that it is impossible for heat to travel of its own accord from a colder to a hotter body. As a result of this, the maximum efficiency of any heat engine is given by the formula

$$\frac{(T_1 - T_2)}{T_1},$$

where T_1 = the temperature (Kelvin) of the reservoir which supplies the working substance, and

T_2 = the temperature of the reservoir to which the working substance is exhausted.

THE THIRD LAW OF THERMODYNAMICS

The Third Law of Thermodynamics states that it is impossible to reduce any system to absolute zero in a finite series of operations. Hence, a reservoir of absolute zero cannot be constructed, and hence, (by the above formula), a heat engine of 100% efficiency cannot be built.

G. ENTROPY

Many volumes have been written about entropy. To sum it up, for the purposes of this book, entropy can be defined as the amount of disorder in a system. By the Second Law of Thermodynamics, this means that entropy will usually increase, or at the best, remain constant. It takes energy to keep things neat! By the Third Law of Thermodynamics, at absolute zero there would be no entropy. Common units of entropy are Joules/Kelvin.

CHAPTER 5

QUANTUM MECHANICS

A. WAVE FUNCTIONS AND EQUATIONS

The wave function ψ has no physical interpretation, but $|\psi|^2$ for a body at a given place and time is proportional to the location of the body at that given time.

Once ψ is determined, the momentum, angular momentum, and Energy of the body can be determined.

Wave Function:

$$\Psi = A + iB$$

where A, B = real functions.

Complex Conjugate:

$$\Psi^* = A - iB$$

If dealing with complex wave functions:

$$|\Psi|^2 = \Psi^* \Psi$$

Conditions for a wave function:

1) $\int_{-\infty}^{\infty} |\psi|^2 dV \neq 0$ (V = Volume)
2) Ψ must be single valued.
3) $\frac{\partial \psi}{\partial x}$, $\frac{\partial \psi}{\partial y}$ and $\frac{\partial \psi}{\partial z}$

   must be finite, single valued and continuous.

Normalization: A wave function is normalized when $|\Psi|^2$ is equal to the probability density, not merely proportional to it.

$$\int_{-\infty}^{\infty} |\psi|^2 dV = 1$$

B. SCHRÖDINGER'S EQUATION

Ψ is not measurable, and therefore may be complex.

Specify Ψ in the x direction:

$$\Psi = Ae^{-i\omega(t-\frac{x}{v})}$$

where $\omega = 2\pi\nu$

$v = \lambda\nu$

then

$$\Psi = Ae^{-2\pi i(\nu t-\frac{x}{\lambda})}$$

$$E = 2\pi\hbar\nu$$

$$\lambda = \frac{2\pi\hbar}{p}$$

For a free particle:

$$\psi = Ae^{-\frac{i(Et-px)}{\hbar}}$$

To obtain Schrödinger's Equation

$$\frac{\partial^2\psi}{\partial x^2} = -\frac{p^2}{\hbar^2}\psi \text{ and } \frac{\partial\psi}{\partial t} = \frac{iE}{\hbar}\psi$$

$$E = \frac{p^2}{2m} + V$$

therefore:

$$E\Psi = \frac{p^2\Psi}{2m} + V\Psi$$

$$E\Psi = -\frac{\hbar}{i}\frac{\partial\Psi}{\partial t} \text{ and } p^2\Psi = -\hbar^2\frac{\partial^2\psi}{\partial x^2}$$

TIME DEPENDENT ONE DIMENSIONAL SCHRÖDINGER'S EQUATION

$$i\hbar\frac{\partial\Psi}{\partial t} = -\frac{\hbar^2}{2m}\left(\frac{\partial^2\Psi}{\partial x^2}\right) + V\Psi$$

In 3 dimensions:

$$i\hbar = -\frac{\hbar^2}{2m}\left(\frac{\partial^2\Psi}{\partial x^2}+\frac{\partial^2\Psi}{\partial y^2}+\frac{\partial^2\Psi}{\partial z^2}\right)+V(x,y,z,t)\Psi$$

STEADY STATE FORM (3-D)

$$\frac{\partial^2\Psi}{\partial x^2}+\frac{\partial^2\Psi}{\partial y^2}+\frac{\partial^2\Psi}{\partial z^2}+\frac{2m}{\hbar^2}(E-V)\Psi=0$$

C. POTENTIAL WELLS AND ENERGY LEVELS

PARTICLE IN A BOX

A particle trapped in a box with infinitely hard walls is the simplest Quantum-Mechanical problem.

Equation (Schrödinger's) in the box:

$$\frac{\partial^2\Psi}{\partial x^2}+\frac{2m}{\hbar^2}E\Psi=0$$

As $V = 0$,

$$\Psi = A\sin\frac{\sqrt{2mE}}{\hbar}x + B\cos\frac{\sqrt{2mE}}{\hbar}x$$

As $\Psi = 0$ at $x = 0$ and $x = L$

$$\frac{\sqrt{2mE}}{\hbar}L = n\pi \quad n = 1, 2, 3, \ldots$$

$$\therefore \quad E_n = \frac{n^2\pi^2\hbar^2}{2mL^2} \quad n = 1, 2, 3, \ldots$$

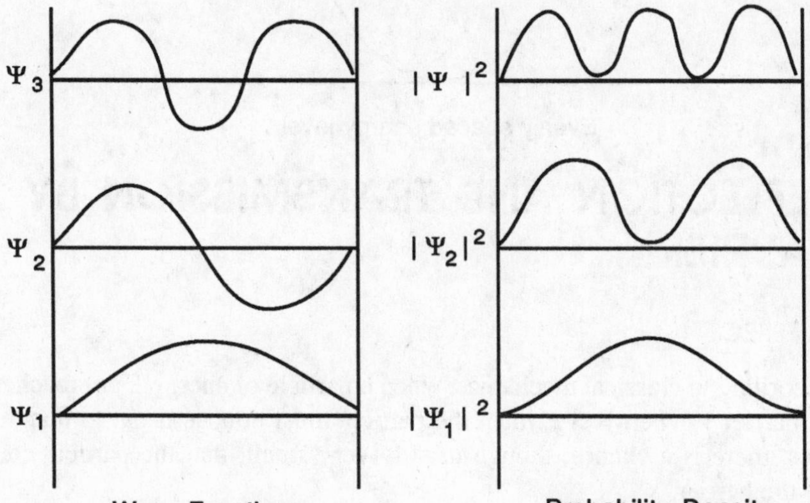

Wave Functions   Probability Density

Normalized wave function of particle in box:

$$\Psi_n = \sqrt{\frac{2}{L}} \sin\frac{n\pi x}{L} \qquad n = 1, 2, 3, \ldots$$

D. HARMONIC OSCILLATOR

There are 3 differences from a classical oscillator:

1. Allowed energies a **discrete** spectrum.
2. Lowest energy not $E = 0$, but $E = E_0$.
3. May go beyond $\pm A$ (tunneling)

The Schrödinger equation for harmonic oscillator:

$$\frac{d^2\Psi}{dx^2} + \frac{2m}{\hbar}\left(E - \frac{1}{2}kx^2\right)\Psi = 0$$

This leads to energy levels

$$E_n = \left(n + \frac{1}{2}\right) h\nu \quad \text{with} \quad E_0 = \frac{1}{2} h\nu.$$

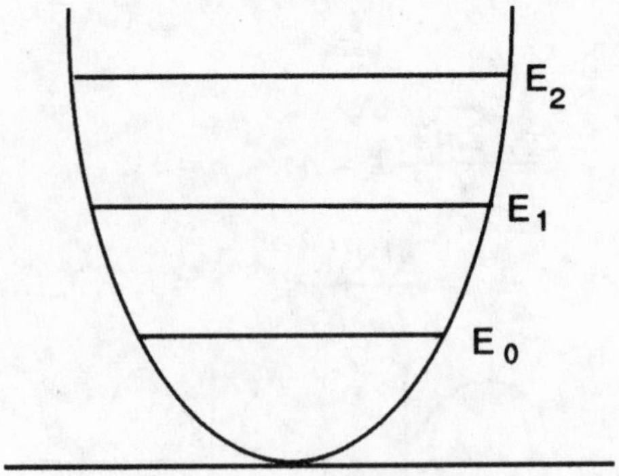

Evenly spaced energy levels

E. REFLECTION AND TRANSMISSION BY A BARRIER

TUNNEL EFFECT

According to classical mechanics, when a particle of energy E approaches a potential barrier V when $V > E$, then the particle must bounce back. In quantum mechanics, there is a chance, though usually very small, that the particle could penetrate the barrier.

According to Heisenberg's uncertainty principle,

$$\Delta x\ \Delta p \geq \frac{\hbar}{2}.$$

If we are 100% certain that the particle is not inside the barrier, then we are saying that $\Delta x = 0$. Therefore, ΔP and E would be infinite, which is impossible. Therefore, there must be some positive finite change of the particle penetrating the barrier.

A particle energy $E > V$ approaches potential barrier:

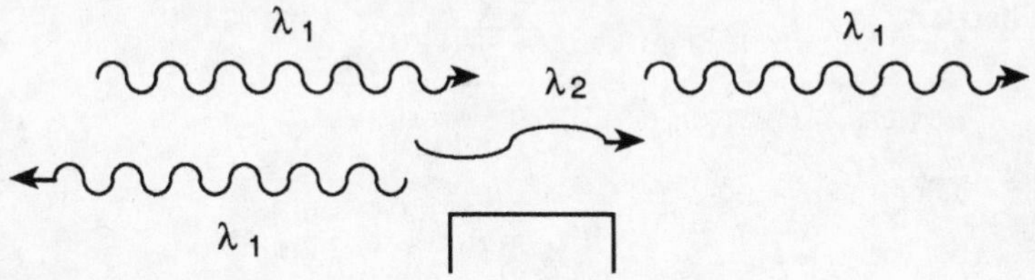

some reflect, others go on.

Wave functions and probability densities of particles in finite potential wells. (Particle can be found in well).

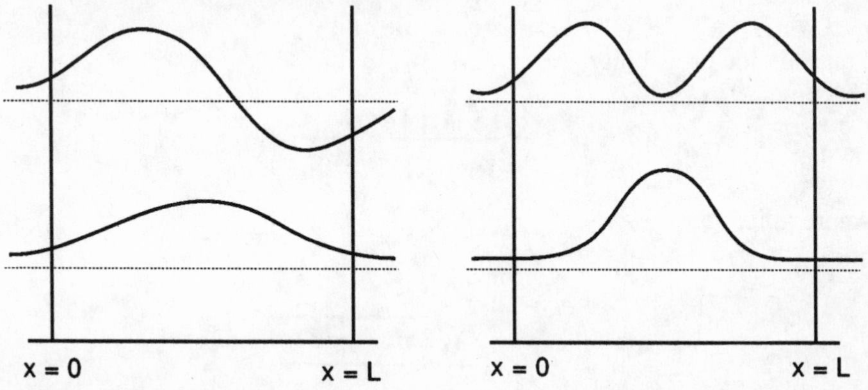

BARRIER PENETRATION

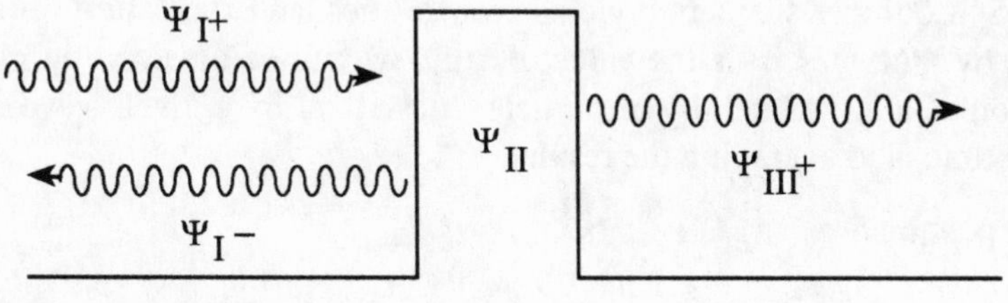

Schrödinger's Equations

$$\frac{\partial^2 \Psi_I}{\partial x^2} + \frac{2m}{\hbar} E\Psi_I = 0$$

$$\frac{\partial^2 \Psi_{III}}{\partial x^2} + \frac{2m}{\hbar} E\Psi_{III} = 0$$

with solutions

$$\Psi_I = Ae^{ik_1 x} + Be^{-ik_1 x}$$

$$\Psi_{III} = Fe^{ik_1 x} + Ge^{-ik_1 x}$$

Outside barrier:

$$k_1 = \frac{\sqrt{2mE}}{\hbar} = \frac{2\pi}{\lambda}$$

Incoming Wave:

$$\Psi_{I+} = Ae^{ik_1 x}$$

Reflected Wave:

$$\Psi_{I-} = Be^{-ik_1 x}$$

Transmitted Wave:

$$\Psi_{III+} = Fe^{ik_1 x}$$

Transmission probability:

$$T = \frac{|\Psi_{III+}|^2 v}{|\Psi_{I+}|^2 v} = \frac{FF^*}{AA^*}$$

Approximation:

$$T \approx e^{-2k_2 L}$$

$$k_2 \frac{\sqrt{2m(V-E)}}{\hbar}$$

EXPECTATION VALUES

As Schrödinger's equation yields probabilities, an expectation value can be described by $\Psi(x, t)$, $<x>$ is the value of x that would be obtained by measuring the position of a large quantity of particles, described by a given wave function, at a given time, and averaging the results.

For position:

$$<x> = \int_{-\infty}^{\infty} x|\Psi|^2 \, dx$$

The expectation value of either quantity such as potential energy, that is dependent on x and described by Ψ, can also be found.

$$<f(x)> = \int_{-\infty}^{\infty} f(x)|\Psi|^2 \, dx$$

CHAPTER 6

SPECIAL RELATIVITY

A. TIME DILATION AND LENGTH CONTRACTION

Time Dilation

$$f = \frac{f_0}{\sqrt{1 - \frac{v^2}{c^2}}}$$

where f_0 = Time passed on clock at rest relative to observer.
f = Time interval on clock in motion relative to observer.
v = Speed of motion relative to observer (relative motion)
c = Speed of light (3×10^8 m/s)

For an object or observer in motion, less time passes in a given interval (to the observer in motion) than for objects or observers relatively at rest.

Length Contraction

$$L = L_0 \sqrt{1 - \frac{v^2}{c^2}}$$

where L_0 = Length of object when at rest relative to observer
L = Length when approaching speed of light relative to observer.

To an observer relatively at rest, as an object approaches the speed of light, its length contracts.

B. DYNAMICS

Relativistic Mass

$$m = \frac{m_0}{\sqrt{1 - \frac{v^2}{c^2}}}$$

Relativistic Momentum

$$P = mv = \frac{m_0 v}{\sqrt{1-\frac{v^2}{c^2}}}$$

Relativistic Newton's 2nd Law

$$F = \frac{d}{dt}\left(\frac{m_0 v}{\sqrt{1-\frac{v^2}{c^2}}}\right)$$

Mass and Energy

Total Energy

$$mc^2 = m_0c^2 + k \text{ (kinetic energy)}$$

Rest Energy

$$E = m_0c^2$$

Total Energy

$$E = mc^2 = \frac{m_0 c^2}{\sqrt{1-\frac{v^2}{c^2}}}$$

$$\therefore \quad E^2 = m_0{}^2c^4 + p^2c^2$$

C. LORENTZ TRANSFORMATIONS

Given two reference frames (x, y, z, t) and (x', y', z', t'), when there is motion of the second frame in the x direction.

Not considering relativity:

$$\text{Galilean Transformation}\begin{cases} x' = x - vt \\ y' = y \\ z' = z \\ t' = t \end{cases}$$

To convert velocities in the "rest" frame to the moving frame, differentiate x', y' and z' with respect to time

$$v'_x = v_x - v, \quad v'_y = v_y, \quad v'_z = v_z$$

If we take v_x to be c, then according to the intuitively correct Galilean transformations, $c' = c - v$, which is impossible since c is an absolute speed.

An alternate transformation can be proposed:

$$x' = k\,(x - vt)$$

which *can* reduce to $x - vt$.

X in terms of x':

$$x = k(x' + vt'), \quad y' = y, \quad z' = z$$

Therefore

$$x = k^2\,(x - vt) + \text{kvt}'$$

and

$$t' = kt + \left(\frac{1 - k^2}{kv}\right)x$$

As light has the same speed for all inertial observers:

$$x = ct \quad \text{and} \quad x = ct'$$

we can evaluate k and solve for x.

$$k(x - vt) = ckt + \left(\frac{1 - k^2}{kv}\right)cx$$

so

$$x = \frac{ckt + vkt}{k - \left(\frac{1 - k^2}{kv}\right)c}$$

$$= ct\left[\frac{1 + \frac{v}{c}}{1 - \left(\frac{1}{k^2} - 1\right)\frac{c}{v}}\right]$$

for x to $= ct$,

$$\frac{1 + \frac{v}{c}}{1 - \left(\frac{1}{k^2 - 1}\right)\frac{c}{v}} = 1$$

$$k = \frac{1}{\sqrt{1 - \frac{v^2}{c^2}}}$$

Lorentz Transformation:

$$x' = k(x - vt)$$

CHAPTER 7

OPTICS AND WAVE PHENOMENA

A. MECHANICAL WAVES

BASIC PROPERTIES

One way of transporting energy from one point to another is through wave motion.

There are two main types of wave motion.

Transverse waves — the disturbance in the medium is transverse, or at right angles, to the line of motion of the wave.

The shape of a transverse wave is a sine wave function, like the one shown below.

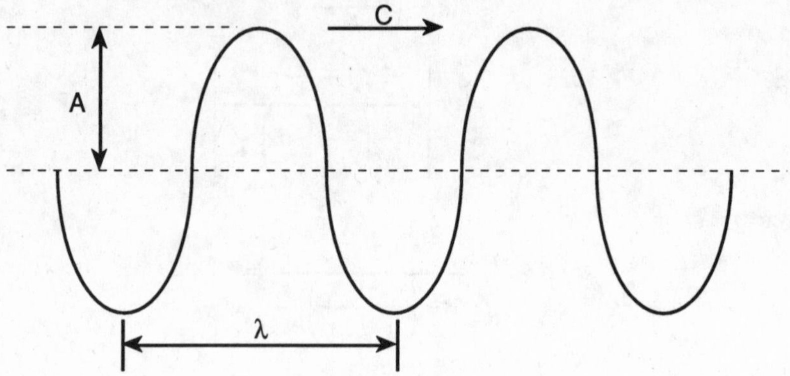

where λ = wavelength (distance between adjacent peaks or valleys).
A = amplitude (distance between the central position and an extreme position).

Longitudinal waves — the disturbance in the medium acts in the same direction that the wave is travelling.

A longitudinal wave appears in a spring as shown on the following page.

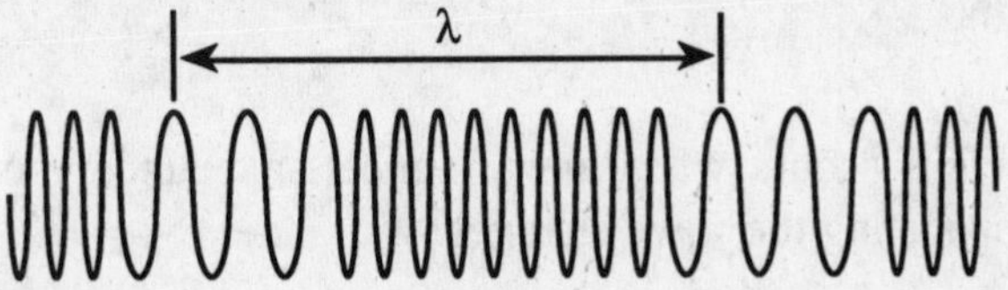

Sound waves are an example of longitudinal waves.

The period, T, is the amount of time to complete one oscillation in all types of waves.

The frequency, ν, is the number of oscillations per second. In other words, frequency is the inverse of T for all types of waves.

$$\nu = \frac{1}{T}$$

For all waves, the waveform travels a distance λ in time T. Therefore, the speed of the wave, c, is

$$c = \frac{\lambda}{T} = \nu\lambda$$

SUPERPOSITION PRINCIPLE

When two wave-forms are travelling in the opposite direction along the same line of motion, and the waveforms collide, the resultant displacement at a point along the line of motion is simply the algebraic sum of the separate wave disturbances. This is referred to as the principle of superposition.

However, the two waves will leave the collision exactly as they were before the meeting.

The superposition of separate waveforms is known as interference.

Constructive interference — The resultant displacement is greater than the individual displacements.

Destructive interference — The resultant displacement is less than the individual displacements.

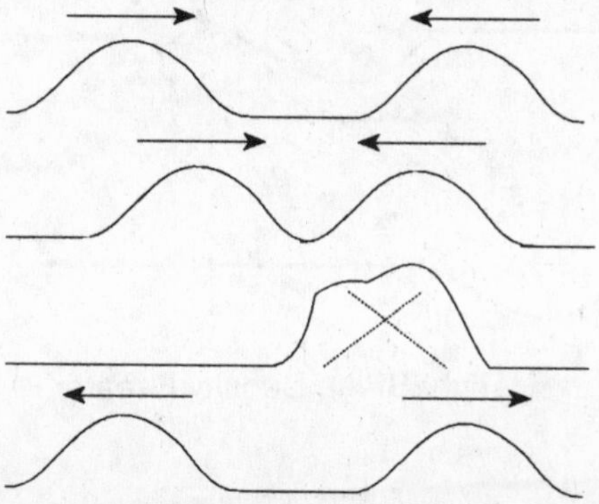

REFLECTION

Reflection occurs when a wave meets a boundary or a place where the medium propagating the wave changes.

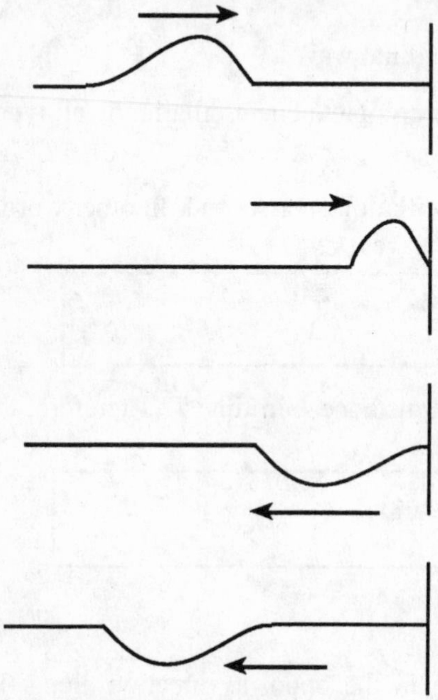

Infinitely Massive Boundary

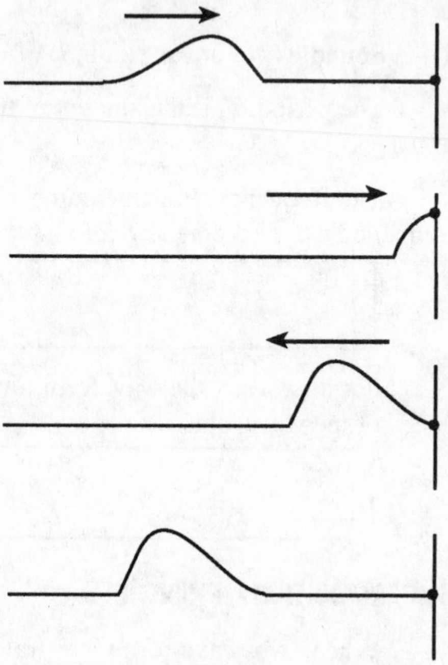

Free End

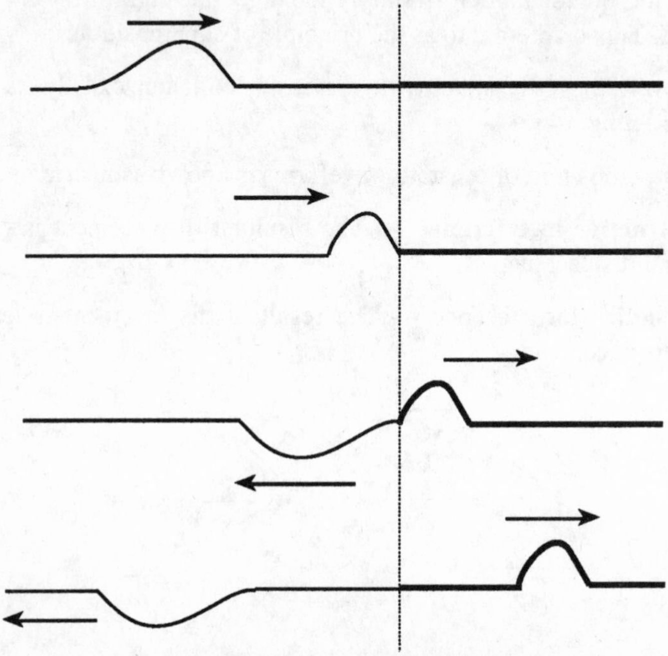

Right String Density Greater

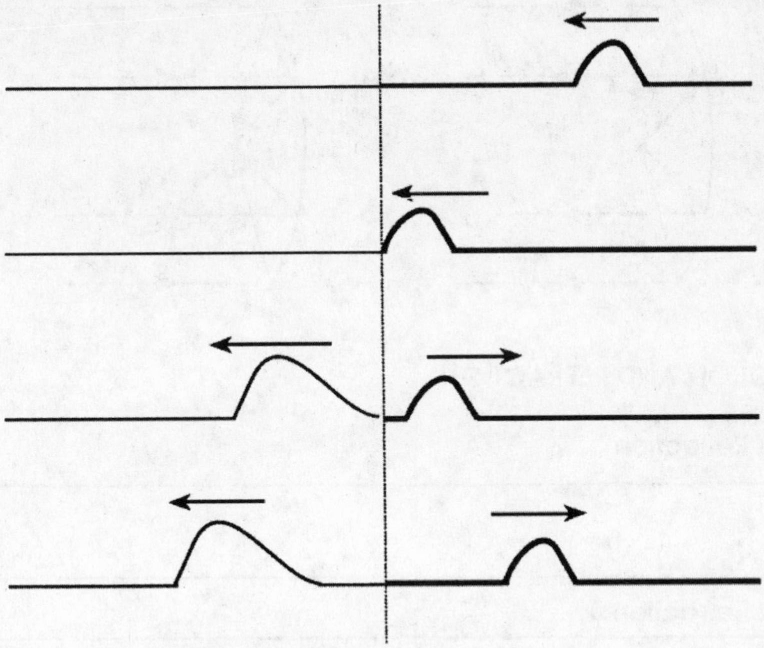

Left String Density Greater

BEATS

When two tones of nearly the same pitch are sounded simultaneously, the human ear encounters a sensation known as beats.

For two sinusoidal waves with frequencies ν_1 and ν_2 and the same amplitude, the equation for displacement (the beat equation) becomes

$$y = \left[2A \cos 2\pi \left(\frac{\nu_1 - \nu_2}{2} \right) t \right] \cos 2\pi \left(\frac{\nu_1 + \nu_2}{2} \right) t$$

The beat frequency, ν_B, is

$$\nu_B = \nu_1 - \nu_2$$

B. RAY OPTICS

RECIPROCITY PRINCIPLE

If a ray travels from 1 to 2, a ray will also travel from 2 to 1 by the same route. (See figure following.)

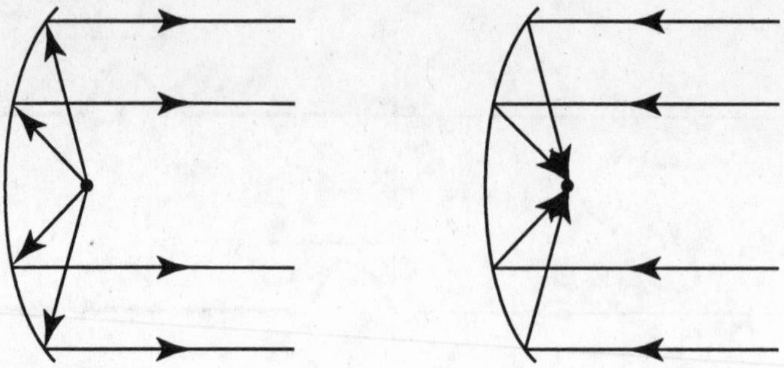

REFLECTION AND REFRACTION

Law of Reflection

$$\theta'_1 = \theta_1$$

Law of Refraction

$$\frac{\sin\theta_1}{\sin\theta_2} = n_{21}$$

where θ'_1 = Angle of Reflection
θ_1 = Angle of Incidence
θ_2 = Angle of Refraction
n_{21} = Index of Refraction of Medium 2 with respect to medium 1.

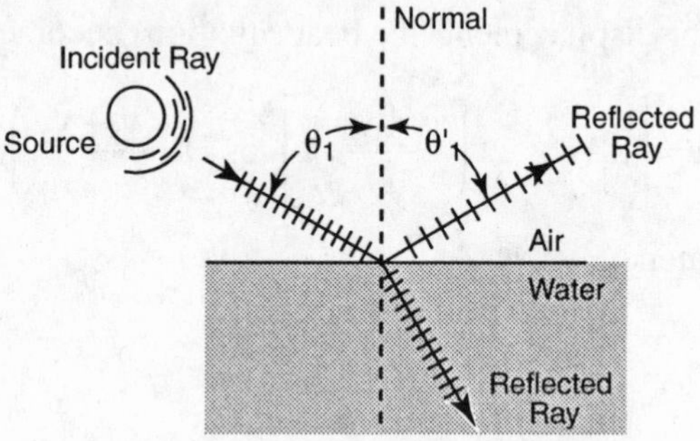

Reflection and Refraction

TOTAL INTERNAL REFLECTION

Critical Angle, θc

$$\sin\theta_c = \frac{n_2}{n_1}$$

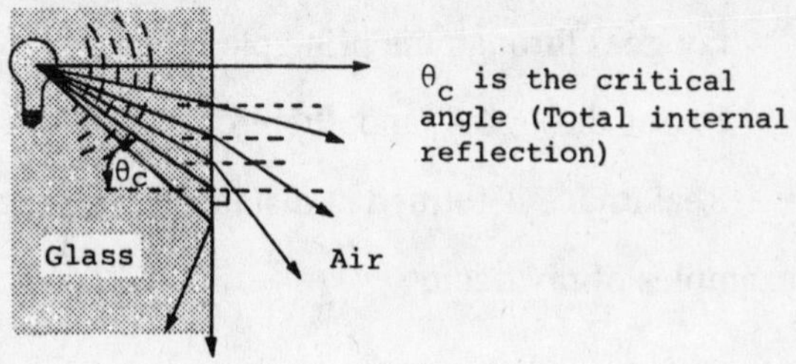

Internal Reflection

C. THIN LENSES

Thin Lens — Any lens whose thickness is small when compared with its radius.

Focal Point — The point at which all rays intersect.

Focal Length — The distance from focal point to the center of the lens.

Real Image — Light rays actually pass through the image location.

Virtual Image — The image is formed by rays which appear to come from the location of the image.

RAY TRACING

Procedure for locating image given object location, lens type, and focal length.

EXAMPLE

Lens tracing using a convex lens

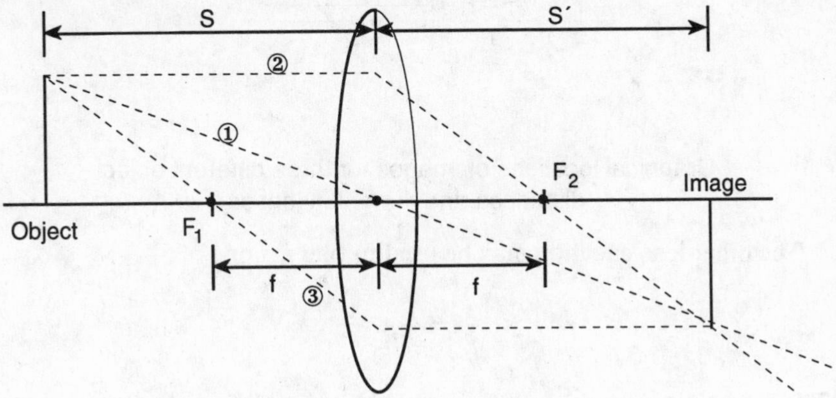

Ray 1: Passes through the center of the thin lens and, therefore, its path is unchanged.

Ray 2: Is parallel to the lens axis and, therefore, is deviated so that the ray goes through the principle focus, F_2.

Ray 3: Passes through F_1 and, therefore, is deviated parallel to lens axis.

Result: Real image is formed at distance s' from lens.

Other examples of ray tracing

Convex Lens with Real Image

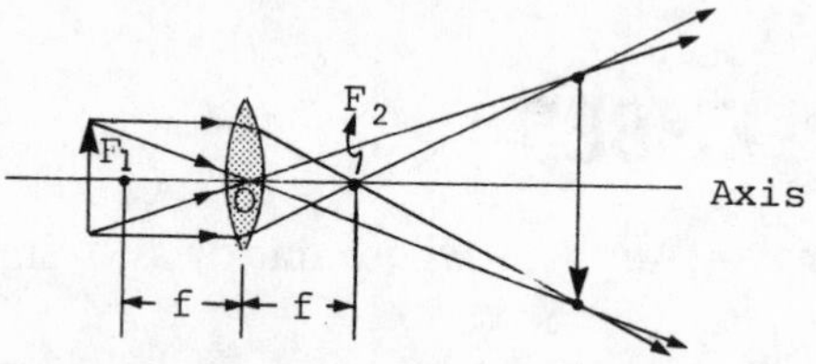

F_1, F_2 = Focal points

f = Focal length

Convex Lens with Virtual Image

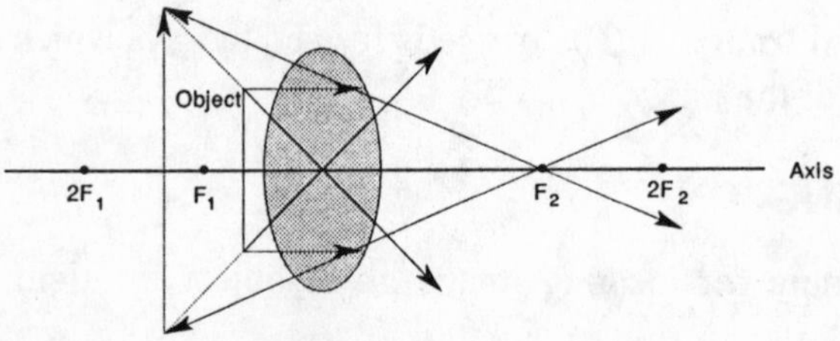

Concave Lens with Virtual Image

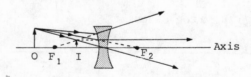

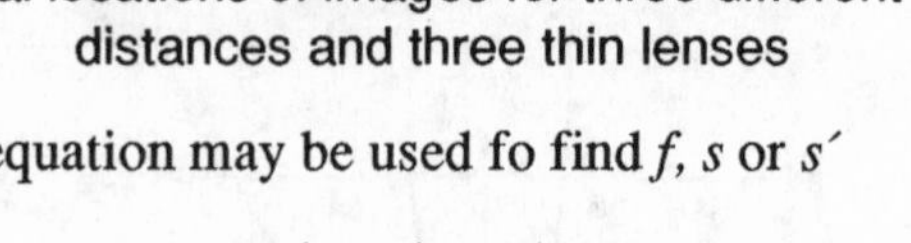

Graphical locations of images for three different object distances and three thin lenses

The other lens equation may be used fo find f, s or s'

$$\frac{1}{f} = \frac{1}{s} + \frac{1}{s'}$$

NOTE: For concave lens $f < 0$; for virtual images $s' < 0$,

The magnification of the image is

$$m = \frac{s'}{s}$$

D. INTERFERENCE

YOUNG'S EXPERIMENT

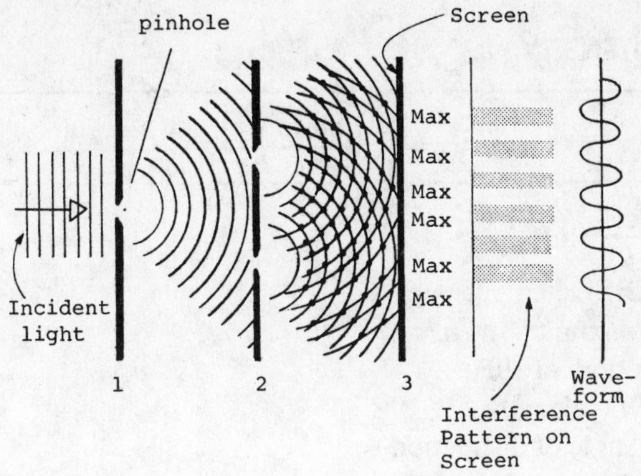

Diffraction wave patterns for Young's Double-slit experiment

INTERFERENCE MAXIMA AND MINIMA

Maxima

$$d \sin \theta = m\lambda$$

where m = 0, 1, 2, … (maxima)

Minima

$$d \sin \theta = (m - {}^1/_2)\, \lambda$$

where m = 1, 2, … (minima)

d = Distance between slits or point sources

θ = Angle between the midpoint of the two slits or point sources and a point on the screen.

λ = Wavelength

E. DIFFRACTION

SINGLE SLIT DIFFRACTION

$$a \sin \theta = m\lambda$$

where m = 1, 2, 3, ... (minima)
a = Width of slit
θ = Angle of diffraction
λ = Wavelength

DIFFRACTED INTENSITY

$$I_\theta = I_m \left(\frac{\sin \alpha}{\alpha} \right)^2$$

where $\alpha = \frac{\pi a}{\lambda} \sin \theta$
I_θ = Diffracted intensity
I_m = Maximum intensity
a = Width of slit
λ = Wavelength
θ = Angle of diffraction

CIRCULAR DIFFRACTION

$$\sin \theta = 1.22 \frac{\lambda}{d}$$

where θ = Angle of diffraction
λ = Wavelength
d = Diameter of circular aperture or lens

DOUBLE SLIT DIFFRACTION

$$I_\theta = I_m (\cos \beta)^2 \left(\frac{\sin \alpha}{\alpha} \right)^2$$

where $\beta = \frac{\pi d}{\lambda} \sin \theta$

$\alpha = \frac{\pi a}{\lambda} \sin \theta$

I_θ = Diffracted intensity
I_m = Maximum intensity
d = Distance between centers of slits
a = Width of slit
λ = Wavelength
θ = Angle of diffraction

MULTIPLE SLIT DIFFRACTION

Maxima

$$d \sin \theta = m\lambda$$

where m = 0, 1, 2, ...
d = Distance between centers of slits
θ = Angle of diffraction
λ = Wavelength

Angular Width

$$\Delta\theta_m = \frac{\lambda}{Nd \cos \theta_m}$$

where $\Delta\theta_m$ = Angular width of the maxima
λ = Wavelength
N = Number of slits
d = Distance between the centers of slits
θ_m = Angle of diffraction for the principal maximum

DIFFRACTION GRATINGS

Dispersion

$$D = \frac{m}{d \cos \theta}$$

where D = Dispersion (Angular Separation)
m = Order of Maxima
θ = Angle of Diffraction

Resolving Power

$$R = \frac{\lambda}{\Delta\lambda} = Nm$$

where R = Resolving power
λ = Mean wavelength
$\Delta\lambda$ = Wavelength difference
N = Number of rulings in the grating
m = Order of maxima

TABLE OF INFORMATION

Rest mass of the electron	m_e	$= 9.11 \times 10^{-31}$ kilogram
		$= 9.11 \times 10^{-28}$ gram
Magnitude of the electron charge	e	$= 1.60 \times 10^{-19}$ coulomb
		$= 4.80 \times 10^{-10}$ statcoulomb (esu)
Avogadro's number	N_0	$= 6.02 \times 10^{23}$ per mole
Universal gas constant	R	$= 8.314$ joules/ (mole· K)
Boltzmann's constant	k	$= 1.38 \times 10^{-23}$ joule/K
		$= 1.38 \times 10^{-16}$ erg/K
Speed of light	c	$= 3.00 \times 10^{8}$ m/s
		$= 3.00 \times 10^{10}$ cm/s
Planck's constant	h	$= 6.63 \times 10^{-34}$ joule·second
		$= 4.14 \times 10^{-15}$ eV·second
Vacuum permittivity	ε_0	$= 8.85 \times 10^{-12}$ coulomb^2/(newton·meter^2)
Vacuum permeability	μ_0	$= 4\pi \times 10^{-7}$ weber/(ampere·meter)
Universal gravitational constant	G	$= 6.67 \times 10^{-11}$ meter^3/(kilogram·second^2)
Acceleration due to gravity	g	$= 9.80$ m/s^2 = 980 cm/s^2
1 atmosphere pressure	1 atm	$= 1.0 \times 10^{5}$ newton/meter^2
		$= 1.0 \times 10^{5}$ pascals (Pa)
1 angstrom	1 Å	$= 1 \times 10^{-10}$ meter
	1 weber/m^2	= 1 tesla = 10^4 gauss

Notations

Vectors — bold letter	**F, v**
Unit vectors — usually the bold letters	**x, y, z**
Planck's constant	$\frac{h}{2\pi} = \hbar$
Derivatives — indicated by primed symbols (Whether the derivative is with respect to time $\frac{d}{dt}$ or position $\frac{d}{dx}$ is apparent from the context of the problem.)	x', x''

The Graduate Record Examination in

PHYSICS

Test 1

THE GRADUATE RECORD EXAMINATION IN

PHYSICS

TEST 1 – ANSWER SHEET

1. Ⓐ Ⓑ Ⓒ Ⓓ Ⓔ
2. Ⓐ Ⓑ Ⓒ Ⓓ Ⓔ
3. Ⓐ Ⓑ Ⓒ Ⓓ Ⓔ
4. Ⓐ Ⓑ Ⓒ Ⓓ Ⓔ
5. Ⓐ Ⓑ Ⓒ Ⓓ Ⓔ
6. Ⓐ Ⓑ Ⓒ Ⓓ Ⓔ
7. Ⓐ Ⓑ Ⓒ Ⓓ Ⓔ
8. Ⓐ Ⓑ Ⓒ Ⓓ Ⓔ
9. Ⓐ Ⓑ Ⓒ Ⓓ Ⓔ
10. Ⓐ Ⓑ Ⓒ Ⓓ Ⓔ
11. Ⓐ Ⓑ Ⓒ Ⓓ Ⓔ
12. Ⓐ Ⓑ Ⓒ Ⓓ Ⓔ
13. Ⓐ Ⓑ Ⓒ Ⓓ Ⓔ
14. Ⓐ Ⓑ Ⓒ Ⓓ Ⓔ
15. Ⓐ Ⓑ Ⓒ Ⓓ Ⓔ
16. Ⓐ Ⓑ Ⓒ Ⓓ Ⓔ
17. Ⓐ Ⓑ Ⓒ Ⓓ Ⓔ
18. Ⓐ Ⓑ Ⓒ Ⓓ Ⓔ
19. Ⓐ Ⓑ Ⓒ Ⓓ Ⓔ
20. Ⓐ Ⓑ Ⓒ Ⓓ Ⓔ
21. Ⓐ Ⓑ Ⓒ Ⓓ Ⓔ
22. Ⓐ Ⓑ Ⓒ Ⓓ Ⓔ
23. Ⓐ Ⓑ Ⓒ Ⓓ Ⓔ
24. Ⓐ Ⓑ Ⓒ Ⓓ Ⓔ
25. Ⓐ Ⓑ Ⓒ Ⓓ Ⓔ
26. Ⓐ Ⓑ Ⓒ Ⓓ Ⓔ
27. Ⓐ Ⓑ Ⓒ Ⓓ Ⓔ
28. Ⓐ Ⓑ Ⓒ Ⓓ Ⓔ
29. Ⓐ Ⓑ Ⓒ Ⓓ Ⓔ
30. Ⓐ Ⓑ Ⓒ Ⓓ Ⓔ
31. Ⓐ Ⓑ Ⓒ Ⓓ Ⓔ
32. Ⓐ Ⓑ Ⓒ Ⓓ Ⓔ
33. Ⓐ Ⓑ Ⓒ Ⓓ Ⓔ
34. Ⓐ Ⓑ Ⓒ Ⓓ Ⓔ
35. Ⓐ Ⓑ Ⓒ Ⓓ Ⓔ
36. Ⓐ Ⓑ Ⓒ Ⓓ Ⓔ
37. Ⓐ Ⓑ Ⓒ Ⓓ Ⓔ
38. Ⓐ Ⓑ Ⓒ Ⓓ Ⓔ
39. Ⓐ Ⓑ Ⓒ Ⓓ Ⓔ
40. Ⓐ Ⓑ Ⓒ Ⓓ Ⓔ
41. Ⓐ Ⓑ Ⓒ Ⓓ Ⓔ
42. Ⓐ Ⓑ Ⓒ Ⓓ Ⓔ
43. Ⓐ Ⓑ Ⓒ Ⓓ Ⓔ
44. Ⓐ Ⓑ Ⓒ Ⓓ Ⓔ
45. Ⓐ Ⓑ Ⓒ Ⓓ Ⓔ
46. Ⓐ Ⓑ Ⓒ Ⓓ Ⓔ
47. Ⓐ Ⓑ Ⓒ Ⓓ Ⓔ
48. Ⓐ Ⓑ Ⓒ Ⓓ Ⓔ
49. Ⓐ Ⓑ Ⓒ Ⓓ Ⓔ
50. Ⓐ Ⓑ Ⓒ Ⓓ Ⓔ
51. Ⓐ Ⓑ Ⓒ Ⓓ Ⓔ
52. Ⓐ Ⓑ Ⓒ Ⓓ Ⓔ
53. Ⓐ Ⓑ Ⓒ Ⓓ Ⓔ
54. Ⓐ Ⓑ Ⓒ Ⓓ Ⓔ
55. Ⓐ Ⓑ Ⓒ Ⓓ Ⓔ
56. Ⓐ Ⓑ Ⓒ Ⓓ Ⓔ
57. Ⓐ Ⓑ Ⓒ Ⓓ Ⓔ
58. Ⓐ Ⓑ Ⓒ Ⓓ Ⓔ
59. Ⓐ Ⓑ Ⓒ Ⓓ Ⓔ
60. Ⓐ Ⓑ Ⓒ Ⓓ Ⓔ
61. Ⓐ Ⓑ Ⓒ Ⓓ Ⓔ
62. Ⓐ Ⓑ Ⓒ Ⓓ Ⓔ
63. Ⓐ Ⓑ Ⓒ Ⓓ Ⓔ
64. Ⓐ Ⓑ Ⓒ Ⓓ Ⓔ
65. Ⓐ Ⓑ Ⓒ Ⓓ Ⓔ
66. Ⓐ Ⓑ Ⓒ Ⓓ Ⓔ
67. Ⓐ Ⓑ Ⓒ Ⓓ Ⓔ
68. Ⓐ Ⓑ Ⓒ Ⓓ Ⓔ
69. Ⓐ Ⓑ Ⓒ Ⓓ Ⓔ
70. Ⓐ Ⓑ Ⓒ Ⓓ Ⓔ
71. Ⓐ Ⓑ Ⓒ Ⓓ Ⓔ
72. Ⓐ Ⓑ Ⓒ Ⓓ Ⓔ
73. Ⓐ Ⓑ Ⓒ Ⓓ Ⓔ
74. Ⓐ Ⓑ Ⓒ Ⓓ Ⓔ
75. Ⓐ Ⓑ Ⓒ Ⓓ Ⓔ
76. Ⓐ Ⓑ Ⓒ Ⓓ Ⓔ
77. Ⓐ Ⓑ Ⓒ Ⓓ Ⓔ
78. Ⓐ Ⓑ Ⓒ Ⓓ Ⓔ
79. Ⓐ Ⓑ Ⓒ Ⓓ Ⓔ
80. Ⓐ Ⓑ Ⓒ Ⓓ Ⓔ
81. Ⓐ Ⓑ Ⓒ Ⓓ Ⓔ
82. Ⓐ Ⓑ Ⓒ Ⓓ Ⓔ
83. Ⓐ Ⓑ Ⓒ Ⓓ Ⓔ
84. Ⓐ Ⓑ Ⓒ Ⓓ Ⓔ
85. Ⓐ Ⓑ Ⓒ Ⓓ Ⓔ
86. Ⓐ Ⓑ Ⓒ Ⓓ Ⓔ
87. Ⓐ Ⓑ Ⓒ Ⓓ Ⓔ
88. Ⓐ Ⓑ Ⓒ Ⓓ Ⓔ
89. Ⓐ Ⓑ Ⓒ Ⓓ Ⓔ
90. Ⓐ Ⓑ Ⓒ Ⓓ Ⓔ
91. Ⓐ Ⓑ Ⓒ Ⓓ Ⓔ
92. Ⓐ Ⓑ Ⓒ Ⓓ Ⓔ
93. Ⓐ Ⓑ Ⓒ Ⓓ Ⓔ
94. Ⓐ Ⓑ Ⓒ Ⓓ Ⓔ
95. Ⓐ Ⓑ Ⓒ Ⓓ Ⓔ
96. Ⓐ Ⓑ Ⓒ Ⓓ Ⓔ
97. Ⓐ Ⓑ Ⓒ Ⓓ Ⓔ
98. Ⓐ Ⓑ Ⓒ Ⓓ Ⓔ
99. Ⓐ Ⓑ Ⓒ Ⓓ Ⓔ
100. Ⓐ Ⓑ Ⓒ Ⓓ Ⓔ

GRE PHYSICS
TEST 1

TIME: 170 Minutes
100 Questions

DIRECTIONS: Each of the questions or incomplete statements below is followed by five answer choices or completions. Choose the best answer to each question.

1. It is possible that the Newtonian theory of gravitation may need to be modified at short range. Suppose that the potential energy between two masses m and m' is given by

$$V(r) = -\frac{Gmm'}{r}(1 - ae^{-r/\lambda}).$$

For short distances $r << \lambda$, calculate the force between m and m'.

(A) $F = -Gmm'/r^2$

(B) $F = -Gmm'(1-a)/r^2$

(C) $F = -Gmm'(1+a)/r^2$

(D) $F = -Gmm'a/\lambda r$

(E) $F = Gmm'(1-a)/r$

2. The Stern Gerlach experiment in quantum physics demonstrates the quantization of spin. Sample data is shown in the figure. The conclusion is that

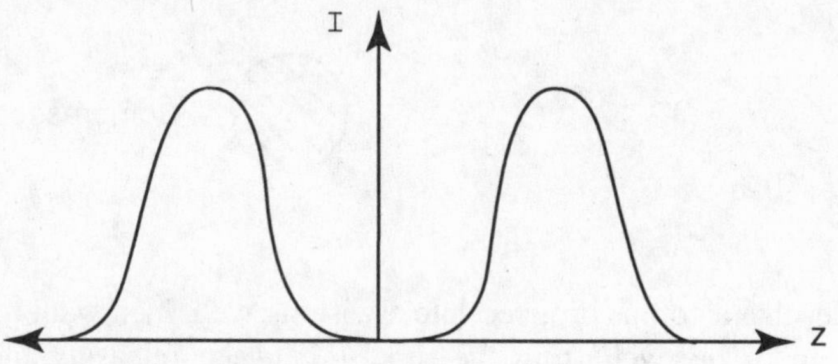

(A) the electron is a fermion and can have spin up or down

(B) the electron has no spin

(C) the electron can only have spin up

(D) the electron can only have spin down

(E) the electron is a fermion and can have spin 3/2, 1/2, – 1/2, or – 3/2

3. By the early 1900's the two major theories of physics were Maxwell's equations and Newton's laws. The transformation from a lab reference frame to a moving reference frame was done by the Galilean transformation ($x' = x - vt$ and $t' = t$). Which of the two major theories was initially thought to be invariant under these transformation equations?

(A) Maxwell's equations

(B) neither Maxwell's equations nor Newton's laws

(C) both Maxwell's equations and Newton's laws

(D) Newton's laws

(E) the invariance is not important

4. In elementary nuclear physics, we learn about the Fermi gas model of the nucleus. The Fermi energy for normal nuclear density ρ_0 is 38.4 MeV. Suppose that the nucleus is compressed, for example in a heavy ion collision. What is the dependence of the Fermi energy on density?

(A) ρ^2

(B) it is independent of density

(C) $\rho^{2/3}$

(D) $\rho^{1/3}$

(E) ρ

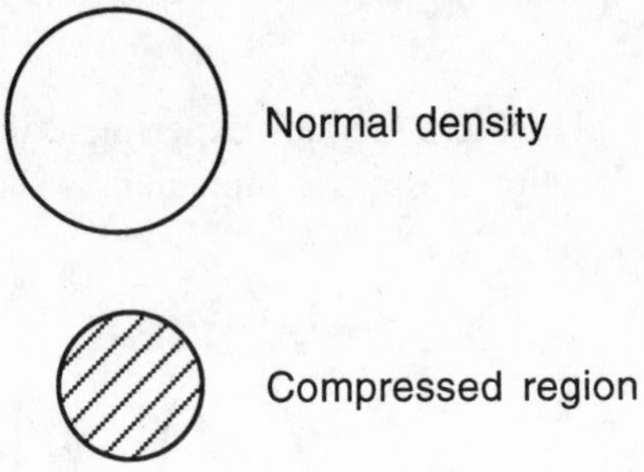

5. Consider that a coin is dropped into a wishing well. You want to determine the depth of the well from the time T between releasing the coin and hearing it hit the bottom. If the speed of sound is 330 m/s, and $T = 2.059$ s, what is the depth h of the well?

(A) 20.77 m

(B) 19.60 m

(C) 23,564 m

(D) 18.43 m

(E) 39.20 m

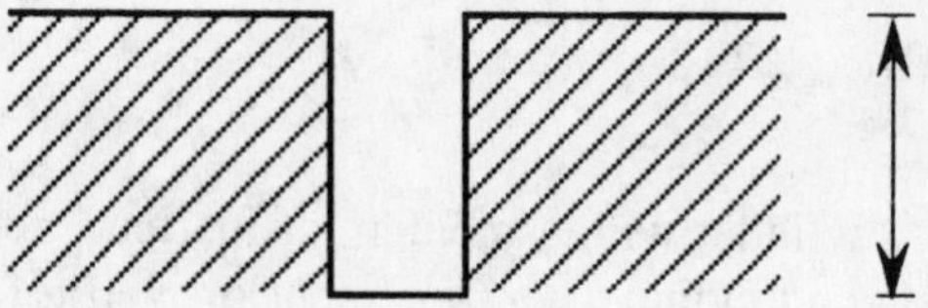

6. A 10 g bullet is fired into a 2 kg ballistic pendulum as shown in the figure. The bullet remains in the block after the collision and the system rises to a maximum height of 20 cm. Find the initial speed of the bullet.

(A) 28.0 m/s

(B) 23.8 m/s

(C) 3.98 m/s

(D) 719 m/s

(E) 398 m/s

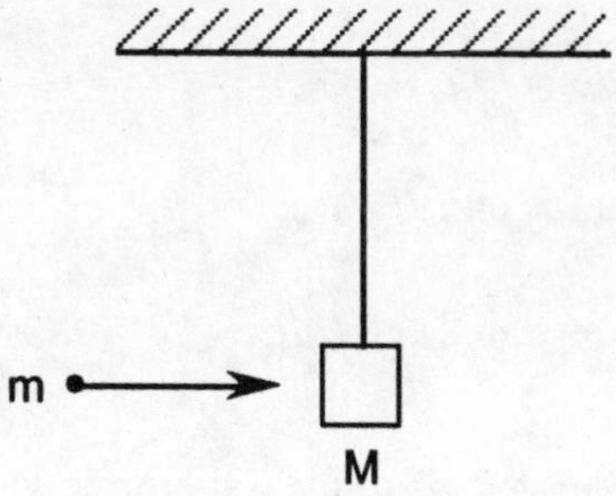

7. A horizontal beam of length 10 m and weight 200 N is attached to a wall as shown. The far end is supported by a cable which makes an angle of 60° with respect to the beam. A 500 N person stands 2 m from the wall. Determine the tension in the cable.

(A) 0 N

(B) 700 N

(C) 500 N

(D) 231 N

(E) 808 N

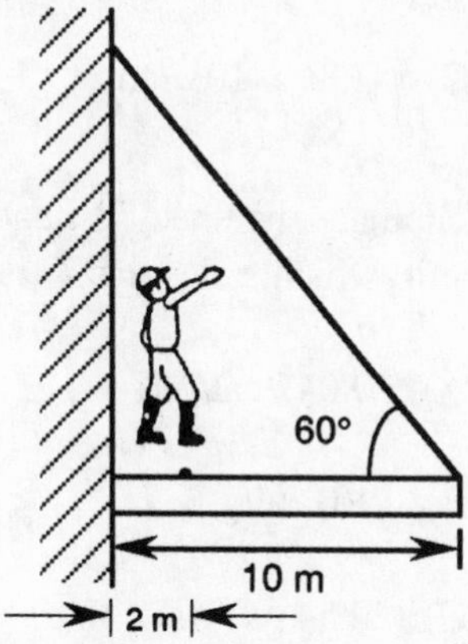

8. When a 4.0 kg mass is hung vertically on a light spring that obeys Hooke's law, the spring stretches 2.0 cm. How much work must an external agent do to stretch the spring 4.0 cm from its equilibrium position?

(A) 1.57 J

(B) 0.39 J

(C) 0.20 J

(D) 3.14 J

(E) 0.78 J

9. A cylinder with a moment of inertia I_0 rotates with angular velocity ω_0. A second cylinder with moment of inertia I_1 initially not rotating drops onto the first cylinder and the two reach the same final angular velocity ω_f. Find ω_f.

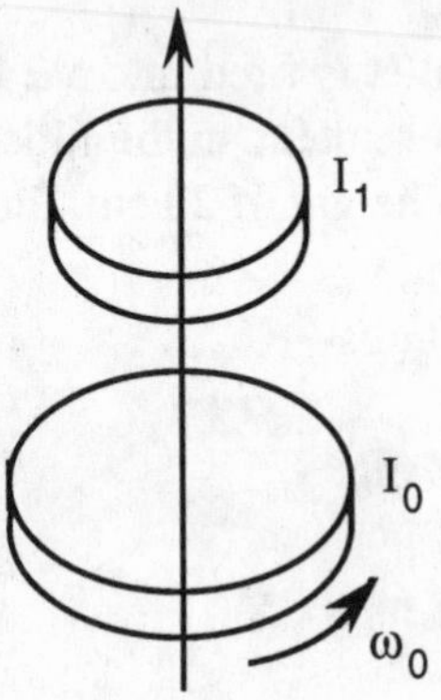

(A) $\omega_f = \omega_0$

(B) $\omega_f = \omega_0\, I_0/I_1$

(C) $\omega_f = I_0\omega_0/(I_0 + I_1)$

(D) $\omega_f = \omega_0\, I_1/I_0$

(E) $\omega_f = \omega_0\,(I_0 + I_1)/I_0$

10. Three moles of an ideal diatomic gas occupy a volume of 20 m^3 at 300 K. If the gas expands adiabatically to 40 m^3, then find the final pressure.

(A) $1.62 \times 10^3 d/\text{cm}^2$

(D) $1.82 \times 10^3 d/\text{cm}^2$

(B) $1.42 \times 10^3 d/\text{cm}^2$

(E) $3.74 \times 10^3 d/\text{cm}^2$

(C) $2.84 \times 10^3 d/\text{cm}^2$

11. Calculate the specific heat of a copper coin using the law of Dulong and Petit, which states that $C_V = 3R$.

(A) 0.047 cal/g.K

(D) 0.27 cal/g.K

(B) 1.0 cal/g.K

(E) 0.094 cal/g.K

(C) 0.54 cal/g.K

12. The tire of an automobile is filled with air to a gauge pressure of 35 psi at 20° C in the summer time. What is the gauge pressure in the tire when the temperature falls to 0° C in the winter time? Assume that the volume does not change and that the atmospheric pressure is a constant 14.70 psi.

(A) 49.7 psi

(B) 35 psi

(C) 14.7 psi

(D) 31.6 psi

(E) 46.3 psi

13. Consider a cone, with a light bulb at the vertex, cut by a plane making an angle of 30° with base. The area of the plane inside the cone has an image of area s on the base. If the area of the base is A and the average light intensity at the base is I, what is the average light intensity on the inclined plane?

(A) $\frac{IA}{2s}$

(B) $\frac{I^2}{As}$

(C) $\frac{\sqrt{3}\,IA}{2s}$

(D) $\frac{\sqrt{3}\,IA}{s}$

(E) $\frac{IA}{s}$

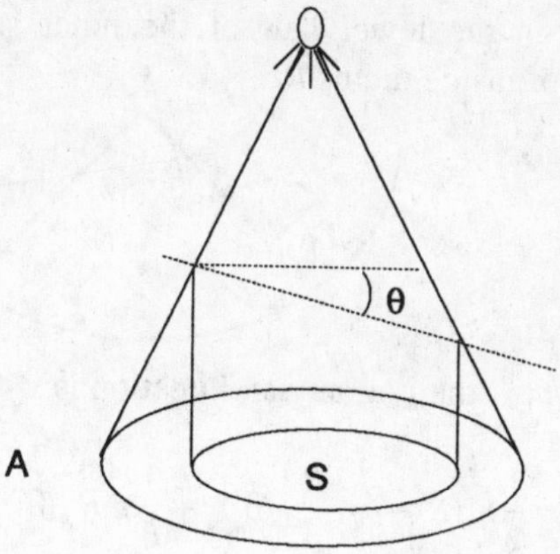

14. One of the following lists the four fundamental forces of nature in order of increasing strength. Choose the correct letter.

(A) gravitational, weak, electromagnetic, nuclear

(B) weak, electromagnetic, nuclear, gravitational

(C) electromagnetic, weak, gravitational, nuclear

(D) weak, gravitational, electromagnetic, nuclear

(E) nuclear, electromagnetic, weak, gravitational

15. A metallic chain of length L and mass M is vertically hung above a surface with one end in contact with it. The chain is then released to fall freely. If x is the distance covered by the end of the chain, how much force (exerted by the bottom surface) will the chain experience at any instance during the process?

(A) $N = Mg - Mx''$

(B) $N = 3Mg$

(C) $N = Mg - 2Mx''$

(D) $N = (3M / L)\, gx$

(E) $N = Mg$

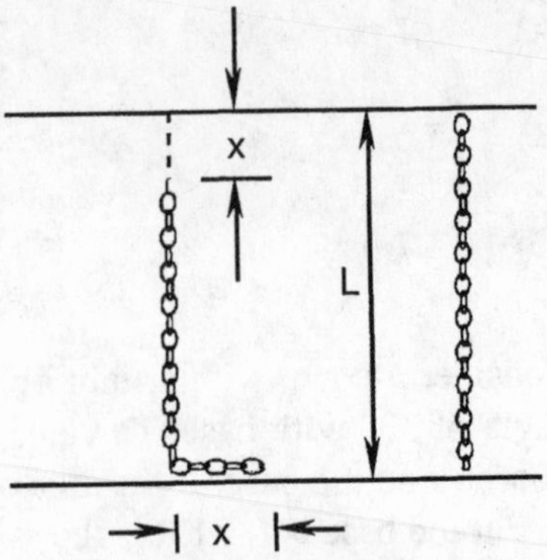

16. A thin-shelled sphere of radius ρ and mass m is constrained to roll without slipping on the lower half of the inner surface of a hollow, stationary cylinder of inside radius R.

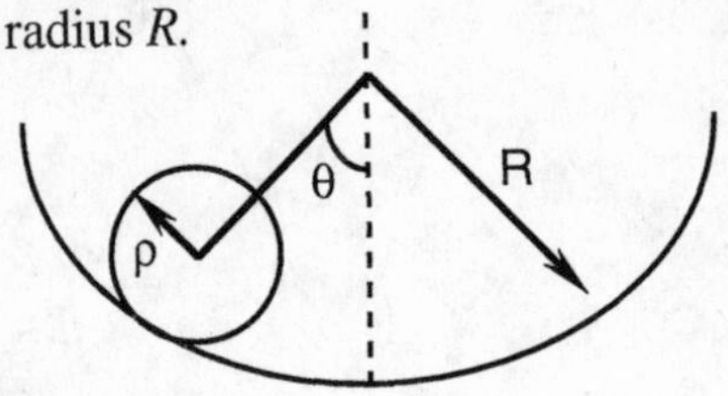

If $I = \frac{2}{3} m\rho^2$, the Lagrangian Function is:

(A) $L = \frac{1}{2} m(R-\rho)^2 \frac{R^2}{\rho^2}(\theta')^2 + \frac{1}{6} mR^2(\theta')^2 + mg(R-\rho)\cos\theta$

(B) $L = \frac{1}{6} mR^2(\theta')^2 + mg(R-\rho)\cos\theta$

(C) $L = \frac{1}{2} m(R-\rho)^2 \frac{R^2}{\rho^2}(\theta')^2 - \frac{1}{6} mR^2(\theta')^2 + mg(R-\rho)\cos\theta$

(D) $L = \frac{1}{2} m(R-\rho)^2 \frac{R^2}{\rho^2}(\theta')^2 + mg(R-\rho)\cos\theta$

(E) $L = \frac{1}{2} m(R-\rho)^2 \frac{R^2}{\rho^2}(\theta')^2 + \frac{1}{6} mR^2(\theta')^2 - mg(R-\rho)\cos\theta$

17. Two equal masses $m_1 = m_2 = m$ are connected by a spring having Hooke's constant k. If the equilibrium separation is l_0 and the spring rests on a frictionless horizontal surface, then derive ω_0 the angular frequency.

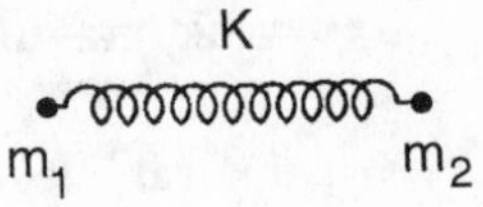

(A) $\sqrt{k/m}$

(B) $\sqrt{2k/m}$

(C) $\sqrt{3k/m}$

(D) $2\sqrt{k/m}$

(E) $\sqrt{g/l_0}$

18. Which of the following defines a conservative force?

(A) $\oint \mathbf{F} \cdot d\mathbf{A} = 0$ or $\nabla \cdot \mathbf{F} = 0$.

(B) The force must be frictional.

(C) The force must be nuclear.

(D) The force must be electromagnetic.

(E) $\oint \mathbf{F} \cdot d\mathbf{r} = 0$ or $\nabla \times \mathbf{F} = 0$.

19. Consider a particle of mass m at temperature T which follows classical Maxwell-Boltzmann statistics. Find the average speed $\langle v \rangle$.

(A) $\sqrt{3kT/m}$

(B) $\sqrt{kT/m}$

(C) $\sqrt{2kT/\pi m}$

(D) $\sqrt{8kT/\pi m}$

(E) $\sqrt{2kT/m}$

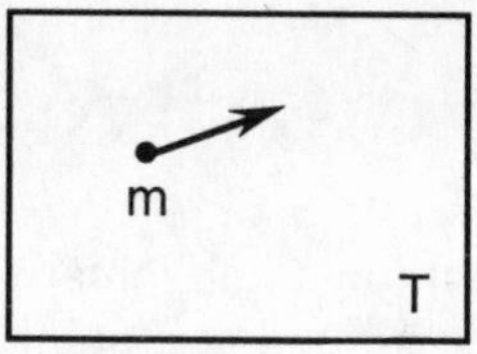

20. A 100 g mass attached to a spring moves on a horizontal frictionless table in simple harmonic motion with amplitude 16 cm and period 2 s. Assuming that the mass is released from rest at $t = 0$ s and $x = -16$ cm, find the displacement as a function of time.

(A) $x = 16 \cos(\pi t)$

(B) $x = -16 \cos(\pi t + \pi)$

(C) $x = 16 \cos(\pi t + \pi)$

(D) $x = -16 \cos(2\pi t + \pi)$

(E) $x = -16 \cos\left(\frac{\pi t}{2}\right)$

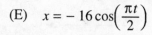

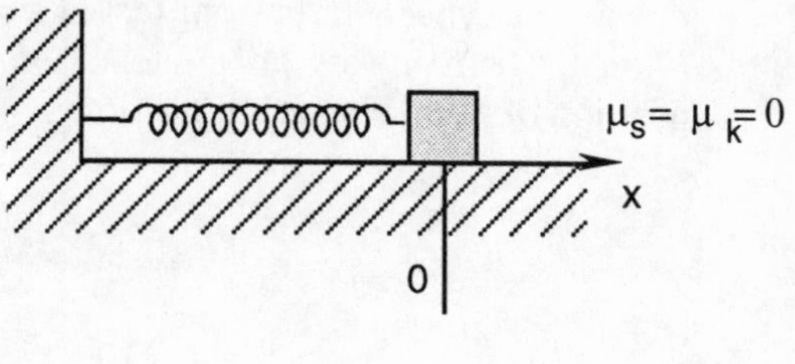

21. Consider a simple laboratory experiment where the length and width of a rectangle are measured $l = 5.45 \pm .05$ cm and $w = 3.86 \pm .02$ cm. Find the uncertainty in the area ΔA.

(A) 0.05 cm^2

(B) 0.02 cm^2

(C) 0.035 cm^2

(D) 0.27 cm^2

(E) 0.12 cm^2

22. Suppose that a man jumps off a building 202 m high onto cushions having a total thickness of 2 m. If the cushions are crushed to a thickness of 0.5 m, what is the man's average acceleration as he slows down?

(A) g

(B) 133 g

(C) 5 g

(D) 2 g

(E) 266 g

23. A ball is thrown horizontally from the top of a tower 40 m high. The ball strikes the ground at a point 80 m from the bottom of the tower. Find the angle that the velocity vector makes with the horizontal just before the ball hits the ground.

(A) 315°

(B) 41°

(C) 0°

(D) 90°

(E) 82°

24. A wheel 4 m in diameter rotates with a constant angular acceleration $\alpha = 4$ rad/s^2. The wheel starts from rest at $t = 0$ *s* where the radius vector to point P on the rim makes an angle of 45° with the x-axis. Find the angular position of point P at arbitrary time t.

(A) 45°

(B) $45 + 2t^2$ degrees

(C) $45 + 114.6t^2$ degrees

(D) $4t^2$ degrees

(E) $229.2t^2$ degrees

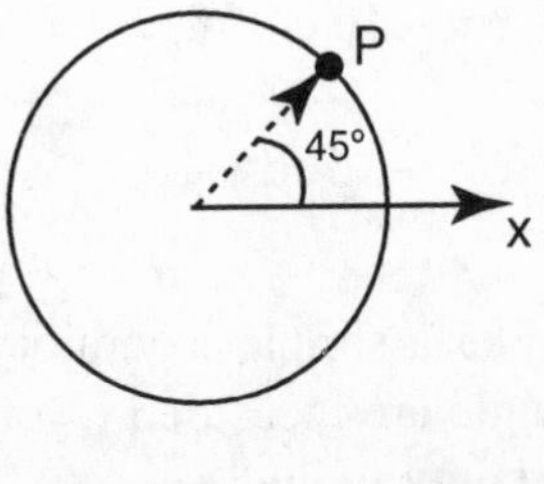

25. A common laboratory experiment involves the thermionic emission of electrons from metal surfaces. Use the Richardson-Dushman law, $J = A_0 T^2 e^{-\phi/kT}$, to estimate the thermionic emission current density for a tungsten filament at 2000 K. Take $\phi = 4.55$ eV as the work function and $A_0 = 120\ A/\text{cm}^2 K^2$ as the Richardson constant.

(A) 0.00083 A/cm^2

(B) 0.00104 A/cm^2

(C) 0.00125 A/cm^2

(D) 0.00146 A/cm^2

(E) 0.00166 A/cm^2

26. A spherically symetric point source emits sound waves with a uniform power of 200 W. At what distance will the intensity be just below the threshold of pain? (Assume $I = 1\ W/\text{m}^2$).

(A) 15.92 m

(B) ∞ m

(C) 7.98 m

(D) 7.07 m

(E) 3.99 m

27. The electric field of a plane EM wave travelling along the z-axis is

$$\mathbf{E} = (E_{0x}\,\mathbf{x} + E_{0y}\,\mathbf{y}) \sin(\omega t - kz + \phi).$$

Find the magnetic field **B**.

(A) $(-E_{0y}\,\mathbf{x} + E_{0x}\,\mathbf{y}) \cos(\omega t - kz + \phi) / c$

(B) $(E_{0x}\,\mathbf{x} + E_{0y}\,\mathbf{y}) \sin(\omega t - kz + \phi) / c$

(C) $(-E_{0y}\,\mathbf{x} + E_{0x}\,\mathbf{y}) \sin(\omega t - kz + \phi) / c$

(D) $(E_{0x}\,\mathbf{x} + E_{0y}\,\mathbf{y}) \cos(\omega t - kz + \phi) / c$

(E) $(-E_{0y}\,\mathbf{x} - E_{0x}\,\mathbf{y}) \sin(\omega t - kz + \phi) / c$

28. Parallel rays from a point object are incident on a prism of index of refraction n (shown) at near normal incidence. Calculate the deviation angle of the rays.

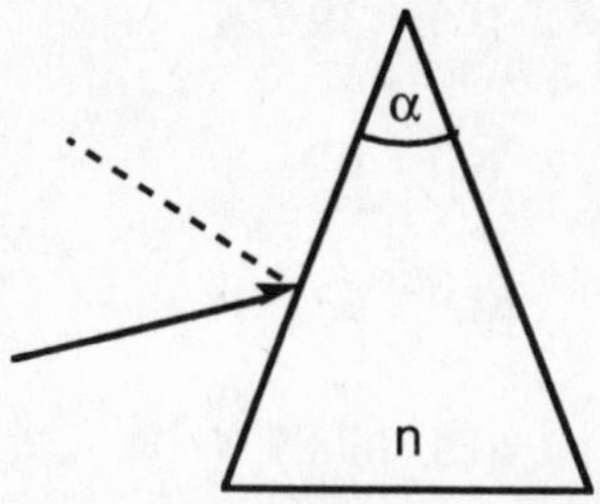

(A) α

(B) $(n-1)\,\alpha$

(C) $(n+1)\,\alpha$

(D) $(n-0.5)\,\alpha$

(E) $(n+0.5)\,\alpha$

29. Find the amount of horizontal deflection of a particle falling freely from height h in the Earth's gravitational field. Let λ be the latitude and ω be the Earth's rotational frequency.

(A) $1/3\omega\cos(\lambda)\sqrt{8h^3/g}$

(B) $2\omega\cos(\lambda)h$

(C) $\omega\cos(\lambda)\sqrt{8hg}$

(D) $\omega R_E\cos(\lambda)\sqrt{2h/g}$

(E) $\omega\cos(\lambda)\sqrt{8h^3/g}$

30. Calculate the centripetal force required to keep a 4 kg mass moving in a horizontal circle of radius 0.8 m at a speed of 6 m/s. (**r** is the radial vector with respect to the center).

(A) 39.2 N tangent to the circle

(B) – 30.0 N tangent to the circle

(C) 144.0 N **r**

(D) – 180 N **r**

(E) 180 N **r**

31. Find the tension T_2 in cord 2 for the system drawn below. The system is in equilibrium.

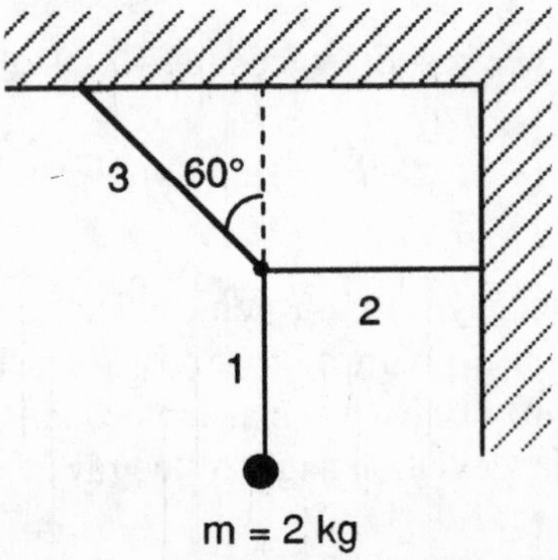

(A) 19.6 N

(B) 39.2 N

(C) 0 N

(D) 17.0 N

(E) 33.9 N

32. Tom has a mass of 70 kg and Susy has a mass of 60 kg. They are separated by a distance of 0.5 m at a wine and cheese party. What is the gravitational potential energy of the Tom-Susy system?

(A) 1.12×10^{-6} J

(B) -1.12×10^{-6} J

(C) 5.60×10^{-7} J

(D) -5.60×10^{-7} J

(E) 2.80×10^{-7} J

33. A wheel 4 m in diameter rotates on a fixed frictionless horizonal axis, about which its moment of inertia is 10 kg m². A constant tension of 40 N is maintained on a rope wrapped around the rim of the wheel. If the wheel starts from rest at $t = 0$ *s*, find the length of rope unwound at $t = 3$ *s*.

(A) 36.0 m

(B) 72.0 m

(C) 18.0 m

(D) 720 m

(E) 180 m

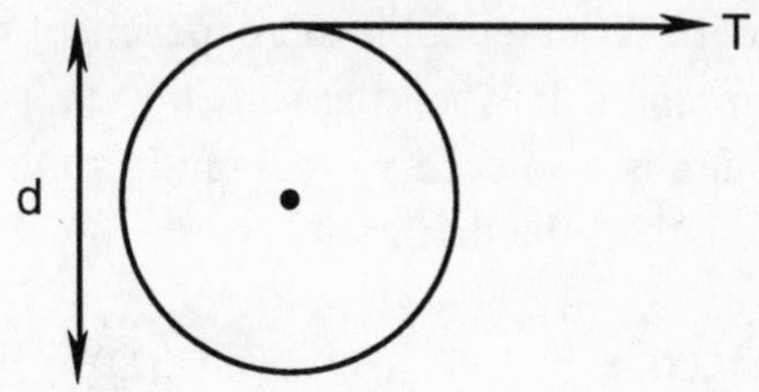

34. In Kepler's problem of planetary motion, various values of the eccentricity and hence the energy *E* classify the orbits according to conic sections. What value of the eccentricity ε and the energy E belongs to a parabolic orbit?

(A) $\varepsilon > 1$ and $E > 0$

(B) $0 < \varepsilon < 1$ and $V_{min} < E < 0$

(C) $\varepsilon = 0$ and $E = V_{min}$

(D) $\varepsilon < 0$ and $E < V_{min}$

(E) $\varepsilon = 1$ and $E = 0$

35. A scientist wants to take a picture of a distant yellow object using a pinhole camera such that the picture is of maximum sharpness. Let λ = wavelength of yellow light, d = diameter of the pinhole, and D = the distance from pinhole to film. Find d.

(A) $\sqrt{2.44\,\lambda D}$

(B) $1.22\lambda^2/D$

(C) $2.44\lambda^2/D$

(D) $\sqrt{\lambda D}$

(E) $\sqrt{1.22\,\lambda D}$

36. A 55-year-old woman has a near point of 100 cm. What lens should be used to see clearly an object at the normal near point of 25 cm? (Find the focal length of the required lens.)

(A) 20.0 cm

(B) – 33.3 cm

(C) 33.3 cm

(D) – 25.0 cm

(E) 100.0 cm

37. Consider a Young double slit experiment where the two slits are spaced $d =$ 0.1 mm apart. If when the screen is at a distance $l = 1$ m, the first bright maximum is displaced $y = 0.5$ cm from the central maximum, then find the wavelength of the light.

(A) 4000 Å

(B) 8000 Å

(C) 10,000 Å

(D) 5000 Å

(E) 5×10^{-7} Å

38. In general, waves have two velocities, the group velocity and the phase velocity. What is the phase velocity of a relativistic particle?

(A) its physical speed v

(B) $c\sqrt{1+(mc^2/\hbar k)^2}$

(C) $\partial\omega/\partial k$

(D) $c^2 p/E$

(E) it is not defined

39. Two infinite nonconducting sheets of charge are parallel to each other. Each sheet has a positive uniform charge density σ. Calculate the value of the electric field to the right of the two sheets.

(A) 0

(B) $\frac{\sigma}{2\varepsilon_0}\mathbf{x}$

(C) $-\frac{\sigma}{2\varepsilon_0}\mathbf{x}$

(D) $-\frac{\sigma}{\varepsilon_0}\mathbf{x}$

(E) $\frac{\sigma}{\varepsilon_0}\mathbf{x}$

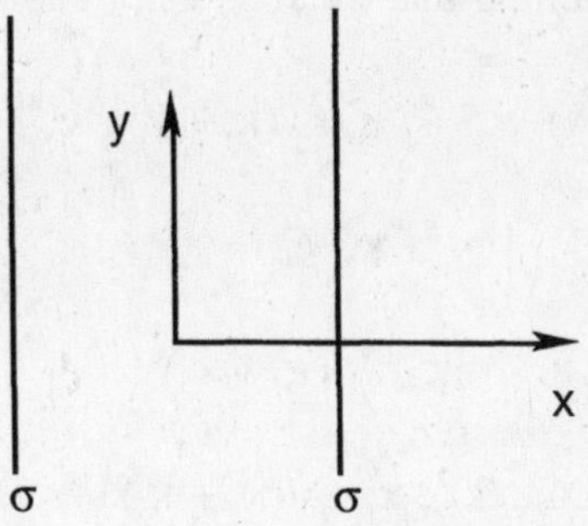

40. Find the potential energy per ion for an infinite one dimensional ionic string of charges of magnitude e and alternating sign. Let the distance between the ions be s.

(A) $-2e^2 1\pi(2)/4\pi\varepsilon_0 s$

(B) 0

(C) $-e^2/4\pi\varepsilon_0 s$

(D) ∞

(E) $e^2/4\pi\varepsilon_0 s$

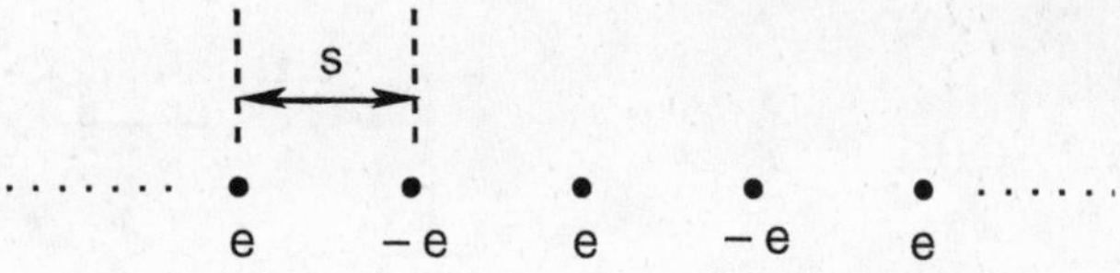

41. A thin rod stretches along the z-axis from $z = -d$ to $z = d$ as shown. Let λ be the linear charge density or charge per unit length on the rod and the points $P_1 = (0, 0, 2d)$ and $P_2 = (x, 0, 0)$. Find the coordinate x such that the potential at P_1 is equal to that at P_2.

(A) 0

(B) d

(C) $\sqrt{3}\,d$

(D) $\sqrt{2}\,d$

(E) $2d$

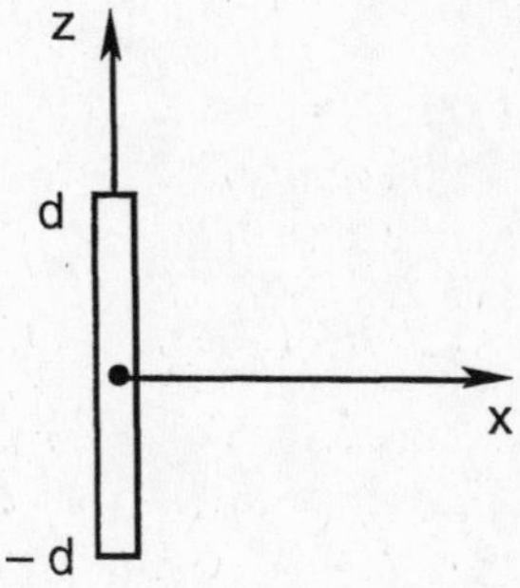

42. A capacitor is constructed from two square metal plates of area L^2 separated by a distance d. One half of the space between the plates is filled with a substance of dielectric constant (κ_1). The other half is filled with another

substance with constant (κ_2). Calculate the capacitance of the device assuming that the free space capacitance is C_0.

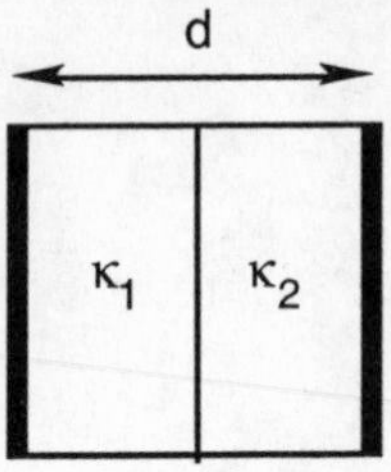

(A) $.5\ C_0\ \kappa_1\ \kappa_2/(\kappa_1 + \kappa_2)$

(B) $(\kappa_1 + \kappa_2)\ C_0$

(C) $\kappa_1 \kappa_2\ C_0/(\kappa_1 + \kappa_2)$

(D) $2\ C_0 \kappa_1 \kappa_2\ /(\kappa_1 + \kappa_2)$

(E) $(\kappa_1 + \kappa_2)\ C_0/2$

43. Consider the circuit shown below. Calculate the effective resistance of the circuit and use this knowledge to find the current in the 4 Ω resistor.

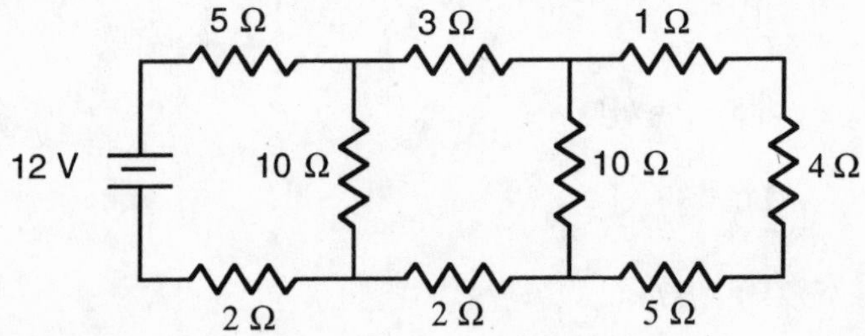

(A) $^1/_4$ A

(B) $^1/_2$ A

(C) $^3/_4$ A

(D) 1 A

(E) $1\ ^1/_4$ A

44. Consider a plane wave travelling in the positive *y*-direction incident upon a block of glass of refractive index $n = 1.6$. Find the transmission coefficient.

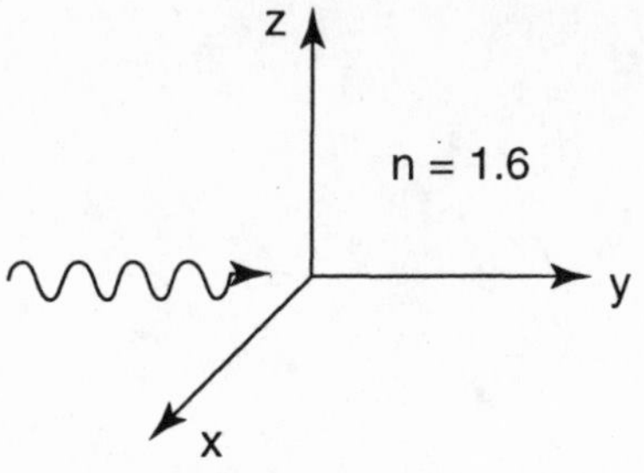

(A) 0.00

(B) 1.00

(C) 0.77

(D) 0.59

(E) 0.15

45. Which one of the following Maxwell equations implies that there are no magnetic monopoles?

(A) $\nabla \cdot \mathbf{E} = \frac{\rho}{\varepsilon_0}$

(B) $\nabla \cdot \mathbf{B} = 0$

(C) $\nabla \times \mathbf{E} = -\frac{\partial \mathbf{B}}{\partial T}$

(D) $\nabla \times \mathbf{B} = \mu_0 \mathbf{J} + \mu_0 \varepsilon_0 \frac{\partial \mathbf{E}}{\partial T}$

(E) magnetic monopoles have recently been found

46. Consider a large ship of volume V_s floating in a square pool of water such that a fraction f of the ship's volume is below the water. Let the cross sectional surface area of the pool be A. How much does the depth h of the pool increase/decrease if the ship sinks?

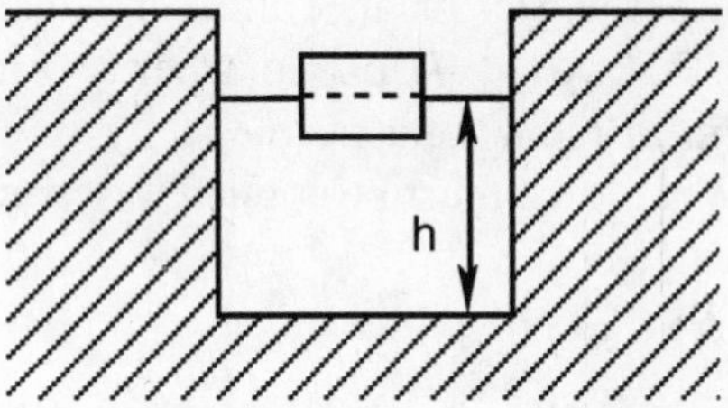

(A) decrease by fV_s/A

(B) increase by fV_s/A

(C) unchanged

(D) increase by V_s/A

(E) decrease by V_s/A

47. Consider an hourglass on a scale pictured below at times $t = 0$, 0.001, and 1 hour. What happens to the scale's measure of weight of the hourglass plus sand combination as the sand falls?

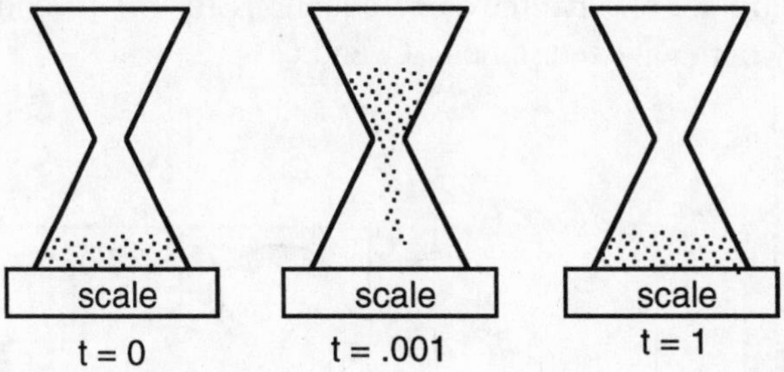

(A) The reading of weight is constant.

(B) The reading of weight decreases and then increases.

(C) The reading of weight increases.

(D) The reading of weight increases and then decreases.

(E) The reading of weight is unchanged.

48. A wire 100 cm in length carries a current of 1.0 Amp in a region where a uniform magnetic field has a magnitude of 100 Tesla in the x-direction. Calculate the magnetic force (including direction) on the wire if $\theta = 45°$ is the angle between the wire and the x axis.

(A) 70.7 **z** N

(B) 141.4 **z** N

(C) –141.4 **z** N

(D) –70.7 **z** N

(E) 0 since I is not parallel to B

49. A permanent magnet alloy of samarium and cobalt has a magnetization $M = 7.50 \times 10^5$ J/Tm^3. Consider two magnetized spheres of this alloy each 1 cm in radius and magnetically stuck together with unlike poles touching. What force must be applied to separate them?

(A) 74 N

(B) 18.5 N

(C) 37 N

(D) 111 N

(E) 9.3 N

50. Recall the equation for a series RLC circuit. Compare this to the parallel resonant circuit shown and find R_p if a series RLC circuit and the parallel RLC circuit are to have the same equations for the potential of capacitor while they both have the same L, C, and Q.

(A) $R_p = R$

(B) $R_p = L$

(C) $R_p = 1/C$

(D) $R_p = L^2/RC^2$

(E) $R_p = L/RC$

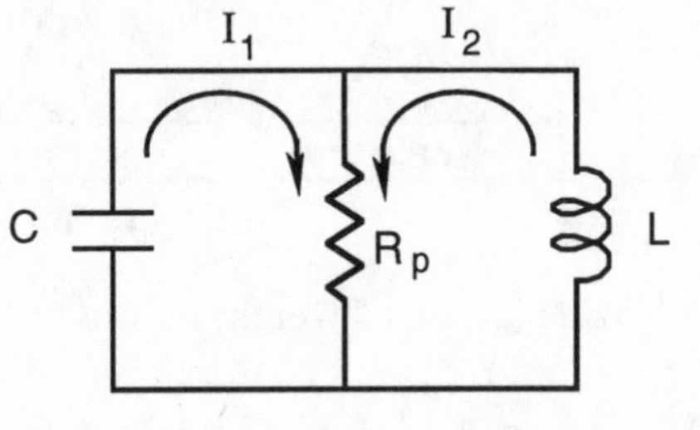

51. In a simple AC circuit involving only a resistor $R = 50\ \Omega$ and a voltage

source V, find the linear frequency of the generator if $V = 0.50\ V_m$ at time $t = 1/720$ s. (Assume $V = 0$ at $t = 0$ also.)

(A) 120 π Hz

(B) 21,600 Hz

(C) 60 Hz

(D) 3400 Hz

(E) 60 π Hz

52. Use Ampere's law to derive for the magnetic field of a toroid (N turns) of inner radius a and outer radius b at a distance r midway between a and b.

(A) $\mu_0 NI / 2\pi(b - a)$

(B) $\mu_0 NI / \pi(b - a)$

(C) $\mu_0 NI / \pi b$

(D) $\mu_0 I/\pi(b - a)$

(E) $4\mu_0 NI / \pi(b - a)$

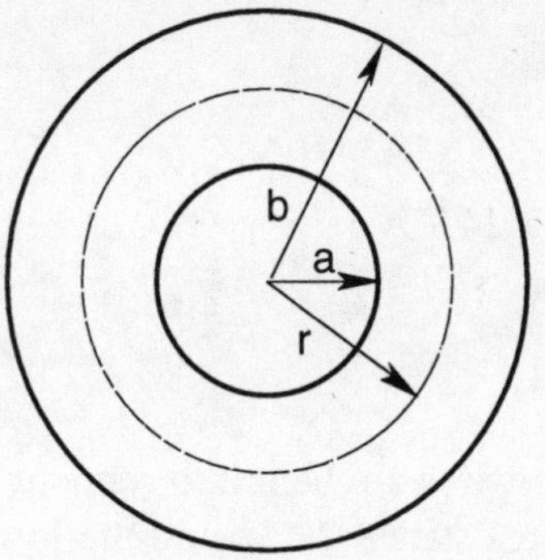

Cross section of toroid seen from the top

53. Two parallel conductors separated by a distance r carry currents I_1 and I_2 in the same direction as shown below. What is the force per unit length exerted on the second conductor by the first?

(A) $(-\mu_0 I_1 I_2/2\pi x)\ \mathbf{x}$

(B) $(\mu_0 I_1 I_2/2\pi x)\ \mathbf{x}$

(C) $(\mu_0 I_1 I_2/\pi x)\ \mathbf{x}$

(D) $(-\mu_0 I_1 I_2/\pi x)\ \mathbf{x}$

(E) $(\mu_0 \pi I_1 I_2/ x)\ \mathbf{x}$

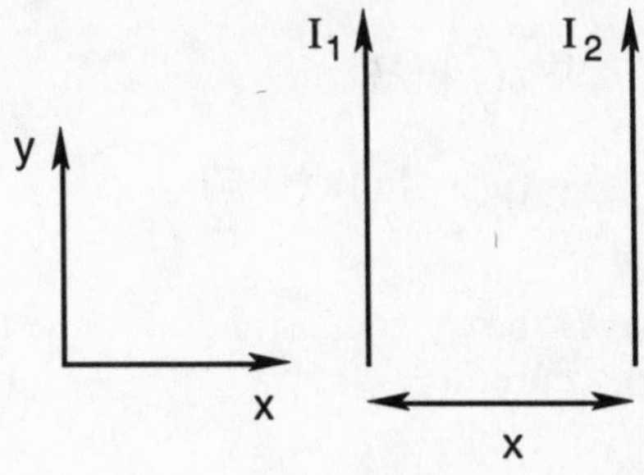

54. Consider a series RL circuit with $R = 10\ \Omega$, $L = 10\ \mu H$, and $V = 30$ volts. Suppose that $I = 0$ at $t = 0$. Find the energy stored in the inductor as $t \to \infty$.

(A) 9.0×10^{-5} J

(B) 90 J

(C) 45 J

(D) 4.5×10^{-5} J

(E) 1.5×10^{-5} J

55. Consider a circuit that consists of four resistors (each with $R = 1\ M\Omega$), a capacitor ($C = 1\ \mu F$), and a battery ($V = 10\ MV$) as shown. If the capacitor is fully charged and then the battery is removed, find the current at $t = 0.5$ s as the capacitor discharges.

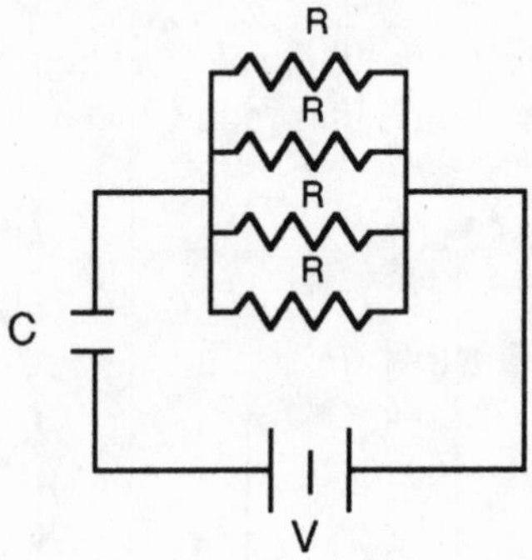

(A) 40 A

(B) 20 A

(C) 24.3 A

(D) 14.7 A

(E) 5.4 A

56. Two wires are bent into semicircles of radius a as shown. If the upper half has resistance $2R\ \Omega$ and the lower half has resistance $R\ \Omega$, then find the magnetic field at the center of the circle in terms of the current I.

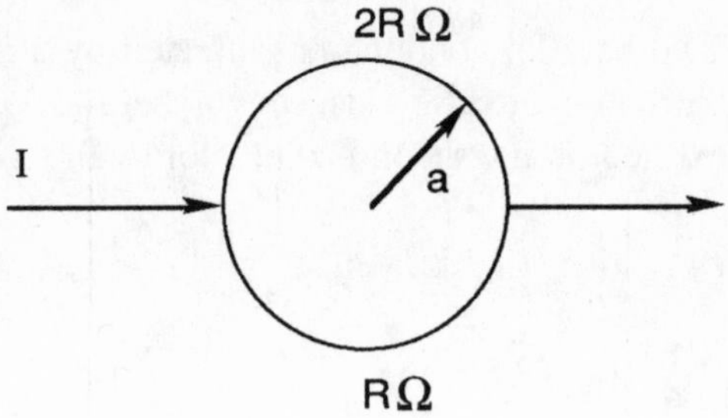

(A) $-(\mu_0 I/12a)\mathbf{z}$

(B) $(\mu_0 I/12a)\mathbf{z}$

(C) $-(\mu_0 I/6a)\mathbf{z}$

(D) $(\mu_0 I/4a)\mathbf{z}$

(E) $-(\mu_0 I/4a)\mathbf{z}$

57. What is the magnetic field at the center of a circular ring of radius r that carries current I?

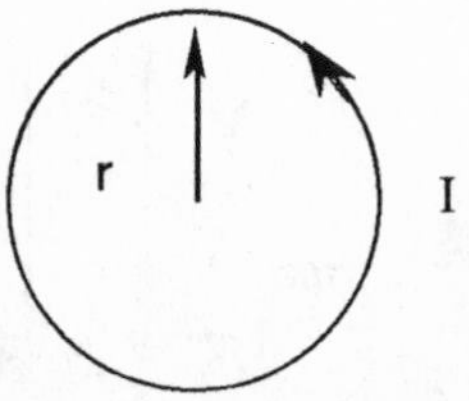

(A) $\mu_0 I/2r$

(B) $\mu_0 I/2\pi r$

(C) $\mu_0 I/r$

(D) $\mu_0 I/\pi r$

(E) it is equal to zero

58. Consider a Fermi gas of electrons at low but non-zero temperature T. How does the thermal energy vary with the temperature?

(A) proportional to T

(B) proportional to ρT

(C) proportional to $T^2 / E_F(\rho)$

(D) proportional to T^2

(E) proportional to $T/E_F(\rho)$

59. How fast must a 2 m stick be moving if its observed length is 1 m as seen from the laboratory frame?

(A) length is the same in every reference frame

(B) 0.866 cm/s

(C) 1.50×10^{10}cm/s

(D) 2.60×10^{10}cm/s

(E) 2.12×10^{8}cm/s

60. In the classic Fizeau experiment to verify the special theory of relativity the speed of light in a moving liquid of refractive index n is measured. If the speed of the liquid is v, then what is the measured speed of light in the laboratory frame?

(A) $c/n + v$

(B) c/n

(C) $(c/n + v)/(1 + v/cn)$

(D) $(c/n + v)/(1 - v/cn)$

(E) c

61. An inertial system K' is moving with a velocity 0.8 c relative to the inertial system K along the xx' axes. A particle in K has velocity

$$\mathbf{v} = (0.5, \sqrt{3}/2)c.$$

Find the velocity of the particle in K'.

(A) $v' = c$ at $\theta = 120°$

(B) $v' = c$ at $\theta = 60°$

(C) $v' = 0.92c$ at $\theta = 109°$

(D) $v' = 0.92c$ at $\theta = 71°$

(E) $v' = 0.5c$ at $\theta = 30°$

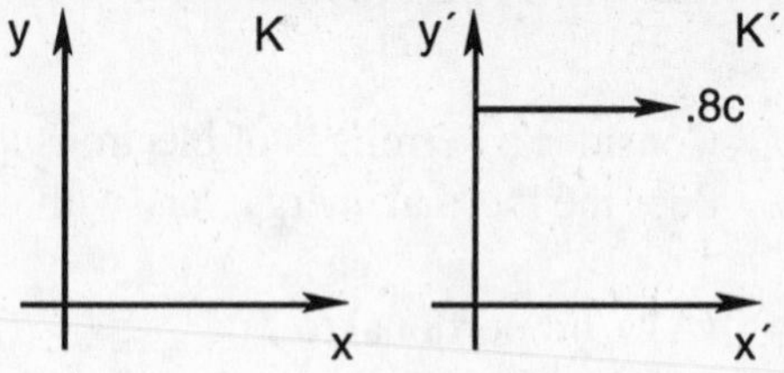

62. Light of wavelength 4500 Å is incident on a Na surface for which the threshold wavelength of the photoelectrons is 5420 Å. Calculate the work function of sodium.

(A) 2.76 eV

(B) 2.29 eV

(C) 0.47 eV

(D) 4.76 eV

(E) 1.00 eV

63. Which of the following would be a true statement about the Franck-Hertz experiment?

(A) the value of Planck's constant was first measured

(B) the charge to mass ratio of the electron was measured

(C) it was proved that atomic energy states are quantized

(D) it was proved that the electron has spin

(E) the quantization of photon energy was discovered

64. In a Rutherford scattering experiment, 10 MeV α particles are scattered by a gold foil 0.1 μm thick into a detector whose sensitive area is 10 cm^2 which is placed 50 cm from the target and makes an angle of 45° with the

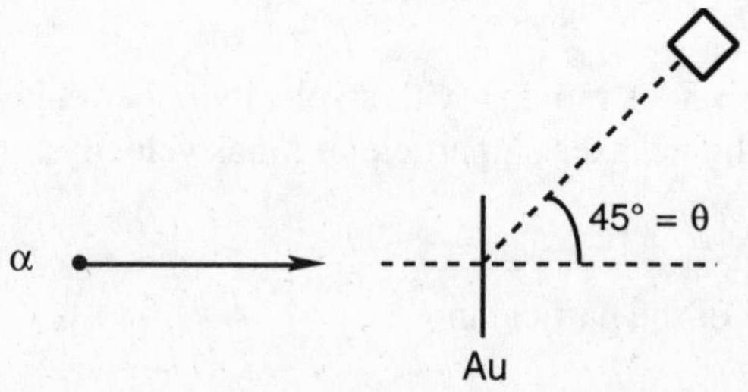

incident beam. Calculate the differential cross section in the center of mass system in barns (b) per steradians (*SR*). (1 millibarn = 10^{-28} square meters.)

(A) 2.65 b/sr

(B) 1.04 b/sr

(C) 3.78 b/sr

(D) 15.1 b/sr

(E) 4.08 b/sr

65. What was achieved by the recent discovery of the *W* and *Z* intermediate vector bosons?

(A) the nuclear force was discovered

(B) the gravitational and nuclear forces were interlinked

(C) the proton will decay in 10^{31} years

(D) there are particles called rishons inside the quarks

(E) the electroweak unification was verified

66. Consider a mechanical model of the proton where the spin is due to its rotation. Assume the proton to be a uniform solid sphere and derive the equatorial velocity. (Assume $m_p = 1.67 \times 10^{-24}$ gr, $r = 10^{-13}$ cm)

(A) 1.58×10^{10} cm/s

(B) 3.00×10^{10} cm/s

(C) 3.94×10^{9} cm/s

(D) 1.87×10^{10} cm/s

(E) 7.88×10^{9} cm/s

67. In quantum mechanics, one may picture a wave function in either momentum space or configuration space. If the wave function in momentum space is $\phi(p) = N/(p^2 + \alpha^2)$, then calculate the wave function in configuration space (aside from a multiplicative constant).

(A) $e^{-a^2x^2/\hbar^2}$

(B) $\cos(px/\hbar)$

(C) $\sin(px/\hbar)$

(D) $e^{-a|x|/\hbar}$

(E) $e^{ipx/\hbar}$

68. Calculate the coefficient of reflection for a particle incident on a step potential with $E > V_0$. Let

$$k = \sqrt{2mE}/\hbar,\ k' = \sqrt{2m(E - V_0)}/\hbar$$

(A) $R = 0$

(B) $R = 1$

(C) $R = \left|\frac{k - k'}{k + k'}\right|^2$

(D) $R = \left|\frac{k - k'}{k + k'}\right|$

(E) $R = \left|\frac{k}{k'}\right|$

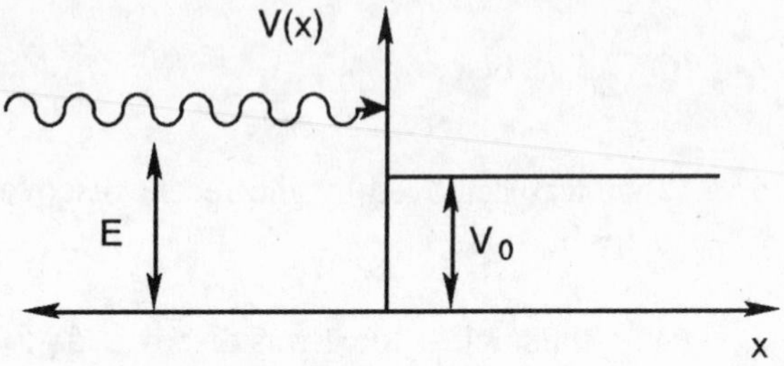

69. Consider the hydrogen molecule H_2 as a rigid diatomic rotor of separation r = 1.0 Å between two protons. Calculate the energy of the $\ell = 3$ level in the rotational spectrum.

($m_p = 938.280 \times 10^6$ eV/c^2

$\hbar = 1973.5$ eV.Å/c

(A) 0.10 eV
(B) 0.05 eV
(C) 0.15 eV
(D) 0.005 eV
(E) 0.10 eV

70. An object of mass 0.4 kg is attached to a spring of Hooke's constant $k = 200$ N/m and subject to a resistive force $-bx'$ where $v = x'$ is the velocity of the object in m/s. If the damped frequency is 0.995 of the undamped frequency, find the value of b.

(A) 3.20 kg/s
(B) 1.79 kg/s
(C) 1.60 kg/s
(D) 0.895 kg/s
(E) 0.00 kg/s

71. In the atom Na, the two levels $^2P_{3/2}$ and $^2P_{1/2}$ are separated by 5.97 Å in wavelength. Transition from these levels involves the emission of light of

wavelengths $\lambda_1 = 5889.95$ Å and $\lambda_2 = 5895.92$ Å. Calculate the value of the constant in the expression for the spin-orbit coupling, $\Delta E = a\Delta(\mathbf{l} \cdot \mathbf{s})$.

(A) 0.1 eV

(B) 0.01 eV

(C) 0.001 eV

(D) 0.0001 eV

(E) 1.0 eV

72. According to classical mechanics the atom will decay in a very short time. Roughly how long does it take for the electron to spiral into the nucleus as it emits electromagnetic radiation?

(A) 10^{-10} s

(B) 10^{-8} s

(C) 10^{-6} s

(D) 10^{-4} s

(E) 10^{-2} s

73. The μ-meson has the same charge as the electron, but a greater mass $m_\mu = 207\ m_e$. Use Bohr theory to find the radius of a μ-mesonic atom with nucleus of charge Ze orbited by the μ^- as compared to the radius of the hydrogen-like atom.

(A) $r_\mu = r_H$

(B) $r_\mu = 207\ r_H$

(C) $r_\mu = 207^2\ r_H$

(D) $r_\mu = r_H / 207$

(E) $r_\mu = r_H / 207^2$

74. X-rays with an energy of 50 keV undergo Compton scattering from a target. If the scattered rays are detected at 45° relative to the incident rays, find the energy of the scattered X-ray.

(A) 51.4 keV

(B) 48.6 keV

(C) 52.8 keV

(D) 47.2 keV

(E) 50.0 keV

75. For collisions between identical particles, what is the relationship between the CM and the laboratory scattering angles?

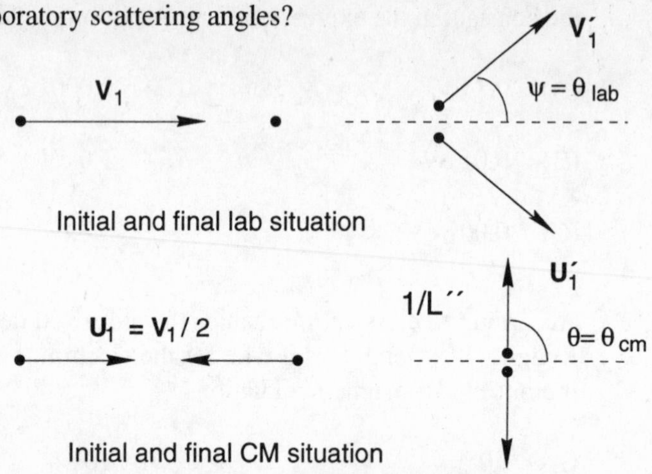

(A) $\theta = \psi$

(B) $\theta = \pi/2 - \psi$

(C) $\theta = \pi/2 + \psi$

(D) $\theta = \psi/2$

(E) $\theta = 2\psi$

76. In the Mossbauer effect, the absorption by the absorber may be destroyed by moving the source. For the case of ^{57}Fe in a lattice where the gamma ray has energy 14.4 keV and lifetime 9.8×10^{-8} s, find the minimum source speed necessary to destroy the resonant absorption.

(A) 0.028 cm/s (D) 0.014 cm/s

(B) 0.010 cm/s (E) 0.007 cm/s

(C) 0.100 cm/s

77. Calculate the speed of a proton of kinetic energy 1 TeV in the Tevatron at Fermilab in Batavia, Illinois. (Use a Taylor expansion.)

(A) 0.999 999 6c (D) 0.999 9c

(B) c (E) 0.999 999 94c

(C) 0.999c

78. Calculate the thermal energy associated with the reaction, Q, in MeV (with negative and positive referring to endothermic and exothermic, respectively) for the nuclear reaction ^{27}Al(d,p)^{28}Al given that $m(^{27}\text{Al}) = 26.98154$, $m_d = 2.01473$, $m_p = 1.00794$, and $m(^{28}\text{Al}) = 27.98154$, all in a.m.u.

(A) –6.32 MeV (D) 6.83 MeV

(B) 0.0 MeV (E) –6.83 MeV

(C) 6.32 MeV

79. The nuclear charge density as found from electron scattering is given by $\rho(r) = \rho_0/(1 + e^{(r-a)/b})$. What is the meaning of the fit parameter b?

(A) $b = 1.12\,A^{1/3}$ gives the half density radius

(B) it is merely a fit parameter and has no physical meaning

(C) it is the classical electron radius $b = e^2/m_e c^2$

(D) generally $b = \infty$ and $r < a$ so that $\rho(r) = \rho_0$

(E) $b = 0.6\,fm$ is related to the surface thickness

80. A simple wave function for the deuteron is given by $\phi(r) = A\sin[k(r-a)]/r$ for $a < r < a + b$ and $\phi(r) = Be^{-kr}/r$ for $r > a + b$. Which of the following expressions can be used to normalize the wave function ψ?

(A) $1 = \int_a^{a+b} A^2 \sin^2 k(r-a)dr$

(B) $1 = \int_a^{a+b} A^2 \sin^2 k(r-a)dr + \int_{a+b}^{\infty} B^2 \frac{e^{-2kr}}{r^2} dr$

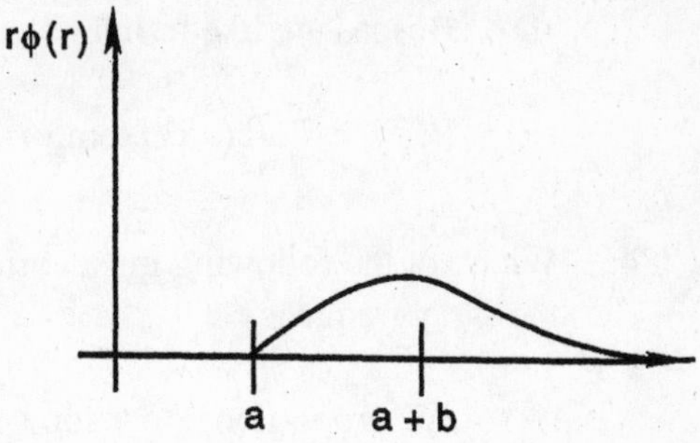

(C) $1 = \int_{a+b}^{\infty} B^2 \frac{e^{-2kr}}{r^2} dr$

(D) $\int_a^{a+b} A^2 \sin^2 k(r-a)dr = \int_{a+b}^{\infty} B^2 \frac{e^{-2kr}}{r^2} dr$

(E) $0 = \int_a^{a+b} A^2 \sin^2 k(r-a)dr + \int_{a+b}^{\infty} B^2 \frac{e^{-2kr}}{r^2} dr$

81. Using the Boltzmann factor, calculate the percentage of hydrogen molecules in the first rotational level relative to the ground state at $T = 300$ K. Assume that $r = 1.06$ Å is the appropriate molecular distance.

(A) 75%

(B) 50%

(C) 25%

(D) 0%

(E) 90%

82. According to the nuclear shell model, what is the proton configuration for the nuclide $^{27}_{13}$Al?

(A) $1s^2 2s^2 2p^6 3s^2 3p^1$

(B) $1s^2 2s^2 2p^6 3s^2 3p^2$

(C) $(1s_{1/2})^2(2s_{1/2})^2(2p_{3/2})^4(3s_{1/2})^2\ (3p_{3/2})^3$

(D) $(1s_{1/2})^2(2p_{3/2})^4(2p_{1/2})^2(3d_{5/2})^6$

(E) $(1s_{1/2})^2(2p_{3/2})^4(2p_{1/2})^2(3d_{5/2})^5$

83. According to Bose-Einstein statistics, there exists a Bose condensate for collections of bosons. What does this mean?

(A) As $T \to \infty$, all particles reside in excited states.

(B) For $T < T_C$ (critical temp.), all particles reside in the ground state.

(C) Bosons are not physically meaningful particles.

(D) Bosons are like fermions.

(E) For $T < T_C$ (critical temp.), bosons dissolve into quarks and gluons.

84. Which of the following most correctly describes Moseley's law (where υ is the x-ray frequency)?

(A) υ is proportional to Z for x-rays.

(B) υ is proportional to $1/Z$ for x-rays.

(C) υ is proportional to Z^2 for x-rays.

(D) υ is proportional to $1/Z^2$ for x-rays.

(E) υ is independent of Z.

85. In the Zeeman effect, the energies corresponding to spectral lines are found to be split into additional lines by an external magnetic field, B. The separation of these lines is proportional to

(A) $eB/2m_e c$

(B) $eB/m_e c$

(C) $\mu_B B$

(D) $2\mu_B B$

(E) $\mu_B B/2$

86. Consider a quantum mechanical two particle system for which the wavefunctions are Ψ (1, 2) and Ψ (2, 1). What is the symmetric eigenstate of the exchange operator P_{12}?

(A) $\frac{1}{\sqrt{2}}$ (Ψ (1,2) + Ψ(2,1))

(B) $\frac{1}{\sqrt{2}}$ (Ψ (1,2 Ψ(2,1))

(C) Ψ (1,2)

(D) Ψ (2,1)

(E) there is none

87. Consider N noninteracting bosons in an infinite potential box of width a. What is the ground state energy?

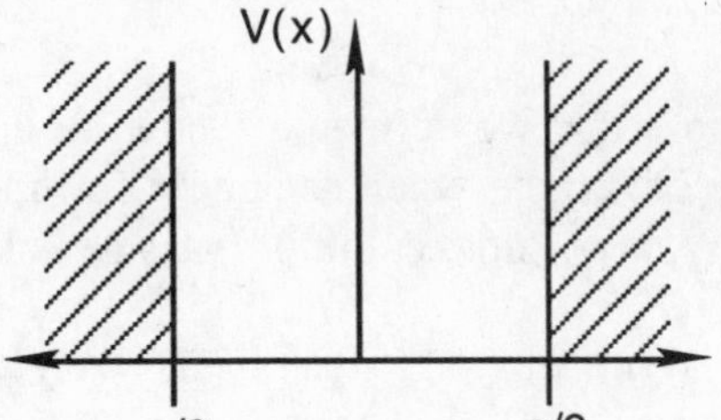

(A) $\hbar^2 \pi^2 N/ma^2$

(B) $\hbar^2 \pi^2/2ma^2$

(C) $\hbar^2 \pi^2/ma^2$

(D) $\hbar^2 \pi^2 N/4ma^2$

(E) $\hbar^2 \pi^2 N/2ma^2$

88. The nuclide ^{232}Th decays by α particle emission with half life $\tau = 4.45 \times 10^{17}$ s. What quantum mechanical model might be used to predict the half life?

(A) the nuclear shell model

(B) the compound nucleus model

(C) the Wentzel-Kramers-Brillouin approximation

(D) the correspondence principle

(E) the Kronig-Penney model

89. The specific heat of solids is explained by the Debye theory, which is in agreement with the Law of Dulong and Petit for

(A) low temperature

(B) high temperature

(C) a critical temperature $T = T_C$ only

(D) metals only

(E) insulators only

90. Use the Maxwell velocity distribution, $<v>=\sqrt{\frac{2kT}{m}}$, to find the ratio of the average speed of an N_2 molecule to the escape speed from the surface of the Earth.

(A) 1.0
(B) 0.44
(C) 0.038
(D) 1.86
(E) 0.056

91. Suppose that we defined a system of units such that 1 unit of mass feels a force of 1 dyne when separated from an identical unit by a distance of 1 cm. What would the unit of mass be in kilograms?

(A) 0.001 kg
(B) 3.87 kg
(C) 2.15 kg
(D) 0.143 kg
(E) 0.521 kg

92. The lowest nucleon resonance state is the Δ which has a mass of 1232 MeV/c^2 and a width of 120 MeV. Calculate the lifetime of this I = 3/2 nucleon state.

(A) 5.5×10^{-24} s
(B) 1.2×10^{-19} s
(C) 3.3×10^{-23} s
(D) 6.9×10^{-9} s
(E) 8.4×10^{-17} s

93. According to the quark model, hadrons are made up of quarks. What is the quark composition of the proton?

(A) the proton is not a hadron
(B) sss
(C) udd
(D) uu
(E) uud

94. For the one-dimensional harmonic oscillator, the potential energy is $U = 1/2\ kx^2$ and the ground state wave function is

$$\psi_0 = Ce^{-ax^2}.$$

Find the constant C. (Note $\int_{-\infty}^{\infty} \frac{1}{\sqrt{2\pi\sigma^2}} e^{-1/2x^2/\sigma^2}$).

(A) $C = \sqrt{2a/\pi}$

(B) $C = \sqrt{a/\pi}$

(C) $C = 1$

(D) $C = (2a/\pi)^{1/4}$

(E) $C = a$

95. Consider the scattering of two identical fermions, for example proton-proton scattering. If the two particles are in a spin singlet state, then how does the differential cross section (σ) relate to the scattering amplitude (Ω)?

(A) $d\sigma/d\Omega = |f(\theta)|^2 + |f(\pi-\theta)|^2$

(B) $d\sigma/d\Omega = |f(\theta)|^2 - |f(\pi-\theta)|^2$

(C) $d\sigma/d\Omega = |f(\theta) + f(\pi-\theta)|^2$

(D) $d\sigma/d\Omega = |f(\theta)|^2 + |f(\pi-\theta)|^2 - f(\theta)f^*(\pi - \theta)$

(E) $d\sigma/d\Omega = |f(\theta) - f(\pi-\theta)|^2$

96. Time dilation may be observed in a jet airplane using an atomic clock. Suppose that the plane moves at 600 mph. If the laboratory time is $\Delta t = 1.00$ s, by what amount is time dilated?

(A) $(1 - 4 \times 10^{-13})$ s

(B) $(1 + 4 \times 10^{-13})$ s

(C) $(1 - 8 \times 10^{-13})$ s

(D) $(1 + 8 \times 10^{-13})$ s

(E) there is not time dilation for such a low speed

97. In an ideal monoatomic adiabatic expansion, if the volume of the gas doubles from V_0 to $2V_0$, then what happens to the temperature?

(A) rises to 1.59 T_0

(B) remains constant

(C) rises to 2 T_0

(D) falls to 0.5 T_0

(E) falls to 0.63 T_0

98. The specific gravity of lead is 11.35 g/cc and the radiation length is 0.53 cm. How much energy is lost by a beam of 10 MeV photons incident on a lead target of 3.00 g/cm² thickness?

(A) 3.03 MeV

(B) 10.0 MeV

(C) 6.07 MeV

(D) 9.01 MeV

(E) 5.34 MeV

99. The bulk modulus of water is $B = 2.04 \times 10^9$ *Pa*. Find the wavelength of a wave with a frequency of 262 Hz. (Note: $v = \sqrt{\frac{\beta}{\rho}}$.)

(A) 10.9 m

(B) 5.45 m

(C) 8.32 m

(D) 4.16 m

(E) 15.3 m

100. Which of the following is NOT true for a converging lens in optics?

(A) A ray parallel to the optic axis passes through the focus.

(B) A ray originating at the focus is bent parallel to the optic axis.

(C) A ray through the center of the lens is bent parallel to the optic axis.

(D) An object placed at the focus has image at infinity.

(E) An object at infinity has image at the focus.

TEST 1

ANSWER KEY

1.	(B)	26.	(E)	51.	(C)	76.	(D)
2.	(A)	27.	(C)	52.	(B)	77.	(A)
3.	(D)	28.	(B)	53.	(A)	78.	(C)
4.	(C)	29.	(A)	54.	(D)	79.	(E)
5.	(B)	30.	(D)	55.	(E)	80.	(B)
6.	(E)	31.	(E)	56.	(B)	81.	(A)
7.	(D)	32.	(D)	57.	(A)	82.	(E)
8.	(A)	33.	(B)	58.	(C)	83.	(B)
9.	(C)	34.	(E)	59.	(D)	84.	(C)
10.	(B)	35.	(A)	60.	(C)	85.	(C)
11.	(E)	36.	(C)	61.	(A)	86.	(A)
12.	(D)	37.	(D)	62.	(B)	87.	(E)
13.	(C)	38.	(B)	63.	(C)	88.	(C)
14.	(A)	39.	(E)	64.	(D)	89.	(B)
15.	(D)	40.	(A)	65.	(E)	90.	(C)
16.	(A)	41.	(C)	66.	(E)	91.	(B)
17.	(B)	42.	(D)	67.	(D)	92.	(A)
18.	(E)	43.	(A)	68.	(C)	93.	(E)
19.	(D)	44.	(D)	69.	(B)	94.	(D)
20.	(C)	45.	(B)	70.	(B)	95.	(C)
21.	(D)	46.	(A)	71.	(C)	96.	(A)
22.	(B)	47.	(B)	72.	(A)	97.	(E)
23.	(A)	48.	(D)	73.	(D)	98.	(C)
24.	(C)	49.	(C)	74.	(B)	99.	(B)
25.	(E)	50.	(E)	75.	(E)	100.	(C)

DETAILED EXPLANATIONS OF ANSWERS

TEST 1

1. **(B)**

The force may be found from the derivative of the potential.

$$V(r) = -\frac{Gmm'}{r}(1 - ae^{-r/\lambda}).$$

$$\frac{dV}{dr} = \frac{Gmm'}{r^2}(1 - ae^{-r/\lambda}) - \frac{Gmm'}{r}\frac{a}{\lambda}e^{-r/\lambda}$$

$$= \frac{Gmm'}{r^2}\left(1 - ae^{-r/\lambda}(1 + \frac{r}{\lambda})\right) \qquad \frac{r}{\lambda} << 1$$

$$F = -\left.\frac{dV}{dr}\right|_{r << \lambda} = -\frac{Gmm'}{r^2}(1 - a)$$

2. **(A)**

The two peaks in the intensity versus z plot verify the quantization of spin. The force exerted upon the electron in the atom is given by

$$F_z = \mu_z \frac{\partial B_z}{\partial z}.$$

Since $\mu_z = \pm {}^1/_2\, \mu_B$, there are two peaks.

3. **(D)**

Newton's laws are invariant under the Galilean transformation equations since

$$x' = x - vt \text{ and } t' = t.$$

Thus $$v' = \frac{dx'}{dt'} = \frac{dx}{dt} - v,$$

and $$a' = \frac{d^2x'}{dt'^2} = \frac{d^2x}{dt^2} = a.$$

However, Maxwell's equations are not invariant. This was one of the clues that brought about the development of the special relativity theory.

4. **(C)**

The differential number of particles is

$$dN = \frac{4V}{(2\pi)^3} d^3K$$

where $g = 4$ is the nuclear degeneracy.

$$P = \hbar K$$

Integrating, we get

$$N = \int_0^N dN = \frac{4V}{(2\pi\hbar)^3} \int_0^{P_F} 4\pi P^2 \, dP$$

$$\rho = \frac{N}{V} = \frac{4}{(2\pi\hbar)^3} \frac{4}{3} \pi P_F^3$$

$$P_F = \hbar \left(\frac{3\pi^2}{2} \rho \right)^{1/3}$$ is the Fermi momentum

and $$E_F = \frac{P_F^2}{2m} = \frac{\hbar^2}{2m} \left(\frac{3\pi^2}{2} \rho \right)^{2/3}$$

is the Fermi energy where $m = 939$ MeV/c^2 is the mass of the nucleon.

5. **(B)**

The total time T is equal to the time t that it takes for the coin to reach the bottom and the time t^* that it takes for the sound waves to travel back to the ground level.

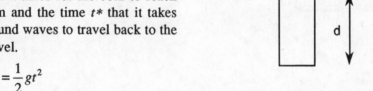

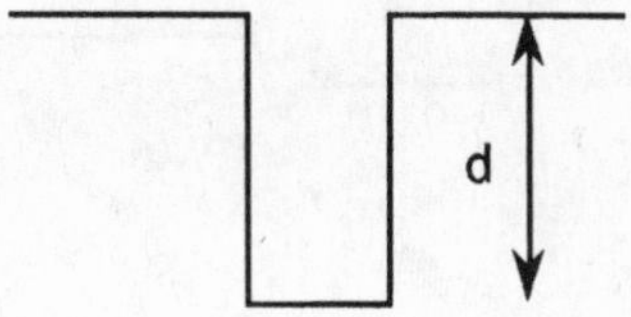

$$d = \frac{1}{2} g t^2$$

$$T = t + t^*, \quad t^* = \frac{d}{v}$$

$$d = \frac{1}{2} g (T - \frac{d}{v})^2$$

$$\frac{1}{2} g T^2 + \frac{1}{2} g \frac{d^2}{v^2} - gT \frac{d}{v} - d = 0$$

$$d^2 - d\left(\frac{2v^2}{g} + 2vT \right) + v^2 T^2 = 0,$$

$$v = 330 \text{ m/s} \quad g = 9.8 \text{ m/s}^2$$

$$d^2 - 23{,}583.4d + 461{,}679.5 = 0$$

$$d = \frac{-b \pm \sqrt{b^2 - 4ac}}{2a} = \frac{23{,}583.4 - 23{,}544.2}{2}$$

$$= 19.6 \text{ m}$$

6. **(E)**

If v' is the velocity of the combined system of the pendulum and the bullet right after the collision, then according to the conservation of linear momentum

$$mv = (m + M)v'$$

From the conservation of energy

$$\tfrac{1}{2}(m + M)(v')^2 = (m + M)gy$$

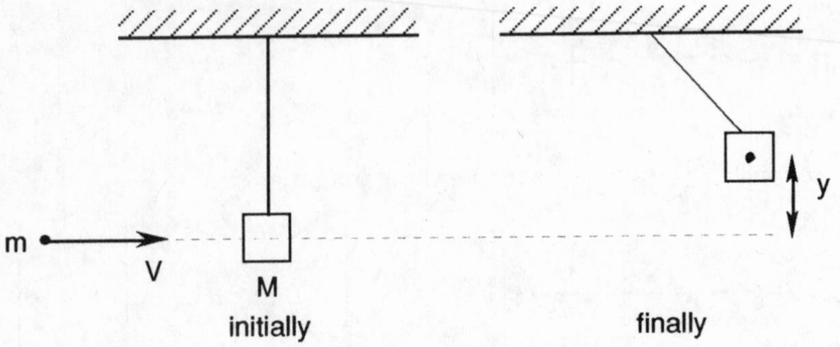

Some energy has been lost during the collision and converted to heat.

$$v = \frac{M + m}{m} v' = \frac{M + m}{m} \sqrt{2gy}$$

$$= \frac{2.010}{.010} \sqrt{2(9.8)(.20)}$$

$$= 398 \text{ m/s}$$

7. **(D)**

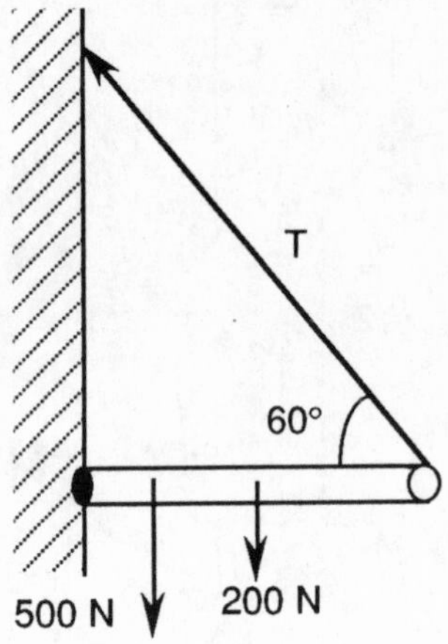

Since the system is in equilibrium, the sum of the torques with respect to any point must be zero. By choosing the point of the beam to the wall as the reference, we can write:

$$\Sigma\tau = 0, \quad \tau = rF \sin \alpha$$

$$(500)(2) \sin(90°) + (200)(5) \sin(90°)$$

$$-(10)(T) \sin(120°) = 0$$

Therefore $T = 231$ N is the desired tension.

8. **(A)**

Work done by the external agent is:

$$W = \int_0^x F \cdot dx$$

$$= \int_0^x kx\, dx$$

$$= \frac{1}{2}kx^2\Big|_0^{x_0}$$

$$= \frac{1}{2}kx^2$$

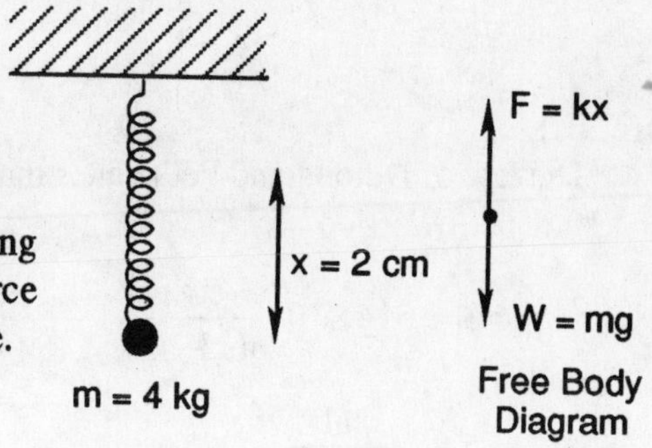

In the free body diagram for the hanging mass, the downward gravitational force is balanced by the upward spring force.

$$F = mg = kx$$

$$k = \frac{mg}{x} = \frac{4(9.8)}{.02}$$

$$= 1960 \text{ N/m}$$

$$W = \frac{1}{2}kx^2$$

$$= \frac{1}{2}(1960)(0.4)^2$$

$$= 1.57 \text{ J}$$

9. **(C)**

From the conservation of angular momentum,

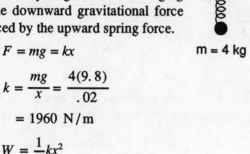

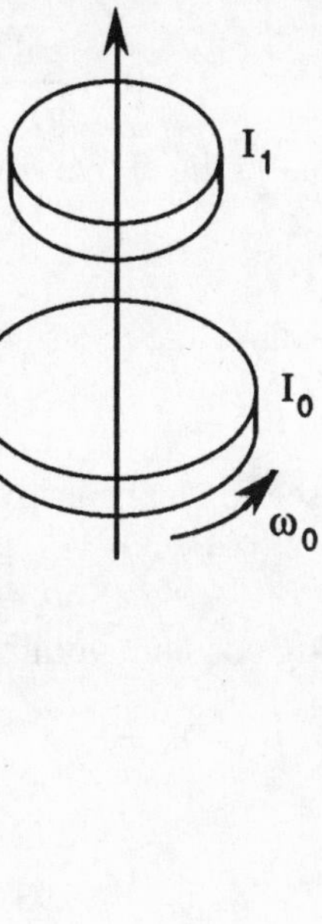

$$(\Sigma L)_0 = (\Sigma L)_f$$

$$I_0\omega_0 = (I_0 + I_1)\omega_f$$

$$\omega_f = \frac{I_0\omega_0}{I_0 + I_1}$$

10. **(B)**

The ideal gas law is

$$pV = nRT$$

Initially, $p_0 = nRT_0 / V_0$

$$= 3(8.314 \times 10^7)(300) / (2 \times 10^7)$$

$$= 3.741 \times 10^3 \text{ d/cm}^2$$

In an adiabatic process $\Rightarrow pV^\gamma = \text{constant}$, thus

$$p_0 V_0^\gamma = p_f V_f^\gamma, \quad p_f = p_0 \left(\frac{V_0}{V_f}\right)^\gamma$$

where the exponent is

$$\gamma = (C_V + R)/C_V = \left(\frac{5}{2}R + R\right) / \left(\frac{5}{2}R\right) = \frac{7}{5}$$

since a diatomic gas has 2 extra degrees of freedom.

$$p_f = (3.741 \times 10^3)\left(\frac{2 \times 10^7}{4 \times 10^7}\right)^{7/5}$$

$$= 1.42 \times 10^3 d / \text{cm}^2$$

11. **(E)**

The law of Dulong and Petit states that the molar heat capacity is

$$C_V = 3R$$

$$= 3\left(8.314 \times 10^7 \frac{\cancel{\text{erg}}}{\text{mol-k}}\right)\left(\frac{\text{cal}}{4.184 \times 10^7 \cancel{\text{erg}}}\right)$$

$$= 5.96 \frac{\text{cal}}{\text{mol-k}}$$

Basically there are six degrees of freedom that contribute to this molar heat capacity. To get the specific heat, we must use the atomic mass of copper

$$C_V = C_V \times \frac{1(\text{mol})}{A(\text{g})}$$

$$= 5.96 \frac{\text{cal}}{\cancel{\text{mol}}-\text{k}} \times \frac{1}{63.5} \frac{\cancel{\text{mol}}}{\text{g}}$$

$$= .094 \frac{\text{cal}}{\text{gK}}$$

Note that in the above equation, A is the mass in grams of Cu.

12. **(D)**

The absolute pressure p is the atmospheric pressure plus the gauge pressure.

$$p = p_A + p_G = 35 + 14.7 = 49.7 \text{ psi} = p_S$$

Now use the ideal gas law

$$pV = nRT, \ \frac{p_w}{p_s} = \frac{T_w}{T_s}$$

assuming constant volume. Thus

$$p_w = p_s \frac{T_w}{T_s}$$

$$= 49.7 \times \frac{273}{293}$$

$$= 46.3 \text{ psi}$$

$$p_{Gw} = p_w - p_G = 46.3 - 14.7 = 31.6 \text{ psi}$$

13. **(C)**

The inclined plane cuts out an area given by:

$$\text{Area} = \frac{s}{\cos\theta} = \frac{s}{\cos 30°} = \frac{2s}{\sqrt{3}}$$

Let the average intensity at the incline be x. Then:

$$(x)\left(\frac{2s}{\sqrt{3}}\right) = (IA) = \quad \text{(constant output power of bulb).}$$

Finally,

$$x = \left(\frac{\sqrt{3}}{2}\right)\left(\frac{IA}{s}\right)$$

14. **(A)**

There are four known forces. In order of increasing strength, these are the gravitational force, the weak force, the electromagnetic force, and the nuclear or strong force.

Also, since Einstein, physicists have been trying to verify the forces in a unified field theory.

15. **(D)**

The net total force exerted on the chain (by both the surface and gravitation) at any time is equal to its mass times the acceleration of its center of mass.

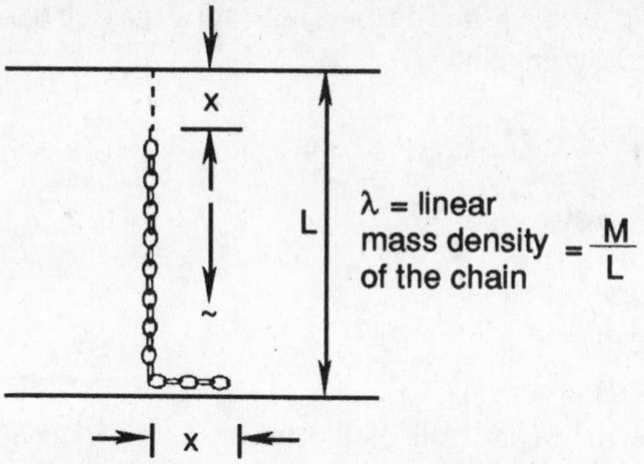

To find the equation of motion of the center of mass, according to the figure, we can write (all the distances are evaluated with respect to the hanging point):

$$x_{cm} = \frac{\Sigma mx}{\Sigma m} = \frac{(x\lambda)L + (L-x)\lambda\left(x + \frac{L-x}{2}\right)}{L\lambda}$$

$$= x + \frac{L^2 - x^2}{2L}$$

$$\Rightarrow x'_{cm} = x' - \frac{xx'}{L}$$

$$x''_{cm} = x'' - \frac{xx'' + x'^2}{L} \Rightarrow Mx''_{cm} = Mg - N = M\left(x'' - \frac{xx'' + x'^2}{L}\right)$$

N: the normal force of the surface

But $x'' = g$ since the chain is falling freely and also we have:

$$x'^2 = 2gx$$

(equation of motion with constant acceleration). So we have

$$N = \frac{M}{L}(xg + 2gx) = \frac{3M}{L}gx$$

16. **(A)**

$L = T - U$, where the Lagrangian L is set equal to the difference of kinetic energy T and potential energy U. $T = (1/2)mV^2 + (1/2)I\omega^2$, with the first term representing translational kinetic energy and the second rotational kinetic energy. Now, V is the velocity of the sphere's center of mass and ω is its angular velocity. They are related by the equation $V = (R - \rho)\omega$. Since $I = (2/3)m\rho^2$, we can write the kinetic energy expression as

$$T = (1/2)m(R-\rho)^2\omega^2 + (1/2)(2/3)m\rho^2\omega^2$$

The potential energy can be written as $U = -mg(R - \rho)\cos\theta$. We wish to find ω in terms of θ, as the Lagrangian involves a single generalized coordinate. To do this we note that when the sphere rolls through a given angle β it traverses a distance of $(\rho\beta)$ along the circumference of the cylinder. Thus, the corresponding θ for that traversal is $\theta = (\rho\beta)/R$. Taking the derivative of both sides and solving for ω we obtain $\omega = (R/\rho)\theta'$, the prime on theta indicating the first derivative. Substituting, we obtain for the Lagrangian:

$$L = \frac{1}{2}m(R-\rho)^2\frac{R^2}{\rho^2}(\theta')^2 + \frac{1}{6}mR^2(\theta')^2 + mg(R-\rho)\cos\theta$$

17. **(B)**

In general

$$x' = \frac{dy}{dx} \quad \text{and} \quad y' = \frac{dy}{dt}$$

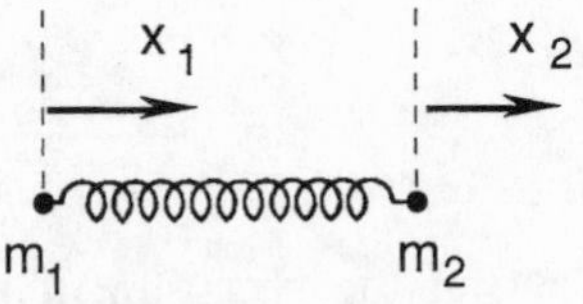

x_1 and x_2 are the separation of the two masses from their equilibrium positions along the respective axis parallel to their path of motion.

$$m_1x_1'' = -kx \quad \text{where } x = x_1 - x_2$$

$$m_2x_2'' = kx$$

Note: x, the total compression or stretching of the spring, is equal to the algebraic difference of x_1 and x_2. Subtract the two equations to get

$$m(x_1'' - x_2'') = -2kx$$

since $\quad m_1 = m_2 = m$ and $x_1'' - x_2'' = x''$

$$mx'' + 2kx = 0, \quad x'' + \frac{2k}{m}x = 0$$

$$\omega_0{}^2 = \frac{2k}{m} \Rightarrow \omega_0 = \sqrt{\frac{2k}{m}}$$

18. **(E)**

A conservative force is a force such that

$$\oint \mathbf{F} \cdot d\mathbf{r} = 0 \quad \text{or} \quad \nabla \times \mathbf{F} = 0$$

these are equivalent conditions since

$$\nabla \times \mathbf{F} = 0$$

$$\int \nabla \times \mathbf{F} \cdot d\mathbf{a} = \oint \mathbf{F} \cdot d\mathbf{r}$$

by Stoke's theorem.

$$\oint \mathbf{F} \cdot d\mathbf{r} = 0$$

Stoke's theorem relates the surface integral of the curl to a line integral of the original vector field.

19. **(D)**

The Maxwell-Boltzmann differential probability for speed is

$$f(v)\,dv = 4\pi c v^2 e^{-mv^2/2kT}\ dV$$

then $$< v >= \int_0^\infty v\, f(v)\,dv \,/ \int_0^\infty f(v)\,dv$$

$$= \int_0^\infty v^3 e^{-\alpha v^2} dv \,/ \int_0^\infty v^2 e^{-\alpha v^2} dv \quad \text{where} \quad \alpha \equiv m/2kt$$

$$= I_3 / I_2$$

Recall $$I_0 = \int_0^\infty e^{-\alpha v^2} dv = \frac{1}{2}\sqrt{\frac{\pi}{2}}$$

and $$I_1 = \int_0^\infty v e^{-\alpha v^2} dv = \frac{1}{2\alpha}$$

We also have:

$$I_n = \int_0^\infty v^n e^{-\alpha v^2} dv$$

Using integration by parts, we can write:

$$\left.\begin{array}{l} u = v^{n-1} \\ dy = v e^{-\alpha v^2} dv \end{array}\right\} \Rightarrow \begin{array}{l} du = (n-1)v^{n-2}dv \\ y = -\dfrac{1}{2\alpha} e^{-\alpha v^2} \end{array}$$

$$\Rightarrow I_n = \frac{-v^{n-1}}{2\alpha} e^{-\alpha v^2} \Bigg|_0^\infty - \int_0^\infty -\frac{1}{2\alpha} e^{-\alpha v^2} (n-1) v^{n-2} dv$$

$$I_n = [0-0] + \frac{(n-1)}{2\alpha} \int_0^\infty e^{-\alpha u^2} v^{n-2}\ dv$$

$$I_n = \frac{n-1}{2\alpha} I_{n-2}$$

Hence we can write:

$$I_2 = \frac{1}{2\alpha} I_0$$

$$I_3 = \frac{2}{2\alpha} I_1$$

Finally,

$$< v >= \frac{\frac{2I_1}{2\alpha}}{\frac{I_0}{2\alpha}} = \frac{2I_1}{I_0} = 2\frac{\frac{1}{2\alpha}}{\frac{1}{2}\sqrt{\frac{\pi}{\alpha}}} = 2\frac{1}{\sqrt{\pi\alpha}} = \sqrt{\frac{8kt}{\pi m}}$$

20. **(C)**

The basic simple harmonic motion equation is

$x = A\cos(\omega t + \delta)$

$A = 16$ cm, $T = 2$ s,

The linear frequency is then

$v = 1/T$ or $v = {}^1/_2$ Hz.

Hence $\omega = 2\pi v = \pi$ rad/s

is the angular frequency. Hence, at $t = 0$:

$$-16 = 16\cos(+\delta)$$

$$\delta = \pi \text{ rad}$$

Therefore:

$$x = 16\cos(\pi t + \pi)$$

21. **(D)**

From the theory of propagation of error:

$$A = lw$$

$$\Delta A = \sqrt{\left(\frac{\partial A}{\partial l}\Delta l\right)^2 + \left(\frac{\partial A}{\partial w}\Delta w\right)^2}$$

$$= \sqrt{(w\Delta l)^2 + (l\Delta w)^2}$$

$$= lw\sqrt{\left(\frac{\Delta l}{l}\right)^2 + \left(\frac{\Delta w}{w}\right)^2}$$

$$= (5.45)(3.86)\sqrt{\left(\frac{.05}{4.35}\right)^2 + \left(\frac{.02}{3.86}\right)^2}$$

$$= 0.27 \text{ cm}^2$$

22. **(B)**

Use basic kinematics.

$$v^2 - v_0 = 2a(x - x_0)$$

$$v = \sqrt{2ax}$$

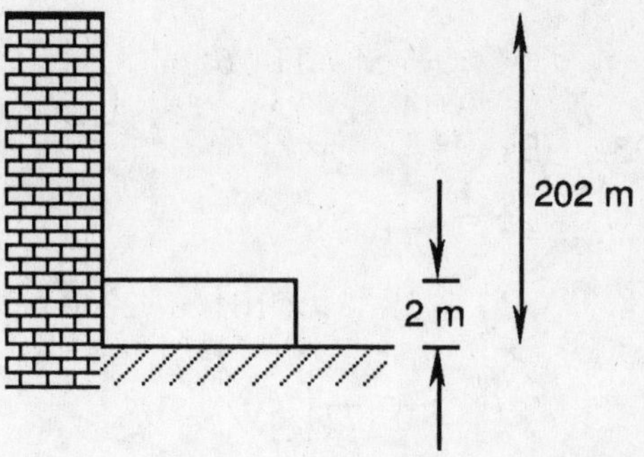

$$= \sqrt{2(9.8)200}$$
$$= 62.61 \text{ m/s}$$
$$v^2 - v_0^2 = 2a(x - x_0)$$
$$0^2 - 62.61^2 = 2a(0.5 - 2)$$
$$a = 1307 \text{ m/s}^2$$
$$a = 133 g$$
using $g = 9.8 \text{ m/s}^2$

23. **(A)**

With standard kinematics, we get

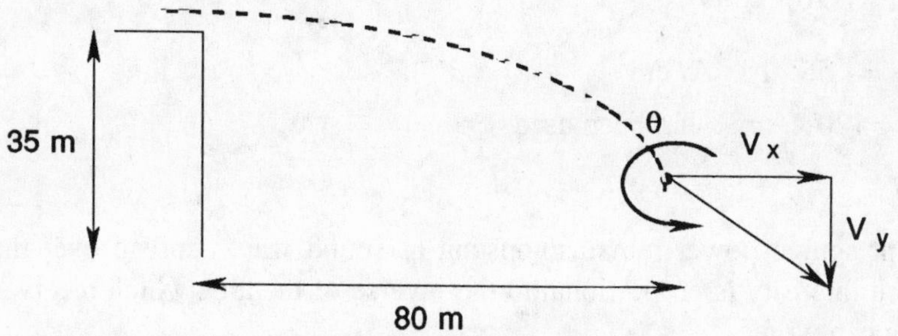

$$y = \frac{1}{2} gt^2, \quad t = \sqrt{2y/g} = \sqrt{80/9.8} = 2.86 s$$
$$x = v_x t, \quad v_x = \frac{x}{t} = \frac{80}{2.86} = 28.0 \text{ m/s}$$
$$v_y^2 - v_0^2 = 2a(y - y_0)$$
$$v_y = -\sqrt{2gy} = -\sqrt{2(9.8)(40)} = -28.0 \text{ m/s}$$
$$\theta = A\tan\left(\frac{v_y}{v_x}\right) = 315°$$

24. **(C)**

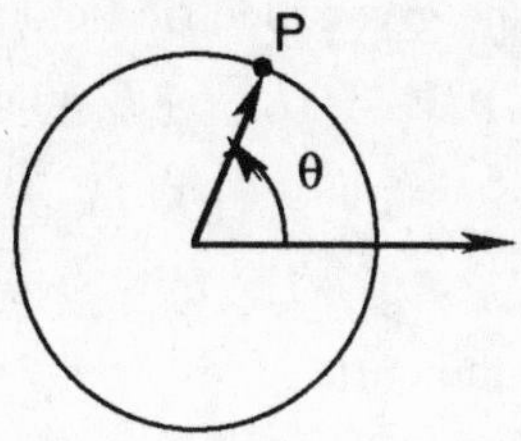

$$\theta_0 = 45°$$
$$\alpha = 4 \text{ rad/s}^2 \times \frac{180°}{\pi \text{ rad}}$$
$$= 720/\pi \text{ deg/s}^2$$
Now
$$\theta = \theta_0 + \omega_0 t + \frac{1}{2}\alpha t^2$$
is one of the basic rotational kinematics equations.

$$= 45° + \frac{360}{\pi} t^2$$

$$= 45° + 114.6° t^2$$

25. **(E)**

$$\phi = 4.55 \text{ eV}$$

$$kT = (1.381 \times 10^{-16})\,(2000)\,\frac{1\,\text{eV}}{1.602 \times 10^{-12}\ \text{erg}}$$

$$= 0.1724 \text{ eV}$$

The Richardson-Dushman Law states that

$$J = A_0 T^2 e^{-\phi/kT}$$

$$= (120)\,(2000)^2\, e^{-4.55/0.172k}$$

$$= 1.56 \times 10^{-3}\, A/\text{cm}^2$$

where $A_0 = 120\ A/\text{cm}^2 k^2$ has been used.

26. **(E)**

Point source power remains constant as sound waves spread over the region. Since intensity is proportional to the inverse of the area which receives the power, we can write:

$$p = 200\ W$$

$$I = P/A$$

$$= P/4\pi r^2$$

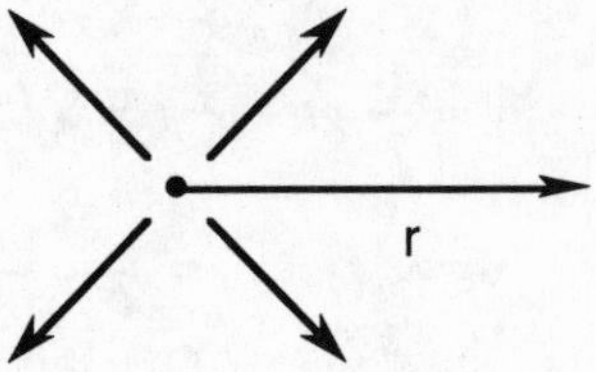

Taking the area as the surface area of a sphere

$$r = \sqrt{P/4\pi I}$$

$$= \sqrt{200/4\pi(1)}$$

$$= 3.99 \text{ m}$$

27. **(C)**

The given electric field vector is

$$\mathbf{E} = (E_{ox}\mathbf{x} + E_{oy}\mathbf{y}) \sin(\omega t - kz + \phi)$$

$$\nabla \times \mathbf{E} = \left(\frac{\partial E_z}{\partial y} - \frac{\partial E_y}{\partial z}\right)\mathbf{x} + \left(\frac{\partial E_x}{\partial z} - \frac{\partial E_z}{\partial x}\right)\mathbf{y}$$

Taking the curl

$$= E_{0y} k \cos(\omega t - kt + \phi)\mathbf{x} - E_{0x} k \cos(\omega t - kt + \phi)\mathbf{y}$$

$$= -\frac{\partial \mathbf{B}}{\partial t}$$

By Faraday's Law

$$\mathbf{B} = -\int (\nabla \times \mathbf{E})\, dt$$

integrating

$$= -E_{0y}\frac{k}{w}\sin(\omega t - kz + \phi)\mathbf{x} + E_{0x}\frac{k}{\omega}\sin(\omega t - kz + \phi)\mathbf{y}$$

$$= (-E_{0y}\mathbf{x} + E_{0x}\mathbf{y})\,\frac{1}{c}\sin(\omega t - kz + \phi)$$

28. **(B)**

Use Snell's law to get:

$$\sin\theta_1 = n\sin\theta_2$$

and $n\sin\theta_3 = \sin\theta_4$

Taking the index of refraction outside of the prism to be 1.

Using the small angle approximation, we get

$$\theta_1 \approx n\,\theta_2$$

and $n\,\theta_3 \approx \theta_4$

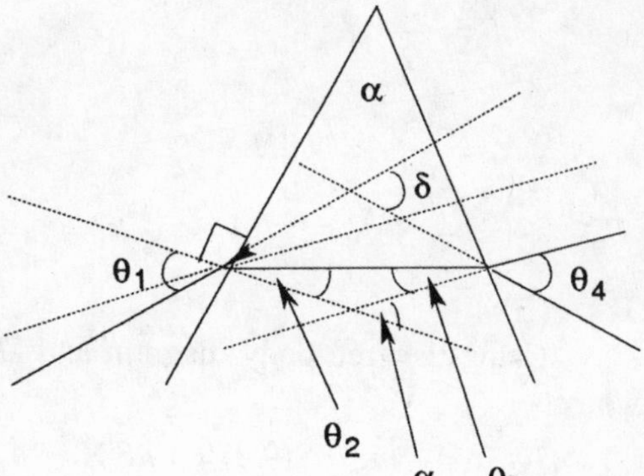

From geometry

$$\alpha = \theta_2 + \theta_3$$

and
$$\delta = (\theta_1 - \theta_2) + (\theta_4 - \theta_3)$$
$$= n\,\theta_2 - \theta_2 + n\,\theta_3 - \theta_3$$
$$= (n-1)\,\alpha$$

Note that δ is the internal angle of the small upper triangle.

29. **(A)**

Breaking ω down into its x and z components

$$\omega = -\omega\cos\lambda\,\mathbf{x} + \omega\sin\lambda\,\mathbf{z}$$

Use $\mathbf{v} \approx -gt\,\mathbf{z}$

to find $\mathbf{a} = \mathbf{g} - 2\,\omega\times\mathbf{v}$

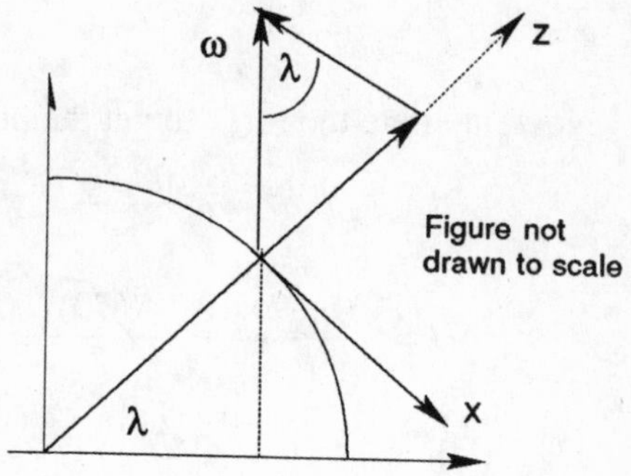

As the acceleration

$$= \mathbf{g} - 2\,\omega\cos(\lambda)\,gt\,\mathbf{x}\times\mathbf{z}$$

and $\mathbf{a}_c = 2\,\omega\,gt\cos(\lambda)\,\mathbf{y}$

is the Coriolis acceleration

then
$$v_y = \int a_y\,\mathrm{dt} = \omega g t^2\cos\lambda$$
$$y = \int v_y\,dt = {}^1/_3\,\omega g t^3\cos\lambda$$

$$h = {}^1/_2\, gt^2 \Rightarrow t = \sqrt{2h/g}$$

thus $$y = {}^1/_3\, \omega \cos \lambda \sqrt{8h^3/g}$$

is the eastward deflection.

30. **(D)**
Use Newton's 2nd Law

$$F = \text{ma}$$

and the centripetal acceleration

$$a = \frac{v^2}{r}$$

to get $$F = \frac{mv^2}{r}$$

$$= \frac{4(6)^2}{0.8} = 180N$$

$$\text{F} = -180N\ \text{r}$$

31. **(E)**
Using the free body diagram and $\Sigma F = 0$, we get

$$T_1 = mg = 2(9.8) = 19.6 \text{ N}$$

A second free body diagram is drawn where the strings meet.

$$T_{3y} = T_1 = 19.6 \text{ N}$$
$$T_3 = T_{3y} / \sin(30°)$$
$$= 39.2 \text{ N}$$
$$T_2 = T_{3x} = T_3 \cos(30°) = 33.9 \text{ N}$$

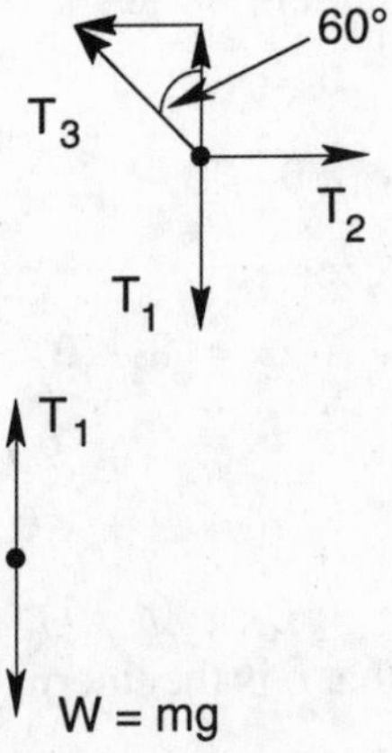

Free body diagram

32. **(D)**
Newton's universal law of gravitation states that

$$F = -\frac{Gm_1m_2}{r^2}$$

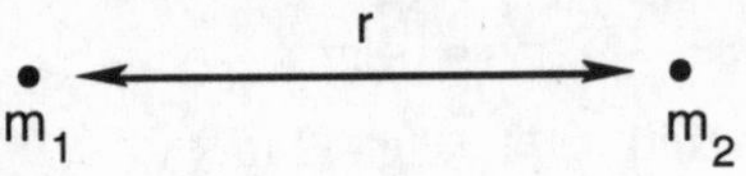

Now integrate the force to get the potential energy.

$$U = -\int F\, dr = -\frac{Gm_1m_2}{r}$$

$$U = -\frac{(6.67\times10^{-11})(70)(60)}{0.5} = -5.60\times10^{-7} \text{ J}$$

33. **(B)**
Use the diameter to find the radius

$$r = \frac{d}{2} = \frac{4}{2} = 2 \text{ m}.$$

Now, Newton's 2nd law for rotation gives

$$\Sigma\tau = rF = rT = I\alpha$$

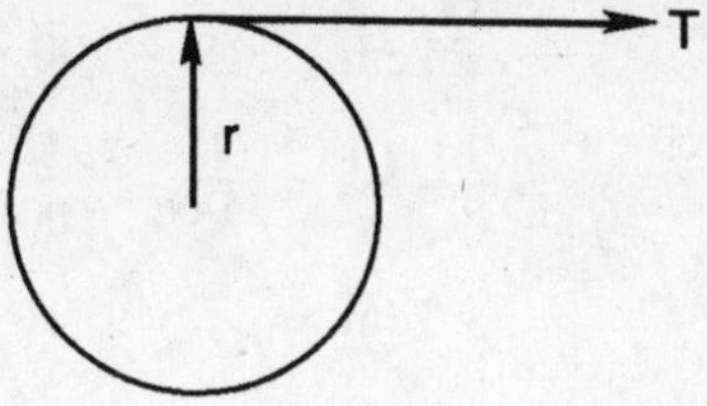

$$\alpha = \frac{rT}{I} = \frac{(2)\,(40)}{10} = 8\,\frac{\text{rad}}{\text{s}^2}$$

$$\theta = \theta_0 + \omega_0\tau + \frac{1}{2}\alpha\tau^2$$

$$s = r\theta = \frac{1}{2}\alpha r\tau^2 = \frac{1}{2}\,(8)(2)(3)^2$$

$$= 72.0 \text{ m}$$

34. **(E)**

The various curves are shown in the figure below.

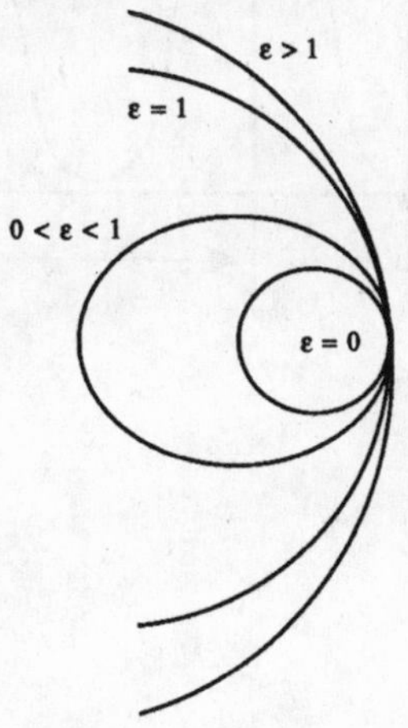

The parabolic orbit has $\varepsilon = 1$ and total energy

$$E = T + U = 0$$

35. **(A)**

Let d be the diameter of the pinhole. When the pinhole is large, then the object is imaged as a disc of diameter $d' = d$. When the pinhole is small, then the Rayleigh criterion gives the image disc diameter in the following way:

$$\sin\theta = 1.22\,\lambda/d$$

$\theta \Rightarrow \measuredangle$ between light ray to the circumference of the image and the maximum intensity of the image.

Now $d/D = 2\,\theta$ and for $\theta << 1$ rad

$$\sin\theta \approx \theta = 1.22\,\lambda/d$$

thus $d\,/\,D = 2 \times 1.22 \times \lambda\,/\,d$

or $d = \sqrt{2.44\,\lambda D}$

36. **(C)**

We would like a lens that brings objects from 25 cm to 100 cm. Note that s' is negative because the image is supposed to be located on the same side of the lens as the object.

$$s = +25\,\text{cm}, \quad s' = -100\ \text{cm}$$

$$\frac{1}{f} = \frac{1}{s} + \frac{1}{s'} = \frac{1}{25} - \frac{1}{100}$$

$$f = 33.3\,\text{cm}$$

37. **(D)**

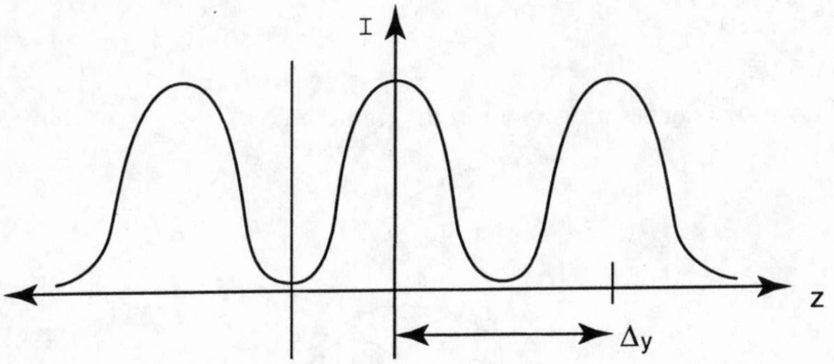

$$\Delta y = l \sin\theta$$

is the distance between the maxima.

$$d \sin\theta = \lambda$$

$$\Delta y = l\frac{\lambda}{d}$$

$$\lambda = \frac{d}{l}\,\Delta y = \frac{10^{-4}}{1}\,0.5\times10^{-2}$$

$$= 0.5\times10^{-6}\ \text{m} = 5000\,\text{Å}$$

38. **(B)**

$$E = \sqrt{p^2c^2 + m^2c^4}$$

$$\hbar\omega = \sqrt{(\hbar kc)^2 + (mc^2)^2}$$

$$\omega = \sqrt{(kc)^2 + (mc^2/\hbar k)^2}$$

$$v_p = \frac{\omega}{k} = \sqrt{c^2 + (mc^2/\hbar)^2}$$

$$= c\sqrt{1 + (mc^2/\hbar k)^2}$$

The group velocity

$$v_g = \frac{\partial \omega}{\partial k}$$

is equal to the physical speed.

39. **(E)**

$$\nabla \cdot \mathbf{E} = \frac{\rho}{\varepsilon_0}$$

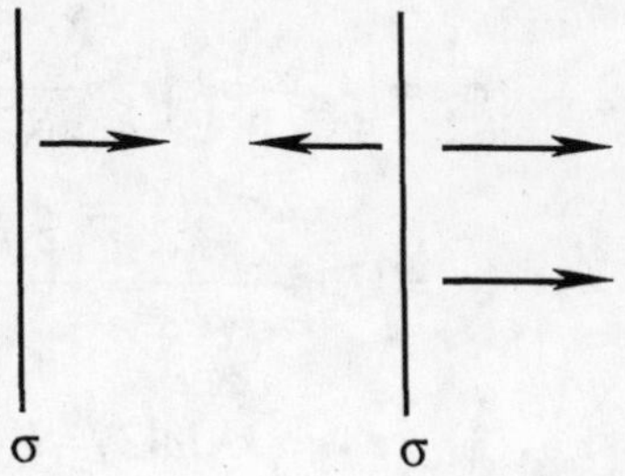

According to superposition principle, we can evaluate the electric field produced by each sheet separately and then add them up, because the presence of each sheet does not have any effect on the charge of the other. Therefore, to find the electric field of one of the sheets we can write:

$$\oint \mathbf{E} \cdot d\mathbf{A} = \frac{q}{\varepsilon_0}$$

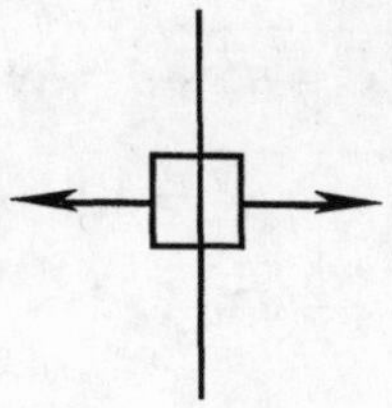

$$2EA = \frac{\sigma S}{\varepsilon_0}$$

Using a Gaussian pillbox

$$E = \frac{\sigma}{2\varepsilon_0}$$

Thus, $\mathbf{E}_{\text{tot}} = \frac{\sigma}{\varepsilon_0}\,\mathbf{x}$

to the right of the sheets.

40. **(A)**

.... • • • • • • ....
e −e e −e e −e

$$F = k\frac{q_1 q_2}{r^2}, \quad V = -\int F \cdot dr = k\frac{q_1 q_2}{r^2}$$

$$V_{\text{tot}} = \Sigma V = -2\left(-\frac{e^2}{s} + \frac{e^2}{2s} - \frac{e^2}{3s} + \ldots\right)k$$

The factor 2 is essential because the string of charges are extended along both directions.

$$= -2(ke^2/s)(1 - \tfrac{1}{2} + \tfrac{1}{3} - \tfrac{1}{4} + \ldots)$$

$$= -2(ke^2/s)\ln(2)$$

since $\ln(1+x) = x - \frac{x^2}{2} + \frac{x^3}{3} + \ldots$

$$V_{\text{tot}} = -2e^2\ln(2)/4\pi\varepsilon_0 s$$

41. **(C)**

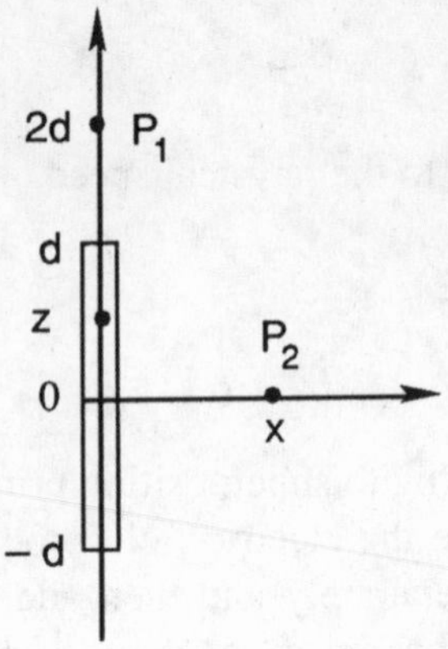

$$\phi_1 = \int k\frac{dq}{r} = k\int_{-d}^{d} \frac{\lambda dz}{\lambda(2d-z)}$$

$$= -k\lambda \ln(2d-z)\Big|_{-d}^{d}$$

$$= k\lambda \ln(3)$$

$$\phi_2 = \int k\frac{dq}{r} = k\int_{-d}^{d} \frac{\lambda dz}{\sqrt{x^2+z^2}}$$

$$= k\lambda \ln\frac{\sqrt{x^2+d^2}+d}{\sqrt{x^2+d^2}-d}$$

$$\phi_1 = \phi_2 \Rightarrow k\lambda\ln(3) = k\lambda\ln(\sqrt{x^2+d^2}+d)/(\sqrt{x^2+d^2}-d)$$

$$\sqrt{x^2+d^2}+d = 3\sqrt{x^2+d^2}-3d$$

$$2\sqrt{x^2+d^2} = 4d, \quad x^2+d^2 = 4d^2$$

$$\Rightarrow x = \sqrt{3}d$$

42. **(D)**

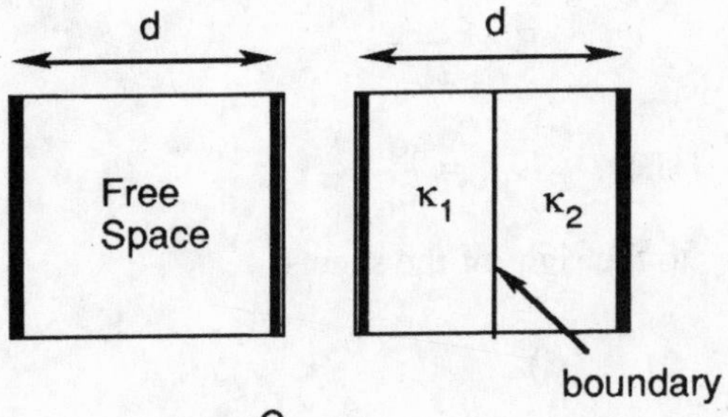

$$C_0 = \frac{\varepsilon_0 L^2}{d}$$

D is continuous across boundary where

$$D = \kappa_0\kappa_1 E_1 = \kappa_0\kappa_2 E_2 = \frac{q}{L^2}$$

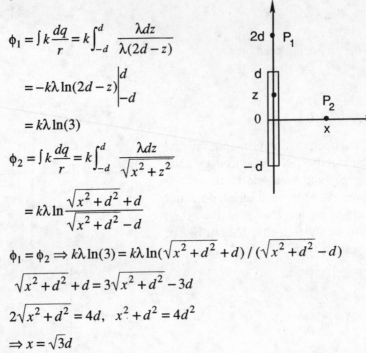

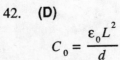

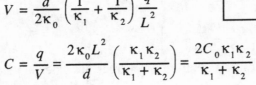

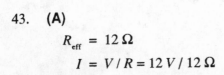

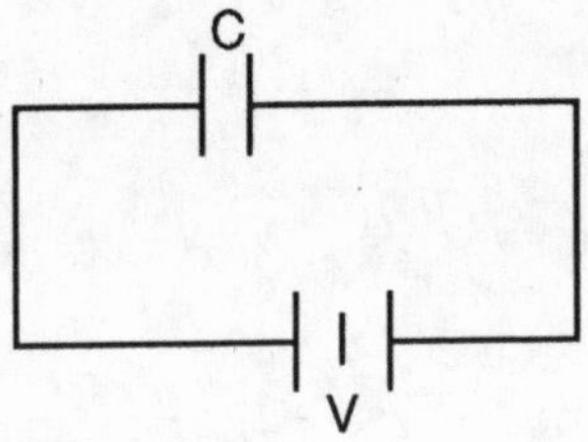

$$V = E_1\frac{d}{2} + E_2\frac{d}{2}$$

$$V = \frac{d}{2\kappa_0}\left(\frac{1}{\kappa_1}+\frac{1}{\kappa_2}\right)\frac{q}{L^2}$$

$$C = \frac{q}{V} = \frac{2\kappa_0 L^2}{d}\left(\frac{\kappa_1\kappa_2}{\kappa_1+\kappa_2}\right) = \frac{2C_0\kappa_1\kappa_2}{\kappa_1+\kappa_2}$$

43. **(A)**

$$R_{\text{eff}} = 12\,\Omega$$

$$I = V/R = 12\,V/12\,\Omega$$

Now working backward the $I = 1\,A$ splits first into

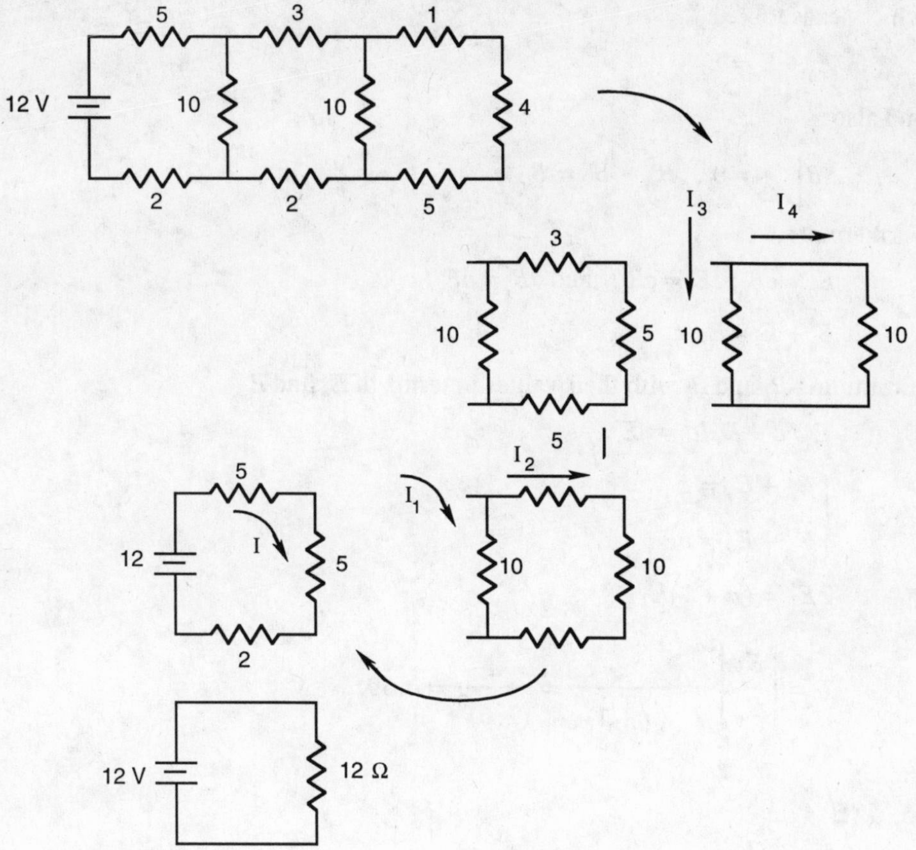

$$I_1 = I_2 = {}^1/_2\, A$$

and then I_2 splits into

$$I_3 = I_4 = {}^1/_4\, A.$$

44. **(D)**

The incident wave is

$$\mathbf{E}_0 = \mathbf{z}\, E_0 \sin(ky - \omega t)$$
$$\mathbf{B}_0 = \mathbf{x}\, B_0 \sin(ky - \omega t)$$

The reflected wave is

$$\mathbf{E}_r = \mathbf{z}\, E_r \sin(ky - \omega t)$$
$$\mathbf{B}_r = -\,\mathbf{x}\, B_r \sin(ky - \omega t)$$

The transmitted wave is

$$\mathbf{E}_t = \mathbf{z}\, E_t \sin(k'y - \omega t)$$
$$\mathbf{B}_t = \mathbf{x}\, B_t \sin(k'y - \omega t)$$

Maxwell's equations require

$$\Delta E\Big|_{y=0} = 0$$

which leads to

$$E_0 + E_r = E_t$$

and also

$$\Delta B\Big|_{y=0} = 0\,,\ B_0 - B_r = B_t$$

Furthermore,

$$E_0 = cB_0,\ E_r = cB_r,\ \text{and}\ B_t = nE_t / c$$

$$E_0 + E_r = E_t\,,$$

substituting B_0 and B_r with their values in terms of E_0 and E_v

$$E_0/c - E_r/c = nE_{t/c}$$

$$\begin{cases} E_0 + E_r = E_t \\ E_0 - E_r = nE_t \end{cases}$$

thus $\quad 2E_0 = (n+1)E_t$

$$T = \left|\frac{E_t}{E_0}\right|^2 = \frac{4}{(n+1)^2} = \frac{4}{(2.6)^2} = 0.59$$

45. **(B)**

$$\nabla \cdot \mathbf{B} = 0$$

implies that there are no magnetic monopoles. If there were, then we would have

$$\nabla \cdot \mathbf{B} = \rho_B$$

with ρ_B a positive or negative magnetic charge density.

It is identical to its integral form which is analogous to Gauss's law for magnetism:

$$\oint \mathbf{B} \cdot d\mathbf{a} = Q_B$$

but we know that the result of the integral is always zero and we cannot have a magnetic monopole.

46. **(A)**

Suppose that a fraction f of the ship is below water when floating. Let V be the volume of the pool without the ship. The buoyant force is

$$B = m_s g = \rho_w f V_s g$$

$$f = \rho_s / \rho_w < 1$$

The floating ship increases the depth by

$$\Delta h = \frac{fV_s}{A}$$

When the ship sinks, it takes in water. Hence the depth now decreases by

$$\frac{fV_s}{A}$$

(the maximum amount of water displaced).

47. **(B)**

Let the initial weight be W_0 then when the hourglass is inverted, the weight must be less than W_0 while the sand is in the air.

As the sand strikes the bottom of the hourglass, it delivers impulsive forces to the scale. The effect is that the scale's measure of weight increases to a value greater than W_0. Therefore (B) is the correct answer. However, the weight decreases to W_0 after all of the sand has fallen.

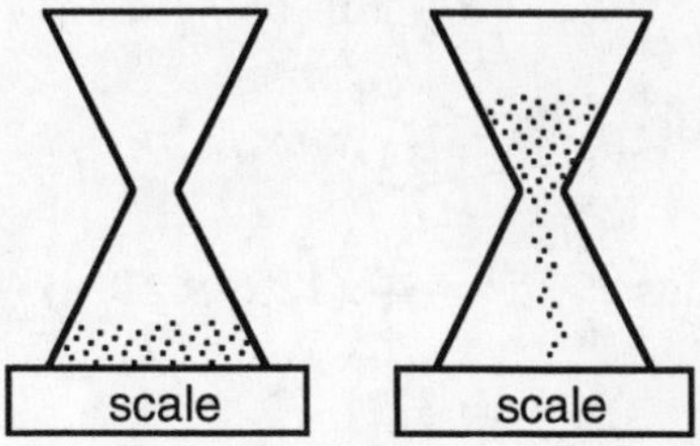

48. **(D)**

$$F = ILB\sin\theta$$

$$= (1)\,(1)\,(100)\left(\frac{1}{\sqrt{2}}\right)$$

$$= 70.7 \text{ Newtons}$$

The direction of **F** is $-$ **z** (Right hand rule).

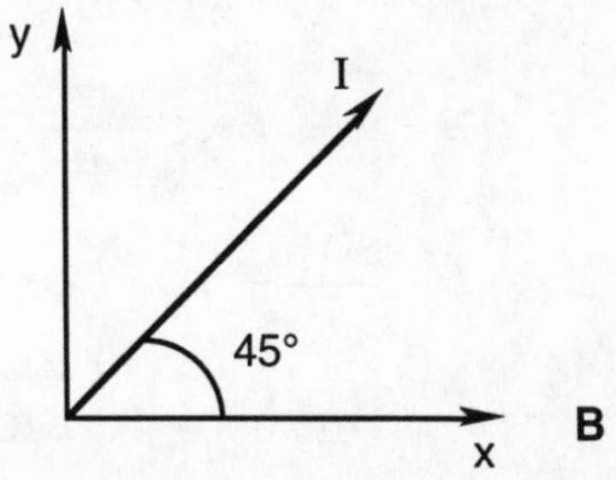

49. **(C)**

First we must find from the given magnetization the amount of the magnetic moment $m = m_1 = m_2$.

$$M = 7.5\times10^{-5}\,\frac{J}{T\cdot m^3} = \frac{m}{V}$$

$$V = \frac{4\pi}{3}r^3$$

$$m = \frac{4\pi}{3}(10^{-2})^3\,(7.5\times10^5)$$

$$= 3.142\ J/T$$

Then the magnetic field may be taken as that of a magnetic dipole.

$$B = (2\ m/r^3)\ (\mu_0/4\pi)$$

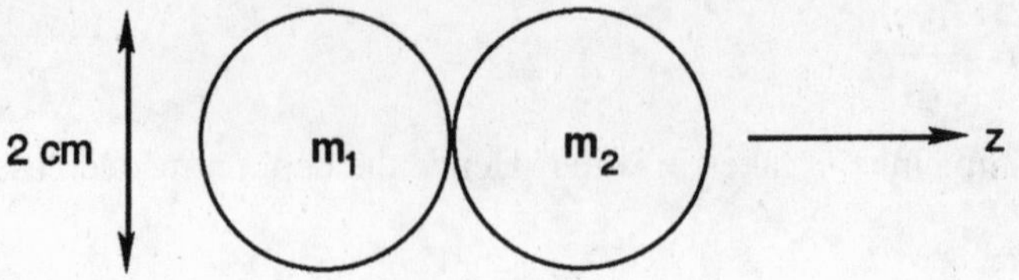

The force is then

$$\mathbf{F} = \mathbf{m} \cdot \nabla \mathbf{B}$$

$$F = m_2 \frac{\partial B_1}{\partial z} = m_2 \frac{\partial}{\partial z}\left(\frac{2m_1}{z^3}\right)\frac{\mu_0}{4\pi}$$

$$= \mu_0 6 m_1 m_2 / z^4 4\pi \ , \quad z = 2r$$

$$= \frac{3}{32}\mu_0 m^2 / r^4 \pi$$

thus $F = \frac{3}{32}(12.6 \times 10^{-7})\left((3.142)^2 / (10^{-2})^4 (3.142)\right)$

$$= 37\,\text{N}$$

50. **(E)**

For a series RLC circuit

$$-L\frac{dI}{dt} - RI - V = 0$$

$$Q = CV \Rightarrow I = C\frac{dV}{dt}$$

$$-LC\frac{d^2V}{dt^2} - RC\frac{dV}{dt} - V = 0$$

or $V'' + \frac{R}{L}V' + \frac{1}{LC}V = 0$

For the parallel RLC circuit shown

$$Q = CV \ , \ I_1 = -\frac{dQ}{dt} = -C\frac{dV}{dt}$$

$$V = R_p(I_1 + I_2) = -L\frac{dI_2}{dt}$$

$$\frac{dV}{dt} = R_p(I'_1 + I'_2)$$

$$= -CR_pV'' - R_p\frac{V}{L}$$

$$V'' + \frac{1}{R_pC}V' + \frac{V}{LC} = 0$$

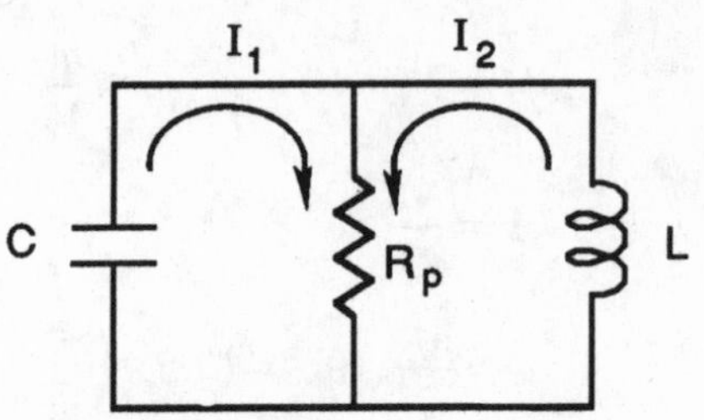

Hence for the same L, C, Q we need

$$\frac{1}{R_pC}=\frac{R}{L}\Rightarrow R_p=\frac{L}{RC}$$

51. **(C)**
The time dependent generator voltage is

$$V = V_m \sin(\omega t)$$
$$\tfrac{1}{2} V_m = V_m \sin(\omega / 720)$$
$$\omega / 720 = A \sin(\tfrac{1}{2}) = \pi/6$$
$$w = 120\,\pi \text{ rad/s}$$

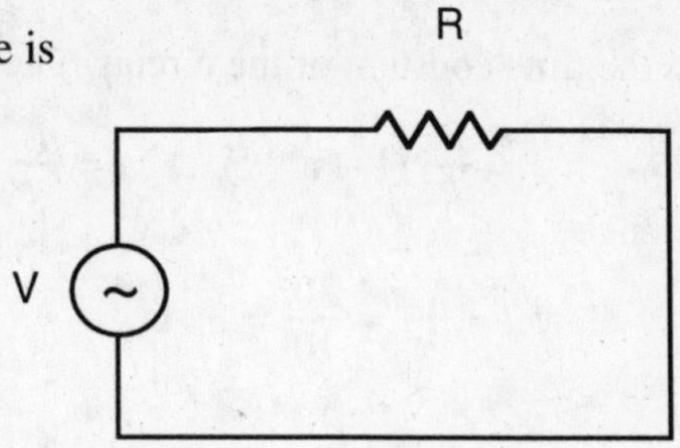

Hence the linear frequency is

$$v = w / 2\pi = 60 \text{ Hz}$$

52. **(B)**
We use Ampere's law

$$\oint \mathbf{B}\cdot dl = \mu_0 I_{in}$$

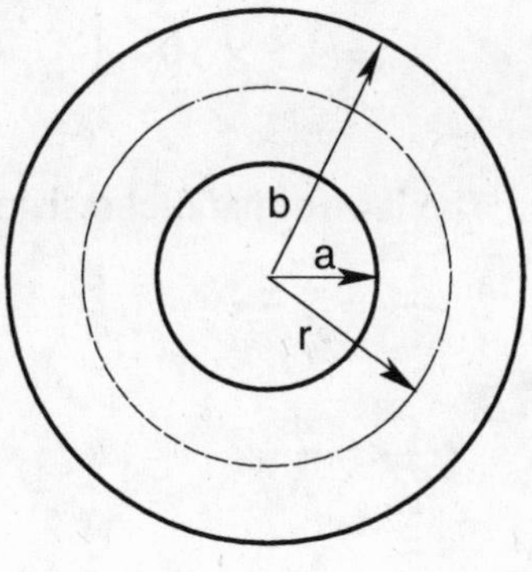

and take the Amperean path as a circle of radius r. Hence

$$B(2\pi r)=\mu_0 NI$$

$$B=\frac{\mu_0}{2\pi}\frac{NI}{r} \quad r=\frac{b-a}{2}$$

$$B=\frac{\mu_0 NI}{\pi(b-a)}$$

53. **(A)**

$$B_1=\frac{\mu_0 I_1}{2\pi x}$$

is the magnetic field produced by I_1 at distance $r = x$. The force that I_1 exerts on I_2 is given by:

$$F_2 = I_2 L B_1$$

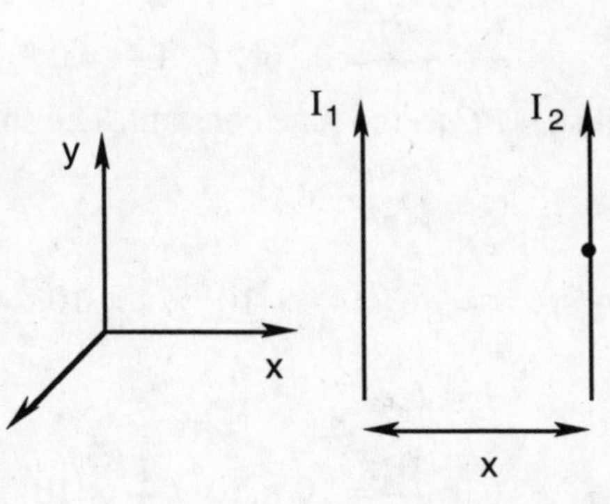

Force per unit length =

$$\frac{F_2}{L}=\frac{\mu_0 I_1 I_2}{2\pi x}$$

in the $-x$ direction.

The force is attractive between like currents.

54. **(D)**
Kirchhoff's law tells us that

$$V - RI - LI' = 0.$$

Differentiating, we get

$$I'' + \frac{I'}{\tau} = 0 \quad \text{where} \quad \tau = \frac{L}{R}$$

is the time constant of the circuit. The solution is

$$I = \frac{V}{R}(1 - e^{-t/\tau}) \;, \quad \tau = \frac{L}{R}$$

Hence

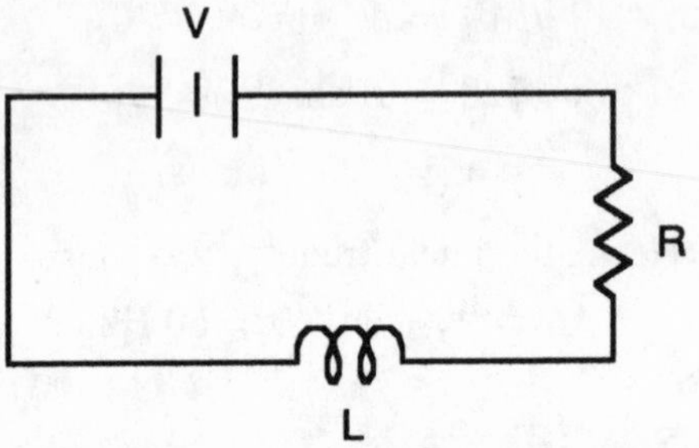

$$I_\infty = \frac{V}{R} = \frac{30}{10} = 3\ A$$

$$U_\infty = \frac{1}{2} L I_\infty^2$$

$$= \frac{1}{2}(10 \times 10^{-6} H)(3A)^2$$

$$= 4.5 \times 10^{-5}\ \text{j}$$

55. **(E)**

The law for parallel resistors is

$$\frac{1}{R_t} = \Sigma \frac{1}{R}$$

Hence

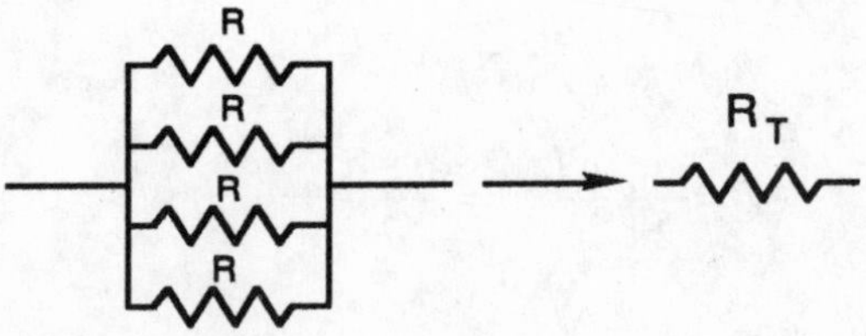

$$\frac{1}{R_T} = \frac{4}{R}$$

$$R_T = \frac{1}{4}R = \frac{1}{4}\ M\Omega$$

The reduced circuit is a basic RC circuit. From Kirchoff's law

$$-RI - \frac{Q}{C} = 0 \quad \text{or} \quad Q' + \frac{Q}{\tau} = 0$$

with $\tau = RC$ as the time constant. The solution is

$$Q = Q_0 e^{-t/\tau}$$

$$\tau = RC = \frac{1}{4} \times 10^6 \times 1 \times 10^{-6} = \frac{1}{4} s$$

$$I = I_0 e^{-t/\tau}$$

$$I_0 = \frac{V}{R} = 10 \times 10^6 / \frac{1}{4} \times 10^6 = 40\text{ A}$$

$$= 40e^{-.5/.25}$$

$$= 5.41\text{ A}$$

56. **(B)**

$$dB = \frac{\mu_0}{4\pi}\frac{I}{r^2}\, dl \times \mathbf{r}$$

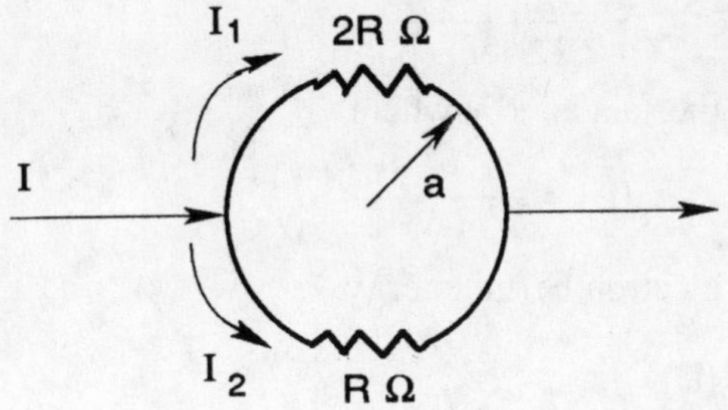

$$\mathbf{B}_1 = \frac{\mu_0}{4\pi}\frac{I_1}{a^2}\int dl(-\mathbf{z})$$

$$= -\frac{\mu_0 I_1}{4\pi a^2}\pi a\mathbf{z}$$

$$= -\frac{\mu_0 I_1}{4a^2}\mathbf{z}$$

Similarly, $\mathbf{B}_2 = \frac{\mu_0}{4a}\mathbf{z}$

Now reduce the series resistor:

$$\frac{1}{R_T} = \frac{1}{R} + \frac{1}{2R} = \frac{3}{2R},\ R_T = \frac{2}{3}R$$

$$V = R_T I = \frac{2}{3}RI$$

$$I_1 = \frac{V}{R_1}, I_1 = \frac{V}{2R} = \frac{1}{3}I,\ I_2 = \frac{V}{R} = \frac{2}{3}I$$

$$\mathbf{B} = \mathbf{B}_1 + \mathbf{B}_2 = \frac{\mu_0}{4a}\mathbf{z}(I_2 - I_1) = \frac{\mu_0 I}{12a}\mathbf{z}$$

57. **(A)**

Use

$$dB = \frac{\mu_0}{4\pi}\cdot\frac{Idl \times \mathbf{r}}{r^2}$$

the Biot-Savart Law where **r** is the unit radial vector. Only the z component of B is non-zero at the origin.

$$(dl \times \mathbf{r})_z = rd\theta$$

$$B_z = \left(\frac{\mu_0 I}{4\pi}\right)\int_0^{2\pi}\frac{d\theta}{r} = \frac{\mu_0 I}{2r}$$

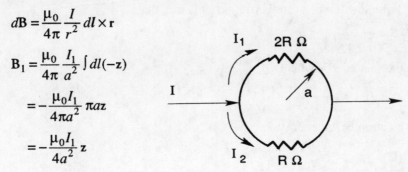

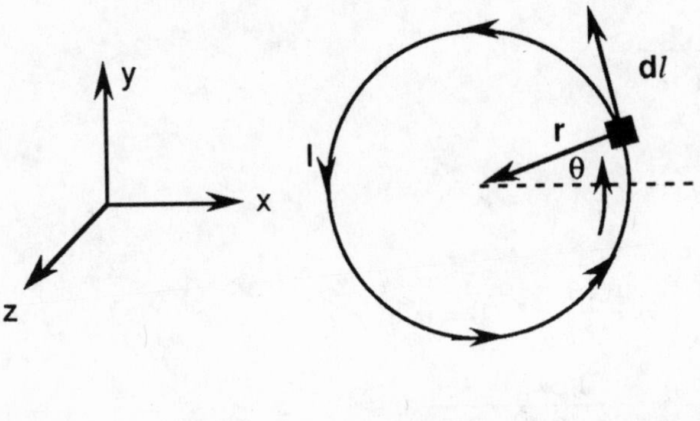

58. **(C)**

For a low temperature Fermi gas, it is true that

$$E_T = \frac{5\pi^2}{12}\frac{T^2}{E_F(\rho)}$$

is the thermal energy where

$$E_F(\rho) = \frac{\hbar^2}{2\,\mathrm{m}}\left(\frac{3\pi^2}{2}\rho\right)^{2/3}$$

is the electron Fermi energy.

59. **(D)**

The Lorentz transformation equation is

$$x' = \gamma(x - vt)$$

or $$\Delta x' = \gamma\Delta x \text{ with } \Delta t = 0.$$

The Lorentz contraction formula is

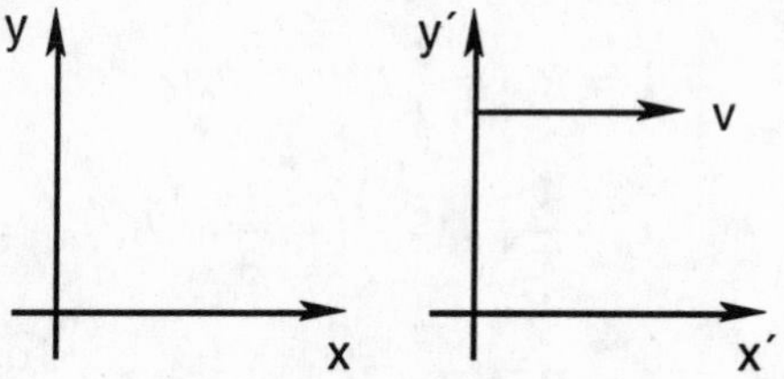

$$l = \gamma l_0$$

$$2 = \gamma 1$$

$$\gamma = 2 = \frac{1}{\sqrt{1-\beta^2}}$$

$$\beta = \sqrt{1-\frac{1}{\gamma^2}} = \sqrt{\frac{3}{4}}$$

$$\beta = \frac{v}{c}$$

$$v = \frac{\sqrt{3}}{2}c = 2.60\times10^{10}\ \text{cm/s}$$

60. **(C)**

The liquid is at rest in K' where the speed of light is $v' = c/n$. In the lab frame we must add the velocity v' to the liquid speed v, relativistically

$$V_3 = \frac{V_1 + V_2}{1 + V_1 V_2/c^2}$$

$$= \frac{c/n + v}{1 + \frac{c}{n}v/c^2}$$

$$= \frac{c/n + v}{1 + v/cn}$$

61. **(A)**

$$v_x = 0.5c\,,\quad v_y = \frac{\sqrt{3}}{2}c\,,\quad \beta = 0.8 \Rightarrow v = 0.8c$$

$$v'_x = \frac{v_x - v}{1 - \frac{vv_x}{c^2}} = \frac{0.5 - 0.8}{1-(0.8)(0.5)}c = -0.5c$$

$$v'_y = \frac{v_y}{\gamma(1 - \frac{vv_x}{c^2})}$$

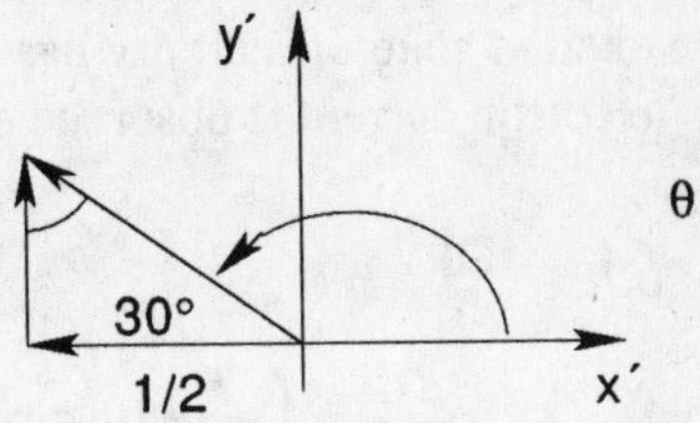

$$\gamma = \frac{1}{\sqrt{1-\beta^2}} = 1.67 = \frac{5}{3}$$

$$v'_y = \frac{\frac{\sqrt{3}}{2}}{\frac{5}{3}(1-(0.8)(0.5))} c = \frac{\sqrt{3}}{2} c$$

$$\theta = A\tan \frac{v'_y}{v'_x}$$

$$= 180 - 60° = 120°$$

Note that

$$v = \sqrt{v'^2_x + v'^2_y} = c$$

since the speed of light is invariant.

62. **(B)**

By conservation of energy

$$h\upsilon = \phi + T$$

At threshold

$$h\upsilon_0 = \phi \text{ and } \upsilon_0 = c/\lambda_0$$

may be used to get

$$\phi = hc / \lambda_0$$
$$= 12{,}400 \text{ eV.Å} / 5420 \text{ Å}$$
$$= 2.29 \text{ eV}$$

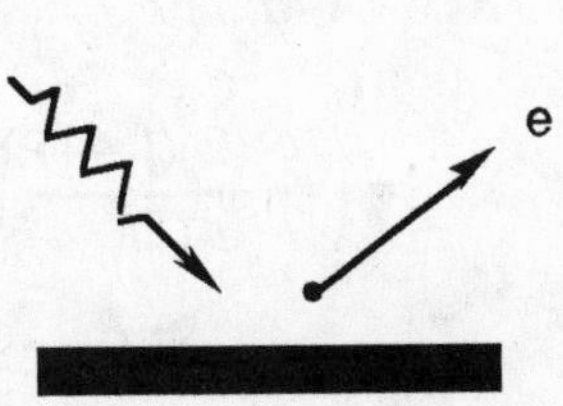

63. **(C)**

The Franck-Hertz experiment definitively established the quantization of atomic energy states. In particular, the data looks like

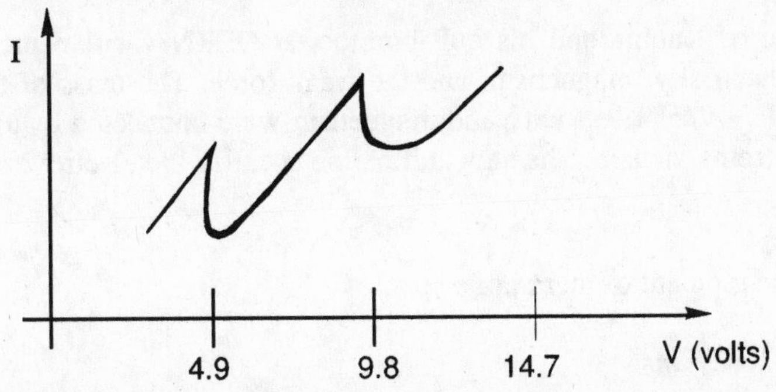

for Hg when one plots the beam current versus the accelerating voltage. The first excited state of mercury has energy 4.9 eV above the ground state. A decrease in electron current is observed every time the potential is increased by 4.9 volts.

64. **(D)**

$$\frac{d\sigma}{d\Omega} = \left(\frac{k}{4T'_0}\right)^2 \left(\sin\left(\frac{\theta}{2}\right)\right)^{-4}$$

$$k = \frac{1}{4\pi\varepsilon_0} Z_1 Z_2 e^2$$

T'_0 is kinetic energy in C.M. system

T_0 is kinetic energy in Lab system

θ is angle in C.M. system

ψ is angle in Lab system.

Given: $\psi = 45°$ and $T_0 = 10$ MeV

Since the mass of an α particle is much smaller than the mass of a gold nucleus,

$$\psi \approx \theta \quad \text{and} \quad t_0 \approx t'_0$$

$$\frac{d\sigma}{d\Omega} \approx \left(\frac{k}{4T_0}\right)^2 \left(\sin\left(\frac{\psi}{2}\right)\right)^{-4}$$

$$\approx \left(\frac{79(2)(1.44)}{4(1)}\right)^2 \sin^{-4}(22.5°)$$

$$\approx 1{,}509 \frac{\text{fm}^2}{\text{sr}} \times \frac{10\,\text{mb}}{1\,\text{fm}^2}$$

$$\approx 15{,}090 \frac{\text{mb}}{\text{sr}}$$

$$\approx 15.09 \frac{\text{b}}{\text{sr}}$$

65. **(E)**

Carlos Rubbia and his collaborators at CERN verified the theory which unifies electricity, magnetism, and the weak force. The mass of the $W^{\pm}$ or Z^0 is about 90 GeV/c². Electricity and magnetism were connected by James Maxwell into electromagnetism. The new unification is called the electroweak theory.

66. **(E)**

The moment of inertia of a sphere is

$$I = \frac{2}{5} mr^2$$

Hence,

$$L = I\omega = \frac{2}{5}mr^2\omega.$$

But also

$$S = \frac{1}{2}\hbar$$

Since the proton is a fermion.

$$\frac{2}{5}mr^2\omega = \frac{1}{2}\hbar$$

$$v = r\omega = \frac{1}{2}\hbar\frac{5}{2}\frac{1}{mr} = \frac{5}{4}\frac{\hbar}{mr}$$

$$= \frac{5}{4}(1.055 \times 10^{-27}) / (1.673 \times 10^{-24})(10^{-13})$$

$$= 7.88 \times 10^{9}\ \text{cm/s}$$

67. **(D)**

$\phi(p) = N/(p^2 + \alpha^2)$

Take the Fourier transform to get

$$\psi(x) = \frac{1}{\sqrt{2\pi\hbar}}\int_{-\infty}^{\infty} dp\, \phi(p) e^{z' px/\hbar}$$

$$= \frac{N}{\sqrt{2\pi\hbar}}\left[\int_{-\infty}^{0} \frac{e^{z' px/\hbar}}{p^2 + \alpha^2} dp + \int_{0}^{\infty} \frac{e^{z' px/\hbar}}{p^2 + \alpha^2} dp\right.$$

$$= \frac{N}{\sqrt{2\pi\hbar}}\int_{0}^{\infty} \frac{e^{z' px/\hbar} + e^{-z' px/\hbar}}{p^2 + \alpha^2} dp$$

Use Euler's theorem

$$e^{i\theta} = \cos\theta + i\sin\theta$$

$$\psi(x) = N\sqrt{\frac{2}{\pi\hbar}}\int_{0}^{\infty} \frac{\cos(px/\hbar)}{p^2 + \alpha^2} dp$$

$$= \sqrt{\frac{2N^2}{\pi\hbar^3}}\int_{0}^{\infty} \frac{\cos kx}{k^2 + \frac{d^2}{\hbar}} dk$$

$$= \frac{N}{\hbar}\sqrt{\frac{2}{\pi\hbar}}\frac{\hbar\pi}{2\alpha} e^{-\alpha|x|/\hbar} = \frac{N}{\alpha}\sqrt{\frac{\pi}{2\hbar}} e^{-\alpha|x|/\hbar}$$

where we have used some knowledge of the Fourier cosine transform. Thus

$$\psi(x) \propto e^{-\alpha|x|/\hbar}$$

68. **(C)**

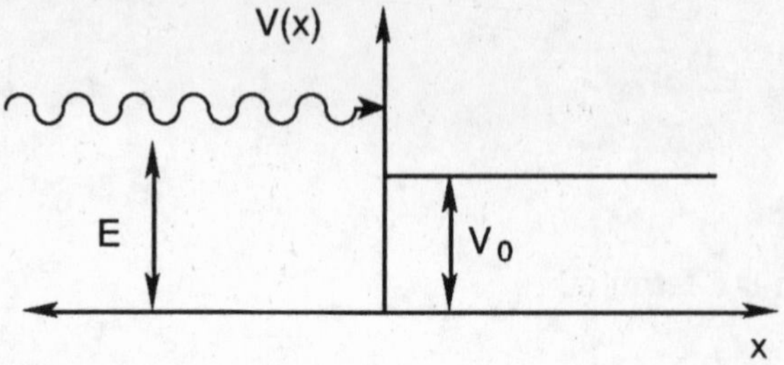

The Schrödinger equation is

$$H\psi = E\psi$$

where $H = T + U$ is the Hamiltonian operator and E is the energy eigenvalue. The solution to this equation is

$$\psi(x) = \begin{cases} e^{ikx} + re^{-ikx}, & x < 0 \quad k = \sqrt{2mE}/\hbar \\ te^{ik'x}, & x > 0 \quad k' = \sqrt{2m(E - V_0)}/\hbar \end{cases}$$

$\psi(0)$ continuous $\Rightarrow 1 + r = t$ or $r = t - 1$

$\psi'(0)$ continuous $\Rightarrow ik - ikr = ik't,$

$$t = \frac{k}{k'} - \frac{k}{k'}r$$

$$r = \frac{k}{k'} - \frac{k}{k'}r - 1$$

Now

$$r(1 + \frac{k}{k'}) = \frac{k}{k'} - 1, \quad r = (k - k')/(k + k')$$

is the amplitude of the reflected wave and

$$R = rr^* = \left|\frac{(k - k')}{(k + k')}\right|^2$$

is the reflection coefficient.

69. **(B)**

The rotational energy eigenvalue is

$$E_l = \hbar^2 \ell(\ell + 1)/2\mu r^2$$

where l is the angular momentum quantum number and r is the relative distance.

$$\hbar = 1973.5 \text{ eV} - \text{Å}/c$$

$$m_p = 938.280 \times 10^6 \text{ eV}/c^2 = m_1 = m_2$$

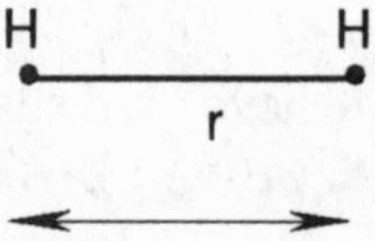

The reduced mass is

$$\mu = m_1 m_2/(m_1 + m_2)$$

$$= m_p/2 = 469.140 \times 10^6 \text{ eV}/c^2$$

$$E_3 = (1973.5)^2\,3(4)\,/\,2\,(469.140 \times 10^6)\,(1)^2$$
$$= 0.05 \text{ eV}$$

70. **(B)**
By Newton's 2nd law,

$$\Sigma F = -kx - bx' = mx''$$

The equation of motion is then

$$x'' + \frac{b}{m}x' + \frac{k}{m}\,x = 0 \quad \text{where} \quad \omega_0^2 = \frac{k}{m}$$

gives the square of the rational frequency

$$x = Ae^{-bt/2m}\cos(\omega t + \phi)$$

is a solution.

$$\omega = \sqrt{\omega_0^2 - \frac{1}{4}\frac{b^2}{m^2}}$$

is the damped frequency

$$0.995\omega_0 = \sqrt{\omega_0^2 - \frac{1}{4}\frac{b^2}{m^2}}$$

$$0.010\omega_0^2 = \frac{1}{4}\frac{b^2}{m^2} = 0.010\frac{k}{m} \quad \text{since} \quad \omega_0^2 = \frac{k}{m}.$$

Hence,

$$b = \sqrt{0.040\,km} = \sqrt{0.040(200)\,(0.4)}$$
$$= 1.789\ kg/s$$

71. **(C)**
Spin orbit coupling results in an energy change

$$\Delta E = a\Delta(\mathbf{l}\cdot\mathbf{s})$$

The total angular momentum is $\mathbf{j} = \mathbf{l} + \mathbf{s}$.

$$j^2 = (\mathbf{l} + \mathbf{s})^2 = l^2 + s^2 + 2\mathbf{l}\cdot\mathbf{s}$$

Now the eigenvalues of *any* angular momentum operator follow the rule

$$j^2\psi = (j(j+1))\psi$$

thus $\quad \mathbf{l}\cdot\mathbf{s} = (j(j+1) - l(l+1) - s(s+1))\,/\,2$

The two states have:

$$(j, l, s) = (\tfrac{3}{2}, 1, \tfrac{1}{2}) \text{ and } (\tfrac{1}{2}, 1, \tfrac{1}{2}) \text{ respectively}$$

Hence,

$$\mathbf{l}\cdot\mathbf{s}=\begin{cases}(\frac{15}{4}-2-\frac{3}{4})/2\\[4pt](\frac{3}{4}-2-\frac{3}{4})/2\end{cases}=\begin{cases}\frac{1}{2}\\[4pt]-1\end{cases}$$

$$\Delta(\mathbf{l}\cdot\mathbf{s})=(\tfrac{1}{2}+1)=\tfrac{3}{2}$$

$$a=\frac{\Delta E}{\Delta\mathbf{l}\cdot\mathbf{s}}$$

$$=\frac{\left(\dfrac{hc}{\lambda_1}-\dfrac{hc}{\lambda_2}\right)}{\left(\dfrac{3}{2}\right)}$$

Using $E=h\nu=hc/\lambda$

$$=(12,400)\,(\tfrac{2}{3})\left(\frac{1}{5889.95}-\frac{1}{5895.92}\right)$$

$$=0.001\ \text{eV}$$

72. **(A)**

Larmor's formula states that an electron circling a nucleus with centripetal acceleration a emits energy with rate

$$p=\frac{1}{4\pi\varepsilon_0}\cdot\frac{2}{3}\cdot\frac{e^2a^2}{c^3}=\frac{dU}{dt}$$

From this it may be shown that the electron will spiral into the nucleus in about 10^{-10} s.

73. **(D)**

Using $F=ma$ with $a=v^2/r$ as the centripetal acceleration and $F=kq_1q_2/r^2$ as the Couloumb force, we have

$$F=\frac{mv^2}{r}=\frac{kZe^2}{r^2}$$

From Bohr theory

$$L=mvr=n\hbar$$

thus $$v=\frac{n\hbar}{mr}$$

$$\frac{m\left(\dfrac{n\hbar}{mr}\right)^2}{r}=\frac{kZe^2}{r^2}$$

$$r_\mu=\frac{n^2\hbar^2}{kZe^2m_\mu}$$

$$r_H=\frac{n^2\hbar^2}{kZe^2m_e}$$

$$r_\mu = \frac{m_e}{m_\mu} r_H = \frac{1}{207} r_H$$

where r_H is the radius of the Hydrogen-like atom in Bohr theory.

74. **(B)**

The Compton shift is

$$\Delta\lambda = \lambda' - \lambda$$

$$\lambda' - \lambda = \lambda_c (1 - \cos\theta)$$

where $\lambda_c = hc/m_e c^2$

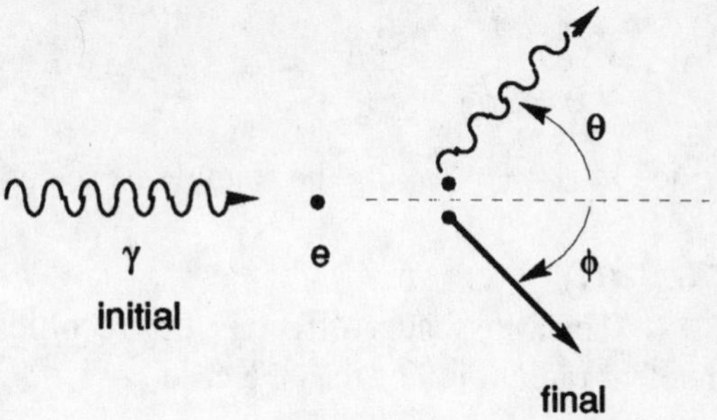

is the Compton wavelength

$$= 12{,}400 / 511{,}000$$

$$= .02426 \text{ Å}$$

$$E = 50 \times 10^3 \text{ eV} = hc/\lambda$$

$$\lambda = hc/E = 12{,}400/50{,}000 = 0.2480 \text{ Å}$$

$$\lambda' = \lambda + \Delta\lambda = .2480 \text{ Å} + .02426 \text{ Å } (1 - \tfrac{1}{\sqrt{2}})$$

$$= .2551 \text{ Å}$$

Thus $E' = hc/\lambda'$

$$= 12{,}400 / .2551$$

$$= 48.6 \text{ keV}$$

is the scattered photon energy. Note that the photon loses energy to the electron.

75. **(E)**

Consider the initial and final states in the two frames:

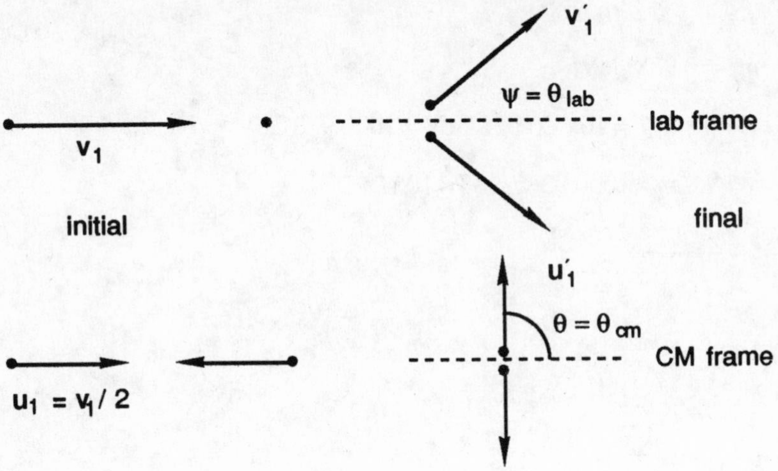

Now $\mathbf{u}_1 = \mathbf{v}_1/2 = \mathbf{v}_1 - \mathbf{v}_1/2$

hence, $\mathbf{u}_1' = \mathbf{v}_1' - \mathbf{v}_1/2$

as in the figure at the right.

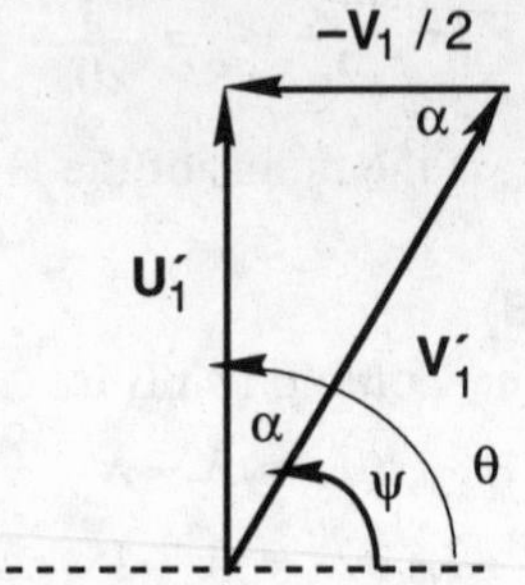

$$\theta = \psi + \alpha$$

by geometry and also

$$\alpha = \psi$$

$$\therefore \quad \theta = 2\psi$$

since $|u'_1| = \frac{v_1}{2}$ making the triangle isosceles.

76. **(D)**

The Mossbauer effect is the recoilless resonance emission/absorption of nuclear radiation. For the ^{57}Fe case

$$E_0 = 14.4 \text{ keV}, \quad t = 9.8 \times 10^{-8} \text{ s}$$

is given. The energy width is

$$\Gamma = \hbar / t = (1.055 \times 10^{-27}) / (9.8 \times 10^{-8}) (1.602 \times 10^{-12} \text{ erg/eV})$$
$$= 6.72 \times 10^{-9} \text{ eV}$$

One destroys resonant absorption in the lattice via the Doppler shift

$$\Delta E \geq \Gamma, \ \frac{v}{c} E_0 \geq \Gamma$$

$$v \geq \Gamma c / E_0 = \frac{(6.72 \times 10^{-9})(2.998 \times 10^{10})}{14.4 \times 10^3}$$

$$v_{\min} = 0.014 \text{ cm/s}$$

77. **(A)**

$$T = 1 \text{ TeV} = 10^3 \text{ GeV}$$

$$m_p = 0.938 \text{ GeV}$$

$$E = m_p + T = 10^3 + 0.938 \text{ GeV} = 1000.938 \text{ GeV}$$

$$\gamma = E / m = 1000.938 / .938 = 1067$$

$$= \frac{1}{\sqrt{1-\beta^2}}$$

$$1 - \beta^2 = \frac{1}{\gamma^2}$$

$$\beta = \sqrt{1 - \frac{1}{\gamma^2}}$$

However,

$$\sqrt{1+x} = f(0) + f'(0)x = 1 + \tfrac{1}{2} x$$

using a Taylor expansion. Hence

$$\beta = 1 - \frac{1}{2\gamma^2} = 1 - 4 \times 10^{-7}$$

$= 0.9999996$, so the answer is $0.9999996c$. It is incredible how close to the speed of light one can get!

78. **(C)**

Consider the reaction

$$I + T \rightarrow E + R$$

Where I = incident particle, T = target, E = emitted particle, and R = residue which is also written

$$T\,(I,\, E)\, R.$$

The *Q–value is*

$$\begin{aligned} Q &= m_I + m_T - m_E - m_R \\ &= (2.01473 + 26.98154 - 1.00794 - 27.98154)\text{ amu} \\ &\quad \times 931.502\text{ MeV / amu} \\ &= 6.32\text{ MeV} \end{aligned}$$

79. **(E)**

The parameter b is a measure of the surface thickness. The falloff distance is approximately the same for all nuclei. R. Hofstadter of Stanford University was awarded the Nobel Prize for these experiments with electron scattering.

80. **(B)**

In general, probability P of finding the particle is $P = \int_V \psi\psi^* \, dV$, where the product of the wave function and its conjugate takes place over volume V. If the integration is carried out over all space, $P = 1$.

Therefore we can write

$$P = 1 = \int_V \psi\psi^* \, dV = \int \phi\phi^* \, r^2 dr \int Y_{00} Y_{00}^* \, d\Omega$$

The first integral on the right represents the radial part of the wave function and the second, its spherical harmonic angular part.

Thus, integrating over all space and substituting, we obtain the expression

$$\text{(B)}\quad 1 = \int_a^{a+b} A^2 \sin^2 k(r-a) dr + \int_{a+b}^{\infty} B^2 \frac{e^{-2kr}}{r^2} dr$$

Note that the normalization constant will be a function of A and B after integration is carried out.

81. **(A)**

The rotational energy eigenvalues of the Schrödinger equation are:

$$E_j = j(j+1)\hbar^2 / 2\,\mu\, r^2$$

The hydrogen atom consists of a proton and an electron:

$$m_H = 938.280 + .511 = 938.791 \text{ MeV}$$

The reduced mass is therefore

$$\mu = m_1 m_2 / (m_1 + m_2) = m_H / 2 = 469.396 \text{ MeV}$$

and $r = 1.06$ Å

is the given relative distance $r = |\mathbf{r}_2 - \mathbf{r}_1|$.

$$kT = (1.38 \times 10^{-16})\,(300) / (1.602 \times 10^{-12}) = .0259 \text{ eV}$$

$$E_0 = 0$$

$$E_1 = \hbar^2 / \mu r^2$$

$$= (1973.50^2 / (469.396 \times 10^6)\,(1.06)^2$$

$$= .00739 \text{ eV}$$

$$N_1 / N_0 = e^{-E_1 / kT}$$

$$= 0.75$$

82. **(E)**

The proton configuration is

$$(1s_{1/2})^2\,(2\,p_{3/2})^4\,(2\,p_{1/2})^2\,(3d_{5/2})^5$$

since there are 13 protons while the neutron configuration is

$$(1s_{1/2})^2\,(2\,p_{3/2})^4\,(2\,p_{1/2})^2\,(3d_{5/2})^6$$

since there are 14 neutrons. Only the open proton shell contributes to the nuclear spin. Hence, the spin of the $^{27}_{13}$Al nuclide may also be deduced to be $j = 5/2$.

83. **(B)**

The Bose condensation phenomenon occurs for low temperatures T less than a critical temperature T_c where all particles reside in the lowest state.

84. **(C)**

Moseley discovered that the frequency of x-ray emission υ is proportional to the square of the atomic number Z of the emitting system. This follows quite naturally from quantum theory since

$$E_n = -13.6 \text{ eV } Z^2 / n^2$$

is the energy eigenvalue for a Hydrogen-like atom and thus the transition energy

$$E_m - E_n = h\upsilon \propto Z^2$$

produces a photon of frequency υ.

85. **(C)**

In the Zeeman effect, the frequency is shifted by an angular frequency

$$\Delta\omega = \pm eB / 2 m_e c$$
$$= \pm \mu_B B / \hbar$$

thus the energy shift is

$$\Delta E = \hbar \Delta\omega$$
$$= \pm \mu_B B$$

86. **(A)**

By definition of the exchange operator,

$$P_{12}\psi(1,2) = \psi(2,1)$$

$$\psi^s(1,2) = \frac{1}{\sqrt{2}}(\psi(1,2) + \psi(2,1))$$

then $\quad P_{12}\psi^s(1,2) = (1)\psi^s(1,2)$

or $\quad P_{12}\psi^s(1,2) = \dfrac{1}{\sqrt{2}}(\psi(1,2) + \psi(2,1))$

87. **(E)**

The potential energy function is

$$V(x) = \begin{cases} \infty & x < -a/2 \\ 0 & -a/2 < x < a/2 \\ \infty & x > a/2 \end{cases}$$

The Schrödinger equation

$$H\psi_n = E\psi_n$$

with Hamiltonian $H = T + U$ has eigenvalues given by

$$\psi_n(x) = \cos(n\pi x/a)$$

since $\quad \dfrac{-\hbar}{2m}\dfrac{d^2\psi_m}{dx^2} = \dfrac{\hbar^2 n^2\pi^2}{2ma^2}\psi_n$

$$E_n = nE = \frac{\hbar^2\pi^2}{2ma^2}n^2$$

for a single boson. In the ground state, $n = 1$. For N such bosons,

$$E_t = NE_1.$$

88. **(C)**

In the WKB approximation, the Schrödinger equation

$$\frac{d^2\psi(r)}{dr^2} + \frac{2m}{\hbar^2}(E - V(r))\psi(r) = 0$$

has a solution

$$\psi(r) = e^{ik(r)/\hbar}$$

where

$$k(r) = \int dr\sqrt{2m(E - V(r))}.$$

This may be used to find the probability for an α particle to tunnel through the Coulomb barrier.

89. **(B)**

The law of Dulong and Petit statues that $C_V = 3\ nR$ where n is the number of moles and $R = N_A k$ is the ideal gas constant. In the Debye theory one finds that C_V increases from zero at $T = 0\ K$ to approach 3 nR at high temperature. Therefore the law of Dulong and Petit is valid only for high temperatures where $C_V \approx 3\ nR$.

90. **(C)**

One may find $<v>$ from

$$\frac{\int vf(v)dv}{\int f(v)dv}$$

using the Maxwell-Boltzmann distribution $f(v)$.

$$<v> = \sqrt{\frac{2kT}{m}}$$

$$= \sqrt{2(1.381 \times 10^{-16})(300)/(28/6.022 \times 10^{23})}$$

$$= 4.22 \times 10^4 \text{ cm/s}$$

The escape speed from the surface of the earth is equal to the velocity of a particle whose kinetic energy is equal to its gravitational potential energy at the surface of the earth. Hence:

$$\frac{1}{2}mv^2 = \frac{GMm}{R}$$

$$v = \sqrt{2GM/R}$$

$$= \sqrt{2\frac{(6.672 \times 10^{-8})(5.98 \times 10^{27})}{6.38 \times 10^8}}$$

$$= 1.12 \times 10^6 \text{ cm/s}$$

thus $<v>/v = .038$ which explains the large presence of N_2 in the atmosphere.

91. **(B)**

$$F = \frac{Gm_1 m_2}{r^2} = \frac{(6.672 \times 10^{-8})m^2}{1^2} = 1$$

$$m = 3.87 \times 10^3 \text{ g}$$

$$= 3.87 \text{ kg}$$

In this convenient gravitational system of units, one could take $G = 1$.

92. **(A)**

$$\Delta E = 120 \text{MeV}$$

$$\tau = \hbar / \Delta E$$

Using the uncertainty principle

$$= 197.35/120$$

$$= 1.64 \frac{fm}{c} \times \frac{10^{-13} \text{ cm}}{3 \times 10^{10} \text{ cm/s}}$$

$$\tau = 5.5 \times 10^{-24} \text{ s}$$

93. **(E)**

The u quark has charge $^2/_3$ and the d quark has charge $- ^1/_3$. Hence the combination

uud

has charge

$$\frac{2}{3} + \frac{2}{3} - \frac{1}{3} = 1$$

the charge of the proton.

94. **(D)**

$$U = \frac{1}{2} kx^2, \ \psi_0 = ce^{-ax^2}$$

are given

$$\int_{-\infty}^{\infty} \psi_0 {}^* \psi_0 \, dx = 1$$

by the normalization condition

$$\int_{-\infty}^{\infty} C^2 e^{-2ax^2} dx = 1$$

Now we know that

$$\int_{-\infty}^{\infty} \frac{1}{\sqrt{2\pi\sigma^2}} e^{-\frac{1}{2}\frac{x^2}{\sigma^2}} dx = 1$$

using the standard Gaussian probability density function. Thus

$$\int_{-\infty}^{\infty} \frac{1}{\sqrt{2\pi}\sqrt{1/4a}} e^{-\frac{1}{2}\frac{x^2}{1/4a}} dx = 1$$

Hence:

$$C^2 = \frac{1}{\sqrt{2\pi}} 2\sqrt{a} = \sqrt{2a/\pi}$$

$$C = (2a/\pi)^{1/4}$$

95. **(C)**

If the two particles are in a spin singlet state, then the spatial wave function is symmetric. Thus

$$\frac{d\sigma}{d\Omega} = |f(\theta) + f(\pi - \theta)|^2$$

96. **(A)**

$$t = \gamma\left(t' + \frac{vx'}{c^2}\right)$$

is one equation of the Lorentz transformation. Hence

$$\Delta t' = \sqrt{1 - \beta^2}\,\Delta t = \Delta t/\gamma \quad \text{using} \quad \Delta x' = 0$$

Now since $\beta << 1$, we may use a Taylor expansion.

$$\sqrt{1 + x} \approx 1 + \frac{1}{2}x$$

and get

$$\Delta t' = (1 - \frac{1}{2}\beta^2)\Delta t$$

converting

$$600 \frac{\text{mi}}{\text{hr}} \Rightarrow 960 \frac{\text{km}}{\text{hr}}$$

$$= \left(1 - \frac{1}{2}\left(960 \frac{\text{km}}{\text{hr}} \frac{1000\ \text{m}}{\text{km}} \frac{\text{hr}}{3600\ \text{s}} \frac{1}{3 \times 10^8\ \text{m/s}}\right)^2\right)(1.00\ \text{s})$$

$$= (1 - 4 \times 10^{-13})\ \text{s}$$

a small but measurable difference!

97. **(E)**

The adiabatic gas law is

$$pV^{\gamma} = p_0 V_0^{\gamma}$$

$$pV = nRT$$

is the ideal gas equation of state for the final situation

$$p_0V_0 = nRT_0$$

and the initial situation.

$$n\frac{RT}{V}V^{\gamma} = n\frac{RT_0}{V_0}V_0^{\gamma}$$

$$\frac{T}{T_0} = \left(\frac{V_0}{V}\right)^{\gamma-1} = \left(\frac{V_0}{V}\right)^{2/3}$$

Taking $\gamma = {}^5/_3$ for a monatomic ideal gas with 3 degrees of freedom. Thus

$$\frac{T}{T_0} = \left(\frac{1}{2}\right)^{2/3} = 0.63$$

98. **(C)**
The particle area density is related to the normal density by

$$\rho_t = \rho_x$$

where x is the physical target thickness.

$$x = \rho_t / \rho = \frac{(3.00 \text{ g/cm}^2)}{(11.35 \text{ g/cm}^3)} = .265 \text{ cm}$$

The kinetic energy loss is exponential:

$$\Delta T = T_0 e^{-x/L}$$
$$= 10e^{-.265/.53}$$
$$= 6.07 \text{ MeV}$$

99. **(B)**

$$B = 2.04 \times 10^9 Pa$$

$$\rho = 1 \text{ g/cm}^3 = 10^3 \text{ kg/m}^3$$

$$v = \sqrt{\frac{B}{\rho}} = \sqrt{\frac{2.04 \times 10^9}{10^3}} = 1430 \text{ m/s}$$

$$\lambda = \frac{v}{f} = \frac{1430}{262} = 5.45 \text{ m}$$

100. **(C)**
A ray through the center of the lens is not bent at all.

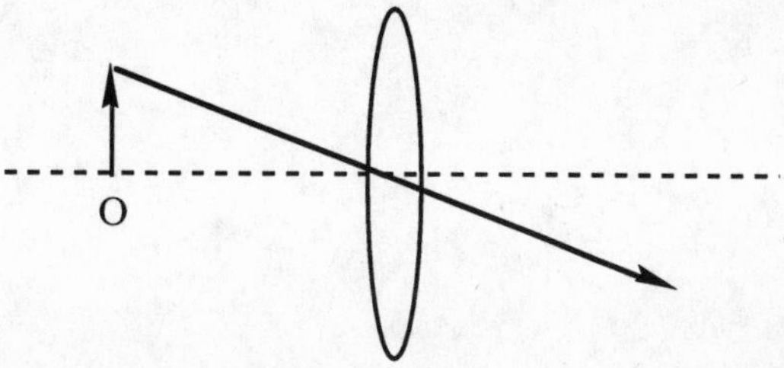

The Graduate Record Examination in

PHYSICS

Test 2

THE GRADUATE RECORD EXAMINATION IN

PHYSICS

TEST 2 – ANSWER SHEET

1. Ⓐ Ⓑ Ⓒ Ⓓ Ⓔ
2. Ⓐ Ⓑ Ⓒ Ⓓ Ⓔ
3. Ⓐ Ⓑ Ⓒ Ⓓ Ⓔ
4. Ⓐ Ⓑ Ⓒ Ⓓ Ⓔ
5. Ⓐ Ⓑ Ⓒ Ⓓ Ⓔ
6. Ⓐ Ⓑ Ⓒ Ⓓ Ⓔ
7. Ⓐ Ⓑ Ⓒ Ⓓ Ⓔ
8. Ⓐ Ⓑ Ⓒ Ⓓ Ⓔ
9. Ⓐ Ⓑ Ⓒ Ⓓ Ⓔ
10. Ⓐ Ⓑ Ⓒ Ⓓ Ⓔ
11. Ⓐ Ⓑ Ⓒ Ⓓ Ⓔ
12. Ⓐ Ⓑ Ⓒ Ⓓ Ⓔ
13. Ⓐ Ⓑ Ⓒ Ⓓ Ⓔ
14. Ⓐ Ⓑ Ⓒ Ⓓ Ⓔ
15. Ⓐ Ⓑ Ⓒ Ⓓ Ⓔ
16. Ⓐ Ⓑ Ⓒ Ⓓ Ⓔ
17. Ⓐ Ⓑ Ⓒ Ⓓ Ⓔ
18. Ⓐ Ⓑ Ⓒ Ⓓ Ⓔ
19. Ⓐ Ⓑ Ⓒ Ⓓ Ⓔ
20. Ⓐ Ⓑ Ⓒ Ⓓ Ⓔ
21. Ⓐ Ⓑ Ⓒ Ⓓ Ⓔ
22. Ⓐ Ⓑ Ⓒ Ⓓ Ⓔ
23. Ⓐ Ⓑ Ⓒ Ⓓ Ⓔ
24. Ⓐ Ⓑ Ⓒ Ⓓ Ⓔ
25. Ⓐ Ⓑ Ⓒ Ⓓ Ⓔ
26. Ⓐ Ⓑ Ⓒ Ⓓ Ⓔ
27. Ⓐ Ⓑ Ⓒ Ⓓ Ⓔ
28. Ⓐ Ⓑ Ⓒ Ⓓ Ⓔ
29. Ⓐ Ⓑ Ⓒ Ⓓ Ⓔ
30. Ⓐ Ⓑ Ⓒ Ⓓ Ⓔ
31. Ⓐ Ⓑ Ⓒ Ⓓ Ⓔ
32. Ⓐ Ⓑ Ⓒ Ⓓ Ⓔ
33. Ⓐ Ⓑ Ⓒ Ⓓ Ⓔ
34. Ⓐ Ⓑ Ⓒ Ⓓ Ⓔ
35. Ⓐ Ⓑ Ⓒ Ⓓ Ⓔ
36. Ⓐ Ⓑ Ⓒ Ⓓ Ⓔ
37. Ⓐ Ⓑ Ⓒ Ⓓ Ⓔ
38. Ⓐ Ⓑ Ⓒ Ⓓ Ⓔ
39. Ⓐ Ⓑ Ⓒ Ⓓ Ⓔ
40. Ⓐ Ⓑ Ⓒ Ⓓ Ⓔ
41. Ⓐ Ⓑ Ⓒ Ⓓ Ⓔ
42. Ⓐ Ⓑ Ⓒ Ⓓ Ⓔ
43. Ⓐ Ⓑ Ⓒ Ⓓ Ⓔ
44. Ⓐ Ⓑ Ⓒ Ⓓ Ⓔ
45. Ⓐ Ⓑ Ⓒ Ⓓ Ⓔ
46. Ⓐ Ⓑ Ⓒ Ⓓ Ⓔ
47. Ⓐ Ⓑ Ⓒ Ⓓ Ⓔ
48. Ⓐ Ⓑ Ⓒ Ⓓ Ⓔ
49. Ⓐ Ⓑ Ⓒ Ⓓ Ⓔ
50. Ⓐ Ⓑ Ⓒ Ⓓ Ⓔ
51. Ⓐ Ⓑ Ⓒ Ⓓ Ⓔ
52. Ⓐ Ⓑ Ⓒ Ⓓ Ⓔ
53. Ⓐ Ⓑ Ⓒ Ⓓ Ⓔ
54. Ⓐ Ⓑ Ⓒ Ⓓ Ⓔ
55. Ⓐ Ⓑ Ⓒ Ⓓ Ⓔ
56. Ⓐ Ⓑ Ⓒ Ⓓ Ⓔ
57. Ⓐ Ⓑ Ⓒ Ⓓ Ⓔ
58. Ⓐ Ⓑ Ⓒ Ⓓ Ⓔ
59. Ⓐ Ⓑ Ⓒ Ⓓ Ⓔ
60. Ⓐ Ⓑ Ⓒ Ⓓ Ⓔ
61. Ⓐ Ⓑ Ⓒ Ⓓ Ⓔ
62. Ⓐ Ⓑ Ⓒ Ⓓ Ⓔ
63. Ⓐ Ⓑ Ⓒ Ⓓ Ⓔ
64. Ⓐ Ⓑ Ⓒ Ⓓ Ⓔ
65. Ⓐ Ⓑ Ⓒ Ⓓ Ⓔ
66. Ⓐ Ⓑ Ⓒ Ⓓ Ⓔ
67. Ⓐ Ⓑ Ⓒ Ⓓ Ⓔ
68. Ⓐ Ⓑ Ⓒ Ⓓ Ⓔ
69. Ⓐ Ⓑ Ⓒ Ⓓ Ⓔ
70. Ⓐ Ⓑ Ⓒ Ⓓ Ⓔ
71. Ⓐ Ⓑ Ⓒ Ⓓ Ⓔ
72. Ⓐ Ⓑ Ⓒ Ⓓ Ⓔ
73. Ⓐ Ⓑ Ⓒ Ⓓ Ⓔ
74. Ⓐ Ⓑ Ⓒ Ⓓ Ⓔ
75. Ⓐ Ⓑ Ⓒ Ⓓ Ⓔ
76. Ⓐ Ⓑ Ⓒ Ⓓ Ⓔ
77. Ⓐ Ⓑ Ⓒ Ⓓ Ⓔ
78. Ⓐ Ⓑ Ⓒ Ⓓ Ⓔ
79. Ⓐ Ⓑ Ⓒ Ⓓ Ⓔ
80. Ⓐ Ⓑ Ⓒ Ⓓ Ⓔ
81. Ⓐ Ⓑ Ⓒ Ⓓ Ⓔ
82. Ⓐ Ⓑ Ⓒ Ⓓ Ⓔ
83. Ⓐ Ⓑ Ⓒ Ⓓ Ⓔ
84. Ⓐ Ⓑ Ⓒ Ⓓ Ⓔ
85. Ⓐ Ⓑ Ⓒ Ⓓ Ⓔ
86. Ⓐ Ⓑ Ⓒ Ⓓ Ⓔ
87. Ⓐ Ⓑ Ⓒ Ⓓ Ⓔ
88. Ⓐ Ⓑ Ⓒ Ⓓ Ⓔ
89. Ⓐ Ⓑ Ⓒ Ⓓ Ⓔ
90. Ⓐ Ⓑ Ⓒ Ⓓ Ⓔ
91. Ⓐ Ⓑ Ⓒ Ⓓ Ⓔ
92. Ⓐ Ⓑ Ⓒ Ⓓ Ⓔ
93. Ⓐ Ⓑ Ⓒ Ⓓ Ⓔ
94. Ⓐ Ⓑ Ⓒ Ⓓ Ⓔ
95. Ⓐ Ⓑ Ⓒ Ⓓ Ⓔ
96. Ⓐ Ⓑ Ⓒ Ⓓ Ⓔ
97. Ⓐ Ⓑ Ⓒ Ⓓ Ⓔ
98. Ⓐ Ⓑ Ⓒ Ⓓ Ⓔ
99. Ⓐ Ⓑ Ⓒ Ⓓ Ⓔ
100. Ⓐ Ⓑ Ⓒ Ⓓ Ⓔ

GRE PHYSICS
TEST 2

TIME: 170 Minutes
100 Questions

DIRECTIONS: Each of the questions or incomplete statements below is followed by five answer choices or completions. Choose the best answer to each question.

1. The displacement vector **r** of a point mass may be expressed in cylindrical coordinates. In that representation, determine the velocity vector **v** = *d***r**/*dt*.

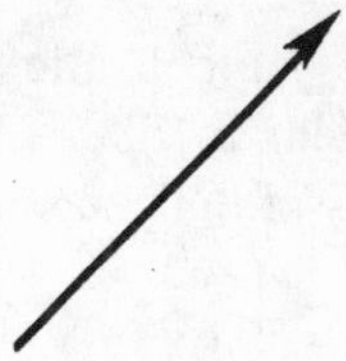

(A) $\mathbf{v} = \dot{x}\hat{x} + \dot{y}\hat{y} + \dot{z}\hat{z}$

(B) $\mathbf{v} = \dot{\rho}\hat{\rho} + \rho\dot{\theta}\hat{\theta} + \dot{z}\hat{z}$

(C) $\mathbf{v} = \dot{\rho}\hat{\rho} + \rho\dot{\theta}\sin\theta\hat{\theta} + \dot{z}\hat{z}$

(D) $\mathbf{v} = \dot{r}\hat{r} + \rho\dot{\theta}\hat{\theta} + r\dot{\phi}\sin\theta\hat{\phi}$

(E) $\mathbf{v} = r\hat{r} + r\dot{\phi}\hat{\theta} + r\dot{\phi}\hat{\phi}$

2. Consider the total energy *E* of a particle. Let *T* be the kinetic energy and *U* the potential energy. What is the total time derivative of that energy if the force acting on the particle is conservative?

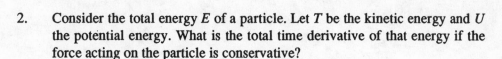

(A) $\partial T / \partial t$

(B) $\mathbf{F} \cdot \mathbf{v}$

(C) ∇U

(D) dU / dt

(E) $\partial U / \partial t$

3. In the realistic fall of a spherical object in fluid air, calculate the magnitude of the viscous force. Given that the Reynolds number is $R_e = 0.5$, the kinematic viscosity is 0.149 cm^2/s, the radius of the sphere is .005 *cm,* and $\rho_{air} = 1.22 \times 10^{-3}$ g/cc.

(A) 1.28 *md*

(B) 5.22 *md*

(C) 1.66 *md*

(D) 3.22 *md*

(E) 2.15 *md*

4. Determine the corrected value for the time of flight of a projectile near the Earth's surface (in two dimensions) subject to a resistive force $\mathbf{F}_R = -b\mathbf{v}$. Let $\gamma = b/m$.

(A) $t = \frac{2v_{0y}}{g}$

(B) $t = \frac{2v_{0y}}{g}(1 - \frac{\gamma v_{0y}}{3g})$

(C) $t = \frac{2v_{0y}}{g}(1 - \frac{\gamma v_{0y}}{g})$

(D) $t = \frac{2v_{0y}}{g}(1 + \frac{2\gamma v_{0y}}{3g})$

(E) $t = \frac{2v_{0y}}{g}(1 + \frac{\gamma v_{0y}}{g})$

5. In the photoelectric effect, the threshold wavelength is 2756 Å. If light of wavelength 1700 Å is incident on a metal substance, determine the kinetic energy of the photoelectrons.

(A) 4.50 eV

(B) 2.25 eV

(C) 3.60 eV

(D) 2.79 eV

(E) 7.29 eV

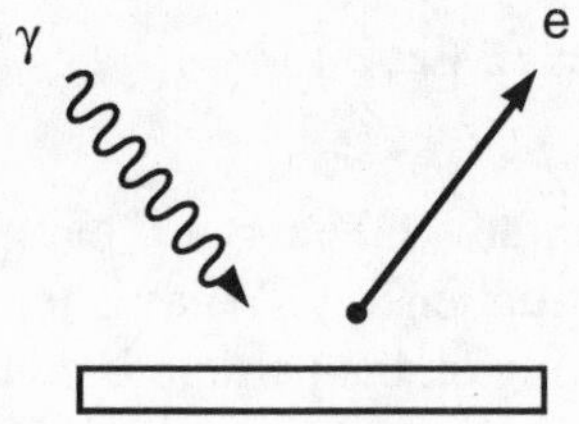

6. X-rays of wavelength 3.00 Å are incident on a substance. The scattered X-rays observed at 45.0° have a different wavelength due to the Compton effect. Find the scattered wavelength.

(A) 3.02Å

(B) 2.98Å

(C) 3.01Å

(D) 2.93Å

(E) 3.07Å

7. In statistical physics, the counting factor N! is very important. Approximate this for large N.

(A) $(N / e)^N$

(B) N^N

(C) N

(D) $(N / \ln 2)^N$

(E) $N(N-1)$

8. The N-step random walk in two dimensions (with step length 1) looks very much like the famous Brownian motion which supported the kinetic theory. What is the root mean square distance from the origin?

(A) $\sqrt{N/4}$

(B) $\sqrt{2N/3}$

(C) $\sqrt{N}$

(D) $\sqrt{N/2}$

(E) $\sqrt{N/3}$

9. Identify the following elementary particle scattering cross section curve. $\sqrt{s}$ is the the total center of mass scattering energy. σ is zero below 2.014 GeV.

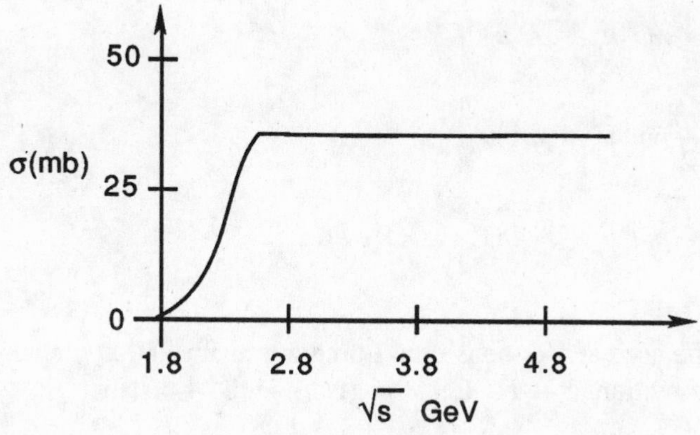

(A) *pp* inelastic cross section

(B) *pp* total cross section

(C) *np* total cross section

(D) *pp* direction cross section

(E) *πp* total cross section

10. Determine the laboratory threshold kinetic energy T_N for the reaction

$$p + p \rightarrow p + p + \pi^0.$$

The target is at rest and the projectile is accelerated to have kinetic energy T_N. Let $m_p = m_N = .938$ GeV and $m_\pi = .140$ GeV.

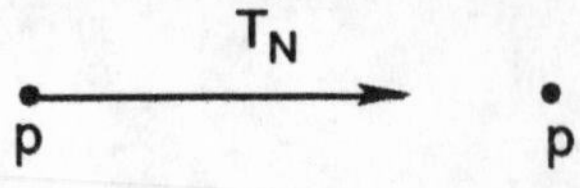

(A) 1.038 GeV

(B) 1.876 GeV

(C) 290 MeV

(D) 140 MeV

(E) 2.016 GeV

11. What is the correct relativistic Lagrangian which yields the Lorentz force law

$$d\mathbf{p}/d\tau = \gamma q(\mathbf{E} + \mathbf{u} \times \mathbf{B})?$$

Let $u^\mu = (\gamma\mathbf{u}, \gamma c)$ be the 4-velocity and $A^\mu = (\mathbf{A}, \phi)$ be the 4-potential where

$$\gamma = 1/\sqrt{1-\beta^2}.$$

(A) $\frac{1}{2}mu^2 + \int q(\mathrm{E} + \upsilon \times \mathrm{B}) \cdot d\rho$

(B) $\frac{1}{2}m\gamma u^2 - \int \gamma q(\mathrm{E} + \upsilon \times \mathrm{B}) \cdot d\rho$

(C) $\frac{1}{2}mu^\mu u_\mu + qA^\mu u_\mu$

(D) $\frac{\gamma}{2}mu^\mu u_\mu + \gamma qA^\mu u_\mu$

(E) $\frac{1}{2}mu^\mu u_\mu - \int \gamma q(\mathrm{E} + \upsilon \times \mathrm{B}) \cdot d\rho$

12. Find the correct 4-dimensional Lorentz transformation matrix for a boost in the y-direction $K \rightarrow K'$. Let $x^\mu = (\mathbf{r}, ct)$ be the 4-distance.

(A) $\begin{pmatrix} \gamma & 0 & 0 & -\beta\gamma \\ 0 & 1 & 0 & 0 \\ 0 & 0 & 1 & 0 \\ -\beta\gamma & 0 & 0 & 0 \end{pmatrix}$

(B) $\begin{pmatrix} 1 & 0 & 0 & 0 \\ 0 & 1 & 0 & 0 \\ 0 & 0 & \gamma & -\beta\gamma \\ 0 & 0 & -\beta\gamma & \gamma \end{pmatrix}$

(C) $\begin{pmatrix} 0 & \gamma & 0 & -\beta\gamma \\ -\beta\gamma & 0 & 0 & \gamma \\ 0 & 0 & 1 & 0 \\ 0 & 0 & 0 & 1 \end{pmatrix}$ (D) $\begin{pmatrix} \gamma & 0 & 0 & \beta\gamma \\ 0 & 1 & 0 & 0\gamma \\ 0 & 0 & 1 & 0 \\ \beta\gamma & 0 & 0 & \gamma \end{pmatrix}$

(E) $\begin{pmatrix} 1 & 0 & 0 & 0 \\ 0 & \gamma & 0 & -\beta\gamma \\ 0 & 0 & 1 & 0 \\ 0 & -\beta\gamma & 0 & \gamma \end{pmatrix}$

13. In the Rutherford scattering of $p + {}^{238}_{92}\text{U}$, the differential cross section at angle θ is measured to be 10 barns. The kinetic energy of the incident proton is 7.6 MeV. Find θ.

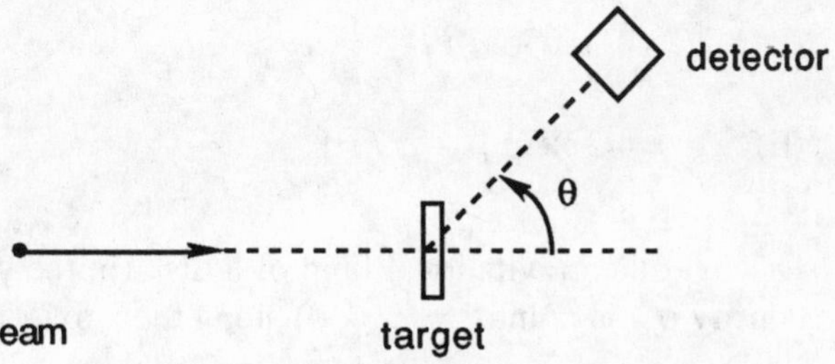

(A) 30.0°

(B) 60.0°

(C) 90.0°

(D) 43.6°

(E) 21.8°

14. Calculate the vector force due to a potential energy $U = kr^n$.

(A) $-knr^{n-2}\,\mathbf{r}$

(B) $-knr^{n-1}\,\mathbf{r}$

(C) $+knr^{n-2}\,\mathbf{r}$

(D) $+knr^{n-1}\,\mathbf{r}$

(E) $+knr^{n}\,\mathbf{r}$

15. Study the problem of a rocket in a constant gravitational field $g = 9.8$ m/s^2. If the initial velocity is 0.40 km/s, the burn time is 100 s, the exhaust velocity is 2.0 km/s, and the mass decreases by a factor of three, find the final velocity.

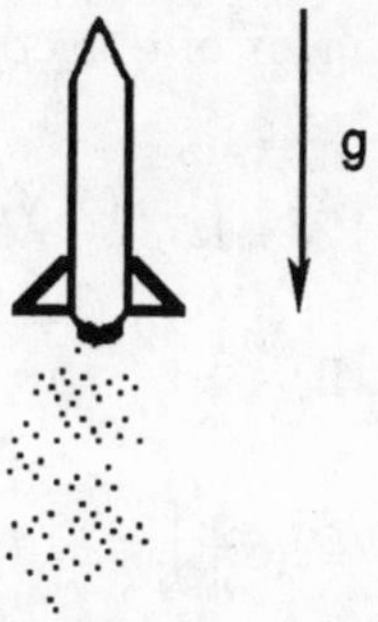

(A) 0.81 km/s

(B) 0.98 km/s

(C) 2.40 km/s

(D) 1.62 km/s

(E) 1.42 km/s

16. The spherical region $a < r < b$ is filled with mass of uniform density ρ. Determine the magnitude of the gravitational field in this region.

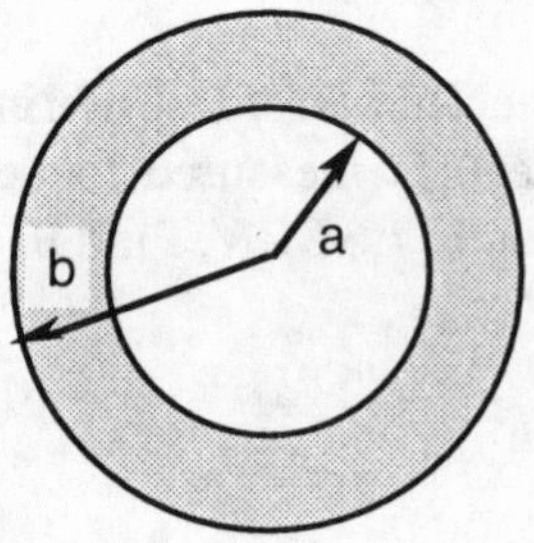

(A) $g = 4/3\ \pi G\rho\ [r - a^3/r^2]$

(B) $g = 4/3\ \pi G\rho\ b^3/r^2$

(C) $g = 4/3\ \pi G\rho\ [b^3 - a^3]/r^2$

(D) $g = 4/3\ \pi G\rho\ a^3/r^2$

(E) $g = 4/3\ \pi G\rho\ [r + a^3/r^2]$

17. Discover the gravitational field of a disk (in the yz plane) of uniform mass density σ at a point $P = (x, 0, 0)$ along the x axis. Let R = disk radius.

(A) $\mathbf{g} = -2\pi\sigma G[1 + x/\sqrt{x^2 + R^2}]\mathbf{x}$

(B) $\mathbf{g} = \pi\sigma G R^2/x^2\mathbf{x}$

(C) $\mathbf{g} = -2\pi\sigma G[1 - x/\sqrt{x^2 + R^2}]\mathbf{x}$

(D) $\mathbf{g} = -\pi\sigma G R^2/x^2\mathbf{x}$

(E) $\mathbf{g} = +2\pi\sigma G[1 - x/\sqrt{x^2 + R^2}]\mathbf{x}$

18. What is the integral quantity that must be minimized to determine the path of a light ray moving from point P to point Q in a medium of variable index of refraction $n(x,y)$? Let the speed of light = c.

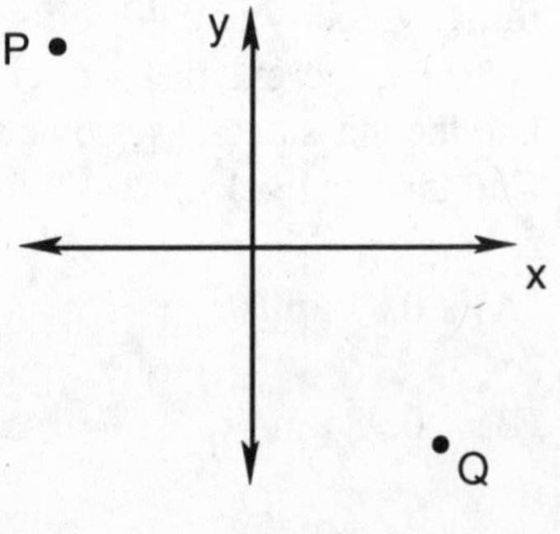

(A) $\int_P^Q n(x,y)\,dx$

(B) $\frac{1}{c}\int_P^Q \sqrt{1+y'^2}\,n(x,y)\,dx$

(C) $\frac{1}{c}\int_P^Q \sqrt{1+y^2}\,n(x,y)\,dx$

(D) $\frac{1}{c}\int_P^Q n(x,y)\,dx$

(E) $\frac{1}{c}\int_P^Q \sqrt{x^2+y^2}\,n(x,y)\,dx$

19. The nuclear reaction ${}^{27}_{13}\text{Al}(\alpha,\text{p})\,{}^{30}_{14}\text{Si}$ has a positive Q-value. Hence energy is given off in the reaction. Determine the minimum kinetic energy needed in the lab system for the *reverse* reaction.

(A) 1.3 MeV

(B) 1.8 MeV

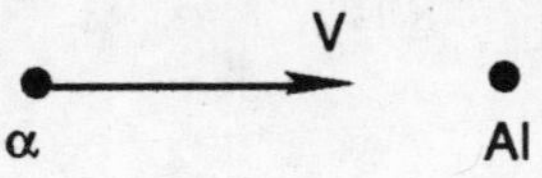

(C) 2.7 MeV

(D) 3.2 MeV

(E) 3.7 MeV

20. The propagation of sound in a gas may be modeled as adiabatic in nature. For a three degree of freedom ideal gas, by what factor does the sound speed change when the pressure is doubled at constant density?

(A) increase by factor $\sqrt{2}$

(B) increase by factor 2

(C) decrease by factor 2

(D) decrease by factor $\sqrt{2}$

(E) stays the same

21. Find the mean square speed at temperature T for particles of mass m that follow Maxwell-Boltzmann statistics.

(A) $2kT/\pi m$

(B) $3kT/m$

(C) $8kT/\pi m$

(D) $2kT/m$

(E) kT/m

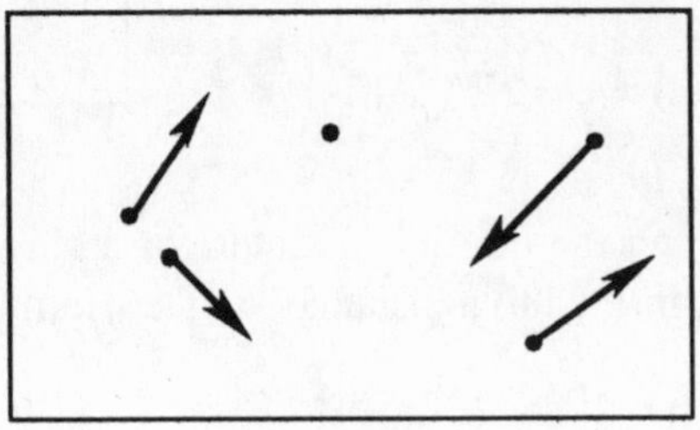

N particles

22. Think about a box of volume 10^8 cm^3 with 10^{27} particles in it. Take a small cubical region of that box of length 100 Å and determine the probability that that region has 0 particles in it.

(A) 4.5×10^{-5}

(B) 0.0

(C) 1.0

(D) 9.0×10^{-5}

(E) 2.2×10^{-5}

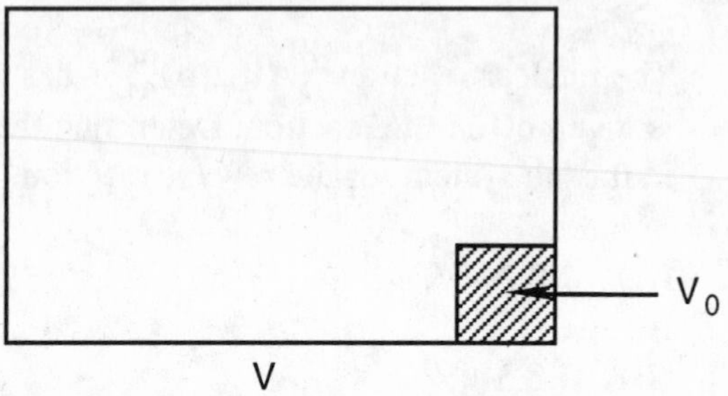

23. In a laboratory experiment to measure the density of a spherical object, the radius of the sphere is measured to be $r = 25.0\ cm \pm 0.1\ cm$ and the mass of the sphere is found to be $m = 183\ g \pm 3\ g$. Use the theory of propagation of error to determine the relative error in ρ given by $\Delta\rho/\rho$.

(A) .016

(B) .004

(C) .012

(D) .020

(E) .008

24. For the Carnot refrigeration cycle shown, determine the efficiency, defined here as work performed divided by heat withdrawn from the cold reservoir.

(A) $e = 1 - T_C/T_H$

(B) $e = 1 - T_H/T_C$

(C) $e = 1 + T_C/T_H$

(D) $e = T_C/T_H - 1$

(E) $e = T_H/T_C - 1$

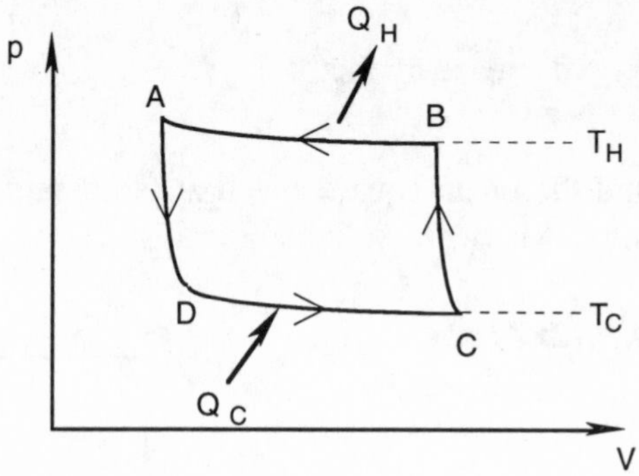

25. Find the density of states for a single particle with one degree of freedom confined to a distance ℓ . The Hamiltonian is $H(x,p) = p^2/2m$.

(A) $\ell\sqrt{2mE^2}\,/\,2\pi\hbar$

(B) $\ell\sqrt{2m\,/\,E}\,/\,2\pi\hbar$

(C) $\ell\sqrt{2mE^{3/2}}\,/\,2\pi\hbar$

(D) $\ell\sqrt{2mE}\,/\,2\pi\hbar$

(E) $\ell\sqrt{2mE}\,/\,2\pi\hbar$

26. Consider a two state system with degeneracies g_1, g_2 and energies $0, \in$. Determine the average total energy for N particles in this system at temperature $T = 1/\beta k$.

(A) $g_2 N\in/[g_2 e^{\beta\in} + g_1]$

(B) $g_1 N\in/[g_2 e^{\beta\in} + g_1]$

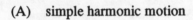

(C) $g_1 N\in/[g_1 e^{\beta\in} + g_2]$

(D) $(g_1 + g_2)N\in/2$

(E) $g_2 N\in/[g_1 e^{\beta\in} + g_2]$

27. It is common to represent many classical mechanics problems and/or differential equations through parametric plots or phase space orbits. Identify the below figure.

(A) simple harmonic motion

(B) gravitational motion (g = constant)

(C) damped motion

(D) Lissajous figure

(E) bifurcation diagram

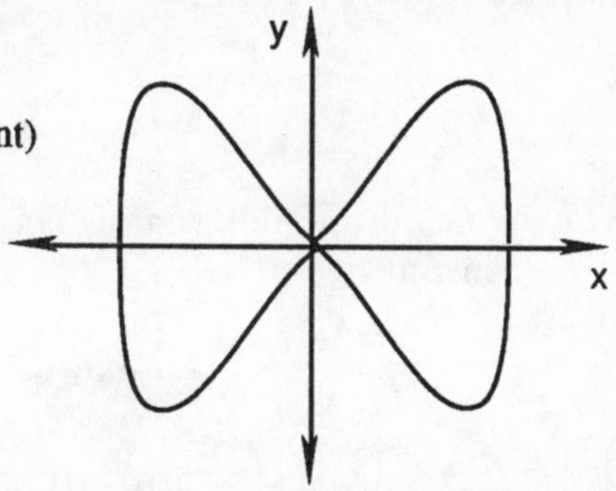

28. What is the solution to the damped motion problem

$$x'' + \gamma x' + \omega_0^2 x = 0 \text{ where } \gamma = b/m, \ \omega_0 = \sqrt{k/m},$$

$$\text{and } \omega = \sqrt{\omega_0^2 - \gamma^2/4}$$

in the light damping case?

(A) $x = A \cos(\omega_0 t + \delta)$

(B) $x = A \cos(\omega t + \delta)$

(C) $x = B e^{-\gamma t/2} \cos(\omega_0 t + \delta)$

(D) $x = B e^{-\gamma t/2} \cos(\omega t + \delta)$

(E) $x = (A + Bt)e^{-\gamma t/2}$

29. Atomic spectoscopy relates the wavelengths of the observed spectral lines of a substance to a mathematical formula. Given the Rydberrg constant for

hydrogen $R = 109{,}677.6\ \text{cm}^{-1}$ find the lower limit for the Paschen series.

(A) 912 Å

(B) 8206 Å

(C) 3646 Å

(D) 2280 nm

(E) 1460 nm

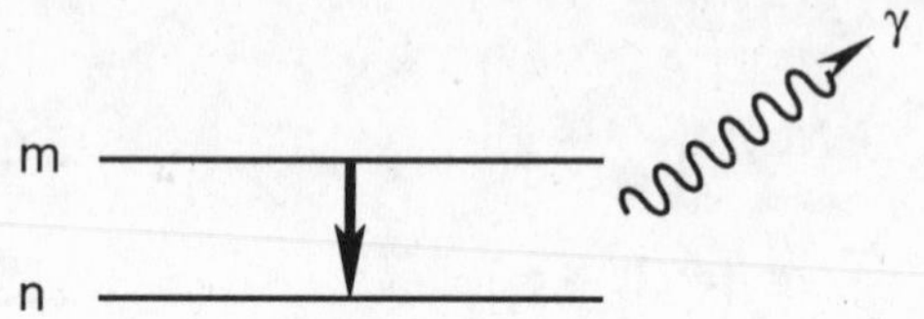

30. Determine the average energy for a photon gas at temperature $T = 1 / k\beta$ where the energy levels are given by $E_j = j\hbar\,\omega$, j = 0,1,2, …

(A) kT

(B) $\hbar\omega / (e^{\hbar\omega\beta} + 1)$

(C) $2kT$

(D) $3/2\ kT$

(E) $\hbar\omega / (e^{\hbar\omega\beta} - 1)$

31. Which of the following is not a true statement about the pictured MOS transistor?

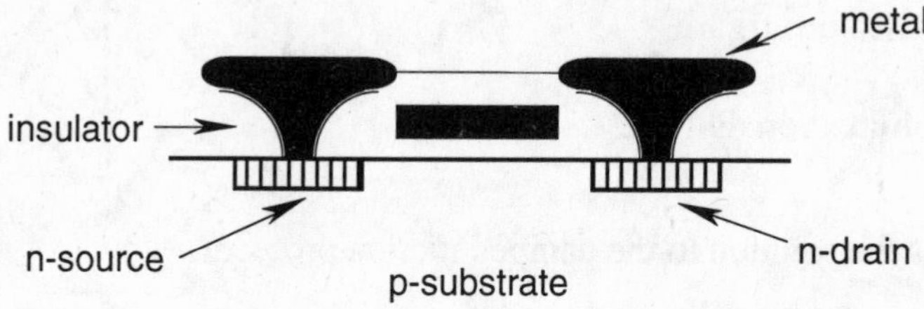

(A) A voltage applied at the metal gate acts like a switch.

(B) The n source and drain are formed by doping.

(C) Electrons from impurity atoms conduct a current.

(D) Positrons from impurity atoms conduct a current.

(E) The p-substrate ordinarily blocks current flow.

32. Determine the electric potential of a circular annulus of inner radius a and outer radius b (in the yz plane) of charge density σ = charge/area < 0 at a distance x along the x-axis.

(A) $\phi = \pi k\sigma[b^2 - a^2]/x$

(B) $\phi = -\,2\pi k\sigma\left[\sqrt{b^2 + x^2} - \sqrt{a^2 + x^2}\right]$

(C) $\phi = -\,2\pi k\sigma\left[\sqrt{b^2 + x^2} - x\right]$

(D) $\phi = +\,2\pi k\sigma\left[\sqrt{b^2 + x^2} - \sqrt{a^2 + x^2}\right]$

(E) $\phi = +\,2\pi k\sigma\left[\sqrt{b^2 + x^2} - x\right]$

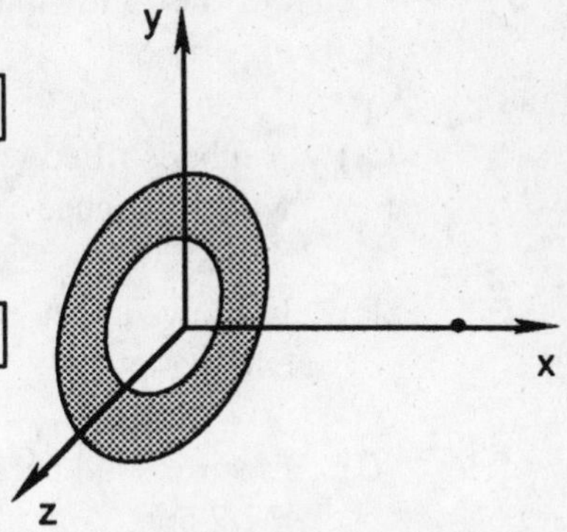

33. What is the intensity (energy per unit volume per unit frequency) distribution that produced the ultraviolet catastrophe in the early theory of black-body radiation? Given that $\beta \equiv 1/kT$.

(A) $u(\omega) = \omega kT / \pi^2 c^3$

(B) $u(\omega) = (\omega / c)^3 e^{-\hbar\omega/kT}$

(C) $u(\omega) = \omega^2 kT / \pi^2 c^3$

(D) $u(\omega) = (\hbar\omega^3/\pi^2 c^3)/(e^{\hbar\omega/kT} - 1)$

(E) $u(\omega) = \omega^3 kT / \pi^2 c^3$

34. The Thomas-Reich-Kuhn sum rule connects the complete set of eigenfunctions and energies of a particle of mass m. What value is assigned by this quantum mechanical rule to

$$\sum_j |x_{j0}|^2 \left[E_j - E_0\right]?$$

(A) $2\hbar^2/m$

(B) $\hbar^2/m$

(C) $3\hbar^2/m$

(D) $\hbar^2/2m$

(E) $\hbar^2/4m$

35. What is the value of the commutator [H, x} for the quantum mechanical Hamiltonian $H = p^2/2m + V(x)$?

(A) $\hbar x'/i$

(B) $2\hbar x'/i$

(C) $3\hbar x'/i$

(D) $4\hbar x'/i$

(E) $\hbar x'/2i$

36. Which of the following is NOT a true statement about the classic Franck-Hertz experiment?

(A) A tube is filled with vapor (e.g. Hg) at high pressure so that electrons will experience a high number of collisions.

(B) It showed that electrons undergo transitions from higher to lower energy levels.

(C) Electrons are accelerated through a potential difference such that $eV_0 = 1/2\, mv^2$.

(D) A tube is fulled with vapor (e.g. Hg) at low pressure so that electrons will experience a low number of collisions.

(E) An electron may lose most of its kinetic energy in an inelastic collision with an atom.

37. The angular wave function for the rigid diatomic rotor with quantum numbers l =1 and m_l =1 is given by Y_{11} $(\theta,\phi) = -N \sin\theta\, e^{i\phi}$. Determine the normalization constant N.

(A) $\sqrt{3/4\pi}$

(B) $\sqrt{3/8\pi}$

(C) $\sqrt{3/2\pi}$

(D) $\sqrt{3/\pi}$

(E) $\sqrt{3/6\pi}$

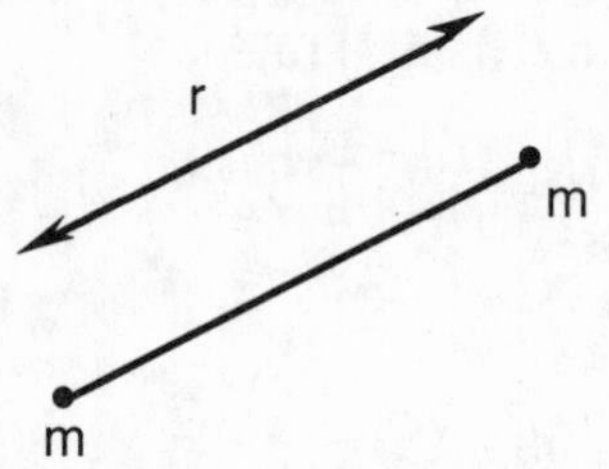

38. Consider the hydrogen-like atom eigenvalue problem: one electron orbits a nucleus of charge Ze. The general wave function is

$$\psi_{nlm_l}(r,\theta,\phi) = R_{nl}(r)Y_{lm_l}(\theta,\phi).$$

Determine the value of r where the radial probability is a maximum for the ground state.

(A) a_0

(B) a_0 / Z

(C) $a_0 / 2Z$

(D) $a_0 / 3Z$

(E) $a_0 / 4Z$

39. The $n = 2$ and $l = 1$ hydrogen-like atom radial wave function is

$$R_{21}(r) = Nre^{-Zr/2a_0}.$$

What is the correct normalization factor N?

(A) $Z/\sqrt{3}a_0$

(B) $(Z/2a_0)^{3/2}$

(C) $(Z/2a_0)^{3/2} Z/\sqrt{3}a_0$

(D) $(Z/2a_0)^3 Z^2/3a_0^2$

(E) $(Z/2a_0)^3$

40. Which of the following is *NOT* a true statement about the Bohr theory of the hydrogen-like atom with nuclear charge Ze and reduced mass μ?

n is the principal quantum number and *l* is the angular momentum quantum number.

(A) The energy eigenvalue is proportional to $1/n^2$.

(B) The energy eigenvalue depends on $\ell(\ell+1)$.

(C) The energy eigenvalue is proportional to μ.

(D) For large values of *Z*, the energy can have magnitude keV.

(E) The radius of the electron orbit is proportional to n^2.

41. Which of the following IS a true statement about the nuclear binding energy in the semi-empirical mass formula model?

(A) The volume term is proportional to A^2.

(B) The Coulomb term is proportional to $A^{-2/3}$.

(C) The symmetry term is proportional to $(A - 2Z)^2/A$.

(D) The area term is proportional to $A^{1/3}$.

(E) The symmetry term is proportional to $(A - 2Z)^2$.

42. Determine the Fermi momentum p_F of nuclear matter of density 0.14 nucleons/fm^3 in the isospin degenerate zero temperature Fermi gas model.

(A) 136 MeV/c

(B) 180 MeV/c

(C) 226 MeV/c

(D) 252 MeV/c

(E) 280 MeV/c

43. Consider the coupled inductor-capacitor circuit shown below. Determine the ratio of the frequency of the anti-symmetric mode to that of the symmetric mode ω_a/ω_s. Let $k = 1/LC$ and $\kappa = 1/L\gamma$.

(A) -1

(B) $\sqrt{1 + k/\kappa}$

(C) $\sqrt{1 + 2k/\kappa}$

(D) $\sqrt{1 + 2\kappa/k}$

(E) $\sqrt{1 + \kappa/k}$

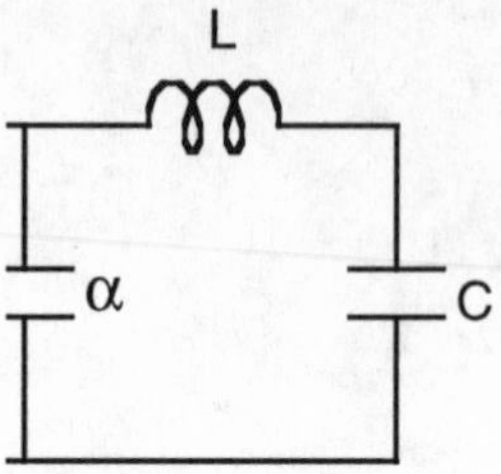

44. A spaceship traveling at 1.50×10^8 m/s leaves the Earth in the year 2050 with John on board. John leaves his twin brother James behind on Earth and goes off to a star 25 light-years away. Upon arrival, he immediately returns. On return, what is the difference in their ages?

(A) 3.3 years

(B) 25 years

(C) 12.5 years

(D) 10.0 years

(E) 13.4 years

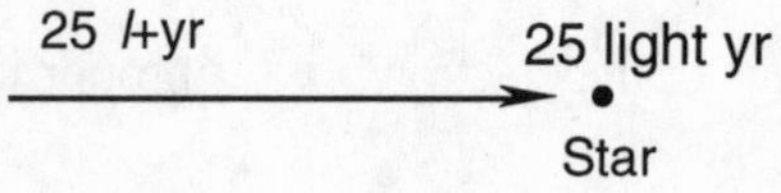

45. Discover for special relativity (and in reality) that it is more difficult to accelerate a particle in a linear accelerator than in a circular accelerator, i.e., compute the ratio $F_{\parallel}/F_{\perp}$ of the parallel force to the perpendicular force given that the desired acceleration is the same $a_{\parallel} = a_{\perp}$.

(A) γ^3

(B) γ^2

(C) β

(D) $\gamma\beta$

(E) γ

46. Find the magnetic field that the electron exerts at the nucleus of the hydrogen atom according to Bohr theory. Assume a size $r = a_0 = 0.529$ Å.

(A) 1.25 T

(B) 125 T

(C) 12.5 T

(D) 1250 T

(E) 12,500 T

47. Consider Maxwell's equations in differential form in media. Now suppose $j = \rho = 0$. If further $\in = \in_0 e^{\alpha t}$ and $\mu = \mu_0 e^{\alpha t}$, then find the relevant wave equation for a plane wave propagated in the x-direction such that **E** = E**y** and **H** = H**z**.

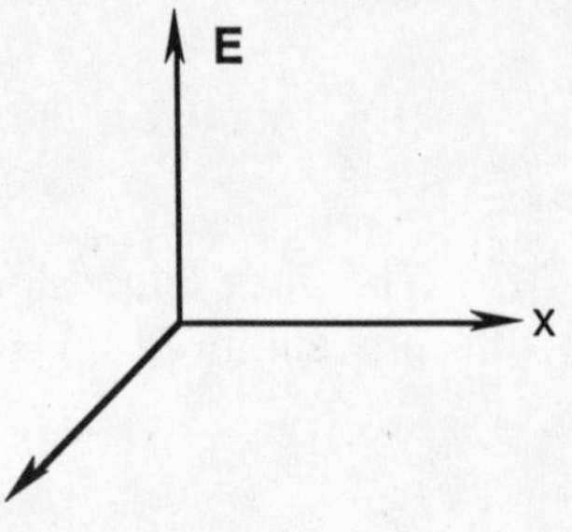

(A) $\partial^2 E / \partial x^2 = \mu \in \partial^2 E / \partial t^2$

(B) $\partial^2 D / \partial x^2 = \mu \in \partial^2 D / \partial t^2$

(C) $\partial^2 D / \partial x^2 = \mu\, \partial^2 D / \partial t^2 + \mu \alpha \partial D / \partial t$

(D) $\partial^2 E / \partial x^2 = \mu\, \partial^2 D / \partial t^2 + \mu \alpha \partial D / \partial t$

(E) $\partial^2 E / \partial x^2 = \mu\, \partial^2 E / \partial t^2 + \mu \alpha \partial E / \partial t$

48. The visual appearance of rapidly moving objects is a fascinating subject. Suppose a circle of radius b is set in motion. Calculate the relativistic speed parameter β (where $\beta = v/c$) such that the circle is seen as an ellipse of semi-minor axis a and semi-major axis b where $a < b$.

(A) $\beta = \sqrt{a/b}$

(B) $\beta = a^2 / b^2$

(C) $\beta = a / b$

(D) $\beta = \sqrt{1 - a^2/b^2}$

(E) $\beta = \sqrt{1 - a/b}$

49. A neutron of kinetic energy $T = 1876$ MeV is incident on a neutron at rest. The neutron scatters elastically at angle θ. Given that $m_n = 938$ MeV/c^2. Find θ.

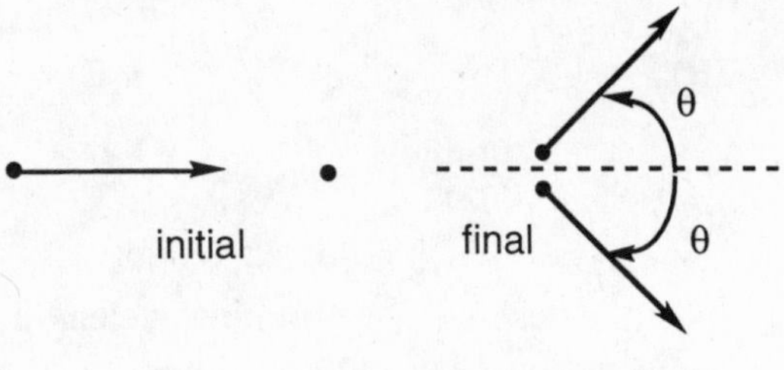

(A) 45.0°

(B) 22.5°

(C) 35.3°

(D) 70.6°

(E) 50.0°

50. A wide range of temperatures is currently accessible in the laboratory and through observation. Which of the following is NOT a true statement about temperature?

(A) 0 K is the absolute zero of temperature.

(B) 20 K is the vaporization point of hydrogen.

(C) 144 K is the vaporization point of nitrogen.

(D) 1234 K is the fusion temperature of silver.

(E) 6000 K is the sun's surface temperature.

51. The three dimensional picture below is of a hydrogen-like orbital, i.e., the probability $P(x,z) = \psi\psi^*(y = 0)$ is shown. What is the wave function?

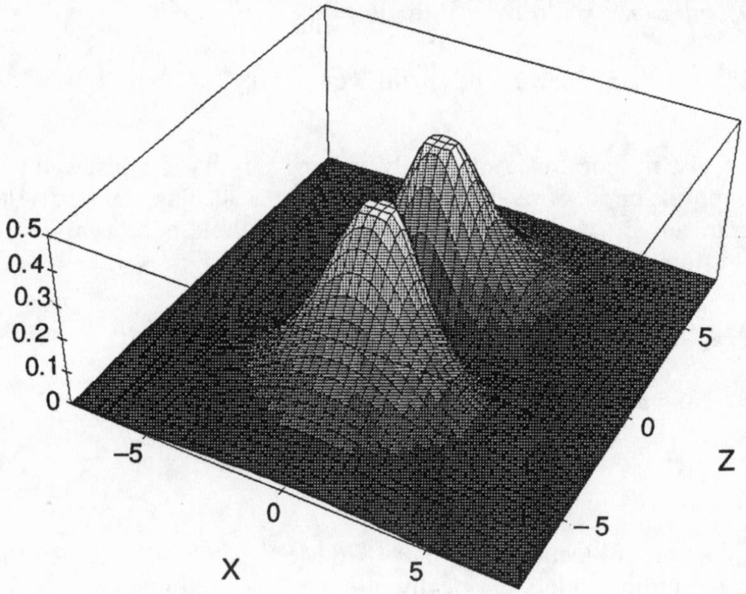

(A) ψ_{100}

(B) ψ_{200}

(C) ψ_{210}

(D) ψ_{211}

(E) $\psi_{21\text{-}1}$

52. One must use the De Broglie wavelength concept to "derive" the Schrödinger equation from the one dimensional wave equation. What De Broglie wavelength must be used to get the general time independent equation?

(A) $\lambda = h / \sqrt{2mE}$

(B) $\lambda = h / \sqrt{2mU}$

(C) $\lambda = h / \sqrt{2m(E-U)}$

(D) $\lambda = h / \sqrt{2m(E+U)}$

(E) $\lambda = h / \sqrt{m(E-U)}$

53. Determine the time dependent total energy for the lightly damped one-dimensional harmonic oscillator in the approximation

$$\gamma << 1 \text{ where } \gamma = b/m \text{ and } \omega_0 = \sqrt{k/m}.$$

Given that $x = B_0 e^{-\gamma t/2} \cos(\omega\tau + \delta)$.

(A) $E(t) \cong \frac{1}{2} kB_0^2 e^{-\gamma t/2}$

(B) $E(t) \cong \frac{1}{2} mB_0^2 e^{-\gamma t}$

(C) $E(t) \cong \frac{1}{2} mB_0^2 e^{-\gamma t/2}$

(D) $E(t) \cong \frac{1}{2} kB_0^2 e^{-\gamma t}$

(E) $E(t) \cong \frac{1}{2} kB_0^2$

54. A particle of energy $E < V_0$ is incident on a step potential of height V_0. k and k´ are wave numbers outside and inside the barrier, respectively, where

$$k = \sqrt{2mE} / \hbar \text{ and } k' = \sqrt{2m(V_0 - E)} / \hbar.$$

Find the transmission coefficient.

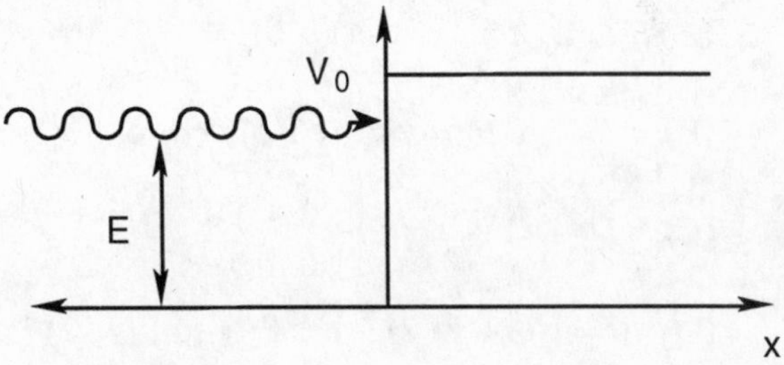

(A) 1

(B) 0

(C) k^2 / k'^2

(D) $4k^2 / (k^2 + k'^2)$

(E) k / k'

55. The particle in a box has a ground state wave function given by

$$\phi(x) = \left(1/\sqrt{a}\right) \cos \pi x / 2a.$$

Calculate the expectation value of x^2.

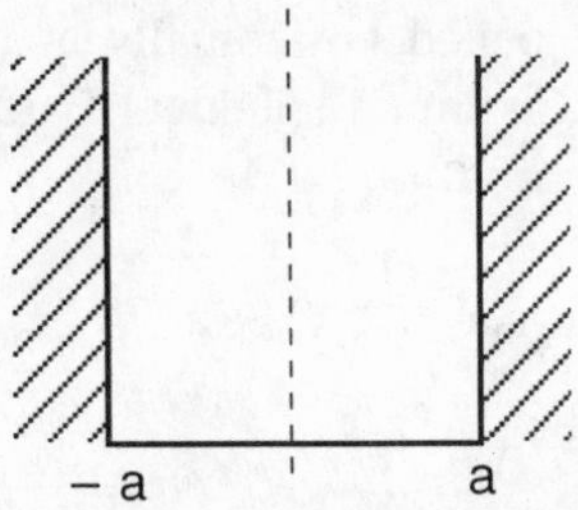

(A) $a^2/3$

(B) $a^2(1/3 - 2/\pi^2)$

(C) $a^2(2/3 - 4/\pi^2)$

(D) $2a^2/\pi^2$

(E) $a^2/4$

56. Many techniques from the physics laboratory appear daily in medical diagnostics and even the legal courtroom. Which of the following is a physics laboratory method now used to see malignant tumors using about 200 Hz waves?

(A) ultrasound

(B) Positron Emission Tomography

(C) Nuclear Magnetic Resonance

(D) the Mössbauer effect

(E) Doppler Vibration Imaging

57. An RLC circuit vibrates subject to the initial conditions $I = I_0$ and $I' = 0$ at $t = 0$. What is the time dependent current in the critical damping case? Let $\gamma = R/L$,

$$\omega_0^2 = 1/LC, \omega = \sqrt{\omega_0^2 - \gamma^2/4}, \text{ and } \tan\delta = -\gamma/2\omega.$$

(A) $I = I_0 e^{-\gamma t/2} \cos(\omega t + \delta)$

(B) $I = I_0 e^{-\gamma t/2} \cos(\omega t + \delta)/\cos\delta$

(C) $I = I_0 (1 + \gamma t/2) e^{-\gamma t/2}$

(D) $I = [(\omega + \gamma/2) I_0 e^{(\omega-\gamma/2)t} + (\omega - \gamma/2) I_0 e^{-(\omega+\gamma/2)t}]/2\omega$

(E) $I = I_0(1 + \gamma t) e^{-\gamma t}$

58. Consider the physical possibility of a shot fired around the world. An object is propelled horizontally at radius r around an assumed spherical Earth. What is the period?

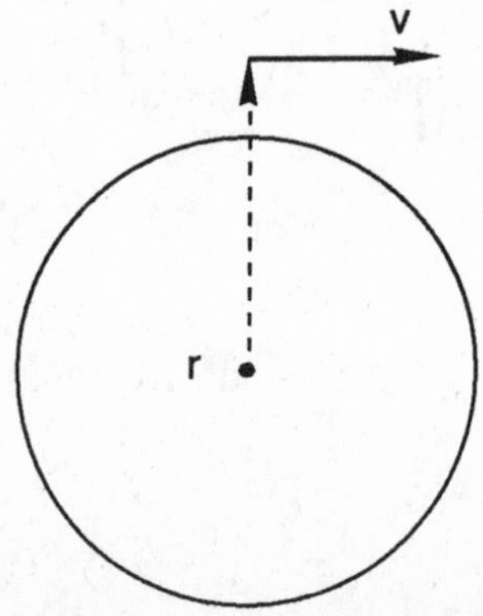

(A) $\frac{1}{2\pi}\sqrt{GM_E/r^3}$

(B) $\frac{1}{2\pi}\sqrt{r^3/GM_E}$

(C) $2\pi\sqrt{GM_E/r^3}$ (D) $2\pi\sqrt{r^3/GM_E}$

(E) 24 hours

59. A pendulum bob of mass *m* is raised to a height *h* and released. After hitting a spring of non-linear force law $F = -kx - bx^3$, calculate the compression distance *x* of the spring.

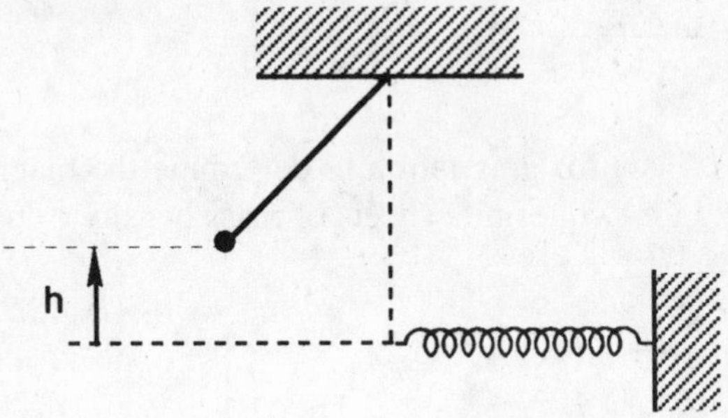

(A) $x = \sqrt{2mgh/k}$

(B) $x = (4mgh/b)^{1/4}$

(C) $x = \left[\sqrt{4mgh/b + k^2/b^2} - k/b\right]^{1/2}$

(D) $x = \left[\sqrt{4mgh/b + k^2/b^2} + k/b\right]^{1/2}$

(E) $x = \sqrt{2k/b}$

60. A frictionless wire connects points *P* and *Q* in a constant gravitational field as shown below. What is the equation that must be solved to find the curve down which a mass will slide in the shortest possible time? Let

$$f = \sqrt{(1 + y'^2)/y}\ ?$$

(A) $f - y'\,\partial f/\partial y' = \text{const.}$

(B) $y' = \text{const.}$

(C) $\partial f/\partial y' = \text{const.}$

(D) $f + f\,\partial f/\partial y' = \text{const.}$

(E) $f - x\,\partial f/\partial x = \text{const.}$

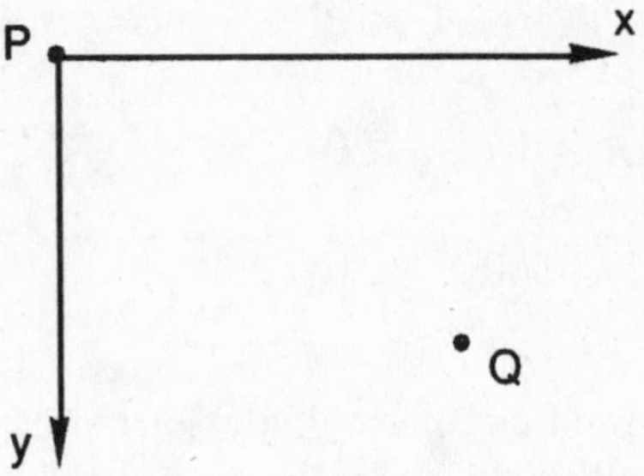

61. A spherical mass is dropped off of a building from rest. Determine the position y = y (*t*) if the mass experiences a resistive force $F_R = -bv$. Take the starting point to be the origin y = 0 as shown below. Let $\gamma = b/m$.

(A) $y = \frac{gt}{\gamma} - \frac{g}{\gamma^2}(1 - e^{-\gamma t})$

(B) $y = \frac{1}{2}gt^2$

(C) $y = \frac{g}{\gamma}(1 - e^{-\gamma t})$

(D) $y = \frac{gt}{\gamma}$

(E) $y = -\frac{g}{\gamma^2}(1 - e^{-\gamma t})$

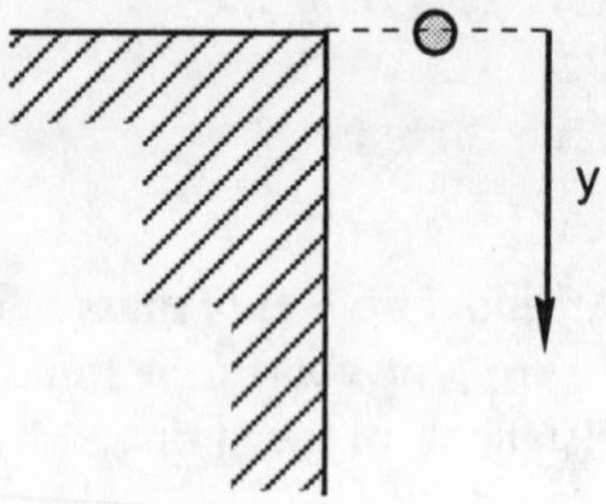

62. Use Gauss' law for gravitation to determine the magnitude of the gravitational field for two infinite sheets of mass density σ in regions I and III.

(A) $4\pi G\sigma$

(B) $2\pi G\sigma$

(C) $\pi G\sigma$

(D) $2\pi G\sigma / \varepsilon_0$

(E) 0

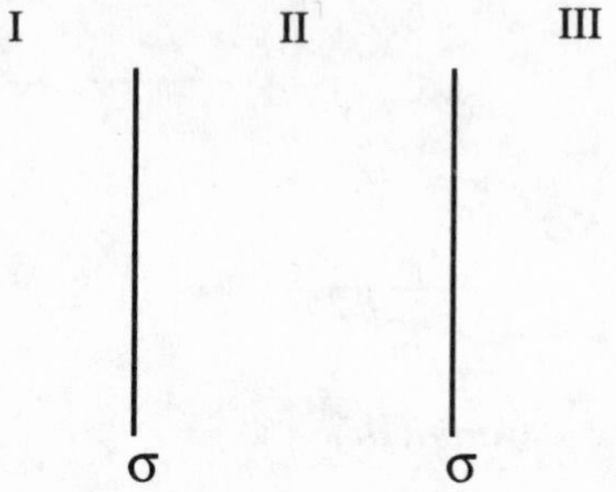

63. A boom is suspended by a cable as shown below. Given that angle $\theta = 45$ and the weight of the boom is $W = 1000\ N$. Find the reaction force **R**.

(A) (1000 N, 45.0°)

(B) (707 N, 30.0°)

(C) (500 N, 60.0°)

(D) (707 N, 45.0°)

(E) (500 N, 30.0°)

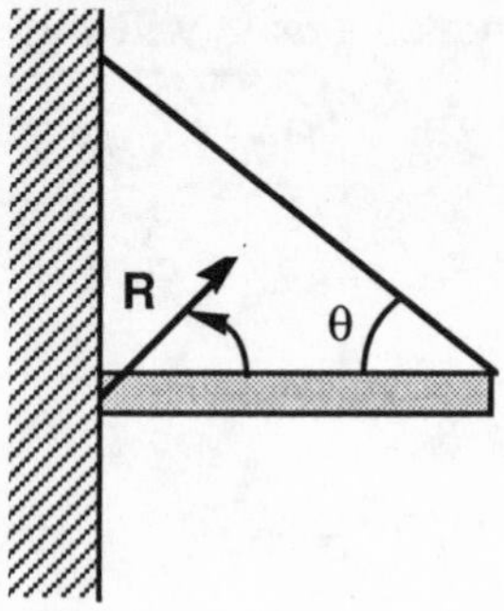

64. A right circular cylinder of radius r rolls down an incline from height h. Determine the ratio of its speed at the bottom to the speed of a point object following the same path. Assume rolling friction, but negligible sliding friction.

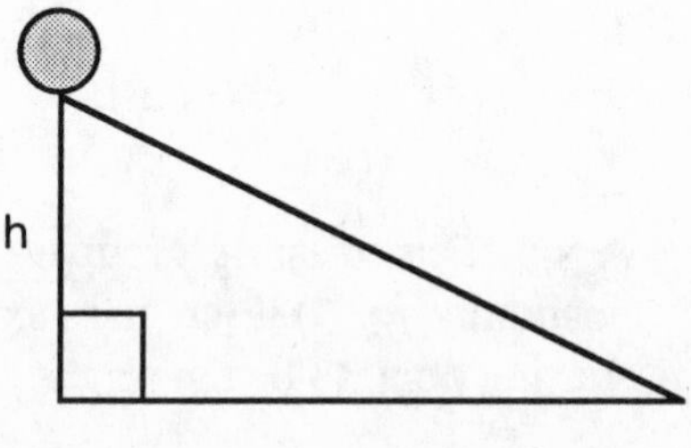

(A) 1

(B) $\sqrt{2}$

(C) $\sqrt{3}$

(D) $\sqrt{2/3}$

(E) 2

65. An object orbits a star in an elliptical orbit. The distance at aphelion is $2a$ and the distance at perihelion is a. Determine the ratio of the objects speed at perihelion to that at aphelion.

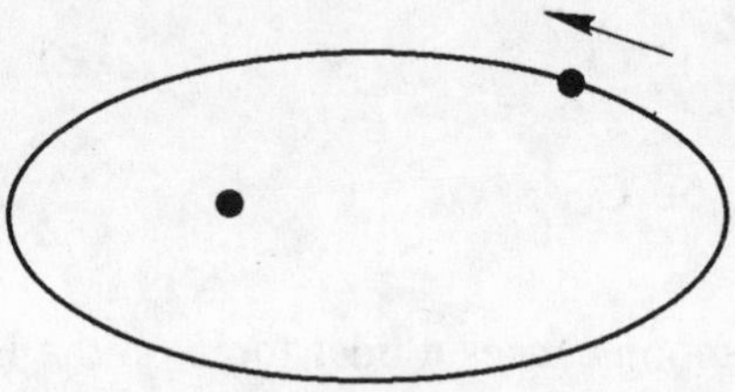

(A) 2

(B) 3

(C) 1

(D) $\sqrt{2}$

(E) $\sqrt{3}$

66. A one-quarter circular line mass of total mass M exerts a gravitational force on a point mass m as shown below. Find the force.

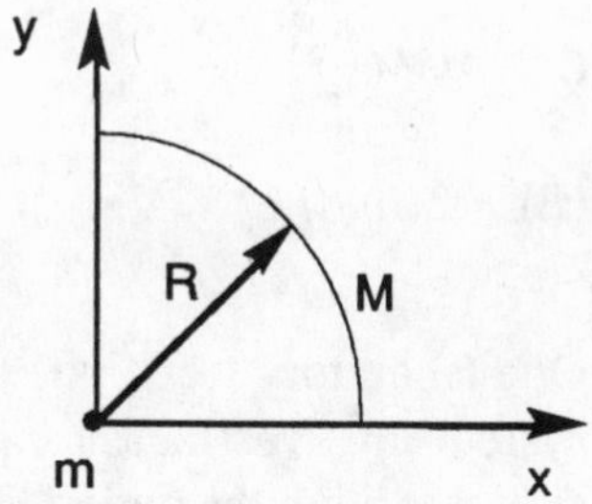

(A) $(2\sqrt{2}GmM / \pi R^2, 45°)$

(B) $(GmM / R^2, 45°)$

(C) $(GmM / \pi R^2, 45°)$

(D) $(2\, GmM / \pi R^2, 45°)$

(E) $(\sqrt{2}GmM / \pi R^2, 45°)$

67. Determine the gravitational field magnitude near the surface of a planet of radius R at altitude h to second order. Take $g(h = 0) = g_0$.

(A) $g_0[\,1 - 2\,h / R\,]$

(B) $g_0[\,1 - h / R + 0.5\,(h / R)^2\,]$

(C) $g_0[\,1 - h / R + (h / R)^2\,]$

(D) $g_0[1 + h/R + (h/R)^2]$

(E) $g_0[1 - 2h/R + 3(h/R)^2]$

68. In the laboratory, two quantities of the same fluid are mixed. The mass of the hotter sample (m_1) is twice that of the cooler one (m_2). The initial temperature of the hotter sample (T_1) is also twice the other initial temperature $T_2 = 30°C$. Find the equilibrium temperature.

(A) 40°C
(B) 45°C
(C) 50°C
(D) 55°C
(E) 35°C

69. The moon causes a tidal force on the Earth's ocean. Determine the differential tidal acceleration. Let $a = r_{earth\ to\ moon}$, $r = r_{earth}$, $m = m_{moon}$, and $M = m_{earth}$.

(A) Gm/a^2
(B) $2Gma/r^3$
(C) $2GMr/a^3$
(D) GM/r^2
(E) $2Gmr/a^3$

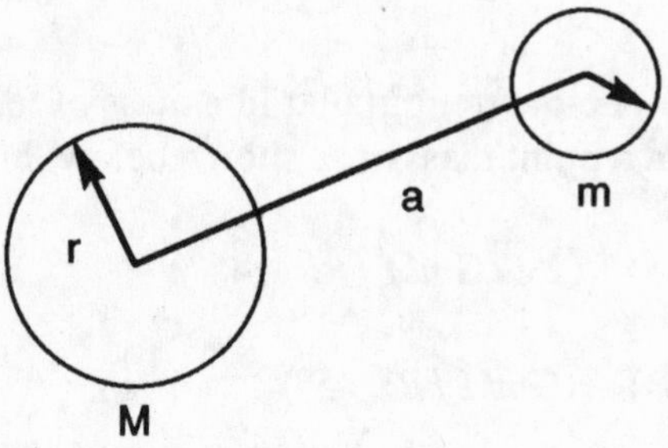

70. One laboratory technique to determine the mass of one star of a binary star system involves measuring the distance a between the stars from parallax and observing the period of revolution T. Suppose $m_1 = m_2 = m$. What is the mass m?

(A) $\pi^2 a^3/T^2$
(B) $2\pi^2 a^3/T^2$
(C) $4\pi^2 a^3/T^2$
(D) $8\pi^2 a^3/T^2$
(E) $4\pi^2 T^2/a^3$

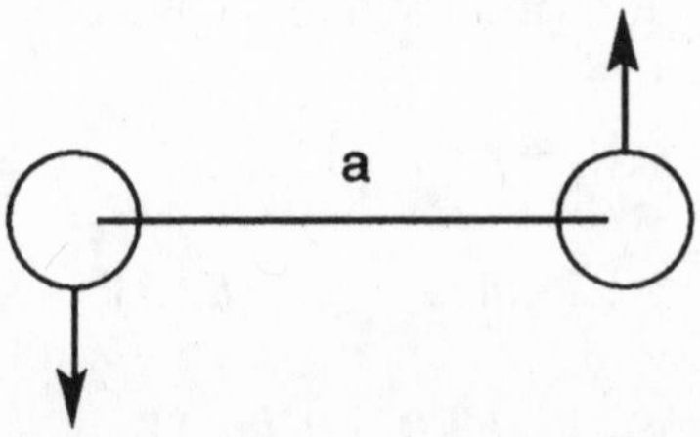

71. In the 3D harmonic oscillator version of the nuclear shell model, what are the nuclear magic numbers?

(A) 1, 4, 16
(B) 1, 4, 9
(C) 4, 12, 24
(D) 4, 16, 40
(E) 2, 8, 20

72. Monochromatic light of wavelength 6000 Å is incident on two slits of spacing .15 mm and the resulting intensity pattern observed 1.5 m away. Determine the location of the first maximum.

(A) 6 mm
(B) 12 mm
(C) 24 mm
(D) 3 mm
(E) 1.5 mm

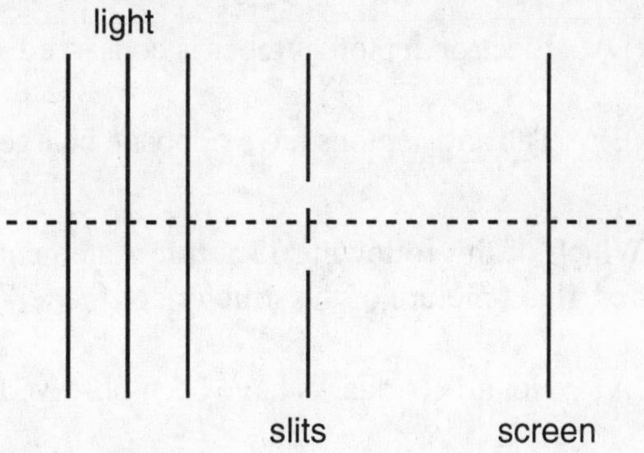

73. Use the Mayer and Jensen nuclear shell model with spin-orbit interaction to figure out the spin of the ${}^{17}_{8}O$ nuclide.

(A) 7 / 2
(B) 5 / 2
(C) 3 / 2
(D) 1
(E) 1 / 2

74. A star may be modeled as a uniform spherical distribution of matter. Let m be the star's mass and V the volume. What is the dependence of the gravitational pressure on volume?

(A) $P \propto V$
(B) $P \propto V^{-1/3}$
(C) $P \propto V^{-2/3}$

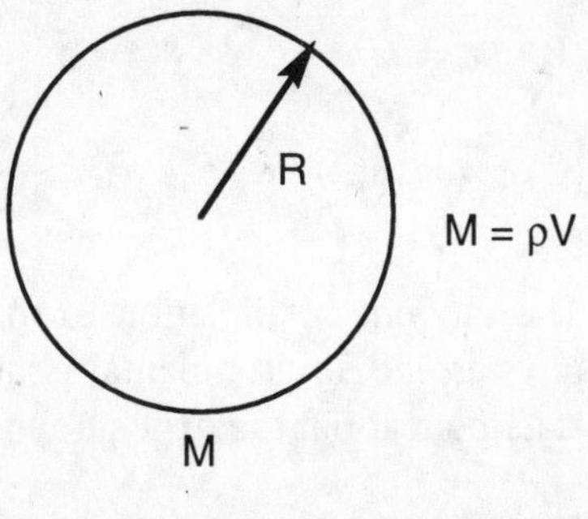

(D) $P \propto V^{-1}$

(E) $P \propto V^{-4/3}$

75. Which of the following is NOT a true statement about the modern particle picture of the structure of matter?

(A) There are only six leptons.

(B) There are only six quarks.

(C) Tau lepton number is not conserved.

(D) Electron lepton number is conserved.

(E) The anti-leptons have opposite charge and lepton number.

76. Which of the following IS a true statement about the modern QCD quark and gluon picture of the structure of matter?

(A) Not all six quarks have been observed in a free unconfined state.

(B) The six quarks are up, down, sideways, charm, bottom, and top.

(C) The s, c, and b quarks have special quantum numbers S, C, B.

(D) The d, s, b quarks have charge 2 / 3 e.

(E) The u, c, t quarks have charge –1 / 3 e.

77. Relate the half-life τ to the decay constant λ in the theory of radioactive decay.

(A) $\tau = 1 / \lambda$

(B) $\tau = \lambda$

(C) $\tau = \ln(2) / \lambda$

(D) $\tau = \lambda / \ln(2)$

(E) $\tau = 1 / \lambda^2$

78. The amount of radiation exposure biological tissue receives is a critical physics and environmental issue. Which of the following is NOT a correct statement about the exposure in mrems?

(A) In a coast-to-coast flight across the U.S., one gets about 2 mrems.

(B) In watching TV for a year, one is exposed to about 20 mrems.

(C) The natural radioactivity of the body produces about 20 mrems per year.

(D) A dental X-ray provides a local exposure of 500 mrems.

(E) Living in Denver, Colo., one receives about 125 mrems per year.

79. A typical Mossbauer effect setup is shown below. For the case of ${}^{191}_{77}\mathrm{Ir}$ where the γ ray energy is 129 keV and the half-life is .14 ns, calculate the normal recoil energy.

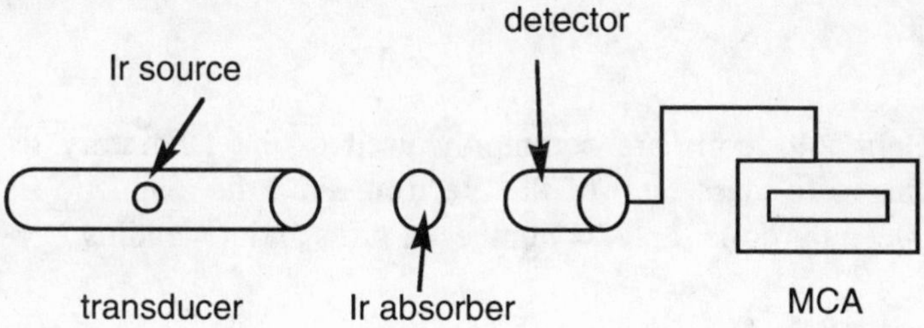

(A) .047 eV

(B) 4.7 μeV

(C) 4.7 meV

(D) 4.7 neV

(E) 4.7 keV

80. An object sits 15 cm to the left of a convex refractive interface of curvature radius 5 cm. The substance to the left has refractive index n = 1.2, while that to the right has index 1.7. Determine the image distance s', primary focal distance f, and secondary focal distance f'. For fat lenses, $-\frac{n}{s}+\frac{n'}{s'}=\frac{n'-n}{R}$.

(A) 3.0, – 2.5, 2.5 cm

(B) 6.0, – 5.0, 5.0 cm

(C) 9.4, 12, 17 cm

(D) 4.7, 6.0, 8.5 cm

(E) 85, – 12, 17 cm

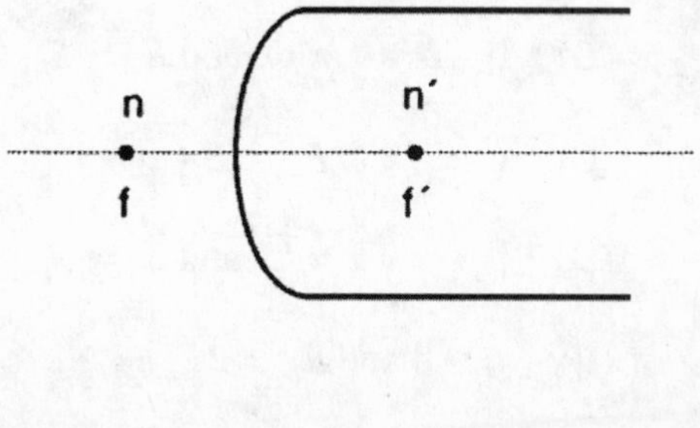

81. A laser operates by light amplification and the stimulated emission of optical radiation. For two molecular states j and i such that $E_j - E_i = \hbar\omega$ in equilibrium in a cavity, we have $N_i/N_j = [A_{ji} + B_{ji}u(\omega)]/B_{ij}u(\omega)$. Use the Boltzmann factor to find u(ω) the energy per unit frequency per unit volume. Given That $\beta = 1/kT$.

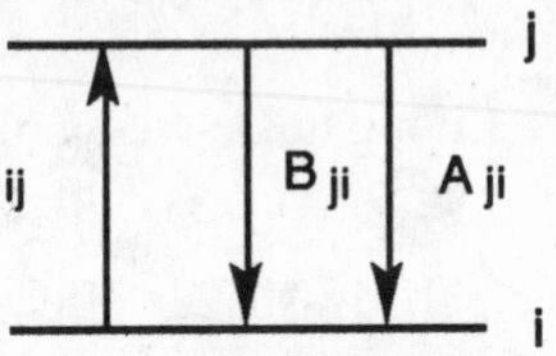

Einstein transition coefficients

(A) $A_{ji}e^{-\hbar\omega b} / B_{ij}$

(B) $A_{ji} / [B_{ij}e^{\hbar\omega b} - B_{ji}]$

(C) A_{ji}/B_{ji}

(D) $A_{ji}/[B_{ij} - B_{ji}]$

(E) $A_{ji} / [B_{ji}e^{-\hbar\omega b} - B_{ij}]$

82. Helmholtz coils are commonly used in the laboratory to determine the charge to mass ratio of the electron. Find the magnetic field directly between the coils. Let N = number of turns and R = radius.

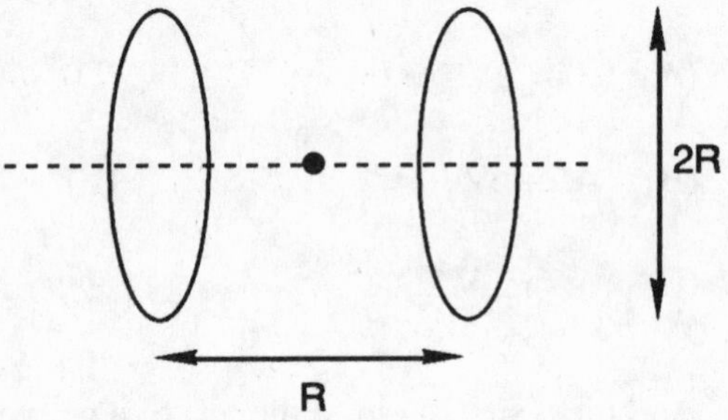

(A) $8N\mu_0 I / 5^{3/2}R$

(B) $4N\mu_0 I / 5^{3/2}R$

(C) $2N\mu_0 I / 5^{3/2}R$

(D) $N\mu_0 I / 2\pi R$

(E) $N\mu_0 I / \pi R$

83. A plane wave solution of the electromagnetic wave equation is

$$\mathbf{E} = \mathbf{y}\, E_{oy} \cos(\omega t - kx + \alpha) + \mathbf{z}\, E_{oz} \cos(\omega t - kx + \beta).$$

Under what conditions is this light wave circularly polarized?

(A) $\beta - \alpha = \pm\pi / 2$

(B) $\beta - \alpha = \pm\pi / 2$ and $E_{oy} = E_{oz}$

(C) $\alpha = \beta$ and $E_{oy} = E_{oz}$

(D) $\beta - \alpha = \pm\pi / 2$ and $E_{oy} = 2E_{oz}$

(E) $\alpha = \beta$ and $E_{oy} = 2E_{oz}$

84. A point charge of magnitude q is located a distance h above an infinite conducting plane (say the xy plane) at coordinates (0, 0, h). Let

$$s = \sqrt{x^2 + y^2}$$

denote the cylindrical distance from (0, 0, 0). Find the electric field in the plane.

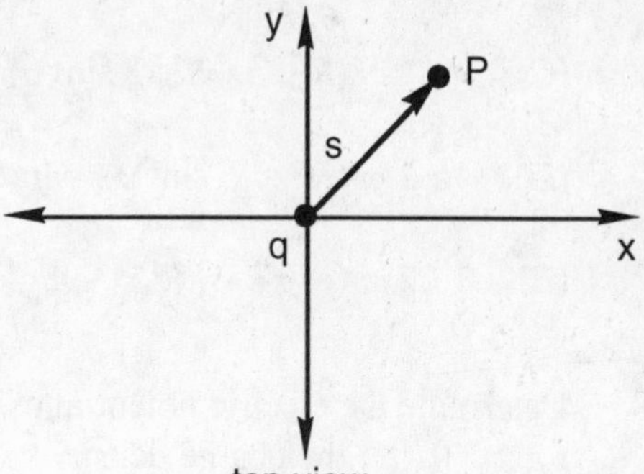

(A) $E = 0$

(B) $E = -q / 2\pi\varepsilon_0$

(C) $E = -q / 2\pi\varepsilon_0 h^2$

(D) $E = -qh / [2\pi\varepsilon_0 (s^2 + h^2)^{3/2}]$

(E) $E = -q / 2\pi\varepsilon_0 s^2$

85. The Fraunhofer single slit diffraction intensity is given by

$$I = I_0 \sin^2(x) / x^2 \text{ where } x = \pi d_w y / \lambda l.$$

d_w is the slit width, y the detector distance, and l the distance from slit to screen. What is the value of the cumulative intensity

$$\int_{-\infty}^{+\infty} I(y)\, dy?$$

(A) 0

(B) $I_0 \lambda l / d_w$

(C) $I_0 \lambda d_w / l$

(D) $I_0 d_w l / \lambda$

(E) I_0

86. Use the fundamental concepts of electromagnetism to determine the electric field of an electric dipole **p** at distance $\mathbf{r} = r\hat{\mathbf{r}}$.

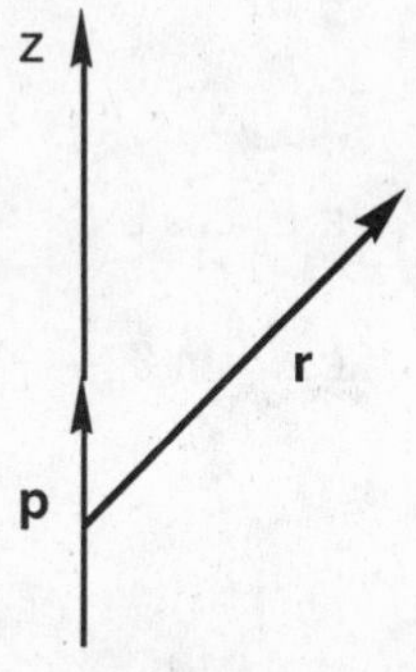

(A) $k[3\hat{\mathbf{r}} \cdot \mathbf{p}\hat{\mathbf{r}} - \mathbf{p}] / r^3$

(B) $k\hat{\mathbf{r}} \cdot \mathbf{p} / r^2$

(C) $k\hat{\mathbf{r}} \cdot \mathbf{p} / r^3$

(D) $k[3\hat{\mathbf{r}} \cdot \mathbf{p}\hat{\mathbf{r}} - \mathbf{p}] / r^2$

(E) $k[2\hat{\mathbf{r}} \cdot \mathbf{p}\hat{\mathbf{r}} - \mathbf{p}] / r^3$

87. A particle is constrained to move on the surface of a sphere of radius R near the Earth's surface. Find the Lagrangian in spherical coordinates.

(A) $1/2\,\mathrm{m}\,(R^2 + R^2 \sin^2\theta) - mgR\cos\theta$

(B) $1/2\,m\,(R^2\theta'^2 + R^2\phi'^2 \sin^2\theta) - mgR\cos\theta$

(C) $1/2\,m\,(R^2\theta'^2 + R^2\phi'^2 \sin^2\theta) + mgR\cos\theta$

(D) $1/2\,m\,(R^2 + R^2 \sin^2\theta) - mgR\cos\theta$

(E) $1/2\,m\,(R^2\theta'^2 + R^2\phi'^2) - mgR\cos\theta$

88. Determine the electric potential of the infinite sheet of charge shown below for $x > 0$. Let the charge density be σ and the x-direction be to the right.

(A) $-\sigma x/\varepsilon_0$

(B) $+\sigma x/2\varepsilon_0$

(C) $-\sigma x/2\varepsilon_0$

(D) $+\sigma x/\varepsilon_0$

(E) $-2\sigma/\varepsilon_0$

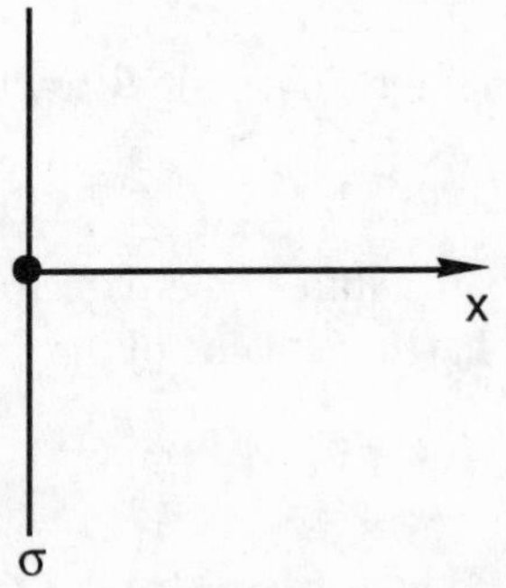

89. The electric potential of a grounded conducting sphere of radius a in a uniform electric field is given as $\varphi(r, \theta) = -E_0 r[1 - (a/r)^3]\cos\theta$. Find the surface charge distribution on the sphere.

(A) $\varepsilon_0 E_0 \sin\theta$

(B) $\varepsilon_0 E_0 \cos\theta$

(C) $2\varepsilon_0 E_0 \cos\theta$

(D) $3\varepsilon_0 E_0 \cos\theta$

(E) $2\varepsilon_0 E_0 \sin\theta$

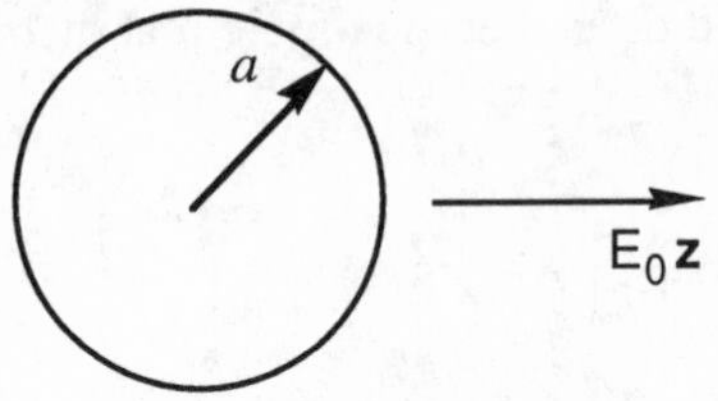

90. What is the distance at which the eye can in principle resolve two truck headlights separated by $d = 2.0$ m? Take the pupil of the eye to be a circular aperture of diameter $D = 3$ mm and the relevant wavelength to be $\lambda = 6000$ Å.

(A) 4.1 km

(B) 8.2 km

(C) 12 km

(D) 16 km

(E) 2.0 km

91. Light is incident at near normal incidence angle on a prism of apex angle α. The prism is made of a substance of refractive index n_r and the light comes from and returns to medium n_i. Find the angle of deviation using the small angle approximation.

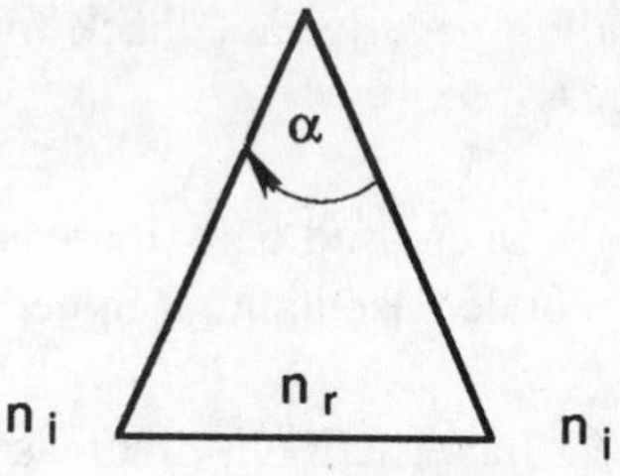

(A) $(n_r / n_i + 1)\,\alpha$

(B) $(n_r / n_i - 1)\,\alpha$

(C) $(n_i / n_r - 1)\,\alpha$

(D) $(n_i / n_r + 1)\,\alpha$

(E) $(n_r - 1)\,\alpha$

92. Which of the following is NOT a correct statement about the optical process of fluorescence?

(A) It is the emission of electromagnetic radiation.

(B) The process takes place in about 10^{-8} s.

(C) Often fluorescence is quenched by collisions.

(D) Ultraviolet photons may thereby be converted to visible photons.

(E) A quantum of light is scattered elastically.

93. Find the output of the circuit (shown on the following page) using only NAND gates.

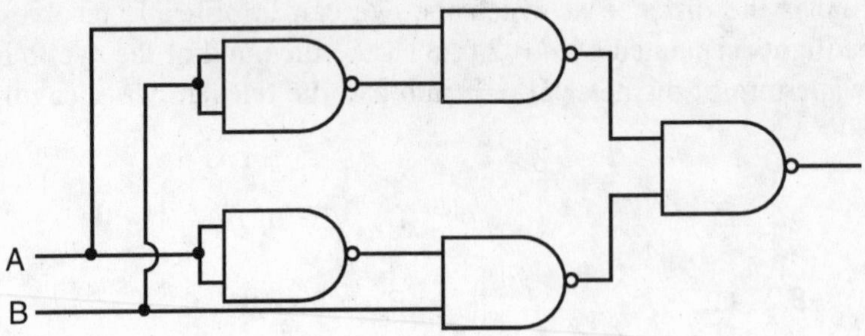

(A) A NAND B

(B) A XOR B

(C) A AND B

(D) A OR B

(E) A NOR B

94. Adding negative feedback to an amplifier results in which of the following?

(A) Decreased gain, increased distortion, increased input impedance, and decreased output impedance.

(B) Increased gain, increased distortion, increased input impedance, and decreased output impedance.

(C) Increased gain, decreased distortion, decreased input impedance, and increased output impedance.

(D) Decreased gain, decreased distortion, increased input impedance, and decreased output impedance.

(E) Decreased gain, decreased distortion, decreased input impedance, and increased output impedance.

95. What waveform appears on the oscilloscope for the following circuit? The zener diode has a breakdown voltage of 5 volts.

(A) 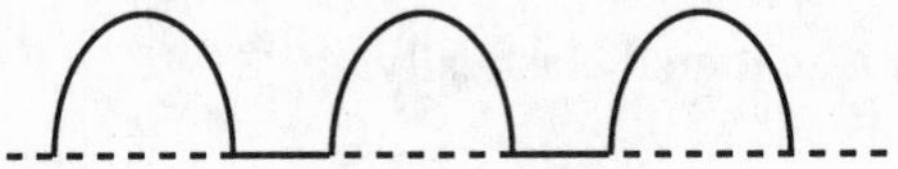

(B) 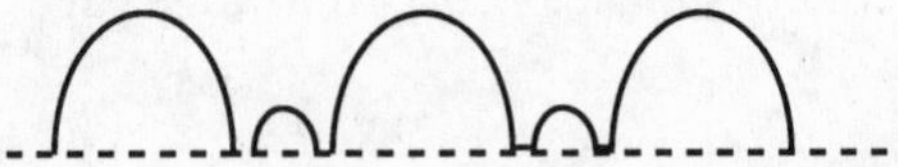

(C) 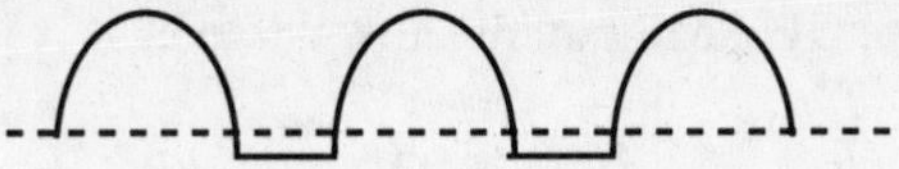

(D) 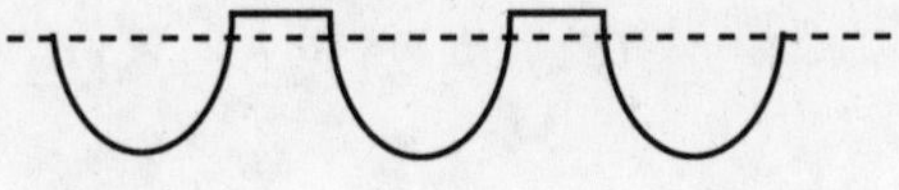

(E) 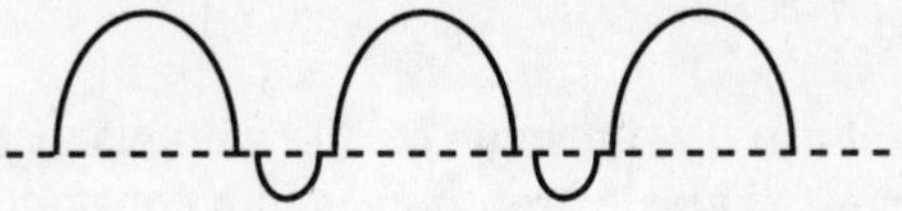

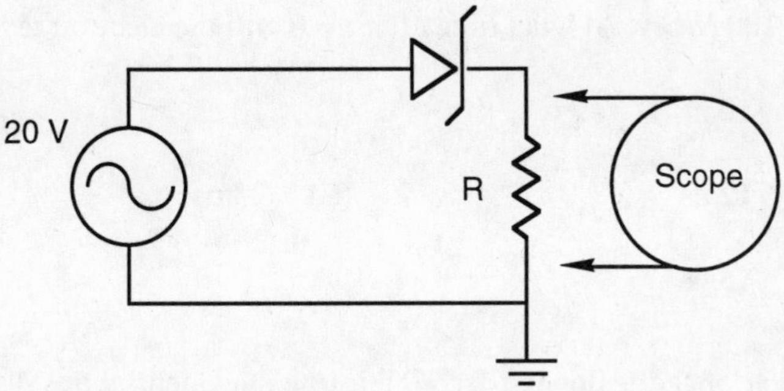

96. Which of the following best describes the way in which a lock-in amplifier improves signal to noise ratio? The amp operates with a reference frequency ω and a time constant RC.

(A) It rejects all noise at frequencies < ω + 1 / *RC*.

(B) It acts like a narrow band amplifier at frequency ω with a bandpass of about 1 / *RC*.

(C) It rejects all noise at frequencies > ω + 1 / *RC*.

(D) It amplifies signals at frequency ω and rejects noise at frequencies > 1 / *RC*.

(E) It amplifies signals at frequency ω and rejects noise at frequencies < 1 / *RC*.

97.

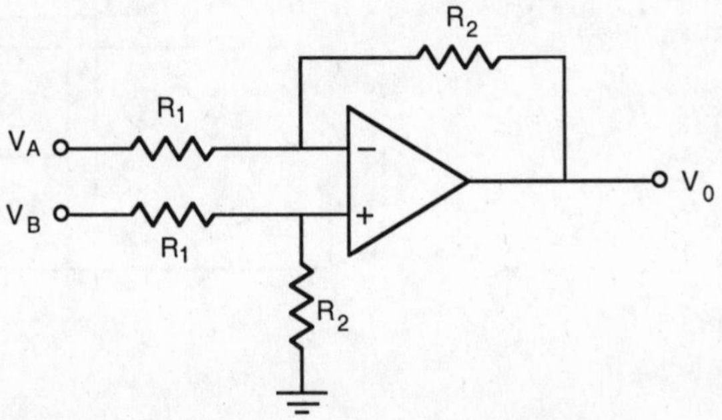

What is the output of the OP AMP circuit shown above?

(A) $R_1(V_A + V_B)/R_2$

(B) $R_2(V_A + V_B)/R_1$

(C) $R_1(V_B - V_A)/R_2$

(D) $R_2(V_B - V_A)/R_1$

(E) $R_2V_A/R_1 - R_1V_B/R_2$

98. An electon is projected at $t = 0$ at an angle of 30° with respect to the x-axis with a speed of 4×10^5 m/s. The electron moves in a constant electric field **E** = 100 *N/C* **y**. At what time after $t = 0$ will the electron recross the x-axis?

(A) 10 ns

(B) 12 ns

(C) 15 ns

(D) 18 ns

(E) 23 ns

99. Which of the following is NOT a true statement about the optical device known as a retarder?

(A) A retarder is used to change the incident wave polarization.

(B) The produced phase difference is $\alpha\ 1/\lambda_{\text{vacuum}}$.

(C) A full wave plate has 2π rad retardance.

(D) A half-wave plate has π rad retardance.

(E) A given wave plate has continuously adjustable retardance.

100. What must the speed of the sliding bar be when the current in the resistor is 0.5 amp? Given that $B = 1\ T$, $R = 2\ \Omega$, and $w = .5$ m.

(A) 2 m/s

(B) 4 m/s

(C) 1 m/s

(D) 3 m/s

(E) 5 m/s

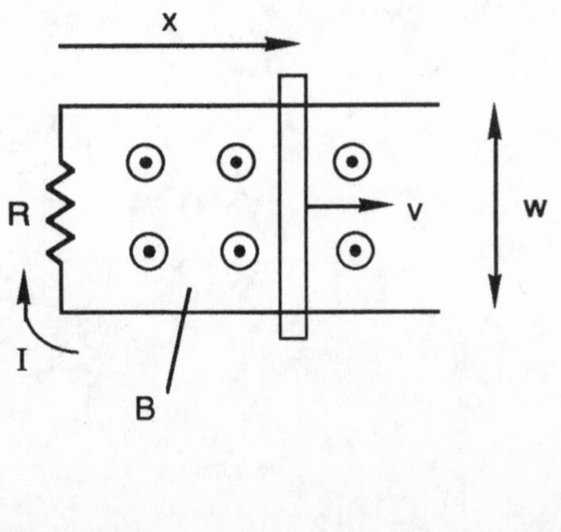

TEST 2

ANSWER KEY

1.	(B)	26.	(E)	51.	(C)	76.	(C)
2.	(E)	27.	(D)	52.	(C)	77.	(A)
3.	(A)	28.	(D)	53.	(D)	78.	(B)
4.	(B)	29.	(B)	54.	(D)	79.	(A)
5.	(D)	30.	(E)	55.	(B)	80.	(E)
6.	(E)	31.	(D)	56.	(E)	81.	(B)
7.	(A)	32.	(D)	57.	(C)	82.	(A)
8.	(C)	33.	(C)	58.	(D)	83.	(C)
9.	(A)	34.	(D)	59.	(C)	84.	(D)
10.	(C)	35.	(A)	60.	(A)	85.	(B)
11.	(C)	36.	(A)	61.	(A)	86.	(A)
12.	(E)	37.	(B)	62.	(A)	87.	(B)
13.	(D)	38.	(B)	63.	(D)	88.	(C)
14.	(A)	39.	(C)	64.	(D)	89.	(D)
15.	(D)	40.	(B)	65.	(A)	90.	(B)
16.	(A)	41.	(C)	66.	(A)	91.	(B)
17.	(C)	42.	(D)	67.	(E)	92.	(E)
18.	(B)	43.	(D)	68.	(C)	93.	(B)
19.	(C)	44.	(E)	69.	(E)	94.	(D)
20.	(A)	45.	(B)	70.	(B)	95.	(E)
21.	(B)	46.	(C)	71.	(D)	96.	(B)
22.	(A)	47.	(D)	72.	(A)	97.	(D)
23.	(D)	48.	(D)	73.	(B)	98.	(E)
24.	(E)	49.	(C)	74.	(E)	99.	(E)
25.	(B)	50.	(C)	75.	(C)	100.	(A)

DETAILED EXPLANATIONS OF ANSWERS
TEST 2

1. **(B)**

This problem involves vectors:

$$\mathbf{r} = x\hat{x} + y\hat{y} + z\hat{z} = \rho\cos\theta\hat{x} + \rho\sin\theta\hat{y} + z\hat{z}$$

The tangent vectors are:

$$\frac{\partial \mathbf{r}}{\partial z} = \hat{z}$$

$$\frac{\partial \mathbf{r}}{\partial \theta} = -\rho\sin\theta\hat{x} + \rho\cos\theta\hat{y}$$

and $$\frac{\partial \mathbf{r}}{\partial \rho} = \cos\theta\hat{x} + \sin\theta\hat{y}$$

The unit vectors are:

$$\hat{z} = (\partial \mathbf{r} / \partial z) \ / \ |\partial \mathbf{r} / \partial z| = \hat{z}$$

and similarly

$$\hat{\theta} = -\sin\theta\hat{x} + \cos\theta\hat{y}$$

and $$\hat{\rho} = \cos\theta\hat{x} + \sin\theta\hat{y}$$

Inverting, one finds

$$\hat{x} = \cos\theta\hat{\rho} - \sin\theta\hat{\theta}$$

$$\hat{y} = \sin\theta\hat{\rho} + \cos\theta\hat{\theta}$$

$\therefore$ $$\mathbf{r} = \rho\hat{\rho} + z\hat{z}$$

Finally $$v = \frac{d\mathbf{r}}{dt} = \dot{\rho}\hat{\rho} + \rho\frac{d\hat{\rho}}{dt} + \dot{z}\hat{z} = \dot{\rho}\hat{\rho} + \rho\dot{\theta}\hat{\theta} + \dot{z}\hat{z}$$

2. **(E)**

$E = T + U$ is the total mechanical energy. Differentiate it to get:

$$\frac{dE}{dt} = \frac{dT}{dt} + \frac{dU}{dt}$$

$$= \mathbf{F}\cdot\mathbf{v} + \frac{\partial U}{\partial t} + \sum_j \frac{\partial U}{\partial x_i} x'_i$$

$$= \mathbf{F}\cdot\mathbf{v} + \frac{\partial U}{\partial t} + \nabla U \cdot \mathbf{v}$$

$$= \frac{\partial U}{\partial t} \text{ since } \mathbf{F} = -\nabla U$$

3. **(A)**
The viscous force is

$$\tfrac{1}{2}\pi r^2 \rho_f \, v \,|\, v \,|\, c_d(v) = F_V.$$

The drag coefficient is

$$c_d(v) = 24 / R_e$$
$$= 24/0.5 = 48$$

here. For a sphere,

$$R_e = 2\,|\,v\,|\,r \,/\, \upsilon$$
$$v = R_e \upsilon / 2r = (.5)\,(.149) / 2\,(.005)$$
$$= 7.45 \text{ cm/s}$$
$$= \tfrac{1}{2}\pi r^2 \rho_f v^2 c_d(v)$$

Then $F_V = \tfrac{1}{2}\pi\,(.005)^2\,(1.22 \times 10^{-3})\,(7.45)^2\,(48)$

$$= 1.28 \; md$$

4. **(B)**
This problem concerns 2D motion. From Newton's 2nd law:

$$\begin{cases} mv'_x = -bv_x \\ mv'_y = -mg - bv_y \end{cases}$$

Now define $\gamma = b/m$. Then the first equation has solution

$$v_x = v_{ox} e^{-\gamma t}$$

and $x = \frac{v_{ox}}{\gamma}(1 - e^{-\gamma t})$

by integration. Similarly,

$$v_y = -g/\gamma + (v_{0y} + g/\gamma)\, e^{-\gamma t}$$
$$y = -gt/\gamma + 1/\gamma\,(v_{0y} + g/\gamma)\,(1 - e^{-\gamma t})$$

by integrating the second equation. At $y = 0$ for positive $t = T$ we find the time of flight:

$$T = \frac{2v_{oy}}{g + v_{oy}\gamma} + \frac{\gamma t^2}{3}$$
$$\approx 2v_{oy}\left(1 - \frac{v_{oy}\gamma}{g}\right)\frac{1}{g} + \frac{\gamma}{3}\left(\frac{2v_{oy}}{g}\right)^2$$
$$= \frac{2v_{oy}}{g}\left(1 - \frac{\gamma v_{oy}}{3g}\right)$$

Where we have used $\frac{1}{1-x} \approx 1-x$.

5. **(D)**

The work function is

$$\phi = h\nu_0 = hc / \lambda_0$$
$$= 12{,}400/2576 = 4.50 \text{ eV}$$

and hence Cu is the substance. The light energy is

$$E = h\nu = hc / \lambda$$
$$= 12{,}400 / 1700 = 7.29 \text{ eV}$$

by conservation of energy

$$t + \phi = h\nu$$

Thus the kinetic energy of the photoelectrons is

$$T = h\nu - \phi$$
$$= 2.79 \text{ eV}$$

6. **(E)**

This is a standard Compton scattering problem. With

$$\lambda = 3.00 \text{ Å}$$

and $\psi = 45.0°$

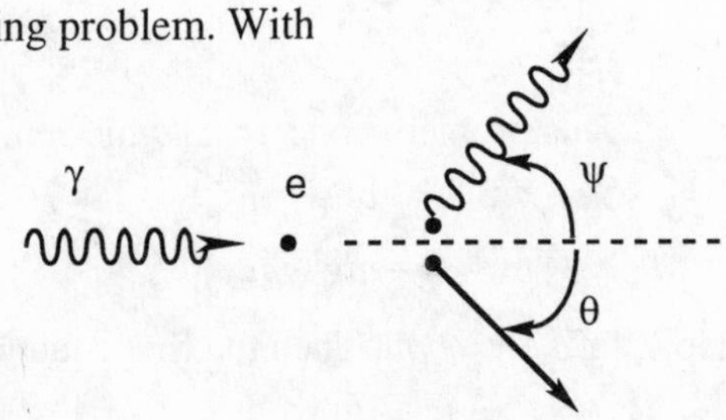

given. The Compton shift is

$$\Delta\lambda = 2\lambda_c \sin^2 \frac{\psi}{2} = \lambda' - \lambda$$

The Compton wavelength is

$$\lambda_C = \frac{h}{m_e c} = \frac{6.626 \times 10^{-34}}{(9.109 \times 10^{-31})(3 \times 10^8)}$$
$$= 2.42 \times 10^{-12} \text{ m} = .0242 \text{ Å}$$

Hence $\Delta\lambda = 2(.0242)(\sin^2 22.5°) = .071 \text{ Å}$

Finally $\lambda' = \lambda + \Delta\lambda = 3.07 \text{ Å}$

7. **(A)**

Stirling's theorem (1st order approximation)

$$\ln N! = \ln N + \ldots + \ln 1$$
$$= \sum_{j=1}^{N} \ln j$$
$$\approx \int_1^N \ln x \, dx$$

$$= x\ln x - x \Big|_1^N$$

$$= N\ln N - N$$

$$\therefore N! = \left(\frac{N}{e}\right)^N$$

8. **(C)**

To get the total displacement, we sum up:

$$x_N = \Sigma x = \Sigma \cos\theta$$

$$y_N = \Sigma y = \Sigma \sin\theta$$

$$r^2 = x_N{}^2 + y_N{}^2$$

$$<r^2>= \frac{\int r^2 d\theta_1 \ldots d\theta_N}{\int d\theta_1 \ldots d\theta_N}$$

$$= \frac{1}{(2\pi)^N}\int \left[(\cos\theta_1 + \ldots + \cos\theta_N)^2 + (\sin\theta_1 + \ldots + \sin\theta_N)^2\right] d\theta_1 \ldots d\theta_N$$

$$= \frac{1}{(2\pi)^N}\int \left[(\cos\theta_1 + U)^2 + (\sin\theta_1 + V)^2\right] d\theta_1 \ldots d\theta_N$$

$$= \frac{1}{(2\pi)^N}\int \left[\cos^2\theta_1 + \sin^2\theta_1 + U^2 + V^2 + 2U\cos\theta_1 + 2V\sin s\theta_1\right] d\theta_1 \ldots d\theta_N$$

$$= \frac{1}{(2\pi)^N}\int \left[\int_0^{2\pi}(1+U^2+V^2)\, d\theta_1\right] d\theta_1 \ldots d\theta_N$$

$$= \frac{1}{(2\pi)^{N-1}}\int \left[(\cos\theta_2 + \ldots + \cos\theta_N)^2 + (\sin\theta_2 + \ldots + \sin\theta_N)^2 + 1\right] d\theta_2 \ldots d\theta_N$$

$$= 1 + \ldots + 1$$

$$= N$$

$$\therefore R_{RMS} = \sqrt{<r^2>} = \sqrt{N}$$

9. **(A)**

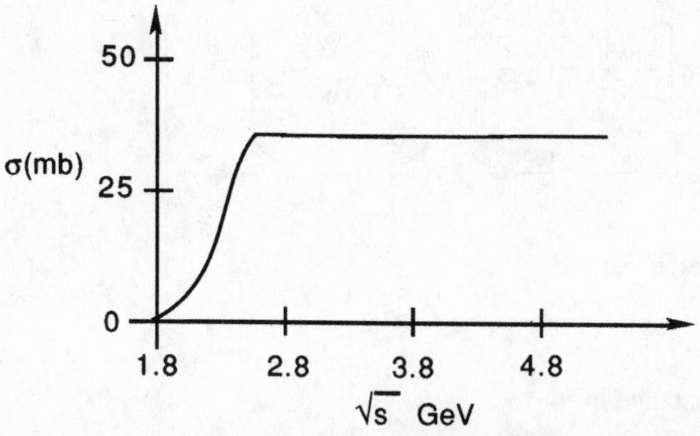

The pp inelastic cross section rises at the pion production threshold

$$\sqrt{s} = 2.014 \text{ MeV}$$

and approaches a constant 30 mb at high energy.

10. **(C)**

$$p + p \rightarrow p + p + \pi^0 \text{ is the given reaction.}$$

The total u-vector momentum squared is

$$(\underline{p}_1 + \underline{p}_2)^2 = -\frac{E_{cm}^2}{c^2} = -m_1{}^2c^2 - m_2{}^2c^2 - \frac{2}{c^2}E_1E_2$$

where each $\underline{p} = (\mathbf{p}, iE/c)$. Now

$$E_1 = T_1 + m_1$$

and $$\sqrt{s} = E_{cm} = \sqrt{m_1{}^2 + m_2{}^2 + 2(T_1 + m_1)m_2}$$

$$2m_N + m_\pi = \sqrt{4m_N{}^2 + 2m_NT_n}$$

Using $m_1 = m_2 = m_N$

$$2(.938) + .140 = \sqrt{4(.938)^2 + 2(.938)T_N}$$

Solve for

$$T_N = .290 \text{ GeV} = 290 \text{ MeV}$$

as the answer.

11. **(C)**

The correct relativistic Langrangian is

$$L = \frac{1}{2}mu^\mu u_\mu + qA^\mu u_\mu$$

To see this, use

$$\frac{d}{dt}\left(\frac{\partial L}{\partial u^\nu}\right) - \frac{\partial L}{\partial x^\nu} = 0$$

which is the relativistic Lagrange/Euler equation

$$\frac{dp^\mu}{dt} = q\left[-\frac{\partial A^\mu}{\partial \tau} - \sum_j \frac{\partial A^\mu}{\partial x^j}u^j + \sum_\nu \frac{\partial A^\nu}{\partial x^\mu}u_\upsilon\right]$$

e.g., $$\frac{dp^1}{dt} = q\left[-\frac{\partial A^1}{\partial \tau} - \frac{\partial \phi}{\partial x^1}u^4 + \gamma(\mathbf{u} \times \mathbf{B})^1\right]$$

$\therefore$ $$\frac{d\mathbf{p}}{dt} = \gamma q(\mathbf{E} + \mathbf{u} \times \mathbf{B})$$

12. **(E)**

The 4-distance is

$$x^{\mu} = (\mathbf{r}, ct)$$

and $$x^{\mu'} = \sum_{\upsilon} \lambda_{\upsilon}^{\mu'} x^{\upsilon}$$

is the transformation equation. The $\mu = 1$ and $\mu = 3$ components are

$$\left.\begin{aligned} x^{1\prime} &= x^{1} \\ x^{3\prime} &= x^{3} \end{aligned}\right\}$$

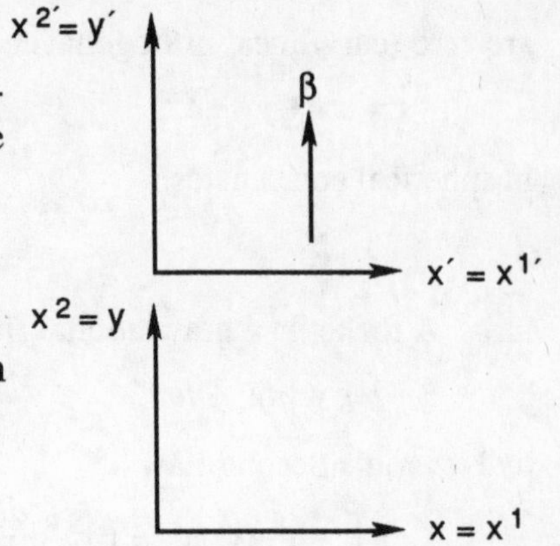

since there is no change in the transverse directions. For the parallel direction and time component, we have

$$x^{2\prime} = \gamma(x^2 - \beta x^4)$$

$$x^{4\prime} = \gamma(x^4 - \beta x^2)$$

The standard forward Lorentz transformation for y and t. Hence

$$\lambda = \begin{pmatrix} 1 & 0 & 0 & 0 \\ 0 & \gamma & 0 & -\beta\gamma \\ 0 & 0 & 1 & 0 \\ 0 & -\beta\gamma & 0 & \gamma \end{pmatrix}$$

is the tranformation matrix and $\underline{x}' = \gamma \underline{x}$ is the matrix equation.

13. **(D)**

$p + {}^{238}_{92}U$ is the elastic Rutherford scattering reaction.

$$\frac{d\sigma}{d\Omega} = \left(\frac{Z_1 Z_2 e^2}{4T}\right)^2 \sin^{-4}\frac{\theta}{2}$$

is the differential cross section.

$$10b \times \frac{1000\ mb}{b} \times \frac{1\ fm^2}{10mb} = 1000\ fm^2$$

$$1000 = \left[\frac{(1)(92)(1.44)}{4(7.6)}\right]^2 \sin^2\frac{q}{2}$$

$$\sin\frac{q}{2} = 0.37 \Rightarrow q = 43.6°$$

14. **(A)**

The given central potential is

$$U = kr^n$$

Hence

$$\mathbf{F} = -\nabla U = -k\left(\hat{r}\frac{\partial}{\partial r} + \hat{\theta}\frac{1}{r}\frac{\partial}{\partial \theta} + \hat{\phi}\frac{1}{r\sin\theta}\frac{\partial}{\partial \phi}\right) r^n$$

Writing the gradient in spherical coordinates.

$$= -k\hat{r}\, nr^{n-1}$$

$$= -kn\, r^{n-2} r\hat{r} = -kn\, r^{n-2}\mathbf{r}$$

since $\frac{\partial r}{\partial \theta}$ and $\frac{\partial r}{\partial \phi}$

are zero (curvilinear orthogonal coordinates). Also

$$\mathbf{r} = x\mathbf{x} + y\mathbf{y} + z\mathbf{z}$$

in spherical coordinates.

15. **(D)**

A rocket in a gravitational field may be understood from

$$-mg = mv' + um'$$

by Newton's Second Law

$$-g\int_0^t dt = \int_{v0}^{v} dv + u\int_{m0}^{m} \frac{dm}{m}$$

$$v = v_0 - gt + u \ln \frac{m_0}{m}$$

$$= 0.4 - 9.8 \times 10^{-3}(100) + 2.0 \ln \frac{3}{1}$$

$$= 1.62 \text{ km/s}$$

16. **(A)**

Use

$$\oint \gamma \cdot d\alpha = -4\pi G m_{in}$$

the integral form of Gauss' law for gravitation. Evaluate the integral in the different regions

$$r < a, \quad \oint \gamma \cdot d\alpha = 0 \Rightarrow g = 0$$

$$r > b, \quad \oint \gamma \cdot d\alpha = -4\pi GM = -g4\pi r^2$$

$$\text{thus} \quad g = \frac{GM}{r^2} \text{ or } \gamma = -\frac{GM\rho}{\mathbf{r}^2}$$

$$a < r < b, \oint \gamma \cdot d\alpha = -4\pi r^2 g = -4\pi G\rho \frac{4\pi}{3}(r^3 - a^3)$$

$$g = \frac{4}{3}\pi G\rho\left(r - \frac{a^3}{r^2}\right)$$

A plot of g versus r is shown in the following figure.

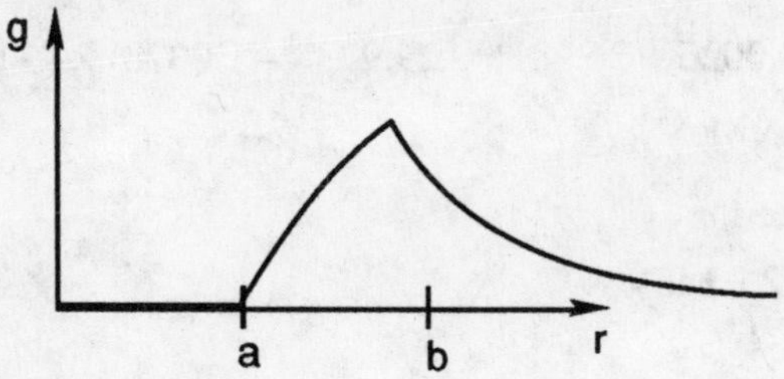

17. **(C)**

The gravitational field of a disk may be found from fundamentals

$$\mathbf{g} = -G\int \frac{dm}{r^2}\mathbf{r}$$

where $dm = \sigma da = 2\pi\sigma s ds.$

$$\mathbf{g} = -G\int \frac{\sigma \mathbf{r} da}{r^2}$$

$$= -2\pi\sigma G\int (s\,ds/r^2)(x/r)\,\mathbf{x}$$

$$\mathbf{g} = -2\pi\sigma Gx\int_0^R \frac{s\,ds}{(x^2+s^2)^{3/2}}\mathbf{x}$$

$$= -2\pi\sigma G\left[1-\frac{x}{\sqrt{x^2+R^2}}\right]\mathbf{x}$$

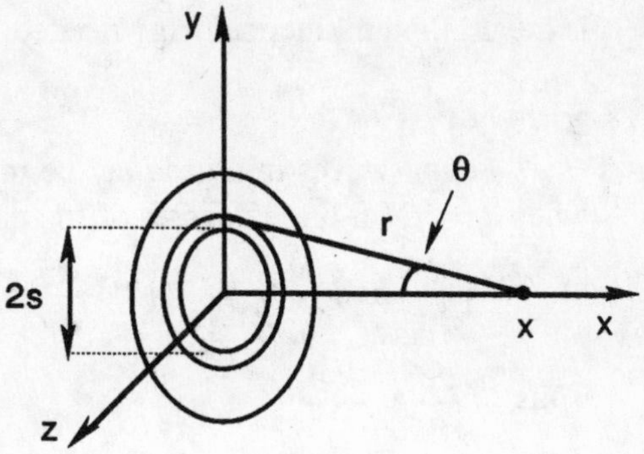

18. **(B)**

Fermat's principle requires that the time be a minimum. The time is given by the action integral

$$A = \int \frac{ds}{v}$$

Using $n = \dfrac{c}{v}$ or $v = \tau / n$

we get $A = \dfrac{1}{c}\int n(x,y)\sqrt{dx^2+dy^2}$

Since $ds = \sqrt{dx^2+dy^2}$

thus $A = \dfrac{1}{c}\int_P^Q \sqrt{1+y'^2}\,n(x,y)\,dx$

19. **(C)**

The nuclear reaction is

$${}^{27}_{13}\mathrm{Al}(\alpha,\mathrm{p})\,{}^{30}_{14}\mathrm{Si} \text{ or } {}^{4}_{2}\alpha + {}^{27}_{13}\mathrm{Al} \rightarrow {}^{1}_{1}p + {}^{30}_{14}\mathrm{Si}$$

with Q-value.

$$Q = m_1 + m_T - m_R - m_E$$

$$= (4.0026 + 26.9815 - 29.9738 - 1.0078) \times 931.502$$
$$= 2.3 \text{ MeV}$$

For the reverse reaction

$$Q = -2.3 \text{ MeV}$$

and

$$T_{\text{lab}} = \left(1 + \frac{m_I}{m_T}\right) |Q|$$
$$= 2.7 \text{ MeV}$$

is the minimum kinetic energy needed.

20. **(A)**

Sound waves in a gas may be modeled as adiabatic. Hence pV^γ = constant where $\gamma = {}^5/_3$ for three degrees of freedom. Differentiate to get

$$\frac{d}{dV}(pV^\gamma) = \gamma pV^{\gamma-1} + V^\gamma \frac{dp}{dV} = 0$$

Thus $\frac{dp}{dV} = -\frac{\gamma p}{V}$

The sound speed is

$$c_1 = \sqrt{\frac{(B + \frac{4}{3}S_m)}{\rho}} = \sqrt{\frac{B}{\rho}}$$

for an ideal fluid which has zero shear modulus and

$$B = -V\frac{dp}{dV} = \gamma p.$$

Finally

$$c_1 = \sqrt{\frac{\gamma p}{\rho}}$$

and hence doubling p changes the sound speed c_1 by a factor of $\sqrt{2}$.

21. **(B)**

The Maxwell-Boltzman distribution is given by

$$dn = gN\left(\frac{1}{2\pi mkT}\right)^{3/2} e^{-E/kT} d^3p$$

where the degeneracy $g = 1$ for classical particles. One can always find the factor $(1/2\,\pi\, mkT)^{3/2}$ by normalization

$$\int_0^N dn = N.$$

Clearly

$$\frac{dn}{N} = p(v)\, dv$$

defines a probability density function $p(v)$. Thus

$$<v^2>= \int_0^\infty v^2 p(v)\, dv$$

$$= \frac{1}{(2\pi mkT)^{3/2}} \int_0^\infty e^{-mv^2/2kT} v^2 4\pi m^2 v^2 m\, dv$$

$$= 4\left(\frac{m}{2\pi kT}\right)^{3/2} \int_0^\infty e^{-at} t^{5/2-1} \frac{dt}{2}, \text{ where } a \equiv \frac{m}{2kT}$$

$$= \frac{1}{\sqrt{2\pi}}\left(\frac{m}{kT}\right)^{3/2} \frac{3}{2}\cdot\frac{\sqrt{\pi}}{2} \Big/ \left(\frac{m}{2kT}\right)^{5/2} = 3kT/m$$

where

$$\left(\frac{3}{2}\right)! = \frac{3}{2}\times\left(\frac{1}{2}\right)! = \frac{3}{2}\frac{\sqrt{\pi}}{2}$$

was used.

22. **(A)**

The situation is governed by the binomial distribution

$$p(n) = \binom{N}{n} p^n (1-p)^{N-n}$$

where $$\binom{N}{n} = \frac{N!}{n!\,(N-n)!}.$$

is the standard binomial coefficient. The probability parameter is

$$p = \frac{V_0}{V} = \frac{10^{-18}\ \text{cm}^2}{1\times 10^8\ \text{cm}^3} = 10^{-26}$$

The desired probability is $p(0)$

$$p(0) = \frac{N!}{0!N!} p^0 (1-10^{-26})^{10^{27}}$$

$$\approx e^{-10} = 4.5\times 10^{-5}$$

where we have used

$$(1-x)^N \approx (e^{-x})^N = e^{-xN}$$

since $x \ll 1$.

23. **(D)**

The standard rule for the propagation of error is

$$\Delta f = \sqrt{\left(\frac{\partial f}{\partial x_1}\Delta x_1\right)^2 + \ldots + \left(\frac{\partial f}{\partial x_N}\Delta x_N\right)^2}$$

the density of a sphere is

$$\rho = \frac{m}{V} = m / \frac{4}{3}\pi r^3$$

Hence

$$\Delta\rho = \sqrt{\left(\frac{\partial \rho}{\partial m}\Delta m\right)^2 + \left(\frac{\partial \rho}{\partial r}\Delta r\right)^2}$$

$$\frac{\Delta\rho}{\rho} = \sqrt{\left(\frac{\Delta m}{m}\right)^2 + 9\left(\frac{\Delta r}{r}\right)^2}$$

$$= \sqrt{\left(\frac{3}{183}\right)^2 + 9\left(\frac{0.1}{25}\right)^2}$$

$$= .020$$

for the solid Al sphere's relative uncertainty.

24. **(E)**

For the entire cycle *ADCBA*

$$\Delta U = 0 = \Delta Q - \Delta W$$

Hence $\Delta Q = Q_C - Q_H = \Delta W$

since Q_C is absorbed and Q_H is ejected. The efficiency is then

$$e = \frac{|\Delta W|}{Q_c} = \frac{Q_H}{Q_c} - 1$$

since $Q_H > Q_C$.

Finally, one needs to use the fact that $Q_H / Q_C = T_H / T_C$ to get

$$e = \frac{T_H}{T_c} - 1$$

where

$$T_H > T_C.$$

25. **(B)**

A single particle with one degree of freedom may be described in a space (x, p) of two dimensions. The cumulative number of states is

$$\Gamma(E) = \frac{\ell}{2\pi\hbar}\int \theta[E - H(x,p)]\, dx\, dp$$

$$= \frac{\ell}{2\pi\hbar}\int_{\left(\frac{p^2}{2m} - E\right)} dp = \frac{\ell}{2\pi\hbar}\int_{-\sqrt{2mE}}^{\sqrt{2mE}} dp$$

$$= \ell\sqrt{2mE} / \pi\hbar$$

The density of states is

$$\frac{d\Gamma}{dE} = \ell\sqrt{2m/E} / 2\pi\hbar$$

26. **(E)**

For the two state system with degeneracies (g_1, g_2) and energies $(E_1, E_2) = (0, \varepsilon)$ the partition function is

$$Z = \Sigma g_j e^{-\beta E_j} = g_1 + g_2 e^{-\beta\varepsilon}.$$

The average energy is then

$$<E> = \frac{-\partial}{\partial\beta} \ln Z = -\frac{1}{Z}\frac{\partial Z}{\partial\beta}$$

$$= g_2 \varepsilon e^{-\beta\varepsilon} / (g_1 + g_2 e^{-\beta\varepsilon})$$

and the total energy for N particles is

$$<E>_N = N <E>$$

$$= g_2 N\varepsilon e^{-\beta\varepsilon} / (g_1 + g_2 e^{-\beta\varepsilon})$$

$$= g_2 N\varepsilon / (g_1 e^{\beta\varepsilon} + g_2)$$

27. **(D)**

Lissajous figures are generated from the coupled harmonic equations

$$\begin{cases} x'' + \omega_x^2 x = 0 \\ y'' + \omega_y^2 y = 0 \end{cases}$$

with solution

$$x = A \cos(\omega_x t + \alpha)$$

$$y = B \cos(\omega_y t + \beta)$$

The figure is thus a parametric plot $(x(t), y(t))$. Let $\delta = \beta - \alpha$ be the phase difference. Then

$$A = B, \omega_y = 2\omega_x, \delta = \pi/2$$

gives the "butterfly." Also

$$\delta = \pm\pi/2, \omega_y = \omega_x$$

gives an ellipse, and

$$\delta = 0 \text{ or } \pm\pi \text{ with } \omega_y = \omega_x$$

is a line.

28. **(D)**

The light damping or underdamped motion solution corresponds to

$$\omega_0^2 > \gamma^2 / 4.$$

The differential equation is

$$mx'' = -kx - bx'$$

$$x'' + \gamma x' + \omega_0^2 x = 0\,, \quad \gamma \equiv b/m\,, \quad \omega_0 \equiv \sqrt{k/m}$$

A solution would be $x = e^{pt}e^{i\delta}$ with auxiliary equation $p^2 + \gamma p + \omega_0^2 = 0$. This implies

$$p_{\pm} = -\frac{\gamma}{2} \pm i\omega \text{ where } \omega \equiv \sqrt{\omega_0^2 - \gamma^2/4}$$

One can write

$$x = x_+ + x_-$$

$$= Ae^{-\gamma t/2}(e^{i(\omega t+\delta)} + e^{-i(\omega t+\delta)})$$

$$= 2Ae^{-\gamma t/2}\cos(\omega t + \delta)$$

$$= Be^{-\gamma t/2}\cos(\omega t + \delta).$$

with $B \equiv 2A$.

29. **(B)**

$$R = 109{,}677.6 \text{ cm}^{-1}$$

is given as the Rydberg constant for hydrogen. The Lyman, Balmer, Paschen, Brackett, and Pfund series result from electronic transitions from level m to $n = 1$, 2, 3, 4, 5 respectively. For the Paschen series $n = 3$ and so

$$\frac{1}{\lambda} = R\left(\frac{1}{n^2} - \frac{1}{m^2}\right)$$

$$= R\left(\frac{1}{9} - \frac{1}{m^2}\right)$$

Clearly $m \to \infty$ gives $\lambda = 8206$Å the lower limit. $m = 4$ gives the upper limit $\lambda =$ 18,760Å.

30. **(E)**

It is desired to find the average energy for a photon gas, i.e., black body radiation. Proceed using Boltzmann factors:

$$E_j = j\hbar w, \ j = 0,1,2,\ldots\infty$$

$$<E> = \Sigma E_j e^{-\beta E_j} / \Sigma e^{-\beta E_j}$$

$$= \hbar\omega \sum_j je^{-jx} / \sum_j e^{-jx}\,, \ x = \hbar\omega\beta$$

$$= \hbar\omega \sum jy^j / \sum y^j\,, \ y \equiv e^{-x}$$

$$= \hbar\omega\,(y/(1-y)^2)/(1/(1-y))$$

$$= \hbar\omega/(e^{\hbar\omega\beta} - 1)$$

We have used the infinite geometric series results

$$1 + y + y^2 + \ldots = 1/(1 - y)$$

and

$$y(1+2y+3y^2+\ldots)=y\frac{d}{dy}(1-y)^{-1}=\frac{y}{(1-y)^2}$$

31. **(D)**

A voltage applied at the metal gate does indeed act as a switch and allows current flow from source to drain. Doping with impurity atoms such as phosphorus and boron determines the formation of the n-source and *p*-substrate in silicon material. The extra P electrons or missing B electrons (holes) can conduct a current. Current flow from the n-source to the n-drain is usually blocked by the p-substrate. A positive voltage applied at the metal gate allows current flow.

32. **(D)**

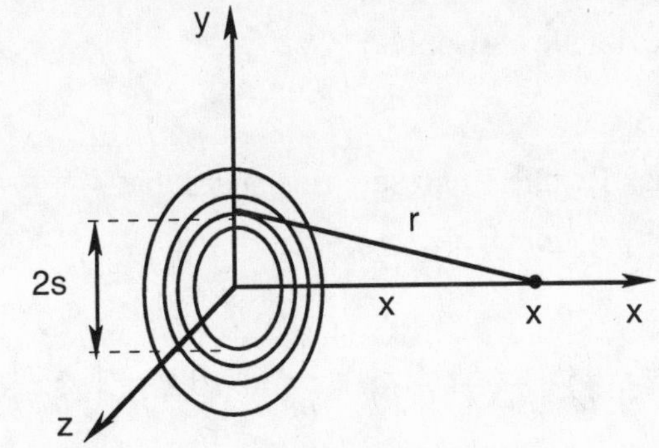

The electric field and electric potential are related by:

$$E=-\nabla\phi=-\frac{d\phi}{dr} \text{ or } \phi=-\int E\cdot dr$$

Another fundamental formula is that

$$\phi=+k\int\frac{dq}{r}.$$

Thus $$\phi=+k\int_a^b\frac{2\pi\sigma s ds}{\sqrt{s^2+x^2}}$$

$$=+2\pi k\sigma\sqrt{s^2+x^2}\Big|_{s=a}^{s=b}$$

$$=+2\pi k\sigma(\sqrt{b^2+x^2}-\sqrt{a^2+x^2})$$

Graphically, this looks like

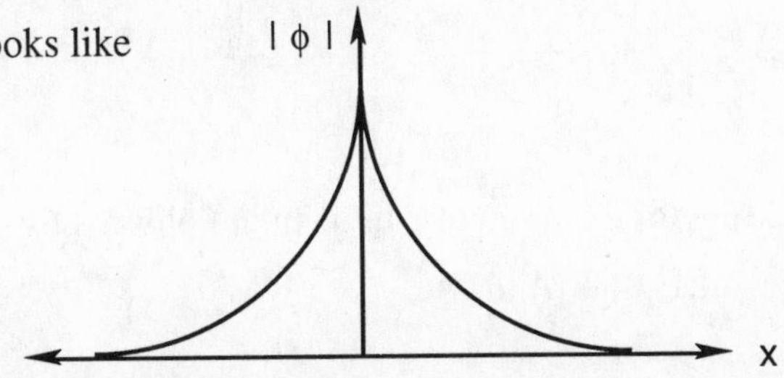

33. **(C)**

The black body distribution is given by

$$U(\omega)=\frac{\hbar\omega^3}{\pi^2c^3}\frac{1}{(e^{\hbar\omega\beta}-1)}$$

For high temperatures or low frequencies, one can make a Taylor expansion of e^x

$$e^x=1+x+\frac{x^2}{2!}+\ldots$$

Hence

$$U(\omega)=\frac{\hbar\omega^3}{\pi^2c^3}\frac{1}{1+\hbar\omega\beta-1}=\omega^2kT/\pi^2c^3$$

If one tried to now calculate the total energy density

$$U=\int_0^{\infty}U(\omega)\,d\omega,$$

one gets the ultraviolet catastrophe.

34. **(D)**

The Thomas-Reiche-Kuhn sum rule states that

$$\sum_j |x_{j0}|^2(E_j-E_0)=\hbar^2/2m$$

Since

$$[H,x]=\frac{\hbar}{i}\frac{p}{m},\quad [x,[H,x]]=\frac{\hbar}{im}[x,p]=\frac{\hbar}{im}\left(\frac{-\hbar}{i}\right)=\frac{\hbar^2}{m^2}$$

Also $\left\langle 0\left|\frac{\hbar^2}{m}\right|0\right\rangle=\frac{\hbar^2}{m}=\langle 0|[x,Hx-xH]|0\rangle$

using a wave function ψ_0 and expanding the commutator

$$\hbar^2/m=\langle 0|2xHx-x^2H-Hx^2|0\rangle$$

Further $<0|xHx|0>=\sum_j <0|x|j><j|x|0>E_j=\Sigma|(x_{j0})|^2E_j$

and $<0|Hx^2|0>=<0|x^2H|0>$

$$=\sum_j <0|x|j><j|x|0>E_0=\sum|x_{j0}|^2E_0$$

Finally we get

$$\frac{\hbar^2}{2m}=\sum_j |x_{j0}|^2(E_j-E_0)$$

35. **(A)**

A general rule for commutators in quantum physics is

$$[A^2,B]=A[A,B]+[A,B]A.$$

This problem involves the operator

$$H = \frac{p^2}{2m} + V(x).$$

Obviously, $[V(x), x] = 0$. Then consider

$$\frac{1}{2m}\left[p^2, x\right] = \frac{1}{2m}\left(p[p,x] + [p,x]\,p\right)$$

$$= \frac{1}{2m}\,2p\,\frac{\hbar}{i}$$

$$= \frac{\hbar x'}{i}$$

using $p = mx'$. Thus

$$[H, x] = \frac{\hbar}{i}\,x'.$$

36. **(A)**

A typical experimental set-up is pictured below.

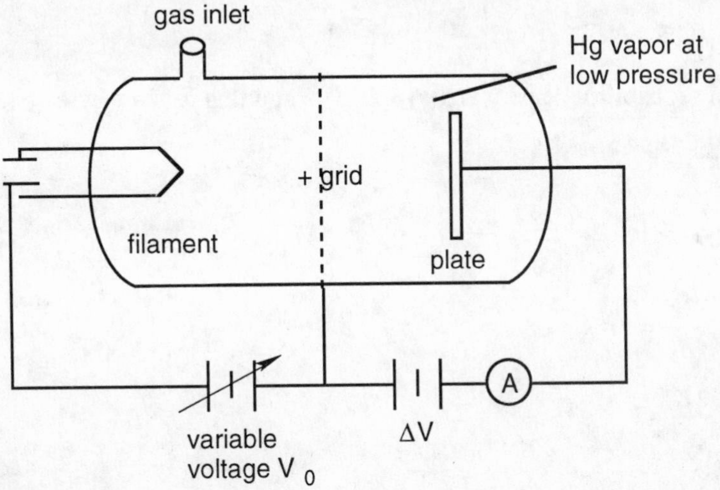

The heated filament supplies electrons which are accelerated by the positive voltage of the grid. The accelerated electrons gain energy so that ($eV_0 = {}^1/_2\, mv^2$) and experience inelastic collisions with Hg atoms. The back voltage ΔV deters some electrons from reaching the plate. The current-voltage curve peaks at the quantum energy levels.

37. **(B)**

For any spherical harmonic, the normalization condition is

$$\int Y_{lm_l} Y_{lm_l} {}^* \, d\Omega = 1$$

where Ω is the solid angle. For the given problem, we have

$$\ell = m_l = 1$$

$$\int Y_{||}Y_{||}{}^{*}\, d\Omega = 1$$

$$\int N^2 \sin^2\theta e^{i\phi} e^{-i\phi}\, d(\cos\theta)\, d\phi$$

where we have used th fact that

$$d\Omega = \sin\theta\, d\theta\, d\phi$$

$$N^2 \int_{-1}^{1} \sin^2\theta\, d(\cos\theta) \int_0^{2\pi} d\phi$$

Use the identity $\sin^2 = 1 - \cos^2\theta$ to get

$$2\pi N^2 \int_{-1}^{1} (1-\cos^2\theta)\, d(\cos\theta) = 2\pi N^2 [2 - \frac{1}{3} 2]$$

$$1 = \frac{8\pi}{3} N^2 \Rightarrow N = \sqrt{3/8\pi}$$

38. **(B)**

The hydrogen radial wave functions come from the associated Laguerre polynomials. The ground state wave function is found from the quantum numbers $n = 1, l = 0, m_l = 0$.

$$R_{10}(Y) = Ne^{-Zr/a_0} = 2\left(\frac{Z}{a_0}\right)^{3/2} e^{-Zr/a_0}.$$

The radial probability density is $p(r) = RR^* r^2$ and this peaks where

$$\frac{d}{dr}(r^2 e^{-2Zr/a_0}) = 0$$

$$2re^{-2Zr/a_0} - r^2 \frac{2Z}{a_0} e^{-2Zr/a_0} = 0$$

$$r^2 \frac{2Z}{a_0} = 2r$$

$$r\frac{2Z}{a_0} = 2$$

Finally

$$r = \frac{a_0}{Z}.$$

One may also show that

$$\frac{d^2 p}{dr^2} < 0 \text{ at } \frac{a_0}{Z}$$

proving that the extremum is a maximum.

39. **(C)**

The $n = 2$ and $l = 1$ radial wave function is under consideration

$$R_{21}(r) = Nre^{-Zr/2a_0}.$$

Use the normalization condition $\int RR^* r^2\, dr = 1$

$$= N^2 \int_0^\infty r^4 e^{-Zr/a_0}\, dr$$

$$= N^2 \int_0^\infty r^{5-1} e^{-Ar/a_0} dr$$

$$= N^2 \Gamma(5)/(Z/a_0)^5 = N^2 4! \times a_o^{\,5}/Z^5$$

Thus $N^2 = \dfrac{Z^3}{8a_0^{\,3}} \dfrac{Z^2}{3a_0^{\,2}} \Rightarrow N = \left(\dfrac{Z}{2a_0}\right)^{3/2} \dfrac{Z}{\sqrt{3}a_0}$

40. **(B)**

The hydrogen-like atom energy is a function of Z, μ, and n

$$E_n = -\,k^2 Z^2 \mu e^4 / 2\hbar^2 n^2$$

$$= -\frac{Z^2}{n^2} \frac{\mu}{m_e} 13.6\ eV$$

This is most easily derived from Bohr theory

$$\left.\begin{aligned} F &= \frac{\mu v^2}{r} = \frac{kZe^2}{r^2} \\ L &= \mu v r = h\hbar \end{aligned}\right\} \Rightarrow r = n^2 a_0 / Z$$

with the Bohr radius as $a_o = \hbar^2 / \mu k e^2$. Then

$$E = T + U = \frac{1}{2}\mu v^2 - \frac{kZe^2}{r}$$

$$= \frac{-kZe^2}{2r}$$

$$= -\frac{kZe^2}{2} \frac{Z}{n^2} \frac{\mu k e^2}{\hbar^2}$$

$$= -\frac{k^2 Z^2 \mu e^4}{2\hbar^2 n^2}$$

41. **(C)**

Experimentally, the nuclear binding energy is

$$BE = 931.50\, A_{el} - 938.28\, Z - 939.57\ \text{N}.$$

neglecting the electron masses. According to the semi-empirical mass formula, we get

$$BE = -C_v A + C_C Z(Z-1)A^{-1/3} + C_A A^{2/3} + C_S \frac{(A-2Z)^2}{A}$$

with parameters

$$C_V = 15.6\ \text{MeV},\ C_C = 0.7\ \text{MeV},\ C_A = 17.2\ \text{MeV},\ C_S = 23.3\ \text{MeV}.$$

42. **(D)**

In the nuclear Fermi gas model, the density of particles in momentum space is constant:

$$\frac{dn}{d^3p} = gV/(2\pi\hbar)^3 = \text{constant}$$

Thus $$\int_0^A \frac{dn}{V} = 4\frac{1}{(2\pi\hbar)^3}\int d^3p = \frac{1}{2\pi^3\hbar^3}\frac{4}{3}\pi p_F{}^3$$

or $$\frac{A}{V} = \rho = \frac{2}{3\pi^3\hbar^3}p_F{}^3$$

Finally, $$p_F = \left(\frac{3}{2}\pi^2\rho\right)^{1/3}\hbar$$

$$= \left(\frac{3}{2}\pi^2 0.14\right)^{1/3} 197.35^*$$

$$= 252\,\text{MeV/c}$$

$$^*\hbar = \frac{h}{2\pi} = \frac{6.63\times10^{-34}\,\text{j}-\text{s}}{2\pi}\times\frac{\text{MeV}}{1.60\times10^{-13}\,\text{j}}\times\frac{1\,\text{fm/c}}{(10^{-15}\,\text{m}/(3\times10^8\,\text{m/s}))}$$
$$= 197.35\,\text{MeV fm/c}$$

43. **(D)**

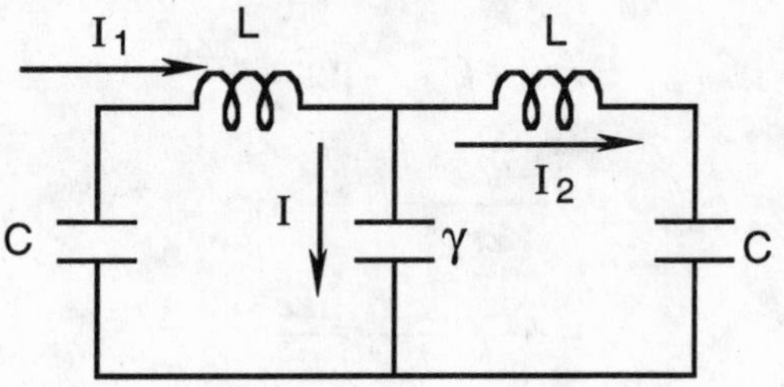

By Kirchhoff's current law

$$I_1 = I + I_2 \Rightarrow I = I_1 - I_2.$$

By Kirchhoff's voltage laws:

$$-q_1/c - LI'_1 - \frac{q_1 - q_2}{\gamma} = 0$$

$$-q_2/c - LI'_2 + \frac{q_1 - q_2}{\gamma} = 0$$

Differentiate and let $K = 1/LC$ and $\kappa = 1/L\gamma$. Then we obtain

$$I_1'' = -I_1K + (I_2 - I_1)\,\kappa$$
$$I_2'' = -I_2K - (I_2 - I_1)\,\kappa$$

Add and subtract the equations letting $y = I_1 + I_2$ and $z = I_2 - I_1$, respectively, to get

$$y'' = -ky \text{ and } z'' = -kz - 2\kappa z.$$

Hence, the ratio $\omega_a/\omega_s = \sqrt{(k+2\kappa)/k} = \sqrt{1+\frac{2\kappa}{k}}$

44. **(E)**

This is the standard twin paradox problem. We are given $v = 1.50 \times 10^8$ *m/s*. Hence,

$$\beta = \frac{v}{c} = \frac{1}{2} \text{ and } \gamma = \frac{1}{\sqrt{1-\beta^2}} = \frac{2}{\sqrt{3}}.$$

The time dilation equation is $t = t_0\gamma$ where t_0 is spaceship time and t is Earth time. We extrapolate that $t_0 = \frac{t}{\gamma}$. We are given $v = 1.50 \times 10^8 m/s$. Hence,

$$\beta = \frac{v}{c} = \frac{1.50 \times 10^8 m/s}{3.0 \times 10^8 m/s} = \frac{1}{2}$$

and $\gamma = \frac{1}{\sqrt{1-\beta^2}} = \frac{2}{\sqrt{3}}$. In terms of Earth years, for a round trip it will take John:

$t = \frac{2}{v} = \frac{2 \times 25}{\frac{1}{2}c} = 100$ years. The time dilation equation is $t = t_0 \times \gamma$, where t_0 is spaceship time and t is Earth time. $t_0 = \frac{t}{\gamma} = \frac{100}{2/\sqrt{3}} = 86.6$ years.

$\Delta t = t - t_0 = 100 - 86.6 = 13.4$ years. **(*light years)**

45. **(B)**
In relativity, $\mathbf{F} = \frac{d\mathbf{p}}{dt}$ just as holds classically.
However, the relativistic momentum is $\mathbf{p} = m\mathbf{v}\gamma$. If $\mathbf{v}$ changes only in direction, then

$$\mathbf{F} = \mathbf{F}_\perp = \frac{d}{dt}(m\mathbf{v}\gamma) = m\gamma\frac{d\mathbf{v}}{dt} = m\gamma\mathbf{a}_\perp$$

If $\mathbf{v}$ changes only in magnitude, then

$$\mathbf{F} = \mathbf{F}_{||} = \frac{d}{dt}(m\mathbf{v}\gamma)$$

$$= m\gamma\frac{d\mathbf{v}}{dt}t + m\beta^2\gamma^3\frac{d\mathbf{v}}{dt}$$

$$= m\frac{d\mathbf{v}}{dt}\gamma^3\left(\frac{1}{\gamma^3} + \beta^2\right)$$

$= m\gamma^3\mathbf{a}_{||}$. For $|\mathbf{a}_\perp| = |\mathbf{a}_{||}|$ we get $\frac{\mathbf{F}_\perp}{\mathbf{F}_{||}} = \gamma^2$.

46. **(C)**

The Biot-Savart Law must be used

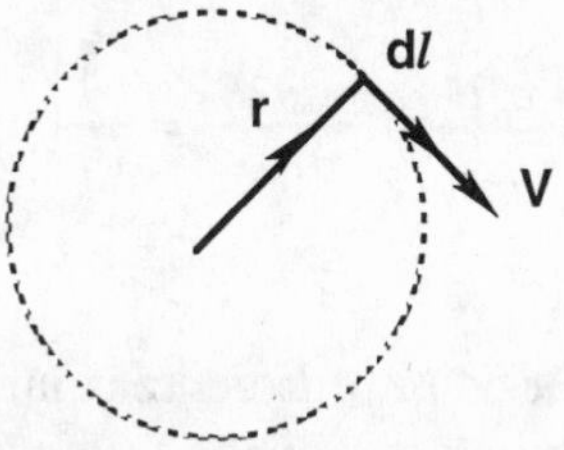

$$d\mathbf{B} = \frac{\mu_0}{4\pi}\frac{Idl \times \mathbf{r}}{r^2}$$

$$B_z = \frac{\mu_0 I}{4\pi}\int_0^{2\pi r}\frac{dl}{r^2} = \frac{\mu_0 I}{2r}$$

The current is

$$I = \frac{q}{t} = \frac{e}{2\pi r/v} = \frac{ev}{2\pi r}$$

and the velocity comes from (in Bohr theory)

$$mv^2/r = ke^2/r^2$$

$$v = \sqrt{ke^2/mr} = \sqrt{\frac{9 \times 10^{9}(1.6 \times 10^{-10})^2}{9.1 \times 10^{-31}(.529 \times 10^{-10})}}$$

$$= 2.19 \times 10^{6} \text{ m/s}$$

Thus $\quad I = (1.60 \times 10^{-19})(2.19 \times 10^{6}) / 2\pi(.529 \times 10^{-10}) = .00105 \text{ A}$

and finally

$$B_z = (4\pi \times 10^{-7})(.00105) / 2(.529 \times 10^{-10})$$

$$= 12.5 \text{ Tesla}$$

47. **(D)**

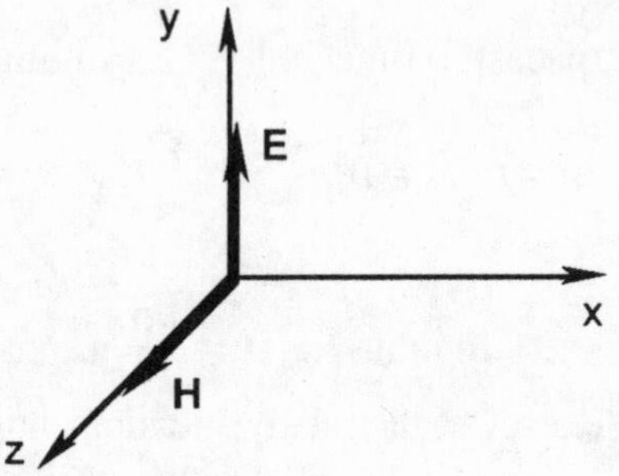

Maxwell's equations are

$$\nabla \cdot \mathbf{D} = 0 \qquad \nabla \cdot \mathbf{B} = 0$$

$$\nabla \times \mathbf{E} = -\frac{\partial \mathbf{B}}{\partial t} \qquad \nabla \times \mathbf{H} = +\frac{\partial \mathbf{D}}{\partial t}$$

where $\mathbf{D} = \varepsilon \mathbf{E}$ and $\mathbf{B} = \mu \mathbf{H}$. Now suppose

$$\mathbf{E} = E\mathbf{y}, \quad \text{and} \quad \mathbf{H} = H\mathbf{z},$$

then $\quad \nabla \times \mathbf{E} = \left(\frac{\partial E_y}{\partial x} - \frac{\partial E_x}{\partial y}\right)\mathbf{z} \equiv \frac{\partial E_y}{\partial x}\mathbf{z}$

since $E_x = 0$ and

$$\nabla \times \mathbf{H} = \left(\frac{\partial H_x}{\partial z} - \frac{\partial H_z}{\partial x}\right)\mathbf{y} \equiv -\frac{\partial H_z}{\partial x}\mathbf{y}$$

since $H_x = 0$. Then we may rewrite the above

$$\frac{\partial H}{\partial x} = -\frac{\partial D}{\partial t} \quad \text{as} \quad \frac{\partial B}{\partial x} = -\mu\frac{\partial D}{\partial t}.$$

Hence, we obtain

$$\frac{\partial E}{\partial x} = -\frac{\partial B}{\partial t} \quad \text{and} \quad \frac{\partial B}{\partial x} = -\mu\frac{\partial D}{\partial t}.$$

If $\quad \varepsilon = \varepsilon_0 e^{\alpha t}$ and $\mu = \mu_0 e^{\alpha t}$,

then we get

$$\frac{\partial^2 E}{\partial x^2} = \frac{-\partial^2 B}{\partial t \partial x} = \frac{\partial}{\partial t}\left(\mu \frac{\partial D}{\partial t}\right) = \mu \frac{\partial^2 D}{\partial t^2} + \mu\alpha \frac{\partial D}{\partial t}.$$

48. **(D)**

Because of Lorentz contraction, the circle becomes an ellipse as seen in the lab frame shown on the following page.

With that proviso, we can find V

$$l = \frac{l_0}{\gamma}$$

$$2a = \frac{2b}{\gamma}$$

$$\frac{a}{b} = \sqrt{1-\beta^2},$$

$$\beta = \sqrt{1 - \frac{a^2}{b^2}}$$

Let k be the lab frame and k' the rest frame of the object.

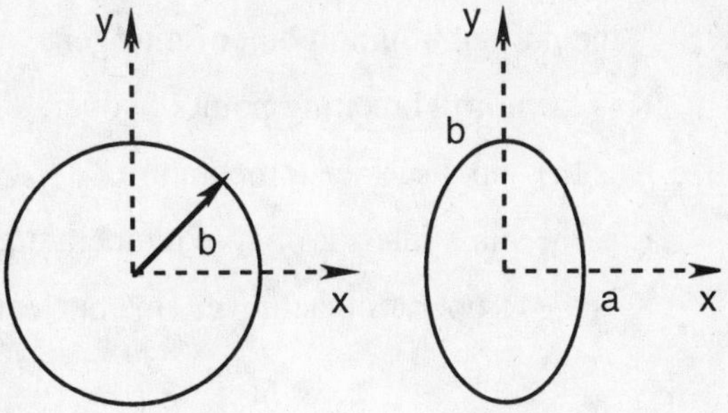

seen in k | seen in k'
$x^2/a^2 + y^2/b^2 = 1$ | $x^2 + y^2 = b^2$

49. **(C)**
The initial picture is

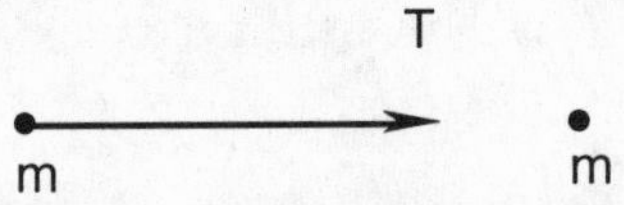

and the final situation is

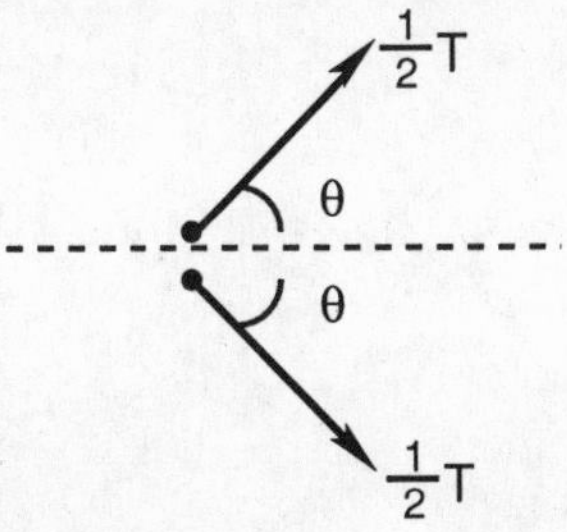

By symmetry, the kinetic energy is evenly split after the collision.

Now:

$$E = T + mc^2 \text{ and } p = \sqrt{E^2 - m^2c^4}$$

give $\quad p^2 = T^2 + 2mc^2T.$

Similarly

$$E' = \frac{1}{2}T + mc^2 \text{and } p' = \sqrt{E'^2 - m^2c^4} \text{ yield } p'^2 = T^2/4 + mc^2T.$$

By conservation of momentum $p = 2p' \cos\theta$ or

$$\cos\theta = \sqrt{T^2 + 2mc^2T} \ / \ \sqrt{T^2 + 4mc^2T}.$$

Plug in $mc^2 = 938$ MeV and $T = 1876$ MeV $= 2\ mc^2$ to get $\theta = A\cos\ (^2/_3) = 35.3$
$\Rightarrow 2\theta = 70.6°$.

50. **(C)**

There is a wide range of temperatures in the physical universe, many accessible in the laboratory.

0 K is the absolute zero or coldest temperature.

20 K is the normal boiling point of hydrogen.

77 K is the normal boiling point of nitrogen.

1234 K is the normal melting point of silver.

6000 K is the sun's surface temperature.

10^6 K is the sun's interior or core temperature.

10^{12} K is the temperature achieved in a nuclear collision.

51. **(C)**

The hydrogen-like atom wave functions have the following functional dependence

$$\psi_{100} \ \alpha \ e^{-Zr/a_0}$$

$$\psi_{200} \ \alpha \ (1 - Zr/2a_0)e^{-Zr/2a_0}$$

$$\psi_{210} \ \alpha \ r\cos\theta e^{-Zr/2a_0}$$

$$\psi_{211} \ \alpha \ r\sin\theta e^{i\phi} e^{-Zr/2a_0}$$

$$\psi_{21-1} \ \alpha \ r\sin\theta e^{-i\phi} e^{-Zr/2a_0}$$

The orbital shown, plotted in 3D at $y = 0$, is that of the 210 state:

$P(x, z) = \psi\psi^* \ (y = 0)$.

52. **(C)**

In order to get from the usual wave equation to the Schrödinger equation, one uses the De Broglie wavelength concept

$$\lambda = \frac{h}{p} = \frac{h}{\sqrt{2m(E-U)}}.$$

Start with the 1-D wave equation

$$\frac{\partial^2 \psi}{\partial x^2} = \frac{1}{v^2}\frac{\partial^2 \psi}{\partial t^2}, \quad \psi(x,t) = \phi(x)e^{i\omega t}$$

Separating variables

$$\frac{d^2\phi}{dx^2} + \frac{\omega^2}{v^2}\phi(x) = 0$$

where $\omega^2 = 4\pi f^2 = 4\pi^2 v^2/\lambda^2 = 4\pi^2 2m(E-U)v^2/h^2$

Substituting

$$\frac{d^2\phi}{dx^2}+\frac{2m(E-U)}{\hbar^2}\phi(x)=0$$

Rearranging

$$-\frac{\hbar^2}{2m}\frac{d^2\phi}{dx^2}+U\phi=E\phi$$

or finally $H\,\phi = E\phi$ in operator form.

53. **(D)**

The damped one-dimensional harmonic oscillator differential equation is

$$x''+\gamma x'+\omega_0^2 x=0$$

where

$$\omega_0=\sqrt{\frac{k}{m}} \text{ and } \gamma=\frac{b}{m}.$$

In the light damping situation $w_0^2 > \gamma^2/4$ and the solution is

$$x=B_0e^{-\gamma t/2}\cos(\omega t+\delta) \text{ where } \omega=\sqrt{\omega_0^2-\gamma^2/4}.$$

If $\gamma << 1$, then

$$x'=-B_0\omega e^{-\gamma t/2}\sin(\omega t+\delta)$$

and $$E=\frac{1}{2}mx'^2+\frac{1}{2}kx^2$$

$$=\frac{1}{2}B_0^{\,2}e^{-\gamma t}\{m\omega^2\sin^2(\omega t+\delta)+k\cos^2(\omega t+\delta))$$

$$=\frac{1}{2}kB_0^{\,2}e^{-\gamma t} \text{ using } \omega\approx\omega_0.$$

54. **(D)**

For $E < V_0$, the two needed wave numbers are

$$k=\sqrt{2mE}/\hbar \text{ and } k'=\sqrt{2m(V_0-E)}/\hbar.$$

The wave function is

$$\phi(x)=\begin{cases} e^{ikx}+re^{-ikx} & x<0 \\ te^{-k'x} & x>0 \end{cases}$$

The boundary conditions give

$$\phi(0) = 1 + r = t$$

$$\phi'(0) = ik - ikr = -k't$$

Solving simultaneously gives $t = -2ik/(k' - ik)$ and the transmission coefficient is

$$T = tt^*$$

$$= (4k^4 + 4k^2 k'^2) / (k^2 + k'^2)^2$$
$$= 4k^2 (k^2 + k'^2) / (k^2 + k'^2)^2$$
$$= 4k^2 / (k^2 + k'^2)$$

55. **(B)**

The given wave function is

$$\phi(x) = \frac{1}{\sqrt{a}} \cos \frac{\pi x}{2a}$$

and we want to find the value of $<x^2>$.

$$<x^2> = \int \phi^* x^2 \phi \, dx$$

$$= \frac{1}{a} \int x^2 \cos^2 \frac{\pi x}{2a} dx$$

Use

$$\cos^2 \theta = \frac{1}{2} + \frac{1}{2} \cos 2\theta$$

to get

$$<x^2> = \frac{1}{a} \int \left(\frac{1}{2} x^2 + \frac{1}{2} x^2 \cos \frac{\pi x}{a}\right) dx$$

Integrate by parts

$$= \frac{1}{a} \left[\frac{1}{6} x^3 + \frac{a}{2\pi} x^2 \sin \frac{\pi x}{a} + \frac{a^2}{\pi^2} x \cos \frac{\pi x}{a} - \frac{a^3}{\pi^3} \sin \frac{\pi x}{a} \right] \Bigg|_{-a}^{a}$$

$$= \frac{1}{a} \left(\frac{1}{3} a^2 + 0 + \frac{-2a^3}{\pi^2} - 0 \right)$$

$$= a^2 \left(\frac{1}{3} - \frac{2}{\pi^2} \right)$$

Note that $<x^2> \neq 0$ but $<x> = 0$.

56. **(E)**

The physics laboratory methods used in medicine and law are quite impressive. Doppler *Vibration Imaging* is based on the Doppler effect. Since malignant tumors are more rigid than nearby healthy tissue, they can be detected by this non-invasive technique. *Ultrasound* uses about 20 KHz sound waves, whereas Doppler vibration imaging uses 200 Hz sound waves. *Positron emission tomography* is commonly used to study brain tissue, the positon is actually anti-matter. Magnetic resonance imaging or *Nuclear Magnetic Resonance* makes use of the flipping of nuclear spins. The *Mössbauer Effect* is the recoil-loss resonance emission or absorption of nuclear radiation (γ-rays).

57. **(C)**

For an RLC circuit, Kirchoff's law gives

$$-RI - LI' - \frac{Q}{C} = 0$$

or differentiating and defining

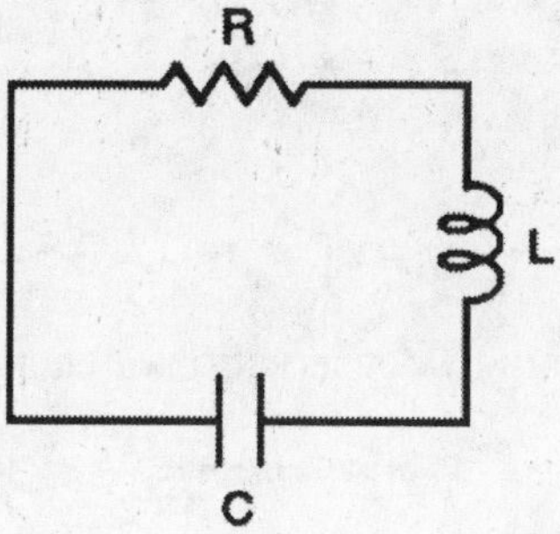

$$\omega_0^{\ 2} = \frac{1}{LC} \text{ and } \gamma = \frac{R}{L}$$

$$I'' + \gamma I' + \omega_0^{\ 2} I = 0$$

for the critical dumping case,

$$\omega_0^{\ 2} = \gamma^2 / 4$$

and the solution is

$$I = (A + Bt)e^{-\gamma t/2}$$

If $I = I_0$ and $I' = 0$ at $t = 0$ then the desired solution is

$$I = I_0(1 + \frac{\gamma}{2}t)e^{-\gamma t/2}.$$

58. **(D)**

An object propelled horizontally at distance r from the center of the Earth into a circular orbit feels a force

$$F = \frac{GmM}{r^2} = \frac{mv^2}{r}$$

Hence

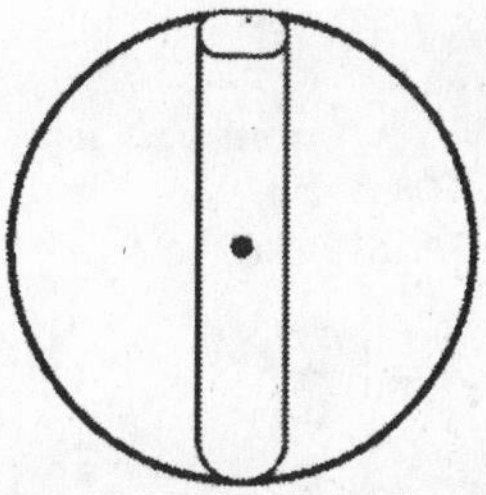

$$v^2 = \frac{GM}{r} \text{ and } v = \sqrt{\frac{GM}{r}} = r\omega$$

The linear frequency is then

$$\nu = \frac{\omega}{2\pi} = \frac{1}{2\pi}\sqrt{\frac{GM}{r^3}}$$

and thus the orbital period is

$$T_r = \frac{1}{\upsilon}$$

$$= 2\pi\sqrt{\frac{r^3}{GM_E}}.$$

It is interesting to note that this is the same as the period of an object dropped from distance $r = r_E$ and falling through a hole in the Earth (see above figure) to execute simple harmonic motion.

59. **(C)**

By conservation of energy

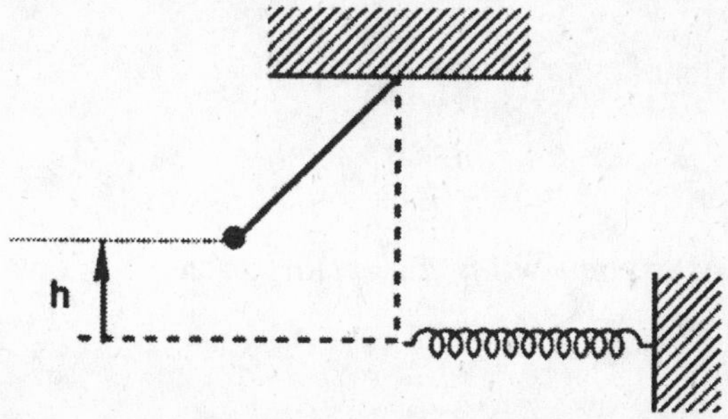

$$mgh = \frac{1}{2}mv^2 \text{ or}$$

$$v = \sqrt{2gh}$$

is the pendulum bob velocity

just before it hits the spring.

The conservative force is

$$F = -kx - bx^3$$

so that

$$U = -\int F\,dx = \frac{1}{2}kx^2 + \frac{1}{4}bx^4.$$

Again by conservation of energy

$$\frac{1}{2}mv^2 = mgh = \frac{1}{2}kx^2 + \frac{1}{4}bx^4$$

Rearranging

$$(x^2 + \frac{k}{b})^2 = \frac{4mgh}{b} + \frac{k^2}{b^2}$$

or $$x = \left(\sqrt{\frac{4mgh}{b} + \frac{k^2}{b^2}} - \frac{k}{b}\right)^{1/2}$$

60. **(A)**

This is Johann Bernoulli's famous brachistochrone problem. By conservation of energy

$$\Delta T = -\Delta V$$

$$\frac{1}{2}mv^2 = mgy \Rightarrow v = \sqrt{2gy}.$$

The action integral

$$A = \int \frac{ds}{v}$$

$$= \int \sqrt{1 + y'^2}\,dx \;/\; \sqrt{2gy}$$

must be minimized. The second form of Euler's equation

$$\frac{\partial f}{\partial x} - \frac{d}{dx}\left(f - y'\frac{\partial f}{\partial y'}\right) = 0$$

is useful since

$$f = \sqrt{1 + y'^2} / \sqrt{y} \neq f(x)$$

Hence $$\frac{d}{dx}\left(f - y'\frac{\partial f}{\partial y'}\right) = 0$$

or $$f - y'\frac{\partial f}{\partial y'} = d$$

After some work, the cycloid equation is obtained.

61. **(A)**

For one-dimensional vertical motion the basic classical mechanics equation is

$$mv' = mg - bv$$

or $$v' = g - \gamma v, \quad \gamma \equiv b/m$$

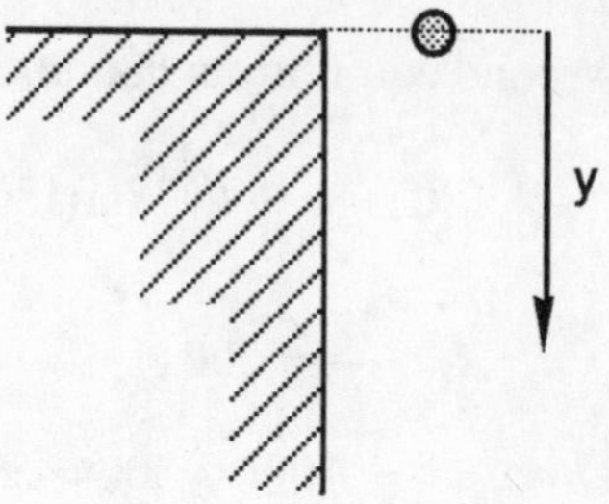

Integrate

$$\int_0^v \frac{dv}{g - \gamma v} = \int_0^t dt$$

by using the u-substitution $u = g - \gamma v$ to get

$$\frac{1}{\gamma}\ln\frac{g-\gamma v}{g} = -t \quad \text{or} \quad v = \frac{g}{\gamma}\left(1 - e^{-\gamma t}\right).$$

Integrate once again to get

$$y = \frac{gt}{\gamma} - \frac{g}{\gamma^2}\left(1 - e^{-\gamma t}\right)$$

Note that $dy / dt = v$.

62. **(A)**

Gauss' law for gravitation is

$$\nabla \cdot \mathbf{g} = -4\pi G\rho$$

in differential form or

$$\oint \mathbf{g} \cdot d\mathbf{a} = -4\pi G m_{in}$$

in integral form. For a single infinite sheet of mass density $\sigma = m / A$ use a Gaussian pillbox as in the figure. Then

$$\oint \mathbf{g} \cdot d\mathbf{a} = -4\pi G m_{in}$$

$$-gA - gA = -4\pi G\sigma A$$

$$2gA = 4\pi G\sigma A$$

$$g = 2\pi G\sigma$$

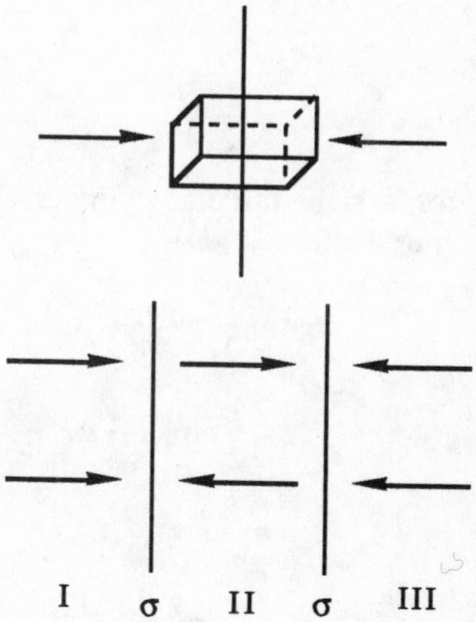

For two sheets, the field will be $4\pi\, G\sigma$ in magnitude in regions I and III and zero in region II.

63. **(D)**

The first condition of equilibrium, that of translational equilibrium, says

$$\Sigma \mathbf{F} = 0.$$

Hence

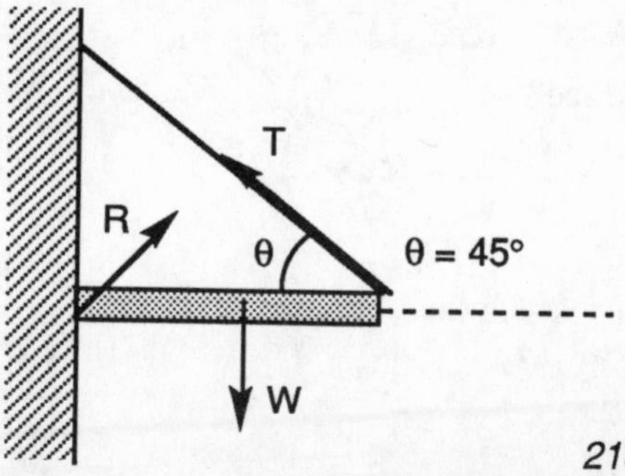

$$\Sigma F_x = R_x - T_x = R_x - \frac{T}{\sqrt{2}} = 0$$

$$\Sigma F_y = R_y + T_y - W$$

$$= R_y + \frac{T}{\sqrt{2}} - mg = 0$$

The second equilibrium condition involves rotation,specifically $\Sigma\tau = 0$. So

$$R(0) - w\frac{l}{2} + Tl\sin(180 - \theta) = 0 \Rightarrow T = \frac{W}{\sqrt{2}}$$

$$R_x = \frac{W}{2} = 500\,\text{N}$$

Thus $\quad R_y = 1000 - 500 = 500\,\text{N}$

In polar coordinate rotation,

$$\mathbf{R} = (707\text{ N}, 45.0°)$$

64. **(D)**

The moment of inertia

$$I = \int r^2\, dm$$

$$= \frac{1}{2}mr^2$$

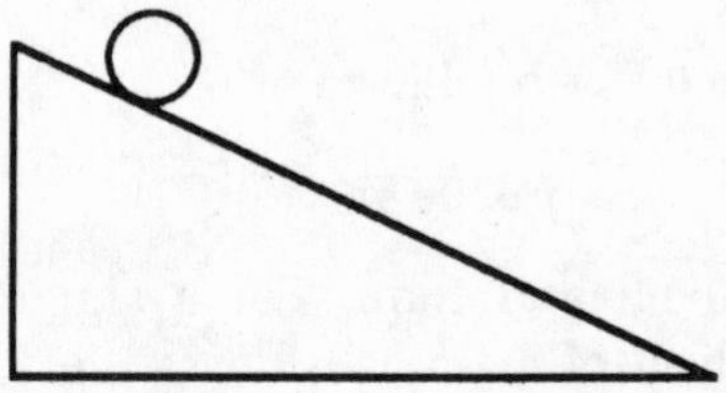

for a right circular cylinder. Then by conservation of energy

$$mgh = \frac{1}{2}mv^2 + \frac{1}{2}I\omega^2\,, \quad v = r\omega$$

$$= \frac{1}{2}mv^2 + \frac{1}{4}mr^2\frac{v^2}{r^2}$$

$$mgh = \frac{3}{4}mv^2$$

$$v_R = 2\sqrt{\frac{gh}{3}}$$

For normal translational motion

$$v_T = \sqrt{2gh}$$

Hence

$$\frac{v_R}{v_T} = \frac{2}{\sqrt{3}} \times \frac{1}{\sqrt{2}}$$

$$= \sqrt{\frac{2}{3}}$$

65. **(A)**

Kepler's Second Law is that the area swept out per unit time by a radius vector from the sun to a planet is constant. By the usual triangle area rule

$$dA = \frac{1}{2}\, r\; rd\theta.$$

Hence

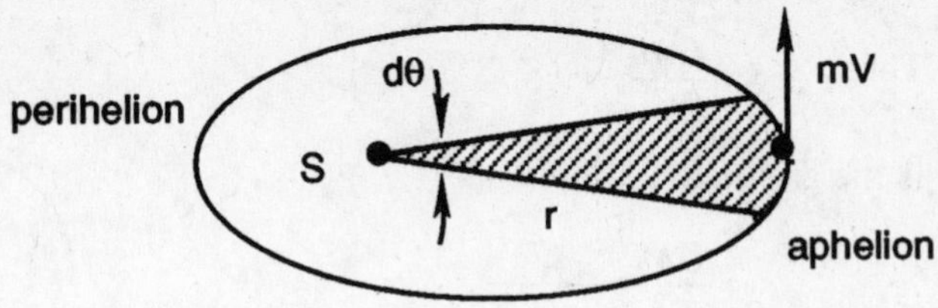

$$\frac{dA}{dt} = \frac{1}{2} r^2 \omega$$

$$= \frac{L}{2m}$$

Since the angular momentum is $L = I\omega = mr^2\omega$. Thus

$$L = \text{constant}$$

$$mv_{ap} 2a = mv_{pe}\, a$$

$$v_{pe} / v_{ap} = 2$$

66. **(A)**

The given mass density is

$$\lambda = M / (\pi R/2)$$

The differential force dF between differential mass element

$$dM = \lambda ds = \lambda R d\theta$$

and m has components

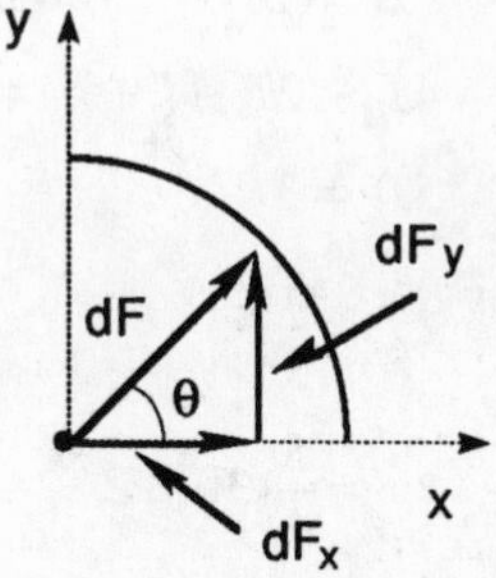

$$dF_x = \frac{Gm\ dM}{R^2} \cos\theta$$

and $dF_y = Gm\ dM \sin\theta / R^2$

Thus $F_x = \dfrac{Gm}{R^2} \lambda R \displaystyle\int_0^{\pi/2} \cos\theta\ d\theta$

$$= Gm \frac{\lambda}{R} = \frac{2GmM}{\pi R^2}$$

and $F_y = \dfrac{Gm}{R^2} \lambda R \displaystyle\int_0^{\pi/2} \sin\theta\ d\theta$

$$= \frac{2GmM}{\pi R^2}$$

Finally $F = \sqrt{F_x^2 + F_y^2} = \dfrac{2\sqrt{2} GmM^2}{\pi R^2}$

and $\mathbf{F} = \left(\dfrac{2\sqrt{2} GmM}{\pi R^2}, 45° \right)$ in polar coordinates.

67. **(E)**

By Newton's universal law of gravitation and the definition of weight

$$\frac{GMm}{r^2} = mg$$

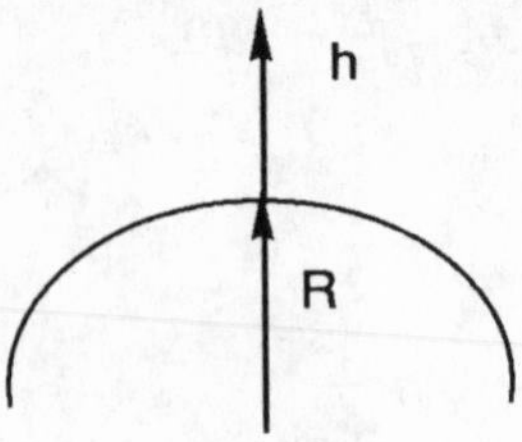

Thus $\quad g = \dfrac{GM}{r^2}$

is the gravitational field.

$$= \frac{GM}{R^2}\frac{1}{(1+x)^2}, \quad x = \frac{h}{R}$$

Use a Taylor expansion to get

$$g = g_0\left[1 - 2\frac{h}{R} + 3\left(\frac{h}{R}\right)^2\right]$$

to 2nd order.

68. **(C)**

The hotter fluid loses heat energy to the cooler one:

Heat lost = heat gained

$$c_1m_1(T_1 - T) = c_2m_2(T - T_2)$$

Assuming equal specific heats $c_1 = c_2 = c$ and with the masses related as given $m_1 = 2m_2$, we get

$$c2m_2(2T_2 - T) = cm_2(T - T_2)$$

$$4T_2 - 2T - T + T_2 = 0$$

$$5T_2 = 3T$$

$$T = \frac{5}{3}T_2$$

$$= \frac{5}{3}(30°)\text{C}$$

$$= 50°\text{C}$$

69. **(E)**

The tide-raising acceleration the moon produces is a differential acceleration between points A and B

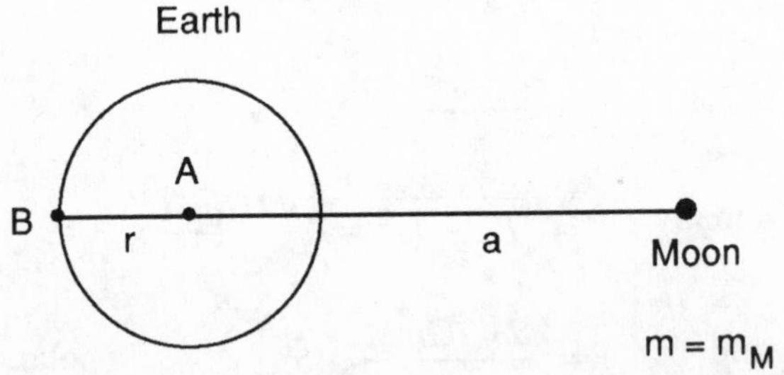

$$\Delta g = g_A - g_B$$

$$= \frac{Gm}{a^2} - \frac{Gm}{(a+r)^2}$$

$$= \frac{Gm}{a^2}\left(1 - \frac{1}{(1+\frac{r}{a})^2}\right)$$

$$= \frac{Gm}{a^2}\left(1 - \left(1 - 2\frac{r}{a}\right)\right)$$

using a series expansion, thus

$$\Delta g = 2Gmr/a^3$$

Tidal acceleration is hence inversely proportional to the distance cubed.

70. **(B)**

Measuring the distance between the two stars in a binary system and knowing the period of revolution allows one to determine the total mass. Kepler's general law (3rd law) is

$$T^2 = 4\pi^2 a^3 / (m_1 + m_2)$$

For the solar system $m_1 = m_0$ and $m_2 = m_{planet}$. Also T = sidereal period. For a binary star system, the period assigned to the system applies to each star. Hence

$$m_T = (m_1 + m_2) = 4\pi^2 a^3 / T^2$$

If $m_1 = m_2 = m$, then

$$m = 2\pi^2 a^3 / T^2$$

gives the mass of one star.

71. **(D)**

The 3-D harmonic oscillator can be used to develop a basic nuclear shell model. Use the Schrödinger equation

$$H\psi = E\psi$$

$$\frac{-\hbar^2}{2m}\nabla^2\psi + U\psi = E\psi$$

with potential energy $U = {}^1/_2\, kr^2$. Because

$$r^2 = x^2 + y^2 + z^2,$$

we get energy eigenvalues

$$E = (n_x + n_y + n_z + \frac{3}{2})\hbar\omega$$

The nucleon has $g = 4$ since we have p, n, and $\uparrow$ and $\downarrow$ spin. For

$$E = \frac{3}{2}\hbar\omega,$$

we get 4 states; for

$$E = \frac{5}{2}\hbar\omega,$$

12 states; and

$$E = \frac{7}{2}\hbar\omega,$$

24 states. Thus 4, 4 + 12 = 16, 4 + 12 + 24 = 40 are magic numbers.

$${}^{4}_{2}\text{He},\ {}^{16}_{8}\text{O},\ \text{and}\ {}^{40}_{20}\text{Ca}$$

are very stable.

72. **(A)**

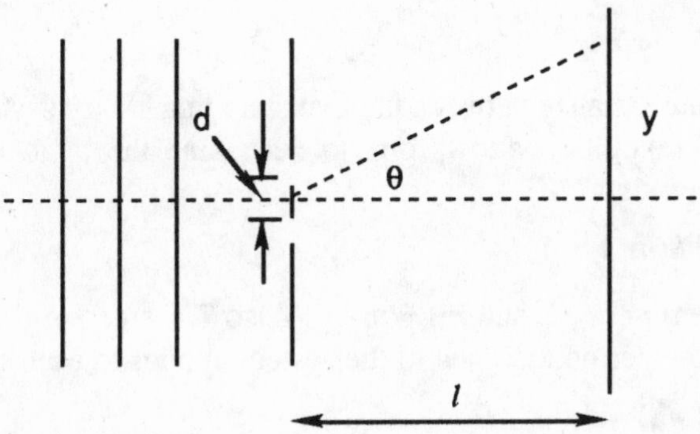

We are given information on the classic Young double slit interference experiment. Plane waves of monochromatic light are incident on the 2 slits. The condition for constructive interference is

$$d \sin\theta = n\lambda.$$

Hence

$$\sin\theta = \frac{\lambda}{d} = \frac{y}{\sqrt{l^2 + y^2}} \approx \frac{y}{l}$$

and $$y = \lambda\frac{l}{d} = \frac{(6000\times10^{-10})(15)}{(0.15\times10^{-3})}$$

$$= .006\text{ m}$$

is the location of the 1st maximum.

73. **(B)**

In the Mayer and Jensen nuclear shell model, the spin-orbit interaction

$$H_{so} = -a\,\mathbf{l}\cdot\mathbf{s}$$

splits levels with the same $\mathbf{l}$ but different

$$\mathbf{j} = \mathbf{s} + \mathbf{l}.$$

For example the $P_{1/2}$ and $P_{3/2}$ states both have $l = 1$ and $s = {}^1/_2$, but the different j values (${}^1/_2$ and ${}^3/_2$) produce different degeneracies (2 and 4). For the nuclide ${}^{17}_{8}\text{O}$, the proton configuration is

$$(1s_{1/2})^2\,(1p_{3/2})^4\,(1p_{1/2})^2$$

and the neutron configuration is

$$(1s_{1/2})^2\,(1p_{3/2})^4\,(1p_{1/2})^2\,(1d_{5/2})^1.$$

The ground state nucleus spin is thus $j = 5/2$ from the unpaired neutron.

74. **(E)**

For a spherical shell, the potential energy is

$$\begin{aligned} dU &= -\frac{G}{r}\left(\frac{4}{3}\pi r^2\rho\right)(4\pi r^2 dr\rho) \\ &= -16\pi^2 G\rho^2 r^4 dr/3 \end{aligned}$$

The stars total gravitational potential energy is then

$$\begin{aligned} U &= -16\pi^2 G\rho^2/3 \int_0^R r^4 dr \\ &= -(16\pi^2 G\rho^2/15)R^5 \end{aligned}$$

Since the volume V and Mass M are

$$V = \frac{4}{3}\pi R^3 \text{ and } M = \frac{4}{3}\pi R^3\rho$$

we may rewrite this as being

$$U = -\frac{3}{5}GM^2/R = -\frac{3}{5}\left(\frac{4\pi}{3}\right)^{1/3} GM^2V^{-1/3}$$

Finally, the gravitational pressure is then

$$\begin{aligned} P &= -\frac{\partial U}{\partial V} = -\frac{1}{5}\left(\frac{4\pi}{3}\right)^{1/3} GM^2V^{-4/3} \\ &= -\left(\frac{4\pi}{375}\right)^{1/3} GM^2 \propto V^{-4/3} \end{aligned}$$

75. **(C)**

There are six leptons:

$$e, \upsilon_e;\ \mu, \upsilon_\mu;\ \text{ and } \tau, \upsilon_\tau.$$

The electron, *mu*, and *tau* increase in mass from 0.511 MeV/c^2 to 105.6 MeV/c^2 to 1784 Mev/c^2; each has charge – e where $e = 1.6 \times 10^{-19}$ C is the fundamental electronic charge. The neutrinos υ_e, υ_μ, and υ_τ are thought to have no mass and and also have zero charge. In nuclear reactions, electron lepton number L_e, mu-lepton number L_μ, and tau-lepton number L_τ are conserved quantities. The antileptons have opposite charge and lepton number: e.g., e has $q = -e$ and $L_e = 1$ but e^+ has $q = +e$ and $L_e = -1$.

76. **(C)**

There are six quarks up, down, strange, charm, bottom, and top or u, d, s, c, b, and t. The up, charm, and top quarks have charges $^2/_3$ e and masses 350, 1800, and ≈ 20,000 MeV/c^2. The down, strange, and bottom quarks have charges $-{}^1/_3$ e and masses 350, 550, and 4500 MeV/c^2. The strange quark has strangeness $S = -1$, the charm quark has charm quantum number $C = 1$, the bottom quark bottomness $B = -1$, and the top quark has top quantum number $T = 1$. Hadrons like the proton and pion are built of quarks and anti-quarks.

77. **(A)**

The theory of radioactive decay proceeds as follows. Let P = probability, then

$$P(1 \text{ decay}) = \lambda dt, \qquad \lambda = \text{decay constant}$$

The differential number of particles decaying is

$$dN = -NP,$$

$$= -\lambda N\, dt$$

$$\int_{N_0}^{N} \frac{dN}{N} = -\int_0^t \lambda\, dt \Rightarrow N = N_0 e^{-\lambda t}$$

The half-life is calculated as an expectation value

$$t = \langle t \rangle = \int_0^\infty te^{-\lambda t}\, dt \,/ \int_0^\infty e^{-\lambda t}\, dt$$

$$= \lambda \left[-\frac{t}{\gamma} e^{-\lambda t} - \frac{1}{\lambda^2} e^{-\lambda t} \right]_0^\infty = \frac{1}{\lambda}$$

where $e^{-\lambda\tau}$ plays the role of a probability function.

78. **(B)**

The Roentgen is the standard unit of radiation exposure. 1 R is the amount of radiation which releases in 1 cc of dry air at STP (.001293 g) one esu of charge (4.803×10^{-20} esu = 1.602×10^{-19} C). The REM or Roentgen-equivalent-man is the amount of radiation which provides the same effect in humans as 1 R of x- or γ-rays. The statements in the problem are in millirems or 10^{-3} REM. Note that a coast-to-coast flight, the natural radioactivity of the body, and living in Denver, Colorado, are natural radiation sources whereas TV (1 mrem per year), a dental x-ray, and a G.I. tract exam (7500 mrem) are obviously human-made radiation sources.

79. **(A)**

The Mössbauer effect, discovered by R. Mössbauer involves the resonance emission or absorption of nuclear radiation without recoil. For the usual emission

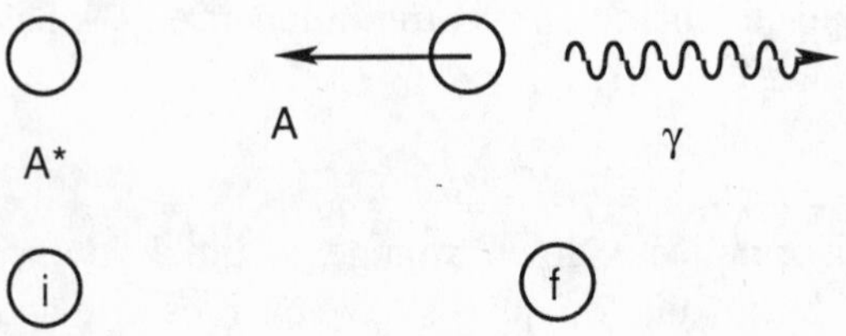

case $A^* \rightarrow A + \gamma$ the initial and final states are shown in the preceding figure. By conservation of momentum the recoil and photon momentum are equal

$$P_R = P_\gamma.$$

Hence the recoil energy is

$$E_R = P_R^2 / 2\,m_A$$
$$= (129 \times 10^3)^2 / 2\,(191)\,(931.5 \times 10^6)$$
$$= .0468 \text{ eV}$$

80. **(E)**

One must use a fat lens formula to solve this kind of problem:

$$-\frac{n}{s}+\frac{n'}{s'}=\frac{n'-n}{R}$$

We are given $n' = 1.7$ and $n = 1.2$. Also $R = 5$ cm and $s = -15$ cm. Thus $s' = 85$ cm.

$$\frac{1.2}{15}+\frac{1.7}{s'}=\frac{0.5}{5} \Rightarrow s'=85\text{ cm}$$

Further

$$s=-\infty \Rightarrow -\frac{n'}{f'}=\frac{n'-n}{R} \text{ or } f'=17\text{ cm and}$$

$$s'=\infty \Rightarrow \frac{-n}{f}-(n'-n)/R \text{ or } f=-12\text{cm}$$

The ray diagram is:

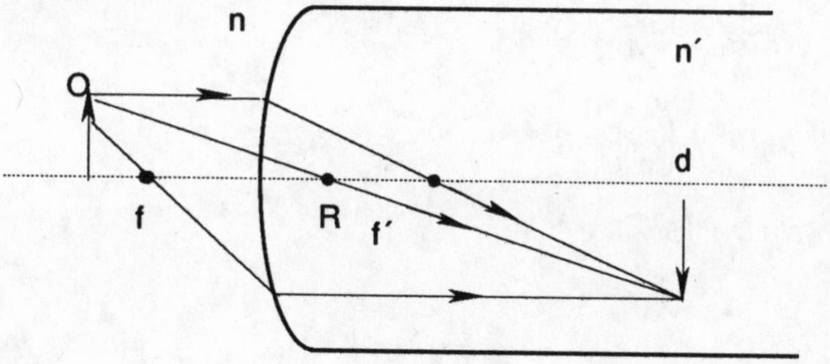

81. **(B)**

Consider transitions between two molecular states i and j. We are usually given that

$$N'_i = N_i B_{ij}\, U(\omega)$$

and $$N'_j = N_j(A_{ji} + B_{ji}\, U(\omega)).$$

Hence

$$\frac{N_i}{N_j} = \left(A_{ji} + B_{ji}U(\omega)\right) / B_{ij}U(\omega)$$

$$E_j - E_i = \hbar\omega$$

But from the Boltzmann factor

$$\frac{N_j}{N_i} = e^{-\hbar\omega B}$$

Thus $$B_{ij}e^{\hbar\omega\beta}U(\omega) = A_{ji} + B_{ji}U(\omega)$$

$$U(\omega) = A_{ji} / (B_{ij}e^{\hbar\omega\beta} - B_{ji})$$

where A_{ji}, B_{ij}, and B_{ji} are the Einstein transition coefficients.

82. **(A)**

The B fields of a single circular current loop may be calculated from the Biot-Savart law

$$d\mathbf{B} = \frac{\mu_0}{4\pi}\frac{Id\mathbf{l}\times\mathbf{s}}{s^2}$$

to be

$$\mathbf{B} = \frac{\mu_0 I r^2}{2(r^2+z^2)^{3/2}}\mathbf{z}$$

along the z-axis.

For Helmholtz coils, we have two such loops, each with N turns, and the field at $z = R/2$ is

$$B = 2N\frac{\mu_0 IR^2}{2\left(R^2+\frac{R^2}{4}\right)^{3/2}}$$

$$= N\mu_0 IR^2 / \left(\frac{5}{4}\right)^{3/2} R^3$$

$$= 8N\mu_0 I / \left(5^{3/2}R\right)$$

83. **(C)**

Consider Faraday's law — Maxwell's 2nd Equation

$$\nabla\times\mathbf{E} = -\frac{\partial\mathbf{B}}{\partial t}$$

A vector identity is

$$\nabla\times(\nabla\times\mathbf{E}) = \nabla(\nabla\cdot\mathbf{E}) - \nabla^2\mathbf{E}$$

Now $\nabla\cdot\mathbf{E} = 0$ in vacuum

$$\Rightarrow -\frac{\partial}{\partial t}\nabla\times\mathbf{B} = -\nabla^2\mathbf{E}.$$

Now use Maxwell's 4th equation

$$\nabla\times\mathbf{B} = \frac{1}{c^2}\frac{\partial\mathbf{E}}{\partial t}$$

to get

$$\nabla^2 E = \frac{1}{c^2}\frac{\partial^2 E}{\partial t^2}.$$

A plane wave solution is

$$\mathbf{E} = \mathbf{y}\, E_{oy} \cos(\omega t - kx + \alpha) + \mathbf{z} \cos(\omega t - kx + \beta)\, E_{oz}$$

If $\alpha = \beta$ and $E_{oy} = E_{oz} = E_o$ then

$$E_x^2 + E_y^2 = E_0^2$$

and we get circular polarization.

84. **(D)**

The potential is that of a real charge q at $z' = h$ and an image charge q at $z'' = -h$

$$\phi = kq\left(\frac{1}{\sqrt{s^2+(z-z')^2}} - \frac{1}{\sqrt{s^2+(z+z')^2}}\right)$$

Note the boundary condition $\phi(z = 0) = 0$ is satisfied. The electric field is then

$$E_z = -\frac{\partial\phi}{\partial z} = kq\left[\frac{z-z'}{(s^2+(z-z')^2)^{3/2}} - \frac{z+z'}{(s^2+(z+z')^2)^{3/2}}\right]$$

$$E(z=0) = -\frac{1}{2\pi\varepsilon_0} qh/(s^2+h^2)^{3/2} \quad \text{using} \quad k = \frac{1}{4\pi\varepsilon_0}$$

and where $s^2 = x^2 + y^2$.

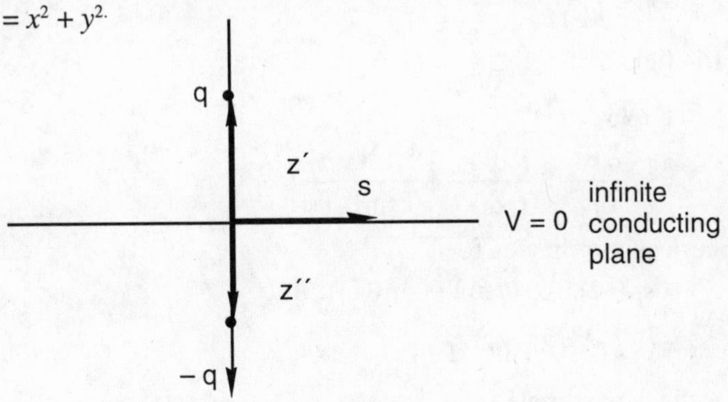

85. **(B)**

The Fraunhofer diffraction intensity pattern is

$$I = I_0 \sin^2\left(\frac{\pi d_w}{\lambda l} y\right) / \left(\frac{\pi d_w}{\lambda l} y\right)^2$$

$$\int_{-\infty}^{\infty} I\, dy = 2\int_0^{\infty} I\, dy$$

$$\frac{\pi d_w}{\lambda l} y = x$$

Let

$$\int_{-\infty}^{\infty} I dy = 2I_0 \int_0^{\infty} \left(\sin^2(x)/x^2\right) dx \frac{\lambda l}{\pi d_w}$$
$$= (2I_0 \lambda l / \pi d_w)(\pi/2)$$
$$= I_0 \lambda l / d_w$$

To do this problem, one needs to know

$$\int_0^{\infty} \frac{\sin x}{x} dx = \int_0^{\infty} \frac{\sin^2 x}{x^2} dx = \frac{\pi}{2}.$$

The physics student should recognize sin (x) / πx as one representation of the Dirac delta function $\delta(x)$.

86. **(A)**

The electric potential is

$$V = k\int \rho d^3 r / r$$
$$= k\hat{r}/r^2 \cdot \int \mathrm{r}\rho \, d^3 r$$
$$= k\hat{r}/r^2 \cdot \mathrm{p}$$

by definition of the dipole moment. Continuing

$$V = k\hat{r} \cdot \mathrm{p}/r^2$$
$$= k\, p \cos\theta / r^2 \cdot$$

for $= \mathrm{p} = p\hat{z}.$

The electric field is

$$\mathrm{E} = -\nabla V$$
$$= -\hat{r}\frac{\partial V}{\partial r} - \hat{\theta}\frac{1}{r}\frac{\partial V}{\partial \theta} - \hat{\phi}\frac{1}{r\sin\theta}\frac{\partial V}{\partial \phi}$$

Using spherical coordinates for ∇

$$= kp((2\cos\theta / r^3)\hat{r} + (\sin\theta / r^3)\boldsymbol{\theta})$$
$$= (k/r^3)(3\hat{r}\cdot\mathbf{p}\hat{r} - \mathbf{p})$$

and this is the usual dipole field.

87. **(B)**

For a particle on the surface of a sphere in spherical coordinates

$$x = r \sin\theta \cos\phi$$
$$y = r \sin\theta \sin\phi$$
$$z = r\cos\theta$$

and $x^2 + y^2 + z^2 = r^2 = R^2.$

The potential energy is

$$U = mg\,z = mg\,R\cos\theta$$

and $\quad v^2 = R^2\theta'^2 + R^2\phi'^2\sin^2\theta$

since $\quad r' = \frac{d}{dt}(R) = 0.$

Hence the Lagrangian function is

$$L = T - U = {}^1/_2\, m(R^2\theta'^2 + R^2\phi'^2\sin^2\theta) - mg\,R\cos\theta.$$

88. **(C)**

The electric field of an infinite sheet of surface charge may be found from Gauss' law.

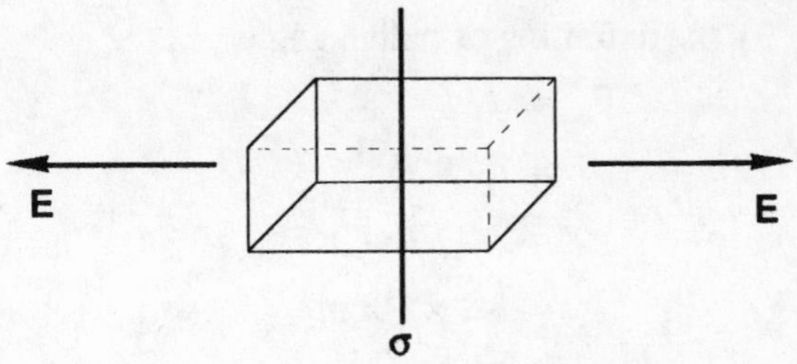

$$\nabla\cdot\mathbf{E} = \rho/\varepsilon_0$$

$$\oint \mathbf{E}\cdot d\mathbf{a} = q_{in}/\varepsilon_0$$

Recognizing that $\mathbf{E}\cdot d\mathbf{a}$ is only non-zero on the left and right side faces of the Gaussian pill box, we get

$$EA + EA = \sigma A/\varepsilon_0$$

or
$$\mathbf{E} = \begin{cases} \sigma/2\varepsilon_0\mathbf{x}, & x > 0 \\ -\sigma/2\varepsilon_0\mathbf{x}, & x < 0 \end{cases}$$

The electric potential must be such that

$$\mathbf{E} = -\nabla V = -\frac{\partial V}{\partial x}\mathbf{x}$$

thus

$$V = -\int \mathbf{E}\cdot d\mathbf{r} = -\int E\,dx$$
$$= -\sigma x/2\varepsilon_0$$

for $x > 0$ as desired.

89. **(D)**

The electric potential of a grounded conducting sphere in a uniform electric field is easily found and given as

$$\Phi(r,\theta) = -E_0 r\left(1 - \left(\frac{a}{r}\right)^3\right)\cos\theta$$

The electric field has two components

$$E_\theta = -\frac{1}{r}\frac{\partial\Phi}{\partial\theta} = -E_0\left(1 - \left(\frac{a}{r}\right)^3\right)\sin\theta$$

(As $r \to a$, clearly $E_\theta \to 0$.) and

$$E_r = -\frac{\partial\Phi}{\partial r} = E_0\left[1 + 2\frac{a^3}{r^3}\right]\cos\theta$$

the surface charge is thus

$$\sigma_\theta = \varepsilon_0 E(r = a) = 3\,\varepsilon_0 E_0 \cos\theta.$$

90. **(B)**

The limiting angle of resolution of a circular aperture is

$$\theta_m = 1.22\frac{\lambda}{\rho}$$

where λ is the light wavelength and D is the lens diameter. We are given λ = 6000 Å and D = 3 mm. Hence

$$\theta_m = 1.22\,\frac{6000 \times 10^{-10}}{3 \times 10^{-3}} = 2.44 \times 10^{-4} \text{ rad}$$

By the definition of radian angle

$$\theta_m = d / l$$

then

$$l = d / \theta_m$$
$$= 2.0 / 2.44 \times 10^{-7}$$
$$= 8.2 \times 10^3 \text{ m}$$
$$= 8.2 \text{ km}$$

Because of smog and haziness, one can rarely see this distance.

91. **(B)**

The deviation angle of a prism at nearly normal incidence is found from Snell's law and geometry

$$n_i \sin\theta_{i1} = n_r \sin\theta_{r1}$$

or

$$n_i\theta_{i1} = n_r\theta_{r1}$$

and

$$n_r\theta_{i2} = n_i\theta_{r2}$$

in the small angle approximation.

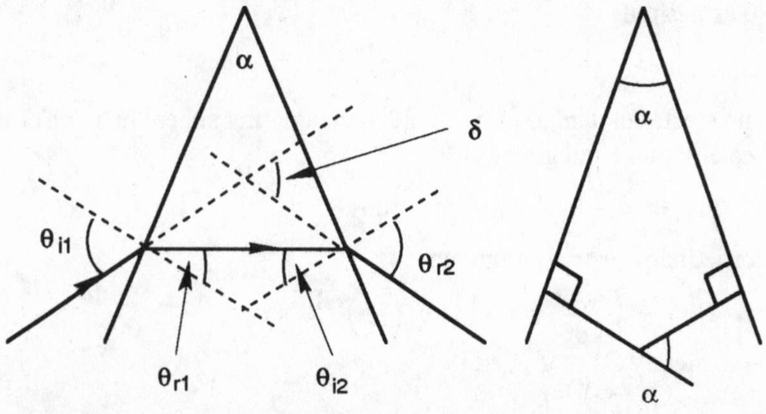

The total deviation angle has 2 parts:

$$\delta = (\theta_{i1} - \theta_{r1}) + (\theta_{r2} - \theta_{i2})$$
$$= \frac{n_r}{n_i}\theta_{r1} - \theta_{r1} + \frac{n_r}{n_i}\theta_{i2} - \theta_{i2}$$
$$= \left(\frac{n_r}{n_i} - 1\right)(\theta_{r1} + \theta_{i2})$$

Observe that

$$\alpha = \theta_{r1} + \theta_{i2}.$$

Thus

$$\delta = \left(\frac{n_r}{n_i} - 1\right)\alpha$$

for θ_{i1} small at near normal incidence.

92. **(E)**

Fluorescence is an emission of electromagnetic radiation which takes place rapidly in $t \sim 10^{-8}$ s. This is the natural lifetime of the molecular or atomic excited state. At STP, a molecule undergoes 100 or more collisions in this time and hence the fluorescence is usually quenched. Ultraviolet photons are commonly used to generate lower energy quanta via the Stokes transition. When there is an appreciable delay $t >> 10^{-8}$ s, the emission is called phosphorescence. A quantum of light is scattered in the Compton effect off of electrons, but no such scattering occurs in fluorescence.

93. **(B)**

The truth tables for circuits are very much related to standard mathematical logic truth tables. Let $T = 1$ and $F = 0$. Then, there are four cases

		A or B	**A and B**		**output**
A	B	$A \vee B$	$A \wedge B$	A NAND B	A XOR B
1	1	1	1	0	0
1	0	1	0	1	1
0	1	1	0	1	1
0	0	0	0	1	0

where we have shown $A \vee B$ and $A \wedge B$ as examples.

94. **(D)**

Adding negative feedback to an amplifier results in decreased gain, decreased distortion, increased input impedance, and decreased output impedance.

95. **(E)**

The oscilloscope measures the voltage across the resistor R and hence the current through R. For positive input voltage, the diode conducts. For negative input voltage, the diode only conducts when the voltage across the diode exceeds 5 volts. Thus the input AC voltage is chopped as shown.

96. **(B)**

A lock-in amplifier is a phase sensitive detector. It detects signals at the same frequency and phase as the reference signal. This produces a DC signal which then goes through a low pass filter with time constant RC. The effect is to reject noise at frequencies more than 1/RC away from ω. That is to say, the lock-in amplifier acts like a narrow band amplifier at frequency ω with bandpass of about 1/RC.

97. **(D)**

This is a simple difference amplifier.

98. **(E)**

This problem is very similar to motion in a constant gravitational field. By the definition of electric field:

$$F = qE = -eE = ma$$

$$\Rightarrow a = -eE/m$$

$$= -(1.6 \times 10^{-19})(100)/(9.1 \times 10^{-31})$$

$$= -1.76 \times 10^{13} \text{ m/s}^2$$

Then from kinematics

$$v_y = v_{oy} + at$$

$$0 = v_o \sin\theta + at$$

$$t = -v_o \sin\theta / a$$

$$T = -2 v_o \sin\theta / a$$

$$= -2(4 \times 10^5)(\sin 30°)/(-1.76 \times 10^{13})$$

$$= 2.3 \times 10^{-8} \text{ s}$$

$$= 23 \text{ ns}$$

since the time of flight is twice the time to reach the apex.

99. **(E)**

A retarder is an optical element used to change the polarization of an incident wave. The phase difference produced $\Delta\phi$ is called the retardance. The optical device is a full wave plate when $\Delta\phi = 2\pi$ rad. The optical device is a half-wave plate when the retardance is π rad. Similarly, the quarter-wave plate causes a phase shift of $\pi/2$ rad. A compensator impresses a controllable retardance on a wave; this retardance can be varied continuously.

100. **(A)**

By Faraday's law or Maxwell's 2nd equation:

$$\nabla \times \mathbf{E} = -\frac{\partial \mathbf{B}}{\partial t}$$

$$\oint \mathbf{E} \cdot d\mathbf{r} = -\frac{d\phi_B}{dt}$$

Thus the induced voltage is

$$V = \frac{d}{dt}\int \mathbf{B} \cdot d\mathbf{a}$$

$$= \frac{d}{dt} B \times w$$

$$= Bwv$$

By Kirchhoff's law

$$V = RI.$$

Thus $Bwv = RI$

$$v = RI / Bw$$

$$= (2\ \Omega)\ (0.5\ \text{A}) / (1T)\ (0.5\ \text{m})$$

$$= 2\ \text{m/s}.$$

The Graduate Record Examination in

PHYSICS

Test 3

THE GRADUATE RECORD EXAMINATION IN PHYSICS

TEST 3 – ANSWER SHEET

1. (A) (B) (C) (D) (E)
2. (A) (B) (C) (D) (E)
3. (A) (B) (C) (D) (E)
4. (A) (B) (C) (D) (E)
5. (A) (B) (C) (D) (E)
6. (A) (B) (C) (D) (E)
7. (A) (B) (C) (D) (E)
8. (A) (B) (C) (D) (E)
9. (A) (B) (C) (D) (E)
10. (A) (B) (C) (D) (E)
11. (A) (B) (C) (D) (E)
12. (A) (B) (C) (D) (E)
13. (A) (B) (C) (D) (E)
14. (A) (B) (C) (D) (E)
15. (A) (B) (C) (D) (E)
16. (A) (B) (C) (D) (E)
17. (A) (B) (C) (D) (E)
18. (A) (B) (C) (D) (E)
19. (A) (B) (C) (D) (E)
20. (A) (B) (C) (D) (E)
21. (A) (B) (C) (D) (E)
22. (A) (B) (C) (D) (E)
23. (A) (B) (C) (D) (E)
24. (A) (B) (C) (D) (E)
25. (A) (B) (C) (D) (E)
26. (A) (B) (C) (D) (E)
27. (A) (B) (C) (D) (E)
28. (A) (B) (C) (D) (E)
29. (A) (B) (C) (D) (E)
30. (A) (B) (C) (D) (E)
31. (A) (B) (C) (D) (E)
32. (A) (B) (C) (D) (E)
33. (A) (B) (C) (D) (E)
34. (A) (B) (C) (D) (E)
35. (A) (B) (C) (D) (E)
36. (A) (B) (C) (D) (E)
37. (A) (B) (C) (D) (E)
38. (A) (B) (C) (D) (E)
39. (A) (B) (C) (D) (E)
40. (A) (B) (C) (D) (E)
41. (A) (B) (C) (D) (E)
42. (A) (B) (C) (D) (E)
43. (A) (B) (C) (D) (E)
44. (A) (B) (C) (D) (E)
45. (A) (B) (C) (D) (E)
46. (A) (B) (C) (D) (E)
47. (A) (B) (C) (D) (E)
48. (A) (B) (C) (D) (E)
49. (A) (B) (C) (D) (E)
50. (A) (B) (C) (D) (E)
51. (A) (B) (C) (D) (E)
52. (A) (B) (C) (D) (E)
53. (A) (B) (C) (D) (E)
54. (A) (B) (C) (D) (E)
55. (A) (B) (C) (D) (E)
56. (A) (B) (C) (D) (E)
57. (A) (B) (C) (D) (E)
58. (A) (B) (C) (D) (E)
59. (A) (B) (C) (D) (E)
60. (A) (B) (C) (D) (E)
61. (A) (B) (C) (D) (E)
62. (A) (B) (C) (D) (E)
63. (A) (B) (C) (D) (E)
64. (A) (B) (C) (D) (E)
65. (A) (B) (C) (D) (E)
66. (A) (B) (C) (D) (E)
67. (A) (B) (C) (D) (E)
68. (A) (B) (C) (D) (E)
69. (A) (B) (C) (D) (E)
70. (A) (B) (C) (D) (E)
71. (A) (B) (C) (D) (E)
72. (A) (B) (C) (D) (E)
73. (A) (B) (C) (D) (E)
74. (A) (B) (C) (D) (E)
75. (A) (B) (C) (D) (E)
76. (A) (B) (C) (D) (E)
77. (A) (B) (C) (D) (E)
78. (A) (B) (C) (D) (E)
79. (A) (B) (C) (D) (E)
80. (A) (B) (C) (D) (E)
81. (A) (B) (C) (D) (E)
82. (A) (B) (C) (D) (E)
83. (A) (B) (C) (D) (E)
84. (A) (B) (C) (D) (E)
85. (A) (B) (C) (D) (E)
86. (A) (B) (C) (D) (E)
87. (A) (B) (C) (D) (E)
88. (A) (B) (C) (D) (E)
89. (A) (B) (C) (D) (E)
90. (A) (B) (C) (D) (E)
91. (A) (B) (C) (D) (E)
92. (A) (B) (C) (D) (E)
93. (A) (B) (C) (D) (E)
94. (A) (B) (C) (D) (E)
95. (A) (B) (C) (D) (E)
96. (A) (B) (C) (D) (E)
97. (A) (B) (C) (D) (E)
98. (A) (B) (C) (D) (E)
99. (A) (B) (C) (D) (E)
100. (A) (B) (C) (D) (E)

GRE PHYSICS
TEST 3

TIME: 170 Minutes
100 Questions

DIRECTIONS: Each of the questions or incomplete statements below is followed by five answer choices or completions. Choose the best answer to each question.

1. Let the point of application of a force **F** = (5, 3, –2) *N* be at position **r** = (–2, 1, –3)*m*. Calculate the torque τ due to this force.

(A) $7\mathbf{x} - 19\mathbf{y} - 11\mathbf{z}\ N-m$

(B) $11\mathbf{x} + 11\mathbf{y} + 1\mathbf{z}\ N-m$

(C) $-10\mathbf{x} + 3\mathbf{y} + 6\mathbf{z}\ N-m$

(D) $-11\mathbf{x} - 11\mathbf{y} - 1\mathbf{z}\ N-m$

(E) $-7\mathbf{x} + 19\mathbf{y} + 11\mathbf{z}\ N-m$

2. Julie, a physics student, stands on top of a 50 m cliff. She releases one stone with a downward speed of 1.0 m/s. With what speed must she project a second stone 0.5 s later at a 35° angle if both stones are to hit the bottom at the same time?

(A) 3.28 m/s

(B) 2.00 m/s

(C) 4.00 m/s

(D) 1.51 m/s

(E) 8.60 m/s

3. A cylindrical bucket of cross sectional area A, initial mass m_0, and initial speed v_0 moves through space, picks up space debris of density ρ (uniformly distributed over A), and slows down. Use Newtonian mechanics to

find the velocity of the bucket as a function of time t.

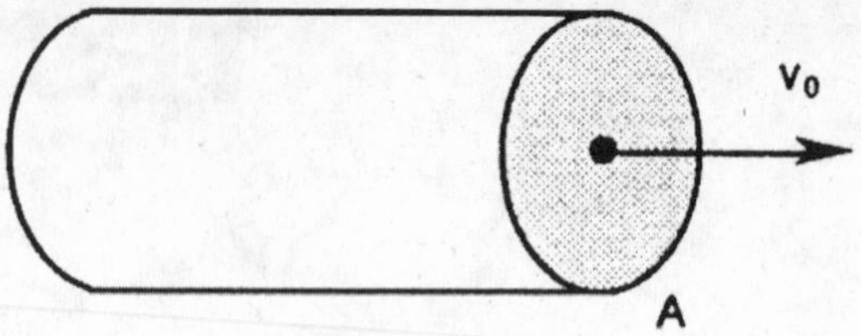

(A) $v = v_0$

(B) $v = v_0 e^{-\rho A v_0 t / m_0}$

(C) $v = v_0 / \sqrt{1 + 2\rho A v_0 t / m_0}$

(D) $v = v_0 e^{-2\rho A v_0 t / m_0}$

(E) $v = v_0 / \sqrt{1 + \rho A v_0 t / m_0}$

4. Consider two reference frames K and K', where K' moves relative to K with speed $v = c(1 - \delta)$ along the xx' axes. Consider a particle moving with speed $u'_x = c(1 - \delta)$ in K'. Find this particle's speed in the lab frame K to order δ^2. Note $\delta << 1$.

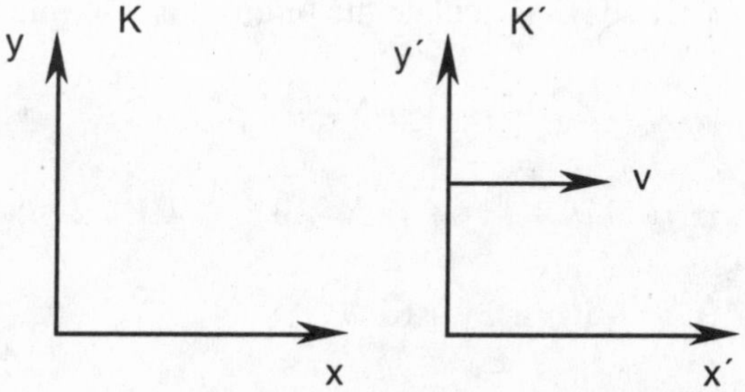

(A) $2c(1 - \delta)$

(B) $c(1-\delta^2/2)$

(C) $c(1 - \delta)$

(D) $c(1 - \delta/2)$

(E) $c(1-\delta^2)$

5. Consider two equal masses $m_1 = m_2 = m$ that are attracted gravitationally. Suppose that the masses are initially a distance $\mathbf{r}_0$ apart and that one mass is given a velocity $\mathbf{v}_0$ perpendicular to $\mathbf{r}_0$. For what values of v_0 will the masses be bound in elliptical motion?

(A) $v_0 > 2\sqrt{Gm / r_0}$

(B) $v_0 > \sqrt{Gm / r_0}$

(C) $v_0 = \sqrt{Gm / r_0}$

(D) $v_0 < 2\sqrt{Gm / r_0}$

(E) $v_0 < \sqrt{Gm / r_0}$

6. According to special relativity, a clock at the North pole must measure a longer time interval than a clock at the equator of the Earth. Suppose that the polar clock reads $T = 100$ years. By how many seconds does the clock at the equator differ? ($r_E = 6.4 \times 10^6$ m)

(A) 1.90×10^{-3} s

(B) 3.79×10^{-3} s

(C) 5.70×10^{-3} s

(D) 7.58×10^{-3} s

(E) 9.48×10^{-3} s

7. Two balls are thrown vertically upward at the same time. Suppose that the balls have initial velocities v_1 = 20 m/s and v_2 = 24 m/s, respectively. Find the distance between the two balls when ball one is at its maximum height.

(A) 20.40 m

(B) 28.56 m

(C) 16.28 m

(D) 8.14 m

(E) 14.28 m

8. Consider two masses m_1 and m_2 moving on a frictionless surface as shown. Find the distance x of maximum compression of the spring.

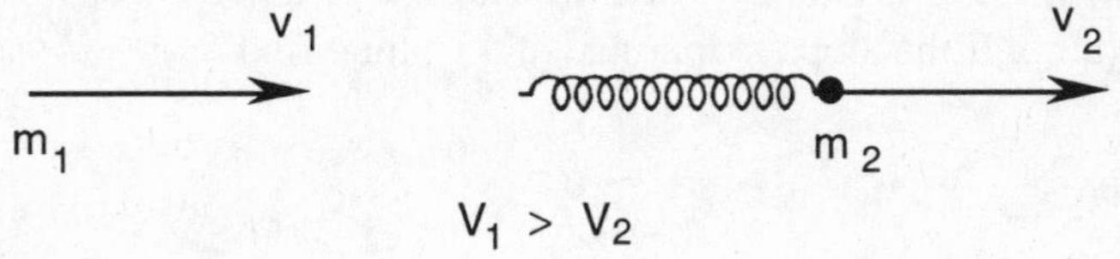

(A) $\sqrt{m_1/k}\,v_1$

(B) $\sqrt{m_2/k}\,v_2$

(C) $\sqrt{(m_1+m_2)/k}\,(v_1-v_2)$

(D) $\sqrt{(m_1+m_2)/k}\,(v_1+v_2)$

(E) $\sqrt{m_1m_2/(m_1+m_2)k}\,(v_1-v_2)$

9. Imagine a type of cylindrical shell as pictured. Initially a solid cylinder of mass M and radius R is rotating with angular velocity ω_0; then the shell, of mass m, collapses onto the cylinder. What is the final angular velocity of the system?

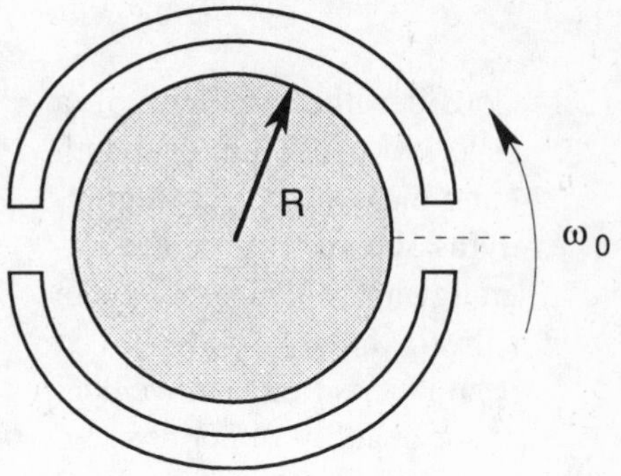

(A) $M\omega_0/(M+m)$

(B) $m\omega_0/(M+m)$

(C) $M\omega_0/(M + 2m)$ (D) $m\omega_0/M$

(E) $M\omega_0/m$

10. A mass m is subject to the gravitational force and attached by a string to a second mass m'. Supposing that the pulley has a finite moment of inertia I, find the acceleration of mass m. Assume friction is negligible.

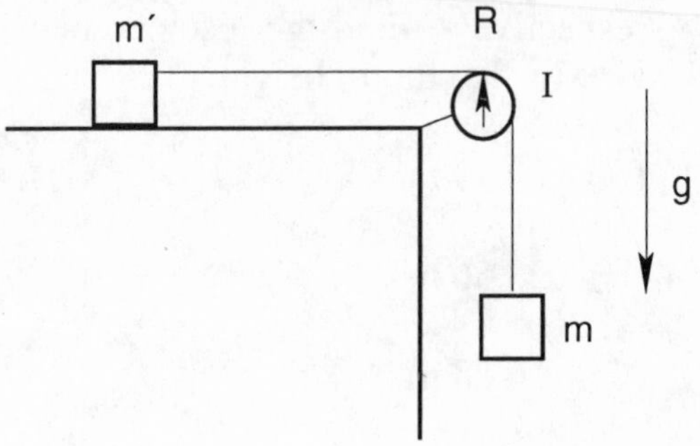

(A) $mg/(I/R^2 + m + m')$

(B) g

(C) mg/m'

(D) $mg/(m + m')$

(E) $(m - m')g/(I/R^2)$

11. A skier leaves a ski jump ramp at an angle of 14° with an initial speed of 11 m/s. Later he lands down the slope a distance l from where he started the jump. If the slope is inclined at 45°, then find l.

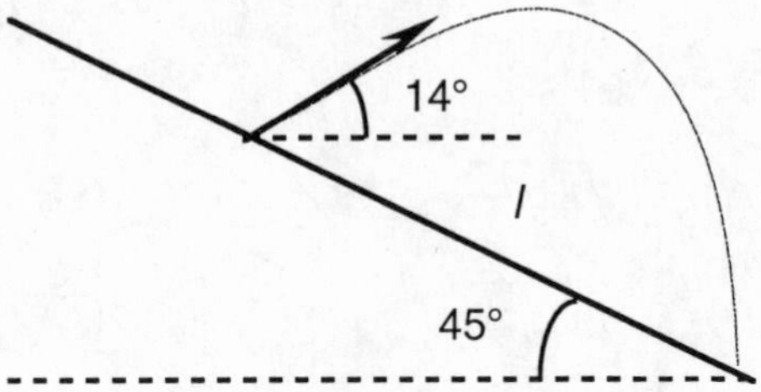

(A) 20.5 m

(B) 41.1 m

(C) 82.0 m

(D) 61.5 m

(E) 10.2 m

12. Consider the problem of a spherical pendulum of length l and mass m subject to gravity as shown. Derive the Lagrangian for this problem in spherical coordinates. The pendulum is free to move both in the x and y directions and would hang (at rest) parallel to the z-axis.

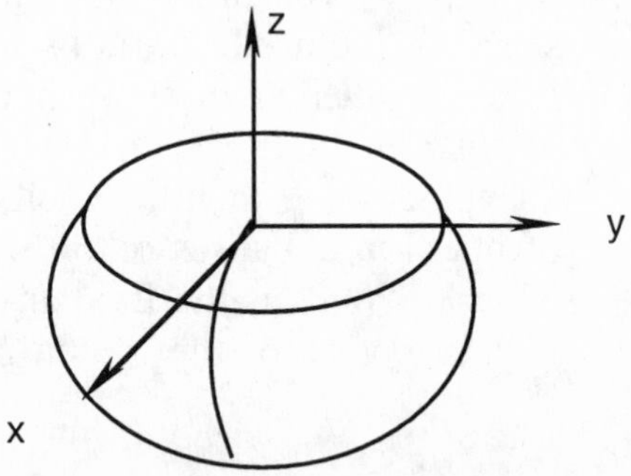

(A) $1/2\, m\, l^2(\theta'^2 + \phi'^2 \sin^2\theta)$ - $mg\, l\, (1 + \cos\theta)$

(B) $1/2\, m\, l^2\, \theta'^2 - mg\, l\, (1 + \cos\theta)$

(C) $1/2\, m\, l^2\, (\theta'^2 + \phi'^2 \sin^2\theta) - mg\, l\, (1 - \cos\theta)$

(D) $1/2\, m\, l^2\, \phi'^2 \sin^2\theta - mg\, l\, (1 + \cos\theta)$

(E) $1/2\, m\, l^2\, (\theta'^2 + \phi'^2) - mg\, l \cos\theta$

13. Picture a particle of mass m that is constrained to move on the surface of a cylinder $x^2 + y^2 = R^2$ and subject to a force $\mathbf{F} = -k\mathbf{r}$. Find the Hamiltonian in the appropriate cylindrical coordinate system.

(A) $H = 1/2\, m\, z'^2 + 1/2\, k\, z^2$

(B) $H = 1/2\, m\, (R^2\theta'^2 + z'^2) + 1/2\, k\, (R^2 + z^2)$

(C) $H = 1/2\, m\, R^2\, (\theta'^2 + \phi'^2 \sin^2\theta) + 1/2\, k\, R^2$

(D) $H = 1/2\, m\, R^2\, \phi'^2 \sin^2\theta + 1/2\, k\, R^2$

(E) $H = 1/2\, m\, R^2\theta'^2 + 1/2\, k\, R^2$

14. Suppose that the disk of radius R shown is in equilibrium. Note that the incline has a coefficient of static friction $\mu_s = \mu$. Find the tension in the cord.

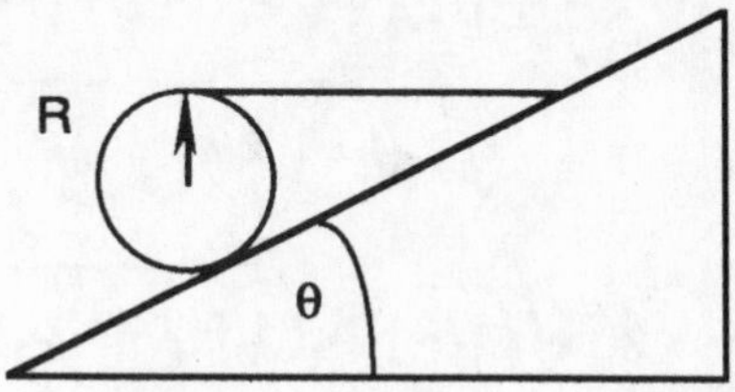

(A) $T = mg \sin\theta$

(B) $T = mg \cos\theta$

(C) $T = mg \sin\theta / (1 + \cos\theta)$

(D) $T = mg \cos\theta / (1 + \sin\theta)$

(E) $T = mg\, (1 + \cos\theta)/\sin\theta$

15. Imagine that an object of mass m (m = 2kg) has position vector $\mathbf{r} = (3t + 5t^3)\mathbf{x}$. Calculate the work done on the particle over the time interval from 0 to 1 s.

(A) 78 J

(B) 157 J

(C) 235 J

(D) 315 J

(E) 393 J

16. Derive Kepler's 3rd law from the assumption that the Earth moves in a circular orbit about the sun of radius $r = 1.50 \times 10^{13}$ cm. Use this information to calculate the mass of the sun.

(A) 2.5×10^{31} g

(B) 5.0×10^{31} g

(C) 3.5×10^{32} g

(D) 1.0×10^{33} g

(E) 2.0×10^{33} g

17. A block of mass m moving at speed v collides with a spring of restoring force $F = -k_1x - k_2x^3$ on a frictionless surface. Find the maximum compression of the spring.

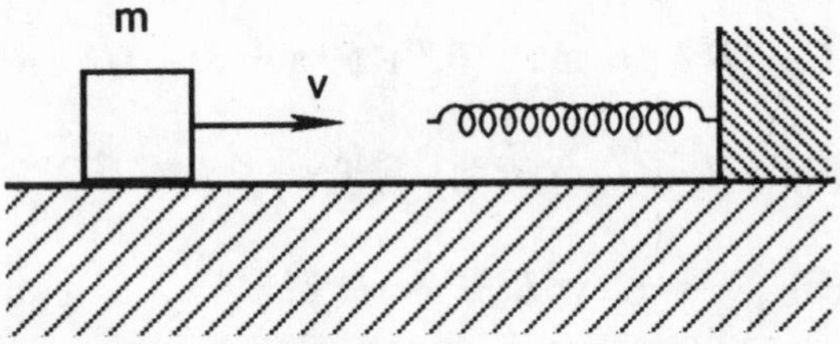

(A) $\sqrt{k_1/k_2}$

(B) $k_1/k_2\left(\sqrt{1 + mv^2k_2/k_1^2} - 1\right)$

(C) $\sqrt{k_1/k_2}\left(\sqrt{1 + mv^2k_2/k_1^2} - 1\right)^{1/2}$

(D) $k_1/k_2\left(\sqrt{1 + 2mv^2k_2/k_1^2} - 1\right)$

(E) $\sqrt{k_1/k_2}\left(\sqrt{1 + 2mv^2k_2/k_1^2} - 1\right)^{1/2}$

18. A dumbbell type molecule is modelled as two spheres of radius r and mass m separated by distance $2l$ as pictured. Suppose that the angular frequency $\omega = \omega_y y + \omega_z z$. Find the angular momentum of the molecule.

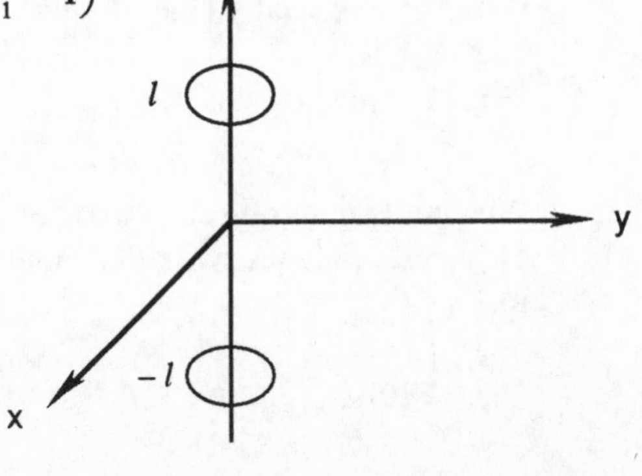

(A) $L_x = 0, L_y = 4/5\ mr^2\omega_y, L_z = 4/5\ mr^2\omega_z$

(B) $L_x = 0, L_y = 2\ m^2\omega_y, L_z = 4/5\ mr^2\omega_z$

(C) $L_x = 2/5\ mr^2\omega_z, L_y = 4/5\ mr^2\omega_y, L_z = 0$

(D) $L_x = 0, L_y = (4/5\ mr^2 + 2ml^2)\omega_y, L_z = 4/5\ mr^2\omega_z$

(E) $L_x = 0, L_y = (2/5\ mr^2 + 2ml^2)\omega_y, L_z = 2/5\ mr^2\omega_z$

19. The executive toy in its simplest form is made of two identical masses hanging from a pivoting rod as shown. If each mass is m and the lengths are L for each arm and l for the pivot, derive the condition under which the toy is stable.

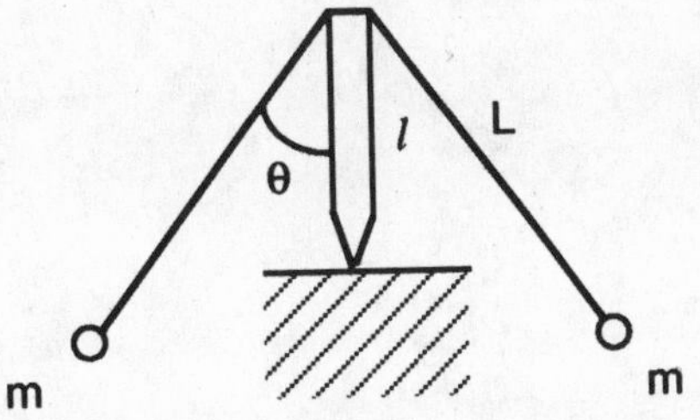

(A) $L \cos\theta > l$

(B) $\theta < 45°$

(C) $L \cos\theta > l$

(D) $\theta < 30°$

(E) $L > l$

20. Consider the flow of an incompressible fluid through a horizontal pipe as shown. Determine the pressure difference $p_2 - p_1$ in terms of the cross sectional areas and the flow velocity v_1 at the left.

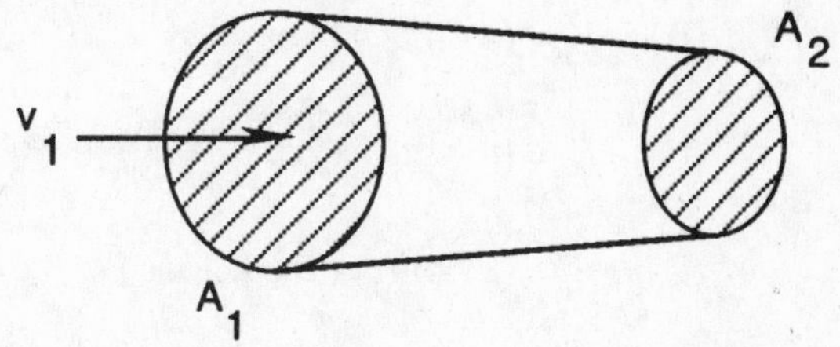

(A) $1/2\rho\, v_1^2\, (1 - A_1^2/A_2^2)$

(B) $1/2\rho\, v_1^2$

(C) $1/2\rho\, v_1^2\, (1 + A_1^2/A_2^2)$

(D) $1/2\rho\, v_1^2\, A_1^2/A_2^2$

(E) $1/2\rho\, v_1^2\, (1 - A_2^2/A_1^2)$

21. Consider the problem of four infinite charged planes situated as shown. Find the electric field in the region $|x| < a/2$. (See figure)

(A) $\sigma / 2\varepsilon_0 \, \mathbf{x}$

(B) $-\sigma / 2\varepsilon_0 \, \mathbf{x}$

(C) $2\sigma / \varepsilon_0 \, \mathbf{x}$

(D) $-2\sigma / \varepsilon_0 \, \mathbf{x}$

(E) 0

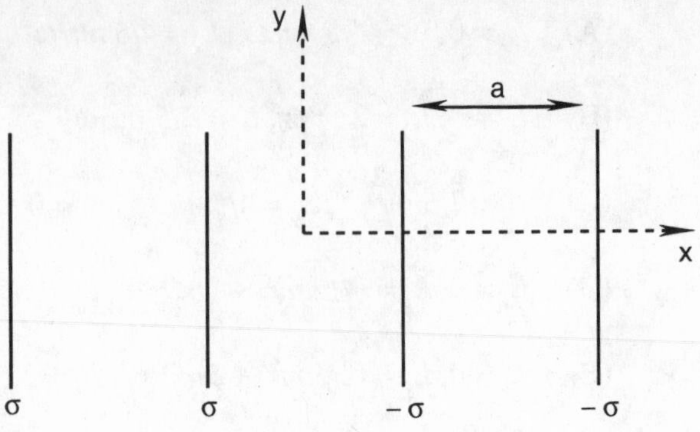

22. A wedge capacitor has potential $\Phi\,(\phi = 0) = 0$ and $\Phi\,(\phi = \alpha) = V_0$. Assume that the two plates are infinite. Find the electric field between the capacitor plates.

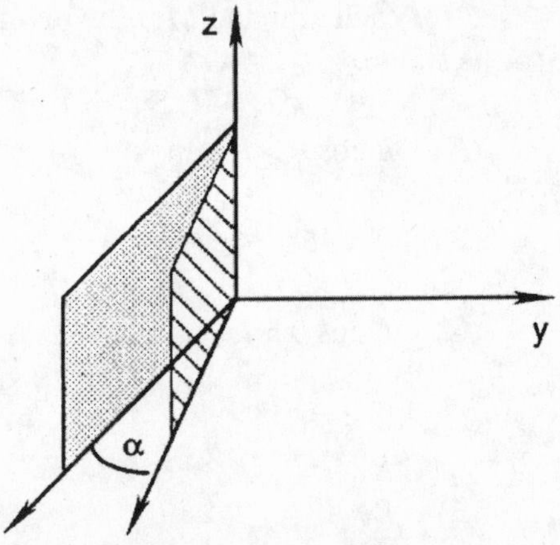

(A) $\mathbf{E} = -\dfrac{V_0\phi}{\alpha\rho}\hat{\phi}$

(B) $\mathbf{E} = -\dfrac{V_0\phi}{\alpha}\hat{\phi}$

(C) $\mathbf{E} = -\dfrac{V_0}{\alpha}\hat{\phi}$

(D) $\mathbf{E} = -\dfrac{V_0}{\alpha\rho}\hat{\phi}$

(E) $\mathbf{E} = -\dfrac{V_0}{\rho}\hat{\phi}$

23. A neutral hydrogen atom may be thought of as a proton orbited by an electron. Supposing that the electron's charge density is $\rho(\mathbf{r}) = e\,(\delta\,(\mathbf{r}) - (\alpha^3 / \pi)\, e^{-2\alpha r})$, calculate the radial electric field E_r.

(A) $E_r = (e / 4\pi\varepsilon_0)\, r^2$

(B) $E_r = (e / 4\pi\varepsilon_0)\, r^2 e^{-2\alpha r}$

(C) $E_r = (e / 4\pi\varepsilon_0)\, (2\alpha/r + 1/r^2)^2 e^{-2\alpha r}$

(D) $E_r = (e / 4\pi\varepsilon_0)\, (2\alpha^2 + 2\alpha/r)\, e^{-2\alpha r}$

(E) $E_r = (e / 4\pi\varepsilon_0)\, (2\alpha^2 + 2\alpha/r + 1/r^2)\, e^{-2\alpha r}$

24. A charged pith ball of mass 2 g is suspended on a massless string in an electric field $\mathbf{E} = (3\mathbf{x} + 4\mathbf{y}) \times 10^5$ N/C. If the ball is in equilibrium at $\theta = 57°$, then find the tension in the string.

(A) .0500 N

(B) .0250 N

(C) .0125 N

(D) .0063 N

(E) .0032 N

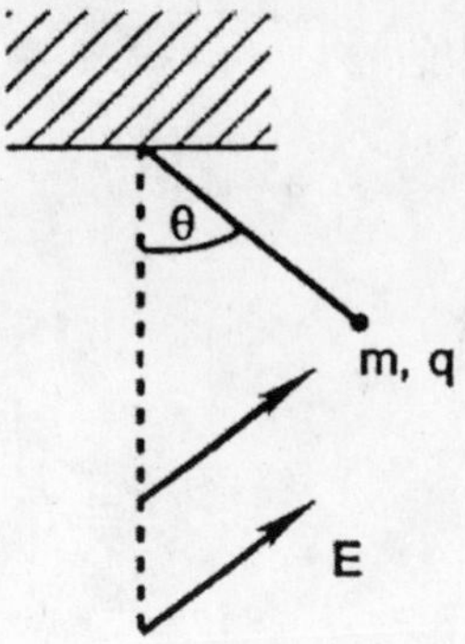

25. A rod 20 cm long has a total charge $q = -75\ \mu C$. Find the electric field along the axis of the rod 10 cm from one end.

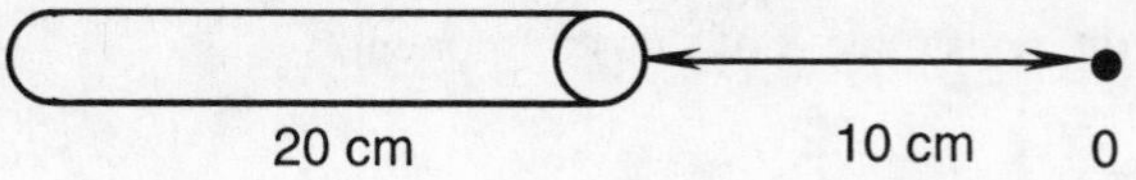

(A) -5.50×10^7 N/C **x**

(B) -2.25×10^7 N/C **x**

(C) 0 N/C

(D) 2.25×10^7 N/C **x**

(E) 5.50×10^7 N/C **x**

26. A capacitor is constructed from two rectangular metal plates of area A separated by a distance d. Suppose that one half of the space between the plates is filled by a dielectric κ_1 and the other half by a dielectric κ_2. Find the capacitance in terms of the free space capacitance C_0, where $C_0 = \varepsilon_0 A/d$.

(A) $2\kappa_1 \kappa_2 C_0 / (\kappa_1 + \kappa_2)$

(B) $(\kappa_1 + \kappa_2) C_0$

(C) C_0

(D) $(\kappa_1 + \kappa_2) C_0 / 2$

(E) $\kappa_1 \kappa_2 C_0 / (\kappa_1 + \kappa_2)$

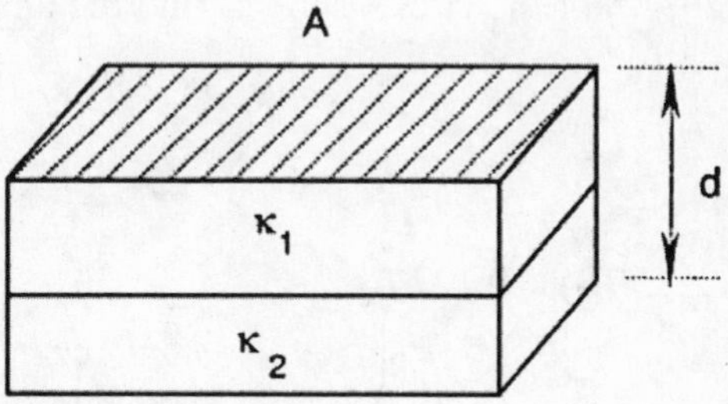

27. Find the electric field of a uniformly charged disk of radius a situated in the yz plane at point P along the x-axis. Let the surface charge density of the disk be σ. (See figure on next page.)

(A) $\sigma / 2\varepsilon_0 \left(1 - x / \sqrt{x^2 + a^2}\right) x$

(B) $\sigma / 2\varepsilon_0 \mathbf{x}$

(C) $\sigma / 2\varepsilon_0 \, x / \sqrt{x^2 + a^2} \, \mathbf{x}$

(D) $\sigma a^2 / 4\varepsilon_0 \, \mathbf{x}$

(E) $\sigma / 2\varepsilon_0 \, (\sqrt{x^2 + a^2} - x) \, \mathbf{x}$

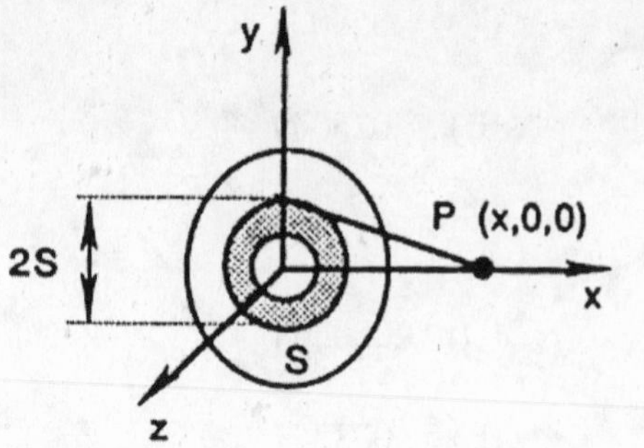

28. A resistor is made from a hollow cylinder of length l, inner radius a, and outer radius b. The region $a < r < b$ is filled with material of resistivity ρ. Find the resistance R of this component

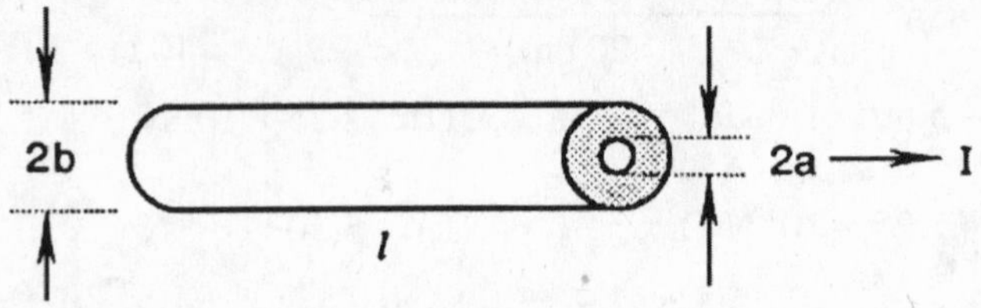

(A) $R = \rho \, l / \pi \, b^2$

(B) $R = \rho \, l / \pi \, a^2$

(C) $R = \rho \, l / \pi \, (b^2 - a^2)$

(D) $R = \pi \, b^2 \, \rho / l$

(E) $R = \pi \, (b^2 - a^2) \, \rho / l$

29. For the circuit shown, find the amount of current that passes through the 5 Ω resistor.

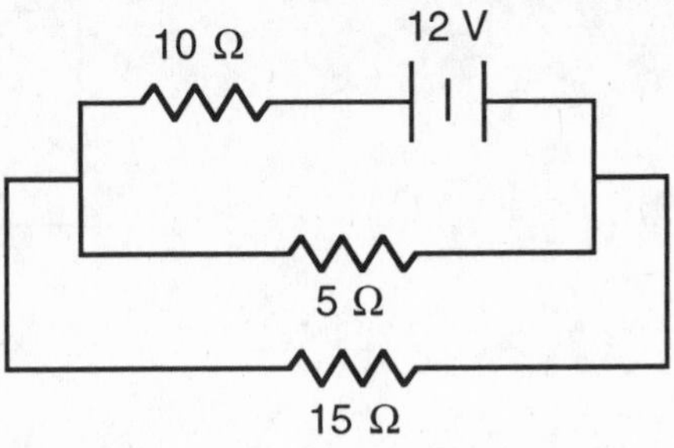

(A) 0.873 A

(B) 0.127 A

(C) 0.346 A

(D) 0.254 A

(E) 0.654 A

30. The Hall effect relates to

(A) the behavior of waves in regularly spaced lattices known as constructive interference.

(B) the generation of a voltage when a current carrying conductor is placed in a magnetic field.

(C) a more sophisticated statement of the consequences of Coulomb's inverse square law.

(D) magnetohydrodynamic waves. (specifically).

(E) the determination of a substance's electric susceptibility.

31. Find the magnetic field of a circular ring of radius r situated in the xy plane for an arbitrary point along the z axis. The ring carries a current I.

(A) $\mu_0 I/2r$

(B) $\mu_0 Ir^2/(r^2+z^2)^{3/2}$

(C) $\mu_0 I/4r$

(D) $\mu_0 Ir^2/2(r^2+z^2)^{3/2}$

(E) $\mu_0 Ir^2/4(r^2+z^2)^{3/2}$

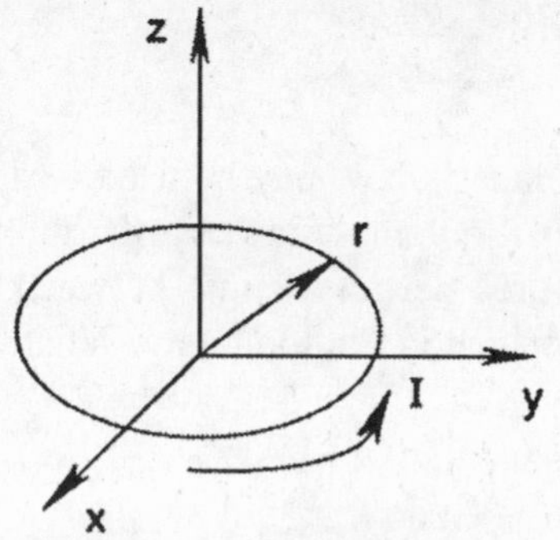

32. The differential statement of Ampere's law is incomplete without the displacement current. In fact, it is implied for the vector current density that $\nabla \cdot \mathbf{j} = 0$. Use Maxwell's equations to find the correct vector whose divergence is zero.

(A) $\mathbf{j} + \partial \mathbf{E}/\partial t$

(B) $\mu_0 \mathbf{j}$

(C) $\mathbf{j} + 1/\mu_0 \varepsilon_0 \partial \mathbf{E}/\partial t$

(D) $\mu_0 \varepsilon_0 \mathbf{j}$

(E) $\mathbf{j} + 1/\varepsilon_0 \partial \mathbf{E}/\partial t$

33. Ampere's law is different in a vacuum than in the presence of matter. In the presence of matter, consider that the total current density consists of a free or vacuum current density and a bound or magnetization current density. Hence derive what vector must have a curl of $\mu_0 \mathbf{j}_{free}$.

(A) $\mathbf{H}$

(B) $\mathbf{B} + \mu_0 \mathbf{M}$

(C) $\mu_0 \mathbf{B} + \mathbf{M}$

(D) $\mathbf{B} - \mu_0 \mathbf{M}$

(E) $\mu_0 \mathbf{B} - \mathbf{M}$

34. In one version of the Millikan oil drop experiment, oil droplets of radius R are allowed to achieve terminal speed first with a downward electric field (v_+) and then with an upward electric field (v_-) Let η be the viscosity of oil in air and E the electric field. Find the electronic charge e.

(A) $\frac{3\pi R\eta}{E}(v_- - v_+)$

(B) $\frac{6\pi R\eta}{E}(v_- - v_+)$

(C) $\frac{3\pi R\eta}{E}(v_- + v_+)$

(D) $\frac{6\pi R\eta}{E}(v_- + v_+)$

(E) $\frac{mg}{E}$

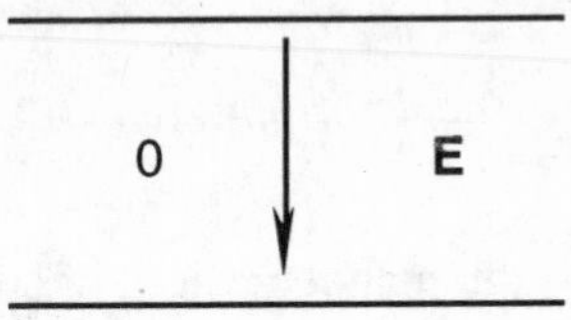

35. Gauss's law may be used to derive Coulomb's law. Let k_E be the constant in Coulomb's law. Furthermore, Ampere's law may be used to derive the force per unit length between two currents. Let k_B be the constant in this magnetic Coulomb law. What is the ratio k_B / k_E ?

(A) c

(B) $2\,\mu_0\,\varepsilon_0$

(C) $2c$

(D) $\mu_0\,\varepsilon_0$

(E) c^2

36. Consider that a sliding conductive bar closes the circuit shown below and moves to the right with a speed $v = 4$ m/s. If $l = 1.5$ *m*, $R = 12\ \Omega$, and $B = 5$ *T*, then find the magnitude of the induced power and the direction of the induced current.

(A) 75 W, counterclockwise

(B) 75 W, clockwise

(C) 2.5 W, counterclockwise

(D) 2.5 W, clockwise

(E) 0 W, there is no current flow

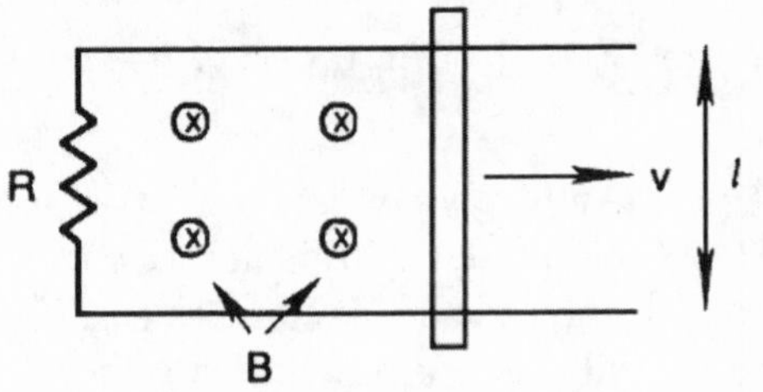

37. A lightly damped RLC circuit has $R = 10\ \Omega$, $L = 10^{-3} H$, and $C = 1\ \mu F$. For this lightly damped circuit, find the ratio of the charge on the capacitor at t

$= 2 \times 10^{-4}$ s to the maximum charge.

(A) 0.732

(B) 0.600

(C) 0.549

(D) 0.400

(E) 0.366

38. As is well known, Maxwell's equations imply the existence of electromagnetic waves. Determine the appropriate wave equation for a magnetic field $\mathbf{B} = B_z (x, y, z)\, \mathbf{z}$.

(A) $\partial^2 B_z / \partial x^2 = \partial^2 B_z / \partial t^2$

(B) $\partial^2 B_z / \partial z^2 = \partial^2 B_z / \partial t^2$

(C) $(\partial^2 / \partial x^2 + \partial^2 / \partial y^2 + \partial^2 / \partial z^2)\, B_z = \mu_0 \varepsilon_0 (\partial^2 B_z / \partial t^2)$

(D) $\partial^2 B_z / \partial y^2 = \partial^2 B_z / \partial t^2$

(E) $(\partial^2 / \partial x^2 + \partial^2 / \partial y^2 + \partial^2 / \partial_z^2)\, B_z = \partial^2 E_y / \partial t^2$

39. An infinite cylinder with charge density λ and current flow I is at rest in reference frame K. Find the speed of reference frame K' where the electric field is zero; i.e., in that frame one observes a pure magnetic field.

(A) $v = \lambda / \varepsilon_0 \mu_0 I$

(B) $v = c / 2$

(C) $v = \lambda \varepsilon_0 \mu_0 / I$

(D) $v = c / 4$

(E) This is impossible

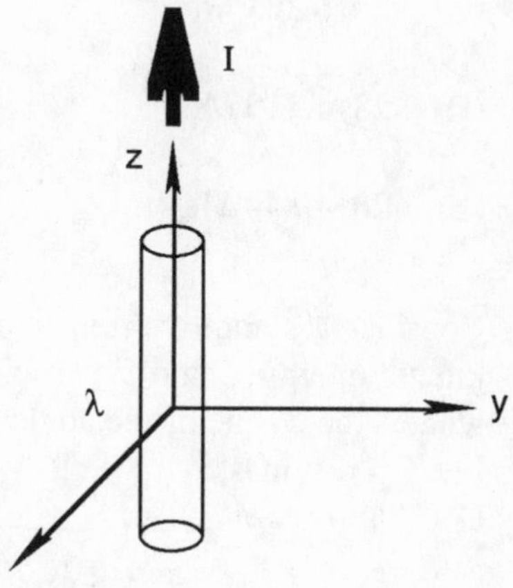

40. The μ-meson has half-life $\tau_{1/2} = 1.5\ \mu$s. These particles are produced by the collision of cosmic rays with gas nuclei 60 km above the surface of the Earth. Find the speed parameter β with which the muons move if only 1/8 of them reach sea level without decaying.

(A) $\beta = 0.975$

(B) $\beta = 0.9975$

(C) $\beta = 0.99$

(D) $\beta = 0.99975$

(E) $\beta = 0.98$

41. Cerenkov radiation is observed from a beam of 700 MeV electrons travelling through air of index of refraction $n = 1.00029$. Find the half angle of the light cone of radiation.

(A) 1.38°

(B) 2.76°

(C) 4.14°

(D) 7.52°

(E) 15.0°

42. A nuclear reaction occurs with 1.808 MeV deuterons incident on a target of deuterium. Protons are observed at $\theta = 90°$ with 3.467 MeV kinetic energy. Given that $m_p = 938.791$ MeV and $m_d = 1876.140$ MeV, find the mass of the triton.

(A) 2814.931 MeV

(B) 2809.462 MeV

(C) 2816.373 MeV

(D) 2814.210 MeV

(E) 2814.840 MeV

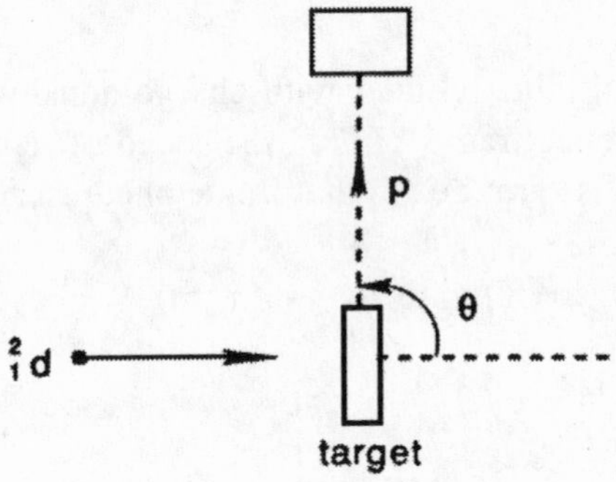

43. Consider a symmetric elastic collision between a particle of mass m and kinetic energy T and a particle of the same mass at rest. Relativistically, what is the cosine of the angle between the two particles after the collision? Let E_0= rest mass.

(A) 1.00

(B) $T/(T+5E_0)$

(C) $T/(T+4E_0)$

(D) $T/(T+3E_0)$

(E) $T/(T+2E_0)$

44. A particle of mass m moves in a delta function potential $V(x) = -g\delta(x)$. Find the energy eigenvalue of the particle.

(A) $-mg^2/8\hbar^2$

(B) $-mg^2/6\hbar^2$

(C) $-mg^2/4\hbar^2$

(D) $-mg^2/2\hbar^2$

(E) $-mg^2/\hbar^2$

45. Consider a particle in a potential $V(x) = -V_0$ for $|x| \leq l/2$ and $V(x) = 0$ otherwise. Determine the equation that must be solved to find the energy eigenvalues. Let

$$\theta = \sqrt{m\,l^2(V_0 - E)/2\hbar^2} \text{ and } \theta_0 = \sqrt{m\,l^2 V_0/2\hbar^2}.$$

(A) $\cot\theta = \sqrt{\theta_0^2/\theta^2 - 1}$

(B) $\sin\theta = \sqrt{\theta_0^2/\theta^2 - 1}$

(C) $\tan\theta = \sqrt{\theta_0/\theta - 1}$

(D) $\sin\theta = \sqrt{\theta_0/\theta - 1}$

(E) $\tan\theta = \sqrt{\theta_0^2/\theta^2 - 1}$

46. A potential well consists of a harmonic oscillator potential $V(x) = 1/2\, m\omega^2 x^2$ for $x > 0$ and an infinite barrier for $x < 0$. In the WKB approximation, what equation must be solved to find the energy eigenvalues? Let $x = a$ specify the classical turning point.

(A) $\int_0^a p\,dx/\hbar = \pi/2,\ 3\pi/2,\ 5\pi/2, \ldots$

(B) $\int_0^a p\,dx/\hbar = 3\pi/4,\ 7\pi/4,\ 11\pi/4, \ldots$

(C) $\int_0^a p\,dx/\hbar = \pi,\ 2\pi,\ 3\pi, \ldots$

(D) $\int_0^a p\,dx/\hbar = \pi/4,\ 3\pi/4,\ 5\pi/4, \ldots$

(E) $\int_0^a p\,dx/\hbar = \pi/4,\ \pi/2,\ 3\pi/4, \ldots$

47. In the Zeeman effect, it is found that a sample of Na placed in a magnetic field B has its spectral D line split into three lines. Find the amount of the shift $\delta\omega$, in cgs units, where ω is the angular frequency of the spectral line.

(A) $\delta\omega = \pm eB/8\,m_e c$

(B) $\delta\omega = \pm eB/4m_e c$

(C) $\delta\omega = \pm eB / 3m_ec$ (D) $\delta\omega = \pm eB / 2m_ec$

(E) $\delta\omega = \pm eB / m_ec$

48. Each hydrogenic spectral series has an upper and a lower limit. Which of the following spectral series has an upper limit $\lambda = 18{,}760$ Å?

(A) Balmer series
(B) Lyman series
(C) Brackett series
(D) Pfund series
(E) Paschen series

49. In the Thomson model of the atom, the electrons are distributed as plums through a positive atomic pudding. What single wavelength of light would a Thomson hydrogen atom emit?

(A) 3550 Å
(B) 2370 Å
(C) 1184 Å
(D) 4740 Å
(E) 7100 Å

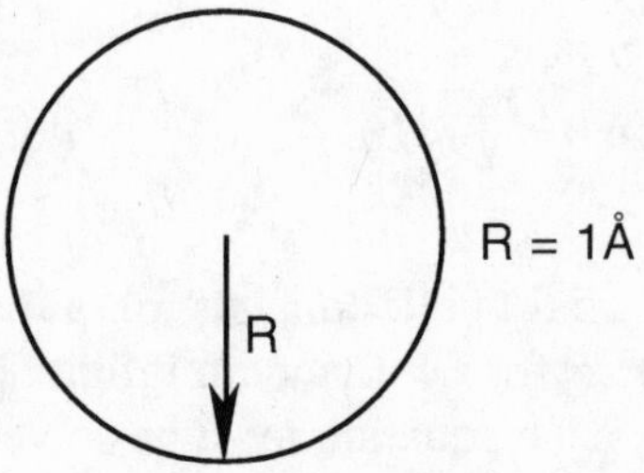

50. Which of the following statements is NOT true about the Franck-Hertz experiment? Specifically, consider the case where the Franck-Hertz tube is filled with Hg vapor at low pressure.

(A) An electron loses most of its kinetic energy in an elastic collision with an atom.

(B) Electrons raise Hg atoms to the first excited state.

(C) The kinetic energy of the electrons may be changed simply by altering the voltage on the grid.

(D) The collected current peaks at multiples of 4.9 volts.

(E) Any monoatomic gas at low pressure may be used.

51. In the photoelectric effect, electromagnetic radiation is incident upon the surface of a metal. Which of the following is NOT a true statement about the photoelectric effect? Let ν = threshold frequency and ν_0 = frequency.

(A) There is no photocurrent unless $\nu > \nu_0$.

(B) ν_0 is characteristic of the cathode material.

(C) Above ν, the flux of electrons per second increases as the intensity of incident light.

(D) The stopping potential V_0 is proportional to ν^2.

(E) The stopping potential is independent of the intensity.

52. A beam of tritons is incident on an Au foil 1μm thick and scattered through an angle of 37° solely through the Coulomb interaction. Find the differential scattering cross section in *b*/sr.

(A) 5.15*b*

(B) 6.23*b*

(C) 7.34*b*

(D) 8.95*b*

(E) 10.30*b*

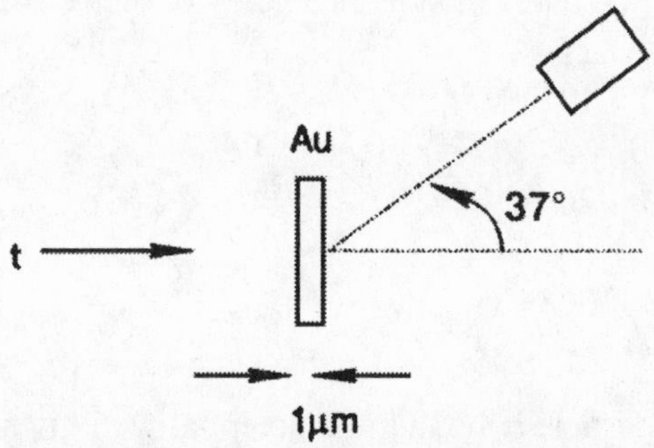

53. Consider a cubical container of volume *V* containing a photon gas in equilibrium. Calculate the differential number of allowable normal modes of frequency ω.

(A) $V\omega^2\, d\omega / 2\pi^2 c^3$

(B) $2V\omega^2\, d\omega / \pi^2 c^3$

(C) $4\, V\omega^2\, d\omega / \pi^2 c^3$

(D) $V\omega^2\, d\omega / \pi^2 c^3$

(E) $8\, V\omega^2\, d\omega / \pi^2 c^3$

54. The black body energy density $u(\omega)$ has a maximum as a function of ω. Find the equation for this maximum, also known as Wien's displacement law. Let *k* be the Boltzmann constant.

(A) $\lambda_{max} T = hc / 2.25k$

(B) $\lambda_{max} T = hc / 4.97k$

(C) $\lambda_{max} T = hc / 3.00k$

(D) $\lambda_{max} T = hc / 3.50k$

(E) $\lambda_{max} T = hc / 4.82k$

55. Photoelectrons are found to be ejected from a metal surface when the wavelength of incident light is below 2300 Å. If the wavelength of incident photons is 1500 Å, then what must be the stopping potential V_0 to stop the photoelectrons?

(A) 8.27 V

(B) 5.39 V

(C) 2.88 V

(D) 2.32 V

(E) 1.56 V

56. X-rays of wavelength 1.50 Å are scattered by a metal through an angle of 90°. What is the kinetic energy of the recoil electrons?

(A) 132 eV

(B) 264 eV

(C) 368 eV

(D) 736 eV

(E) 822 eV

57. A particle is bound in a potential well given by $V(x) = \infty$ for $x \leq 0$ and $V(x) = cx$ for $x > 0$. Estimate the ground state energy of this system.

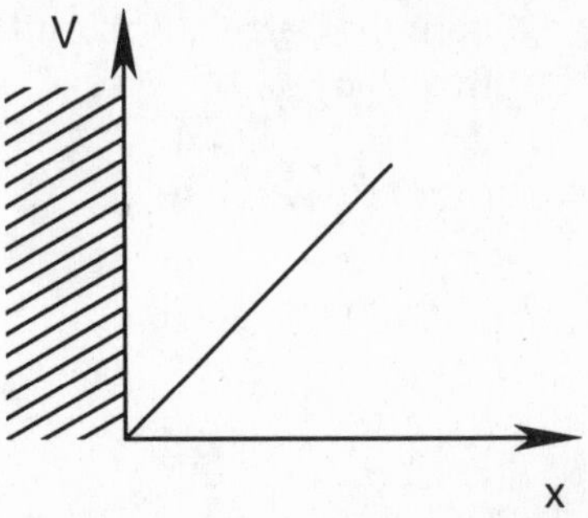

(A) $(\hbar c/2\sqrt{2m})^{2/3}$

(B) $\hbar^2/2m + c$

(C) $(\hbar^2 c^2/m)^{1/3}$

(D) $(\hbar c/\sqrt{2m})^{2/3} + (\hbar^2 c^2/2m)^{1/3}$

(E) $(\hbar c/2\sqrt{2m})^{2/3} + (\hbar^2 c^2/m)^{1/3}$

58. A ball with a mass of 2 g and a kinetic energy of 10^4 erg is incident upon a potential barrier 20 cm in height and 2 cm in width. What is the probability that the ball will quantum-mechanically tunnel through the potential barrier and appear on the other side?

(A) $10^{-5.6\times10^{29}}$

(B) $10^{-1.3\times10^{30}}$

(C) 10^{-4}

(D) 10^{-6}

(E) $10^{-3.2\times10^{28}}$

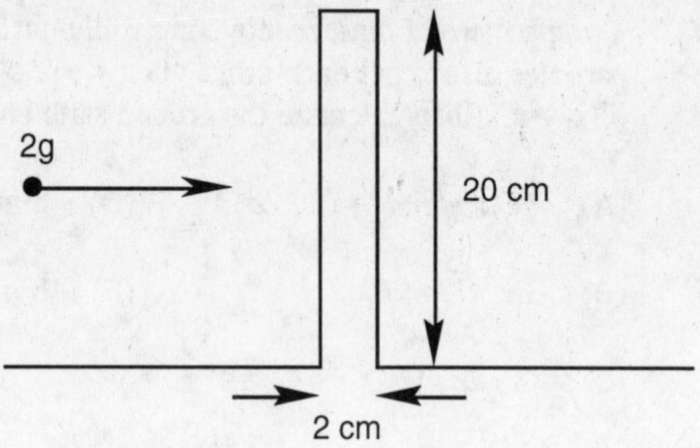

59. Which of the following is a FALSE statement?

(A) A wave function can be found that is a simultaneous eigenfunction of H, L^2, and L_y.

(B) $[L_t, L_z] = 0$ where L_+ is the raising operator.

(C) $L_t Y_{lm}(\theta, \phi)$ is an eigenfunction of L^2

(D) A wave function can't be constructed that is a simultaneous eigenfunction of H, L_x, and L_z.

(E) Exact energy eigenfunctions are obtainable for the case of three identical fermions interacting with an external potential well, but not with each other.

60. What is the transmission probability due to the tunnel effect of a 1 eV electron incident on a barrier .5 nm wide and 5 eV high.

(A) 1.4×10^{-4}

(B) 3.6×10^{-14}

(C) 8.6×10^{-20}

(D) 4.5×10^{-5}

(E) 3.2×10^{-30}

61. Calculate the Fermi energy for relativistic electrons in a neutron star. The density of the electrons is $\rho = 0.01\ /\ \text{fm}^3$.

(A) 16.9 GeV

(B) 8.45 GeV

(C) 38.4 MeV

(D) 65.77 MeV

(E) 131.54 MeV

62. Two particles of mass m move in a 3-dimensional cubical box of side a. If the particles also repel each other via a weak short range force $V(\mathbf{r}_1 - \mathbf{r}_2) = V_0 \, \delta^3(\mathbf{r}_1 - \mathbf{r}_2)$, then calculate the ground state energy using perturbation theory.

(A) $3\hbar^2 \pi^2 / ma^2 + (3/2a)^3 V_0$
(B) $3\hbar^2 \pi^2 / ma^2$
(C) $(3/2a)^3 V_0$
(D) $\hbar^2 \pi^2 / ma^2 + (3/2\,a)^3 V_0$
(E) $\hbar^2 \pi^2 / ma^2$

63. An atom has three valence electrons in a p shell. Determine the total number of states in this configuration. That is, how many distinct three electron states can be constructed from the orbits in a p shell?

(A) 8
(B) 20
(C) 12
(D) 4
(E) 3

64. Let the potential energy of the NaCl molecule be described by

$$V(r) = -\,e^2/r + k\,e^{-r/r_0}$$

where r is the internuclear separation. If the equilibrium separation is $r^* = 2.50$ Å and the dissociation energy is $V(r^*) = 3.60$ eV, then find the constants r_0 and k.

(A) $r_0 = 2.50$ Å, $k = 3.60$ eV
(B) $r_0 = 1.25$ Å, $k = 7.20$ eV
(C) $r_0 = 0.94$ Å, $k = 30.94$ eV
(D) $r_0 = 1.88$ Å, $k = 15.47$ eV
(E) $r_0 = 2.50$ Å, $k = 5.76$ eV

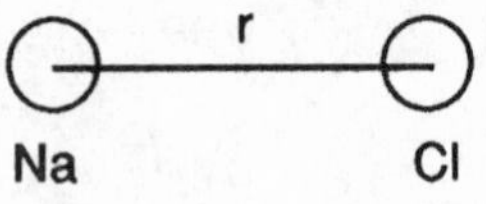

65. Scientists use the Lennard-Jones 6 – 12 potential $V(r) = A/r^{12} - B/r^6$ to describe the interaction between the atoms in a diatomic molecule. For small departures from the equilibrium separation r_0, find the angular frequency of oscillation. Let m be the mass of each atom.

(A) $\omega = \sqrt{312A/mr_0^{14} - 84B/mr_0^8}$

(B) $\omega = \sqrt{A/mr_0^{14} + B/mr_0^8}$

(C) $\omega = \sqrt{A/mr_0^{14} - B/mr_0^8}$

(D) $\omega = \sqrt{312A/mr_0^{14} + 84B/mr_0^8}$

(E) $\omega = \sqrt{156A/mr_0^{14} - 42B/mr_0^8}$

66. An object of mass 6.0 kg oscillates harmonically with negligible damping with a frequency of 1.0 Hz. With a small magnetic damping, the amplitude decreases from 0.25 m to 0.125 m after 10 seconds. Find the angular frequency for the damped system.

(A) 6.28 rad/s

(B) 3.14 rad/s

(C) 1.07 rad/s

(D) 4.21 rad/s

(E) 5.28 rad/s

67. The bobs of two simple pendula each have mass *m* and are attached to a string of length *l* as shown. If the two pendula are coupled by a massless spring of constant *k*, then find the higher frequency of oscillation of the system. String tension can be neglected, as oscillations about equilibrium are small.

(A) $\omega = \sqrt{g/l + k/m}$

(B) $\omega = \sqrt{2g/l + k/m}$

(C) $\omega = \sqrt{2g/l + 3k/m}$

(D) $\omega = \sqrt{g/l + 2k/m}$

(E) $\omega = \sqrt{g/l + 3k/m}$

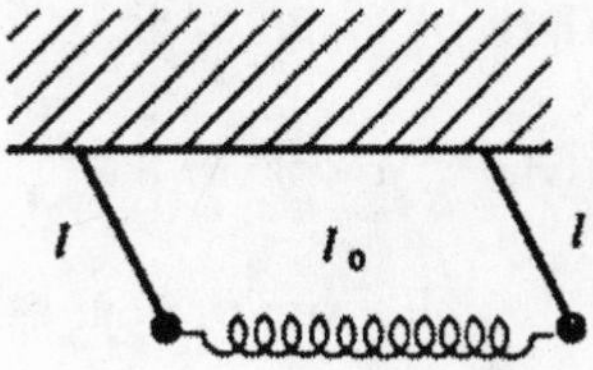

68. The ionosphere may be viewed as a dielectric medium of refractive index $n = n(\omega_p)$, where ω_p is the plasma frequency. Calculate the group velocity of a radio wave of frequency $\omega = \sqrt{2}\omega_p$.

(A) $c/\sqrt{2}$

(B) $c/\sqrt{3}$

(C) $c/2$ (D) $c/4$

(E) $\sqrt{2}c$

69. In a laboratory experiment, two quantities x and y are measured. Then the formula

$$f = c\sqrt{x/y}$$

is used to calculate a third quantity f. If Δx and Δy are the uncertainties in x and y, respectively, then what is the uncertainty in f?

(A) $\Delta f = \sqrt{(\Delta x)^2 + (\Delta y)^2}$

(B) $\Delta f = f\sqrt{(\Delta x/2x)^2 + (\Delta y/y)^2}$

(C) $\Delta f = \frac{f}{2}\sqrt{(\Delta x/x)^2 + (\Delta y/y)^2}$

(D) $\Delta f = f\sqrt{(\Delta x/x)^2 + (\Delta y/2y)^2}$

(E) $\Delta f = f\sqrt{(\Delta x/x)^2 + (\Delta y/y)^2}$

70. A point charge initially at rest at the origin experiences an acceleration a for a very short time and then proceeds to move with speed $u = a\,\Delta t$. What is the magnitude of the Poynting flux of this accelerated charge at distance r and angle θ?

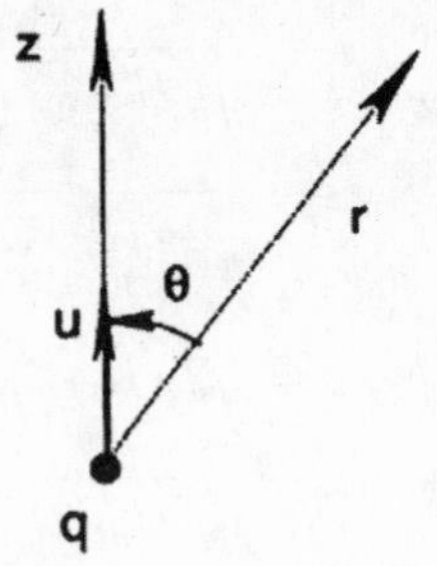

(A) $q^2 a^2 \cos^2\theta / 16\pi^2 \varepsilon_0 r^2 c^3$

(B) $q^2 a^2 \sin^2\theta / 8\pi^2 \varepsilon_0 r^2 c^3$

(C) $q^2 a^2 \cos^2\theta / 8\pi^2 \varepsilon_0 r^2 c^3$

(D) $q^2 a^2 \sin^2\theta / 16\pi^2 \varepsilon_0 r^2 c^3$

(E) $q^2 a^2 \sin^2\theta\cos^2\theta / 4\pi^2 \varepsilon_0 r^2 c^3$

71. The nitrogen molecules in the atmosphere have an ultraviolet transition at $\lambda_0 = 750$ Å. The density of N_2 there is $\rho_t = 1.68 \times 10^{29}$ particles / m^2. Find the fraction of blue sunlight $\lambda = 4500$ Å scattered out of the atmosphere.

(A) .43% (B) .86%

(C) 1.29%

(D) 1.72%

(E) 2.15%

72. Consider the field of a point charge q moving with constant velocity. What must the speed β of the charge be for its field in the lab frame at $\theta' = 90°$ to be twice the normal non-relativistic value?

(A) $c/4$

(B) $c/3$

(C) $c/2$

(D) $c/\sqrt{2}$

(E) $\sqrt{3}c/2$

73. A particle of mass m follows the Maxwell-Boltzmann distribution at temperature T. Find the most probable speed for this particle.

(A) $\sqrt{2kT/m}$

(B) $\sqrt{kT/m}$

(C) $\sqrt{8kT/\pi m}$

(D) $\sqrt{3kT/m}$

(E) $\sqrt{3kT/\pi m}$

74. Consider the validity of the classical theory of the ideal gas. Let ρ be the number of particles per unit volume, m the particle mass, and T the temperature. Derive a condition for the classical Maxwell-Boltzmann distribution to be valid.

(A) $h\rho^{1/3}/\sqrt{2mkT} << 1$

(B) $h\rho^{1/3}/\sqrt{mkT} >> 1$

(C) $\rho^{-1/3} >> 1$ Å

(D) $\rho^{-1/3} << 1$ Å

(E) $h\rho^{1/3}/\sqrt{mkT} << 1$

75. Consider a Helmholtz resonator of neck length L and area A as shown. Find

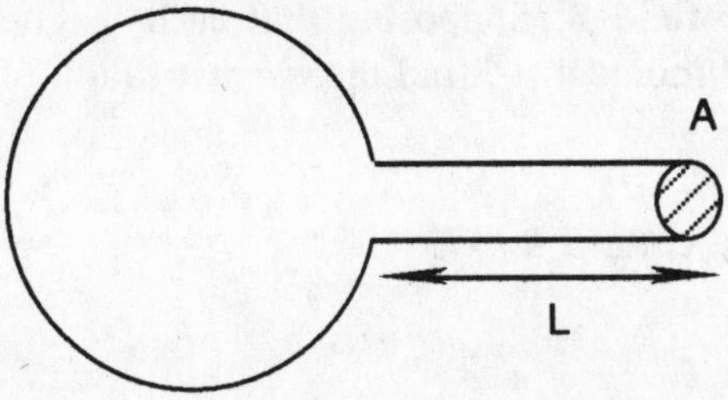

the frequency of oscillation if the volume of the container is V_0. Let v_s be the speed of sound at the ambient temperature and pressure and γ be the adiabatic coefficient.

(A) $\sqrt{2\gamma p_0 A / \rho_0 V_0 L}$

(B) $\sqrt{\gamma p_0 A / 2\rho_0 V_0 L}$

(C) $v_s^{-1}\sqrt{V_0 L / A}$

(D) $v_s\sqrt{A / V_0 L}$

(E) $v_s\sqrt{L^3 / V_0 L}$

76. Consider the oscillations of an electron in a plasma of electrons. Let N be the number of electrons per cubic meter. Calculate the oscillation frequency υ_p in Hz.

(A) $17.96\sqrt{N}$

(B) $13.47\sqrt{N}$

(C) $2.25\sqrt{N}$

(D) $4.49\sqrt{N}$

(E) $8.98\sqrt{N}$

77. A square wave $f(t) = a$ for $0 < t < T/2$ and $f(t) = -a$ for $-T/2 < t < 0$ is generated on a laboratory oscilloscope. Decompose this wave into a Fourier series.

(A) $f(t) = 4a/\pi \sum_{j=0}^{\infty} \cos(j\omega t)/(2j+1)$

(B) $f(t) = 2a/\pi \sum_{j=0}^{\infty} \cos(2j+1)\omega t/(2j+1)$

(C) $f(t) = 4a/\pi \sum_{j=0}^{\infty} \sin(2j+1)\omega t/(2j+1)$

(D) $f(t) = 2a/\pi \sum_{j=0}^{\infty} \sin(2j+1)\omega t/(2j+1)$

(E) $f(t) = 4a/\pi \sum_{j=0}^{\infty} \sin(j\omega t)/(2j+1)$

78. Consider a system which contains N magnetic atoms per unit volume in a magnetic field **B**. Supposing that each magnetic atom has spin 1/2 and magnetic moment μ_0, find the magnetization of the system at temperature T.

(A) $N\mu_0 \coth(\mu_0 B / kT)$

(B) $N\mu_0(e^{\mu_0 B/kt} + e^{-\mu_0 B/kT})$

(C) $N\mu_0 \tanh(\mu_0 B / kT)$

(D) $N\mu_0 (e^{\mu_0 B / kt} - e^{-\mu_0 B / kT})$

(E) $N\mu_0 \sinh(\mu_0 B / kT)$

79. In the derivation of the Stefan-Boltzmann law from the Planck distribution, one must evaluate the integral

$$\int_0^\infty z^3 \, dz / (e^z - 1)$$

where $z = h\upsilon / kT$. What is the value of this integral?

(A) $\pi^4 / 15$

(B) $\pi^3 / 90$

(C) $\pi^2 / 40$

(D) $\pi^3 / 15$

(E) $\pi^4 / 90$

80. A typical commercially available diatomic gas will actually consist of a diatomic and a monatomic portion. Let the degree of disassociation be $\delta = m_1/m$ where m_1 is the mass of the monatomic portion and m the total system mass. Use Dalton's law of partial pressures to obtain the equation of state of the gas. The monatomic mass has a mass of A g per mole.

(A) $pV = m(1 + \delta)RT / A$

(B) $pV = m(1 + \delta)RT / 2A$

(C) $pV = m_1 RT / A$

(D) $pV = mRT / 2A$

(E) $pV = m_l(1 + \delta)RT / A$

81. For a gas with a van der Waals equation of state, calculate the coefficient of cubical expansion β, where $\beta = \frac{1}{V}\left(\frac{\partial V}{\partial T}\right)_p$.

(A) $\beta = RV^2 (V - b) / (RTV^3 - 2a(V - b)^2)$

(B) $\beta = 1 / T$

(C) $\beta = RV^2 (V - a) / (RTV^3 - b(V - a)^2)$

(D) $\beta = T$

(E) $\beta = RV (V - b) / (RTV^2 - a(V - b)^2)$

82. A cubical box of edge length L contains n molecules per cc of radius a. Estimate the mean number of collisions that an ideal gas molecule will undergo in crossing the box. Let $L = 100\ m$ and $a = 1$ Å.

(A) 10^{20}

(B) 10^{17}

(C) 10^{8}

(D) 10^{10}

(E) 10^{24}

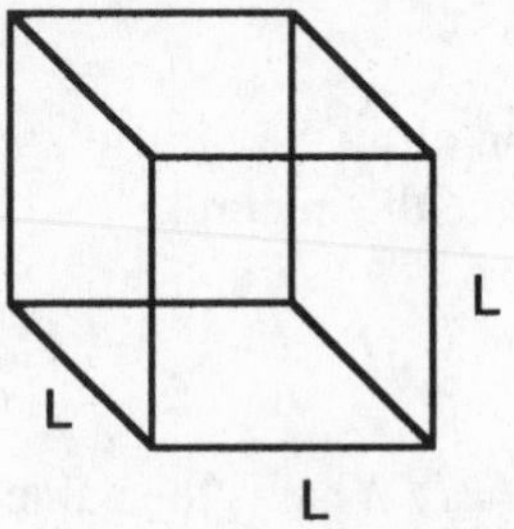

83. Consider a one dimensional anharmonic oscillator of energy

$$E = p^2 / 2m + bx^4.$$

Find the mean total energy of this oscillator at a temperature T.

(A) $1/2\ kT$

(B) kT

(C) $3/4\ kT$

(D) $3/2\ kT$

(E) $7/4\ kT$

84. A thermally insulated ideal gas is compressed quasi-statically from an initial macrostate of volume V_0 and pressure p_0 to a final macrostate of volume V_f and pressure p_f. Calculate the work done on the gas in this process.

(A) $p_fV_f - p_0V_0$

(B) 0

(C) $(c_p - c_V)/R\ (p_fV_f - p_0V_0)$

(D) $c_V/R\ (p_fV_f - p_0V_0)$

(E) $c_p/R\ (p_fV_f - p_0V_0)$

85. The pictured one dimensional system is in equilibrium at temperature T. The normal mode frequencies are $a\omega_0$, $b\omega_0$, and $c\omega_0$ where $a = 1.0$, $b = 0.54$, $c =$

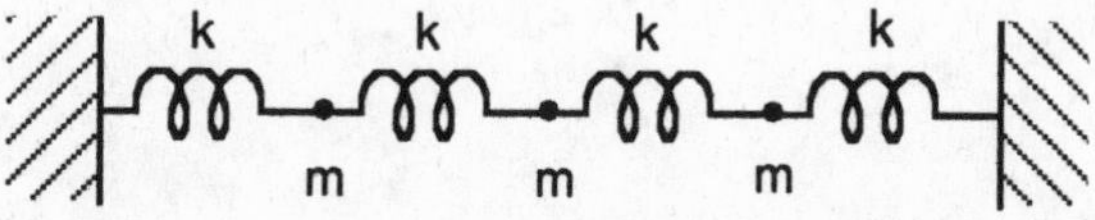

1.3, and $\omega_0 = \sqrt{2k/m}$. Compute the total average energy of the system including quantum mechanical effects.

(A) $\hbar\omega_0\,(an_a + bn_b + cn_c)$

(B) $\hbar\omega_0\,(an_a + bn_b + cn_c + 3/2)$

(C) $\hbar\omega_0\,[ae^{-\hbar\omega_0/kT} + be^{-\hbar\omega_0/kT} + ce^{-\hbar\omega_0/kT}]$

(D) $\hbar\omega_0\,[a/(e^{\hbar\omega_0/kT}+1) + b/(e^{\hbar\omega_0/kT}+1) + c/(e^{\hbar\omega_0/kT}+1)]$

(E) $\hbar\omega_0\,[a/(e^{\hbar\omega_0/kT}-1) + b/(e^{\hbar\omega_0/kT}-1) + c/(e^{\hbar\omega_0/kT}-1)]$

86. A K_α x-ray emitted by one hydrogen atom strikes a second hydrogen atom and undergoes photoelectric absorption with an L shell electron. What energy does the ejected electron have?

(A) 13.6 eV

(B) 10.2 eV

(C) 4.6 eV

(D) 3.4 eV

(E) 6.8 eV

87. In deriving the Rayleigh-Jeans law, it is necessary to count the number of modes dn corresponding to a wave number k for a photon gas in a cubical box. Consider this same problem, but in two dimensions for a square of side length L What is the number of modes dn? Let $A = L^2$.

(A) $\dfrac{A}{2\pi}\,k\,dk$

(B) $\dfrac{2A}{\pi}\,k\,dk$

(C) $\dfrac{4A}{\pi}\,k\,dk$

(D) $\dfrac{A}{\pi}k\,dk$

(E) $\dfrac{A}{4\pi}k\,dk$

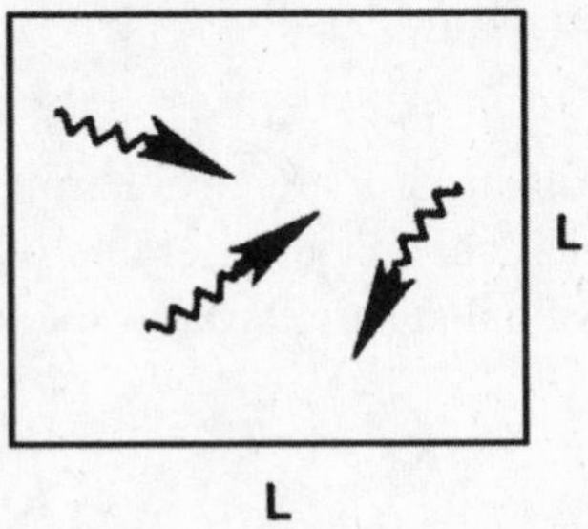

88. Consider that the energy of an incident photon becomes very large. The photon is then scattered by an electron as shown here in the initial state. Find the upper limit of energy for the Compton scattered photon.

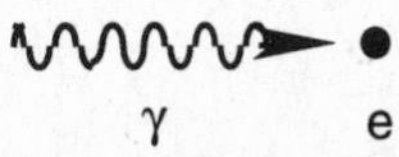

(A) $m_e c^2$

(B) E

(C) $1/2\ m_e c^2$

(D) $E/2$

(E) $E/2 + 1/2\ m_e c^2$

89. Suppose that the parameters in J.J. Thomson's $e\ /\ m$ apparatus are: path length of deflecting plates = 5 cm, plate separation = 1.5 cm, potential between deflecting plates = 50 volts, and deflection of the beam when the magnetic field is off = 1.25 mm. Further suppose that no deflection is observed when B = 1.2 gauss. Find $e\ /\ m$.

(A) 4.62×10^{11} coul/kg

(B) 2.31×10^{11} coul/kg

(C) 1.76×10^{11} coul/kg

(D) 3.52×10^{11} coul/kg

(E) 2.04×10^{11} coul/kg

90. A deuteron is incident on a lead nucleus at Brookhaven National Laboratory. The terminal voltage of the accelerator is 15 MegaVolts. Find the distance of closest approach in a head on collision.

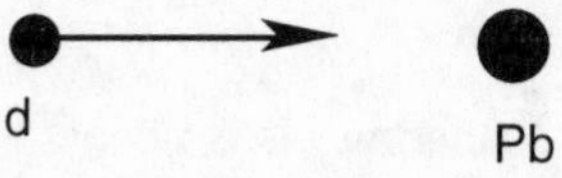

(A) 7.87 fm

(B) 15.74 fm

(C) 5.32 fm

(D) 10.64 fm

(E) 13.20 fm

91. The problem of n identical harmonic oscillators with negligible interactions in a microcanonical ensemble of energy E is solved by considering an n-dimensional sphere. What is the volume of such a sphere?

(A) $4\ /\ 3\ \pi\ R^n$

(B) $\pi\ R^2$

(C) $\pi^{n/2}\ /\ (n\ /\ 2)!\ R^n$

(D) $\pi^n\ /\ n!\ \ R^n$

(E) $\pi^{n-1}\ /\ (n-1)!$ RREV MZ 12/2/02^n

92. Consider an ensemble of systems consisting of N harmonic oscillators of total energy $E = 1/2\ \hbar\ \omega\ N + \hbar\ \omega\ M$ subject to the constraint

$$\sum_{i=1}^{N} n_i = M.$$

Find the number of microstates $\Omega(E)$ and from that the entropy in Stirling's approximation.

(A) $S = (M + N) \ln(M + N)$

(B) $S = \mathrm{M} \ln M$

(C) $S = N \ln N$

(D) $S = (M + N) \ln (M + N) - M \ln M - N \ln N$

(E) $S = (M + 2N) \ln (M + 2N) - M \ln M - 2N \ln 2N$

93. A solid at absolute temperature T contains N negative impurity ions per cm^3 with lattice spacing a. An equal number of positive ions are free to propagate throughout the solid. If a small electric field E is applied along the x direction, then find the electric polarization P_x.

(A) $\frac{Nea}{2} \tanh \left(\frac{eEa}{2kT}\right)$

(B) Nea

(C) $2Nea \sinh \left(\frac{2eEa}{kT}\right)$

(D) $\frac{Nea}{2}$

(E) $Nea \tanh \left(\frac{eEa}{kT}\right)$

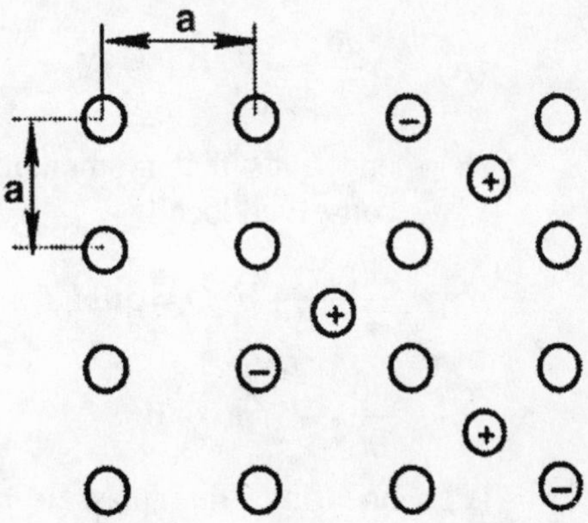

94. An ion of mass m and electric charge e is moving in a dilute gas of molecules experiencing collisions. Suppose that the mean time between collisions is τ and that a uniform electric field E is applied in the x direction. What is the mean distance $\langle x \rangle$ that the ion travels between collisions?

(A) $1/2\, eE\tau^2 / m$

(B) $eE\tau^2 / m$

(C) $\sqrt{2} eE\tau^2 / m$

(D) $eE\tau^2 / \sqrt{2m}$

(E) $eE\tau^2 / \sqrt{3m}$

95. A hollow cube has conducting walls defined by six planes: $x = 0$, $y = 0$, $z = 0$, $x = a$, $y = a$, and $z = a$. The walls at $z = 0$ and $z = a$ are held at constant potential V_0 whereas the other sides have $\phi = 0$. (See Diagram) Find the potential at the center ϕ_c.

(A) $V_0/6$

(B) $V_0/4$

(C) V_0

(D) $V_0/2$

(E) $V_0/3$

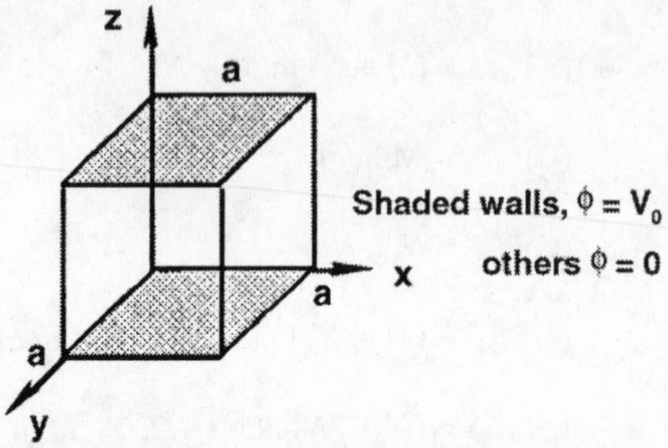

96. If the Boltzmann equation, which describes the scattering of two particles with initial momenta **p** and $\mathbf{p}_2$ to final momenta $\mathbf{p}'_1$, and $\mathbf{p}'_2$, is integrated with a weight of the mass, then what is the result? Let ρ be the local density, **u** the local mean velocity, ***P*** the pressure tensor, **Q** the general energy flux, and **F** the external force.

(A) $\rho\frac{d\mathbf{u}}{dt} = -\nabla\cdot \boldsymbol{P} + \frac{\rho}{m}\mathbf{F}$

(B) one finds that momentum is not conserved locally

(C) $\frac{\partial(\rho E)}{\partial t} + \nabla\cdot\mathbf{Q} = \rho\mathbf{u}\cdot\mathbf{F}/m$

(D) $\frac{\partial\rho}{\partial t} + \nabla\cdot(\rho\mathbf{u}) = 0$

(E) one finds that mass is not conserved locally

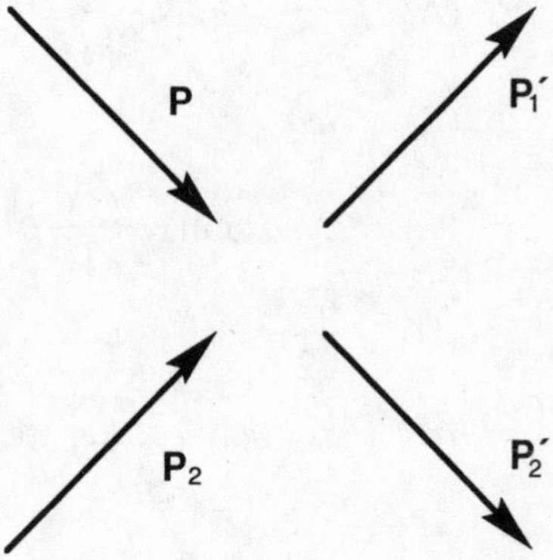

97. Consider a sphere of radius R whose surface is held at a potential given by $\psi(R, \theta, \phi) = B \sin\theta \sin\phi$. Find the charge density on the sphere.

(A) $\frac{B\varepsilon_0}{R}$

(B) $\frac{3B\varepsilon_0}{R}\sin\theta\sin\phi$

(C) $\frac{2B\varepsilon_0}{R}\sin\theta\sin\phi$

(D) $\frac{B\varepsilon_0}{R}\cos\theta\sin\phi$

(E) $\frac{B\varepsilon_0}{R}\sin\theta\sin\phi$

98. A beam of singly ionized boron is accelerated through a potential difference of 4 kilovolts and then passed through a mass spectrometer with magnetic field $B = 0.5$ Tesla. What is the radius R through which the boron is bent? Note $A = 10.0129$ amu for boron.

(A) 5.76 cm

(B) 2.88 cm

(C) 8.64 cm

(D) 11.52 cm

(E) 14.40 cm

99. A nuclear magnetic resonance experiment is performed with protons. The frequency may be adjusted so as to resonate when the sweeping field crosses its zero value. What resonance frequency is expected for a magnetic field of 6642 gauss?

(A) 7.02 MHz

(B) 28.1 MHz

(C) 14.0 MHz

(D) 21.1 MHz

(E) 3.51 MHz

100. Radiation safety is an important laboratory issue. Consider a whole body exposure of 10 rem received in a few hours. What is the average effect on the human body?

(A) results in quick death

(B) causes injury

(C) causes detectable blood changes

(D) results in a 50% death probability in 30 days

(E) causes no damage

TEST 3

ANSWER KEY

1.	(A)	26.	(A)	51.	(D)	76.	(E)
2.	(E)	27.	(A)	52.	(E)	77.	(C)
3.	(C)	28.	(C)	53.	(D)	78.	(C)
4.	(B)	29.	(E)	54.	(B)	79.	(A)
5.	(D)	30.	(B)	55.	(C)	80.	(B)
6.	(B)	31.	(D)	56.	(A)	81.	(A)
7.	(D)	32.	(E)	57.	(E)	82.	(B)
8.	(E)	33.	(D)	58.	(A)	83.	(C)
9.	(C)	34.	(C)	59.	(B)	84.	(D)
10.	(A)	35.	(B)	60.	(D)	85.	(E)
11.	(B)	36.	(A)	61.	(E)	86.	(E)
12.	(A)	37.	(E)	62.	(A)	87.	(D)
13.	(B)	38.	(C)	63.	(B)	88.	(C)
14.	(C)	39.	(A)	64.	(C)	89.	(B)
15.	(D)	40.	(D)	65.	(A)	90.	(A)
16.	(E)	41.	(A)	66.	(A)	91.	(C)
17.	(E)	42.	(B)	67.	(D)	92.	(D)
18.	(D)	43.	(C)	68.	(A)	93.	(A)
19.	(C)	44.	(D)	69.	(C)	94.	(B)
20.	(A)	45.	(E)	70.	(D)	95.	(E)
21.	(C)	46.	(B)	71.	(B)	96.	(D)
22.	(D)	47.	(D)	72.	(E)	97.	(B)
23.	(E)	48.	(E)	73.	(A)	98.	(A)
24.	(C)	49.	(C)	74.	(A)	99.	(B)
25.	(B)	50.	(A)	75.	(D)	100.	(C)

DETAILED EXPLANATIONS OF ANSWERS

TEST 3

1. **(A)**

$$\mathbf{r} = -2\mathbf{x} + \mathbf{y} - 3\mathbf{z}\ m$$

$$\mathbf{F} = 5\mathbf{x} + 3\mathbf{y} - 2\mathbf{z}\ N$$

One must evaluate the cross product as a determinant.

$$\tau = \mathbf{r} \times \mathbf{F} = \left| \begin{array}{ccc|cc} \mathbf{x} & \mathbf{y} & \mathbf{z} & \mathbf{x} & \mathbf{y} \\ -2 & 1 & -3 & -2 & 1 \\ 5 & 3 & -2 & 5 & 3 \end{array} \right.$$

$$= \mathbf{x}(-2+9) + \mathbf{y}(-15-4) + \mathbf{z}(-6-5)$$

$$= 7\mathbf{x} - 19\mathbf{y} - 11\mathbf{z}\ \ N-m$$

2. **(E)**

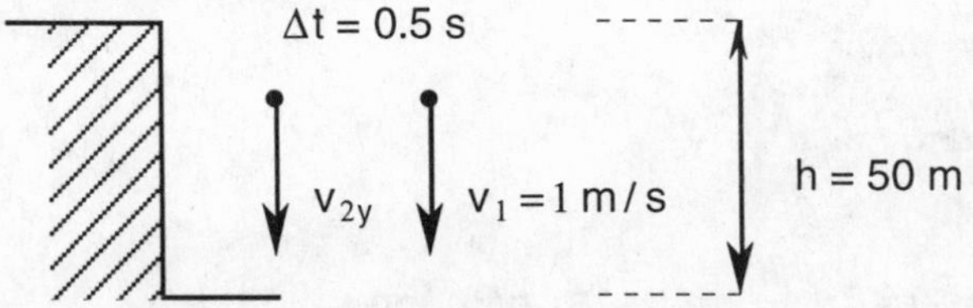

Using basic translational kinematics, we have

$$y_1 = y_0 + v_0 t + {}^1/_2 at^2 = v_1 t + {}^1/_2 gt^2 = t + 4.9t^2$$

thus $\quad h = t + 4.9t^2$

for the first stone,

$$50 = t + 4.9t^2$$

$$t^2 + .204t = 10.204$$

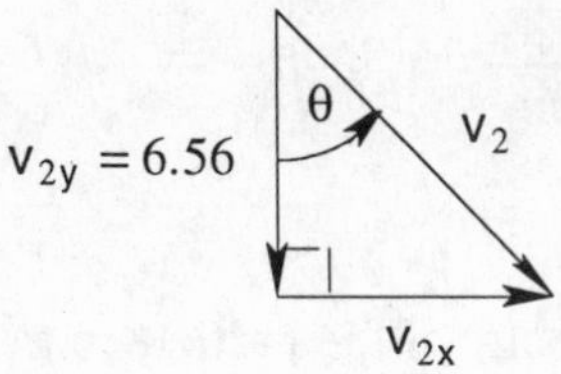

Completing the square, we get

$$(t + .102)^2 = 10.204 + (.102)^2$$

So $\quad t = 3.094s$

is the time for the first stone.

The key here is to find the time from the first stone and then use that information. Again, we apply the basic 1-D kinematics formula with $x_0 = 0$. But now there is a time delay $\Delta t = 0.5$s.

$$y_2 = v_2(t-.5) + 4.9\,(t-.5)^2$$
$$50 = v_2(2.594) + 4.9\,(2.594)^2$$
$$v_2 = 17.028 / 2.594$$
$$v_2 = 6.56 \text{ m/s}$$

The initial velocity of the second stone in the y–direction must therefore be 6.56 m/s.

$$v_{2y} = 6.56 \text{ m/s}$$

$$\frac{6.56}{v_2} = \cos\theta$$

$$v_2 = \frac{6.56}{\cos\theta} = \frac{6.56}{\cos(35°)} = 8.60 \text{ m/s}$$

3. **(C)**

Conservation of momentum means that

$$mv = m_0 v_0.$$

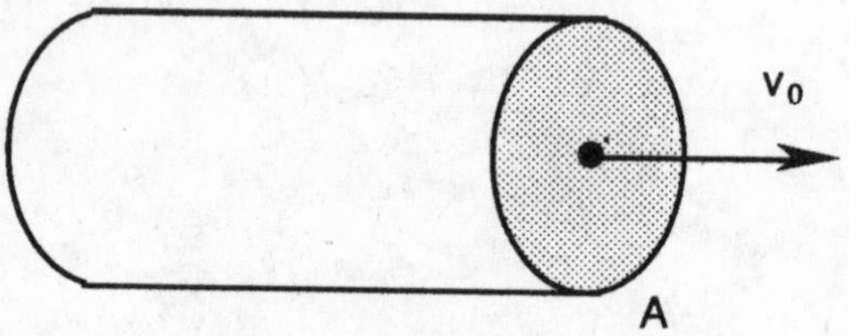

Yet there is a mass increase of the bucket system

$$\frac{dm}{dt} = \rho A v$$

Note $\quad m\frac{dm}{dt} = \frac{1}{2}\frac{d}{dt}(m^2)$

thus $\quad \frac{d}{dt}(m^2) = 2m\frac{dm}{dt} = 2m\rho Av = 2\rho Amv = 2\rho Am_0v_0$

$$\int_{m_0}^{m} d(m^2) = \int_0^t 2\rho Am_0v_0\,dt,$$

Integrating, we obtain

$$m^2 = m_0^{\,2} + 2\rho Am_0v_ot$$

$$v = \frac{m_0v_0}{m} = v_o \Big/ \sqrt{1 + \frac{2\rho Av_0}{m_0}t}$$

4. **(B)**

The velocity of the particle in the rest frame K' is

$$u'_x = c(1-\delta), \quad \delta \ll 1.$$

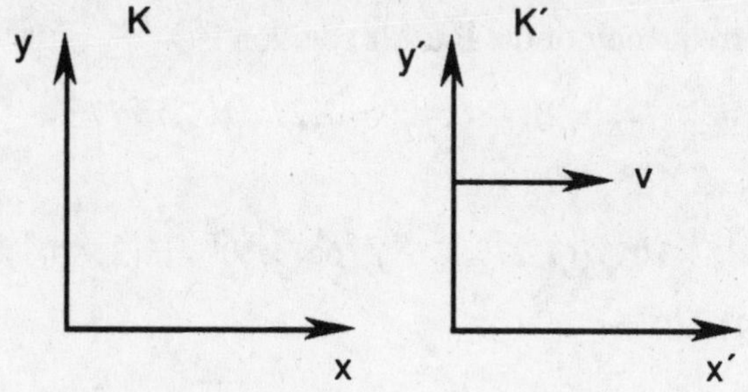

The Lorentz addition of velocities formula is

$$v_3 = \frac{v_1 + v_2}{1 + \frac{v_1 v_2}{c^2}} = \frac{c(1-\delta) + c(1-\delta)}{1 + (1-\delta)^2} = \frac{2c(1-\delta)}{1+(1-\delta)^2}$$

$$= 2c\,\frac{1-\delta}{2 - 2\delta + \delta^2} = \frac{c}{1 + \frac{\delta^2}{2(1-\delta)}}$$

$$\approx c\left(1 - \frac{\delta^2}{2(1-\delta)}\right) \approx c\left(1 - \frac{\delta^2}{2}\right)$$

to order δ^2.

5. **(D)**

The motion is elliptical when the mechanical energy is negative:

$$E = K + U = \frac{1}{2}\mu v_0^{\,2} - \frac{Gm_1 m_2}{r_0} < 0$$

Now the reduced mass is $\mu = m_1 m_2 / (m_1 + m_2) = m/2$. Thus

$$E = \frac{1}{4} m v_0^{\,2} - \frac{Gm^2}{r_0} < 0$$

$\Rightarrow Gm^2 / r_0 > {}^1/_4\, m v_0^2,\ v_0 < 2\sqrt{Gm/r_0}$

6. **(B)**

The clock at the North pole is at rest in an approximate inertial system. The equatorial clock moves with speed $v = \omega R_E$.

Now $T = T_0 \gamma$ is the time at the pole and

$$T = 100\,yr\,\frac{365\,dy}{yr}\,\frac{86{,}400\,s}{dy} = 3.15 \times 10^9\,s$$

$$\Delta T = T - T\sqrt{1-\beta^2}$$

$$\approx T - T(1 - \tfrac{1}{2}\beta^2)$$

$$= T\tfrac{1}{2}\frac{v^2}{c^2} = \frac{T}{2}\frac{\omega^2 R_E^{\,2}}{c^2}$$

Now the angular frequency of the Earth's rotation is

$$\omega = 2\pi v = 2\pi / t_E = 2\pi / 86,400 = 7.27 \times 10^{-5} rad / s$$

Hence

$$\Delta T = \tfrac{1}{2}(3.15 \times 10^9)((7.27 \times 10^{-5})^2 (6.4 \times 10^6)^2 / (3 \times 10^8)^2)$$
$$= 3.79 \times 10^{-3} s$$

7. **(D)**

The two balls have velocities

$v_1 = 20$ m/s and $v_2 = 24$ m/s at time $t = 0$.

For the first object:

$$v^2 = v_0^2 + 2a(y - y_0)$$
$$0 = 20^2 - 2(9.8)h$$

Since the velocity reduces to zero at the maximum height

$$h = 20^2 / 2(9.8) = 20.41\ m = y_1$$

Also $v = v_0 + at$

$$0 = 20 - 9.8t$$
$$t = 2.04s$$

For the second object:

$$y = y_0 + v_0 t + {}^1/_2\, at^2$$
$$= 24t - 4.9t^2$$
$$= 24(2.04) - 4.9(2.04)^2$$
$$= 28.55\ m = y^2$$
$$\Delta y = y_2 - y_1 = 8.14\ \text{m}$$

8. **(E)**

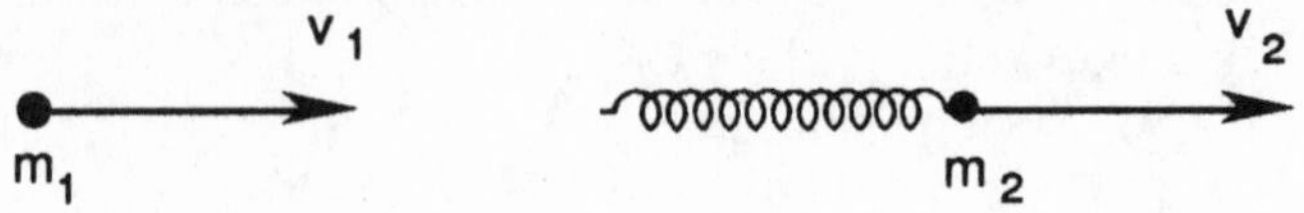

$V_1 > V_2$

We must use both conservation of momentum and energy. By the law of conservation of energy:

$$\tfrac{1}{2} m_1 v_1^2 + \tfrac{1}{2} m_2 v_2^2 = \tfrac{1}{2}(m_1 + m_2)v^2 + \tfrac{1}{2}kx^2$$

By the law of conservation of momentum:

$$m_1 v_1 + m_2 v_2 = (m_1 + m_2)v \Rightarrow v = \frac{m_1 v_1 + m_2 v_2}{m_1 + m_2}$$

$$m_1v_1^2 + m_2v_2^2 = (m_1 + m_2)\left(\frac{m_1v_1 + m_2v_2}{m_1 + m_2}\right)^2 + kx^2$$

$$kx^2 = \frac{(m_1v_1^2 + m_2v_2^2)(m_1 + m_2) - m_1^2v_1^2 - m_2^2v_2^2 - 2m_1m_2v_1v_2}{m_1 + m_2}$$

$$= m_1m_2(v_1 - v_2)^2 / (m_1 + m_2)$$

$$x = \sqrt{m_1m_2 / [(m_1 + m_2)k]}\ (v_1 - v_2)$$

$$= \sqrt{\frac{\mu}{k}}(v_1 - v_2)$$

where $\mu = m_1m_2 / (m_1 + m_2)$

9. **(C)**

The cylindrical shell has moment of inertial $I_2 = mR^2$ while the solid cylinder has $I_1 = {}^1/_2\, MR^2$.

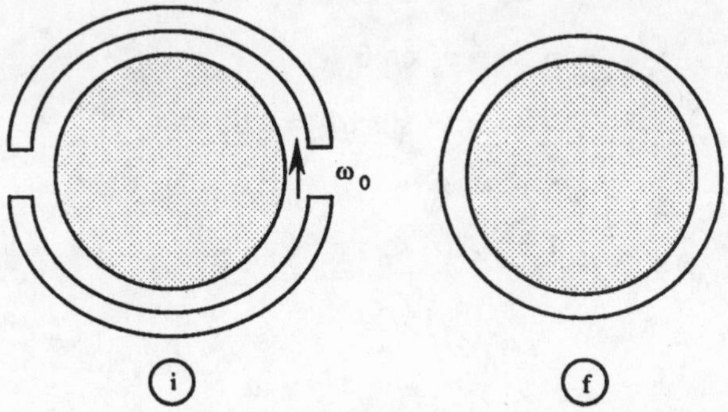

We must use the conservation of angular momentum.

$$\Sigma L = I_1\, \omega_0 = (I_1 + I_2)\, \omega_f$$

Since initially only the cylinder is rotating while finally the cylinder and shell rotate with the same angular velocity.

$$\omega_f = I_1\, \omega_0 / (I_1 + I_2) = {}^1/_2\, Mr^2\, \omega_0 / ({}^1/_2\, Mr^2 + mr^2)$$

$$= M\omega_0 / (M + 2m)$$

Note that energy is *not* conserved in this inelastic interaction.

10. **(A)**

This is a basic dynamics problem. Applying Newton's 2nd law to the hanging mass m and then the second mass m' we get:

$$\Sigma\tau = (T_1 - T_2)\, R = I\mathrm{a},$$

$$mg - T_1 = ma$$

$T_2 = m'a$

Applying Newton's 2nd law for rotation, we obtain:

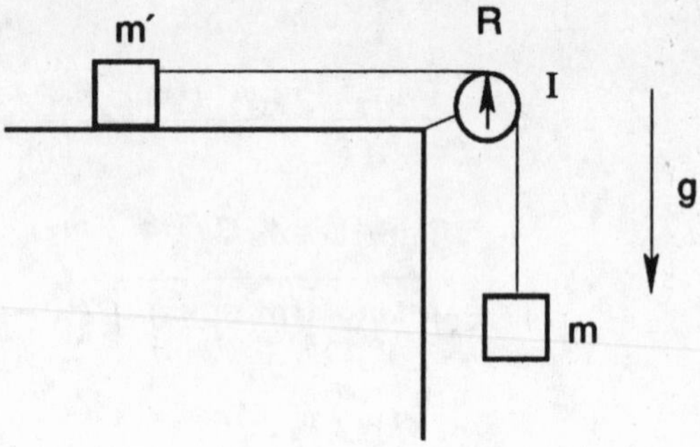

$$v = R\omega \Rightarrow a = R\alpha$$

$$(T_1 - T_2)R = Ia / R$$

$$m(g - a) - m'a = Ia / R^2$$

$$mg - (m + m')\, a = Ia / R^2$$

$$a\,(I/R^2 + m + m') = mg$$

$$\Rightarrow a = mg / (I/R^2 + m + m')$$

11. **(B)**

$$v_{0x} = v_0 \cos\theta$$

$$= 11 \cos 14° = 10.67 \text{ m/s}$$

$$v_{0y} = v_0 \sin\theta$$

$$= 11 \sin 14° = 2.66 \text{ m/s}$$

$$x = v_{0x} t$$

$$l \cos 45° = 10.67\, t$$

$$t = l/15.09$$

$$y = y_0 + v_{0y}\, t + {}^1/_2\, a_y t^2$$

$$-l \sin 45° = 2.66t - 4.9t^2 = .1763\, l - .02152\, l^2$$

$$.02152\, l^2 - 0.8834\, l = 0$$

$$l = 0.8834 / .02152 = 41.05 \text{ m}$$

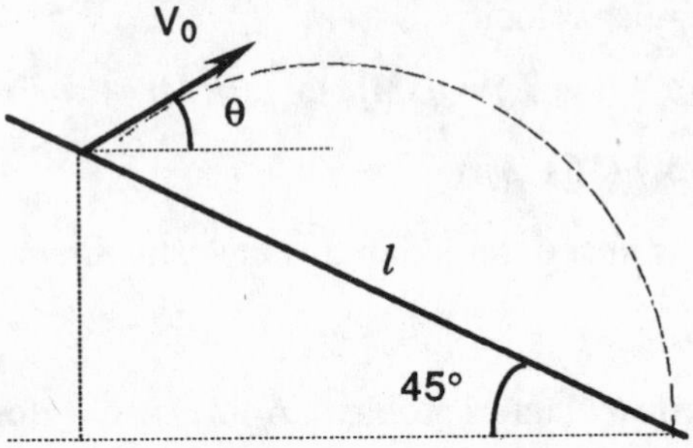

12. **(A)**

Consider the usual spherical coordinates (r, θ, ϕ). The velocity then has two components

$$v_\theta = l\frac{d\theta}{dt} \text{ and } v_\phi = l\sin\theta\frac{d\phi}{dt}$$

Hence the kinetic energy is

$$K = {}^1/_2 ml^2(\theta'^2 + \phi'^2 \sin^2 \theta).$$

Also the potential energy comes solely from the z coordinate

$$z = r\cos\theta = l\cos\theta$$

$$U = mg\,l\,(1 + \cos\theta),$$

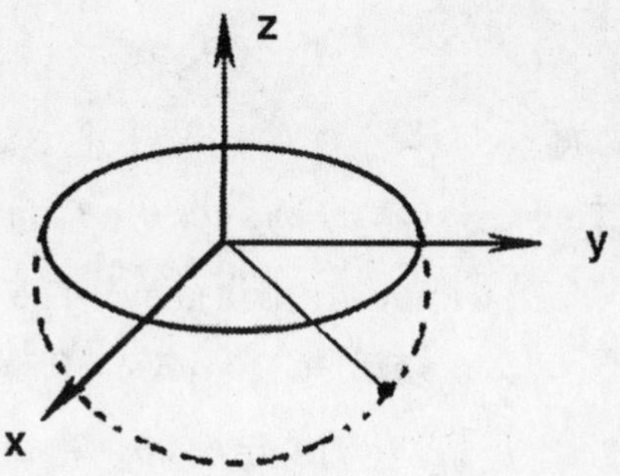

Note that

$$\theta = 180° \Rightarrow U = 0$$

Hence the Lagrangian is

$$L = K - U = {}^1/_2\, ml^2(\theta'^2 + \phi'^2 \sin^2\theta) - mg\,l(1 + \cos\theta)$$

13. **(B)**

The potential is

$$U = -\int \mathbf{F}\cdot d\mathbf{r} = \int kr\,dr = {}^1/_2\,kr^2$$

$$= {}^1/_2\,k(R^2 + z^2)$$

In cylindrical coordinates the velocity is

$$\mathbf{v} = r'\hat{r} + r\theta'\hat{\theta} + z'\hat{z}$$

Thus

$$K = {}^1/_2\,mv^2$$

$$= {}^1/_2\,m\,(r'^2 + r^2\theta'^2 + z'^2)$$

Since $r = R$ = constant

$$= {}^1/_2\,m(R^2\,\theta'^2 + z'^2)$$

Hence

$$H = K + U = {}^1/_2 m(R^2\,\theta'^2 + z'^2) + {}^1/_2 k(R^2 + z^2)$$

14. **(C)**

This is a static equilibrium problem.

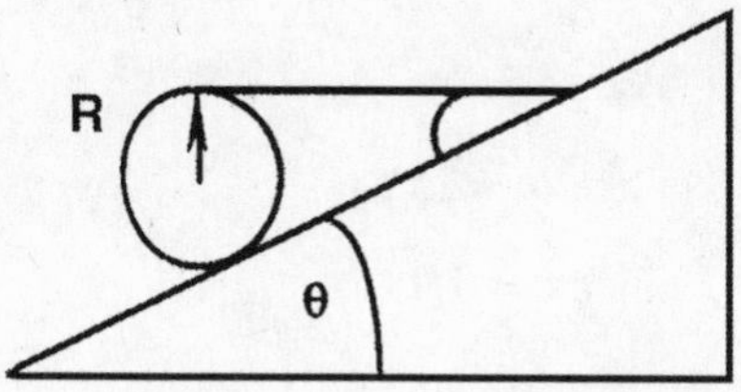

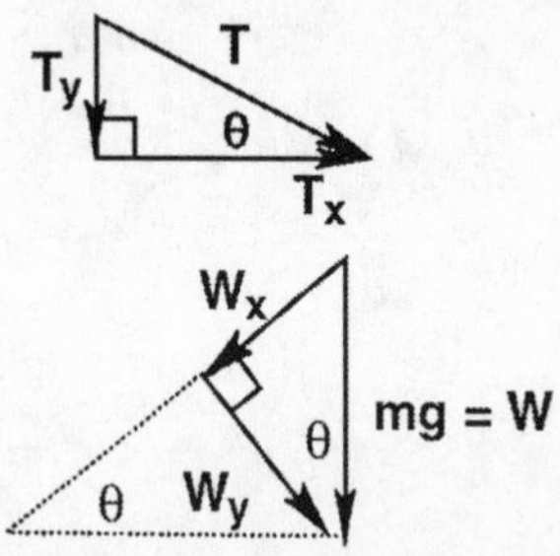

The first condition of equilibrium gives:

$$\Sigma F_x = T_x + \mu N - W_x = 0$$

$$T\cos\theta + \mu(mg\cos\theta + T\sin\theta) - mg\sin\theta = 0$$

and $\quad \Sigma F_y = N - T_y - W_y = 0$

Thus $\quad N = mg\cos\theta + T\sin\theta$

which we already used above. The second condition of equilibrium is:

$$\Sigma\tau = RT - \mu NR = 0 \Rightarrow \mu N = T$$

$$\Rightarrow \mu(mg\cos\theta + T\sin\theta) = T$$

$$T\cos\theta + T = mg\sin\theta$$

Finally $\quad T = mg\sin\theta / (1 + \cos\theta).$

15. **(D)**

The given position vector is:

$$r = (3t + 5t^3)\mathbf{x} \quad \text{or} \quad x = 3t + 5t^3$$

$$v = \frac{dx}{dt} = 3 + 15t^2$$

$$a = \frac{dv}{dt} = 30t \Rightarrow F = ma = 60t$$

since $m = 2kg$ is given. The power is

$$P = \mathbf{F}\cdot\mathbf{v} = 180\,t + 900\,t^3$$

The work is then

$$W = \int_0^1 P\,dt = \int_0^1 (180t + 900t^3)\,dt$$

$$= 90t^2 + 225t^4\Big|_0^1 = 315J$$

16. **(E)**

If the motion is circular, the gravitational force causes centripetal acceleration so that

$$F = mv^2/r$$

$$\Sigma F = ma$$

$$G\,mm_s/r^2 = m\omega^2 r \qquad \text{using } v = \omega r$$

$$= 4\pi^2 m\upsilon^2 r \qquad \text{since } \omega = 2\pi\upsilon$$

$$= 4\pi^2 mr / T^2 \qquad \text{since } \upsilon = 1/T$$

$$G\,mm_s/r^2 = 4\pi^2 mr/T^2$$

$$T^2 = (4\pi^2/Gm_s)r^3$$

Hence $$m_s = (4\pi^2/G)\, r^3 / T^2$$

$$= (4\pi^2/6.673 \times 10^{-8})\,(1.50 \times 10^{13})^3 / (\pi \times 10^7)^2$$

$$= 2.0 \times 10^{33} \text{ g}$$

17. **(E)**

The given spring force is nonlinear but conservative.

$$F = -k_1x - k_2x^3$$

Using the work-energy theorem:

$$W = \Delta K$$

$$W = -\int \boldsymbol{F}\cdot d\boldsymbol{x} = {}^1/_2\, k_1x^2 + {}^1/_4\, k_2x^4 = {}^1/_2\, mv^2$$

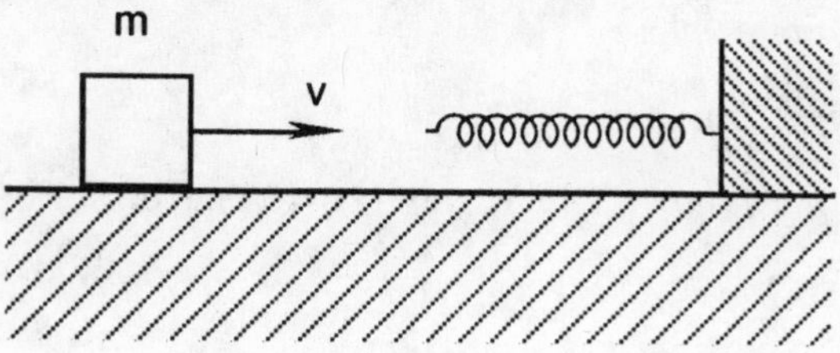

$$x^4 + 2\frac{k_1}{k_2}x^2 = \frac{2m}{k_2}v^2$$

$$\left(x^2 + \frac{k_1}{k_2}\right)^2 = 2\frac{m}{k_2}v^2 + \left(\frac{k_1}{k_2}\right)^2$$

$$x^2 = -\frac{k_1}{k_2} + \sqrt{2\frac{m}{k_2}v^2 + \frac{k_1^2}{k_2^2}}$$

$$x = \sqrt{k_1/k_2}\left(\sqrt{1 + \frac{2mv^2k_2}{k_1^2}} - 1\right)^{1/2}$$

18. **(D)**

The products of inertia or off diagonal elements of the inertia tensor vanish for a symmetric body, e.g., $I_{xy} = -\Sigma mxy = 0$. Thus

$$L_x = I_{xx}\omega_x,\ L_y = I_{yy}\,\omega_y \text{ and } L_z = I_{zz}\,\omega_z$$

I_{zz} just comes from the moment of inertia of the two spheres:

$$I_{zz} = {}^2/_5\, mr^2 + {}^2/_5\, mr^2 = {}^4/_5\, mr^2$$

I_{yy} comes from the parallel axis theorem:

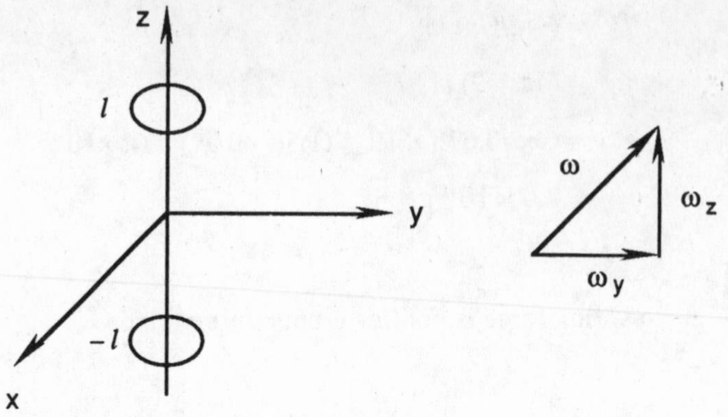

$I_{yy} = 2(I_{cm} + md^2)$

where $d = l$ has been used

$= 2(^2/_5\, mr^2 + ml^2)$

$= ^4/_5\, mr^2 + 2ml^2$

thus $\quad L_x = 0,\, L_y = (^4/_5\, mr^2 + 2ml^2)\,\omega_y$ and $L_z = ^4/_5\, mr^2\omega_z$

19. **(C)**

Consider that the executive toy is tilted at angle α

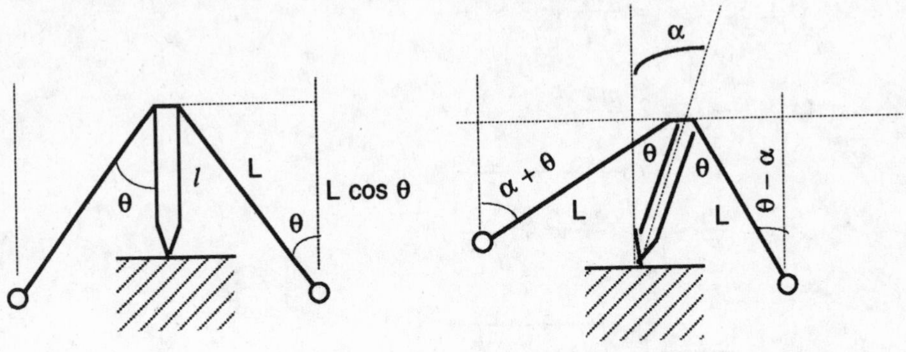

$$U = mg(l\cos\alpha - L\cos(\alpha + \theta)) + mg\,(l\cos\alpha - L\cos(\theta - \alpha))$$
$$= 2mg\,(l - L\cos\theta)\cos\alpha$$

Equilibrium occurs at

$$\frac{dU}{d\alpha} = -2mg(l - L\cos\theta)\sin\alpha = 0$$

As we expect, $\Rightarrow \alpha = 0$ so that stability at equilibrium requires

$$\left.\frac{d^2U}{d\alpha^2}\right|_{\alpha=0} = -2mg(l - L\cos\theta)\cos\alpha > 0$$

Thus $L\cos\theta > l$ which means that the masses must hang below the pivot.

20. **(A)**

Bernoulli's equation is

$$\tfrac{1}{2}\rho v^2 + p + \rho g h = \text{constant}$$

Here we may take $h = 0$ so that

$$\tfrac{1}{2}\rho v_1^2 + p_1 = \tfrac{1}{2}\rho v_2^2 + p_2.$$

Now the equation of continuity implies that

$$A_1 v_1 = A_2 v_2.$$

Hence $p_2 = p_1 + \frac{1}{2}\rho v_1^2\left(1 - \frac{A_1^2}{A_2^2}\right)$

Note that $A_1 > A_2 \Rightarrow p_2 < p_1$.

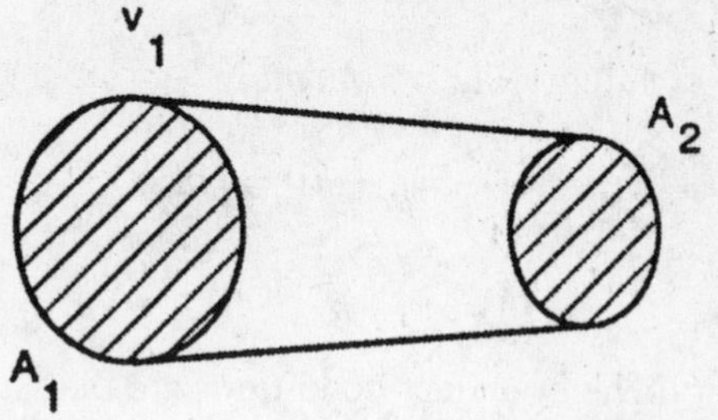

21. **(C)**

For an infinite charged plane

$$\int \mathbf{E} \cdot d\mathbf{a} = q / \varepsilon_0$$

by Gauss' law or Maxwell's 1st equation:

$$EA + EA = \sigma \cdot A / \varepsilon_0$$

$$E = \sigma / 2\varepsilon_0$$

In between the planes where $-a/2 < x < a/2$, there are four identical contributions

$$\mathbf{E} = 4\,\sigma/2\varepsilon_0\,\mathbf{x} = 2\,\sigma/\varepsilon_0\,\mathbf{x}.$$

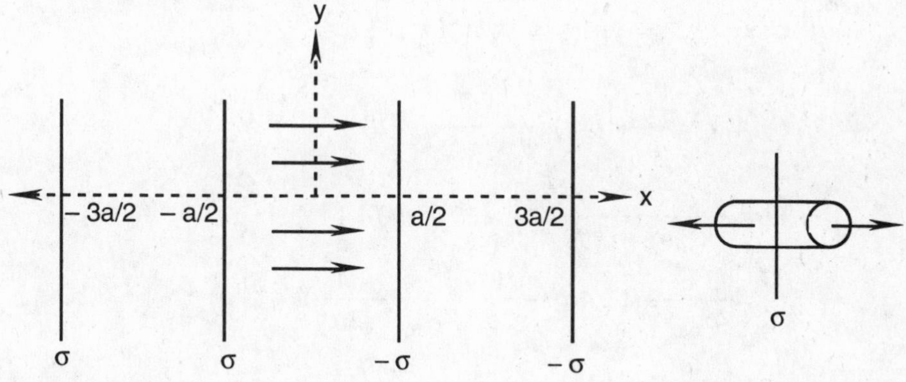

22. **(D)**

Here cylindrical coordinates are appropriate. Laplace's equation is:

$$\nabla^2 \Phi = 0$$

and

$$\nabla^2 = \frac{1}{\rho}\frac{\partial}{\partial \rho}\left(\rho\frac{\partial}{\partial \rho}\right) + \frac{1}{\rho^2}\frac{\partial^2}{\partial \phi^2} + \frac{\partial^2}{\partial z^2}$$

in orthogonal curvilinear cylindrical coordinates. By symmetry $\Phi = \Phi(\phi)$ only. Thus

Laplace's equation is

$$\frac{1}{\rho^2}\frac{d^2\Phi}{d\Phi^2}=0$$

Integrating we obtain

$$\frac{d\Phi}{d\Phi}=a, \int d\Phi=\int a d\phi$$

$$\Phi=a\phi+b$$

The boundary conditions are that at

$$\phi=0, \Phi=0 \Rightarrow b=0$$

and at

$$\phi=\alpha, \Phi=V_0 \Rightarrow a=V_0/\alpha,$$

$$\Phi=\frac{V_0}{\alpha}\phi$$

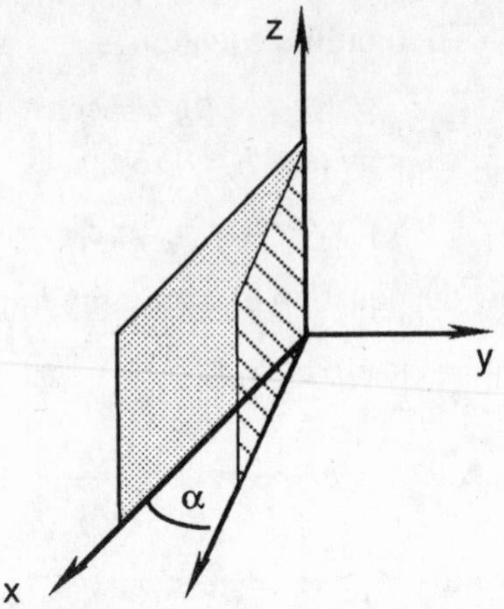

Finally

$$\mathrm{E}=-\nabla\Phi=-\frac{1}{\rho}\frac{\partial\Phi}{\partial\phi}\hat{\phi}=-\frac{V_0}{\alpha\rho}\hat{\phi}$$

23. **(E)**

The given charge density is:

$$\rho(\mathbf{r})=e(\delta(\mathbf{r})-\frac{\alpha^3}{\pi}e^{-2\alpha r})$$

Now we use Gauss' law.

$$\nabla\cdot\mathbf{E}=\frac{\rho}{\varepsilon_0} \text{ or } \oint \mathrm{E}\cdot da=\int\nabla\cdot \mathrm{E}dV$$

$$E_r\cdot 4\pi r^2=\frac{e}{\varepsilon_0}(\int\delta(\mathbf{r})dV-\frac{\alpha^3}{\pi}\int e^{-2\alpha r}dV)$$

$$E_r=\frac{e}{4\pi\varepsilon_0 r^2}(1-\frac{\alpha^3}{\pi}4\pi\int_0^r e^{-2\alpha r}r^2dr)$$

$$=\frac{e}{4\pi\varepsilon_0 r^2}(1-4\alpha^3[-\frac{1}{2\alpha}(r^2+\frac{r}{\alpha}+\frac{1}{2\alpha^2})e^{-2\alpha r}\Big|_0^r])$$

$$=\frac{e}{4\pi\varepsilon_0 r^2}(2\alpha^2r^2+2\alpha r+1)e^{-2\alpha r}$$

$$=\frac{e}{4\pi\varepsilon_0}(2\alpha^2+\frac{2\alpha}{r}+\frac{1}{r^2})e^{-2\alpha r}$$

24. **(C)**

We are given that

$$m = 2g,$$

$$\mathbf{E} = (3\mathbf{x}+4\mathbf{y})\times10^5 \text{ N/C},$$

and $\theta = 33°$.

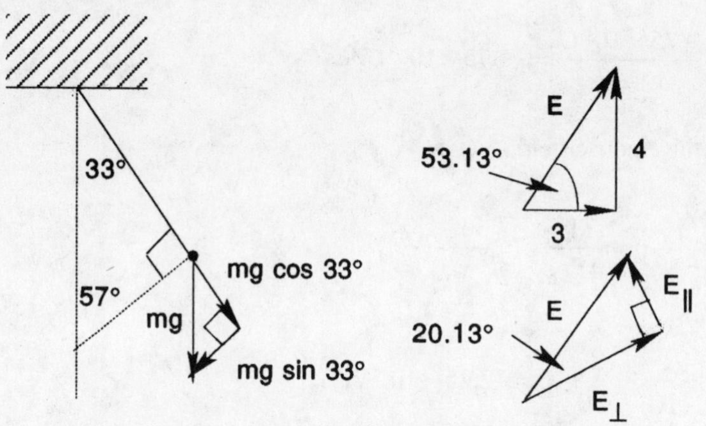

The angle **E** makes with respect to the horizontal is found from

$$\tan\theta = \frac{E_y}{E_x}$$

$$= \frac{4}{3}$$

$$\Rightarrow \theta = 58.13°$$

We resolve **E** into parallel and perpendicular components:

$$E_{\parallel} = 5 \times 10^5 \sin 20.13 = 1.72 \times 10^5 \text{ N/C}$$

$$E_{\perp} = 5 \times 10^5 \cos 20.13 = 4.70 \times 10^5 \text{ N/C}$$

Since the pith ball is in equilibrium

$$qE_{\perp} = mg \sin\theta$$

$$q = (.002)(9.8) \sin(33°) / 5 \times 10^5 \cos(20.13°)$$

$$= 2.27 \times 10^{-8} \text{ C}$$

$$T = mg\cos\theta - qE_{\parallel}$$

$$= (.002)(9.8)\cos(33°) - (2.27 \times 10^{-8})\, 1.72 \times 10^{5)}$$

$$= 0.0125 \text{ N}$$

25. **(B)**

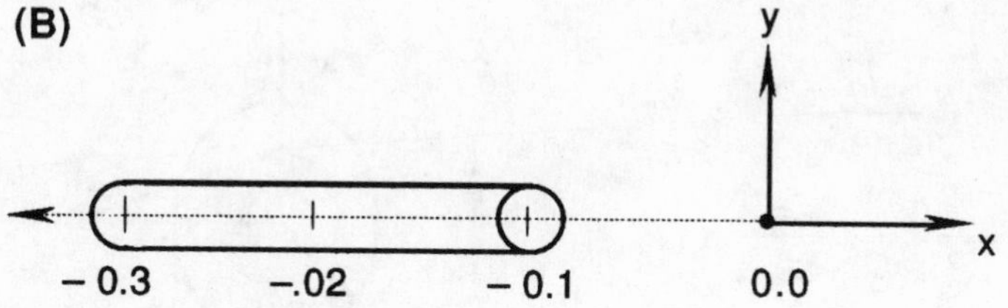

The given charge is

$$q = -75\ \mu C.$$

Therefore the linear charge density is

$$\lambda = \frac{q}{l} = \frac{-75 \times 10^6 C}{.20M} = -3.75 \times 10^{-4} C/m$$

Now calculate the electric field

$$\mathrm{E} = \int \frac{dq}{4\pi\varepsilon_0 r^2}\mathbf{r} = \frac{1}{4\pi\varepsilon_0}\int_{-.30}^{-.10} \frac{\lambda dx}{x^2}(-x)$$

$$= \frac{-\lambda}{4\pi\varepsilon_0}\left(\frac{1}{.10} - \frac{1}{.30}\right)x, = -2.25 \times 10^7 N/Cx$$

Substituting

$$\varepsilon_0 = 8.85 \times 10^{-12}$$

26. **(A)**

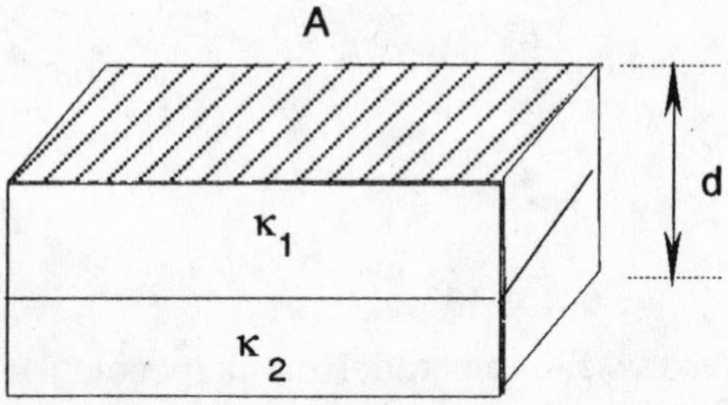

In vacuum,

$$C_0 = \varepsilon_0 A/d.$$

In a dielectric,

$$C = \kappa \varepsilon_0 A/d.$$

Here we really have two capacitors in series.

$$C_1 = \frac{\kappa_1 \varepsilon_0 A}{d/2}, \quad C_2 = \frac{\kappa_2 \varepsilon_0 A}{d/2}$$

The rule for adding capacitance in series is:

$$C = C_1 C_2 / (C_1 + C_2)$$

Hence, $= \kappa_1 \kappa_2 (2\,\varepsilon_0 A/d)^2 / (\kappa_1 + \kappa_2)(2\,\varepsilon_0 A/d)$

$$= 2\,\kappa_1 \kappa_2 C_0 / (\kappa_1 + \kappa_2)$$

27. **(A)**

Using the symmetry of the disk, the differential change element of an annulus is

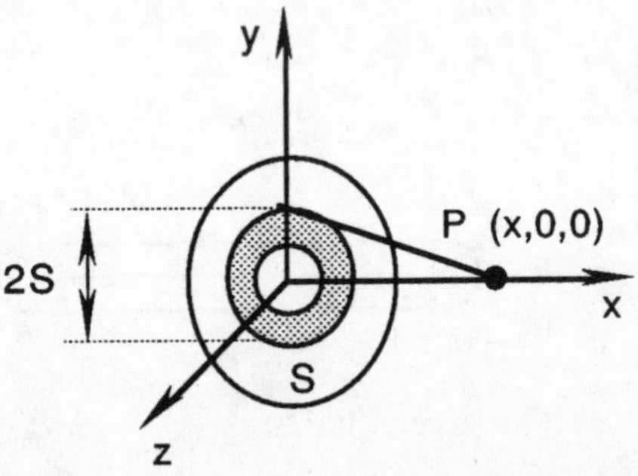

$$\sigma = \frac{dq}{da}$$

$$V(x) = \int \frac{dq}{4\pi\varepsilon_0 r}$$

$$= \int \frac{2\pi\sigma s}{\sqrt{s^2 + x^2}} \frac{ds}{4\pi\varepsilon_0}$$

$$= \frac{1}{4\pi\varepsilon_0} 2\pi\sigma\sqrt{x^2 + s^2}\Bigg|_{s=0}^{s=a}$$

$$V(x) = \frac{\sigma}{2\varepsilon_0}(\sqrt{x^2 + a^2} - x), x > 0$$

Now the electric field is the negative gradient of the electric potential.

$$\mathbf{E} = -\nabla V = \frac{\sigma}{2\varepsilon_0}\frac{\partial}{\partial x}(\sqrt{x^2+a^2} - x)\mathbf{x}$$

$$= \frac{\sigma}{2\varepsilon_0}(\frac{1}{2}(x^2+a^2)^{-1/2}2x - 1)\mathbf{x}$$

$$= \frac{\sigma}{2\varepsilon_0}\left(\frac{x}{\sqrt{x^2+a^2}} - 1\right)\mathbf{x}$$

28. **(C)**

Now the current density is

$$j = I/A = I/\rho\,(b^2 - a^2)$$

and by Ohm's law

$$j = \sigma E = \frac{1}{\rho}E = \frac{1}{\rho}\frac{V}{l}$$

where s is the conductivity and r is the resistivity. Hence

$$\frac{1}{\rho}\frac{V}{l} = \frac{I}{\pi(b^2 - a^2)}$$

Finally

$$R = V/I = \rho l/\pi\,(b^2 - a^2).$$

29. **(E)**

The bottom two resistors are in parallel

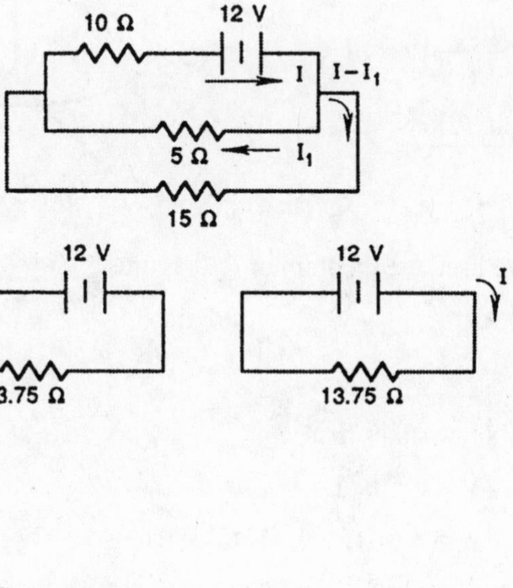

Thus

$$R = \frac{R_1 R_2}{R_1 + R_2} = \frac{15(5)}{15+5} = 3.75\Omega$$

The last two resistors now add up since they are in series:

$$R = R_1 + R_2$$
$$= 10 + 3.75$$
$$= 13.75\ \Omega$$

The current in the reduced circut is then

$$I = V/R = 12/13.75 = .873\ \text{A}$$

Applying Kirchhoff's voltage law to the second circuit, we get:

$$12\ V = 5I_1 + 10\,I = 5I_1 + 8.73$$

thus $I_1 = 3.27/5 = 0.654$ A.

30. **(B)**

If a magnetic field is applied to a current-carrying conductor perpendicularly, an electrical potential difference is generated. This physical phenomenon was discovered by E. H. Hall in 1879 and, consequently, is known as the Hall effect.

31. **(D)**

The Biot-Savart law states that:

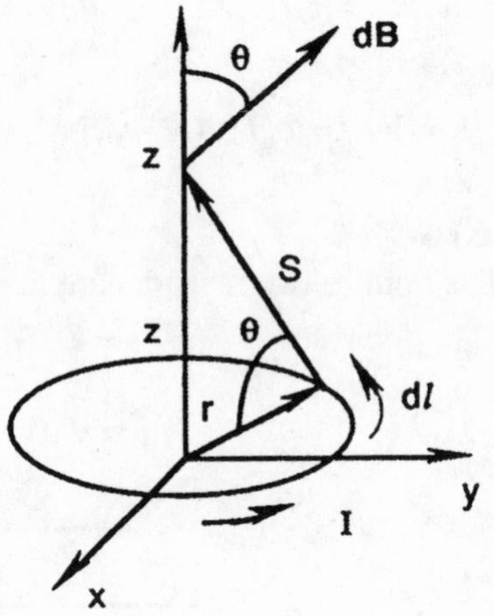

$$dB = \frac{\mu_0}{4\pi} I \frac{dl \times s}{s^2}$$

$$dB_z = dB \cos\theta$$

$$= \frac{\mu_0 I dl}{4\pi s^2} \cos\theta = \frac{\mu_0 I dl}{4\pi s^2} \frac{r}{s}$$

$$B_z = \frac{\mu_0 I r}{4\pi s^2} \int_0^{2\pi r} dl$$

$$= \frac{\mu_0 I 2\pi r^2}{4\pi s^3}$$

$$= \mu_0 I r^2 / 2(r^2 + z^2)^{3/2}$$

Where we have used the theorem of Pythagoras

$$s^2 = r^2 + z^2$$

32. **(E)**

Ampere's law states that

$$\nabla \times \mathbf{B} = \mu_0\, \mathbf{j}.$$

Since $\mathbf{A} \cdot (\mathbf{A} \times \mathbf{B}) = 0,\ \nabla \cdot (\nabla \times \mathbf{B}) = 0 \Rightarrow \nabla \cdot \mathbf{j} = 0.$

But really $\nabla \cdot \mathbf{j} + \frac{\partial \rho}{\partial t} = 0$

is the continuity equation. Now

$$\nabla \cdot \mathbf{E} = \frac{\rho}{\varepsilon_0}$$

is Gauss' Law. Hence

$$\nabla \cdot \mathbf{j} + \frac{\partial}{\partial t} \nabla \cdot (\varepsilon_0 \cdot \mathrm{E}) = 0$$

$$\nabla \cdot \left(\mathbf{j} + \varepsilon_0 \frac{\partial \mathrm{E}}{\partial t} \right) = 0$$

33. **(D)**

In a vacuum $\nabla \times \mathbf{B} = \mu_0 \mathbf{j}$. But really $\mathbf{j} = \mathbf{j}_{free}$. In the presence of matter

$$\mathbf{j} = \mathbf{j}_{free} + \mathbf{j}_{bound}.$$

Hence $\nabla \times \mathbf{B} = \mu_0 (\mathbf{j}_{free} + \mathbf{j}_{bound})$

$$\nabla \times \mathbf{B} - \mu_0 \mathbf{j}_{bound} = \mu_0 \mathbf{j}_{free}$$

Defining the magnetization vector by

$$\nabla \times (\mathbf{B} - \mu_0 \mathbf{M}) = \mu_0 \mathbf{j}_{free}$$

where $\nabla \times \mathbf{M} \equiv \mathbf{j}_{bound}$,

the problem is solved.

34. **(C)**

The electron drifts in a different direction depending on the direction of the electric field. When the electron drifts upward:

$$mg = eE - 6\pi R\eta v_+.$$

When the electron drifts downward:

$$mg = -eE + 6\pi R\eta v_-$$

Subtracting the two equations we obtain:

$$0 = 2eE - 6\pi R\eta (v_+ + v_-)$$

or $$e = \frac{3\pi R\eta}{E}(v_- + v_+)$$

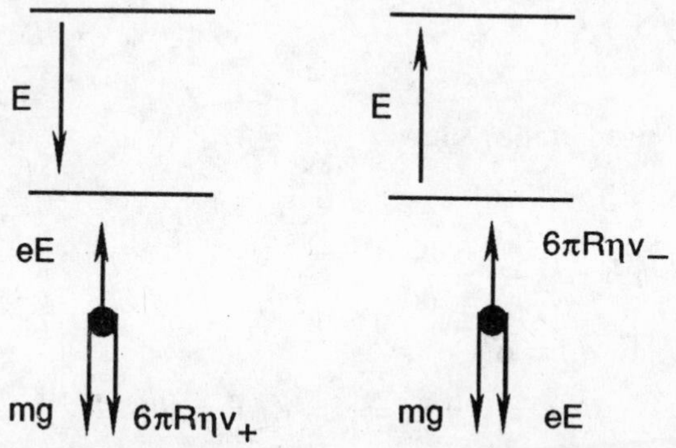

35. **(B)**

Derivation of Coulomb's law from Gauss's law:

$$\nabla \cdot \mathbf{E} = \rho / \varepsilon_0$$

$$\oint \nabla \cdot \mathbf{E}\, dV = \oint \mathbf{E} \cdot d\mathbf{a}$$

by the divergence theorem.

$$\oint \mathbf{E} \cdot d\mathbf{a} = \oint \rho dV / \varepsilon_0$$

For a point charge

$$E \cdot 4\pi r^2 = q / \varepsilon_0$$

$$E = q/4\pi\varepsilon_0 r^2$$

for a charge $q = q_1$

$$E_1 = q_1 / 4\pi\varepsilon_0 r^2$$

$$F = q_2 E_1 = q_1 q_2 / 4\pi \varepsilon_0 r^2 = k_E q_1 q_2 / r^2$$

for the force on another charge q_2 due to q_1.

Using Ampere's law:

$$\nabla \times \mathbf{B} = \mu_0 \mathbf{j}$$

$$\int \nabla \times \mathbf{B} \cdot d\mathbf{a} = \oint \mathbf{B} \cdot d\mathbf{l}$$

by Stoke's theorem.

$$\int (\nabla \cdot (\mathbf{B}) \cdot d\mathbf{a} = \mu_0 \int \mathbf{j} \cdot d\mathbf{a}$$

For a line current

$$2\pi r B = \mu_0 I$$

$$B = \mu_0 I / 2\pi r$$

$$B_1 = \mu_0 I_1 / 2\pi r$$

For a current $I = I_{1.}$

The Lorentz force is

$$\mathbf{F} = q_2 \mathbf{v} \times \mathbf{B} = I_2 \mathbf{l} \times \mathbf{B},$$

$$F / l = \mu_0 I_1 I_2 / 2 \pi r = k_B I_1 I_2 / r$$

Hence:

$$k_B / k_E = \frac{\mu_0}{2\pi} 4\pi\varepsilon_0$$

$$= 2 \mu_0 \varepsilon_0$$

36. **(A)**

We must use Faraday's law:

$$\nabla \times \mathbf{E} = -\partial \mathbf{B} / \partial t$$

$$V = \int \mathbf{E} \cdot d\mathbf{l} = -\frac{\partial \Phi}{\partial t},$$

where $\Phi = \int \mathrm{B} \cdot da = Blx$

$$V = -Blv \text{ and } V = RI \Rightarrow I = V / R = Blv / R$$

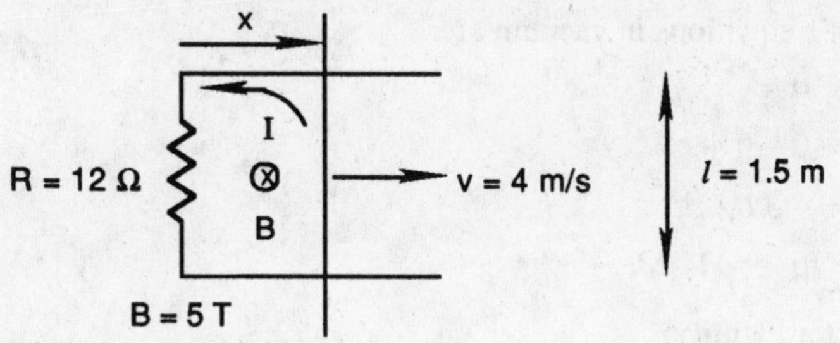

The power is

$$P = VI$$
$$= (Blv)^2 / R$$
$$= (5 \cdot 1.5 \cdot 4)^2 / 12 = 75\ W$$

Furthermore, I must be *counterclockwise* by Lenz's law to counteract the increase of magnetic flux due to the motion of the bar.

37. **(E)**

By Kirchoff's voltage law,

$$\Sigma V = 0.$$

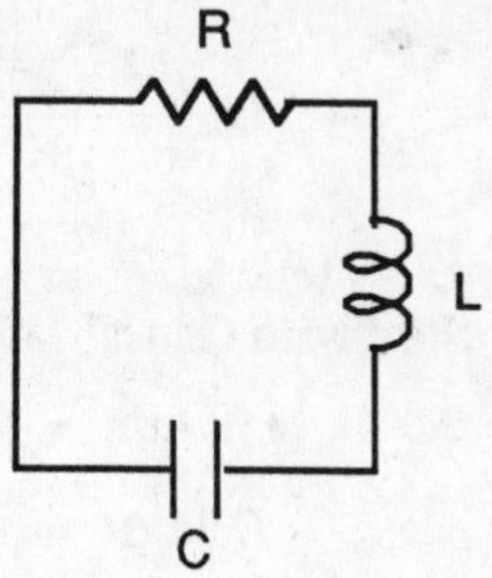

So

$$-RI - LI' - \frac{Q}{C} = 0$$

$$Q'' + \frac{R}{L}Q' + \frac{1}{LC}Q = 0$$

$$\omega_0 = \sqrt{1/LC}, \gamma = R/L, \omega = \sqrt{\omega_0^2 - \gamma^2/4}$$

$$Q'' + \gamma Q' + \omega_0^2 Q = 0$$

Then for the light damping case, the solution is

$$Q = Q_m e^{-1/2\gamma t}\cos(\omega t + \delta)$$
$$= Q_m e^{-1/2\gamma t}\cos\omega t \quad \text{if} \quad \delta = 0;$$

$$R = 10\,\Omega, L = 10^{-3}\,H, C = 10^{-6}\,F$$

$$\omega_0 = 1/\sqrt{LC} = 1/\sqrt{10^{-9}} = 31,620\ \text{rad/s}$$

$$\omega = \sqrt{\omega_0^2 - \frac{1}{4}\frac{R^2}{L^2}}$$

$$= \sqrt{31,620^2 - \frac{1}{4}\frac{10^2}{10^{-6}}} = 31,220\ \text{rad/s}$$

$$\frac{Q}{Q_m} = e^{-\frac{1}{2}\times\frac{10}{10^{-3}}\times 2\times 10^{-4}} \cos(31,220 \times 2 \times 10^{-4}) = 0.366$$

38. **(C)**

Maxwell's equations in vacuum are:

$$\nabla \cdot \mathbf{E} = 0$$

$$\nabla \cdot \mathbf{B} = 0$$

$$\nabla \times \mathbf{E} = -\partial \boldsymbol{B} / \partial t$$

$$\nabla \times \mathbf{B} = \mu_o \varepsilon_o \partial \mathbf{E} / \partial t$$

Now use a vector identity:

$$\nabla \times (\nabla \times \mathbf{B}) = \nabla (\nabla \cdot \mathbf{B}) - \nabla^2 \mathbf{B}$$

$$\nabla \times (\mu_o \varepsilon_o \partial \mathbf{E} / \partial t) = -\nabla^2 \mathbf{B} \text{ since } \nabla \cdot \mathbf{B} = 0$$

$$\mu_0 \varepsilon_0 \frac{\partial}{\partial t} \frac{\partial \mathbf{B}}{\partial t} = \nabla^2 \mathbf{B}$$

$$\nabla^2 \mathbf{B} = \mu_0 \varepsilon_0 \frac{\partial^2 \mathbf{B}}{\partial t^2}$$

is the general wave equation. For

$$\mathbf{B} = B_z(x, y, z)\mathbf{z}$$

we get $\left(\frac{\partial^2}{\partial x^2} + \frac{\partial^2}{\partial y^2} + \frac{\partial^2}{\partial z^2}\right) B_z = \mu_0 \varepsilon_0 \frac{\partial^2 B_z}{\partial t^2}$

39. **(A)**

Start with Gauss' law in integral form:

$$\oint \mathbf{E} \cdot d\mathbf{a} = q / \varepsilon_o$$

$$E\, 2\pi \rho l = q / \varepsilon_o$$

$$\mathbf{E} = (\lambda / 2\pi \rho \varepsilon_o)\, \hat{\rho}$$

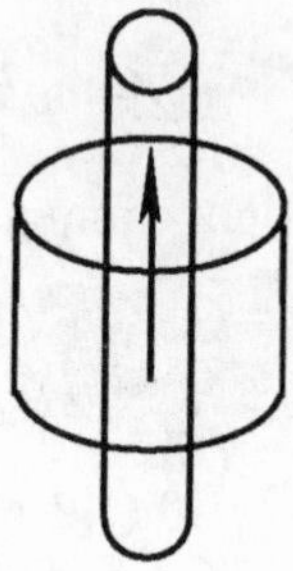

Now use Ampere's law:

$$\oint \mathbf{B} \cdot d\mathbf{a} = \mu_o \mathrm{I}$$

$$2 \pi \rho B = \mu_o I$$

$$\mathbf{B} = (\mu_o I / 2\pi \rho)\, \hat{\phi}$$

By the Lorentz transformation,

$$E'_\rho = \gamma(E_\rho - vB_\phi)$$

$$= \gamma\left(\frac{\lambda}{2\pi\rho\varepsilon_0} - v\frac{\mu_0 I}{2\pi\rho}\right) = \frac{\gamma}{2\pi\rho}\left(\frac{\lambda}{\varepsilon_0} - v\mu_0 I\right)$$

Hence

$$E'_\rho = 0 \text{ if } v\mu_0 I = \frac{\lambda}{\varepsilon_0}, \Rightarrow v = \frac{\lambda}{\varepsilon_0 \mu_0 I}$$

40. **(D)**

The altitude is

$$x = 60 \text{ km}$$

Also $\quad x = ct$

so that $\quad t = \dfrac{60\times10^3}{3\times10^8} = 2\times10^{-4}\,s$

Every half-life, one loses one-half of the particles

$$(\frac{1}{2})^3 = \frac{1}{8} \Rightarrow t_0 = 3\times1.5\times10^{-6} = 4.5\times10^{-6}\,s$$

three half-lives. Using time dilation:

$$t = t_0\gamma \Rightarrow \gamma = \frac{2\times10^{-4}}{4.5\times10^{-6}} = 44.44$$

$$\gamma = \frac{1}{\sqrt{1-\beta^2}},$$

$$\beta = \sqrt{1-\frac{1}{\gamma^2}} = 0.99975$$

$$1-\beta = 0.00025$$

41. **(A)**

The kinetic energy of the electron is

$$K = 700 \text{ MeV}.$$

Hence the total relativistic energy is

$$E = K + m = 700.511 \text{ MeV}$$

The γ parameter is thus

$$\gamma = E/m = 700.511 / 5.11 = 1371$$

$$\beta = \sqrt{1-\frac{1}{\gamma^2}} = 1-\frac{1}{2\gamma^2} = 0.9999997$$

Now we must use the index of refraction:

$$n = c/v = 1.00029$$

The Cerenkov radiation formula is needed

$$\beta' = 1/n = 0.9997100$$

$$\cos\phi = \beta'/\beta = 0.9997100/0.9999997$$

$$= 0.9997104$$

$$\phi = 1.38°.$$

42. **(B)**

The nuclear reaction is

$${}^2_1\text{H} + {}^2_1\text{H} \rightarrow {}^1_1\text{H} + {}^3_1\text{H} \quad or \quad d + d \rightarrow p + t$$

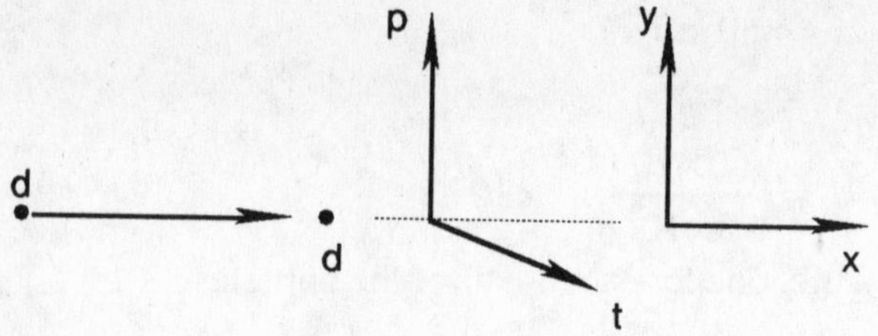

$T_2 = 1.808\text{MeV}$

and $\quad T_1 = 3.467 \text{ MeV}$

The relativistic 4-momentum must be conserved

$$(\underline{p})_0 = (\underline{p})_f \Rightarrow (\mathbf{p}_1\ i\ E/c)_0 = (\mathbf{p}_1\ i\ E/c)_f$$

The 4th component of the 4-momentum is the total energy:

$$E_2 + m_2 = E_1 + E_3$$

The momenta components are assumed to be in the *xy* plane.

$$p_{2x} = p_{3x}$$

$$p_{1y} = -p_{3y}$$

$$m_3^2 = E_3^2 - \mathbf{p}_3^2 = (E_2 + m_2\ E_1)^2 - p_{2x}^{\ 1} - p_{1y}^{\ 2}$$

$$= E_2^2 - p_{2x}^2 + E_1^2 - p_{1y}^2 - 2E_1\ E_2 + m_2^2 + 2m_2\ (E_2 - E_1)$$

$$= 2m_2^2 + m_1^2 + 2m_2\ (E_2 - E_1) - 2E_1\ E_2$$

We are given the mass of the deuteron and the mass of the proton:

$$m_2 = 1876.140 \text{ MeV},$$

$$m_1 = 938.791 \text{ MeV}$$

Hence $\quad E_2 = T_2 + m_2 = 1877.948 \text{ MeV}$

and $\quad E_1 = T_1 + m_1 = 942.258 \text{ MeV}$

$$m_3^2 = 2\,(1876.140)^2 + (938.791)^2 + 2(1876.140)\,(1877.948 - 942.258)$$
$$-2\,(1877.948)\,(942.258)$$

Finally $\quad m_3 = 2809.462 \text{ MeV}$

43. **(C)**

Classically $2\theta = 90°$.

In a relativistic equation, rest energy (mass, E_0) must be considered as part of the total energy of the system. The total initial energy is thus:

$$E = T + E_0$$

By symmetry, the total final energy of each particle is:

$$E' = \frac{1}{2}T + E_0$$

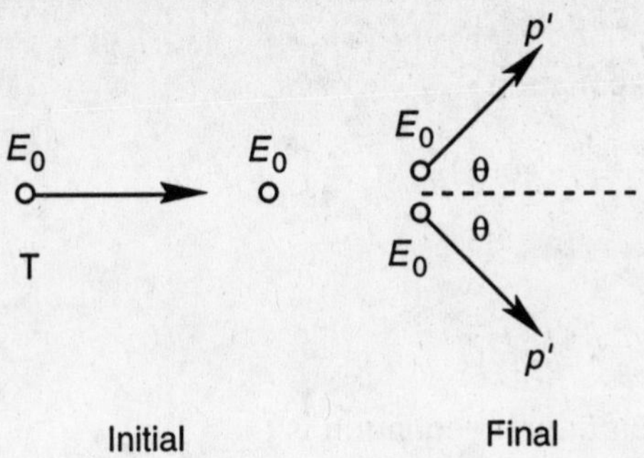

The relativistic momentum must then be:

$$p = \sqrt{E^2 - E_0^{\,2}}$$

$$p' = \sqrt{E'^2 - E_0^{\,2}}$$

$$= \sqrt{\frac{1}{4}T^2 + E_0^{\,2} + E_0 T - E_0^{\,2}}$$

$$= \sqrt{\frac{1}{4}T^2 + E_0 T}$$

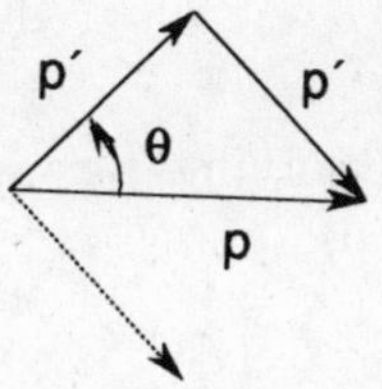

Using the 3-momentum triangle,

$$2p'\cos\theta = p.$$

Thus, $$\cos^2\theta = \frac{p^2}{4p'^2}$$

$$= \left(T^2 + 2E_0 T\right)/\left(T + 4E_0\right)$$

Using a trigonometric identity,

$$\frac{1}{2}(1 + \cos 2\theta) = \left(T + 2E_0 /\left(T + 4E_0\right)\right.$$

$$\cos(2\theta) = \left(2T + 4E_0 - T - 4E_0\right)/\left(T + 4E_0\right)$$

$$= T/\left(T + 4E_0\right)$$

44. **(D)**

Where the Schrödinger equation is $H\Psi = E\Psi$

$$H = T + U$$

$$= \frac{p^2}{2m} - g\delta(x)$$

$$= \frac{-\hbar^2}{2m}\frac{d^2\Psi}{dx^2} - g\delta(x)$$

We now integrate the equation

$$\int_{-\varepsilon}^{\varepsilon}\left(-\frac{\hbar^2}{2m}\frac{\partial^2\psi}{\partial x^2}-g\delta(x)\psi\right)dx=\int_{-\varepsilon}^{\varepsilon}E\Psi\,dx$$

to get

$$\frac{-\hbar^2}{2m}\frac{d\Psi}{dx}\Bigg|_{-\varepsilon}^{\varepsilon}-g\psi(0)=0$$

The solution to the Schrödinger equation is

$$\psi(x)=\begin{cases}Ae^{kx}, & x<0\\ Ae^{-kx}, & x>0\end{cases}$$

thus

$$\psi'(x)=\begin{cases}k\Psi(x), & x<0\\ -k\Psi(x), & x>0\end{cases}$$

Upon substitution, we obtain

$$\frac{\hbar^2 k}{m}=g, \text{ and thus } E=-\frac{\hbar^2 k^2}{2m}=-\frac{1}{2}\frac{mg^2}{\hbar^2}$$

45. **(E)**

Upon solving the Schrödinger equation, one obtains the following eigenfunctions:

$$\psi(x)=\begin{cases}Ae^{k_1x} & x<-l/2\\ B\cos k_2x & |x|<l/2\\ Ae^{-k_1x} & x>l/2\end{cases}$$

The continuity of ψ ($\pm\, l/2$) gives the condition that

$$Ae^{-k_1l/2}=B\cos(k_2l/2)$$

The continuity of ψ' ($\pm\, l/2$) gives the further condition that

$$k_1Ae^{-k_1l/2}=k_2B\sin(k_2l/2)$$

Dividing produces the equation

$$k_2\tan(k_2\,l/2)=k_1$$

or $\quad \tan(k_2\,l/2)=k_1/k_2$

Substituting the appropriate wave number values, one obtains

$$\tan\left(\sqrt{2m(V_0-E)}\,l/2\hbar\right)=\sqrt{2mE}/\hbar/\sqrt{2m(V_0-E)}/\hbar$$

$$\tan\sqrt{ml^2(V_0-E)/2\hbar^2}=\sqrt{E/(V_0-E)}$$

$$\tan\theta=\sqrt{\theta_0^{\,2}/\theta^2-1}$$

or

with $\theta = \sqrt{ml^2(V_0 - E)/2\hbar^2}$

and $\theta_0 = \sqrt{ml^2 V_0 / 2\hbar^2}$

46. **(B)**

The given potential energy is:

$$V(x) = \begin{cases} \frac{1}{2} m\omega^2 x^2 & x > 0 \\ \infty & x < 0 \end{cases}$$

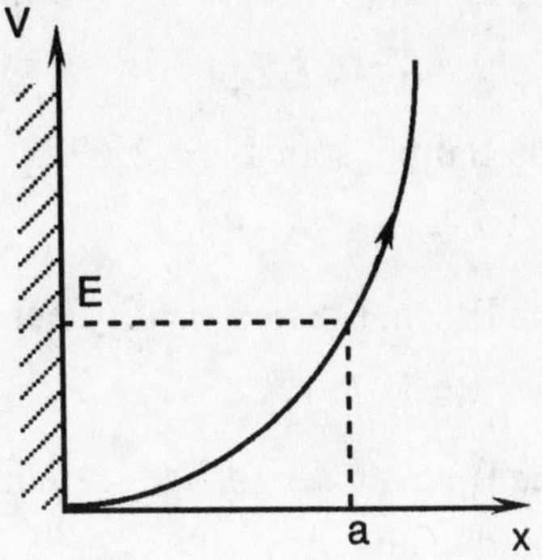

The WKB or Wentzel-Knowes–Brillouin approximation may be used. This approximon is valid for a slowly changing potential energy.

$$\int_0^a p\frac{dx}{\hbar} = n\frac{\pi}{2} + \frac{\pi}{4}, \quad n = 1, 3, 5\ldots$$

$$\int_0^a p\,dx = \left(\frac{3\pi}{4}, \frac{7\pi}{4}, \frac{11\pi}{4}, \ldots\right)\hbar$$

where $p = \sqrt{2m(E - V)}$

$$= \sqrt{2m(E - \frac{1}{2}m\omega^2 x^2)}$$

Note that for the case of the full harmonic oscillator, the WKB solution is exact.

47. **(D)**

The Zeeman effect may be explained semi-classically. Consider an electron orbiting in a circular orbit. The centripetal force is

$$F_0 = m\omega_0^2 r \text{ with } B = 0$$

and

$$F = m\omega_0^2 r \pm \frac{evB}{c} = m\omega^2 r \text{ with finite } B$$

Combining the two equations, one gets

$$m(\omega^2 - \omega_0^2)\, r = \pm e\omega r B / c$$

or

$$(\omega + \omega_0)(\omega - \omega_0) = \pm eB\omega / mc$$

$$2\omega\delta\omega = \pm eB\omega / mc$$

Using the approximation that

$$\omega = \omega_0$$

thus

$$\delta\omega = \pm eB / 2mc$$

48. **(E)**

According to the Bohr Theory

$$1/\lambda = R\,(1/n^2 - 1/m^2)$$

$$=1.0977373 \times 10^{-3}(1/n^2 - 1/m^2)/\text{Å}$$

Where R is the Rydberg constant

$$R = 1.097 \times 10^7 m^{-1}$$
$$= 1.097 \times 10^{-3} \text{Å}^{-1}$$

For the Lyman series, $n = 1$. For the series upper limit, $m = n + 1 = 2$. Hence

$$\lambda = 1216 \text{ Å}.$$

For the Balmer series, $n = 2$. Thus

$$\lambda = 6565 \text{ Å}.$$

For the Paschen series, $n = 3$. Therefore

$$\lambda = 18760 \text{ Å}.$$

For the Brackett series, $n = 4$. Hence

$$\lambda = 40520 \text{ Å}.$$

For the Pfund series, $n = 5$. Thus

$$\lambda = 74600 \text{ Å}.$$

Clearly the Paschen series, discovered in 1908, is the answer.

49. **(C)**

In the Thomson atom, the electrons are dispersed throughout a positive nuclear fluid. Applying Gauss' law:

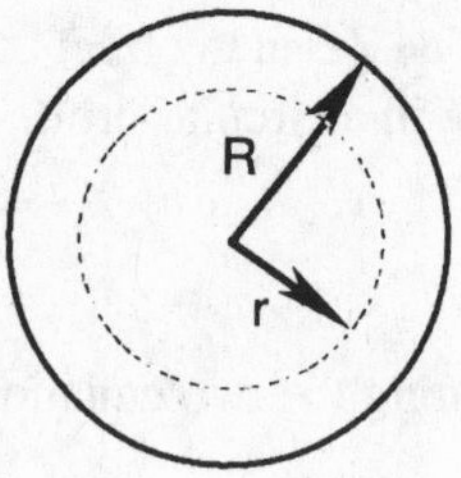

$$\nabla \cdot \text{E} = \frac{\rho}{\varepsilon_0}$$

$$\oint \text{E} \cdot d\mathbf{a} = \frac{q}{\varepsilon_0}$$

Integrating over the inner sphere, we obtain

$$E \cdot 4\pi r^2 = \rho \frac{4}{3}\pi r^3 / \varepsilon_0$$

$$E = \frac{e}{\frac{4}{3}\pi R^3} \frac{4}{3}\pi r^3 / 4\pi r^2 \varepsilon_0 \Rightarrow \text{E} = \frac{e}{4\pi\varepsilon_0 R^3}\mathbf{r}$$

The electron vibrates in this positively charged fluid so that

$$\mathbf{F} = \left(-e^2/4\pi\varepsilon_0 R^3\right)\mathbf{r} = \text{m}r''$$

$$\mathbf{r}'' + \frac{e^2}{4\pi\varepsilon_0 R^3 m}\mathbf{r} = 0$$

$$\mathbf{r}'' + \omega_0{}^2\mathbf{r} = 0$$

$$\omega_0 = \sqrt{e^2 / 4\pi\varepsilon_0 R^3 m}$$

$$= \sqrt{(1.602 \times 10^{-19})^2 / 4\pi(8.84 \times 10^{-12})(10^{-10})^3(9.108 \times 10^{-31})}$$

$$= 1.592 \times 10^{16} \text{ rad/s}$$

$$\lambda = 2\pi c / \omega = 2\pi(3 \times 10^8) / (1.592 \times 10^{16}) = 1184\text{Å}$$

50. **(A)**

In the Franck-Hertz experiment, an electron loses most of its kinetic energy in an *inelastic* collision with an atom. The electrons raise Hg atoms to the 1st excited state 4.9 eV above the ground state. Any monatomic gas can be used in the Franck-Hertz experiment. Of course, the excited state energy will be different for other gases.

51. **(D)**

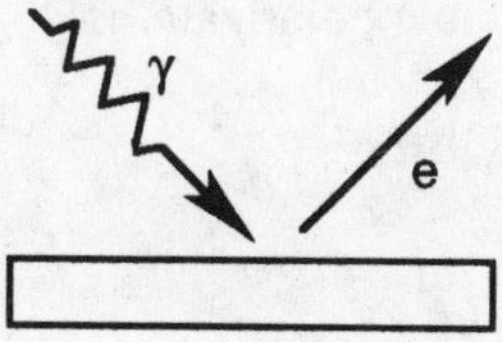

In the photoelectric effect , by conservation of energy

$$h\upsilon = {}^1/_2\, mv^2 + \phi$$

where ϕ is the work function of the metal. Furthermore,

$$eV_0 = {}^1/_2\, mv^2.$$

Thus the stopping potential V_0 is directly proportional to the incident light frequency υ:

$$eV_0 = h\nu - \phi \quad \text{or} \quad V_0 = \frac{h}{e}\nu - \frac{\phi}{e}$$

In fact, this is one way of determining Planck's constant.

52. **(E)**

The Rutherford scattering differential cross section is

$$\frac{d\sigma}{d\Omega} = \left(\frac{Z_1 Z_2 e^2}{4K}\right)^2 \sin^{-4}\left(\frac{\theta}{2}\right)$$

$$Z_1 = 1, Z_2 = 79, K = 8.8 \text{ MeV}$$

$$\frac{d\sigma}{d\Omega} = \left(\frac{(1)(79)(1.44)}{(4)(8.8)}\right)^2 \sin^{-4}\left(\frac{37°}{2}\right)$$

$$= 1030\, fm^2 \times \frac{10mb}{fm^2} \times \frac{1b}{1000mb}$$

$$= 10.30\, b$$

53. **(D)**

For a cavity of volume

$$V = l^3$$

$$k_x l = n_x \pi$$

or $$n_x = l/\pi\, k_x$$

thus $$dn_x = l/\pi\, dk_x.$$

Also, the same is true for the y and z directions. But

$$dn = dn_x\, dn_y\, dn_z$$

$$= (l/\pi)^3\, d^3k$$

However, only the 1st octant of number space is physically meaningful

$$dn = (l/2\pi)^3\, d^3\, k$$

Finally, photons have two possible polarizations

$$dn = 2\frac{V}{(2\pi)^3}d^3k \quad \text{and} \quad k = \frac{\omega}{c}$$

$$= \frac{2}{8\pi^3}\mathrm{V}\,4\pi(\frac{\omega}{c})^2 d(\frac{\omega}{c})$$

$$= \mathrm{V}\,\omega^2\pi^2\frac{d\omega}{c^3} = \frac{\mathrm{V}\omega^2 d\omega}{\pi^2 c^3}$$

54. **(B)**

The black body energy density is

$$u(\omega) = \frac{\hbar\omega^3}{\pi^2 c^3}1/(e^{\hbar\omega/kt} - 1)$$

The functional dependence is that

$$u(\omega) \propto x^3/(e^x - 1), \; x \equiv \frac{\hbar\omega}{kT}$$

We use the first derivative test to find the maximum.

$$\frac{du}{dx} = 3x^2/(e^x - 1) - (x^3/(e^x - 1)^2)e^x = 0$$

$$3x^2(e^x - 1) - x^3 e^x = 0$$

$$3e^x - 3 - xe^x = 0$$

$$e^x(3 - x) = 3$$

By inspection or recollection,

$$\lambda_{\max}T = \frac{hc}{4.965k} = 0.002898$$

55. **(C)**

The threshold wavelength allows us to determine the work function ϕ of the metal:

$$\phi = h\upsilon_0 = hc / \lambda_0$$
$$= 12{,}400 / 2300 = 5.39 \text{ eV}$$

The incident light has energy

$$h\upsilon = hc / \lambda = 12{,}400 / 1500$$
$$= 8.27 \text{ eV}$$

Hence, the kinetic energy of the photoelectrons is

$$K = h\upsilon - \phi$$
$$= 8.27 - 5.39 = 2.88 \text{ eV}$$

Finally $eV_0 = K \Rightarrow V_0 = 2.88$ Volts

56. **(A)**

In the Compton effect, photons scatter from electrons.

$$\gamma + e \rightarrow \gamma' + e.$$

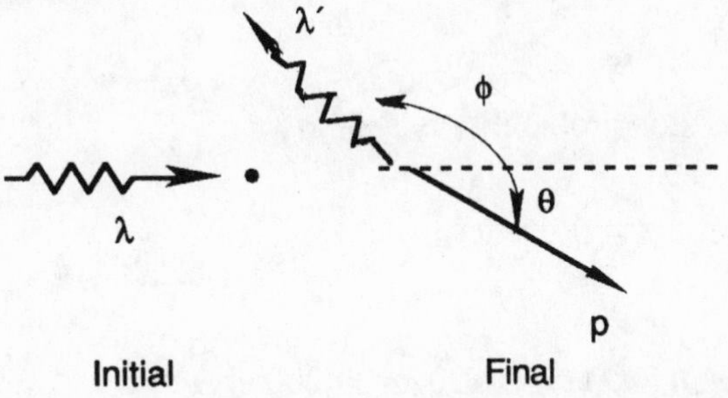

The given wavelength is:

$$\lambda = 1.50\text{Å}$$

then $\Delta\lambda = 2\lambda_c \sin^2 \phi/_2$ is the Compton shift

where the Compton Wavelength

$$\lambda_c = h / m_e c = (6.626 \times 10^{-27}) / (9.109 \times 10^{-28})\,(3 \times 10^{10})$$
$$= 2.43 \times 10^{-10} \text{ cm} = 0.0243 \text{ Å}$$

thus $\Delta\lambda = 2(.0243) \sin^2 90° / 2 = .0243$ Å

and $\lambda' = \lambda + \Delta\lambda = 1.5243$ Å

Finally the electron kinetic energy is

$$K = hc / \lambda - hc / \lambda' = 12{,}400\,(1/1.50 - 1/1.5243)$$
$$= 131.8 \text{ eV}$$

57. **(E)**

The given potential energy is

$$V(x) = \begin{cases} \infty & x \leq 0 \\ cx & x > 0 \end{cases}$$

$$E = p^2 / 2m + cx$$

Using the uncertainty principle:

$$\Delta p \, \Delta x = \hbar$$

or

$$px = \hbar$$

$$p = \hbar / x$$

$$E = (\hbar / x)^2 / 2m + cx$$

$$= \hbar^2 / 2mx^2 + cx$$

Now we look for the minimum energy value:

$$dE/dx = \hbar^2 / mx^3 + c = 0$$

$$\Rightarrow x_o = (\hbar^2 / cm)^{1/3}$$

$$E_0 = (\hbar^2 / 2m)(cm / \hbar^2)^{2/3} + c(\hbar^2 / cm)^{1/3}$$

$$= (\hbar c/2\sqrt{2m})^{2/3} + (\hbar^2 c^2/m)^{1/3}$$

58. **(A)**

The transmission probability is

$$T = e^{-2kl}$$

where $k = \sqrt{(2m/\hbar^2)(V_0 - E)}$

Note that

$$V_0 = mgh = (2)(980)(20) = 39{,}200 \text{ erg.}$$

Hence $k = \sqrt{[2(2)/(1.054 \times 10^{-27})^2](39{,}200 - 10{,}000)}$

$$k = 3.24 \times 10^{29}$$

Finally

$$T = e^{-2(3.24 \times 10^{29})(2)}$$

$$= e^{-1.30 \times 10^{30}}$$

$$= 10^{-1.30 \times 10^{30} \log e}$$

$$= 10^{-5.63 \times 10^{29}}$$

which is very, very small.

59. **(B)**

(A) The Hamiltonian and the angular momentum operators all commute.

(B) The raising operator is

$$L_+ = L_x + iL_y$$
$$[L_+, L_z] = [L_x + iL_y, L_z] = [L_x, L_z] + i[L_y, L_z]$$
$$= -i\hbar L_y + i[i\hbar L_x] = -\hbar L_+$$

(C) This is true since $[L^2, L_+] = 0$. Hence

$$L^2 L_+ Y_{lm} = L_+ L^2 Y_{lm} = l(l+1)\hbar^2 L_+ Y_{lm}$$

(D) L_x and L_z do not commute.

(E) The three body problem has been solved for this case. In fact, the solution is given by the Slater determinant.

60. **(D)**
The transmission probability

$$T = e^{-2kl}$$

where $$K = \frac{\sqrt{2m(V_0 - E)}}{\hbar}$$

$$l = 5\times10^{-10}\,m, \quad m_e = 9.10\times10^{-31}\ \text{kh},$$

$$V_0 = 5\ \text{eV}, \quad E = 1\ \text{eV}, \quad \hbar = 1.054\times10^{-34}\ \text{J}\cdot\text{s}$$

$$K = \frac{\sqrt{(2)(9.1\times10^{-31})(4)(1.6\times10^{-19}\ \text{J/eV})}}{1.054\times10^{-34}} = 1\times10^{10}\ \text{m}^{-1}$$

$$T = e^{-2(1\times10^{10})(5\times10^{-10})} = 4.5\times10^{-5}$$

61. **(E)**
The number counting is still the same relativistically

$$dn = g\frac{V}{(2\pi)^3}d^3k$$

and g = 2 for electrons. Integrating,

$$N = 2\frac{V}{(2\pi)^3}\int_0^{k_F} 4\pi k^2 dk$$

then $$k_F = (3\pi^2\rho)^{1/3}, \quad \rho = \frac{N}{V}$$

Now $$E^2 = p^2 + m^2, \quad \text{hence } E_F = \sqrt{(\hbar k_F)^2 + m_e^2}$$

$$\hbar k_F = (3\pi^2 0.01)^{1/3}(197.35) = 131.54\ \text{MeV}/c$$

Thus $$E_F = \sqrt{131.54^2 + 0.511^2}$$
$$= 131.54\ \text{MeV}$$

is the Fermi energy.

62. **(A)**

The Schrödinger equation is for the two particle system is

$$\left(-\frac{\hbar^2}{2m}(\nabla_1^{\ 2}+\nabla_2^{\ 2})+V_0\delta^3(r_1-r_2)\right)\psi(r_1,r_2)=E\psi(r_1,r_2)$$

For $V_0 = 0,$

$$W_0 = (\hbar k_1)^2 / 2m + (\hbar k_2)^2 / 2m$$
$$= (\hbar^2 / 2m)\,(3+3)\,\pi^2 / a^2$$
$$= 3\hbar^2 \pi^2 / ma^2$$

Where we have used the fact that

$$\mathbf{k}_1 = \pi/a\,(n_x\mathbf{x} + n_y\mathbf{y} + n_z\mathbf{z}) \text{ and } n_x = n_y = n_z = 1$$

for the ground state. (Similarly for $\mathbf{k}_2$.)

$$W_1 = \langle 0\,|V|\,0\rangle$$
$$= (2/a)^6 \int V_0\, \delta^3\,(r_1 - r_2)\, \sin^2(\pi/a\, x_1) \ldots \sin^2(\pi/a\, z_2)\, d^3r_1,\, d^3r_2$$
$$= (2/a)^6\, V_0 \int \sin^4(\pi/_a\, x_1)\, \sin^4(\pi/_a\, y_1)\, \sin^4(\pi/_a\, z_1)\, \delta^3\, r_1$$

where we have used the fact that

$$\psi_0 = (2/_a)^3 \sin(\pi/_a x_1)\, \sin(\pi/_a x_2)\, \sin(\pi/_a y_1)\, \sin(\pi/_a y_2)$$
$$\sin(\pi/_a z_1)\, \sin(\pi/_a z_2)$$

Thus $W_1 = (2/_a)^6\, V_0\, (\int \sin^4(\pi/_a\, x_1)\, dx_1)^3$

$$= (2/_a)^6\, V_0\, (3/_8\, \pi\, a/_\pi)^3 = (3/_{2a})^3\, V_0$$

Finally $E_0 = W_0 + W_1 = 3\,\hbar^2\, \pi^2 / ma^2 + (3/_{2a})^3\, V_0$

63. **(B)**

The s shell has $l = 0$ and the p shell has $l = 1$. Hence $m_l = -1, 0, 1$. The possible states taking each electron separately are then

−1	↑	↓	↓	↑	↑	↑	↓	↓	
0	↑	↓	↑	↓	↑	↓	↑	↓	8 states
1	↑	↓	↑	↑	↓	↓	↓	↑	

Where the first electron is on the first line, the second electron on the second line, and the third electron on the third line.

Now we count states with two electrons in one state and the other electron separate.

−1	–	–	–	–	↑	↓	↑↓	↑↓	↑	↓	↑↓	↑↓	
0	↑	↓	↑↓	↑↓	–	–	–	–	↑↓	↑↓	↑	↓	12 states
1	↑↓	↑↓	↑	↓	↑↓	↑↓	↑	↓	–	–	–	–	

Hence, there are a total of 20 states, as one expects from the binomial coefficient

$$\binom{6}{3} = \frac{6!}{3!3!} = 20.$$

64. **(C)**

The given potential energy is

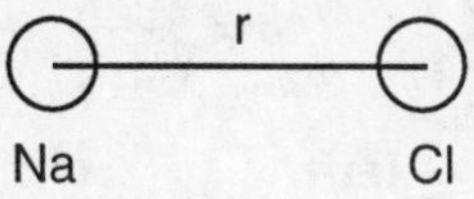

$$V(r) = -e^2 / r + k\, e^{-r/r0},\ V(r^*) = -3.60eV$$

$$\frac{dU}{dr} = e^2 / r^2 - \frac{k}{r_0} e^{-r/r0} = 0$$

when $r = r^* = 2.5\text{Å}$

$$e^2 = 1.44 M_e V - fm = 14.4 eV - \text{Å}$$

Plugging into the two equations, we get

$$\begin{cases} 14.4/(2.5)^2 - k/r_0 e^{-2.5/r0} = 0 \\ -14.4/2.5 + k e^{-2.5/r0} = -3.60 \end{cases}$$

Adding we get

$$2.30\, r_0 - 5.76 = -3.60 \text{ and so } r_0 = 0.94\ \text{Å}$$

Substituting in the second equation,

$$-5.76 + ke^{-2.5/.94} = -3.6$$

thus $k = 30.94$ eV.

65. **(A)**

The Lennard-Jones potential is

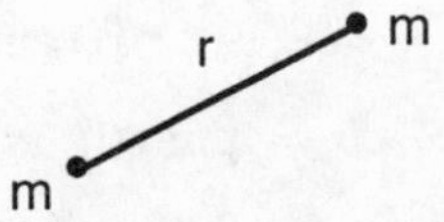

$$V(r) = \frac{A}{r^{12}} - \frac{B}{r^6}$$

We wish to find the minimum.

$$\frac{d}{dr} V(r) = \frac{-12A}{r^{13}} + \frac{6B}{r^7} = 0 \Rightarrow r_0 = \sqrt[6]{2A/B}$$

Using a Taylor expansion, we have

$$V(r) \approx V(r_0) + \frac{d}{dr} U(r)\Big|_{r=r_0} + \frac{1}{2}\frac{d^2}{dr^2} U(r)\Big|_{r=r_0} (r - r_0)^2$$

$$V(r) = \frac{A}{r_0^{12}} - \frac{B}{r_0^{12}} + \frac{1}{2}\left(\frac{156A}{r_0^{14}} - \frac{42B}{r_0^{8}}\right)(r - r_0)^2$$

The constant may be eliminated by redefining the energy zero.

$$V(r) = \frac{1}{2} k (r - r_0)^2$$

The angular frequency and reduced mass are

$$\omega = \sqrt{k/\mu} \text{ and } \mu = m/2.$$

so $$\omega = \sqrt{2/m}\sqrt{\frac{156A}{r_0^{14}} - \frac{42B}{r_0^{8}}}$$

$$\omega = \sqrt{\frac{312A}{mr_0^{14}} - \frac{84B}{mr_0^{8}}}$$

66. **(A)**

We are given that

$$m = 6.0 \text{ kg} \quad \text{and} \quad \upsilon_0 = 1 \text{ Hz.}$$

According to Newton's 2nd law

$$F = -kx - bx' = mx''$$

The differential equation is then

$$x'' = \beta x' + \omega_0^2 x = 0,$$

where

$$\omega_0 = \sqrt{k/m} \text{ and } \beta = b/m$$

The solution is

$$x = c\,e^{-\beta t/2} \cos \omega t$$

We are also given that

$$x_0 = x(t=0) = c = 0.25\ m$$

$$x_{10} = {}^1/_2\, c = ce^{-5\beta}$$

thus $$e^{5\beta} = 2, \quad 5\beta = \ln 2$$

$$b = \beta m = {}^1/_5\, m \ln 2$$

$$= 0.83 \text{ kg/sec}$$

Also $$\omega = \sqrt{\omega_0^{\,2} - \beta^2/4} = \sqrt{4\pi^2 - .139^2/4} = 6.283 \text{ rad/s}$$

67. **(D)**

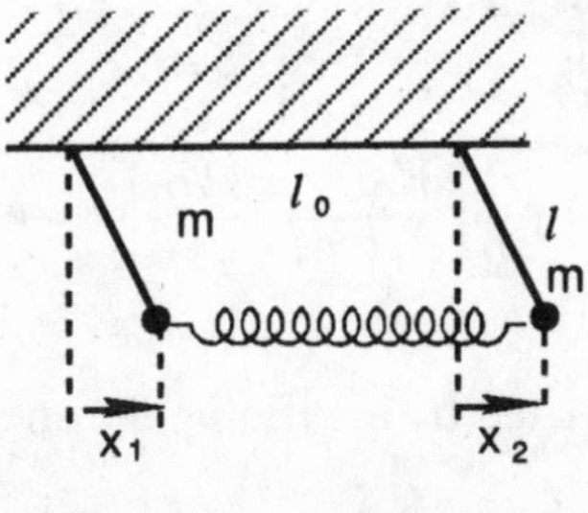

From Newton's 2nd law, we obtain two equations

$$mx_1'' = -mg\frac{x_1}{l} + k(x_2 - x_1)$$

$$mx_2'' = -mg\frac{x_2}{l} + k(x_1 - x_2)$$

Assuming sinusoidal solutions, we get

$$x_1'' = -\omega^2 x_1 \text{ and } x_2'' = -\omega^2 x_2$$

The coupled equations then become:

$$\begin{cases} m\omega^2 x_1 - mg\frac{x_1}{l} + k(x_2 - x_1) = 0 \\ m\omega^2 x_2 - mg\frac{x_2}{l} - k(x_2 - x_1) = 0 \end{cases}$$

or $\quad (\omega^2 - g/l)\,(x_2 - x_1) - 2k/m\,(x_2 - x_1) = 0$

Combining the equations there are two solutions, the symmetric mode

$$\omega_+ = \sqrt{g/l}$$

and the antisymmetric mode

$$\omega_- = \sqrt{g/l + 2k/m}$$

68. **(A)**

The refractive index is given by

$$n = \sqrt{1 - \omega_p{}^2/\omega^2}$$

The wave number is

$$k = \frac{\omega}{v_p} = \frac{\omega n}{c} \quad \text{since} \quad n = c/v_p$$

$$= \frac{\omega}{c}\sqrt{1 - \omega_p{}^2/\omega^2}$$

The phase velocity is easy

$$v_p - \frac{\omega}{K} = c\Big/\sqrt{1 - \omega_p{}^2/\omega^2} = \sqrt{2}c$$

The group velocity requires differentiation

$$v_g = \frac{d\omega}{dk} = 1\Big/\left(\frac{dk}{d\omega}\right)$$

$$= 1\Big/\frac{d}{d\omega}\left(\frac{\omega}{c}\sqrt{1 - \omega_p{}^2/\omega^2}\right)$$

$$= 1\Big/\left[\frac{1}{c}\sqrt{1 - \omega_p{}^2/\omega^2} + \frac{\omega}{c}(1 - \omega_p{}^2/\omega^2)^{-1/2}\frac{\omega_p{}^2}{\omega^3}\right]$$

$$= c\Big/(\sqrt{1/2} + \frac{1}{2}\sqrt{2}) = c/\sqrt{2}$$

69. **(C)**
The observable is

$$f = c\sqrt{x/y}$$

and the standard error propagation formula is

$$\Delta f = \sqrt{\left(\frac{\partial f}{\partial x}\Delta x\right)^2 + \left(\frac{\partial f}{\partial y}\Delta y\right)^2}$$

$$= \sqrt{\left(\frac{c}{\sqrt{y}}\frac{1}{2\sqrt{x}}\Delta x\right)^2 + \left(c\sqrt{x}\,\frac{1}{2}\frac{1}{\sqrt{y^3}}\Delta y\right)^2}$$

$$= \sqrt{\left(c\sqrt{x/y}\right)^2\left[\left(\frac{\Delta x}{2x}\right)^2 + \left(\frac{\Delta y}{2y}\right)^2\right]}$$

$$= \frac{1}{2}f\sqrt{\left(\frac{\Delta x}{x}\right)^2 + \left(\frac{\Delta y}{y}\right)^2}$$

70. **(D)**
By similar triangles

$$\frac{E_\perp}{E_{||}} = \frac{v_\perp t}{c\Delta t}$$

$$= \frac{a_\perp \Delta t\, t}{c\Delta t}.$$

thus $E_\perp = E_{||}\dfrac{a_\perp r}{c^2}$

since $r = ct$ or $t = r/c$. But

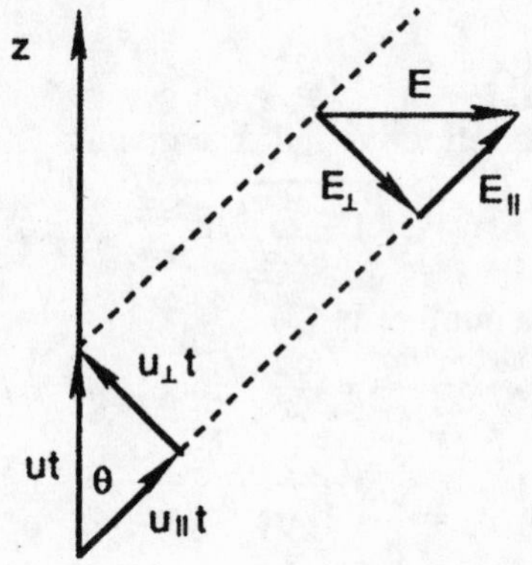

$$E_{||} = \frac{q}{4\pi\varepsilon_0 r^2}$$

is just the radial Coulomb field. Hence

$$E_\perp = \frac{qa_\perp}{4\pi\varepsilon_0 rc^2} = \frac{qa\sin\theta}{4\pi\varepsilon_0 rc^2}$$

Also $\mathrm{B} = \mathrm{r} \times \mathrm{E}_\perp / c$.

Hence $|\mathrm{S}| = |\mathrm{E} \times \mathrm{B}| / \mu_0$

$$= q^2 a^2 \sin^2\theta / 16\pi^2 \varepsilon_0 r^2 c^3$$

is the magnitude of the Poynting flux.

71. **(B)**

The scattering cross section is

$$\sigma_R = \sigma_T \left(\frac{\lambda_0}{\lambda}\right)^4$$

where $\sigma_T = \dfrac{8\pi}{3}\left(\dfrac{e^2}{4\pi\varepsilon_0 m_e c^2}\right)^3$

is the Thomson cross section

$$\sigma_T = 6.65 \times 10^{-29}\ m^2.$$

The reduction in intensity is

$$\begin{aligned} F &= 1 - e^{-\rho_l \sigma_R} \\ &= 1 - \exp\left(-(1.68 \times 10^{29})(6.65 \times 10^{-29})(750/4500)^4\right) \\ &= .0086 \\ &= .86\% \end{aligned}$$

72. **(E)**

In the rest frame of the charge $E = q/4\pi\varepsilon_0 r^2$. In the lab frame where the charge is moving

$$E' = \frac{q}{4\pi\varepsilon_0 r'^2}\frac{1-\beta^2}{(1-\beta^2\sin^2\theta')^{3/2}}$$

$$= \frac{q}{4\pi\varepsilon_0 r'^2}\frac{1-\beta^2}{(1-\beta^2)^{3/2}} \quad \text{at} \quad \theta' = 90°$$

We are given that $E' = 2E$, thus

$$\frac{1-\beta^2}{(1-\beta^2)^{3/2}} = 2, \quad \frac{1}{1-\beta^2} = 4$$

$$\beta = \sqrt{1-\tfrac{1}{4}} = \frac{\sqrt{3}}{2}, \quad v = \frac{\sqrt{3}}{2}c$$

73. **(A)**

The Maxwell Boltzmann probability density for speed is

$$p(v) = 4\pi c v^2 e^{-mv^2/2kT}$$

$$\frac{dp}{dv} = 4\pi c\left(2ve^{-mv^2/2kT} - v^2\frac{2mv}{2kT}e^{-mv^2/2kT}\right) = 0$$

$$2v = \frac{m}{kT}v^3$$

Thus $\quad v = \sqrt{2kT/m}$

is the most probable speed.

74. **(A)**

The typical magnitude of p is

$$p = mv = \sqrt{2mkT}$$

Using the most probable speed for v. This corresponds to

$$\lambda = \frac{h}{p} = \frac{h}{\sqrt{2mkT}}$$

The classical description is valid for $s >> \lambda$ where s is the typical separation between particles. Now

$$\rho = \frac{N}{V} \Rightarrow s^3 = \frac{1}{\rho}$$

taking $N = 1$ and $V = s^3$.

Hence $\left(\frac{1}{\rho}\right)^{1/3} >> \frac{h}{\sqrt{2mkT}}$

$$\frac{h\rho^{1/3}}{\sqrt{2mkT}} << 1$$

The classical description is thus valid for low density and/or high temperature.

75. **(D)**

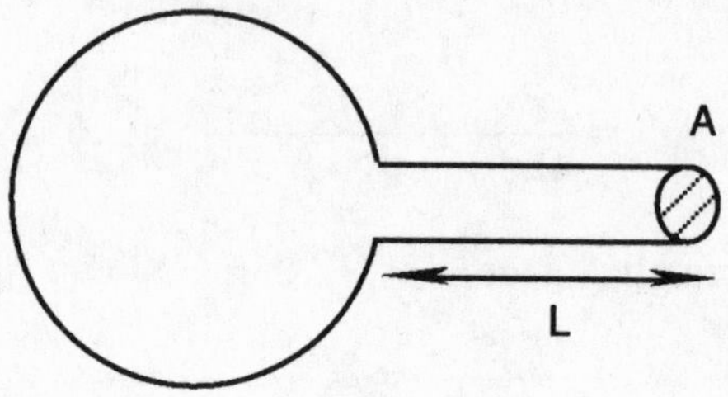

In the oscillation $V \approx V_0$.

$$F_x = A\Delta p = A\left(\frac{dp}{dV}\right)_0 Ax$$

For an adiabatic process

$$pV^\gamma = constant,$$

and so $\frac{dp}{dV} = -\gamma V^{-\gamma-1}\ constant$

$$= -\gamma p_0 V_0^\gamma / V_0^{\gamma+1} = -\gamma \frac{p_0}{V_0}$$

thus $F_x = -A^2\gamma \frac{p_0}{V_0} x = AL\rho_0 x''$

Using Newton's Second Law

$$x'' + A\gamma \frac{p_0}{\rho_0 L V_0} x = 0$$

$$\omega = \sqrt{\gamma \frac{p_0}{\rho_0} \frac{A}{V_0 L}} = v_s \sqrt{\frac{A}{V_0 L}}$$

where $v_s = \sqrt{\gamma\, p_o/\rho_0}$ is the sound speed.

76. **(E)**

The field in the plasma is

$$\mathbf{E} = \frac{\sigma}{\varepsilon_0} = -\frac{Ne}{\varepsilon_0}\mathbf{x}$$

where N is the density of electrons. hence an electron oscillates according to

$$mx'' = \frac{-Ne^2}{\varepsilon_0}x$$

The differential equation is then

$$x'' + \frac{Ne^2}{m\varepsilon_0}x = 0$$

$$\nu_p = \frac{\omega_p}{2\pi} = \frac{1}{2\pi}\sqrt{N}\frac{e}{\sqrt{m_e\varepsilon_0}}$$

$$= \sqrt{N}\frac{1.602\times10^{-19}/2\pi}{\sqrt{9.109\times10^{-31}\times8.854\times10^{-12}}}$$

$$= 8.98\sqrt{N}\ \text{Hz}$$

77. **(C)**

The given wave form is

$$f(t) = \begin{cases} a & 0 < t < t/2 \\ -a & -t/2 < 0 < t \end{cases}$$

The square wave is an odd function $\Rightarrow A_m = 0$

$$B_m = \frac{1}{\pi}\int_{-\pi}^{\pi} f(x)\sin(mx)\,dx\,, \quad x = \omega t$$

$$= \frac{\omega}{\pi}\int_{-T/2}^{T/2} f(t)\sin(m\omega t)\,dt$$

$$= \frac{\omega}{\pi}2\int_0^{T/2} a\sin(m\omega t)\,dt$$

$$= \frac{2a}{m\pi}(1-\cos m\pi) = \frac{4a}{\pi},\ 0,\ \frac{4a}{3\pi},\ 0,\ \ldots$$

Hence

$$f(t) = \frac{4a}{\pi}(\sin(\omega t) + \frac{1}{3}\sin(3\omega t) + \ldots)$$

78. **(C)**

The energy of interaction is

$$E = -\mu\cdot\mathbf{B} \Rightarrow E_+ = -\mu_0 B,\ E_- = \mu_0 B$$

Now we must find the probabilities

$$p_+ = Ce^{-\beta E_+} = Ce^{\beta\mu_0 B}\ ,\ \beta = 1/kT$$

$$p_- = Ce^{-\beta E_-} = Ce^{-\beta\mu_0 B}$$

$$p_+ + p_- = 1 \Rightarrow C = 1/(e^{\beta\mu_0 B} + e^{-\beta\mu_0 B})$$

$$<\mu>= p_+\mu_0 + p_-(-\mu_0)$$

$$= (e^{\beta\mu_0 B} - e^{-\beta\mu_0 B})\,\mu_0 / (e^{\beta\mu_0 B} + e^{-\beta\mu_0 B})$$

$$= \mu_0 \tanh(\mu_0 B / kT)$$

The magnetiziation is

$$m = N <\mu>= N\mu_0 \tanh(\mu_0 B / kT)$$

79. **(A)**

We are asked to evaluate

$$\int_0^\infty \frac{z^3}{e^z - 1} dz$$

Rewrite the integral as

$$= \int z^3 \frac{e^{-z}}{1 - e^{-z}} dz$$

$$= \int z^3 \sum_{n=1}^{\infty} e^{-nz} dz$$

$$= \sum_{n=1}^{\infty} \int_0^\infty z^{4-1} e^{-nz} dz$$

$$= \sum_{n=1}^{\infty} \frac{\Gamma(4)}{n^4}$$

$$= \sum_{n=1}^{\infty} \frac{3!}{n^4} = \frac{\pi^4}{90} \times 6 = \frac{\pi^4}{15}$$

80. **(B)**

By Dalton's Law

$$p = p_1 + p_2$$

$$= (n_1 + n_2)\frac{RT}{V}$$

Using the ideal gas law

$$= \left(\frac{m_1}{A} + \frac{m_2}{2A}\right)\frac{RT}{V}$$

Hence

$$pV = (m_1 + \frac{1}{2}(m - m_1))RT/A$$

$$= \frac{1}{2}m(1 + \frac{m_1}{m})RT/A$$

$$= \frac{1}{2A} m(1+\delta)RT$$

Thus each component acts as an ideal gas, but the mixture does not!

81. **(A)**

The coefficient of cubical expansion

$$\beta = \frac{1}{V}\left(\frac{\partial V}{\partial T}\right)_p = -\frac{1}{V}\frac{(\partial P/\partial T)_V}{(\partial P/\partial V)_T}$$

Use Van Der Waals equation of state

$$(p+\frac{a}{V^2})(V-b) = RT$$

to get $p = \dfrac{RT}{V-b} - \dfrac{a}{V^2}$.

Then $\left(\dfrac{\partial P}{\partial T}\right)_V = \dfrac{R}{V-b}$, $\left(\dfrac{\partial P}{\partial V}\right)_T = \dfrac{-RT}{(V-b)^2} + \dfrac{2a}{V^3}$

Hence $\beta = -\dfrac{1}{V}\dfrac{R/(V-b)}{-RT/(V-b)^2 + 2a/V^3} = \dfrac{RV^2(V-b)}{RTV^3 - 2a(V-b)^2}$

82. **(B)**

The mean free path is

$$\lambda = \frac{1}{\sqrt{2}n\pi(2a)^2}$$

Where the factor $\sqrt{2}$ comes from the motion of the molecules. Now

$$L = \sqrt{N}\,\lambda$$

for a random walk. So

$$\begin{aligned} N &= L^2/\lambda^2 \\ &= L^2\, 2n^2\, \pi^2\, 16a^4 \\ &= 32\,\pi^2\, n^2\, a^4\, L^2 \\ &= 32\,\pi^2\,(2.69\times10^{19})^2\,(10^{-8}\text{cm})^4\,(10^4)^2 \\ &= 2.28\times10^{17} \approx 10^{17} \end{aligned}$$

where we have used the fact that

$$n = \frac{6.022\times10^{23}}{22.4\times10^{3}\,cm^3} = 2.69\times10^{19}\,/cc$$

83. **(C)**

We are given that

$$E = \frac{p^2}{2m} + bx^4$$

Now $<KE> = \left\langle \frac{p^2}{2m} \right\rangle = \frac{1}{2} kT$

by the equipartition theorem. Also

$$<PE> = -\frac{d}{d\beta} \ln \int_{-\infty}^{\infty} e^{-\beta b x^4}\, dx,$$

since $y^4 = \beta x^4$, $y = \beta^{1/4} x$ and $dy = \beta^{1/4}\, dx$

$$<PE> = -\frac{d}{d\beta} \ln \beta^{-1/4} \int_{-\infty}^{\infty} e^{-by^4}\, dy$$

$$= -\frac{d}{d\beta}\left(-\frac{1}{4} \ln \beta + \ln \int (\ldots)\, dy \right) = \frac{1}{4} \beta = \frac{kT}{4}$$

Hence $<E> = \frac{1}{2} kT + \frac{1}{4} kT = \frac{3}{4} kT$

84. **(D)**

The gas is thermally insulated

$\Rightarrow dQ = 0$

and hence the expansion is adiabatic.

$$W = -\int_{V_0}^{V_f} p\, dV = -\int_{V_0}^{V_f} kV^{-\gamma}\, dV \quad \text{since} \quad pV^{\gamma} = k$$

$$= \frac{k}{-\gamma+1} V^{-\gamma+1} \Bigg|_{V_f}^{V_0} = \frac{k}{\gamma - 1}\left(\frac{V_f}{V_f^{\gamma}} - \frac{V_0}{V_0^{\gamma}} \right)$$

$$= \frac{1}{\gamma - 1}(p_f V_f - p_0 V_0)$$

Now $\gamma - 1 = \frac{C_p}{C_V} - 1 = \frac{C_p - C_V}{C_V} = \frac{R}{C_V}$

$$W = \frac{C_V}{R}(p_f V_f - p_0 V_0)$$

85. **(E)**

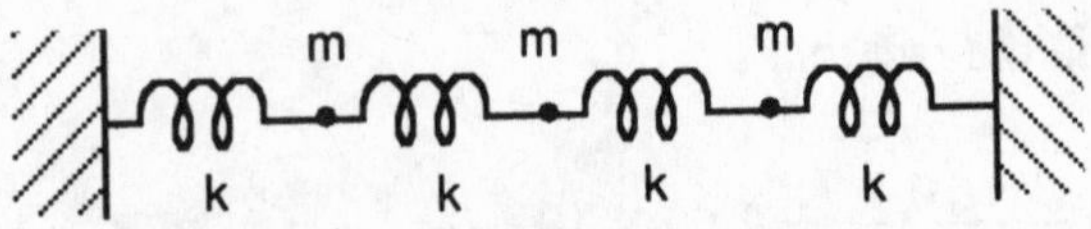

Quantum mechanically, the energies are

$E_a = n_a \hbar a \omega_0,$

$E_b = n_b \hbar b \omega_0,$

$$E_c = n_c \hbar c \omega_0$$

combine to give total energy

$$E = E_a + E_b + E_c.$$

Hence the partition function is

$$Z = \Sigma e^{-E\beta} = \Sigma e^{-E_a\beta} \Sigma e^{-E_b\beta} \Sigma e^{-E_c\beta}$$

$$= \frac{1}{1-e^{-\hbar\omega_0 a\beta}} \frac{1}{1-e^{-\hbar\omega_0 b\beta}} \frac{1}{1-e^{-\hbar\omega_0 c\beta}}$$

This gives rise to a sum of Planck distributions with average energy

$$< E >= \hbar\omega_0 \left(\frac{a}{e^{\hbar\omega_0 a\beta} - 1} + \frac{b}{e^{\hbar\omega_0 b\beta} - 1} + \frac{c}{e^{\hbar\omega_0 c\beta} - 1} \right)$$

86. **(E)**

For the hydrogen atom

$$E_n = -\ 13.6\,\text{eV} \frac{1}{n^2}$$

The K_α *x*-ray energy has energy

$$E_\alpha = -13.6\,\text{eV}\left(\frac{1}{2^2} - \frac{1}{1^2}\right) = 10.2\,\text{eV}$$

The initial energy of an *l*-shell electron is

$$E = -\ 13.6\ \text{eV}\ \frac{1}{2^2} = -\ 3.4\,\text{eV}$$

After absorbing the photon and escaping, the kinetic energy of the electron is

$$K = 10.2 - 3.4 = 6.8\ \text{eV}$$

87. **(D)**

This is a mode counting problem.

$$dn = dn_x dn_y = \left(\frac{l}{\pi}\right)^2 dk_x dk_y$$

$$n_x \frac{\lambda_x}{2} = l,\ n_y \frac{\lambda_y}{2} = l$$

$$\pi n_x \frac{\lambda_x}{2\pi} = l,\ \pi n_y \frac{\lambda_y}{2\pi} = l$$

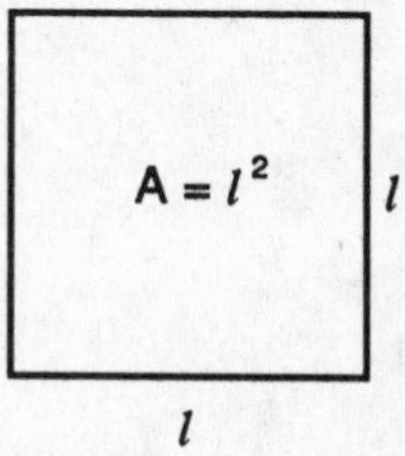

Thus $\quad n_x = \frac{l}{\pi} k_x$ and $n_y = \frac{l}{\pi} k_y$.

But since only the first quadrant in number space is physically meaningful

$$dn = \left(\frac{l}{2\pi}\right)^2 2\pi k\ dk$$

Finally the photon has two possible polarizations so that

$$dn = \frac{A}{\pi} k\, dk$$

88. **(C)**

In the Compton effect

$$\Delta\lambda = \lambda' - \lambda = 2\lambda_c \sin^2 \frac{\phi}{2}$$

For $\phi = \pi$

$$\lambda' = \lambda + 2h / m_e c$$

High incident photon energy $E = hc/\lambda$ means small wavelength λ. Nevertheless

$$\lambda' \geq \frac{2h}{m_e c}$$

and $$E' = \frac{hc}{\lambda'} \leq \frac{1}{2} m_e c^2$$

89. **(B)**

In the Thomson experiment, the electric force balances the magnetic force

$$eE = evB.$$

Thus $$v = E/B.$$

In the absence of B, the deflection is

$$s = \frac{1}{2} a t^2$$

$$= \frac{1}{2} \frac{eE}{m} \left(\frac{l}{V} \right)^2$$

$$s = \frac{1}{2} \frac{eE}{m} \frac{l^2 B^2}{E^2} = \frac{1}{2} \frac{e}{m} \frac{l^2 B^2}{V / d}$$

Hence

$$\frac{e}{m} = 2(1.25 \times 10^{-3})(50 / 1.5 \times 10^{-2}) / (5 \times 10^{-2})^2 (1.2 \times 10^{-4})^2$$

$$= 2.31 \times 10^{11} \text{ coul}/kg$$

90. **(A)**

$${}^{2}_{1}\text{d} + {}^{208}_{82}\text{Pb}$$

is the reaction. We are given that $K = 15$ MeV.

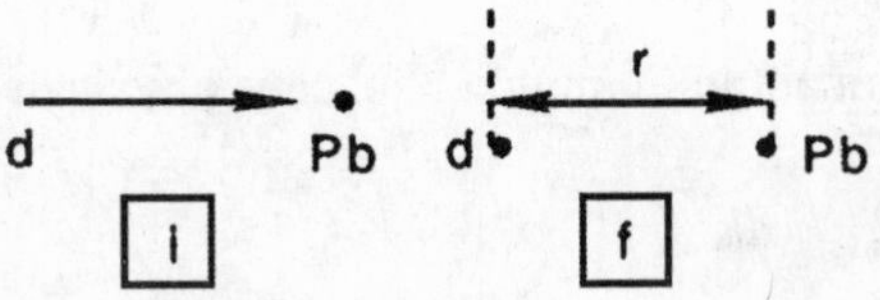

$$K=\frac{1}{2}mV^2=\frac{q_1q_2}{r}=\frac{82e^2}{r}$$

$$r=82e^2/K=82(1.44)/15$$

$$=7.87\ fm$$

In a head on collision, the *KE* is transformed into *PE* at the distance of closest approach.

91. **(C)**

$$V_n=\int dx_1\int dx_2\ldots\int dx_n=C_nR^n$$

Where the integrals are all subject to the constraint that

$$x_1{}^2+x_2{}^2+\ldots+x_n{}^2<R^2$$

where R is the radius of the n-dimensional sphere. Now consider a different integral

$$\int dx_1\ldots\int dx_n e^{-(x_1{}^2+\ldots+x_n{}^2)}=(\int dx\, e^{-x^2})^n=\left(\sqrt{\pi}\right)^n$$

$$\int dV_n e^{-R^2}=\pi^{n/2}$$

$$\int nC_nR^{n-1}e^{-R^2}dR=\pi^{n/2}$$

Make a substitution $R^2=t$ so that

$$dR=\frac{dt}{2\sqrt{t}}$$

$$\frac{n}{2}C_n\int_0^\infty t^{n/2-1}e^{-t}dt=\pi^{n/2}$$

$$\frac{n}{2}C_n\left(\frac{n}{2}-1\right)!=\pi^{n/2}$$

Thus $\quad C_n=\pi^{n/2}/\left(\frac{n}{2}\right)!$

92. **(D)**

Ω(E) can be thought of as the number of ways of putting M indistinguishable balls (the quanta) among $N-1$ partitions along a line. For example,

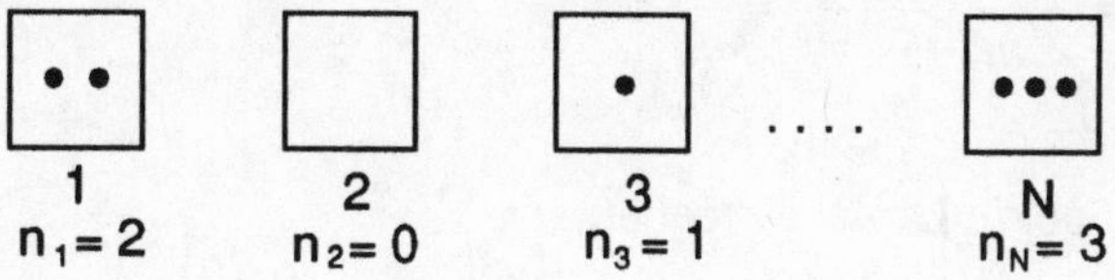

Hence

$$\Omega=\binom{M+N-1}{M}\approx\frac{(M+N)!}{M!N!}$$

The entropy is

$$\begin{aligned} S &= k \ln \Omega \\ &= k \ln (M+N)! - \ln M! - \ln N! \\ &\approx (M+N) \ln (M+N) - M \ln M - N \ln N \end{aligned}$$

Using Sterling's approximation

93. **(A)**

The polarization is $\mathbf{P} = Ne\mathbf{r}$ where $\mathbf{r}$ is the vector from negative to positive ion. The positive ions tend to be found at $\pm a/2$ with respect to the negative ions (by symmetry). The positive ion can thus have energy

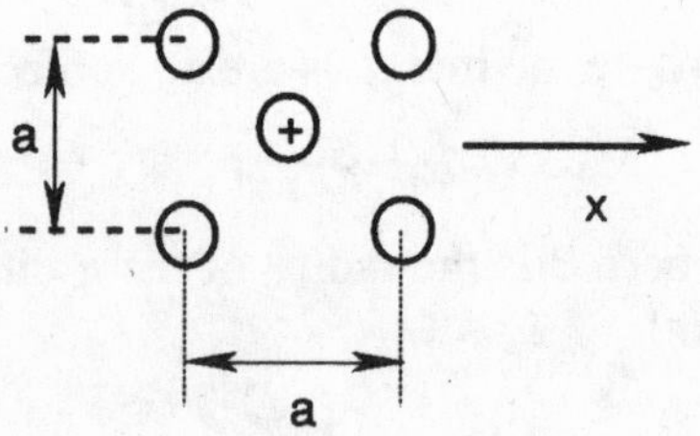

$$E_{\pm} = e\,E\,a/2$$

Thus the polarization is

$$P_x = \frac{Ne\frac{a}{2}e^{eEa/2kT} - Ne\frac{a}{2}e^{-eEa/2kT}}{e^{eEa/2kT} + e^{-eEa/2kT}}$$

$$= (Ne\,a/2)\tanh(eEa/2kT)$$

94. **(B)**

According to Newton's 2nd law

$$F = eE = mx''$$

with Solution

$$x = \frac{1}{2}\frac{eE}{m}t^2$$

$$P(t) = \frac{e^{-t/\tau}}{\tau}$$

is the probability that a particle after surviving without collisions for a time t suffers one collision by time $t + dt$. The mean distance is

$$\langle x \rangle = \int_0^\infty \frac{1}{2}\frac{eE}{m}t^2 \frac{1}{\tau}e^{-t/\tau}\,dt$$

$$= \frac{1}{2}\frac{eE}{m\tau}\frac{\Gamma(3)}{(1/\tau)^3} = \frac{eE}{m}\tau^2$$

95. **(E)**

We must solve Laplace's equation

$$\nabla^2\phi = 0.$$

Use separation of variables

$$\phi = XYZ$$

$$\frac{1}{X}\frac{d^2X}{dX^2}+\frac{1}{Y}\frac{d^2Y}{dY^2}+\frac{1}{Z}\frac{d^2Z}{dZ^2}=0$$

$$\frac{X''}{X}=\text{constant}=-\alpha^2,\ -\alpha^2-\beta^2+\gamma^2=0$$

$$X=a_m\sin(\alpha_m x),\ \ \alpha_m=\frac{m\pi}{a}$$

$$Y=b_n\sin(\beta_n y),\ \ \beta_n=\frac{n\pi}{a}$$

$$Z=c_{nm}^{\pm}\,e^{\pm\gamma_{nm}z},\ \gamma_{nm}=\frac{\pi}{a}\sqrt{m^2+n^2}$$

To get the potential of the center, we can use symmetry. If all six sides had $\phi = V_0$, then $\phi_C = V_0$. The potential is the superposition of contributions from three pairs of opposing sides. With $\phi = V_0$ for just one pair, $\phi_c = {}^1/_3\, V_0$.

96. **(D)**

The Boltzmann equation is

$$\frac{\partial f}{\partial t}+\frac{\mathbf{p}}{m}\cdot\frac{\partial f}{\partial \mathbf{r}}+\mathbf{F}\cdot\frac{\partial f}{\partial \mathbf{p}}$$
$$=\int(f_1'f_2-f\,f_2)\sigma v\,d\Omega\,d^3p_2'$$

The scattering process is

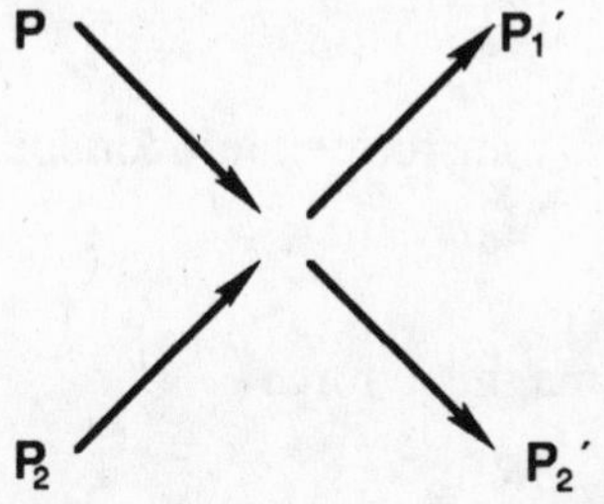

Integrating

$$\int d^3p\frac{\partial f}{\partial t}m=\int d^3p\frac{\partial(mf)}{\partial t}=\frac{\partial}{\partial t}\int d^3p\,mf=\frac{\partial\rho}{\partial t}$$

$$\int d^3p\frac{\mathbf{p}}{m}\cdot\frac{\partial f}{\partial\rho}m=\frac{\partial}{\partial\rho}\int d^3p f\mathbf{p}=\frac{\partial}{\partial\mathbf{r}}(\rho\mathbf{u})$$

$$\int d^3p\,\mathbf{F}\cdot\frac{\partial f}{\partial\mathbf{p}}m=\int d^3p\frac{\partial}{\partial p_i}(F_i fm)=F_i fm\Big|_{-\infty}^{\infty}=0$$

Likewise, the collision integral contributes zero since the net mass does not change in the collision between two particles. Hence we get the conservation of mass equation.

$$\frac{\partial\rho}{\partial t}+\frac{\partial(\rho\mathbf{u})}{\partial\mathbf{r}}=0$$

97. **(B)**

The general potential is

$$\psi(r,\theta,\phi)=\sum_{l,m}\left(A_{lm}r^{l}+\frac{B_{lm}}{r^{l+1}}\right)Y_{lm}(\theta,\phi)$$

The boundary condition is $\Psi(R, \theta, \phi) = B \sin\theta \sin\phi$. Now

$$Y_{1,1} = \sin\theta\, e^{i\phi},$$

and $$Y_{1,-1} = \sin\theta\, e^{-i\phi}.$$

Hence

$$\psi(r,\theta,\phi)=\begin{cases}\dfrac{Br}{R}\sin\theta\sin\phi & r<R\\ \dfrac{BR^2}{r^2}\sin\theta\sin\phi & r>R\end{cases}$$

The charge density is

$$\sigma=\varepsilon_0\left(\left.\frac{\partial\psi}{\partial r}\right|_{\text{in}}-\left.\frac{\partial\psi}{\partial r}\right|_{\text{out}}\right)$$

$$=\varepsilon_0 B\left(\frac{1}{R}\sin\theta\sin\phi+\frac{2R^2}{R^3}\sin\theta\sin\phi\right)$$

$$=\frac{3B\varepsilon_0}{R}\sin\theta\sin\phi$$

98. **(A)**

The potential energy is transformed into kinetic energy

$$\frac{1}{2}mv^2=qV_0$$

The centripetal force is the magnetic force

$$\frac{mv^2}{R}=qvB\Rightarrow v=q\frac{BR}{m}$$

Thus

$$\frac{q}{m}=v^2/2V_0=(qBr/m)^2/2V_0$$

$$q/m=2V_0/B^2R^2$$

$$R=\sqrt{2V_0m/B^2q}$$

$$=\sqrt{2(4000)(10.0129)(1.66\times10^{-27})/(.5^2\cdot1.602\times10^{-19})}$$

$$=0.0576\,\text{m}$$

$$=5.76\,\text{cm}$$

99. **(B)**

The energy splitting is

$$\Delta E = 2g\,\mu_N\,BI$$

where g is the Lande g factor and $\mu_N = e\hbar / 2m_p$ is the nuclear magneton. Also $I = {}^1/_2$ is the intrinsic proton spin. Hence

$$\Delta E = h\upsilon_L = 2\,g\,\mu_N\,BI$$

where υ_L is the resonant Larmor frequency

$$\upsilon_L = 2g\mu_N BI / h$$

$$= \frac{(5.56)(0.5050\times10^{-26})(0.6642)(1/2)}{(6.626\times10^{-34})}$$

$$= 2.81\times10^{7}\,\text{Hz}$$

$$= 28.1\,M\text{Hz}$$

100. **(C)**

Radiation damage is caused by the ionization and excitation of charged particles in the body.

1 rem causes no damage

10 rem causes detectable blood changes

100 rem causes injury

400 rem results in 50% deaths in 30 days

100,000 rem results in quick death

The Graduate Record Examination in

PHYSICS

Test 4

THE GRADUATE RECORD EXAMINATION IN
PHYSICS
TEST 4 – ANSWER SHEET

1. (A) (B) (C) (D) (E)
2. (A) (B) (C) (D) (E)
3. (A) (B) (C) (D) (E)
4. (A) (B) (C) (D) (E)
5. (A) (B) (C) (D) (E)
6. (A) (B) (C) (D) (E)
7. (A) (B) (C) (D) (E)
8. (A) (B) (C) (D) (E)
9. (A) (B) (C) (D) (E)
10. (A) (B) (C) (D) (E)
11. (A) (B) (C) (D) (E)
12. (A) (B) (C) (D) (E)
13. (A) (B) (C) (D) (E)
14. (A) (B) (C) (D) (E)
15. (A) (B) (C) (D) (E)
16. (A) (B) (C) (D) (E)
17. (A) (B) (C) (D) (E)
18. (A) (B) (C) (D) (E)
19. (A) (B) (C) (D) (E)
20. (A) (B) (C) (D) (E)
21. (A) (B) (C) (D) (E)
22. (A) (B) (C) (D) (E)
23. (A) (B) (C) (D) (E)
24. (A) (B) (C) (D) (E)
25. (A) (B) (C) (D) (E)
26. (A) (B) (C) (D) (E)
27. (A) (B) (C) (D) (E)
28. (A) (B) (C) (D) (E)
29. (A) (B) (C) (D) (E)
30. (A) (B) (C) (D) (E)
31. (A) (B) (C) (D) (E)
32. (A) (B) (C) (D) (E)
33. (A) (B) (C) (D) (E)
34. (A) (B) (C) (D) (E)
35. (A) (B) (C) (D) (E)
36. (A) (B) (C) (D) (E)
37. (A) (B) (C) (D) (E)
38. (A) (B) (C) (D) (E)
39. (A) (B) (C) (D) (E)
40. (A) (B) (C) (D) (E)
41. (A) (B) (C) (D) (E)
42. (A) (B) (C) (D) (E)
43. (A) (B) (C) (D) (E)
44. (A) (B) (C) (D) (E)
45. (A) (B) (C) (D) (E)
46. (A) (B) (C) (D) (E)
47. (A) (B) (C) (D) (E)
48. (A) (B) (C) (D) (E)
49. (A) (B) (C) (D) (E)
50. (A) (B) (C) (D) (E)
51. (A) (B) (C) (D) (E)
52. (A) (B) (C) (D) (E)
53. (A) (B) (C) (D) (E)
54. (A) (B) (C) (D) (E)
55. (A) (B) (C) (D) (E)
56. (A) (B) (C) (D) (E)
57. (A) (B) (C) (D) (E)
58. (A) (B) (C) (D) (E)
59. (A) (B) (C) (D) (E)
60. (A) (B) (C) (D) (E)
61. (A) (B) (C) (D) (E)
62. (A) (B) (C) (D) (E)
63. (A) (B) (C) (D) (E)
64. (A) (B) (C) (D) (E)
65. (A) (B) (C) (D) (E)
66. (A) (B) (C) (D) (E)
67. (A) (B) (C) (D) (E)
68. (A) (B) (C) (D) (E)
69. (A) (B) (C) (D) (E)
70. (A) (B) (C) (D) (E)
71. (A) (B) (C) (D) (E)
72. (A) (B) (C) (D) (E)
73. (A) (B) (C) (D) (E)
74. (A) (B) (C) (D) (E)
75. (A) (B) (C) (D) (E)
76. (A) (B) (C) (D) (E)
77. (A) (B) (C) (D) (E)
78. (A) (B) (C) (D) (E)
79. (A) (B) (C) (D) (E)
80. (A) (B) (C) (D) (E)
81. (A) (B) (C) (D) (E)
82. (A) (B) (C) (D) (E)
83. (A) (B) (C) (D) (E)
84. (A) (B) (C) (D) (E)
85. (A) (B) (C) (D) (E)
86. (A) (B) (C) (D) (E)
87. (A) (B) (C) (D) (E)
88. (A) (B) (C) (D) (E)
89. (A) (B) (C) (D) (E)
90. (A) (B) (C) (D) (E)
91. (A) (B) (C) (D) (E)
92. (A) (B) (C) (D) (E)
93. (A) (B) (C) (D) (E)
94. (A) (B) (C) (D) (E)
95. (A) (B) (C) (D) (E)
96. (A) (B) (C) (D) (E)
97. (A) (B) (C) (D) (E)
98. (A) (B) (C) (D) (E)
99. (A) (B) (C) (D) (E)
100. (A) (B) (C) (D) (E)

GRE PHYSICS
TEST 4

TIME: 170 Minutes
100 Questions

DIRECTIONS: Each of the questions or incomplete statements below is followed by five answer choices or completions. Choose the best answer to each question.

1. Consider the motion of a relativistic particle of mass m, momentum p, and energy E. Find the group velocity.

(A) $v_g = pc^2 / E$ (B) $v_g = E / p$

(B) $v_g = E / p$ (E) $v_g = 0$

(C) $v_g = p / mc$

2. Each of the hydrogen atom quantum mechanical wave functions has a characteristic symmetry. In the below 3D picture where we have plotted $\Psi\Psi^*$ ($y = 0$), what is the quantum state?

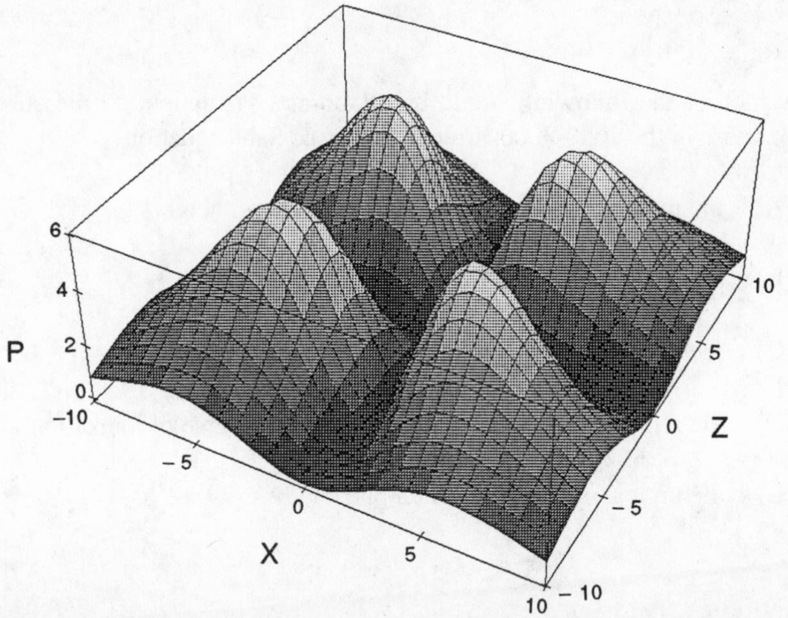

(A) ψ_{100}

(B) ψ_{321}

(C) ψ_{200}

(D) ψ_{210}

(E) ψ_{300}

3. Which of the following is NOT a true statement about quantum physics?

(A) The wave function is always a real quantity.

(B) The wave function represents the complete physical state.

(C) ψ, ψ', and ψ'' are finite, single-valued, and continuous.

(D) For every observable, there is a Quantum Mechanical operator.

(E) In one dimension that $\int_{-\infty}^{+\infty} \psi^* \psi \, dx = 1$ is required.

4. The first excited state of the one dimensional harmonic oscillator has eigenfunction

$$\phi(x) = Nxe^{-\alpha^2 x^2/2}.$$

Find N.

(A) $(\alpha^2/\pi)^{1/4}$

(B) α/π

(C) $2\alpha^3/\sqrt{\pi}$

(D) $(\alpha^2/\pi)^{1/2}$

(E) $\sqrt{2\alpha^3/\sqrt{\pi}}$

5. Which of the following would be a laboratory technique to measure temperature in the 2000-3000 K range using the Saha equation?

(A) the mercury thermometer (measure a liquid height)

(B) the standard thermocouple (measure an EMF)

(C) the resistance thermometer (measure resistance)

(D) the ionization thermometer (measure the degree of ionization)

(E) the optical pyrometer (match blackbody spectra)

6. The dispersion relationship for deep water waves is given by $\omega^2 = gk + ak^3$ where g and a are constants. Find the phase velocity in terms of λ.

(A) $\sqrt{g\lambda/2\pi + 2\pi a/\lambda}$

(B) $\sqrt{g\lambda/2\pi}$

(C) $\sqrt{g\lambda/2\pi + 2a/\lambda}$

(D) $\sqrt{2\pi a/\lambda}$

(E) $\sqrt{g\lambda/\pi + \pi a/\lambda}$

7. An important part of experimental physics involves the use of high vacuum technology. Which of the following is an INCORRECT statement?

(A) Mechanical pumps pump down to about 10^{-3} torr.

(B) Ion pumps are generally useful as roughing pumps.

(C) Molecular diffusion pumps take the system to 10^{-7} torr.

(D) Ion pumps can evacuate a chamber to 10^{-9} torr.

(E) Several different types of pumps are usually needed to get a high vacuum.

8. The potential energy of a particle moving in one dimension is given by $U(x) = 1/2\, kx^2 + 1/4\, bx^4$. Determine the force.

(A) $-kx - bx^3$

(B) $kx + bx^3$

(C) $1/6\, kx^3 + 1/20\, bx^5$

(D) $-1/6\, kx^3 - 1/20\, bx^5$

(E) $-kx - bx^2$

9. A particular curve connected from points P to Q and revolved about the *x-axis* generates the surface of minimum surface energy. What is the name of the surface of revolution?

(A) conic section

(B) catenoid

(C) portion of a sphere

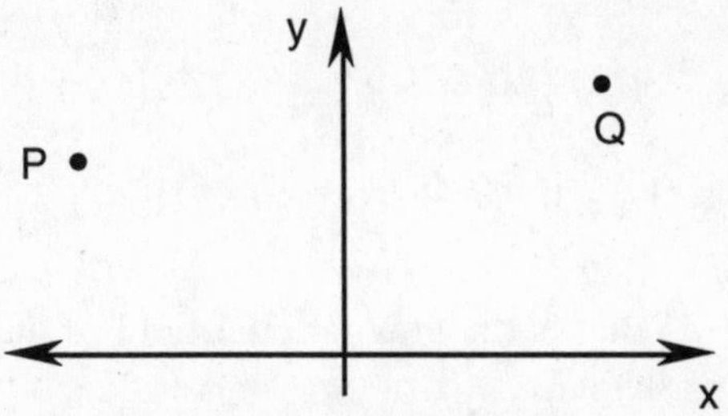

(D) cycloid

(E) geodesic

10. A pendulum of length l is attached to the roof of an elevator near the surface of the Earth. The elevator moves upward with acceleration $a = 1/2$ g. Determine the linear frequency of the pendulum's vibration.

(A) $\frac{1}{2\pi}\sqrt{3g/2l}$

(B) $\frac{1}{2\pi}\sqrt{2g/3l}$

(C) $\frac{1}{2\pi}\sqrt{g/l}$

(D) $\frac{1}{2\pi}\sqrt{g/l}$

(E) $\frac{1}{2\pi}\sqrt{2g/l}$

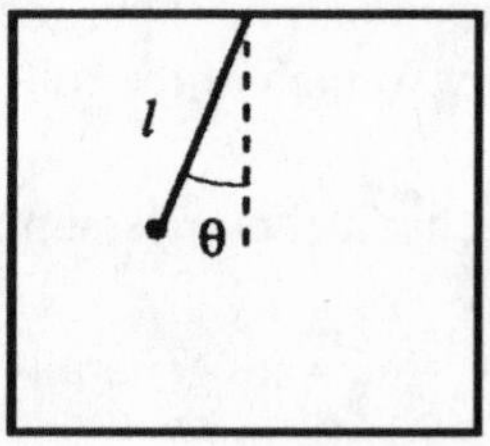

11. A room of dimensions $h = 2.5$ m by $w = 5.0$ m by $l = 5.0$ m contains 10^{27} air molecules. If all of the molecules in the room statistically conglomerated in a small corner of dimensions $h = 2.5$ cm by $w = 5.0$ cm by $l = 5.0$ cm, then a person in the room would be unable to breathe. Calculate the logarithm $\log_{10}$ of the probability that this will happen.

(A) $\log p = 0$

(B) $\log p = -27$

(C) $\log p = -6 \times 10^{27}$

(D) $\log p = -6$

(E) $\log p = -162$

12. An object is projected upward near the surface of the Earth, but also subject to a resistive force $-bv$. Determine the time taken to reach the maximum height. Let $\gamma \equiv b/m$ (for simplicity).

(A) v_0 / g

(B) $2g_0 / g$

(C) $(1/\gamma) \ln(1 + v_0\gamma/g)$

(D) $\ln(1 + v_0\gamma / g)$

(E) $(1/\gamma) \ln(1 - v_0\gamma / g)$

13. What is the gravitational field of an infinite line mass of linear mass density λ?

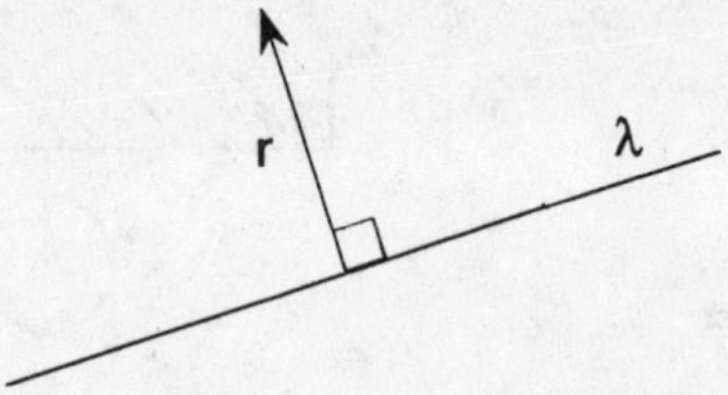

(A) $-(\lambda G / r)\,\mathbf{r}$

(B) $-(2\lambda G / r^2)\,\mathbf{r}$

(C) $(2\lambda G / r)\,\mathbf{r}$

(D) $-(\lambda G / r^2)\,\mathbf{r}$

(E) $-(2\lambda G / r)\,\mathbf{r}$

14. A circular annulus $a < r < b$ of uniform mass density σ is situated with center at the origin in the yz plane. Determine the gravitational potential at distance x.

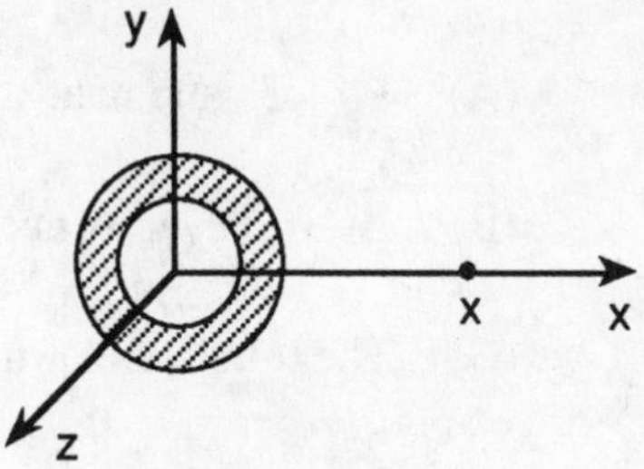

(A) $-2\pi\sigma G\sqrt{b^2 + x^2}$

(B) $-2\pi\sigma G\left[\sqrt{b^2 + x^2} - \sqrt{a^2 + x^2}\right]$

(C) $+\pi\sigma\,[b^2 - a^2]\,/\,x$

(D) $-\pi\sigma\,[b^2 - a^2]\,/\,x$

(E) $+2\pi\sigma G\left[\sqrt{b^2 + x^2} - \sqrt{a^2 + x^2}\right]$

15. A stunt plane flies a loop-the-loop circle at uniform speed v. The pilot experiences an apparent weight at the bottom that is twice his apparent weight at the top of the circular path. What is the radius of the path?

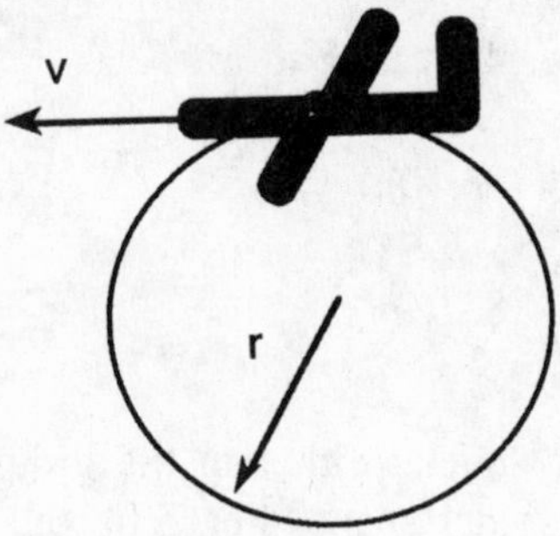

(A) v^2 / g

(B) $2v^2 / g$

(C) $3v^2 / g$

(D) $4v^2 / g$

(E) $5v^2 / g$

16. In an Atwood's machine where the one hanging mass is four times the other, find the acceleration.

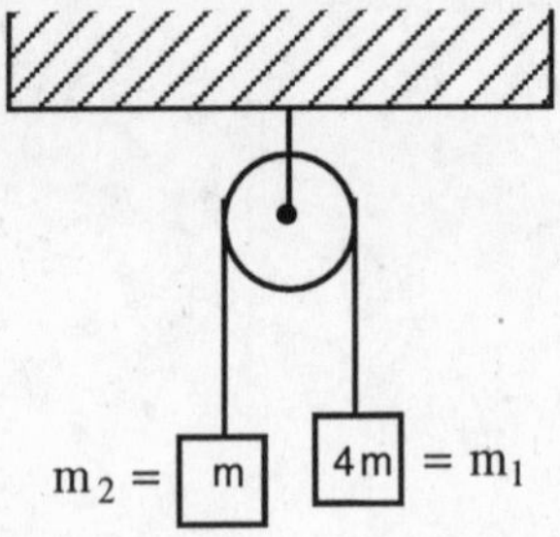

(A) $g/2$

(B) $2g/3$

(C) $3g/5$

(D) $3g/4$

(E) $4g/5$

17. Which of the following is NOT a true statement about nucleons?

(A) Protons and neutrons are fermions.

(B) Even Z even N nuclei have zero total angular momentum.

(C) The total angular momentum is integral for nuclei with even A.

(D) Protons and neutrons have integer spin.

(E) The total angular momentum is half-integral for nuclei with odd A.

18. The Roche limit for the earth-moon system is the distance at which the tidal action of the earth would start to rip the moon apart. Let a = earth-moon distance (assumed variable), r = radius of moon, M = earth's mass, and m = moon's mass. Find the Roche limit a.

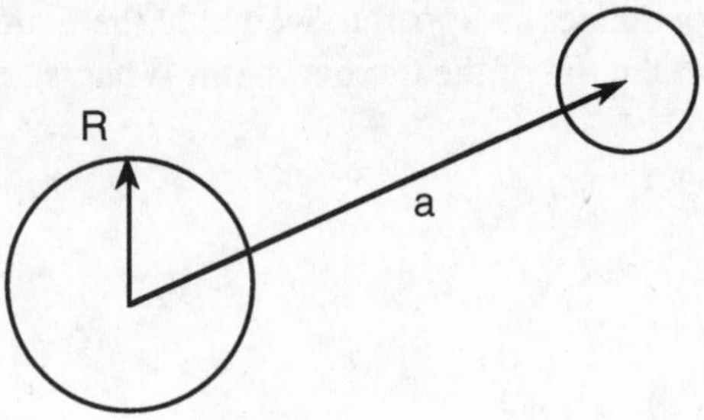

(A) $(4m/M)^{1/3}r$

(B) $(4M/m)^{1/3}r$

(C) $(4M/m)^{1/3}R$

(D) $(8m/m)^{1/3}R$

(E) $(8M/m)^{1/3}r$

19. Many nuclei either in the ground state or in an excited state assume an ellipsoidal shape. Let Z be the number of protons in the nucleus, N the number of neutrons, e the eccentricity, a the semi-major axis, and b the semi-minor axis of the ellipse. What is the quadrupole moment Q?

(A) $1/5\ Z\ e^2a^2$

(B) $1/5\ Z\ e^2b^2$

(C) $3/5\ N\ e^2a^2$

(D) $2/5\ Z\ e^2a^2$

(E) $3/5\ Z\ e^2b^2$

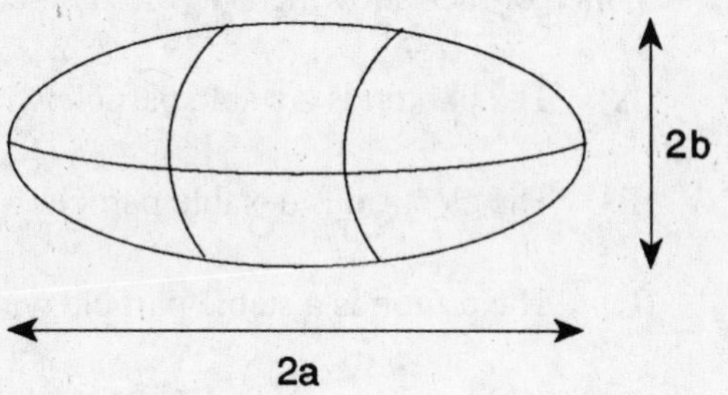

20. The meson theory of nuclear forces suggests a nucleon-nucleon potential of the form

$$U(r) = V_R e^{-k_R r}/r - V_A e^{-k_A r}/r.$$

Determine the form of the repulsive part of the force, the so-called hard core.

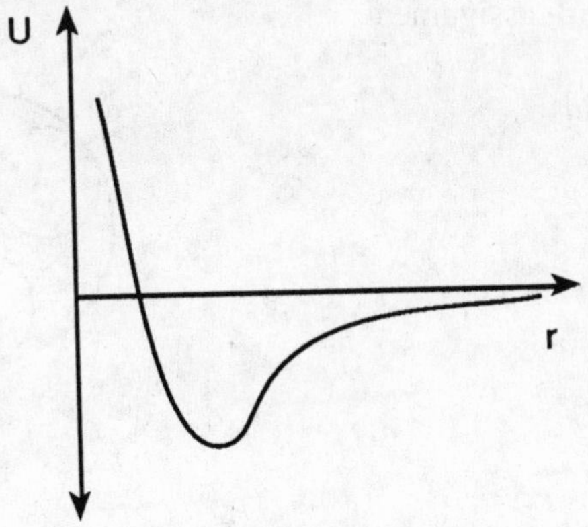

(A) $\left(V_R e^{-k_R r}/r\right)[k_R + 1/r] - \left(V_A e^{-k_A r}/r\right)[k_A + 1/r]$

(B) $V_A k_A e^{-k_A r}/r$

(C) $V_R k_R e^{-k_R r}/r$

(D) $\left(V_R e^{-k_R r}/r\right)[k_R + 1/r]$

(E) $\left(V_A e^{-k_A r}/r\right)[k_A + 1/r]$

21. Use the nuclear shell model to determine the ground state spin of ${}^{67}_{30}\mathrm{Zn}$.

(A) 1 / 2

(B) 3 / 2

(C) 0

(D) 1

(E) 5 / 2

22. Which of the following is a true statement about the elementary particles?

(A) The photon is a stable particle with non-zero mass and spin one.

(B) The electron is a stable particle with mass .511 MeV / c^2 and spin 3/2.

(C) The proton is a stable particle with mass 1836 MeV / c^2 and spin 1/2.

(D) The kaon has mass 134.96 MeV / c^2, lifetime longer than that of the pion, spin zero, and strangeness one.

(E) None of the above.

23. Hadrons consist of baryons and mesons and their structure is investigated using quantum chromo-dynamics or QCD. Which of the following is NOT a correct quark assignment?

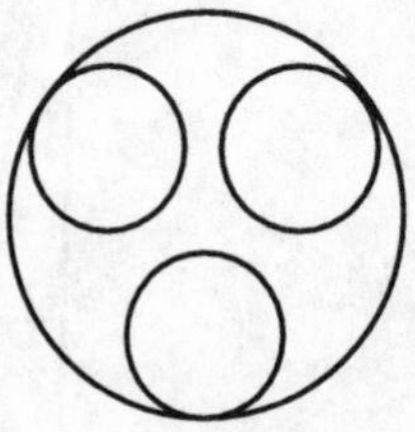

(A) $p = uud$

(B) $n = udd$

(C) $\pi^+ = us$

(D) $K^- = \underline{u}s$

(E) $J = cc$

24. Consider the elastic scattering of two identical atoms. Let the scattering angles in the lab frame be $(\theta_{lab}, \phi_{lab})$ and those in the center of mass (cm) frame be (θ, ϕ). If the differential cross section is isotropic is the CM with value $\sigma_0 / 4\pi$, then what is the lab cross section?

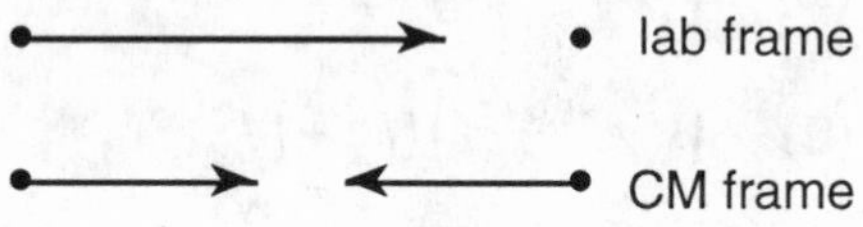

(A) $\sigma_0 / 4\pi$

(B) $\sigma_0 / 2\pi$

(C) $\sigma_0 / 8\pi$

(D) $\sigma_0 \cos\theta_{lab} / 2\pi$

(E) $\sigma_0 \cos\theta_{lab} / \pi$

25. Much of radioactive dating is based on the nuclear reaction

$${}^{14}_{6}C \rightarrow {}^{14}_{7}N + e^- + \overline{\upsilon}_e$$

which has a half-life of 5760 years. What is the mean life for this reaction?

(A) 11,520 years (B) 5760 years

(B) 7985 years (E) 3993 years

(C) 8310 years

26. The laboratory operation of a LASER is related to the atomic transition problem. Let $E_2 - E_1 = \hbar\,\omega$ for two atomic states, $u(\omega)$ be the radiation density, N_1 be the number of atoms in state 1, and N_2 that in state 2. B_{12} is the Einstein coefficient for absorption, B_{21} the transition probability for emission, and A_{21} the spontaneous emission coefficient. Find N_2 / N_1 for thermal equilibrium.

(A) $B_{12}u(\omega) / A_{21}$

(B) $A_{21}u(\omega) / B_{21}$

(C) $B_{12}u(\omega) / B_{21}$

(D) $B_{12}/ [A_{21} + B_{21}]$

(E) $B_{12}u(\omega) / [A_{21} + B_{21}u(\omega)]$

27. Which of the following is NOT a true statement about the Raman effect? Let $\hbar\omega$ be the energy per incident photon.

(A) A quantum of monochromatic light is scattered inelastically.

(B) Energy $\hbar\omega'$ is exchanged with a molecule.

(C) The frequency of the scattered radiation is $\omega'' = \omega \pm \omega'$.

(D) Raman scattering occurs as a result of the induced dipole moment.

(E) A quantum of monochromatic light is scattered elastically.

28. Find the magnetic field due to the finite current carrying wire pictured at point P. (See figure on following page.)

(A) $\dfrac{\mu_0 I}{2\pi r}$ (B) $\dfrac{\mu_0 I}{4\pi r}$

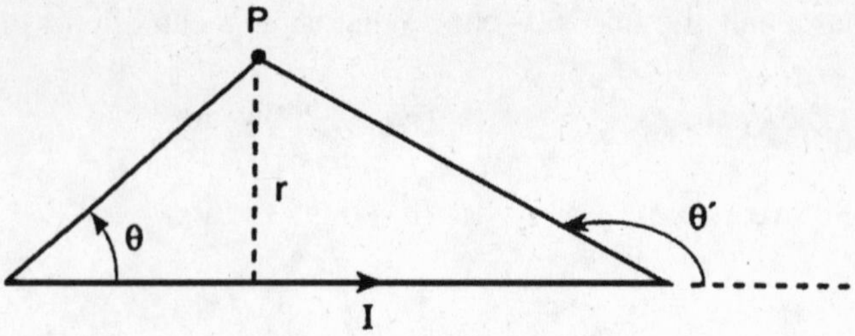

(C) $\frac{\mu_0 I}{4\pi r}[\cos\theta - \cos\theta']$

(D) $\frac{\mu_0 I}{4\pi r}[\cos\theta + \cos\theta']$

(E) $\frac{\mu_0 I}{2\pi r}[\cos\theta - \cos\theta']$

29. Figure out the total electric potential energy of a *single* spherical object of uniform charge density ρ, total charge Q, and radius R. Let $k = 1/4\,\pi\varepsilon_0$ as usual.

(A) 0

(B) kQ^2/R

(C) $1/2\; kQ^2/R$

(D) $3/5\; kQ^2/R$

(E) $2/3\; kQ^2/R$

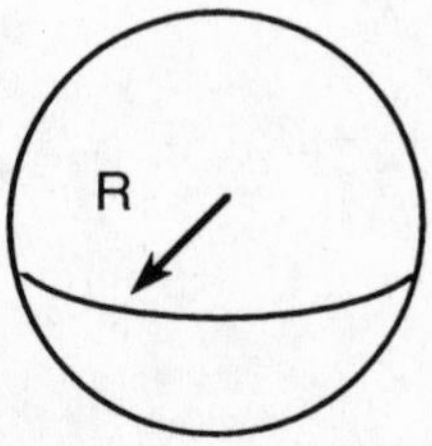

30. A plane wave solution of Maxwell's equations in free space is

$$\mathbf{E} = \mathbf{y}\,E_{oy}\cos(\omega t - kx + \alpha) + \mathbf{z}\,E_{oz}\cos(\omega t - kx + \beta).$$

Let $\delta = \beta - \alpha$ be the phase difference. Under what conditions do we get elliptic polarization?

(A) $\delta = \pm\pi/2$

(B) $\delta = 0$

(C) $\delta = \pm\pi/4$ and $E_{oy} = E_{oz}$

(D) $\delta = \pm\pi/2$ and $E_{oy} = E_{oz}$

(E) $\delta = \pm\pi$

31. A toroidal substance of inner radius *a*, outer radius *b*, and magnetic permeability μ is wrapped with *N* turns in which current *I* flows. Find the magnetic field *B* at the center of the toroid's cross-section.

(A) $N\mu_0 I / \pi (a + b)$

(B) $N\mu_0 I / \pi$

(C) $N\mu I / \pi (a + b)$

(D) $N\mu I / \pi a$

(E) $NI / \pi (a + b)$

32. Monochromatic light waves of wavelength λ are incident on a single slit of width d and observed on a screen a distance l away and a height y above the slit optical axis. If the distance y is halfway to the first minimum, then what is the relative intensity $I(y) / I_0$? For destructive interference, $d \sin \theta = n\lambda$.

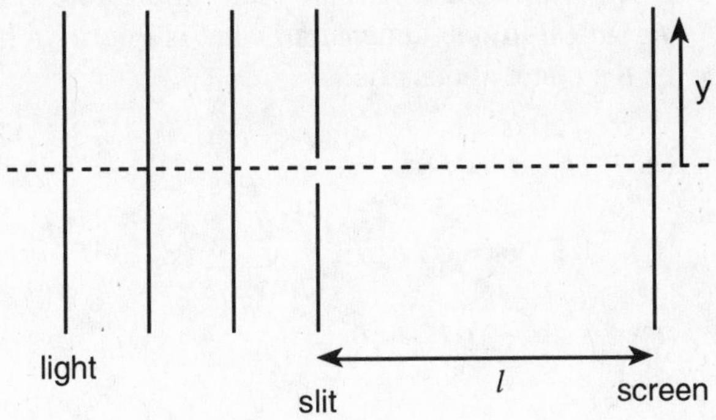

(A) $1 / 2$

(B) $1 / e$

(C) $2 / \pi$

(D) $4 / \pi^2$

(E) $1 / e^2$

33. A point charge of magnitude q is situated a distance h above an infinite conducting xy plane, as shown. What is the charge density σ on top of the plane as a function of the cylindrical radius s?

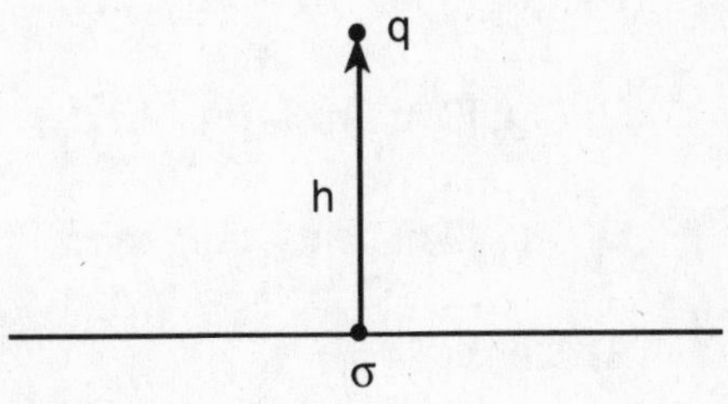

(A) $-qh / 2\pi(s^2 + h^2)^{3/2}$

(B) $-q / (s + h)$

(C) $+q / (s + h)$

(D) $+qh / 4\pi (s^2 + h^2)^{3/2}$

(E) zero since the plane is conducting

34. An infinite conducting xy plane is maintained at zero voltage everywhere except within a circular region $s < r$ where the voltage is V_0. Given that the voltage along the z-axis is

$$\phi(z) = \frac{V_o z}{2\pi} \int s\, ds\, d\phi \,/\, (s^2 + z^2)^{3/2} ,$$

determine the electric field along this axis.

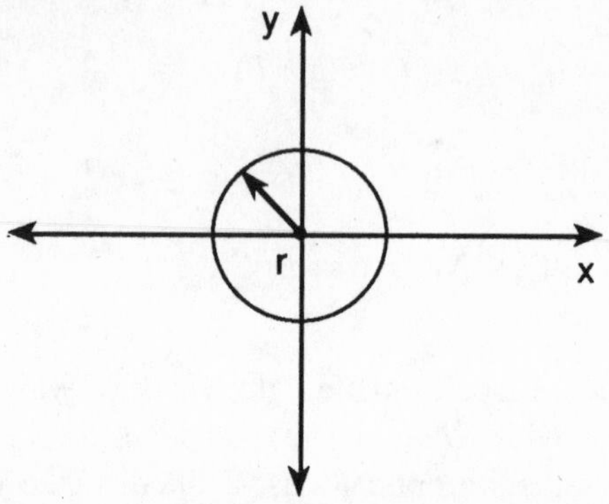

(A) $V_0 / (r + z)$

(B) $V_0 r^2 / (r^2 + z^2)^{3/2}$

(C) V_0 / r

(D) V_0 / z

(E) $V_0 r^2 / z^3$

35. In the fundamentals of heat transfer the energy flux j, the thermal conductivity σ, the specific heat c_v, the temperature T and the time t are important variables. In one dimension, what is Fourier's law for heat transfer? Let ρ be the material density.

(A) $j = -\sigma\, \partial T / \partial x$

(B) $\partial T / \partial t = \sigma / c_v\, \partial^2 T / \partial x^2$

(C) $j = +\sigma\, \partial T / \partial x$

(D) $\partial j / \partial t = \sigma / c_v\, \partial^2 T / \partial x^2$

(E) $\partial T / \partial t = \sigma / \rho\, \partial^2 T / \partial x^2$

36. The magnetic vector potential can be used to derive the magnetic dipole **m** field. What is the resultant field at distance **r**?

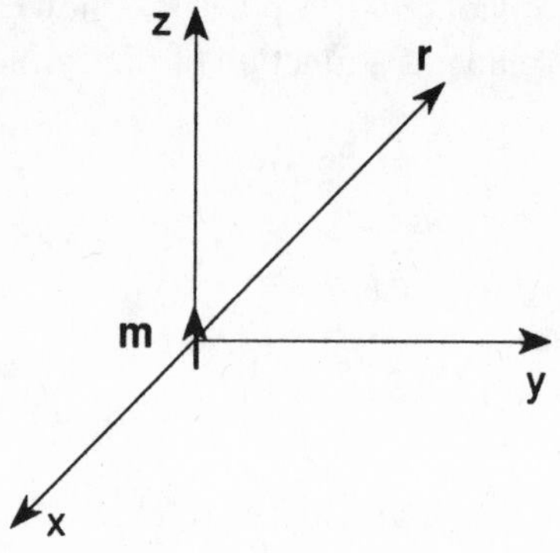

(A) $\mu_0 [3 (\mathbf{m} \cdot \mathbf{r})\, \mathbf{r} - \mathbf{m}] / 4\pi r^3$

(B) $\mu_0 [3\, \mathbf{m} \cdot \mathbf{r}\, \mathbf{r} - \mathbf{m}] / 4\pi r^2$

(C) $\mu_0 [2\, \mathbf{m} \cdot \mathbf{r}\, \mathbf{r} - \mathbf{m}] / 4\pi r^3$

(D) $\mu_0 [3\, \mathbf{m} \cdot \mathbf{r}\, \mathbf{r} - \mathbf{m}] / 4\pi r^2$

(E) $\mu_0\, \mathbf{m} / 4\pi r^2$

37. A particle is constrained to move on the surface of a sphere of radius R near the surface of the earth. What is the Lagrangian in cylindrical coordinates (ρ, θ, z)?

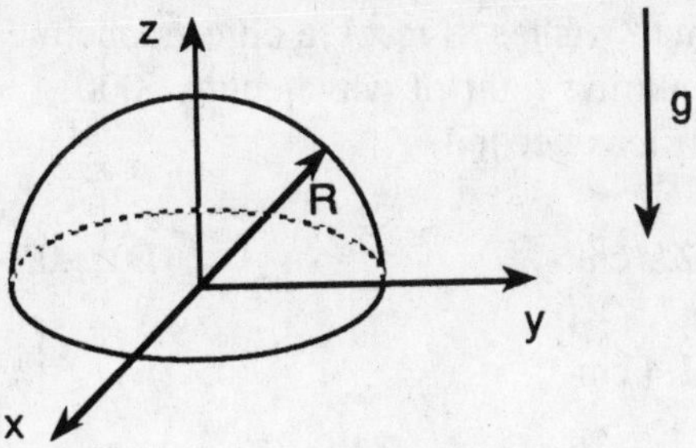

(A) $1/2\, m\, (\rho'^2 + \rho^2\theta'^2 + z'^2) - mgz$

(B) $1/2\, m\, (\rho'^2 + \rho^2\theta'^2) - mgz$

(C) $1/2\, m\, (\rho'^2 + z'^2) - mgz$

(D) $1/2\, m\, (\rho^2\theta'^2 + z'^2) - mgz$

(E) $1/2\, m\, (\rho'^2 + \rho^2\theta'^2 \sin^2\theta + z'^2) - mgz$

38. A grounded conducting sphere is placed in a uniform electric field $\mathbf{E} = E_0\mathbf{z}$. Determine the electric potential $\Phi(r, \theta)$ given that

$$\Phi(r, \theta) = [Ar + B/r^2] \cos\theta.$$

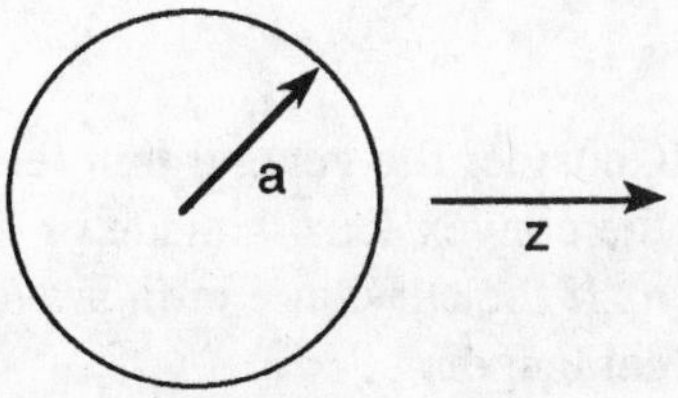

(A) $-E_0 r \cos\theta$

(B) $-E_0 r\, [1 - (a/r)^3] \cos\theta$

(C) $-E_0 r\, (a/r)^3 \cos\theta$

(D) $-E_0 r\, [1 + (a/r)^3] \cos\theta$

(E) $+E_0 r\, (a/r)^3\,] \cos\theta$

39. What is the differential statement of Poynting's theorem? Let **S** be the Poynting vector, *u* be the field energy density, and **j** be the current density.

(A) $\nabla \cdot \mathbf{S} + \mathbf{j} \cdot \mathbf{E} = 0$

(B) $\nabla \cdot \mathbf{S} + \partial u / \partial t + \mathbf{j} \cdot \mathbf{E} = 0$

(C) $\nabla \cdot \mathbf{S} + \partial u / \partial t = 0$

(D) $\nabla \cdot \mathbf{S} + \partial u / \partial t + \mathbf{j} \cdot \mathbf{E} + IR = 0$

(E) $\nabla \cdot \mathbf{S} = 0$

40. A woman wishes to resolve objects one meter apart at a distance of 10,000 m. Assuming light of wavelength 6000 Å, what is the minimum diameter circular lens needed?

(A) 2.9 cm
(B) 1.4 cm
(C) 0.7 cm
(D) 0.3 cm
(E) 0.1 cm

41. Light is incident on a prism of apex angle $\alpha = 60°$ at angle of incidence $\theta_{i1} = 30°$. The prism is made of a substance of refractive index $n_r = 1.5$ and is surrounded by a near vacuum. Determine the net angle of deviation of the light due to passage through the prism.

(A) 30°
(B) 60°
(C) 23°
(D) 47°
(E) 70°

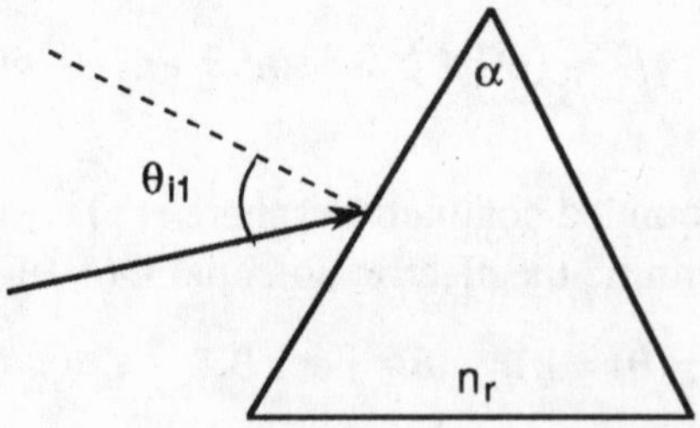

42. Consider the general thin lens problem where the object sits in medium n_0, the convex lens is made of material n_r, and the image is found in medium n_i. If the curvature radii are R_1 and R_2 as shown, then find the secondary focal length f'.

(A) $f' = -n_0 / [(n_r - n_0)/R_1 + (n_i - n_r)/R_2]$
(B) $f' = n_i / [(n_r - n_0)/R_1 + (n_i - n_r)/R_2]$
(C) $f' = n_i / [(n_i - n_r)/R_1 + (n_r - n_0)/R_2]$
(D) $f' = -n_0 / [(n_i - n_r)/R_1 + (n_r - n_0)/R_2]$
(E) $f' = -4/(R_1 + R_2]$

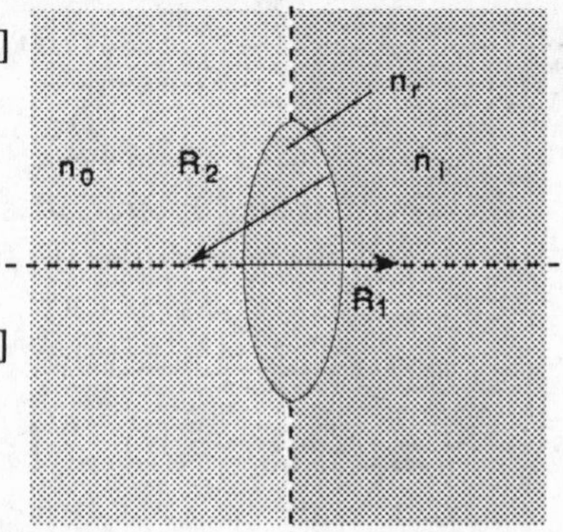

43. Determine the logic statement for the CMOS gate shown, where Q_1 and Q_4 are *n*-channel MOSFET and Q_2 and Q_3 are *p*–channel MOSFET. Assume positive logic.

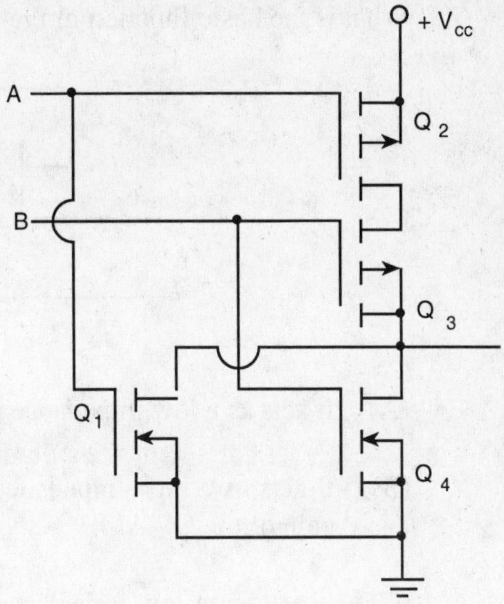

(A) NAND

(B) AND

(C) OR

(D) XOR

(E) NOR

44. A TTL logic gate is designed to be a NAND gate using positive logic. What is the logical statement assuming negative logic?

(A) NAND

(B) NOR

(C) AND

(D) OR

(E) XOR

45. For the below circuit, determine the waveform which appears at point *A*.

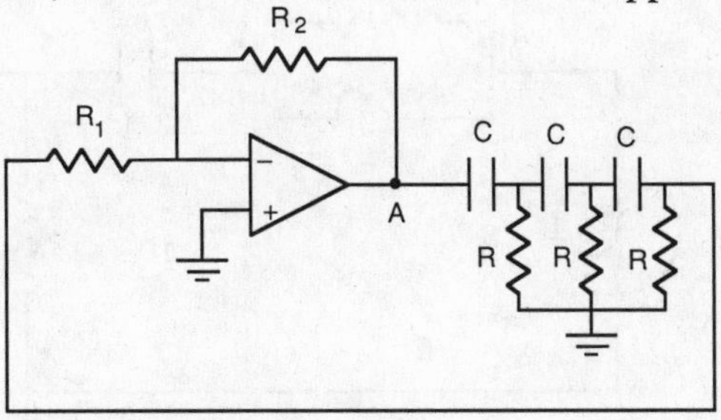

(A) sine wave of frequency $\frac{1}{3}RC$

(B) sine wave of frequency $\frac{1}{\sqrt{6}}RC$

(C) square wave of frequency $\frac{1}{RC}$

(D) square wave of frequency $\frac{1}{\sqrt{6}}RC$

(E) triangle wave of frequency $\frac{1}{RC}$

46. What is the basic function of the below OP AMP circuit?

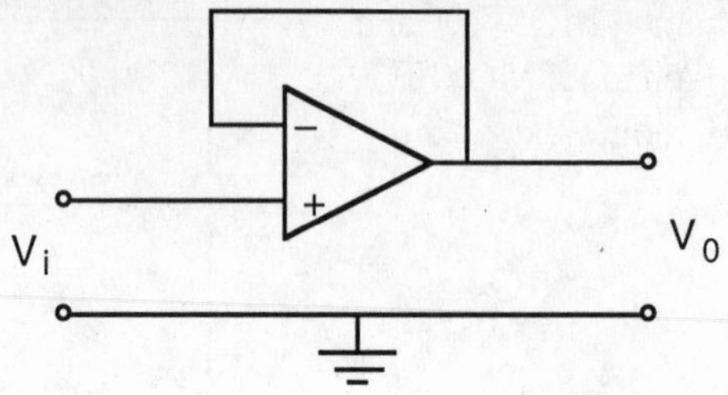

(A) It acts as a low impedance buffer with unity gain.

(B) It acts as a high impedance b uffer with gain equal to the open loop gain of the OP AMP.

(C) It acts as a low impedance buffer with gain equal to the open loop gain of the OP AMP.

(D) It acts as a low impedance buffer with gain equal to the closed loop gain of the OP AMP.

(E) It acts as a high impedance buffer with unity gain.

47. For the shown circuit, what best describes the output voltage compared to the input voltage at very high frequencies?

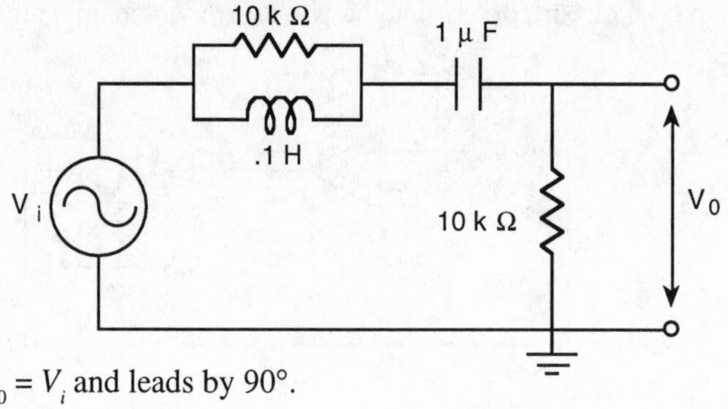

(A) $V_0 = V_i$ and leads by 90°.

(B) $V_0 = 1/2\ V_i$ and lags by 90°.

(C) $V_0 << V_i$ and is in phase.

(D) $V_0 = 1/2\ V_i$ and is in phase.

(E) $V_0 << V_i$ and lags by 90°.

48. Which of the following is NOT a correct statement about the phenomenon of optical activity?

(A) The vibration plane of light undergoes rotation when passed through a substance like turpentine.

(B) The electric field of the incident plane wave rotates about the optic axis.

(C) Quartz is only dextro-rotatory.

(D) A substance that causes clockwise rotation (looking in the source direction) is dextro-type.

(E) A substance that causes counter-clockwise rotation is levo-type.

49. Consider a plane transmission diffraction grating. Let d be the distance between ruled lines, m the order number, and θ the observation angle. Find the angular dispersion $d\theta/d\lambda$ for incident light of wavelength λ.

(A) $\sin\theta / \lambda$

(B) $\cos\theta / \lambda$

(C) $\cot\theta / \lambda$

(D) $\tan\theta / \lambda$

(E) $\sec\theta / \lambda$

50. Newton's rings are observed with a plano-convex lens resting on a plane glass surface. If R is the lens radius or curvature, m is the order number, and λ is the incident light wavelength, then find the radii of dark interference rings r, such that $r << R$.

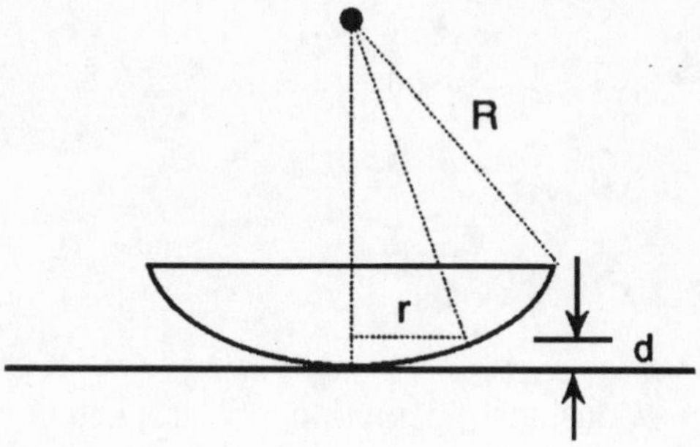

(A) $\sqrt{(m+1)\lambda R}$

(B) $\sqrt{(m\lambda)} / R$

(C) $\sqrt{m\lambda R}$

(D) $\sqrt{m\lambda / R}$

(E) $\sqrt{(m+1/2)\lambda R}$

51. Determine the speed of the photoelectrons ejected from a metal surface. The threshold wavelength is 2638 Å and the wavelength of incident light is 1600 Å.

(A) 5.2×10^5 m/s
(B) 2.6×10^5 m/s
(C) 2.08×10^6 m/s
(D) 1.66×10^6 m/s
(E) 1.04×10^6 m/s

52. Electromagnetic radiation of wavelength 6.20 Å is incident on a substance and back-scattered at an angle of 180°. Determine the Compton energy shift of the radiation.

(A) 31.0 eV
(B) 15.5 eV
(C) 2.0 keV
(D) 4.0 keV
(E) 1.0 keV

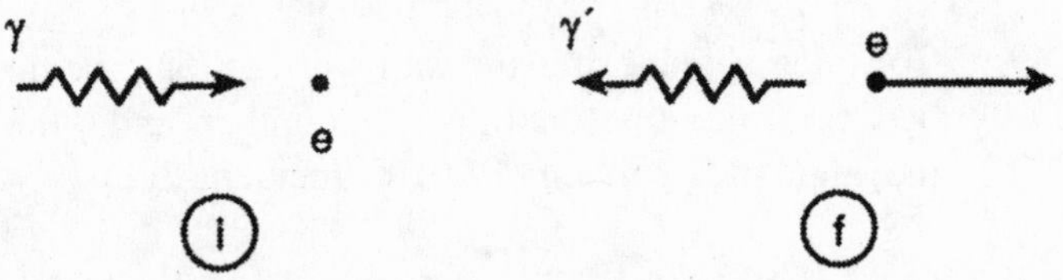

53. A particle of mass m moves in one dimension subject only to a resistive force $F_R = -bv$. Let $\gamma = b/m = 2.0\ s^{-1}$ and the initial speed be 100 m/s. Determine the distance moved at $t = 2.5\ s$.

(A) 50.0 m
(B) 25.0 m
(C) 12.5 m
(D) 49.7 m
(E) 24.8 m

54. Consider the motion of a rocket in free space. If the rocket starts with initial velocity 0.5 km/s and its mass decreases by a factor of two due to exhaust emitted with speed 1.0 km/s, then find the final velocity of the rocket.

(A) 1.5 km/s

(B) 0.5 km/s

(C) 0.6 km/s

(D) 1.7 km/s

(E) 1.2 km/s

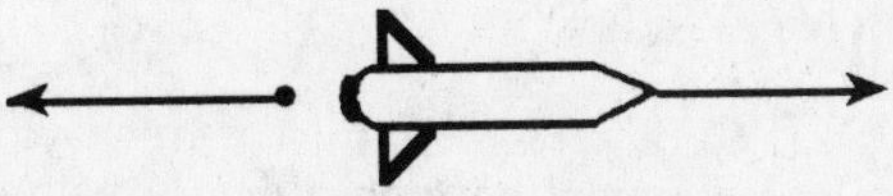

55. Obtain the expression for the acceleration of a mass in cylindrical coordinates. (Hint, find **r** then use to get **v** in cylindrical coordinates.)

(A) $(\rho'' + \rho\theta'^2)\,\hat{\rho} + (\rho\theta'' - 2\rho'\theta'')\hat{\theta} + z''\hat{z}$

(B) $\rho''\hat{\rho} + \rho\theta''\,\hat{\theta} + z''\hat{z}$

(C) $(\rho'' - \rho\theta'^2)\,\hat{\rho} + (\rho\theta'' - 2\rho'\theta')\hat{\theta} + z''\hat{z}$

(D) $(\rho'' - \rho\theta'^2)\,\hat{\rho} + (\rho\theta'' + 2\rho'\theta')\hat{\theta} + z''\hat{z}$

(E) $\rho''\hat{\rho} - \rho\theta''\,\hat{\theta} + z''\hat{z}$

56. The position of a particle is given by $P = (1.0, 1.0)\ m$ in standard Cartesian coordinates. What is the position of this particle with respect to a frame rotated by 30°?

(A) (1.00, 1.00)

(B) (1.37, 0.37)

(C) (0.37, 1.37)

(D) (1.37, 1.37)

(E) (0.37, 0.37)

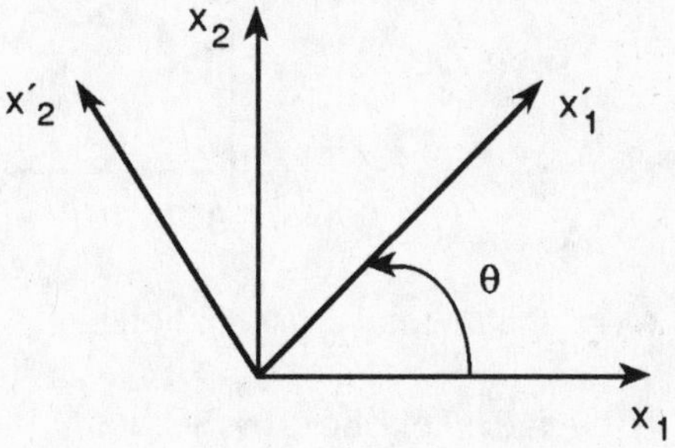

57. Stirling's approximation for $N!$ may be found for large N by using the gamma function. What is the approximation to second order?

(A) $(N / e)^N$

(B) N^N

(C) $(N/e)^N \sqrt{2\pi}$ (D) $(N/e)^N \sqrt{2\pi N}\,[1 - 1/12N]$

(E) $(N/e)^N \sqrt{2\pi N}$

58. The microcanonical ensemble theory value for the cumulative number of states (ideal gas) is

$$\Gamma(E) = \frac{\pi^{3N/2}}{N!\left(\frac{3N}{2}\right)!(2\pi\hbar)^{3N}} V^N P^{3N} \text{ where } P = \sqrt{2mE}.$$

Use this information to determine the entropy, i.e., the Sackor-Tetrode equation. Let $g = m / 2\pi\hbar^2$ and $T = 2E/3N$.

(A) $S = Nk \ln [(gT)^{3/2} V / N] + 5/2\, Nk$

(B) $S = Nk \ln [(gT)^{3/2} V / N] + 3/2\, Nk$

(C) $S = 3/2\, Nk \ln T + Nk \ln V + 5/2\, Nk$

(D) $S = 3/2\, Nk \ln T + Nk \ln V + 3/2\, Nk$

(E) $S = 3/2\, Nk \ln T - Nk \ln V / N + 5/2\, Nk$

59. Use your knowledge of nuclear and particle physics to determine which elementary cross section the below curve represents.

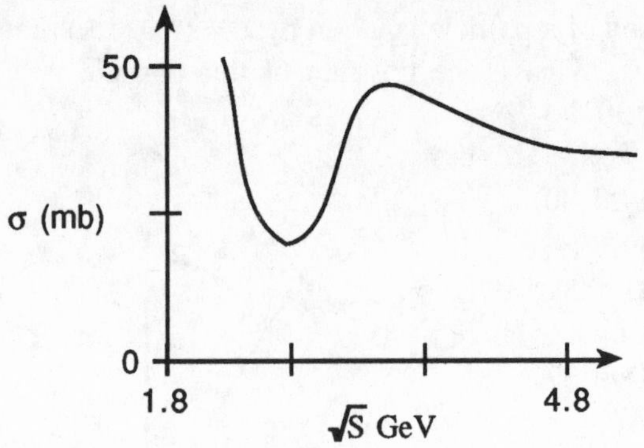

(A) the pp total cross section

(B) the nn elastic cross section

(C) the nn inelastic cross section

(D) the direct pn cross section

(E) the $\pi\, n$ cross section

60. Determine the threshold kinetic energy to produce proton-antiproton pairs in positron-electron collisions. The positron *KE* is T_e and the target electrons are at rest.

(A) 1.876 GeV

(B) 0.938 GeV

(C) 1.72 TeV

(D) 3.44 TeV

(E) 0.86 TeV

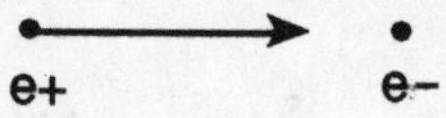

61. Obtain the correct classical Lagrangian for a particle subject to an electric field **E** due to potential ϕ and a magnetic field due to vector potential **A** such that $\mathbf{B} = \nabla \times \mathbf{A}$.

(A) $L = 1/2\, mv^2 + q\phi - q\mathbf{A} \cdot \mathbf{v}$

(B) $L = 1/2\, mv^2 - \int (q\mathbf{E} + \mathbf{v} \times \mathbf{B}) \cdot d\mathbf{r}$

(C) $L = 1/2\, mv^2 - q\phi + q\mathbf{A} \cdot \mathbf{v}$

(D) $L = 1/2\, mv^2 + \int q\mathbf{E} \cdot d\mathbf{r}$

(E) $L = 1/2\, mv^2 + q\phi + q\mathbf{A} \cdot \mathbf{v}$

62. Find the distance of closest approach for the elastic nuclear reaction

$${}^{7}_{3}\text{Li} + {}^{208}_{82}\text{Pb}.$$

Assume that only the Coulomb force is important. The Li nucleus is accelerated to a kinetic energy of 50.0 MeV.

(A) 1.12 fm

(B) 2.24 fm

(C) 3.54 fm

(D) 7.08 fm

(E) 8.20 fm

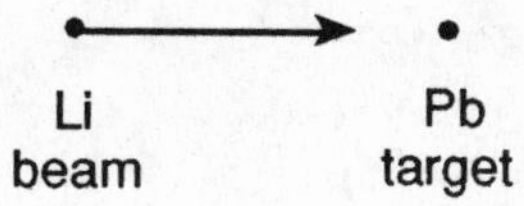

63. A charge q is distributed throughout a sphere of radius R with uniform charge density ρ. Given that the potential is

$$\phi = -\rho r^2 / 6\varepsilon_o + A/r + B \text{ for } r < R,$$

determine the constants A and B and hence ϕ.

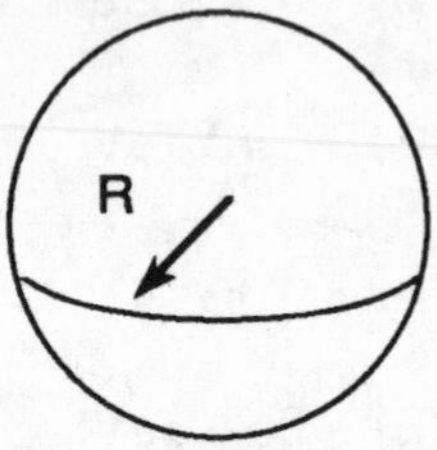

(A) $\phi = -\rho r^2 / 6\varepsilon_o + \rho R^3 / 3\varepsilon_o r$

(B) $\phi = -\rho r^2 / 6\varepsilon_o$

(C) $\phi = -(\rho / 2\varepsilon_o)\,[2R^2 - r^2/3]$

(D) $\phi = 0$

(E) $\phi = (\rho / 2\varepsilon_o)\,[R^2 - r^2/3]$

64. Two small spheres are half immersed in a substance of conductivity σ as shown below. Find the resistance of the two sphere system for $r_1 = r_2 = r$. $d >> r$.

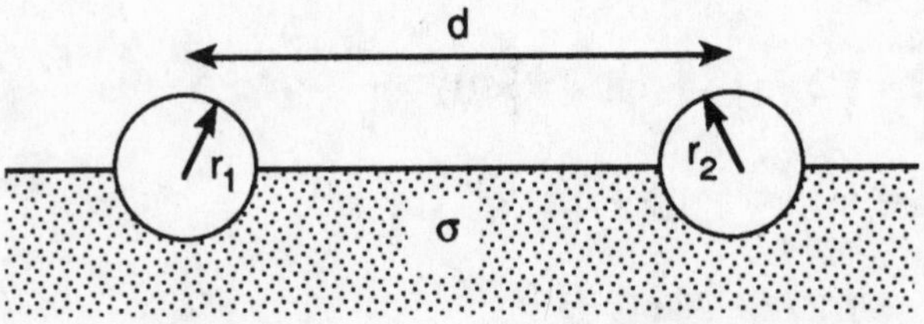

(A) $R = [1/r + 1/d]/\pi\sigma$

(B) $R = [2/r + 2/d]/\pi\sigma$

(C) $R = d/\pi\sigma r^2$

(D) $R = [1/r - 1/d]/\pi\sigma$

(E) $R = [2/r - 2/d]/\pi\sigma$

65. The nature of the gravitational field and the electric field are alike in that both are inverse square. Use this analogy to develop a differential Gauss' law for gravitation. Let ρ be the mass/volume.

(A) $\nabla \cdot \mathbf{g} = -4\pi G\rho / \varepsilon_o$

(B) $\nabla \cdot \mathbf{g} = -G\rho$

(C) $\nabla \cdot \mathbf{g} = -4\pi\rho$

(D) $\nabla \cdot \mathbf{g} = -\rho / G$

(E) $\nabla \cdot \mathbf{g} = -4\pi G\rho$

66. The first variation

$$\delta f = \frac{\partial f}{\partial x}\,\delta x + \frac{\partial f}{\partial x}\,\delta x'$$

is used to determine the Lagrange equation. What is the second variation of the integrand of the action integral

$$A = \int_{t_1}^{t_2} f(t, x, x')\,dt?$$

(A) $\frac{\partial^2 f}{\partial x^2}(\delta x)^2 + 2\frac{\partial^2 f}{\partial x \partial x'}\,\delta x \delta x' + \frac{\partial^2 f}{\partial x'^2}(\delta x')^2$

(B) $\frac{\partial^2 f}{\partial x^2}(\delta x)^2 + \frac{\partial^2 f}{\partial x'^2}(\delta x')^2$

(C) $\frac{\partial^2 f}{\partial x^2}(\delta x)^2 + 2\frac{\partial^2 f}{\partial x \partial x'}\,\delta x \delta x'$

(D) $2\frac{\partial^2 f}{\partial x \partial x'}\,\delta x \delta x' + \frac{\partial^2 f}{\partial x'^2}(\delta x')^2$

(E) $\frac{\partial^2 f}{\partial x^2}(\delta x)^2$

67. What is the fundamental physics basis of Snell's law?

(A) the first postulate of special relativity

(B) the Pauli principle

(C) the uncertainty principle

(D) Newton's first law

(E) Fermat's principle of least time

68. Determine the two-dimensional Lorentz transformation matrix $K \rightarrow K'$ using the rapidity variable $y = i\phi$.

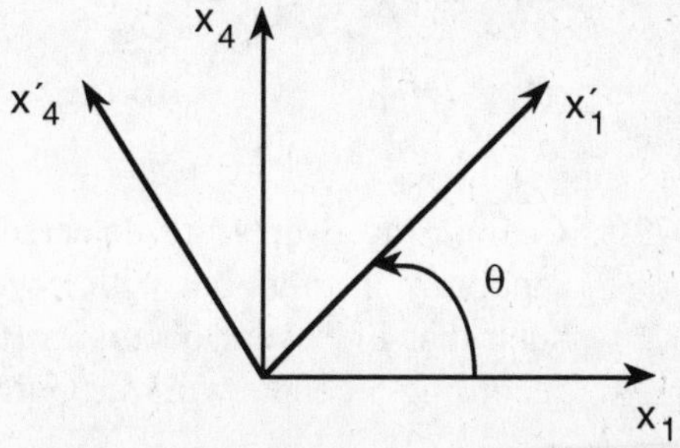

(A) $\begin{pmatrix} \cosh y & -i\sinh y \\ i\sinh y & \cosh y \end{pmatrix}$

(B) $\begin{pmatrix} \cosh y & i\sinh y \\ i\sinh y & \cosh y \end{pmatrix}$

(C) $\begin{pmatrix} \cosh y & i\sinh y \\ -i\sinh y & \cosh y \end{pmatrix}$

(D) $\begin{pmatrix} \cosh y & -i\sinh y \\ -i\sinh y & \cosh y \end{pmatrix}$

(E) $\begin{pmatrix} \cosh y & \sinh y \\ \sinh y & \cosh y \end{pmatrix}$

69. Discover the first correction term for the classical kinetic energy as relativistic effects become important.

(A) $1/2\ mv^2\gamma^2$

(B) $3/4\ mv^2\beta^2$

(C) $1/2\ mv^2\beta^2$

(D) $3/8\ mv^2\beta^2$

(E) $1/2\ mv^2\beta^2\gamma^2$

70. Consider the standard two body nuclear reaction $^{14}N\ (\alpha, p)^{17}O$ and determine the minimum kinetic energy needed (in the center of mass frame) for the reaction to occur. Given:

$m_p = 1.0078$, $m_\alpha = 4.0026$, $m_N = 14.0031$, and $m_O = 16.9991$ all in amu.

(A) 0.0 MeV

(B) 1.1 MeV

(C) 2.2 MeV

(D) 0.6 MeV

(E) 1.6 MeV

71. An ideal system of N spins each of magnetic moment μ_0 is under consideration. Each spin can either point up or down only, where $P(\uparrow) = p$ and $P(\downarrow) = q = 1 - p$. Find the variance of the mean magnetic moment.

(A) $Npq\mu_0^2$

(B) $2Npq\mu_0^2$

(C) $4Npq\mu_0^2$

(D) $6Npq\mu_0^2$

(E) $8Npq\mu_0^2$

72. Cosmic ray events are detected with a Geiger counter. The events occur randomly in time, but with a well defined mean rate r = 1 Hz = 1 event/s such that P[1 event occurs in (t,t + dt)] = rdt. What is the probability of recording 5 counts with the Geiger counter?

(A) .009

(B) .019

(C) .038

(D) .047

(E) .057

73. The second law of thermodynamics is intimately connected with the transfer of heat and the operation of machines. Which of the following is NOT a correct statement in light of this law?

(A) It is not possible to *only* transform heat into work extracted from a uniform temperature source.

(B) It is impossible to construct a perpetuum mobile of the second kind.

(C) It is impossible to *only* transfer heat from a body at high temperature to one at lower temperature.

(D) If heat flows by conduction from body A to body B, then it is impossible to *only* transfer heat from body B to body A.

(E) It is not possible to *only* transform work into heat where the body is at a uniform temperature.

74. In a centripetal motion laboratory experiment, g is computed from spinning a bob of mass $m = 50$ grams in a circle of radius $r = 20 \pm 1$ cm. The rotational period is measured to be $T = .638 \pm .016$ *s*. The body stretches a spring a distance equivalent to the force of a weight Mg where $M = 100$ grams. If the working equation is $g_{exp} = 4\pi^2 mr/MT^2$, then find the uncertainty Δg.

(A) 24 cm/s^2

(B) 39 cm/s^2

(C) 49 cm/s^2

(D) 69 cm/s^2

(E) 59 cm/s^2

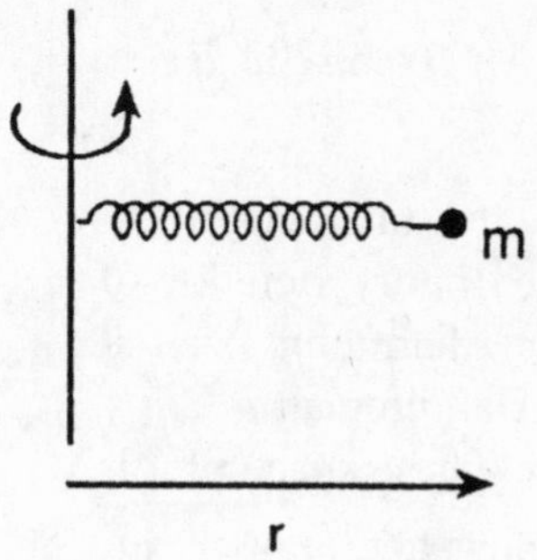

75. For one mole of ideal gas and the Carnot cycle pictured on the following page, find $Q_H - Q_C$.

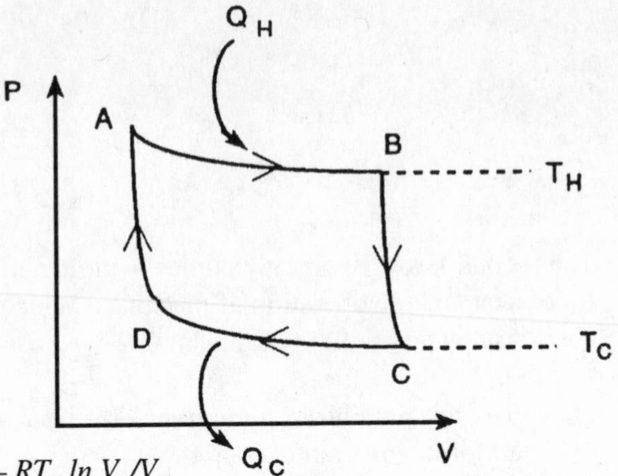

(A) $RT_H \ln V_A/V_B - RT_C \ln V_C/V_D$

(B) $RT_H \ln V_B/V_A - RT_C \ln V_D/V_C$

(C) $RT_H \ln V_A/V_B - RT_C \ln V_D/V_C$

(D) $R[T_H - T_C]$

(E) $RT_H \ln V_B/V_A - RT_C \ln V_C/V_D$

76. Use the Boltzmann factor to study the thermodynamics of N independent particles of a spin system in a magnetic field where the energies are $E_\pm = \mp\mu_o B$. Find the total average energy at temperature $T = 1/\beta k$.

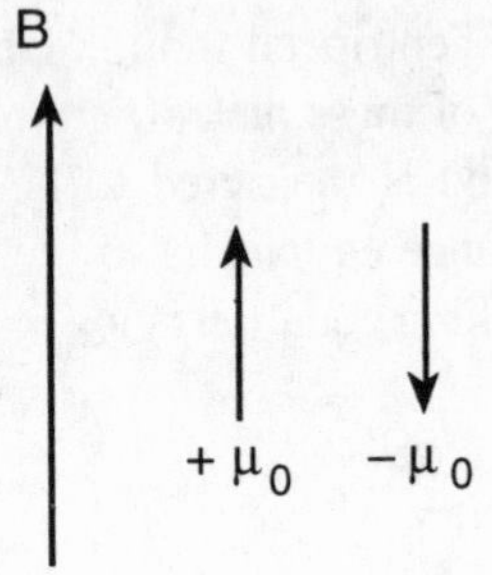

(A) $-N\mu_o B \coth(\beta\mu_o B)$

(B) $+N\mu_o B \coth(\beta\mu_o B)$

(C) $-N\mu_o B \tanh(\beta\mu_o B)$

(D) $-N\mu_o B \sinh(\beta\mu_o B)$

(E) $+N\mu_o B \tanh(\beta\mu_o B)$

77. Evaluate the microcanonical ensemble theory density of states for a harmonic oscillator with Hamiltonian $p^2/2m + kx^2/2$. The phase space plot is shown below. Let $\omega = \sqrt{k/m}$.

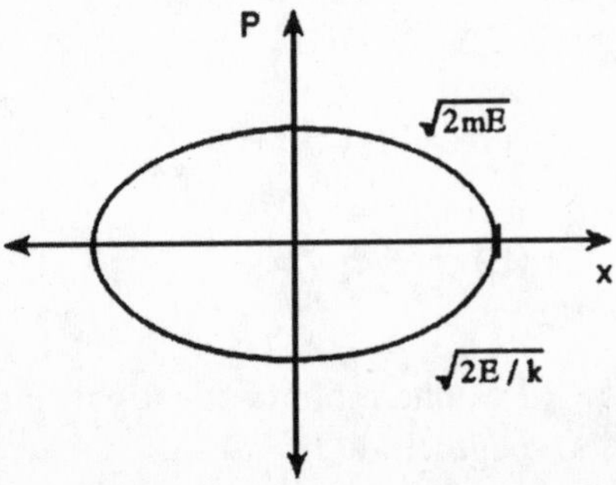

(A) $E/\hbar\omega$

(B) $1/\hbar\omega$

(C) $E^2/\hbar\omega$

(D) $\sqrt{E}/\hbar\omega$

(E) $E^{3/2}/\hbar\omega$

78. Identify the below phase space orbit.

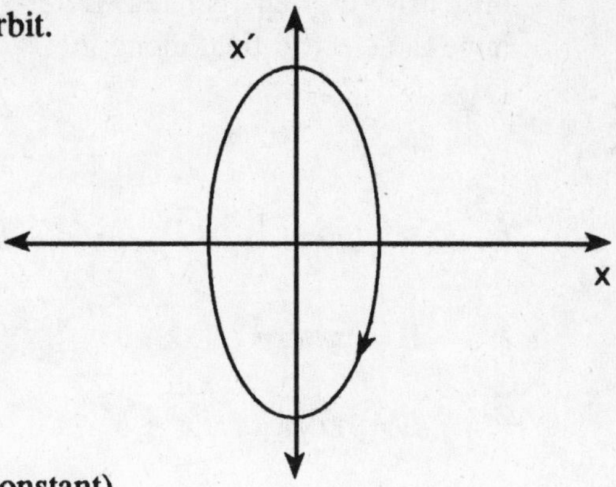

(A) Lissajous figure

(B) damped motion.

(C) simple harmonic motion

(D) gravitational motion (g = constant)

(E) logistic difference equation

79. Consider the spectroscopy of the hydrogen atom in Bohr theory. Determine the upper limit for the Brackett series. Given that $R = 109{,}677.6\ \text{cm}^{-1}$.

(A) 1216 Å

(B) 6563 Å

(C) 4050 nm

(D) 1880 nm

(E) 7450 nm

80. By looking at an empty glass along the ray path shown (angle = θ), one sees the lower left hand corner. Now when the glass is filled with a clear liquid of refractive index $n = 1.3$, one sees the middle of the bottom of the glass again looking along angle θ. Given the width is 5.0 cm, find the height y.

(A) 2.73 cm

(B) 5.46 cm

(C) 1.35 cm

(D) 4.08 cm

(E) 6.33 cm

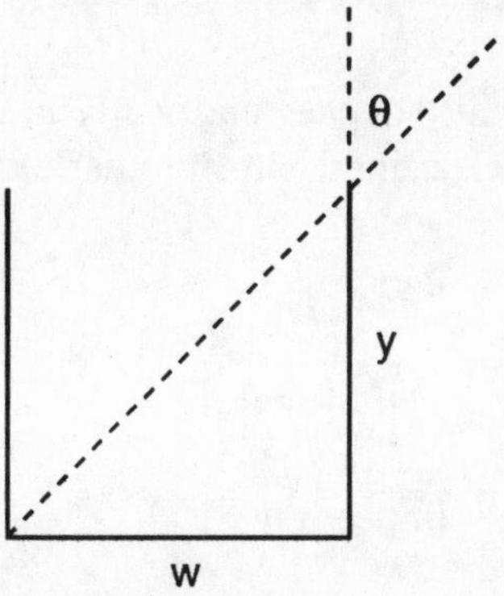

81. A circular annulus of inner radius a and outer radius b is centered at the origin in the yz plane. The annulus is filled with positive charge of density σ = charge/area. Determine the electric field along the x-axis.

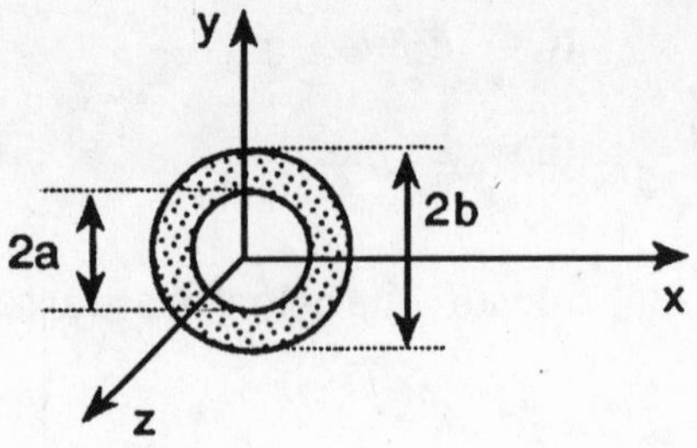

(A) $\mathbf{E} = 2\pi\sigma kx\left[1/\sqrt{x^2+a^2} - 1/\sqrt{x^2+b^2}\right]\mathbf{x}$

(B) $\mathbf{E} = 2\pi\sigma kx\,\mathbf{x}/\sqrt{x^2+a^2}$

(C) $\mathbf{E} = 2\pi\sigma kx\,\mathbf{x}/\sqrt{x^2+b^2}$

(D) $\mathbf{E} = \pi\sigma\left[b^2 - a^2\right]\mathbf{x}/x^2$

(E) $\mathbf{E} = -2\pi\sigma kx\left[1/\sqrt{x^2+a^2} - 1/\sqrt{x^2+b^2}\right]\mathbf{x}$

82. The surface temperature of a blackbody such as the sun or any star can be found from plotting the intensity $u(\lambda)$ versus the wavelength λ. Generally, $u(\lambda)$ is proportional to $1/[\lambda^5(e^x - 1)]$ where $x = hc\beta/\lambda$. Find the equation for x which one could use to find the temperature.

(A) $e^x(5 - x) = 5$

(B) $e^x(4 - x) = 4$

(C) $e^x(3 - x) = 3$

(D) $e^x(2 - x) = 2$

(E) $e^x(1 - x) = 1$

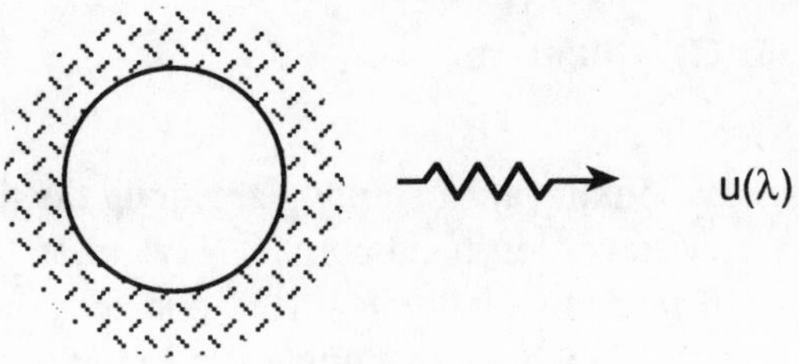

83. A ball bounces elastically in the vertical y direction. Calculate the energy levels using Bohr-Summerfeld quantization.

(A) $ng\hbar m$

(B) $[9n^2\pi^2g^2\hbar^2m]^{2/3}$

(C) $[n^2\pi^2g^2\hbar^2m/8]^{1/3}$

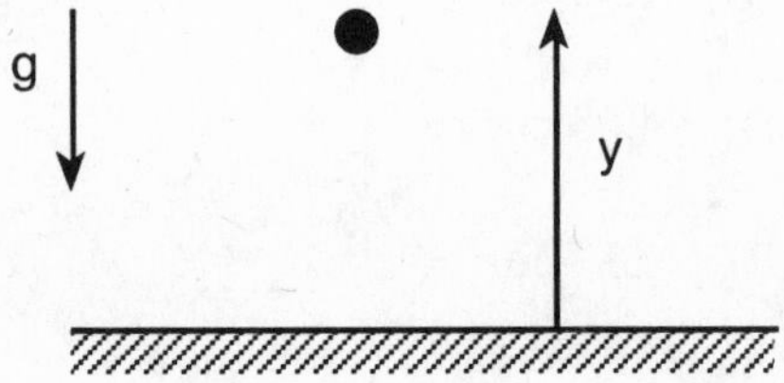

(D) $[9n^2\pi^2 g^2\hbar^2 m/8]^{1/3}$

(E) $[9n^2\pi^2 g^2\hbar^2 m/8]^{2/3}$

84. A metal ball is dropped into a deep well with water on the very bottom. The time taken between dropping the ball from rest to hearing it splash the water is 6.83 s. Calculate the depth of the well assuming $v_s = 330$ m/s.

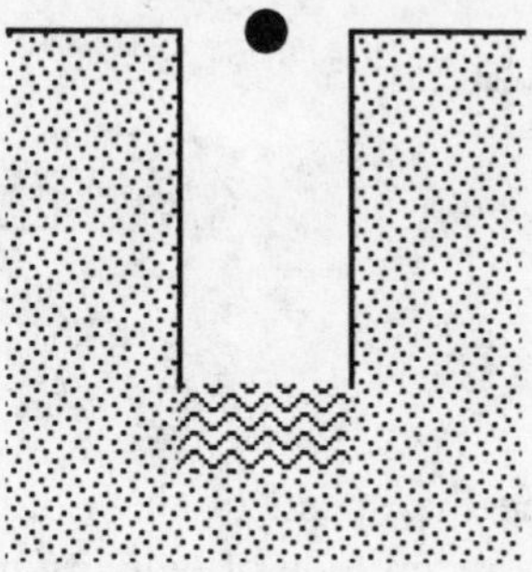

(A) 229 m

(B) 219 m

(C) 201 m

(D) 191 m

(E) 181 m

85. Consider a quantum mechanical problem where the eigenfunction is the spherical harmonic

Y_{lm_l} with $l = 1$ and $m_l = 0$, i.e., $Y_{10}(\theta, \phi) = N \cos\theta$.

Find the normalization constant N.

(A) $\sqrt{3/6\pi}$

(B) $\sqrt{3/\pi}$

(C) $\sqrt{3/8\pi}$

(D) $\sqrt{3/2\pi}$

(E) $\sqrt{3/4\pi}$

86. What is the degeneracy of the energy for a Hydrogen like atom with principal quantum number n and orbital quantum number l?

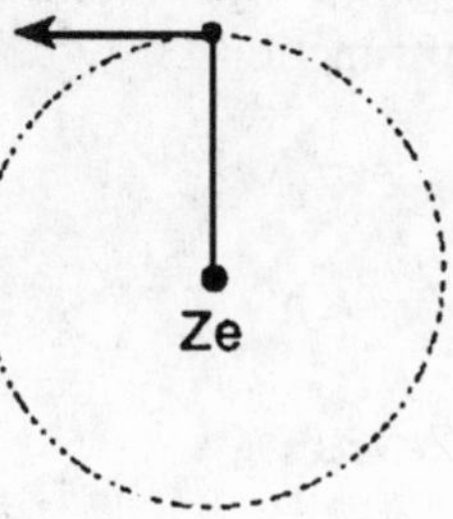

(A) n

(B) n^2

(C) n^3

(D) $l(l + 1)$

(E) $2l + 1$

87. Study the ballistic pendulum problem where a bullet of mass m = 5 g hits and becomes embedded in a block of mass 1000 g. Given that the initial velocity of the bullet is 20,000 cm/s, determine the height the ballistic pendulum rises.

(A) 5.05 cm

(B) 10.1 cm

(C) 15.15 cm

(D) 20.2 cm

(E) 25.25 cm

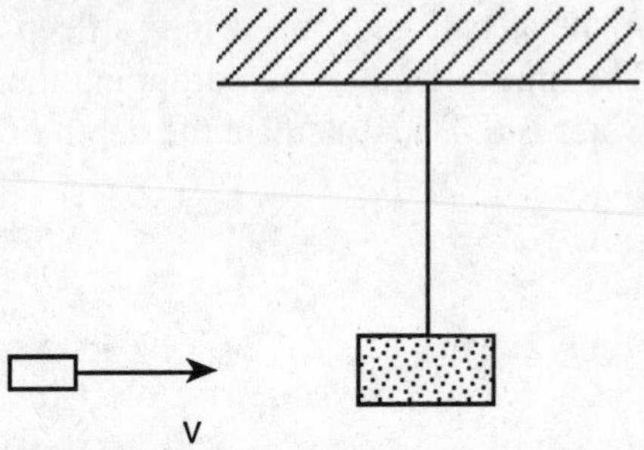

88. Determine the speed of the Lorentz transformation in the x-direction for which the magnitude of velocity in frame K of a particle is

$$\mathbf{u} = (c/\sqrt{2}, c/\sqrt{2})$$

and the magnitude of velocity in frame K′ is seen as

$$\mathbf{u}' = (-c/\sqrt{2}, c/\sqrt{2})$$

(A) 1.4×10^8 m/s

(B) 2.8×10^8 m/s

(C) 7.0×10^7 m/s

(D) 3.5×10^7 m/s

(E) 1.2×10^7 m/s

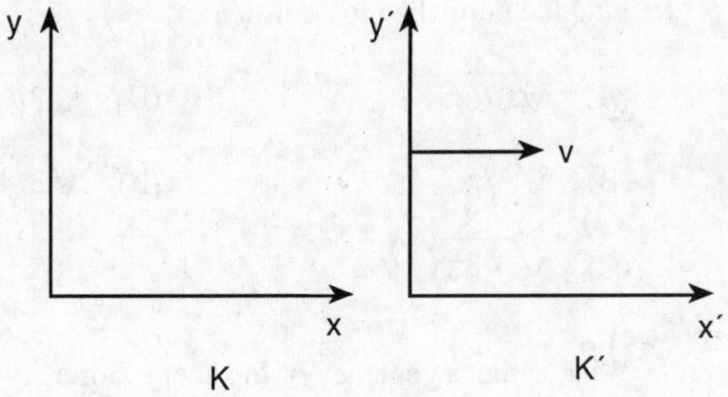

89. In the quantum theory approach to the hydrogen-like atom for l = 0 using the Schrödinger equation, find the energy eigenvalue for the ground state radial wavefunction

$$R_{10}(r) = Ne^{-Zr/a_0}.$$

(A) $-k^2 Z \mu e^4 / 2\hbar^2$

(B) $-k^2 Z e^4 / 2\mu\hbar^2$

(C) $-k^2 Z^2 \mu e^4 / 2\hbar^2$

(D) $k^2 Z^2 \mu e^4 / 2\hbar^2$

(E) $k^2 Z e^4 / 2\mu\eta\hbar$

90. Two events occur in the space-time continuum. Event A has coordinates (1m, 2m, 3m, 0s) and event B occurs at (2m, 3m, 4m, $1/c$) where the 4th coordinate gives the time in seconds. Calculate the proper distance between these two events.

(A) 1 m

(B) 2 m

(C) $\sqrt{3}$ m

(D) $\sqrt{2}$ m

(E) $\sqrt{5}$ m

91. Use the Fermi gas model for electrons in a metal to determine the Fermi momentum $k_F = p_F/\hbar$ for electrons in a metal of density .971 g/cm³ and molar mass 22.99 g/mol.

(A) 0.11 Å^{-1}

(B) 0.22 Å^{-1}

(C) 0.45 Å^{-1}

(D) 0.91 Å^{-1}

(E) 1.82 Å^{-1}

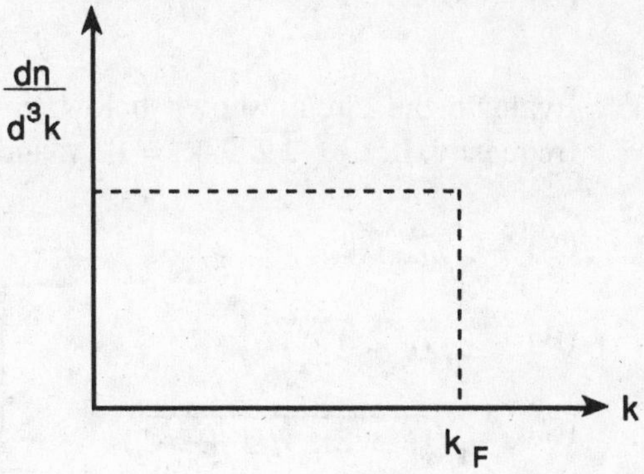

92. The complete wavefunction for a particular state of a hydrogen-like atom is

$$\psi(r,\theta,\phi) = Nr^2 e^{-Zr/3a_0} \sin^2\theta\, e^{2i\phi}.$$

Determine the eigenvalue of the angular momentum operator L_z.

(A) $\hbar$

(B) $2\hbar$

(C) $3\hbar$

(B) $4\hbar$

(E) $\hbar$

93. Study the coupled harmonic oscillator problem pictured below. Find the anti-symmetric mode frequency.

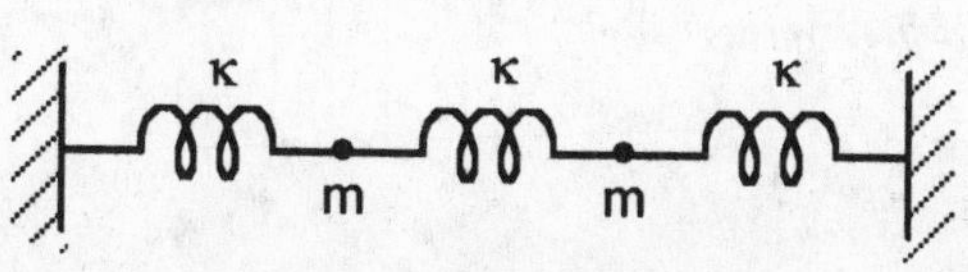

(A) $\sqrt{k/m}$

(B) $\sqrt{\kappa/m}$

(C) $\sqrt{(k+2\kappa)/m}$

(D) $\sqrt{(\kappa+2k)/m}$

(E) $\sqrt{(k+\kappa)/m}$

94. Determine the electric current due to two electrons in a $1s^2$ quantum state orbiting a central nucleus at distance 1.0 Å in a circular orbit.

(A) .0004 A

(B) .0008 A

(C) .0012 A

(D) .0016 A

(E) .0020 A

95. Evaluate the circuit shown below to determine the anti-symmetric mode frequency. Let $k = 1/LC$, $\kappa_1 = 1/L\gamma$, and $\kappa_2 = \beta/L$.

(A) $\sqrt{k}$

(B) $\sqrt{(k+2\kappa_1)}$

(C) $\sqrt{(k+2\kappa_1)/(1+2\kappa_2)}$

(D) $\sqrt{(1+2\kappa_2)}$

(E) $\sqrt{(k+\kappa_1)/(1+\kappa_2)}$

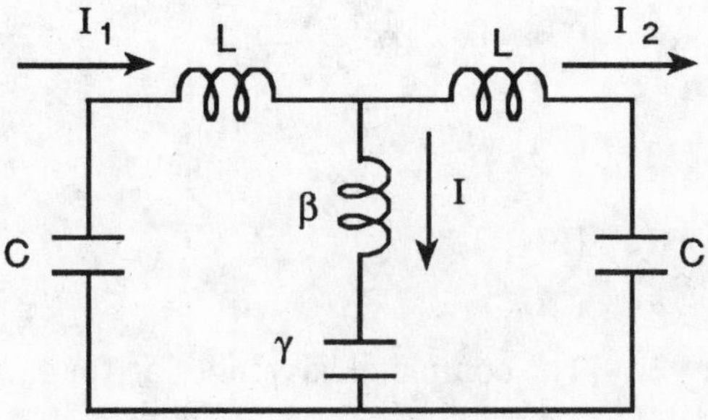

96. F. London and H. London in 1935 explained a superconductor as a single wave function describing a coherent collective state. Use the London equation $\mathbf{j} = -\mathbf{A}/\mu_o\lambda_L^2$ to determine the equation for the B field as a function of distance into the superconductor. Hence explain the Meissner effect.

(A) $B = 0$ inside

(B) $B = B_0 e^{-x/\lambda_L}$

(C) $B = B_o(1 - x/\lambda_L)$

(D) $B = B_o$ inside

(E) $B = B_o\delta(x)$

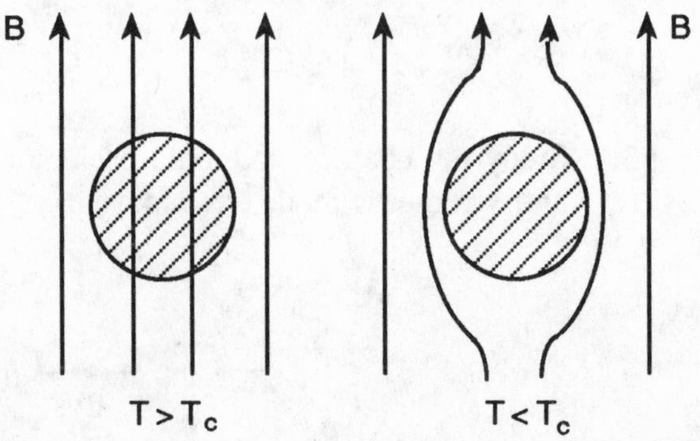

97. Consider a reversible isothermal expansion of a photon gas. Determine the entropy S for this gas at temperature T and volume V.

(A) $\sigma T^4 V$

(B) $\sigma T^3 V$

(C) $1/3\ \sigma T^3 V$

(D) $2/3\ \sigma T^3 V$

(E) $4/3\ \sigma T^3 V$

98. The problem of the rigid diatomic rotor is of fundamental importance in physics and physical chemistry. What is the differential equation for the θ part of the wave function $\psi(\theta,\phi) = P(\theta)\, Q(\phi)$?

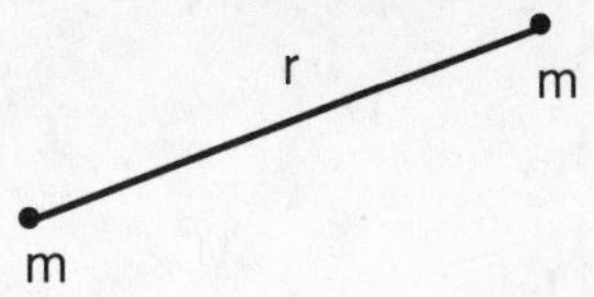

(A) $\frac{1}{\sin\theta}\frac{d}{d\theta}(\sin\theta\ \frac{dP}{d\theta}) = 0$

(B) $\frac{1}{Q}\frac{d^2Q}{d\phi^2} = -m_l^2$

(C) $\frac{1}{\sin\theta}\frac{d}{d\theta}(\sin\theta\ \frac{dP}{d\theta}) + [l(l+1) - \frac{m_l^2}{\sin^2\theta}]\ P = 0$

(D) $\frac{d}{d\theta}(\sin\theta\ \frac{dP}{d\theta}) + [l(l+1) - \frac{m_l^2}{\sin^2\theta}]\ P = 0$

(E) $[l(l+1) - \frac{m_l^2}{\sin^2\theta}]\ P = 0$

99. Which of the following is NOT a true statement about the general theory of relativity?

(A) True physical laws hold only in an inertial coordinate system.

(B) The gravitational equations can be applied to any coordinate system.

(C) The gravitational equations are structure laws describing the changes of the gravitational field.

(D) The universe is not Euclidean.

(E) The ellipse of the planet Mercury rotates with respect to the sun.

100. Choose the correct dynamics equation for the relativistic rocket (of initial mass m_1) problem. A mass element m is ejected with speed υ to the left and the remaining mass of the rocket m_2 moves with velocity u to the right.

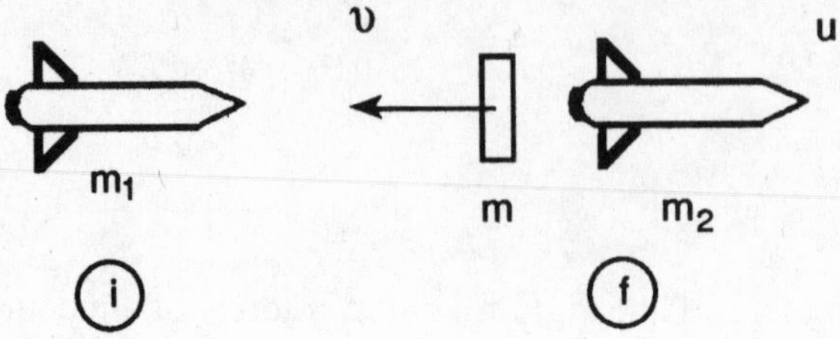

(A) $m_1c^2 = m\,\gamma_\upsilon\, c^2 + m_2\,\gamma_u\, c^2$

(B) $m_1c^2 = m\,\gamma_\upsilon\, c^2$

(C) $m_1\,\gamma_\upsilon\, \upsilon = m_2\,\gamma_u\, u$

(D) $m_1c^2 = m_2\,\gamma_u\, c^2$

(E) $m\,\gamma_\upsilon\, \upsilon = m_2\,\gamma_u\, u$

TEST 4

ANSWER KEY

1.	(A)	26.	(E)	51.	(E)	76.	(C)
2.	(B)	27.	(E)	52.	(B)	77.	(B)
3.	(A)	28.	(C)	53.	(D)	78.	(C)
4.	(E)	29.	(D)	54.	(E)	79.	(C)
5.	(D)	30.	(A)	55.	(D)	80.	(A)
6.	(A)	31.	(C)	56.	(B)	81.	(A)
7.	(B)	32.	(D)	57.	(E)	82.	(A)
8.	(A)	33.	(A)	58.	(A)	83.	(D)
9.	(B)	34.	(B)	59.	(A)	84.	(D)
10.	(A)	35.	(A)	60.	(D)	85.	(E)
11.	(C)	36.	(A)	61.	(C)	86.	(B)
12.	(C)	37.	(A)	62.	(D)	87.	(A)
13.	(E)	38.	(B)	63.	(E)	88.	(B)
14.	(B)	39.	(B)	64.	(D)	89.	(C)
15.	(C)	40.	(C)	65.	(E)	90.	(D)
16.	(C)	41.	(D)	66.	(A)	91.	(D)
17.	(D)	42.	(B)	67.	(E)	92.	(B)
18.	(E)	43.	(E)	68.	(A)	93.	(C)
19.	(D)	44.	(B)	69.	(D)	94.	(B)
20.	(D)	45.	(B)	70.	(B)	95.	(C)
21.	(E)	46.	(E)	71.	(C)	96.	(B)
22.	(E)	47.	(D)	72.	(C)	97.	(E)
23.	(C)	48.	(C)	73.	(E)	98.	(C)
24.	(E)	49.	(D)	74.	(D)	99.	(A)
25.	(C)	50.	(C)	75.	(E)	100.	(E)

DETAILED EXPLANATIONS OF ANSWERS TEST 4

1. **(A)**

The total relativistic energy is found from

$$E^2 = p^2c^2 + m^2c^4.$$

Hence, $$E = \sqrt{p^2c^2 + m^2c^4}.$$

Using QM, $$\hbar\omega = \sqrt{(\hbar kc)^2 + m^2c^4}$$

$$\omega = \sqrt{(kc)^2 + (mc^2/\hbar)^2}$$

By definition $$V_g = \frac{\partial\omega}{\partial k} = \frac{1}{2}\left((kc)^2 + (mc^2/\hbar)^2\right)^{-1/2} c^2 2k$$

$$= \frac{\hbar kc^2}{\sqrt{p^2c^2 + m^2c^4}}$$

$$= \frac{pc^2}{E} = \frac{mv\gamma c^2}{m\gamma c^2} = v$$

2. **(B)**

Several of the Hydrogen-like atom quantum mechanical wave functions are

$$\psi_{100} = \frac{2}{\sqrt{4\pi}}\left(\frac{Z}{a_0}\right)^{3/2} e^{-Zr/a_0}$$

$$\psi_{200} = \frac{2}{\sqrt{4\pi}}\left(\frac{Z}{2a_0}\right)^{3/2}\left(1 - \frac{Zr}{2a_0}\right) e^{-Zr/2a_0}$$

$$\psi_{210} = \sqrt{\frac{3}{4\pi}} \cos\theta \left(\frac{Z}{2a_0}\right)^{3/2} \frac{Zr}{\sqrt{3}a_0} e^{-Zr/2a_0}$$

$$\psi_{300} = \frac{2}{\sqrt{4\pi}}\left(\frac{Z}{3a_0}\right)^{3/2}\left(1 - \frac{2Zr}{3a_0} + \frac{2(Zr)^2}{27a_0^2}\right) e^{-Zr/3a_0}$$

$$\psi_{321} = -\sqrt{\frac{15}{8\pi}} \sin\theta\cos\theta\, e^{i\phi} \frac{2\sqrt{2}}{27\sqrt{5}}\left(\frac{Z}{3a_0}\right)^{3/2}\left(\frac{Zr}{a_0}\right)^2 e^{-Zr/3a_0}$$

In the 3-D picture, we have plotted

$$P(x, z) = \psi\psi^* \ (y = 0)$$

where $\cos\theta = z/r$ and $\sin\theta = x/r$. Only ψ_{321} has the rich structure pictured.

3. **(A)**

In quantum mechanics $\psi(x, t)$ represents the physical state of the particle/system. Usually ψ, ψ', and ψ'' are finite, single valued, and continuous. For every observable x, p, E, etc. there is an operator

$$\hat{x}, \hat{p} = \frac{\hbar}{i}\frac{\partial}{\partial x}, \quad \hat{E} = i\hbar\frac{\partial}{\partial t}, \text{ etc.}$$

The expectation value of the observable is a real number:

$$\langle F\rangle = \int \phi^* \hat{F}\phi \, dx.$$

$\psi(x, t) = \phi(x)\, e^{-iEt/\hbar}$ is the usual separation of variables technique. $\phi(x)$ is normalized such that $\int \phi^*\phi \, dx = 1$. Also, the operator follows an eigenvalue equation $\hat{F}\,\psi = F\psi$.

4. **(E)**

The quantum mechanical harmonic oscillator has energy eigenvalues.

$$E_n = \hbar\omega_0\left(n + \frac{1}{2}\right) \text{ where } \omega_0 = \sqrt{\frac{k}{m}}$$

and wave functions

$$\phi(x) = \eta(x)e^{-\alpha^2 x^2/2} \text{ where } \alpha = (mk/\hbar^2)^{1/4}$$

is a constant and the $\eta(x)$ are Hermite polynomials. For $n = 1$,

$$E_1 = \frac{3}{2}\hbar\omega_0 \text{ and } \phi_1 = Nxe^{-\alpha^2 x^2/2}$$

By the normalization condition

$$N^2\int_{-\infty}^{\infty} x^2 e^{-\alpha^2 x^2} dx = 1$$

Let $t = x^2$. Then

$$1 = N^2 2\int_0^{\infty} t^{3/2-1} e^{-\alpha^2 t}\, dt/2$$

$$= N^2\Gamma\left(\frac{3}{2}\right)/(\alpha^2)^{3/2}$$

$$1 = N^2\frac{1}{2}!/\alpha^3$$

$$N^2 = \alpha^3/\left(\sqrt{\pi}/2\right)$$

$$= 2\alpha^3/\sqrt{\pi}$$

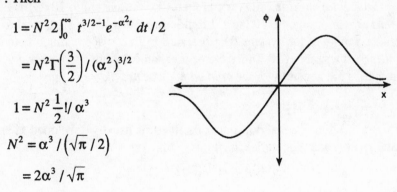

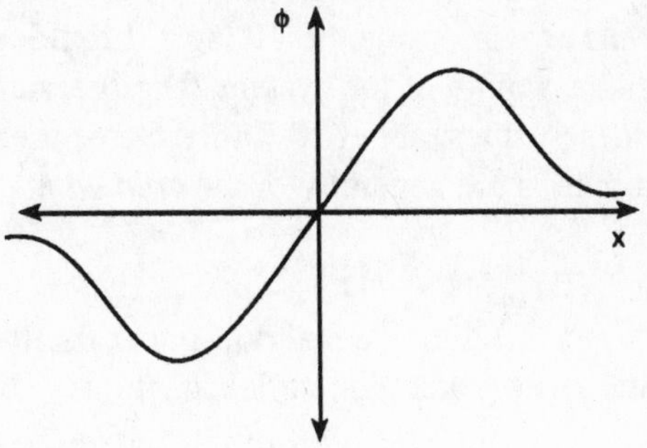

Finally $N = \sqrt{2\alpha^3/\sqrt{\pi}}$.

5. **(D)**

There are numerous ways to measure temperature in the laboratory. The standard *thermometer* uses the expansion properties of a liquid $\Delta l \propto \Delta T$. A *thermocouple* uses an electromotive force measured with a potentiometer. The *resistance thermometer* uses the resistance of a fine wire measured with a Wheatstone bridge. In a *constant volume gas thermometer*, the gas pressure is the thermometric property. The *optical pyrometer* matches the brightness of a filament to that of the background; it is useful for high temperatures not easily accessed by thermocouples. The *Saha equation* involves the degree of ionization of a substance and is useful for temperatures $T = 2{,}000 - 3{,}000$ K.

6. **(A)**

The given dispersion relationship for deep water ocean waves is

$$\omega^2 = gk + ak^3.$$

Solving for ω, we get

$$\omega = \sqrt{gk + ak^3}$$

The phase velocity is

$$v_p = \frac{\omega}{k}$$

$$= \sqrt{\frac{g}{k} + ak}$$

$$= \sqrt{\frac{g\lambda}{2\pi} + \frac{2\pi a}{\lambda}},$$

using the definition of wave number $k = 2\pi/\lambda$.

7. **(B)**

The use of vacuum techniques is essential in many laboratory experiments. *Mechanical pumps* pump down to about 10^{-3} torr (about the same as 10^{-3} mm Hg). *Molecular diffusion pumps* can then take the system to 10^{-7} torr. Finally, *ion pumps* are used to get to 10^{-9} torr. Liquid nitrogen cold traps are used to condense volatile vapors in the system. The pressure in free space is much better than any of these values, about 10^{-16} torr. Some mechanical pumps are *two stage* in design. Ion pumps are generally of the *cold cathode* or *hot filament* type.

8. **(A)**

A one dimensional non-linear oscillator is usually developed as an approximation to a general potential function

$$U(x) = U(0) + U'(0)x\ {}^1/_2\ U''(0)x^2 + \ldots$$

using a Taylor series. In the given problem

$$U(x) = {}^1/_2\ kx^2 + {}^1/_4\ bx^4.$$

Constant terms like $U(0)$ do not affect the results. For stable equilibrium in a symmetric potential, the odd terms are zero. The force is

$$\mathbf{F} = -\nabla U$$

or

$$F = \frac{-\partial U}{\partial x} \quad \text{in } 1-\text{D}$$

$$= -kx - bx^3$$

9. **(B)**

This is basically the soap film problem. A film has a certain surface energy per unit area γ. The total energy is then just γ * area. Hence minimizing the energy is tantamount to minimizing the action integral

$$A = \int 2\pi y \, ds$$

$$= \int 2\pi y \sqrt{1 + y'^2} \, dx.$$

Since

$$f = y\sqrt{1+y'^2} = f(y, y'),$$

the 2nd form of Euler's equation is needed.

$$\frac{\partial f}{\partial x} - \frac{d}{dx}\left(f - y' \frac{\partial f}{\partial y'}\right) = 0 \Rightarrow f - y' \frac{\partial f}{\partial y'} = c.$$

After a little work, we get

$$y = c \cosh\left(\frac{x-d}{c}\right) = \text{catenoid.}$$

10. **(A)**

This is the standard pendulum problem, but in an effective local gravitational field

$$g_e = g + \frac{1}{2} g$$

$$= \frac{3}{2} g.$$

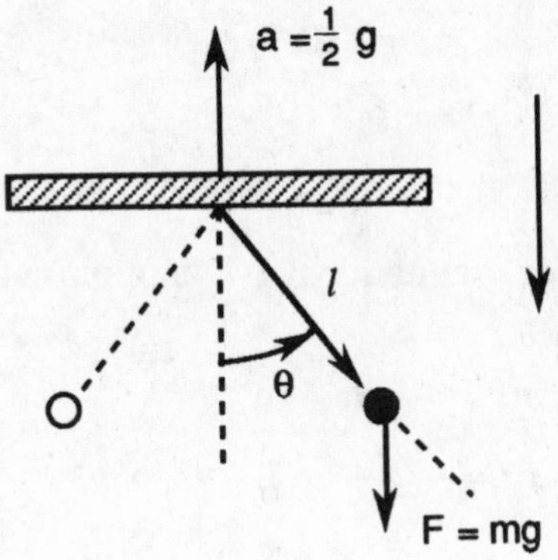

By Newton's 2nd law for rotational motion

$$\Sigma\tau = I\alpha$$

$$-mg_e l \sin\theta = I\theta''$$

$$= ml^2\theta''$$

thus

$$\theta'' + \frac{g_e}{l}\sin\theta = 0$$

is the equation of motion. For $\theta \ll 1$, a Taylor expansion gives $\sin\theta \approx \theta$.

Thus $\theta'' + \omega_0^2 \theta = 0$

where $\omega_0 = \sqrt{\frac{g_l}{l}} = \sqrt{\frac{3g}{2l}}$

is the angular frequency. Also

$$\upsilon_0 = \frac{\omega_0}{2\pi} = \frac{1}{2\pi}\sqrt{\frac{3g}{2l}}.$$

is the linear frequency. In other words, the problem may be solved by substituting g_e for g.

11. **(C)**

The room volume is

$$V = lwh = (2.5\text{ m})(5\text{ m})(5\text{ m})$$
$$= 62.5\text{ m}^3$$

The smaller volume is

$$V_0 = (.025\text{ m})(.05\text{ m})(.05\text{ m})$$
$$= 6.25 \times 10^{-5}\text{ m}^3.$$

The probability parameter is

$$p = \frac{V_0}{V} = 10^{-6}.$$

The situation under consideration is binomial in nature

$$p(n) = \binom{N}{n} p^n (1-p)^{N-n}.$$

The desired probability is

$$p(N) = \frac{N!}{N!\,0!} p^N (1-p)^0$$

$$= (10^{-6})^{10^{27}}$$

or $\log_{10} p(N) = -6 \times 10^{27}$.

12. **(C)**

For gravitational 1-D motion with a resistive force the equation of motion is

$$mx'' = -mg - bx'$$

or $x'' = -(g + \gamma x'), \quad \gamma \equiv b/m.$

Integrate

$$\int_{v_0}^{v} \frac{dv}{g + \gamma v} = -\int_0^t dt$$

to get

$$\frac{1}{\gamma}\ln\frac{g+\gamma v}{g+\gamma v_0}=-t.$$

Exponentiate to get

$$g+\gamma v=(g+\gamma v_0)e^{-\gamma t}$$

or $$v=\left(\frac{g}{\gamma}+v_0\right)e^{-\gamma t}-\frac{g}{\gamma}.$$

The maximum height occurs when $v = 0$ so that

$$e^{\gamma t}=\left(\frac{g}{\gamma}+v_0\right)/\left(\frac{g}{\gamma}\right)$$

or $$t=\frac{1}{\gamma}\ln\left(1+\frac{v_0\gamma}{g}\right).$$

Note for $\gamma << 1$, we get using a Taylor expansion

$$t=\frac{1}{\gamma}\frac{v_0\gamma}{g}=\frac{v_0}{g}$$

the vacuum value.

13. **(E)**

Gauss' law for gravitation is

$$\nabla\cdot\mathbf{g}=-4\pi G\rho$$

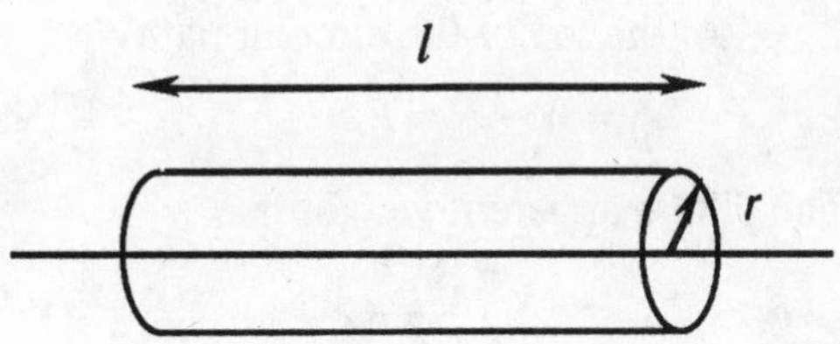

where G = the universal constant of gravitation. Applying the divergence theorem, we get

$$\oint\gamma\cdot d\alpha=-4\pi Gm_{in}.$$

For an infinite line mass, the mass density is $\lambda = m/l$. Use a Gaussian cylinder for integration to get

$$\oint\mathbf{g}\cdot d\mathbf{a}=-4\pi G\lambda l$$

$$-g2\pi rl=-4\pi G\lambda l$$

or $$\mathbf{g}=-(2\lambda G/r)\mathbf{r}.$$

14. **(B)**

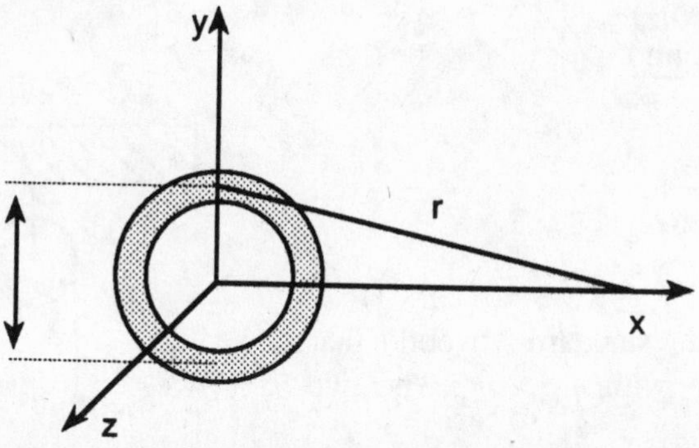

The basic equation to find the gravitational potential is

$$\phi = -G\int \frac{dm}{r}$$

$$= -G\int_a^b \frac{2\pi\sigma s ds}{r}$$

using the definition of mass density σ so that

$$dm = 2\pi\sigma s\, ds$$

$$= -2\pi\sigma G\int_a^b \frac{s\, ds}{\sqrt{s^2+x^2}}$$

using the theorem of Pythagoras. Integrating, we obtain

$$\phi = -2\pi\sigma G\sqrt{s^2+x^2}\Big|_a^b$$

$$= -2\pi\sigma G\left[\sqrt{b^2+x^2}-\sqrt{a^2+x^2}\right].$$

Note that one could also find **g** since

$$\mathbf{g} = -\nabla\phi = -\frac{d\phi}{dx}\mathbf{x}.$$

15. **(C)**

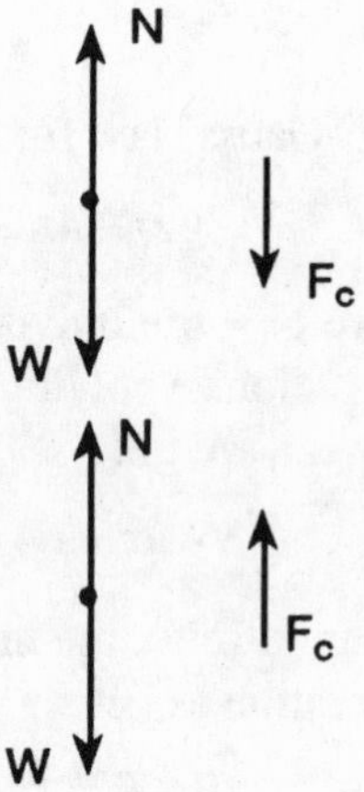

At the top of the circular path

$$\Sigma F = W - N = F_c$$

The pilot's apparent weight is

$$N_T = mg - \frac{mv^2}{r}$$

At the bottom of the loop

$$\Sigma F = N - W = F_c$$

and the pilot's apparent weight is

$$N_B = mg + \frac{mv^2}{r}$$

We want

$$N_B = 2N_T \Rightarrow mg + \frac{mv^2}{r} = 2mg - 2\frac{mv^2}{r}$$

or $$mg = 3\frac{mv^2}{r}$$

$$r = 3\frac{v^2}{g}$$

16. **(C)**

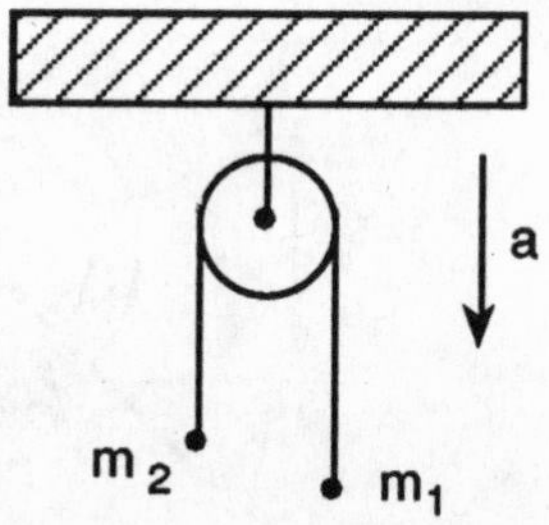

This is the standard Atwood's machine problem with $m_1 > m_2$. The two free body diagrams shown here.

By Newton's Second law

$$m_1g - T = m_1a \text{ and } T - m_2g = m_2a$$

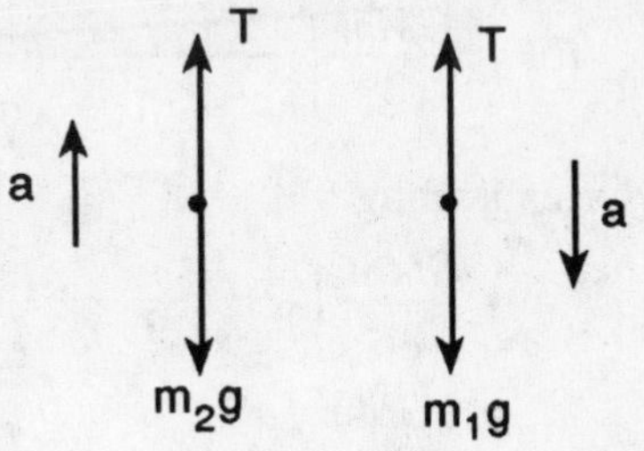

Solving the Second equation

$$T = m_2a + m_2g$$

and substituting in the first:

$$m_1g - m_2a - m_2g = m_1a$$

$$(m_1 - m_2)\,g = (m_1 + m_2)a$$

$$a = (m_1 - m_2)\,g\,/\,(m_1 + m_2)$$

For $m_1 = 4m$ and $m_2 = m$, we obtain.

$$a = \frac{3}{5}\,g.$$

17. **(D)**

This question concerns some of the basic properties of nucleons and nuclei. Protons and neutrons are nucleons. They are also fermions since they have spin $s = {}^1/_2\hbar$. Their orbital angular momentum is integral $l = 0, 1, 2, \ldots$ The total angular momentum of collections of nucleons in nuclei is

$$J = \sum_{i=1}^{A} J_i$$

and is

(i) integral for even A nuclei
(ii) half integral for odd A nuclei
and (iii) zero for even z, even N nuclei.

18. **(E)**

We are given that

$$m = m_m\,,\ r = r_m$$

$$a = r_{EM}\,,\ M = M_E$$

The Roche limit is the Earth-moon centers distance at which the tidal action of the Earth would rip the moon apart. Consider the moon as being composed of two halves. Then the attractive force is

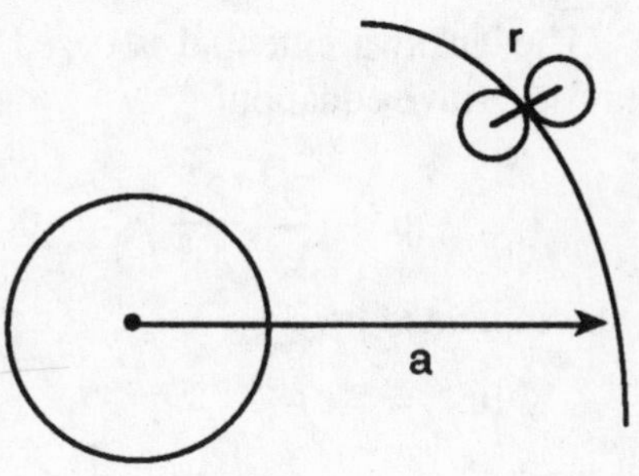

$$F_A = G\,\frac{m}{2}\,\frac{m}{2}\,/r^2$$

$$= Gm^2/4r^2$$

and the disruptive tidal force is

$$F_R = \frac{GMm}{2}\left[\frac{1}{(a-r)^2} - \frac{1}{(a+r)^2}\right]$$

Taylor expanding

$$= \frac{GMm}{2a^2}\left[1 + 2\,\tfrac{r}{a} - \left(1 - 2\,\tfrac{r}{a}\right)\right]$$

$$= 2GMmr/\,a^3$$

Set $F_A = F_R$ to get the Roche limit distance

$$Gm^2 \,/\, 4r^2 = 2\,GMmr/a^3$$

$$a^3 = 8Mr^3/m$$

thus $a = (8M/m)^{1/3}\, r \approx 16{,}000$ km.

19. **(D)**

The electric quadrupole moment of a charge distribution is

$$Q = \frac{2}{5}\,z(a^2 - b^2)$$

where Z = the number of protons in the nucleus,

a = the nuclear semi-major axis,

and b = the ellipse semi-minor axis.

Clearly this factor is a measure of how elliptical the nuclear charge distribution is. The eccentricity is

$$e = \sqrt{a^2 - b^2}\,/\,a \Rightarrow e^2 = (a^2 - b^2)/\,a^2.$$

Thus

$$Q = \frac{2}{5}\,Ze^2a^2.$$

For a circle $e = 0$. The deuteron, for example, has $Q = .003$ barn.

20. **(D)**

The Tukawa potential is based in the meson theory of nuclear forces. The relativistic wave equation

$$\left(\nabla^2 - \mu^2 - \frac{1}{c^2}\frac{\partial^2}{\partial t^2}\right)\Phi = 0$$

may be separated by

$$\Phi(\mathbf{r},t) = \phi(\mathbf{r})e^{-iEt/\hbar}.$$

to get

$$(\nabla^2 - \mu^2)\,\phi = 0$$

for a virtual particle. The radial solutions are $\phi \sim e^{-\mu r} / r$. The Tukawa potential has the same form

$$U(r) = V_R e^{-k_R r} / r - V_A e^{-K_A r} / r$$

The repulsive part is

$$V_R e^{-k_R r} / r$$

with force

$$F = \frac{-\partial}{\partial r} V_R \frac{e^{-k_R r}}{r}$$

$$= \frac{V_R e^{-k_R r}}{r}\left(k_R + \frac{1}{r}\right)$$

21. **(E)**

It is desired to use the nuclear shell model to find the ${}^{67}_{30}$Zn spin. The proton configuration is

$$(1s_{1/2})^2\,(1p_{3/2})^4\,(1p_{1/2})^2\,(1d_{5/2})^6\,(2s_{1/2})^2\,(1d_{3/2})^4\,(1f_{7/2})^8\,(2p_{3/2})^2$$

and the neutron configuration is

$$(1s_{1/2})^2 \ldots (2p_{3/2})^4\,(1f_{5/2})^5.$$

One looks for unpaired nucleons to determine *j*. Only one $1f_{5/2}$ neutron is unpaired. Thus $j = 5/2$.

22. **(E)**

The photon is a stable particle with zero mass, infinite lifetime, and spin $j = 1$. The electron is a stable particle with mass 0.511 MeV/c^2, infinite lifetime, and spin $j = {}^1/_2$. The proton is a stable particle with mass 938.28 MeV/c^2, lifetime greater than 10^{32} years (perhaps infinite), and spin 1/2. The pion π^0 has mass 134.96 MeV/c^2, half-life $t = -8 \times 10^{-17}$ s, spin 0, and commonly decays to $\gamma\gamma$. The kaon K^+ has mass 493.67 MeV/c^2, lifetime 10^{-8} s, spin zero, strangeness S = 1, and commonly decays to $\mu^+\upsilon$.

23. **(C)**

Hadrons are built of quarks whereas leptons are fundamental particles. Quarks have spin $j = 1/2$ and baryon number $B = 1/3$. Antiquarks have the same spin, but opposite baryon number, electric charge, and isospin. u, d, s, c, b and t are the flavors of quarks: up, down, strange, charm, bottom, and top. Some common hadron configurations are

$p = u\,u\,d$	$\overline{p} = \overline{u}\,\overline{u}\,\overline{d}$	
$n = u\,d\,d$	$\overline{n} = \overline{u}\,\overline{d}\,\overline{d}$	$\Delta^{++} = u\,u\,u$
$\pi^+ = u\,\overline{d}$	$\pi^- = \overline{u}\,d$	$J = c\,\overline{c}$
$K^+ = u\,\overline{s}$	$K^- = \overline{u}\,s$	

24. **(E)**
In the lab frame the atomic scattering looks like

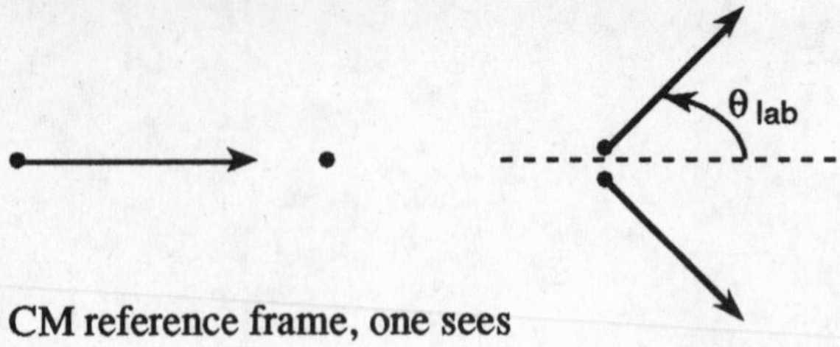

whereas in the CM reference frame, one sees

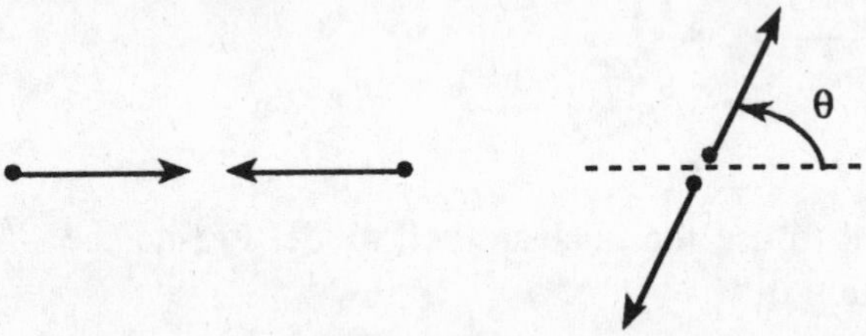

where $\theta = 2\theta_{lab}$ and $\phi = \phi_{lab}$ (not shown). Particle number is conserved so that

$$\sigma(\theta_{lab})\, d\Omega_{lab} = \sigma(\theta) d\Omega$$

$$\sigma(\theta_l) 2\pi \sin\theta_l\, d\theta_l = \frac{\sigma_0}{4\pi} 2\pi \sin\theta\, d\theta$$

$$= \sigma_0 2 \sin\theta_l \cos\theta_l 2d\theta_l / 2$$

$$\sigma(\theta_l) = \sigma_0 \cos\theta_l / \pi$$

The differential cross section is thus not isotropic in the lab!

25. **(C)**
In radioactive decay

$$N = N_0\, e^{-\lambda t}$$

follows from the assumption that the decay is a random process where the probability of one decay is λdt. (This means $dN = -\lambda N\, dt$.) The half-life is related to the decay constant

$$N_0 / 2 = N_0 e^{-\lambda t_{1/2}} \Rightarrow t_{1/2} = \ln(2)/\lambda$$

as is the mean life

$$\tau = \langle t \rangle = \frac{\int_0^\infty t e^{-\lambda t} dt}{\int_0^\infty e^{-\lambda t} dt}$$

$$= \lambda \left[-\frac{t}{\lambda} e^{-\lambda t} - \frac{1}{\lambda^2} e^{-\lambda t} \right]\Bigg|_0^\infty = \frac{1}{\lambda}$$

Hence $\tau = \frac{1}{\lambda} = t_{1/2} / \ln(2) = 5760 \text{ yr} / \ln(2) = 8310 \text{ yrs}$

26. **(E)**

Since the discovery of lasers in 1955, this laboratory technology has found diverse uses in the cutting and welding of metals, the research study of nuclear fusion, dermatology, and even art/music/entertainment. A small CO_2 laser can radiate at 10^5 times the solar intensity. The basic idea is that of optical pumping or to produce a population inversion. Suppose the atoms have 2 quantum states E_1 and E_2. Then $\hbar\omega = E_2 - E_1$. Also, according to Einstein

$$\frac{dN_1}{dt} = N_1 B_{12} u(\omega)$$

$$\frac{dN_2}{dt} = N_2 A_{21} + N_2 B_{21} u(\omega)$$

At equilibrium $N'_1 = N'_2$ so that

$$N_1 B_{12} u = N_2 A_{21} + N_2 B_{21} u$$

thus $$\frac{N_2}{N_1} = B_{12} u(\omega) / (A_{21} + B_{21} u(\omega)).$$

27. **(E)**

In the Raman effect, an incident beam of monochromatic light of frequency ω induces a dipole moment in a molecule. This inelastic interaction results in scattered radiation of frequency

$$\omega'' = \omega \pm \omega'$$

depending on whether $\hbar\omega'$ of energy is given to or taken from the molecule. The electric field of the light interacts with the molecule. The incident light can be of any frequency whereas in fluorescence, the incident photon must be at the proper molecular absorptive frequency.

28. **(C)**

One can use the Biot-Savart law

$$d\mathbf{B} = \frac{\mu_0}{4\pi} I d\mathbf{l} \times \mathbf{s} / s^2$$

$$= \frac{\mu_0 I}{4\pi} \frac{dx \sin\theta}{s^2} \mathbf{z}$$

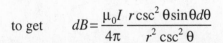

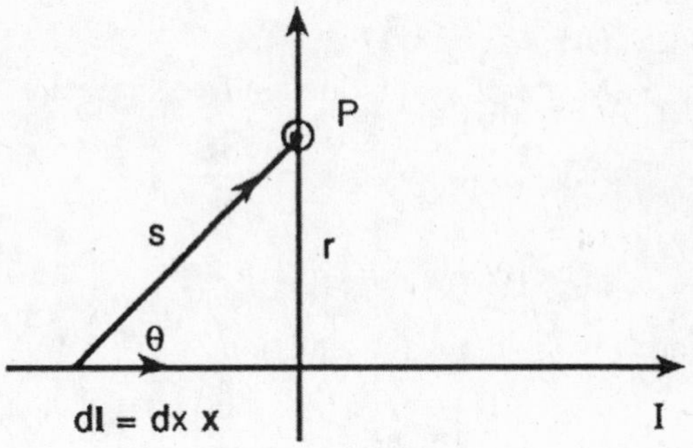

and plug in the trigonometric facts

$$s = r \csc\theta$$

and $$\cot\theta = \frac{-x}{r}$$

so that $$dx = r\csc^2\theta \, d\theta$$

to get $$dB = \frac{\mu_0 I}{4\pi} \frac{r\csc^2\theta \sin\theta d\theta}{r^2 \csc^2\theta}$$

Integrating, one obtains

$$B=\frac{\mu_0 I}{4\pi r}\int_{\theta}^{\theta'} \sin\theta\, d\theta = \frac{\mu_0 I}{4\pi r}\cos\theta\Big|_{\theta'}^{\theta}$$

$$=\frac{\mu_0 I}{4\pi r}(\cos\theta - \cos\theta')$$

29. **(D)**

Consider the electric potential energy between the spherical shell of differential charge

$$dq = 4\pi r^2 dr\rho$$

and the central charge

$$q=\frac{4}{3}\pi r^3\rho.$$

The differential potential energy is

$$dU = kq dq / r$$

$$=16\pi^2 k\rho^2 r^4 dr/3$$

The spherical charge distribution is total electric potential energy is then

$$U=\frac{16\pi^2 k\rho^2}{3}\int_0^R r^4\, dr$$

$$=\frac{16}{15}\pi^2 k\rho^2 R^5$$

Since

$$Q=\int \rho d^3 r = \frac{4}{3}\pi R^3\rho,$$

we rearrange to get

$$U=\frac{3}{5}kQ^2/R.$$

30. **(A)**

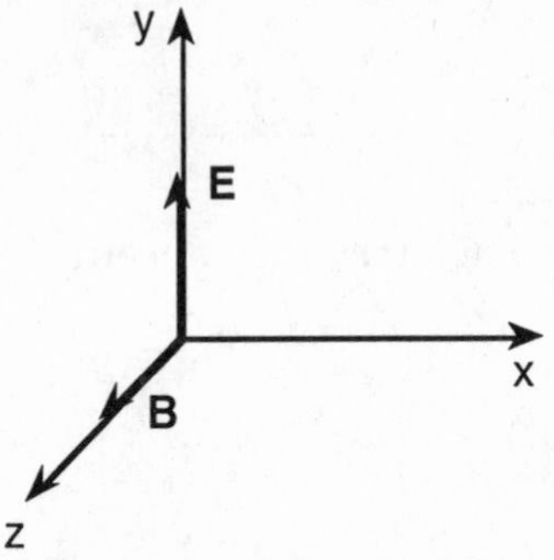

Maxwell's equations in free space are

$$\nabla\cdot\mathbf{E}=0 \quad \nabla\times\mathbf{E}=-\frac{\partial\mathbf{B}}{\partial t}$$

$$\nabla\cdot\mathbf{B}=0 \quad \nabla\times\mathbf{B}=\mu_0\varepsilon_0\frac{\partial\mathbf{E}}{\partial t}$$

and they yield a wave equation

$$\nabla^2\begin{pmatrix}\mathbf{E}\\ \mathbf{B}\end{pmatrix}=\mu_0\varepsilon_0\frac{\partial^2}{\partial t^2}\begin{pmatrix}\mathbf{E}\\ \mathbf{B}\end{pmatrix}$$

where

$$c^2=\frac{1}{\mu_0\varepsilon_0}$$

A plane wave solution is

$$\mathbf{E} = \mathbf{y}\, E_{0y} \cos (\omega t - kx + \alpha) + \mathbf{z}\, E_{0z} \cos (\omega t - kx + \beta)$$

and

$$\mathbf{B} = -\mathbf{y}\frac{E_{0z}}{c}\cos(\omega t - kx + \beta) + \mathbf{z}\frac{E_{0y}}{c}\cos(\omega t - kx + \alpha)$$

since $c = \omega/k$. Now if $\delta \equiv \beta - \alpha$, then

$$\left(\frac{E_y}{E_{0y}}\right)^2 + \left(\frac{E_z}{E_{0z}}\right)^2 = \cos^2\phi + \cos^2(\delta + \phi)$$

where $\phi \equiv \omega t - kx + \alpha$. Clearly for $\delta = \pm\pi/2$, we get elliptic polarization

$$\left(\frac{E_y}{E_{0y}}\right)^2 + \left(\frac{E_z}{E_{0z}}\right)^2 = 1$$

31. **(C)**

Ampere's law in medium is

$$\nabla \times \mathbf{H} = \mathbf{j}.$$

By Stokes Theorem

$$\oint \mathrm{H} \cdot d\mathbf{r} = \int \nabla \times \mathrm{H} \cdot d\mathbf{a}$$

Thus

$$\oint \mathbf{H} \cdot d\mathbf{r} = \int \mathbf{j} \cdot d\mathbf{a} = I_{\text{in}}$$

Integrate around a circular loop to get

$$2\pi r H = NI$$

Solve for

$$H = NI / [2\pi(a+b)/2] \text{ since } r = \frac{a+b}{2}$$

$$= NI / \pi(a+b)$$

Thus $B = \mu H = N\mu I / \pi(a+b)$

since the magnetic field B is related to the field H. Note that in the vacuum case

$$B_0 = N\mu_0 I / \pi(a+b).$$

32. **(D)**

The Fraunhofer diffraction pattern results from monochromatic light waves incident on a single slit. The condition for destructive interference is

$$d \sin\theta = n\lambda$$

Hence

$$\sin\theta = \frac{\lambda}{d} = \frac{y}{\sqrt{y^2 + l^2}} \approx \frac{y}{l}$$

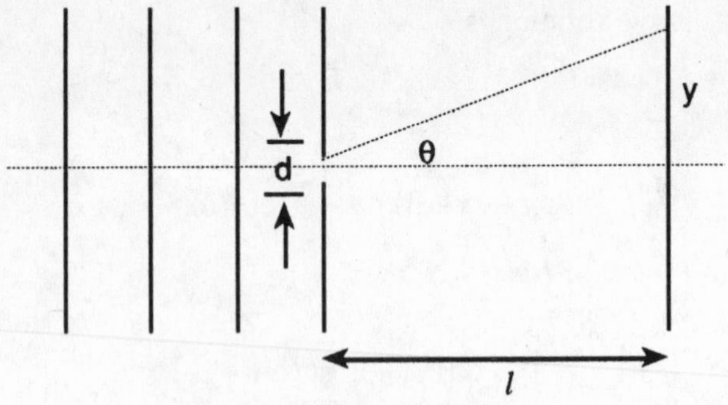

and

$$y = \frac{\lambda l}{d}$$

gives the first minimum. The intensity pattern is

$$I = I_0 \sin^2\left(\frac{\pi d}{\lambda l} y\right) / \left(\frac{\pi d}{\lambda l} y\right)^2$$

$$= I_0 \sin^2\left(\frac{\pi}{2}\right) / \left(\frac{\pi}{2}\right)^2 \text{ at } y = \frac{\lambda l}{2d}$$

Finally $\frac{I}{I_0} = \frac{4}{\pi^2}$.

33. **(A)**

The electric field is that of the given charge and an image charge of equal and opposite magnitude. Hence

$$E_z = kq\left[\frac{z - z'}{\left(s^2 + (z - z')^2\right)^{3/2}} - \frac{z + z'}{\left(s^2 + (z + z')^2\right)^{3/2}}\right]$$

The charge density is

$$\sigma = \varepsilon_0 E_z \Big|_{z=0} = -\frac{qh/2\pi}{(s^2 + h^2)^{3/2}}$$

Note that

$$\int_0^\infty \sigma s\, ds \int_0^{2\pi} d\phi = -qh\int_0^\infty s\, ds/(s^2 + h^2)^{3/2}$$

$$= qh(s^2 + h^2)^{-1/2}\Big|_0^\infty$$

$$= -q$$

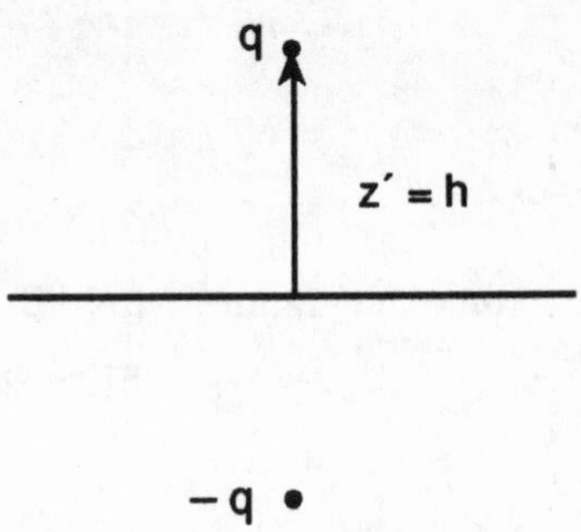

The infinite sheet has charge $-q$ on top, as it must.

34. **(B)**

The given voltage boundary condition is

$$V(s) = \begin{cases} V_0 & s < r \\ 0 & s > r \end{cases}$$

for $z = 0$ with along the z–axis.

$$f(z)=\frac{V_0 z}{2p}\int \frac{s\,ds\,df}{(s^2+z^2)^{3/2}}$$

$$=V_0 z(s^2+z^2)^{-1/2}\Big|_{s=r}^{s=0}$$

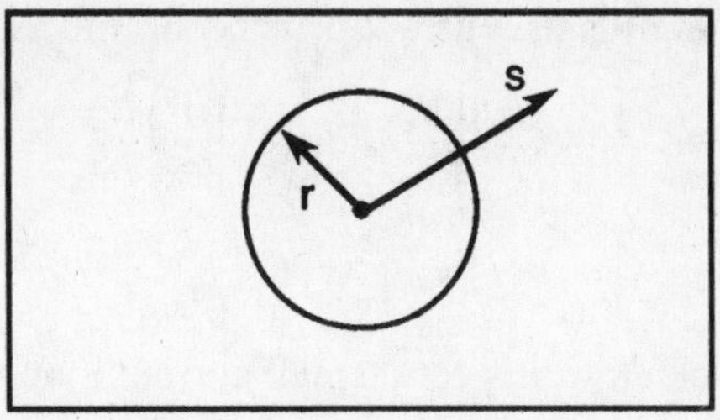

taking $\int_0^{2\pi} d\phi = 2\pi$

$$\phi(z)=V_0 z\left(\frac{1}{z}-\frac{1}{\sqrt{r^2+z^2}}\right)$$

$$=V_0\left(1-\frac{z}{\sqrt{r^2+z^2}}\right)$$

Now we calculate the electric field.

$$E_z=-\frac{\partial f}{\partial z}=\frac{\partial}{\partial z}\left(\frac{V_0 z}{\sqrt{r^2+z^2}}\right)$$

by the definition of the electric field $\mathbf{E} = -\nabla\phi$. Differentiate to get

$$E_z=V_0\frac{(1)\sqrt{r^2+z^2}-z(z(r^2+z^2)^{-1/2})}{r^2+z^2}$$

$$=V_0\frac{r^2}{(r^2+z^2)^{3/2}}$$

a dipole field.

35. **(A)**

Let j be the energy flux or energy per unit area per unit time. The energy flow is in the x-direction and the temperature decreases in that direction. This is just the 0th law of thermodynamics: heat flows from high to low temperature. Fourier's law then says

$$j=-\sigma\frac{\partial T}{\partial x}$$

where σ is the material's thermal conductivity. Consideration of energy gain gives

$$\rho c_V\frac{\partial T}{\partial t}=-\frac{\partial j}{\partial x},$$

where c_v is the specific heat. Using Fourier's law, we obtain

$$\frac{\partial T}{\partial t}=\frac{\sigma}{\rho c_V}\frac{\partial^2 T}{\partial x^2}.$$

36. **(A)**

The magnetic vector potential is

$$\mathbf{A} = \frac{\mu_0}{4\pi}\int \mathbf{j}d^3r/r = \frac{\mu_0}{4\pi}\int \frac{Idl}{r}$$

where **j** is the current density. By the Stokes theorem

$$\mathbf{A} = \frac{\mu_0 I}{4\pi}\int d\mathbf{a}\times\nabla\left(\frac{1}{r}\right)$$

$$= \frac{\mu_0 I}{4\pi}\int d\mathbf{a}\times\frac{\mathbf{r}}{r^2}$$

since $d\mathbf{m} = Id\mathbf{a}$ for a small current loop.

$$= \frac{\mu_0}{4\pi}\int d\mathbf{m}\times\frac{\mathbf{r}}{r^2}$$

$$= \frac{\mu_0}{4\pi}\mathbf{m}\times\frac{\mathbf{r}}{r^2}$$

Finally

$$\mathbf{B} = \nabla\times\mathbf{A}$$

$$= \frac{\mu_0}{4\pi}\nabla\times\left(\frac{\mathbf{m}\times\mathbf{r}}{r^2}\right)$$

$$= \frac{\mu_0}{4\pi r^3}\left[3(\mathbf{m}\cdot\mathbf{r})\mathbf{r}-\mathbf{m}\right]$$

which is the standard form for any dipole field.

37. **(A)**

This problem is best treated in cylindrical coordinates, as suggested. Therefore

$$x^2 + y^2 = \rho^2$$

and $x = \rho\cos\theta, y = \rho\sin\theta$, and $z = z$.

The potential energy is $U = mgz$ taking $U = 0$ at $z = 0$. Also,

$$v^2 = \rho'^2 + \rho^2\theta'^2 + z'^2$$

in cylindrical coordinates. Hence the Lagrangian is

$$L = T - U = {}^1\!/_2\, mv^2 - mgz$$

$$= {}^1\!/_2\, m(\rho'^2 + \rho^2\theta'^2 + z'^2) - mgz.$$

38. **(B)**

The problem of a grounded conducting sphere in a uniform electric field has potential Φ which satisfies Laplace's equation:

$$\nabla^2\Phi = 0 \text{ for } a < r < \infty.$$

Also the boundary conditions are

$$\Phi_{r=a} = 0 \text{ and } \mathbf{E}_{r=\infty} = E_0\,\mathbf{z}.$$

Thus $\Phi_{r=\infty} = -E_0 z$ or $-E_0\, r\cos\theta$.

since $E_z = -\dfrac{\partial\Phi}{\partial z}$.

The given solution is

$$\Phi = \left(Ar + \frac{B}{r^2}\right)\cos\theta .$$

Applying the boundary conditions

$$\Phi(r=\infty) = Ar\cos\theta = -E_0 r\cos\theta$$

$$\Rightarrow A = -E_0$$

$$\Phi(r=a) = \left(Aa + \frac{B}{a^2}\right)\cos\theta = 0$$

$$\Rightarrow B = -Aa^3 = a^3 E_0$$

Hence the electric potential is

$$\Phi(r,\theta) = \left(-E_0 r + \frac{a^3 E_0}{r^2}\right)\cos\theta$$

$$= -E_0 r\left(1 - \left(\frac{a}{r}\right)^3\right)\cos\theta$$

39. **(B)**

Consider a system of charges and an **E** field. Then since power = **F** · **v**

$$\frac{dE_{\text{mech}}}{dt} = \Sigma q\mathbf{v}\cdot\mathbf{E}$$

where $\mathbf{F} = q\mathbf{E}$ has been used

$$= \int \rho\mathbf{v}\cdot\mathbf{E}d^3r$$

passing to the continuous case

$$= \int \mathbf{j}\cdot\mathbf{E}d^3r \equiv \int \frac{\partial W}{\partial t}d^3r$$

where

$$\frac{\partial W}{\partial t} = \mathbf{j}\cdot\mathbf{E}$$

is the mechanical power density and $\mathbf{j} = \rho\mathbf{v}$ is the current density. Let

$$u = u_E + u_M = \frac{1}{2}(\mathbf{E}\cdot\mathbf{D} + \mathbf{B}\cdot\mathbf{H})$$

be the field energy density and $\mathbf{S} = \mathbf{E}\times\mathbf{H}$ the Poynting vector. Then

$$\nabla\cdot\mathbf{S} + \frac{\partial u}{\partial t} + \mathbf{j}\cdot\mathbf{E} = 0$$

is the differential statement of Poynting's theorem. In integral form, we have

$$\oint \mathbf{s}\cdot d\mathbf{a} + \int \frac{\partial v}{\partial t}d^3r + \int \mathbf{j}\cdot\mathbf{E}d^3r = 0$$

which is just the conservation of energy.

40. **(C)**

The minimum angle of resolution for a circular lens is

$$\theta_m = \frac{d}{l} = 1.22\frac{\lambda}{D}.$$

The relationship $d = l\theta_m$ follows from the radian definition of angle. We are given

$$d = 1m \text{ and } l = 10{,}000 \text{ m}.$$

Thus $\quad \theta_m = 10^{-4}$ rad

and using $\lambda = 6000$ Å

$$D = 1.22\,\lambda / \theta_m$$
$$= 1.22 \times 6000 \times 10^{-10} / 10^{-4}$$
$$= 7.3 \times 10^{-3} \text{ m}$$
$$= 0.73 \text{ cm}$$

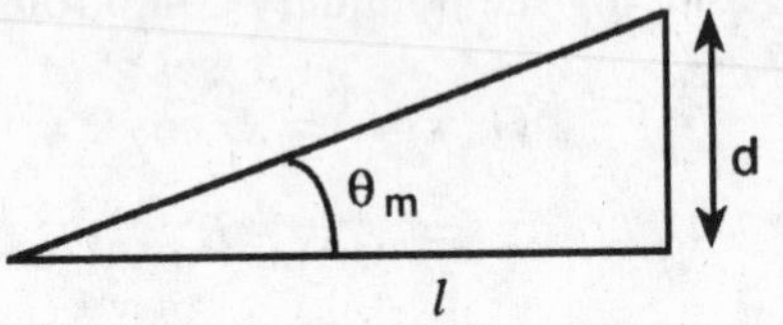

41. **(D)**

We are given $\alpha = 60°$ and $\theta_{i1} = 30°$. By Snell's law

$$n_i \sin\theta_i = n_r \sin\theta_r$$

$$(1)\sin 30° = 1.5 \sin\theta_r \Rightarrow \theta_{r1} = 19.47°$$

By geometry

$$\alpha = \theta_{r1} + \theta_{i2} \Rightarrow \theta_{i2} = 60 - 19.47 = 40.53°.$$

Again apply Snell's law to get

$$1.5 \sin 40.53° = 1 \sin\theta_r \Rightarrow \theta_{r2} = 77.10°.$$

Now the total deviation angle is

$$\delta = (\theta_{i1} - \theta_{r1}) + (\theta_{r2} - \theta_{i2})$$
$$= \theta_{i1} + \theta_{r1} - \alpha$$
$$= 30 + 77.1 - 60 = 47.1°.$$

Note that the near normal incidence prism formula *cannot* be used here.

42. **(B)**

This is the general thin lens problem. Applying the optics equation for going from one medium to another

$$-\frac{n}{s} + \frac{n'}{s'} = \frac{n' - n}{R}$$

we get

$$-\frac{n_0}{s_0} + \frac{n_r}{s'} = \frac{n_r - n_0}{R_1}$$

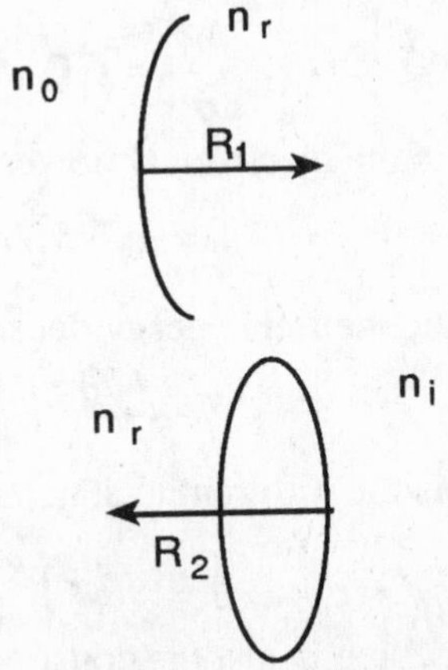

and $$-\frac{n_r}{s'}+\frac{n_i}{s'_i}=\frac{(n_i-n_r)}{R_2}$$

Add the equations to get

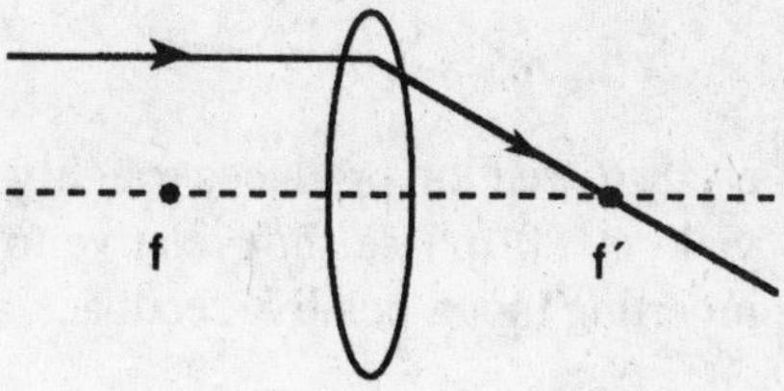

$$-\frac{n_0}{s_0}+\frac{n_i}{s'_i}=\frac{(n_r-n_0)}{R_1}+\frac{(n_i-n_r)}{R_2}.$$

To find the secondary focal length, set $s_0=-\infty$

$$\frac{n_i}{f'}=\frac{n_r-n_0}{R_1}+\frac{n_i-n_r}{R_2}$$

or $$f'=\frac{n_i}{(n_r-n_0)/R_1+(n_i-n_r)/R_2}$$

43. **(E)**

n-channel MOSFET's conduct for positive gate to source voltage. p-channel MOSFET's conduct for negative gate to source voltage. The gate may be understood by constructing a truth table. Considering all possible combinations of input, we have:

A	B	Q_1	Q_2	Q_3	Q_4	output
0	0	off	on	on	off	1
0	1	off	on	off	on	0
1	0	on	off	on	off	0
1	1	on	off	off	on	0

The output is seen to be the same as the definition of A NOR B.

44. **(B)**

Positive logic means that the high voltage state is 1 whereas the low voltage state represents 0. The assignments are reversed for negative logic. The voltage truth table for NAND is

A	B	output
lo	lo	hi
lo	hi	hi
hi	lo	hi
hi	hi	lo

For negative logic, this becomes

A	B	output
1	1	0
1	0	0
0	1	0
0	0	1

which is A NOR B.

45. **(B)**

The circuit is a phase shift oscillator. At a frequency of

$$\omega = \frac{1}{\sqrt{6}} RC$$

each RC section produces roughly a 60° phase shift. Hence the three RC sections yield a 180° phase shift relative to the output at A. When this is put back into the inverting input, positive feedback and oscillations are achieved.

46. **(E)**

This is one of the standard OP AMP circuits. It is the voltage follower configuration. The circuit has unity gain and a high input impedance.

47. **(D)**

At high frequency the inductive reactance

$$X_L = \omega L$$

is very much greater than the 10 kΩ resistance. Thus most of the current then goes through that resistor:

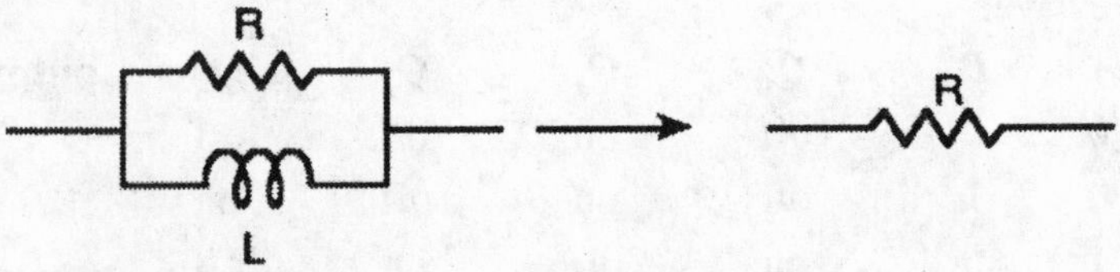

Also at high frequency the capacitive reactance

$$X_c = 1/\omega C$$

acts like a short. The equivalent circuit is a voltage divider.

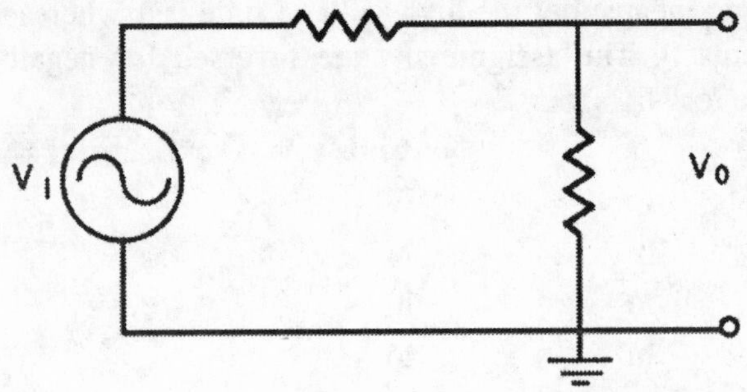

48. **(C)**

Arago first discovered optical activity in 1811 in France. The plane of vibration of light undergoes a continuous rotation when passed through a number of substances (quartz, turpentine, benzil, etc.). The **E** field of the incident linear plane wave rotates about the optic axis. With respect to the source direction, a substance that causes clockwise rotation is dextro type or right handed. Levo type means left handed. Crystal quartz can be either dextro or levo depending on the crystallography.

49. **(D)**

For a plane transmission diffraction grating the condition for maxima (constructive interference) is

$$d \sin \theta = m\lambda$$

where $m = 0, 1, 2, 3, \ldots$ gives the order of the spectrum. Note that for $m = 0$, all wavelengths are indistinguishable since $\theta = 0$ for each of them. Differentiating, we get

$$d \cos \theta \, d\theta = m d\lambda \quad \text{or} \quad \frac{d\theta}{d\lambda} = \frac{m}{d \cos \theta}$$

Since $m / d = \sin \theta / \lambda$, the angular dispersion is

$$\frac{d\theta}{d\lambda} = \frac{1}{\lambda} \tan\theta$$

50. **(C)**

The radii of the dark interference rings of various orders is given by

$$r = \sqrt{m\lambda R}$$

where m is the order of the spectrum, λ is the wavelength, and R is the radius of curvature of the plano-convex lens. This result follows from the thin film destructive interference condition.

$$2\,nd = m\lambda \quad \text{where } n = 1 \text{ for air}$$

$$\Rightarrow d = m\lambda/2$$

and geometry

$$R^2 = (R - d)^2 + r^2$$

$$r^2 = 2Rd - d^2 \approx 2\,Rd$$

Thus $r = \sqrt{2Rd}$

$$= \sqrt{m\lambda R}$$

51. **(E)**

Note that Ag is the substance. We find its work function

$$\phi = h\upsilon_0 = hc / \lambda_0$$

$$= 12{,}400 \text{ eV.Å} / 2638 \text{ Å} = 4.70 \text{ eV}$$

The energy of the incident light is

$$E = h\upsilon = hc / \lambda = 12{,}400 / 1600 = 7.75 \text{ eV}$$

Thus the kinetic energy of the photoelectrons is

$$T = h\upsilon - \phi = 7.75 - 4.70 = 3.05 \text{ eV}$$

Finally

$$T = \frac{1}{2}mv^2 \Rightarrow v = \sqrt{(3.05)(2)/(511{,}000)}c$$

$$= 1.04 \times 10^6 \ m/s$$

52. **(B)**

This is a standard Compton scattering problem

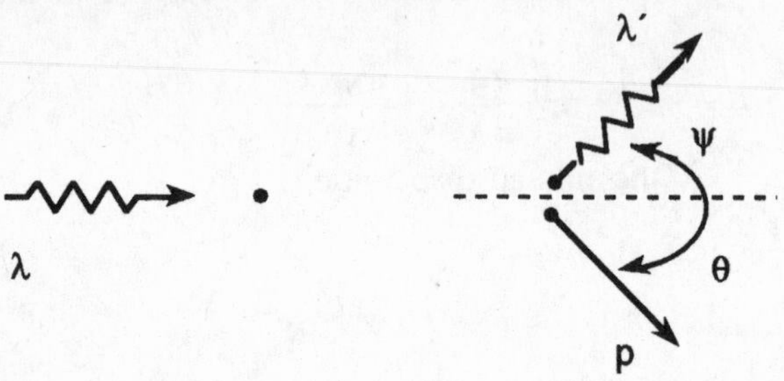

We are given that:

$$\lambda = 6.20\text{Å}.$$

Hence

$$E = \frac{hc}{\lambda} = \frac{12.4\,\text{keV}-\text{Å}}{6.2\text{Å}} = 2.0\,\text{keV}$$

The Compton Shift is

$$\phi = 180° \Rightarrow \Delta\lambda = 2\lambda_c \sin^2\frac{\phi}{2}$$

$$= 2(.0242)(1) = .484\,\text{Å}$$

thus the photon wavelength and energy in the final state is

$$\lambda' = \lambda + \Delta\lambda = 6.2484\text{Å},\ E' = \frac{hc}{\lambda'} = 1.985\,\text{keV}$$

The Compton energy shift is then

$$\Delta E = E - E' = .015\,\text{keV} = 15.5\,\text{eV}.$$

53. **(D)**

Apply Newton's Second Law to get

$$mv' = -bv$$

and integrate:

$$\int_{v_0}^{v} \frac{dv}{v} = -\int_0^t \frac{b}{m}dt,\ \ln\frac{v}{v_0} = -\frac{b}{m}t$$

$$\gamma \equiv \frac{b}{m} \Rightarrow v = v_0 e^{-\gamma t} = \frac{dx}{dt}$$

Integrate again to get

$$x = \frac{v_0}{\gamma}(1 - e^{-\gamma t})$$

$$= \frac{100}{2}(1 - e^{-5})$$

$$= 49.7\ m$$

substituting the given information

$$t = 2.5s,\ \gamma = 2s^{-1},\ v_0 = 100\text{m/s}$$

54. **(E)**

This is a rocket problem. By the conservation of momentum

$$m d\text{v} = -\text{v} dm$$

Integrating, we obtain

$$\int_{m_0}^{m} -\frac{dm}{m} = \frac{1}{0}\int_{\text{v}_0}^{\text{v}} d\text{v}$$

$$\text{v} = \text{v}_0 + \text{v} \ln \frac{m_0}{m}$$

$$= 0.5 + 1.0 \ln \frac{2}{1}$$

$$= 1.2\ \text{km/s}$$

55. **(D)**

In cylindrical coordinates

$$\mathbf{r} = \rho\hat{\rho} + z\hat{z}$$

and $\mathbf{v} = \frac{d\mathbf{r}}{dt} = \rho'\hat{\boldsymbol{\rho}} + \rho\boldsymbol{\theta}'\hat{\theta} + z'\hat{z}$ where $\frac{d\hat{\boldsymbol{\rho}}}{dt} = \theta'\hat{\boldsymbol{\theta}}$

is used. Now by differentiating, one gets

$$\mathbf{a} = \frac{d\mathbf{v}}{dt} = \rho''\hat{\boldsymbol{\rho}} + \rho'\theta'\hat{\boldsymbol{\theta}} + \rho'\theta'\hat{\boldsymbol{\theta}} + \rho'\theta''\hat{\boldsymbol{\theta}} + \rho'\theta'\frac{d\hat{\boldsymbol{\theta}}}{dt} + z''\hat{z}$$

then use

$$\frac{d\hat{\theta}}{dt} = -\theta'\hat{\rho}$$

and collect terms

$$\mathbf{a} = (\rho'' - \rho\theta'^2)\ \hat{\rho} + (\rho\theta'' + 2\rho'\theta')\ \hat{\theta} + z''\hat{z}$$

to get the desired answer.

56. **(B)**

The given vector is

$$\mathbf{r} = \mathbf{x} + \mathbf{y} = \boldsymbol{x}_1 + \boldsymbol{x}_2$$

The rotational transformation is

$$\begin{pmatrix} x'_1 \\ x'_1 \end{pmatrix} = \begin{pmatrix} \lambda_{11} & \lambda_{12} \\ \lambda_{21} & \lambda_{22} \end{pmatrix} \begin{pmatrix} x_1 \\ x_1 \end{pmatrix}$$

$$= \begin{pmatrix} \cos\theta & \sin\theta \\ -\sin\theta & \cos\theta \end{pmatrix} \begin{pmatrix} x_1 \\ x_1 \end{pmatrix}, \quad \theta = 30°$$

$$= \begin{pmatrix} \frac{\sqrt{3}}{2} & \frac{1}{2} \\ -\frac{1}{2} & \frac{\sqrt{3}}{2} \end{pmatrix} \begin{pmatrix} 1 \\ 1 \end{pmatrix}$$

$$= \begin{pmatrix} 1.37 \\ .37 \end{pmatrix}$$

$$\mathbf{r}' = 1.37\,\mathbf{x}'_1 + .37\,\mathbf{x}'_2 = (1.37, .37)\,m$$

which may be confirmed geometrically using cos 15° and sin 15°.

57. **(E)**

Stirling's approximation to second order is desired. Use the definition of the Γ function:

$$N! = \Gamma(N+1) = \int_0^\infty e^{-t} t^N dt = \int_0^\infty e^{f(t)} dt$$

$$f(t) = N \ln t - t$$

Now we wish to do a Taylor expansion

$$f' = \frac{N}{t} - 1 = 0 \Rightarrow t = N \text{ maximum}$$

$$f'' = -\frac{N}{t^2}\bigg|_{t=N} = -\frac{1}{N}$$

$$f(t) \approx f(N) + f'(N)(t-N) + \frac{1}{2!} f''(N)(t-N)^2$$

$$N! = e^{N \ln N - N} \int_0^\infty e^{-(t-N)^2/2N} dt$$

$$= \left(\frac{N}{e}\right)^N \sqrt{2\pi N}$$

58. **(A)**

In microcanonical ensemble theory, the cumulative number of states for an ideal gas is

$$\Gamma(E) = \frac{\pi^{3N/2}}{N!\left(\frac{3N}{2}\right)!(2\pi\hbar)^{3N}} V^N (2mE)^{3N/2}$$

The factors of

$$\pi^{3N/2}\left(\sqrt{2mE}\right)^{3N} / (3N/2)!$$

come from the volume of a $3N$ dimensional sphere in momentum space. Using the 1st order Stirling approximation, we have

$$N! = \left(\frac{N}{e}\right)^N \quad \text{and} \quad \left(\frac{3N}{2}\right)! = \left(\frac{3N}{2e}\right)^{3N/2}$$

The entropy is

$$S = k \ln \Gamma$$

$$= Nk \ln \frac{V}{N}\left(\frac{m}{2\pi\hbar^2}\frac{2}{3}\frac{E}{N}\right)^{3/2} + \frac{5}{2}Nk$$

which is the Sackor-Tetrode equation:

$$S = Nk \ln\left(gT\right)^{3/2}\frac{V}{N} + \frac{5}{2}Nk$$

59. **(A)**

The pp total cross section is high at low energy, has a minimum of about 24 mb, and is about 40 mb at high energies.

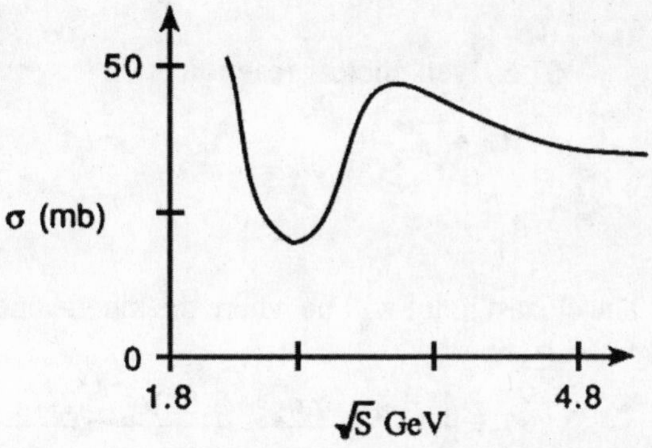

60. **(D)**

The total rest and kinetic energy of the electron-positron pair must be sufficient to account for the rest energy of the resultant proton-antiproton pair. The particle reaction is

$$e^- + e^+ \to p + \overline{p}$$

$$\sqrt{s} = E_{cm} = c^2\sqrt{(m_I + m_T)^2 + 2T_{\text{lab}}m_T}$$

$$m_p + m_{\overline{p}} = \sqrt{(m_e + m_{\overline{e}})^2 + 2T_e m_{\overline{e}}}$$

$$2 \times 9.38 = \sqrt{(2 \times .511)^2 + 2T_e(.511)}$$

$$T_e = 3.44 \times 10^6\ \text{MeV} = 3440\ \text{GeV}$$

$$= 3.44\ \text{TeV}$$

61. **(C)**
The given Lagrangian $L = T - U$ is

$$L = \frac{1}{2}mv^2 - q\phi + q\mathbf{A}\cdot\mathbf{v}.$$

The Lagrange/Euler equation is

$$\frac{d}{dt}\left(\frac{\partial L}{\partial x'_j}\right) - \frac{\partial L}{\partial x_j} = 0$$

From this, we obtain

$$mx''_j = +q\left[-\frac{\partial \phi}{\partial x_j} - \frac{\partial A_j}{\partial t} - \sum_k \left(\frac{\partial A_j}{\partial x_k} - \frac{\partial A_k}{\partial x_j}\right)x'_k\right]$$

or

$$F_j = q\left[E_j + (\mathbf{v}\times\mathbf{B})_j\right]$$

$$\mathbf{F} = q(\mathbf{E} + \mathbf{v}\times\mathbf{B})$$

which is the Lorentz force law.

62. **(D)**
The given nuclear reaction is

$${}^{7}_{3}\text{Li} + {}^{208}_{82}\text{Pb}$$

The closest point will be where the kinetic energy of the Li is converted entirely to potential energy.

$$T = \frac{1}{2}mv^2 = \frac{q_1 q_2}{r} = \frac{3(82)e^2}{r} = \frac{246e^2}{r}$$

$$r = 246e^2 / T$$

$$= 246(1.44\,\text{MeV} - fm) / (50\,\text{MeV})$$

$$= 7.08\ fm$$

In the head on collision, we thus see a transformation of KE into PE.

63. **(E)**
Gauss' law and the definition of electric field give

$$\nabla\cdot\mathrm{E} = \frac{\rho}{\varepsilon_0},\ \mathrm{E} = -\nabla\phi \Rightarrow \nabla^2\mathrm{E} = \begin{cases} -\dfrac{\rho}{\varepsilon_0} & r < R \\ 0 & r > R \end{cases}$$

In Spherical coordinates

$$\nabla^2 = \frac{1}{r^2}\frac{\partial}{\partial r}\left(r^2\frac{\partial}{\partial r}\right) = \frac{1}{r^2}\frac{\partial^2}{\partial r^2}(r).$$

We are given that

$$\phi = -\rho r^2/6\varepsilon_0 + A/r + B, r < R.$$

For $r > R$, we guess by symmetry $\phi = C/r + D$. The boundary conditions then give

$$\phi(r \to \infty) = 0 \Rightarrow D = 0,$$

$$\phi\ (r \to 0) \text{ finite} \Rightarrow A = 0$$

$$\phi(r = R) \text{ continuous} \Rightarrow B - \rho R^2/6\varepsilon_0 = C/R$$

Gauss' law in integral form gives

$$\oint \mathbf{E} \cdot d\mathbf{a} = \frac{C}{R^2} 4\pi R^2 = \frac{q}{\varepsilon_0} \Rightarrow C = \frac{q}{4\pi\varepsilon_0}$$

Thus $\quad B = \dfrac{q}{4\pi\varepsilon_0 R} + \dfrac{\rho R^2}{G\varepsilon_0}$

and $\quad \phi = \dfrac{\rho}{6\varepsilon_0}(R^2 - r^2) + \dfrac{q}{4\pi\varepsilon_0 R}$

$$= \frac{\rho}{2\varepsilon_0}\left(R^2 - \frac{r^2}{3}\right)$$

64. **(D)**

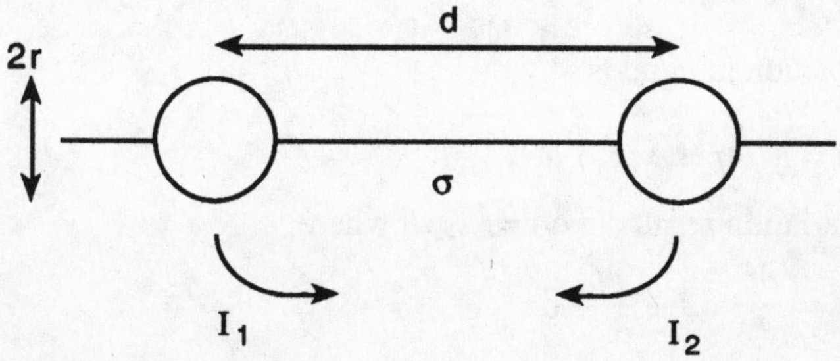

A matrix approach is appropriate here.

$$\begin{pmatrix} \phi_1 \\ \phi_2 \end{pmatrix} = \begin{pmatrix} R_{11} & R_{12} \\ R_{21} & R_{22} \end{pmatrix} \begin{pmatrix} I_1 \\ I_2 \end{pmatrix}$$

If $\quad I_2 = 0 \Rightarrow R_{11} = 1/(2\pi\sigma r_1) = 1/(2\pi\sigma r)\ \{I_1 \neq 0\}$

$\quad I_1 = 0 \Rightarrow R_{22} = 1/(2\pi\sigma r_2) = 1/(2\pi\sigma r)\ \{I_2 \neq 0\}$

In the same way $R_{12} = R_{21} = 1/(2\pi\sigma d)$

$$\begin{pmatrix} \phi_1 \\ \phi_2 \end{pmatrix} = \frac{1}{2\pi\sigma} \begin{pmatrix} \frac{1}{r} & \frac{1}{d} \\ \frac{1}{d} & \frac{1}{r} \end{pmatrix} \begin{pmatrix} I_1 \\ I_2 \end{pmatrix}$$

Now use $I_2 = I = -I_1$. By Ohm's law

$$\frac{(\phi_2 - \phi_1)}{I} = \frac{1}{\pi\sigma}\left(\frac{1}{r} - \frac{1}{d}\right) = R$$

65. **(E)**

Newton's law of universal gravitation is

$$\mathbf{F} = -\frac{GmM}{r^2}\mathbf{r} = m\,\mathbf{g}$$

We can write this as a Gauss' law for gravitation:

$$\oint \mathbf{g} \cdot d\mathbf{a} = -\frac{GM}{r^2}4\pi r^2 = -4\pi GM \equiv -4\pi G m_{in}$$

The divergence theorem is

$$\oint \nabla \cdot \mathbf{g} d^3 r = \oint \mathbf{g} \cdot d\mathbf{a}$$

and hence

$$\nabla \cdot \mathbf{g} \frac{4}{3}\pi r^3 = -4\pi G m_{in} \Rightarrow \nabla \cdot \mathbf{g} = -4\pi G\rho$$

This is analogous to the electric field law

$$\nabla \cdot \mathbf{E} = 4\pi k_e \rho_q$$

with $k_e = 1/4\pi\varepsilon_0$.

66. **(A)**

The action integral is

$$A = \int_{t_1}^{t_2} f(t, x, x')\, dt$$

The first variation results in $\delta A = \int \delta t\, dt$ where

$$\delta f = \frac{\partial f}{\partial x}\delta x + \frac{\partial f}{\partial x'}\delta x'$$

gives the usual Euler-Lagrange equation.

In a similar manner, the second variation is

$$\delta^2 f = \frac{\partial^2 f}{\partial x^2}(\delta x)^2 + 2\frac{\partial^2 f}{\partial x \partial x'}\delta x \delta x' + \frac{\partial^2 f}{\partial x'^2}(\delta x')^2$$

where $\delta^2 A = \int \delta^2 f\, dt$ and the total variation is

$$\Delta A = \alpha \delta A + \frac{\alpha^2}{2}\delta^2 A + \ldots$$

67. **(E)**

Snell's law follows from Fermat's principle of least time. The action integral

$$A = \int \frac{ds}{V}$$

is just the time t to go from P to Q.

$$A = \frac{l_1}{v_1} + \frac{l_2}{v_2} = \frac{n_1 l_1}{c} + \frac{n_2 l_2}{c}$$

$$= \frac{n_1}{c}\sqrt{a^2 + x^2} + \frac{n_2}{c}\sqrt{b^2 + (d-x)^2}$$

The first derivative condition $dA / dx = 0$ gives

$$n_1 \frac{x}{\sqrt{a^2 + x^2}} = n_2 \frac{d - x}{\sqrt{b^2 + (d-x)^2}}$$

or $\quad n_1 \sin\theta_1 = n_2 \sin\theta_2$.

68. **(A)**

The usual Lorentz transformation is Minkowski space (**r**, ict) is

$$\begin{pmatrix} x'_1 \\ x'_4 \end{pmatrix} = \begin{pmatrix} \cos\phi & \sin\phi \\ -\sin\phi & \cos\phi \end{pmatrix} \begin{pmatrix} x_1 \\ x_4 \end{pmatrix}$$

Using Euler's formula

$$e^{i\phi} = \cos\phi + i \sin\phi$$

one easily proves

$$\cos\phi = \frac{e^{i\phi} + e^{-i\phi}}{2} = \cosh(i\phi) = \cosh y$$

$$\sin\phi = (e^{i\phi} - e^{-i\phi}) / 2i = -i \sinh(y)$$

Thus, the desired result is

$$\begin{pmatrix} x'_1 \\ x'_4 \end{pmatrix} = \begin{pmatrix} \cosh y & -i \sinh y \\ i \sinh y & \cosh y \end{pmatrix} \begin{pmatrix} x_1 \\ x_2 \end{pmatrix}$$

69. **(D)**

The total relativistic energy is

$$E = T + mc^2 = m\gamma c^2$$

where T is the relativistic kinetic energy

$$T = mc^2(\gamma - 1) = mc^2\left(\frac{1}{\sqrt{1 - \beta^2}} - 1\right)$$

Now we use a Taylor series expansion

$$\frac{1}{\sqrt{1 - x}} = 1 + \frac{1}{2}x + \frac{3}{8}x^2 + \ldots$$

with $x = \beta^2$ to get

$$T = mc^2\left(\frac{1}{2}\beta^2 + \frac{3}{8}\beta^4\right)$$

$$= \frac{1}{2}mv^2 + \frac{3}{8}mv^2\,\beta^2$$

70. **(B)**

The standard two-body nuclear reaction is

$$I + T \rightarrow E + R$$

where I is the incident nucleus, T is the target, E is the emitted particle, and R is the residual nucleus. Here the reaction is

$$\alpha + {}^{14}\mathrm{N} \rightarrow \mathrm{p} + {}^{17}\mathrm{O}$$

with Q-value

$$\begin{aligned} Q &= m_I + m_T - m_R - m_E \\ &= (4.0026 + 14.0031 - 1.0078 - 16.9991)\text{ amu} \\ &\quad \times 931.502\text{ MeV/amu} \\ &= -1.1\text{ MeV} \end{aligned}$$

In the center of mass reference frame, this is the minimum kinetic energy needed for the reaction to occur.

71. **(C)**

The ideal system of N spins is an example of the binomial distribution where

$$p = P(\uparrow) \text{ and } q = 1 - p = P(\downarrow)$$

The mean magnetic moment for one spin is

$$<\mu> = p\mu_0 + (1-p)(-\mu_0) = (2p-1)\,\mu_0$$

and the single spin variance is

$$\begin{aligned} \sigma^2 &= <(\mu - <\mu>)^2> = <\mu^2> - <\mu>^2 \\ &= p\mu_0^{\,2} + (1-p)\mu_0^{\,2} - (2p-1)\mu_0^{\,2} \\ &= 4pq\mu_0^{\,2} \end{aligned}$$

Hence for N spins,

$$<M> = N(2p-1)\mu_0 \text{ and } \sigma_M^{\,2} = 4\,Npq\mu_0^{\,2}.$$

72. **(C)**

We are given that

$$p[1 \text{ event occurs in } (t, t+dt)] = r\,dt$$

with $r = 1$ Hz. One must know that the distribution is Poisson with $\lambda = rt = 10$

being the expected number of counts in $t = 10$ s. Thus, the probability of 5 counts is found from

$$p(n) = \lambda^n e^{-\lambda}/n!$$

or is

$$p(5) = \lambda^5 e^{-\lambda} / 5!$$
$$= 10^5 e^{-10} / 5!$$
$$= .038.$$

73. **(E)**

Answer (A) is the postulate of Lord Kelvin and is a statement of the second law

$$\Delta S \geq 0.$$

Answer (B) is simply a restatement of choice (A). Selection (C) is the postulate of Clausius and is a statement of the second law. Answer (D) is a restatement of (C). An easy counterexample for (E) is the heating of a body, no matter what its temperature, by frictional work. Clearly also electric energy can do work and be transformed into heat in a toaster (resistor).

74. **(D)**

For this centripetal motion laboratory experiment

$$g = 4\pi^2 mr / T^2M.$$

The standard rule for the propagation of error is

$$\Delta g = \sqrt{\left(\frac{\partial g}{\partial r}\Delta r\right)^2 + \left(\frac{\partial g}{\partial T}\Delta T\right)^2}$$
$$= \sqrt{\left(g\frac{\Delta r}{r}\right)^2 + \left(2g\frac{\Delta T}{T}\right)^2}$$

Hence the relative error is

$$\frac{\Delta g}{g} = \sqrt{\left(\frac{\Delta r}{r}\right)^2 + 4\left(\frac{\Delta T}{T}\right)^2} = \sqrt{\left(\frac{1}{20}\right)^2 + 4\left(\frac{.016}{.638}\right)^2}$$
$$= .071$$

The experimental g-value is thus 970 ± 69 cm/s^2.

75. **(E)**

For the two isothermal parts of the cycle

$$\Delta U = 0.$$

Hence, by the first law of thermodynamics

$$\Delta Q = \Delta W$$

or $$-Q_C = W_{CD} - \int_C^D p\,dV$$

$$= \int_{V_C}^{V_D} \frac{RT_C}{V}\,dV = -RT_C \ln \frac{V_C}{V_D}$$

Therefore

$$Q_C = RT_C \ln \frac{V_C}{V_D}$$

and in the same way we find

$$Q_H = RT_H \ln \frac{V_B}{V_A}.$$

Thus, the total amount of heat absorbed is

$$Q_H - Q_C = RT_H \ln \frac{V_B}{V_A} - RT_c \ln \frac{V_C}{V_D}$$

76. **(C)**

For the simple two level system, there are only two relevant energies

$$E_- = \mu_0 B \text{ and } E_+ = -\mu_0 B.$$

The partition function for the system is

$$Z = \Sigma e^{-\beta E_j}$$

$$= e^{-\beta\mu_0 B} + e^{\beta\mu_0 B}$$

$$= 2\cosh(\beta\mu_0 B)$$

The single particle average energy is

$$<E> = -\frac{\partial}{\partial\beta} \ln Z$$

$$= -2\mu_0 B \sinh(\beta\mu_0 B) / 2\cosh(\beta\mu_0 B)$$

$$= -\mu_0 B \tanh(\beta\mu_0 B)$$

Hence the total or N-particle energy is

$$<E>_N = N<E>$$

$$= -N\mu_0 B \tanh(\beta\,\mu_0\,B)$$

77. **(B)**

The Hamiltonian of the system is

$$H(x, p) = p^2 / 2m + kx^2 / 2 = E.$$

The cumulative number of states is found in the usual way

$$\Gamma(E) = \frac{1}{2\pi\hbar} \int \theta(E - H)\,dx\,dp$$

$$= \frac{1}{2\pi\hbar}\int dx \int_{-p}^{p} dp,\ p = \sqrt{2mE - mkx^2}$$

$$= \frac{1}{2\pi\hbar}\int_0^{\sqrt{2E/k}} 2\sqrt{2mE}\sqrt{1 - kx^2/2E}\,dx$$

$$= \frac{E}{\hbar\omega}$$

Using $\omega = \sqrt{k/m}$

and a u-substitution

$$u = \sin\theta = \sqrt{k/2E}\,x.$$

Finally, the density of states is

$$\frac{d\Gamma}{dE} = \frac{1}{\hbar\omega}$$

Note that $\int \theta\,(E - H)\,dx\,dp$ could also be found from the ellipse area formula

$$\pi ab = \pi\sqrt{\frac{2E}{k}}\sqrt{2mE} = 2\pi E/\omega.$$

78. **(C)**

The phase space orbit is easily identified as that of simple harmonic motion

$$\Sigma F = -kx = mx''$$

$$x'' = \omega_0^2 x = 0,\ \omega_0 = \sqrt{k/m}$$

$$x'x' + \omega_0^2 xx' = 0$$

$$\frac{d}{dt}\left(\frac{1}{2}x'^2 + \frac{1}{2}\omega_0^2 x^2\right) = 0$$

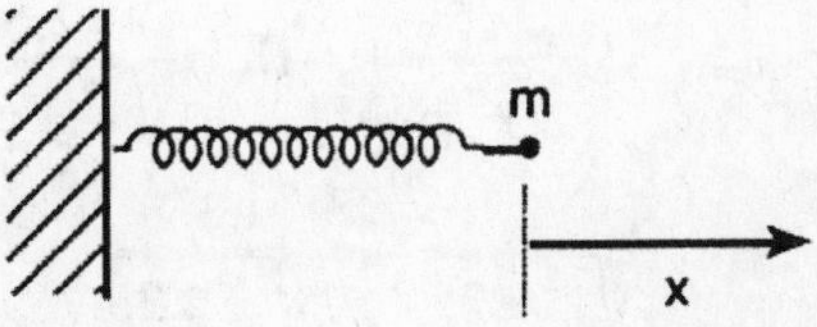

$$\frac{d}{dt}\left(\frac{1}{2}mx'^2 + \frac{1}{2}kx^2\right) = 0$$

The constant is the energy

$$E = \frac{1}{2}mx'^2 + \frac{1}{2}kx^2$$

which may be written as

$$\left(\frac{x'}{A}\right)^2 + \left(\frac{x}{B}\right)^2 = 1$$

with $A = \sqrt{2E/k}$ and $B = \sqrt{2E/m}$.

Thus the phase space plot is an ellipse.

79. **(C)**

The Brackett series in hydrogen involves transitions from energy level m to energy level n = 4 resulting in the emission of a photon. The wavelength is found from

$$1/\lambda = R(1/n^2 - 1/m^2)$$

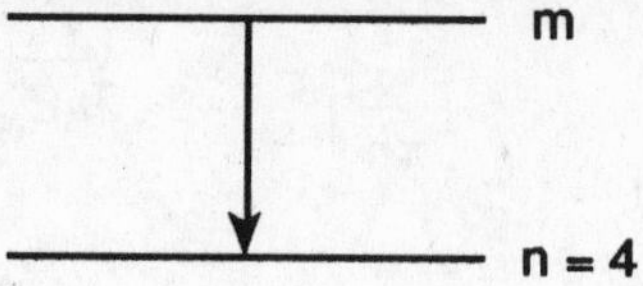

where R is the Rydberg constant.

The upper limit comes from $m = 5$

$$1/\lambda = 109{,}677.6\ (^1/_{16} - ^1/_{25})$$

which gives $\lambda = 40{,}500$ Å $= 4050$ nm.

80. **(A)**

Applying Snell's law to the second figure, we get

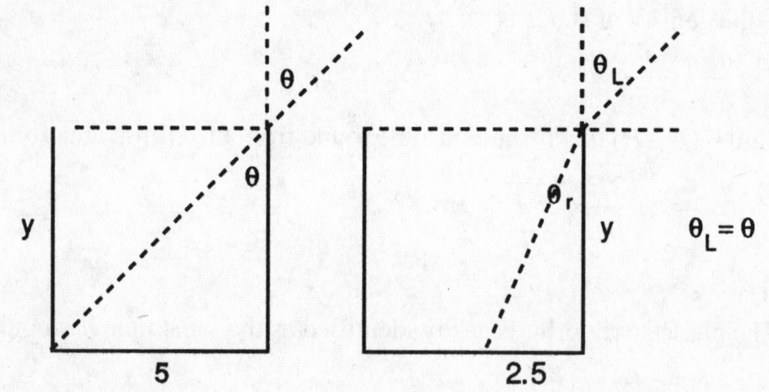

$$n_i \sin\theta_i = n_r \sin\theta_r$$

$$(1)\frac{5}{\sqrt{y^2+25}} = (1.3)\frac{2.5}{\sqrt{y^2+6.25}}$$

$$\frac{2}{\sqrt{y^2+25}} = \frac{1.3}{\sqrt{y^2+6.25}}.$$

Multiplying means and extremes and squaring, we get

$$4y^2 + 25 = 1.69y^2 + 42.25$$

$$2.31y^2 = 17.25$$

$$y = 2.73\text{cm}$$

81. **(A)**

The continuous charge distribution approach is:

$$\mathbf{E} = k\int \frac{dq}{r^2}\mathbf{r}$$

where $dq = \sigma da = 2\,\pi\sigma s ds$

$$= k\int \frac{2\pi\sigma s ds}{r^2}\,\frac{x}{r}\,\mathbf{x}$$

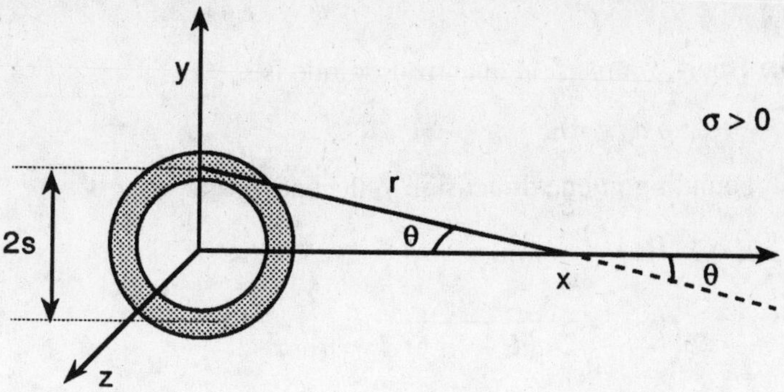

Using

$$\cos\theta = \frac{x}{r}$$

Since by symmetry only the x-component contributes.

$$\mathbf{E} = 2\pi\sigma kx \int_a^b \frac{s\,ds}{(s^2+x^2)^{3/2}}\,\mathbf{x}$$

$$= 2\pi\sigma kx\,\mathbf{x}\left.\frac{1}{\sqrt{x^2+s^2}}\right|_{s=b}^{s=a}$$

$$= 2\pi\sigma kx\left[\frac{1}{\sqrt{x^2+a^2}} - \frac{1}{\sqrt{x^2+b^2}}\right]\mathbf{x}$$

82. **(A)**

The blackbody distribution may be expressed in various ways

$$u(\omega)\,d\omega = u(\lambda)d\lambda$$

$$\frac{\hbar\omega^3}{\pi^2 c^3}\frac{1}{e^{\hbar\omega\beta}-1}\,d\omega = \frac{16\pi^2\hbar c}{\lambda^5}\frac{1}{e^{hc\beta/\lambda}-1}\,d\lambda$$

since $$\omega = 2\pi\upsilon = 2\pi\frac{c}{\lambda}.$$

The intensity $u(\lambda)$ has a maximum when

$$du(\lambda)/d\lambda = 0$$

$$-\frac{5}{\lambda^6}\frac{1}{e^x-1} + \frac{1}{\lambda^5}\frac{e^x}{(e^x-1)^2}\frac{hc\beta}{\lambda^2} = 0,\ x \equiv hc\beta/\lambda$$

Rearranging terms, we get $e^x(5 - X) = 5$ which has solution $x = 4.965$ so that

$$\lambda_{max}T = hc/4.97\ \text{K}.$$

83. **(D)**

The Bohr-Sommerfeld quantization rule is

$$\frac{1}{2\pi}\int p\,dy = n\hbar.$$

For a ball bounding in one dimension y, the energy is

$$E = T + U = \frac{p^2}{2m} + mgy$$

Thus $$\frac{1}{2\pi}\cdot 2\int_0^{E/my} \sqrt{2m(E-mgy)}\,dy = n\hbar$$

$$n\hbar = \frac{-2}{2\pi}\sqrt{2mE}\,\frac{2}{3}\left(1-\frac{mgy}{E}\right)^{3/2}\frac{E}{my}\Bigg|_{y=0}^{y=\frac{E}{mg}}$$

Simplifying, we get

$$\frac{2}{3\pi g}\sqrt{\frac{2}{m}}E^{3/2} = n\hbar \text{ or } E_n = \left(9\pi^2 g^2 n^2 \hbar^2 m/8\right)^{1/3}$$

84. **(D)**

The total time is a combination of the fall time plus the time for the sound wave to propagate.

$$t = \sqrt{2h/g} + h/v_s$$

$$h + v_s\sqrt{2/g}\sqrt{h} - v_s t = 0$$

$$h + 149.08\sqrt{h} - 2253.90 = 0$$

Completing the square

$$(\sqrt{h} + 74.54)^2 = 2253.90 + 5556.12$$

$$\sqrt{h} = -74.54 + 88.37$$

thus $$h = 191\text{m}.$$

85. **(E)**

The normalization constant for any spherical harmonic is found from the condition

$$\int \left|Y_{lm_l}\right|^2 d\Omega = 1.$$

Thus or $l = 1$ and $m_l = 0$

$$1 = \int Y_{10}Y_{10}{}^*\,d\Omega = N^2\int_{-1}^{1}\cos^2\theta\, d(\cos\theta)\int_0^{2\pi} d\phi$$

$$= N^2(2\pi)\frac{1}{3}\cos^3\theta\Bigg|_{\theta=\pi}^{\theta=0}$$

$$= \frac{2\pi}{3} N^2 (1-(-1)) = \frac{4\pi}{3} N^2$$

Hence

$$N = \sqrt{\frac{3}{4\pi}}.$$

86. **(B)**

The degeneracy for the *H*-like atom problem is found from thinking about the quantum numbers which describe a state. $n = 1, 2, 3, \ldots$ is the principal quantum number. $l = 0, 1, 2, \ldots, n-1$ is the orbital quantum number. $m_l = -l, -(l-1), \ldots -1, 0, 1, \ldots, l-1$ is the magnetic quantum number. Hence the degeneracy g is the number of states that have the same energy E_n

$$g = \sum_{l=0}^{n-1} (2l+1)$$

$$= 2\sum_{l=0}^{n-1} l + \sum_{l=0}^{n-1} 1$$

$$= 2\frac{(n-1)(n)}{2} + n$$

$$= n^2$$

87. **(A)**

An initial, intermediate, and final picture is helpful to solve the problem.

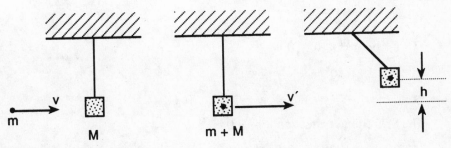

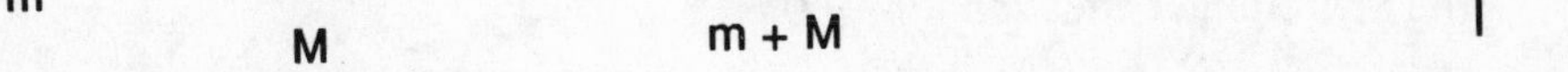

By momentum conservation:

$$mv = (m+M)v'$$

$$v = \frac{m+M}{m}\sqrt{2gh},$$

By energy conservation:

$$\frac{1}{2}(m+M)v'^2 = (m+M)gh$$

$$v' = \sqrt{2gh}$$

$$h = \left(\frac{m}{m+M}v\right)^2 / 2g$$

$$= \left[\frac{5}{1005}20{,}000\right]^2 / 2(980)$$

$$= 5.05 \text{ cm}$$

88. **(B)**

The Lorentz transformation for coordinates is

$$x' = \gamma(x - vt)$$

$$y' = y,$$

$$z' = z$$

$$t' = \gamma\left(t - \frac{v}{c^2}x\right).$$

By differentiation one finds the velocity transformation

$$u_x' = (u_x - v)/(1 - u_x v/c^2)$$

$$u_y' = u_y/\gamma(1 - u_x v/c^2)$$

$$u_z' = u_z/\gamma(1 - u_x v/c^2)$$

We are given that

$$\mathbf{u} = \left(\frac{1}{\sqrt{2}}c, \frac{1}{\sqrt{2}}c\right) \text{ and } \mathbf{u}' = \left(-\frac{1}{\sqrt{2}}c, \frac{1}{\sqrt{2}}c\right).$$

Hence

$$-\frac{1}{\sqrt{2}} = \left(\frac{1}{\sqrt{2}} - \beta\right)\Big/\left(1 - \frac{1}{\sqrt{2}}\beta\right)$$

$$-\frac{1}{\sqrt{2}} + \frac{\beta}{2} = \frac{1}{\sqrt{2}} - \beta$$

$$\Rightarrow \beta = \frac{4}{3\sqrt{2}} = 0.94$$

$$v = \beta c = (3\times10^8)(0.94)$$

$$= 2.8\times10^8 \text{ m/s}$$

89. **(C)**

The Schrödinger equation for $l = 0$ is

$$\frac{1}{R}\frac{d}{dr}\left(r^2\frac{dR}{dr}\right) + \frac{2\mu r^2}{\hbar^2}(E - U) = 0.$$

Now the wavefunction is given as

$$R_{10}(r) = Ne^{-Zr/a_0}$$

and the potential energy is $U(r) = -kZe^2/r$. Differentiating, one obtains

$$\frac{d}{dr}\left(r^2\frac{dR}{dr}\right) = -\frac{Z}{a_0}R\left(2r - \frac{Z}{a_0}r^2\right).$$

Hence we have

$$\left(-\frac{2Z}{a_0} + \frac{2\mu kZe^2}{\hbar}\right)r + \left(\frac{Z^2}{a_0^2} + \frac{2\mu E}{\hbar}\right)r^2 = 0.$$

Thus the Bohr radius is

$$a_0 = \frac{\hbar^2}{k\mu e^2}$$

and the energy eigenvalue is

$$E = -\hbar^2 Z^2 / 2\mu a_0^{\ 2} = -k^2 Z^2 \mu e^4 / 2\hbar^2 .$$

90. **(D)**

The proper distance squared is

$$ds^2 = \sum_{\mu=1}^{4} dx^\mu dx_\mu$$

or $\quad dx^2 + dy^2 + dz^2 - c^2\, dt^2.$

Hence we have

$$\Delta s^2 = \Delta x^2 + \Delta y^2 + \Delta z^2 - c^2 \Delta t^2$$

and since $\underline{x}(A) = (1, 2, 3, 0)$ and $\underline{x}(B) = (2, 3, 4, {}^1/c)$ we get

$$\Delta s^2 = (2-1)^2 + (3-2)^2 + (4-3)^2 - \left(\frac{1}{c} - 0\right)^2 c^2$$

$$= 3 - 1$$

$$= 2$$

or finally

$$\Delta s = \sqrt{2}\,\text{m}.$$

91. **(D)**

In the Fermi gas model at zero temperature

$$\frac{dn}{d^3k} = g\,\frac{V}{(2\pi)^3} = \text{const.}$$

Integrate to obtain

$$\int_0^N \frac{dn}{V} = 2\,\frac{1}{(2\pi)^3} \int_0^{k_F} 4\pi k^2\, dk$$

where the degeneracy $g = 2$ for electrons.

$$\rho = \frac{N}{V} = \frac{1}{\pi^2}\frac{1}{3} k_F^{\ 3}$$

or $\quad k_F = (3\pi^2 \rho)^{1/3}\,\text{Å}^{-1}$

where $\quad \rho = d \times N_A / A = .971\ \text{g/cm}^3 \times \dfrac{6.02 \times 10^{23}\ /\text{mol}}{22.99\ \text{g/mol}} \times \left(\dfrac{10^{-8}\ \text{cm}}{1\text{Å}}\right)^3$

$$= .0254\text{Å}^{-3}$$

Thus $\quad k_F = .910\ \text{Å}^{-1}.$

92. **(B)**

The angular part of the wave function is a spherical harmonic

$$Y_{lm_l} = Y_{22} = \frac{1}{4}\sqrt{\frac{15}{2\pi}} \sin^2\theta e^{2i\phi}$$

and the radial part is

$$R_{nl} = R_{32} = \frac{2\sqrt{2}}{27\sqrt{5}}\left(\frac{Z}{3a_0}\right)^{3/2}\left(\frac{Zr}{a_0}\right)^2 e^{-Zr/3a_0}.$$

The complete wavefunction is

$$\psi_{nlm_l}(r,\theta,\phi) = R_{nl}(r)\,Y_{lm_l}(\theta,\phi).$$

Fortunately, L_z only operates on the ψ component

$$L_z\psi = \frac{\hbar}{i}\frac{\partial}{\partial\phi}\psi$$

$$= \frac{\hbar}{i}2i\psi$$

$$= 2\hbar\psi$$

Hence the angular momentum eigenvalue is $2\hbar = m_l\hbar$.

93. **(C)**

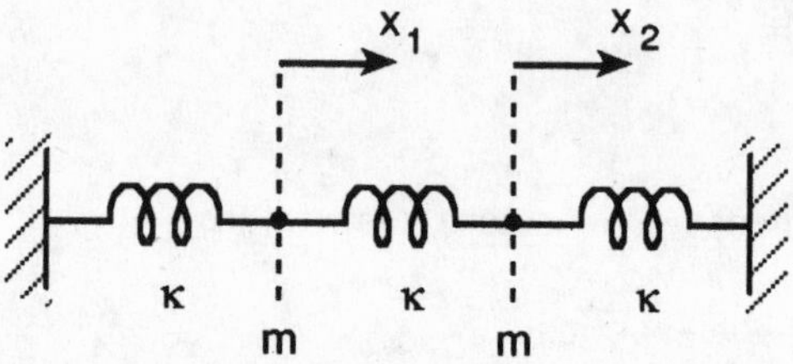

Newton's Second law states:

$$F_1 = mx_1'' = -kx_1 - \kappa x_1 + \kappa x_2 = -kx_1 + \kappa(x_2 - x_1)$$

$$F_2 = mx_2'' = -kx_2 - \kappa x_2 + \kappa x_1 = -kx_2 - \kappa(x_2 - x_1)$$

The solutions are

$$x_1 = A\cos(\omega t + \delta)$$

and $\quad x_2 = B\cos(\omega t + \delta)$

The easiest way to find the frequencies is to add and subtract the equations to get

$$my'' = -ky,\quad y = x_1 + x_2$$

$$mz'' = -(k + 2\kappa)\,z,\quad z = x_2 - x_1.$$

The symmetrical mode frequency is thus

$$\omega_s = \sqrt{\frac{k}{m}}$$

and the anti-symmetrical one is

$$\omega_a = \sqrt{(k+2\kappa)/m}.$$

94. **(B)**

Two electrons can form an $l = 0$ quantum state by the Pauli principle, e.g., a $1s^2$ configuration. The current is then

$$I = \frac{q}{t} = \frac{2e}{(2\pi r/v)} = \frac{ev}{\pi r}$$

and the velocity comes from Newton's 2nd law $F = ma$ or

$$\frac{mv^2}{r} = \frac{ke^2}{r^2}$$

$$v = \sqrt{\frac{ke^2}{mr}}$$

$$= \sqrt{(9\times10^9)(1.6\times10^{-19})^2/(9.1\times10^{-31})(1\times10^{-10})}$$

$$= 1.59\times10^6 \text{ m/s}$$

Therefore the electric current is

$$I = (1.6\times10^{-19})(1.59\times10^6)/\pi(1\times10^{-10})$$

$$= 8.1\times10^{-4} A$$

95. **(C)**

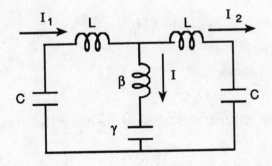

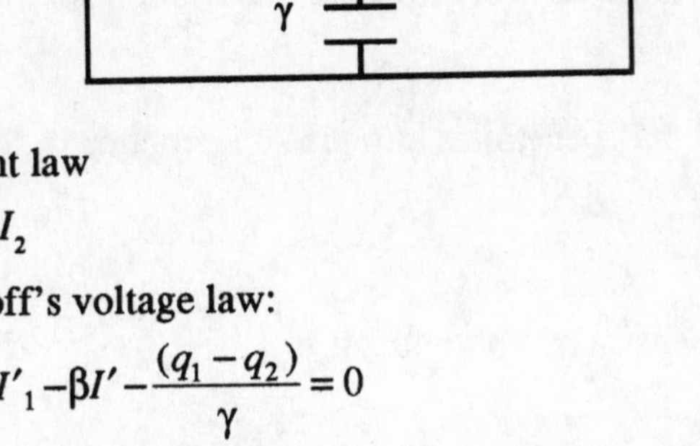

By Kirchoff's current law

$$I = I_1 - I_2$$

According to Kirchoff's voltage law:

$$-\frac{q_1}{C} - LI'_1 - \beta I' - \frac{(q_1 - q_2)}{\gamma} = 0$$

$$-\frac{q_2}{C} - LI'_2 + \frac{(q_1 - q_2)}{\gamma} + \beta I' = 0$$

Differentiate and set

$$\kappa = 1/LC, \quad \kappa_1 = 1/L\gamma, \quad \kappa_2 = \beta / L.$$

Note that κ_2 is dimensionless. Then we find

$$I_1''(1+\kappa_2) - \kappa_2 I_2'' + (k+\kappa_1) I_1 - \kappa_1 I_2 = 0$$

$$I_2''(1+\kappa_2) - \kappa_2 I_1'' + (k+\kappa_1) I_2 - \kappa_1 I_1 = 0$$

Add and subtract the equations letting

$$y = I_1 + I_2 \text{ and } z = I_2 - I_1$$

to obtain

$$y'' + ky = 0 \text{ and } z'' + \frac{k+2\kappa_1}{1+2\kappa_2} z = 0$$

thus

$$w_a = \sqrt{(k+2\kappa_1)/(1+2\kappa_2)}\,.$$

96. **(B)**
Maxwell's Fourth equation is

$$\nabla \times \mathbf{B} = \mu_0 \mathbf{j}.$$

The London equation

$$\mathbf{j} = -\mathbf{A} / \mu_0 \lambda_L^2$$

is given. Hence

$$\nabla \times \mathbf{j} = -\nabla \times \mathbf{A} / \mu_0 \lambda_L^2 = -\mathbf{B} / \mu_0 \lambda_L^2.$$

Also

$$\nabla \times (\nabla \times \mathbf{B}) = \nabla(\nabla \cdot \mathbf{B}) - \nabla^2 \mathbf{B}$$

$$\nabla \times \mu_0 \mathbf{j} = -\nabla^2 \mathbf{B}$$

since $\nabla \cdot \mathbf{B} = 0$ by Gauss' law.

Thus $\qquad \nabla^2 \mathbf{B} = \mathbf{B} / \lambda_L^2.$

One solution is obviously $\mathbf{B} = 0$. However, the desired solution is

$$B = B_0 e^{-x/\lambda_L}$$

The magnetic field thus penetrates into the superconductor to a penetration depth, typically $\lambda_L \approx 200$ Å,

97. **(E)**
The energy density of a photon gas is

$$U = \sigma T^4.$$

Thus the energy is

$$E = \int U\, d^3r = \sigma V T^4$$

Now use the first law of thermodynamics

$$dE = dQ - dW$$

$$dQ = dE + dW = dE + pdV$$

$$= \sigma T^4 dV + \frac{1}{3}\sigma T^4 dV$$

$$= \frac{4}{3}\sigma T^4 dV$$

$$dS = \frac{dQ}{T} = \frac{4}{3}\sigma T^3 dV$$

$$S = \int dS = \frac{4}{3}\sigma T^3 V$$

We have used the fact $p = {}^1/_3\, E/V$, the relativistic Virial theorem.

98. **(C)**

The motion of two particles of masses $m_1 = m_2 = m$ separated by a distance r is equivalent to that of a reduced mass particle μ as shown. The Schrödinger equation is

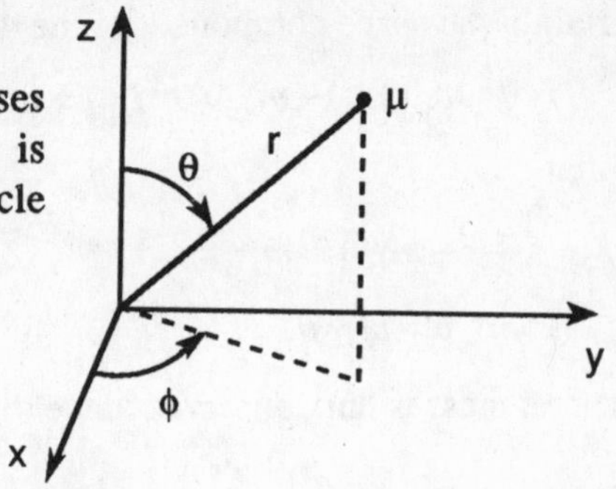

$$H\psi = E\psi\,,\ H = \frac{-\hbar^2}{2\mu}\nabla^2 + U(r)$$

where $U(r) = 0$ for fixed r

In spherical coordinates, we get

$$\frac{1}{r^2 \sin\theta}\frac{\partial}{\partial\theta}\left(\sin\theta\frac{\partial\psi}{\partial\theta}\right) + \frac{1}{r^2\sin^2\theta}\frac{\partial^2\psi}{\partial\phi^2}$$

$$+\frac{2\mu E}{\hbar^2}\psi = 0.$$

The standard separation of variables technique using $\psi(\theta,\phi) = P(\theta)\, Q(\phi)$ gives

$$Q(\phi) = \frac{1}{\sqrt{2\pi}} e^{im_l\phi}$$

and $$\frac{1}{\sin\theta}\frac{d}{d\theta}\left(\sin\theta\frac{dP}{d\theta}\right) + \left[l(l+1) - \frac{m_l^2}{\sin^2\theta}\right]P = 0$$

where $P = P_l^{m_l}(\theta)$

is the associated Legendre function.

99. **(A)**

The two postulates of special relativity are:

(1) True physical laws are the same in all inertial reference frames;

(2) The speed of light is a constant in vacuo regardless of source and observer relative motion.

This was Einstein's 1905 theory. In 1915, he went beyond this with the general theory of relativity for which (B) – (E) in the question are true statements.

100. **(E)**

This is the usual relativistic rocket problem. The four momentum is

$$\begin{aligned} p^{\mu} &= mu^{\mu} \\ &= (m\gamma \mathbf{u}, m\gamma c). \end{aligned}$$

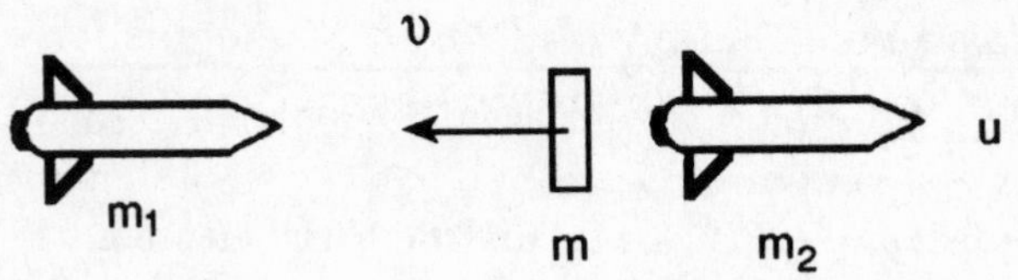

Certainly the space component of the 4-momentum is conserved

$$(0, m_1\, c) = (-\, m\gamma_{\upsilon}\upsilon, m\gamma_{\upsilon}c) + (m_2\gamma_u u, m_2\gamma_u c)$$

so that

$$0 = -\, m\gamma_{\upsilon}\upsilon + m_2\gamma_{\upsilon}u$$

or $\quad m\gamma_{\upsilon}\upsilon = m_2\gamma_u u.$

The rest mass is not conserved since this is an inelastic collision in reverse.

REA's Test Prep Books Are The Best!

(a sample of the hundreds of letters REA receives each year)

"I am writing to congratulate you on preparing an exceptional study guide. In five years of teaching this course I have never encountered a more thorough, comprehensive, concise and realistic preparation for this examination."

Teacher, Davie, FL

"I have found your publications, *The Best Test Preparation...*, to be exactly that."

Teacher, Aptos, CA

"I used your *CLEP Introductory Sociology* book and rank it 99% — thank you!"

Student, Jerusalem, Israel

"Your *GMAT* book greatly helped me on the test. Thank you."

Student, Oxford, OH

"I recently got the *French SAT II* Exam book from REA. I congratulate you on first-rate French practice tests."

Instructor, Los Angeles, CA

"Your *AP English Literature and Composition* book is most impressive."

Student, Montgomery, AL

"The REA *LSAT* Test Preparation guide is a winner!"

Instructor, Spartanburg, SC

(more on next page)

REA's Test Prep Books Are The Best!

(a sample of the hundreds of letters REA receives each year)

" I did well because of your wonderful prep books... I just wanted to thank you for helping me prepare for these tests. "

Student, San Diego, CA

" My students report your chapters of review as the most valuable single resource they used for review and preparation. "

Teacher, American Fork, UT

" Your book was such a better value and was so much more complete than anything your competition has produced — and I have them all! "

Teacher, Virginia Beach, VA

" Compared to the other books that my fellow students had, your book was the most useful in helping me get a great score. "

Student, North Hollywood, CA

" Your book was responsible for my success on the exam, which helped me get into the college of my choice... I will look for REA the next time I need help. "

Student, Chesterfield, MO

" Just a short note to say thanks for the great support your book gave me in helping me pass the test... I'm on my way to a B.S. degree because of you! "

Student, Orlando, FL

(more on previous page)